# THE
## —— COMPENSATION ——
# HANDBOOK

# THE
# COMPENSATION
# HANDBOOK

### SIXTH EDITION

## A STATE-OF-THE ART GUIDE TO COMPENSATION STRATEGY AND DESIGN

## LANCE A. BERGER
## DOROTHY R. BERGER

NEW YORK   CHICAGO   SAN FRANCISCO
ATHENS   LONDON   MADRID   MEXICO CITY
MILAN   NEW DELHI   SINGAPORE
SYDNEY   TORONTO

2 3 4 5 6 7 8 9 10    DOC    21 20 19 18 17 16

ISBN: 978-0-07-183699-9
MHID: 0-07-183699-3

e-ISBN: 978-0-07-183823-8
e-MHID: 0-07-183823-6


**Library of Congress Cataloging-in-Publication Data**

The compensation handbook : a state-of-the-art guide to compensation strategy and design / [edited by] Lance Berger and Dorothy Berger. -- Sixth edition.
    pages cm
  ISBN 978-0-07-183699-9 (alk. paper) -- ISBN 0-07-183699-3 (alk. paper)  1.  Compensation management--Handbooks, manuals, etc.  I. Berger, Lance A. II. Berger, Dorothy R.
   HF5549.5.C67H36 2015
   658.3'2--dc23
                                2015001213

McGraw-Hill Education books are available at special quantity discounts to use as premiums and sales promotions, or for use in corporate training programs. To contact a representative, please visit the Contact Us page at www.mhprofessional.com.

# Contents

# Preface

*The Compensation Handbook* has been recognized as the most authoritative reference book in the field of compensation for over 40 years. The secret of the book's success has been:

- Identifying the most significant issues impacting compensation and human resources' practitioners.

- Providing the best straightforward, comprehensive, and understandable solutions to deal with issues.

- Utilizing respected and prestigious leaders in the field to provide solutions.

- Putting forward unique and innovative approaches not found elsewhere.

- Building on the strong knowledge foundation of past editions.

Each edition of this book has its own novel structure. The first three editions focused on the evolution of new compensation techniques and methodologies as they applied to the business and social environment of their era. The fourth edition was based on a framework of compensation diagnostics. The fifth edition showed compensation and human resources professionals how to use reward systems to address a dramatically changing set of human capital issues arising from changes in business economics, workforce demographics, and employee culture.

The sixth edition helps practitioners use compensation programs to address five strategic human capital issues:

- Creating and maintaining a culture of innovation, engagement, leadership, and performance.

- Employing novel ways to win the battle for external talent, retain internal talent, and develop mission-critical competencies.

- Using "big data" to make compensation decisions that lead to greater business success.

- Implementing total compensation programs that adapt to rapidly changing business and workforce scenarios.

- Creating compensation programs that create competitive business advantage.

The sixth edition has all new, updated, or revised chapters. Each one links to one or more specified human capital issues cited above. It also ensures that compensation and human resources professionals will continue to utilize the best historical and new compensation tools, methods, and diagnostics to align their programs with the key issues. In the sixth edition, we have added an entirely new section devoted to the role and use of "big data" in the compensation practice.

Thanks to the contributions of 63 compensation professionals, 26 of whom are new authors to *The Compensation Handbook*, this edition contains new, updated, or revised chapters. As we did for the fifth edition, we again dedicate this book with appreciation and affection to Milton L. Rock, consummate compensation and business guru, whose vision spearheaded the first three editions of *The Compensation Handbook*.

The sixth edition is also dedicated to the children and grandchild of the editors: Adam and Alejandra Gimenez Berger; Craig and Alexandra Block Berger; Nancy Berger; and Cheryl, Steve, and Hailey Rose McGuire.

—Lance A. Berger and Dorothy R. Berger

# THE
## ─── COMPENSATION ───
# HANDBOOK

# PART I

# INTRODUCTION

# The State of the Compensation Practice

Lance A. Berger
*Lance A. Berger & Associates, Ltd.*

The first edition of *The Compensation Handbook* was a snapshot of the compensation practice as it had evolved prior to 1972. Each subsequent edition was a time capsule containing a rich trove of information representing the cumulative successes of its predecessors as well as the best new practices, issues, procedures, and processes that would be useful in the future. This sixth edition extends this evolution of knowledge to the current time. It shows that today's successful compensation practice has evolved into five blended elements:

1. Expertise

2. Codified methodologies

3. Decision-making tools

4. Databases

5. Monitoring

## Expertise

*Expertise* refers to a particular knowledge or skill in specific practices or disciplines. Every organization needs a designated group of people with a sufficient level of expertise in compensation practice to develop and implement or outsource effectively their pay programs. This group could include any combination of compensation professionals, human resources generalists, and line managers.

Because most organizations in the United States are small firms, the overwhelming number of people involved in directing compensation programs are line managers.

Level of expertise can be classified in many ways, including basic, operational, tactical, and strategic.

1. *Basic.* Knows the fundamental principles, terminology, concepts, issues, applications, and vendors associated with the compensation discipline. This is the minimal level of expertise expected for a line manager.

2. *Operational.* Able to implement compensation programs provided by, and with guidance from, others with higher levels of expertise. This is a realistic level of expertise for most managers, entry-level compensation professionals, and human resources generalists.

3. *Tactical.* Develops and implements compensation programs with minimal assistance from outsiders. Can coach others in implementing a compensation program. This is the expected level of an experienced compensation professional.

4. *Strategic.* Creates, implements, provides guidance, troubleshoots, and answers questions related to the compensation discipline. This is a recognized expert in the compensation discipline.

Over the course of time, the various editions of *The Compensation Handbook* have shown that readers have been seeking guidance in moving toward the strategic level of expertise. The chapters in this book seek to provide a context relevant to all four levels of expertise.

The expansion of formal and disciplined knowledge in the compensation practice was accelerated by the growth of WorldatWork, particularly its certification programs. It did so through workshops, seminars, webinars, and formal credit and noncredit courses. WorldatWork programs were supplemented by additional offerings conducted by consulting firms, universities, software companies, and other organizations with stakeholders associated with the compensation practice.

Chapter 5, written by WorldatWork professionals Brian Moore and Sue Holloway, outlines six professional training and technical skills that represent the building blocks for growth in the profession:

1. Designing and administering base-pay programs

2. Designing and administering variable-pay programs

3. Integrating compensation programs with business strategy

4. Complying with legal and regulatory requirements

5. Communicating compensation information

6. Designing and administering other total rewards programs

The "WorldatWork 2012 Total Rewards Professionals' Career Census" revealed eight key differentiators of top total rewards performers:

1. Technical mastery

2. Strategic business understanding

3. Analytical skills and attention to detail

4. Communication and connection

5. Adaptability and flexibility

6. Passion and proactivity

7. Continuous learning

8. Development support system

Collectively, the six building blocks and eight differentiators create a framework for viewing the role of compensation practitioners. The four levels of expertise descibed previously can be applied to this framework to generate a profile of the level of compensation practioner required by the organization.

## Codified Methodologies

Codified methodologies are the documented processes, practices, and policies that enable organizations to define, replicate, adapt, and effectively implement compensation programs. Codification emerged from the experience of the successful compensation programs of the organizations themselves; the shared best practices of several organizations, consulting firms, and associations; WorldatWork publications; and materials produced by vendors. Codified methodologies embrace and combine within one place the goals, objectives, programs, processes, databases, and analytical and decision-making tools associated with specific compensation goals, strategies, and outcomes. Since the first edition of *The Compensation Handbook*, the most codified methodologies include job evaluation, market pricing, and salary administration. Chapters addressing these issues can be found in Part II of this book.

Each new edition of *The Compensation Handbook* has reflected only small changes in codified salary administration practices. Since the last edition, one important change in this edition, noted by Michael Armstrong in Chapter 8, is that "progressively ... the original concept of broad banding was eroded as more structure was introduced and job evaluation became more prominent to define the structure. ... Job evaluation was used not only to define the boundaries of the band but to size jobs as a basis for deciding where reference points should be placed in conjunction with market pricing."

Perhaps the newest tweak adopted by some organizations is alternative merit pay plans. Performance increases under these plans are not frozen into base pay each year but rather are earned annually. These "variable merit" plans more heavily incent and reward employee achievement and/or the demonstration of success competencies. They are budgeted as part of an affordable merit increase pool. The acceptance of this type of pay plan, described by Dorothy Berger in Chapter 4, is evolving gradually.

The evolution of the compensation practice indicates that a successful compensation practice must codify three major elements: philosophy, strategy, and administration.

### 1. Compensation Philosophy

A compensation philosophy contains a widely publicized set of core principles, values, and mutual expectations that are the foundations of employee pay. It is the basis of an organization's pay strategy. Organizations align their compensation philosophy with their business and human resources requirements. Most commonly, an organization's compensation philosophy focuses on delivering pay, based on institutional affordability, in a way that enables the organization to attract, retain, and reward employee performance in an equitable, competitive, and legal way.

## 2. Compensation Strategy

Compensation strategies tell the organization how it will allocate employee pay based on its compensation philosophy. Tom Wilson in Chapter 3 writes, "A strategy helps to focus goal setting, guidelines, policies, practices, behaviors, and investments." Steve Gross and Mandy Rook in Chapter 2 describe compensation strategy as the allocation of total rewards in both holistic (recognizing all the tools in a rewards toolkit) and customized (using the right tool for the right job) approach. A typical compensation strategy consists of five codified components. They are affordability, pay markets, competitive level, mix of compensation elements, and employee contribution.

*Affordability.* Every organization must determine the overall level of base pay and all other forms of compensation that it can afford to pay in at least two successive years based on its current and projected growth level. Two-year intervals are always selected to gauge the multiyear impact of changes in proposed annual compensation adjustments. Because base salaries represent the largest amount of employee pay, the aggregate cost of base salary midpoints (the salary structure) is the starting point for the determination of affordability. Once this is accomplished, the organization can establish the potential funding pools for annual salary increases and for variable pay programs.

*Pay markets.* In order to determine the competitiveness of pay associated with a given position, an organization must survey its talent market. A talent market consists of incumbents who have been or can be a source of recruitment for or candidates for "pirating" by other organizations. Surveyed compensation for people in benchmark (commonly found) jobs in a chosen talent market should be the basis for an organization establishing pay. The best surveys are those that accurately measure a pay market derived from current and projected sources of recruitment and exit interviews. Positions within a talent market that have no survey counterpart can derive their value from a comparison of relative internal organizational worth with the jobs that can be surveyed. Note that talent market competitors may not necessarily be in the same business as your company. Most companies will have multiple talent markets. Chapter 11 describes the use of surveys in pay market measurement.

*Competitive level.* Within each market and within the organization as a whole, management must determine the competitive level of total human resources costs the organization can afford and is willing to pay to attract, retain, and reward employees. Competitive level is generally expressed as a percentile level of pay in positions in surveys associated with a given talent market (25th, 50th, 75th). The total affordable pot of money is the basis of pay allocation. It is possible that the characteristics of different pay markets (supply and demand) will necessitate different pay structures and competitive levels.

*Mix.* The percentage of total pay targeted for each pay component (base salary, annual incentives, and long-term incentives) defines its mix. Furthermore, within a total pay package, there may be different competitive levels targeted for base pay, annual incentives, long-term incentives, and total compensation. The mix of compensation, as well as competitive level, could be different for different pay markets. The greater the amount of variable or nonbase pay, the more leverage (upside opportunity) or risk (nonguaranteed pay) becomes a factor in an employee's compensation package. In general, the level of risk or leverage decreases in employee pay packages as an organization evolves from that of a precarious startup to that of a secure establishment. Within an organization, the amount of leverage in a pay package also reflects the risk and accountability associated with a given position. Senior management and line positions typically have more variable pay than staff positions. Generally, codified methodologies for risk-oriented variable pay also have evolved slowly since the first edition of this book. Part III of this edition covers codified methodologies for variable pay.

*Employee contribution.* Compensation strategies typically consider the actual and projected levels of employee contribution. Compensation philosophies and strategies state the organization's approach to allocating pay packages that it judges to be best to incent, engage, ensure retention, reinforce advancement, and facilitate recruitment of employees who are high achievers, deemed to have high potential, and/or are backups for key positions. Once compensation is allocated to employees in these critical categories, it is distributed for the remaining employee population. Employees in this group must at least meet organizational expectations for performance. Andrew Rosen in Chapter 7 and Myrna Hellerman and James Kochanski in Chapter 9 link employee contribution to pay programs.

### 3. Salary Administration

Salary administration is the packaged set of policies, methods, and procedures that guides professionals and line managers in the implementation of their compensation strategy. Salary administration elements that characteristically have been codified include compensation philosophy (discussed previously), responsibilities of compensation professionals and managers in salary administration, employee communication, and basic components, including

1. Position descriptions
2. Job evaluation
3. Salary surveys
4. Salary structures
5. Performance evaluation
6. Merit increases
7. Promotions and promotional increases

The details of each component of codified salary administration programs are covered in Part II.

Regardless of the reader's approach to codification, Tom Wilson in Chapter 3 provides a useful lesson. He recommends that every reward program must have a stated purpose that must answer three critical questions:

1. Why does the program exist?
2. Why is it meaningful to employees?
3. How does it give the organization a competitive advantage?

## Decision-Making Tools

Decision-making tools enable compensation practitioners to determine the kinds of processes that will best help them to develop, implement, and monitor their own compensation philosophy, strategy, and administrative and monitoring programs. Decision-making tools have become integral to selecting appropriate compensation methodologies and to converting information in "big databases" to high-value accurate, quick, and timely decisions. They are also critical to monitoring the actual outcomes of targeted compensation programs.

In Chapter 33, Martin Wolf helps readers to make a choice of the best performance appraisal methodologies for their organization. Michael Armstrong and Paul Thompson, in Chapter 10, describe the best options in job evaluation methodology, whereas Linda Amuso, in Chapter 15, and Erin Packwood, in Chapter 16, cover requirements for selecting different types of variable compensation programs. Dorothy Berger, in Chapter 4, helps readers to identify the pay plans that are useful for supporting desired organizational culture, whereas Deborah Rees, in Chapter 39, suggested novel compensation approaches based on type of employee.

This book is replete with other decision-making tools that will help practitioners to select and use methodologies to determine the type of compensation program that is best for their organizations.

## Databases

Data have been central to the compensation practice since its inception. Data on jobs, employee pay, market pay, and numerous other areas of talent management have now exploded with the advancement of technology and data-collection devices into what we refer to as *big data*. Big data combines multiple data elements into a cogent process that enables better compensation decisions faster and more accurately. It is now easier to combine business, culture, talent management, and compensation data elements into understandable decision points. Although big data is becoming an integral part of business operations for a growing number of organizations, many compensation practitioners and line managers find it to be ambiguous, confusing, and intimidating. It appears to them that big data is an insurmountable barrier. This barrier, however, is not insurmountable, and Part IX of this edition is designed to help readers find and use the level of big data that is appropriate to their organizations.

In Chapter 46, I suggest that most organizations can use big data simply by linking readily available information on compensation policies and practices and business data to talent management and/or employee culture data. Every organization can develop a scorecard that will tell it whether

1. Organization-wide employee evaluation and total salary increases based on performance appraisal systems correlate with organization and unit performance.

2. Compensation is appropriately distributed to critical groups (high performers, high potentials, backups for key positions, and employees with demonstrated high levels of key competencies).

3. Pay is not a cause of turnover in critical employee groups.

4. Pay is perceived as fair and consistent with organization values.

5. Compensation strategies are administered effectively.

According to David Turetsky (Chapter 48), "'big data' leverages the 'small data' and the 'data' platforms to build a more complete picture of the enterprise. It leverages disparate system data together to form a union of unlikely confederations into a symphony of knowledge and intelligence. The value of the big data effort is greater than the sum of the parts of the lower-level interconnections." Turetsky also talks about the role of big data in analyzing outcomes such as those identified in Table 1.1.

| Base Salary | Incentives | Pay Equity |
| --- | --- | --- |
| • Is our merit increase program effective?<br><br>• If we increased our merit budget by 1 percent, can we expect a 1 percent increase in performance? | • Are we rewarding the right behaviors?<br><br>• Do our goals reflect the organizational objectives? | • Do we pay too much for certain roles?<br><br>• What does pay equity mean for our organization? |
| **Market Position** | **Succession** | **Grades/ Structures** |
| • Do we know how much it would cost in salary and incentive to get everyone to the market on total cash compensation?<br><br>• Do the reward programs, as currently designed, achieve the goals of the organization? | • Are our high potentials on track to be able to achieve the minimum of the range for the job for which they are successors?<br><br>• Are we compensating the right people? | • Do our grade levels represent the appropriate groupings of job responsibility and impact to the organization?<br><br>• Do our salary structures represent the market for the current job market? |

Table 1.1

Dan Weber, in Chapter 47, suggests that compensation professionals will continue to be called on to respond to business inquiries. To prepare for these types of inquiries, such professionals should be familiar with four areas:

1. Where and how the business currently generates value (current operations)

2. Where the business anticipates growth, expansion, and change (strategic plan)

3. The data currently available within company compensation and human resources information systems (HRIS)

4. External sources of data, such as market surveys, government agencies, and other organizations

Weber also suggests that readers consider three approaches to big-data issues:

1. Understanding the issues to be addressed, including the potential for big data to solve an issue, specific desired outcomes, and the perceptions and concerns of stakeholders

2. Understanding the full range of forces that can influence the desired outcome

3. Thinking beyond the numbers because many decision factors cannot be easily tracked or accounted for in a statistical analysis

Ezra Schneier, in Chapter 49, states that big data can help an organization to achieve three broad goals:

1. Enhanced engagement and retention
2. Better alignment of individual efforts and organizational goals
3. Improved business results

He cites the following big-data processes that can help to achieve these organizational goals:

- Evaluating compensation along with other elements of rewards to determine what matters to employees
- Increasing the frequency of evaluating compensation and the mix of factors considered in determining compensation levels and awards
- Communicating total rewards and walk-away value to improve retention and engagement

It is clear from the big-data section that the expansion of big-data technologies and their pervasive adoption by organizations of all sizes and practitioners at all levels will be an integral component of state-of-the-art compensation practices in the future.

## Monitoring

Monitoring compensation practices means anticipating, creating, and/or responding to change triggers that can affect compensation programs. These change triggers include business, environmental, cultural, and talent-management factors. Monitoring compensation practices is a change-management program.

Steve Gross and Mandy Rook, in Chapter 2, allude to the need for clearly defining the organization's total rewards principles in order to assess their current and future state against these principles. A gap analysis then can be conducted to assess misalignments between the existing rewards programs and the desired overarching principles. A blueprint then can be created to define the extent of change management required to migrate to the desired state. When an organization seeks change, it may be a difficult undertaking. Systems, processes, and people must adapt. Compensation management systems may need to accommodate multiple base pay and incentive programs, compensation, training, and development; recruiting may need to make tradeoffs across historically siloed budgets, and managers will need to handle more challenging conversations about an individual's compensation, benefits, and career. Once an organization has changed, it must be prepared to change again. Business strategies evolve continuously. If the total rewards strategy does not keep pace, costly misalignments can occur, hindering business progress and diminishing return on investment. Maintaining the total rewards principles and frequently reviewing their appropriateness, effectiveness, and applicability are suggested preventive measures to avoid having an established total rewards program become disconnected from the internal requirements (both employer and employee) and the external market. When programs are disconnected, they threaten the competitive advantage of the organization that was created initially with the development and implementation of its total rewards strategy. Overcoming these challenges, according to Gross and Rook, requires leadership support, pragmatic segmentation (recognizing meaningful differences in workforce segments), and comprehensive implementation and communication change management with an eye on both the present and the future.

In Chapter 6, Joe Martocchio talks about anticipating compensation issues that are "a mix of complex economic, social, and demographic dynamics. Each of these challenges will require that compensation professionals anticipate policy and compensation system design features that will serve the interests of shareholders and employees."

Organizations should have a formal audit program that uses credible, high-quality, reliable, timely, and cost-effective information to assess whether their codified metholdogies, decision-making tools, and databases are yielding the targeted business, culture, and talent-management outcomes.

# 2

# Using a Total Rewards Strategy to Achieve Competitive Advantage

Steven E. Gross
*Mercer LLC*

Mandy Rook
*Mercer LLC*

A total rewards strategy can create continuous competitive advantage for your business. This chapter will address the following questions:

- Why is a total rewards strategy essential for creating a continuing competitive business advantage?

- What elements of a total rewards program are essential for consideration today?

- How does an organization design a total rewards program?

## Why is a total rewards strategy essential for creating a continuing competitive business advantage?

Creating a competitive business advantage starts with recognizing the role that total rewards plays in organizations today. This role has emerged as a result of both external and internal influences. Among the external influences is the changing employment model. The evolving employment model is driven not by one dominant perspective, as in the past—a perspective typically founded on the employer's capacity to draw from a deep labor pool and rely on long-tenured workers who are happy to have jobs—but by multiple perspectives. Now the employer perspective recognizes an emerging shortage of labor skills, knowledge, and experience (in part, driven by the aging of the baby boomer population in mature economies) in a less company-loyal, more geographically mobile workforce. The employee perspective is marked by changing cultural and generational attitudes, needs, and wants when it comes to work, driven by a newfound awareness on the levels of pay and availability of benefits as communicated through social media and Internet outlets that previously did not exist. The cost perspective is that of increasing employment costs and their sustainability—driven largely by the ever-inflating cost of healthcare (primarily) and other benefits, along with the competitive cost of paying for skilled talent in a tightening global job market.

Although operating in an increasingly global marketplace, employers are often recruiting from a smaller qualified workforce because statistics show that the level and quantity of technical education are not keeping pace with demand. At the same time, there is loss of experienced workers to retirement—a phenomenon that will only accelerate as the baby boomer generation moves out of the workforce en masse in the coming years, especially in the United States, where healthcare reform provides baby boomers with more freedom to elect an early retirement (whereas prior to healthcare reform, workers were working to age 65 for Medicare because few employers offered preretirement health insurance). This results in a loss of institutional knowledge that cannot be easily replaced simply by adding new hires. Not only do less-experienced workers need more on-the-job training, forcing organizations to invest more energy and resources, but today's and tomorrow's employees also question a one-company career while demanding a competitive rewards package.

The mismatch between available talent and available skills is evident in the findings from the collaboration of Mercer and the World Economic Forum in 2013, which indicated that 34 percent of employers are unable to fill available jobs, whereas 205 million people are unemployed across the globe. On closer examination in North America, human resources professionals cited attracting and retaining the "right" talent as the number one rewards challenge in both the 2008 and 2014 "Total Rewards Snapshot Surveys" conducted by Mercer. Labor dynamics suggest that employers will continue to face the daunting task of engaging a diverse new workforce that grows its own institutional knowledge, and stays with the organization.

As employers face the external influences and identify appropriate responses to the changing employment rules, uneven labor supply and demand, and retiring baby boomers, they are left with one other external challenge—uneven business cycles. The inability to predict the ups and downs in our global economy can raise havoc in trying to sustain a business advantage over competitors as unemployment declines and the economy continues to grow slowly. At the same time, establishing a total rewards framework can be the glue that sustains the competitive advantage when the external pressures surmount. In addition, the total rewards framework also will provide support when internal challenges test an organization's ability to manage the workforce and respond to employees. Even if an organization can withstand the pressures from the outside, responding to its workforce and providing an environment that promotes productivity, health, and satisfaction can be extremely difficult. The ability to manage employee expectations starts with a transparent total rewards philosophy that speaks to the specific daily challenges in the job that each employee deals with.

Myriad employee perspectives of this diverse workforce are illustrated in Mercer's 2011 "What's Working" global employee survey of workers' perceptions and attitudes toward their organizations. Unlike prior "What's Working" surveys, the 2011 study showed that employee engagement is eroding. The global economic downturn that started in 2008 led to layoffs, cuts in pay and benefits, reduced job security, and more limited training and advancement opportunities. As organizations made smaller investments in their workforces, over one-third of employees globally have responded that they are seriously considering leaving their employers at the present time. Equally alarming, about 20 to 25 percent of employees in the 17 surveyed markets have no definite plans to leave but are apathetic and even more negative about work than employees who are considering an exit. Given these developments, employers are faced with a critical question: How do you redefine the employee value proposition to meet today's business requirements and employee needs?

Among the challenges organizations face as they redefine the employee value proposition is engaging the so-called generation Y, or millennials (ages 18 to 29), in a manner that provides purpose. In Mercer's "What's Working" survey, an astonishing contradiction was presented: the youngest members of the global workforce tended to be more satisfied with both their organizations and their jobs compared with the overall workforce and are more likely to recommend their organizations as good places to work. At the same time, these workers, especially those under age 25, are far more likely to be seriously considering leaving their organizations at the present time, as revealed in the scores, which were 10 points higher for workers under age 25 than for the overall workforce. Another interesting insight from Mercer's survey is that the youngest members of the global workforce are more likely today to view work similarly to their same-age counterparts in other countries than they are to view work like their older colleagues in the same country. For the first time, data suggest that workforce views and attitudes may be changing globally—at least among the youngest members of the workforce.

Balancing the attitudes, wants, and needs of a diverse employee population adds complexity and cost to workforce management. In fact, assessing the sustainability of current costs for employers points disturbingly to the escalating price of providing total rewards. For example, ongoing volatility in pension plan funded status and in the markets results in fluctuating plan expenses, making budgeting a difficult and frustrating endeavor for plan sponsors. Mercer's 2012–2013 "Spotlight on Benefits" report indicates a 34 percent decrease in organizations offering a defined-benefit plan to their employees in the last five years because of risk-adverse employers concerned with pension plans posing material balance sheet risks for U.S. companies. These remaining plans tend to be more poorly funded and are material compared with the size of the organization (Mercer defines a "risky" plan as having a funded status of less than 75 percent and pension liability greater than 40 percent of market capitalization). Plan sponsors continue to explore risk-management strategies ranging from retaining and managing the pension risk to transferring the risk either to employees (via a cash-out) or to insurers (via a buy-out). U.S. organizations seek solutions to pension plan volatility because the alternative points to the very real risk employment costs pose to an organization's sustained financial success.

As organizations attempt to balance a desired workforce with one that is affordable, the employee value proposition becomes increasingly important so that employers can articulate the competitive advantage they want to build among their organizations. Eroding employee loyalty, widespread apathy, generational differences, and cost constraints are the reasons why employers not only should review their total rewards framework now but also should raise several fundamental questions as to what employers should consider when they take the plunge to develop a total rewards program.

## What elements of a total rewards program are essential for consideration today?

Total rewards is not a new concept, but the role that it is playing within organizations is evolving. Employees are no longer considering their jobs as long-time commitments but rather as experiences within their "portfolio." Employees are also taking on greater accountability for managing their own careers, health, and wealth, even if they do not know how. As employers think about how to respond to these changes, the following questions are key considerations for the foundation of a total rewards program:

- What are effective attraction, engagement, and retention policies?
- What is the most effective way to allocate limited resources?
- What is the best way to balance employee preferences with cost constraints?
- What is the impact of creating a build-versus-buy approach to talent?
- Should all employees be governed by the same rewards philosophy?
- What role should recognition plans play?
- How should reward plan effectiveness be measured?

While the answers to these questions are unique to each organization, there are common considerations that organizations can think through to identify what is best for them. Let's start with workforce segmentation.

Businesses require a strategic solution to managing their workforces—one that encompasses the realities of generations and geographies, emerging nontraditional staffing models, and pressure to produce return on human capital investments. Such a strategy begins with the identification of unique workforce segments. There are four important aspects of segmentation to consider:

- *Business life cycle.* A company's position on the business life-cycle curve: whether it is experiencing rapid, moderate, or declining growth. A young startup will have different characteristics than a mature firm in a flat market.
- *Business design.* A company's business model: how the entity is organized and the types of competencies required to create value. There may be one overall design or different emphases for units or divisions within the company.
- *Geography.* A company's geographic breadth and complexity, as well as its need for cross-border interconnectedness and mobility: mature versus emerging markets.
- *Brand reputation.* The extent to which a company's brand is an asset or liability in attracting and retaining both customers and employees.

Once the portfolio of workforce segments is identified, it is important to assess the contribution that each segment makes to organization success. Segments may include

- *Performance drivers.* Segments that create value for the organization, such as marketing in consumer products companies, research scientists in pharmaceutical organizations, and logistics in an emerging market for a globally expanding manufacturing firm.
- *Performance enablers.* Segments that support value creation, such as staff (human resources, accounting, supply chain, etc.) and workers who play an important role in facilitating the efficiency of performance drivers (such as information technology in the creation of electronic medical records).

- *Legacy drivers.* Segments (skill sets) that historically created value for the organization but no longer drive competitive advantage. For example, production and distribution functions in a media organization may become legacy drivers as content is increasingly delivered online.

It is critical to emphasize that those different job families, geographies, and skill sets are not universally categorized as performance drivers, performance enablers, or legacy drivers because their role in value creation depends on organization and even business-unit profit models. A good example would be a single group of information technology (IT) professionals that might play different roles in value creation for different organizations. How? To a buyer of IT outsourcing services that rely on IT to support its operations, those IT professionals function as performance enablers, but to an IT outsourcing vendor that sells their services, they are performance drivers. In other words, workforce segmentation requires an organization-specific view of value creation. As organizations consider the role that each workforce segment plays and, more specifically, the role that each job plays, they can categorize jobs by their criticality and scarcity, as shown in Figure 2.1.

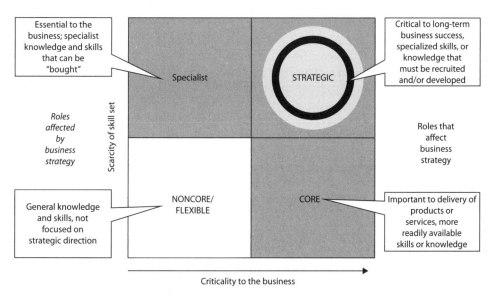

**Figure 2.1  Workforce segmentation driven by strategic importance.**

The rewards challenge for each workforce segment is often different. For performance drivers, the value proposition must succeed in attracting, engaging, and retaining these value creators through an optimal mix of base pay, incentive compensation, benefits, and career-development offerings. For performance enablers, the rewards mix must ensure that these workers continue to effectively support the business. And for legacy drivers, appropriate rewards depend on the value of retaining their institutional knowledge.

Complex organizations are multifaceted compilations of workforce segments. If an organization does not rigorously identify and qualify its workforce populations, it cannot act on differences in relative value contribution or design programs that reflect varying workforce needs and performance goals. Workforce segmentation is required to ensure that total rewards resources can be intentionally allocated strategically across the organization to promote the greatest opportunity for success.

Organizations also need to think beyond workforce segmentation, especially as they consider the cost implications of the segments. Once an organization can identify what the workforce segments are, the question becomes, what is the most affordable way to staff these roles? Adding to the cost dilemma is the fact that for most businesses—especially those operating in a global context—workforce requirements vary over time and location. For example, the traditional model of permanent, full-time employees is not flexible or cost efficient in addressing periods of under- or overcapacity of staff. Cost and flexibility pressures, changing employee demands, and the challenges employers face in attracting, engaging, and motivating talent that will create value for the organization promote the growth of alternative employment arrangements.

The workforce of the future demands a suite of employment arrangements that meets employer, employee, external, and cost concerns. Traditional long-term, permanent, full-time positions will always have a role delivering organizational success, but employers and employees will see an expanded range of work arrangements from long-term to contingent. Long-term employment is typically traditional permanent, full-, or part-time work. The visible shift in long-term arrangements is the demand for flexible work plans. Contingent employment is a more varied mix of nonlinear multicompany work experiences, including short-term employment that may be structured as temporary/full or part time, temporary-to-hire, specific-project employment structured as temporary/full or part time, and contractor arrangements such as consultants and the self-employed. Including contingent workers in an organization's staffing model allows it to optimize the number and cost of permanent headcount while adding resources as required to meet fluctuating capacity demands.

Long-term employment with flexible work options can include flextime, telecommuting, job sharing, compressed workweek, sabbaticals, and generally a greater level of employee autonomy in scheduling and delivering work. Growth of flexible work plans speaks to what employees want and need and how employers are rising to the challenge. Mercer's 2014 "Total Rewards Snapshot Survey" reveals that flexible hours and telecommuting are the most prevalent flexible work options, with 76 percent of surveyed organizations allowing professional employees the ability to flextime and 70 percent offering professional employees the option to telecommute. These percentages are up in the last 15 years because surveys on workplace policies and practices conducted by Mercer over the years have revealed that only about 30 percent of surveyed companies had telecommuting arrangements in 1999.

Taking flexible one step further, the employment of a temporary workforce is an accepted practice among consumer goods employers in North America and Latin America. Mercer's 2013 "Workforce Composition Metrics Regional Report for the Americas Consumer Goods Industry" showed that, on average, temporary workers represent 6 percent of the total workforce (permanent and temporary). When broken down between North America and Latin America, the averages are 4 and 7 percent, respectively. Besides the variations by region, Mercer's report also indicated that across the Americas, the percentage of temporary workers is highest in companies with more than 500 employees and less than US$350 million in revenue. The conclusion that can be drawn is that employers with limited funds are employing a larger temporary workforce when headcount is a requirement to the business operation as a means to mitigate their overall cost of total rewards to their full-time populations.

As employers consider the use of a temporary workforce to mitigate the cost of total rewards, evidence from Accenture's 2013 article entitled, "The Rise of the Extended

Workforce," indicates that outsourcing contracts with Fortune 100 companies have more than doubled since 2000, with about 20 percent of global organizations using outsourced or off-shored workers. What is interesting about this shift is that the profile of the temporary worker is changing from primarily low skilled and uneducated to increasingly high skilled, well educated, and globally accessible. The recent emergence of online independent contractor talent platforms enables companies to access "talent in the cloud," and currently, more than 1 million workers make up this workforce. The contingent-workforce phenomenon will modify such traditional patterns as those seen, for example, in career paths where long-term career growth is predicated on a typically linear progression from job A to jobs B, C, and ultimately D. Contingent-workforce careers tend to move nonlinearly from job A to modified work arrangements (lateral jobs B1 and then B2, for example) before acceding to next-level jobs C or D. Ultimately, organizations will have to recognize this portfolio of experience and respond to different views of career path—that of permanent, long-term workers who see a career path within the firm and contingent workers who see a career path moving from firm to firm.

Increasing demands for alternative employment arrangements such as flexible work plans and contingent staffing, along with the changing view of "career path," require organizations to rethink workforce management for the future. Understanding the workforce segments within an organization, as well as the best approach to staffing, is a key ingredient to creating a competitive business advantage and building a total rewards program that will resonate with the workforce.

## How does an organization design a total rewards program?

Strategic allocation of total rewards means taking both a holistic (recognizing all the tools in a rewards toolkit) and a customized (using the right tool for the right job) approach. Mercer's 2014 "Total Rewards Survey" examines the practices organizations are using to align compensation, benefits, training, and career development with today's business priorities. This survey found that while more than half (55 percent) of organizations made a significant change to their total rewards strategy in the past three years, less than one-third (32 percent) said that their total rewards and business strategies fully align.

A balanced approach to total rewards—one that acknowledges the needs of the business, the changing environment, the aspirations and demographics of employees, the local culture, and the current and future cost constraints—is both essential and challenging. Approaching total rewards begins with a top-down review of the business strategy and the human capital strategy, identifying the implications that each of these has on the total rewards philosophy (Figure 2.2).

Considerable strides have been made in shifting both employee and employer focus from disparate pay components to a holistic total rewards approach that encompasses

- *Compensation.* This includes base pay, short- and long-term incentives, guaranteed allowances, and financial recognition awards.
- *Benefits.* This includes health and other group benefits, retirement plans, life insurance, disability, and accident coverage.
- *Careers.* This includes training and development, stretch assignments and other career opportunities, and formal career and succession planning.

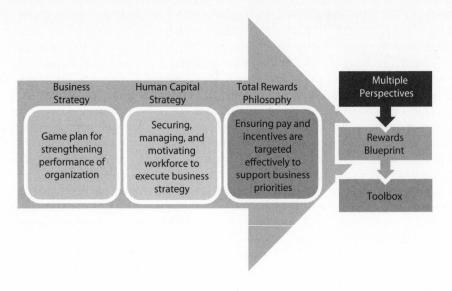

**Figure 2.2  Developing a total rewards philosophy.**

- *Work life.* This includes programs such as flexible working arrangements, telecommuting, dependent care, wellness programs, commuter programs, and other nonfinancial recognition.

Among these components, the value of the specific reward elements to employees varies by country. In Mercer's 2011 "What's Working" global employee survey of workers' perceptions and attitudes toward their organizations, base pay ranked as the most important reward element in mature markets, for example, the United States, United Kingdom, and Germany, whereas career advancement ranked as the most important element in emerging markets, for example, Brazil, China, and India, where advancement meets both employees' personal and financial needs. A ranking of the top six reward elements is provided in Figure 2.3.

Clearly, a universal or "one-company" holistic approach can lead to over- or underrewarding specific workforce segments—or, worse, inappropriately rewarding all segments. Strategic total rewards means that organizations must consider the external influences on their workforces, such as the countries in which they operate, to provide rewards that will be meaningful to each of their respective geographic segments.

However, as mentioned previously, geography is not the sole differentiator among segments. Other unique factors specific to an organization require employers to make tactical decisions in customizing programs. A good example is the case of the global energy company that identified multiple business models: in one, profit was generated through a premium, long-term position in global exploration, and in another, profit was generated through low-margin, intensely competitive local retail market-share transactions. This organization needed to distinguish two workforce segments and build tailored total rewards approaches. One design, relating to the firm's global organization, involved paying above-market salaries for "hot" skills; building talent from within the organization through a total rewards program that emphasized career-based rewards, nondifferentiated corporate performance awards, and a focus on learning and development; and centralized decision making. The other approach, keyed to the local retail end of the business, involved paying market price for talent (and "buying" it on the open market rather than "building"

| Rank | China | India | UK | Germany | Brazil | USA |
|------|-------|-------|-----|---------|--------|-----|
| 1 | Career advancement | Career advancement | Base pay | Base pay | Career advancement | Base pay |
| 2 | Base pay | Base pay | Type of work | Type of work | Base pay | Retirement savings or pension plan |
| 3 | Supplemental retirement savings plan | Training opportunities | Bonus/other incentives | Bonus/other incentives | Training opportunities | Type of work |
| 4 | Training opportunities | Type of work | Retirement savings or pension | Flexible work schedule | Type of work | Low healthcare costs |
| 5 | Bonus/other incentives | Working for respectable organization | Flexible work schedule | Working for respectable organization | Health ins. with broad coverage | Bonus/other incentives |
| 6 | Supplemental medical ins. coverage | Bonus/other incentives | Paid time off | Training opportunities | Flexible work schedule | Working for respectable organization |

**Figure 2.3  Employee perception varies from country to country.**

*Source:* Mercer's 2011 "What's Working" survey (between 2,000 and 2,400 respondents per country).

it from within the organization), spot rewards and differentiated performance awards, less emphasis on learning and development, and entrepreneurial decision making. While this may seem like a mix-and-match, one-from-column-A, two-from-column-C approach to total rewards, it reflects the need for a holistic yet customized total rewards strategy that aligns with different business models. Segmentation helps organizations to understand where customization of total rewards will drive business performance, but organizations cannot forget that in the new employment reality, there are likely to be multiple work arrangements across and/or even within workforce segments. This dimension further refines how and where a company should target rewards spent to attract, engage, and retain diverse employee populations. Mercer's observations from its 2008 and 2014 "Total Rewards Snapshot Survey" revealed that in general, more organizations are using some form of internal and/or external analysis to establish the facts about their total rewards strategy. Consistent with Mercer's 2008 results, affordability is the most prevalent internal analysis used, and one in four participants says that it is highly effective. However, in comparison with the 2008 results, the prevalence of using external analyses has increased, along with the method. In 2008, the most prevalent external analysis used was to assess common rewards practices among other companies, and in 2014, it is to use external benchmarking of a specific peer group.

Typically, there are four perspectives an organization should seek to understand when it wants to identify reward strategies that will be meaningful to employees while aligning with the broader business strategy:

1. *Employer perspective.* Conducting discussions (i.e., interviews) with key organization leaders is important for understanding how the reward programs should be structured to secure the desired workforce outcomes.

2. *Employee perspective.* There are two suggested approaches for understanding the value an employee places on his or her reward package. A more qualitative approach is to conduct focus groups with select employees. The focus groups

should be thoughtfully planned so that employees can speak freely, and they should be structured to represent specific homogeneous workforce segments. Organizing the focus groups allows for a comparison to be made among the segments. The alternative approach is more quantitative, although both approaches can be conducted to provide some of the informal employee commentary behind the numerical analysis. The quantitative approach involves conducting a conjoint analysis, which is a type of survey where employees can rank reward elements by their importance and their derived satisfaction. This type of analysis can be meaningful to organizations with limited budgets seeking to understand where to allocate their dollars and seeking to understand differences in how workforce segments value their rewards.

3. *External perspective.* Benchmarking compensation and benefits is an important activity in understanding the value of the rewards package being offered to employees. The external perspective provides insight into how the rewards stack up against those of other similar companies and can provide insight on how to weight the employer and employee perspectives when considering changes to make to the rewards program. For example, if benchmarking of compensation reveals that employees are underpaid compared with the market and employees have been complaining about their pay, then the employees have a legitimate gripe. Adjusting salaries may be the key to refining the total rewards package. However, if benchmarking reveals that employees are paid competitively with their pay market and employees have been complaining about pay, a deeper issue needs to be addressed. What components of the pay are employees unhappy with? What information do they have that leads them to think that they are underpaid? Are there requirements of the job for which employees think they should be paid more?

4. *Internal cost perspective.* At the end of the day, organizations want to do right by their employees. However, they need to balance what they offer with what they can afford. Typical internal cost analysis involves examining several metrics, including but not limited to payroll cost as a percent of revenue, benefit cost as a percent of revenue, benefit costs per capita, year-over-year trends of payroll and benefit costs, retirement plan contributions and expenses reported on accounting disclosures, any incentive plan budgeting and payout analysis, and so on. The metrics that an organization uses need to be meaningful to the organization's determination of what is affordable and sustainable in the long run.

Each of these four perspectives will provide insight into the success of the total rewards program, but it is the combination of these perspectives that will provide the direction for an organization to make decisions related to the elements within the total rewards package.

All the elements of total rewards play a role. The question is where to place the greatest emphasis. For example, long-term, permanent performance drivers should be engaged by career opportunity, offered through access to quality training and development, leading-edge projects, international assignments, and so on. Contrast this with long-term, permanent legacy drivers. Unfortunately, these employees operate in an area of the business that is no longer a growth engine or source of competitive advantage. The organization should not invest in career opportunities or promote career opportunities as a means of motivating or retaining these employees. Emphasis on short-term incentives that reap the remaining benefits of legacy market share or transferred institutional knowledge is a better and more realistic allocation of funds. For contingent workers, current cash is often the driving factor. This is particularly true for traditionalist or baby boomer employees, who may consider cash the primary reason to remain in the workforce because they may be unable to retire in the lifestyle they desire. Contingent gen X and millennial employees may be more forward-looking. For performance drivers in this group, the opportunity for potential full-time employment holds significant appeal (Figure 2.4).

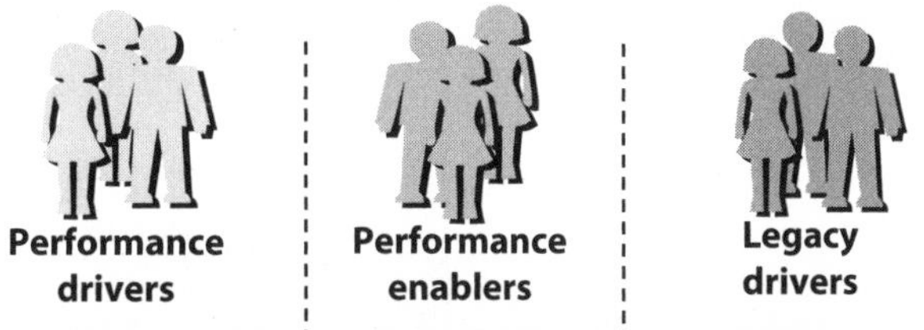

| | | Performance drivers | Performance enablers | Legacy drivers |
|---|---|---|---|---|
| **Employment Arrangement** | | **Permanent** | **Contingent** | **Permanent** |
| **Long Term** | | ▪ Career<br>▪ Alternate work arrangements | ▪ Base pay<br>▪ Benefits | ▪ Short-term incentives<br>▪ Alternate work arrangements |
| **Contingent** | ▪ Traditionalists<br>▪ Baby Boomers | ▪ Cash<br>▪ Benefits | ▪ Cash<br>▪ Benefits | ▪ Cash |
| | ▪ Generation X<br>▪ Millennials | ▪ Cash<br>▪ Potential full-time employment | | ▪ Short-term incentives |

**Figure 2.4  Fluctuating capacity requirements (rewards offered by work arrangement and workforce segment).**

Addressing alternative employment arrangements and unique workforce segments requires significantly more sophisticated total rewards strategies than those of the past. Today's strategies need to reflect the desired outcomes. For some workforce segments, the need may be more focused on attraction, whereas others have a greater focus on retention—yet all organizations require a productive and engaged workforce. In building a total rewards strategy, one needs to think about the rewards components and how they fit together while considering the value of those components as revealed by multiple perspectives (e.g., employer, employee, cost, and external) to understand the impact on the desired outcomes. Thinking holistically, considering all rewards elements drawing on multiple perspectives, and considering outcomes before design constitute a best-practice approach to laying the groundwork for guiding principles to serve as the total rewards framework (Figure 2.5).

Executing strategic, customized total rewards means coming to grips with institutional attitudes and operations that need to change—and change again. One of the most widespread struggles is addressing organizational views of equity and fairness. By definition, segmented, differentiated total rewards programs treat people differently—some perhaps better than others. And although organizations often vary rewards in response to market pressures, skill shortages, and so on, a strategy of explicit differentiation-based employment arrangement and/or value creation is a difficult approach for organizations to adopt and

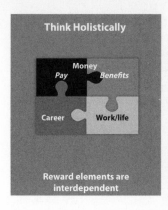
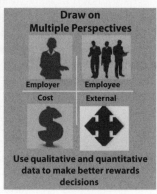

**Figure 2.5 Guiding principles for making program-specific rewards decisions.**

communicate. Developing an overarching total rewards framework is most easily accomplished when considering the following global principles:

1. The degree of segmentation within the organization (e.g., geography, tenure, level, etc.)

2. The role of each rewards element for each segment (e.g., attraction, engagement, retention, etc.)

3. The appropriate external comparator groups (e.g., industry, geography, ownership, etc.)

4. The consistent application of the rewards strategy (internal equity) (i.e., overarching principles are the same but the details vary by segment)

5. The competitive positioning of each element in the pay mix (i.e., at what percentile will base pay be targeted against various markets?)

6. The degree of performance orientation (e.g., amount of pay at risk and performance against various metrics)

7. The affordability and sustainability of the rewards programs (i.e., ability to manage current and future costs)

8. The framework for decision making and cascade within the organization (i.e., governance)

9. The approach and vehicles for communicating rewards (e.g., e-mails, portals and social media, etc.)

10. The extent of the administration needed to maintain programs (i.e., amount of automation and manager self-service)

11. The monitoring process and measures to evaluate the ongoing success of the programs (e.g., employee sensing, behaviors and actions, leadership input, return-on-investment analyses)

After defining the organization's total rewards principles, the organization then can assess their current state against these principles. A gap analysis can be conducted to assess misalignments between existing rewards programs and the desired overarching principle, and a blueprint can be created that defines the extent of the change management required to migrate to the desired state. When an organization seeks change, it may be a difficult undertaking. Systems, processes, and people must adapt; compensation-management systems may need to accommodate multiple base pay and incentive programs, compensation, training, and development; recruiting may need to make tradeoffs across historically siloed budgets; and managers will need to handle more challenging conversations about an individual's compensation, benefits, and career. Once an organization has changed, it must be prepared to change again. Business strategies evolve continuously. If the total rewards strategy does not keep pace, costly misalignments can occur, hindering business progress and diminishing return on investment. Maintaining the total rewards principles and frequently reviewing their appropriateness, effectiveness, and applicability are suggested preventive measures to avoid an established total rewards program from becoming disconnected from the internal desires (both employer and employee) and external market and ultimately failing to sustain the organization's competitive advantage that was created initially by implementation of the total rewards strategy. Overcoming these challenges requires leadership support, pragmatic segmentation (recognizing meaningful differences in workforce segments), and comprehensive implementation and communication change management with an eye on both today's and tomorrow's changes.

## Summary

The workforce of the future is taking shape now because the new employment model continues to evolve to address changing employer, employee, and cost dynamics. More and more, today's and tomorrow's employees will be rethinking traditional employment arrangements and taking a nonlinear, multicompany, individually driven attitude toward career success. Organizations need to take steps to better understand both their existing workforce and the future talent they seek to employ inclusive of the cultural and generational differences, the emerging alternative work arrangements such employees demand, and the relative value creation of unique workforce segments in the business models they advance: best fit versus best practice. A global workforce of the future is one that demands that an employer invest its thought leadership, time, and precious employment budget in building a customized total rewards program that considers fairness and sustainability—but most important, engagement. An employer willing to make such an investment is one that understands how a total rewards program can evolve with the times and create a sustained competitive business advantage.

# 3

# Aligning Total Compensation Programs with Organization Values and Strategy

THOMAS B. WILSON
*Wilson Group*

This chapter provides a new way to look at compensation. Although it is always important to know *how much* you should pay, it is actually more important to know *how* you should pay. Although there are many approaches and best practices in the marketplace, this chapter will examine how to align total compensation and rewards programs with the strategy and core values of your organization. The principles developed will not tell you how to develop a plan with a particular set of features but rather will show you how to ensure that the plans align with what your organization needs today and in the future. What is most important is that there are different approaches appropriate to different situations. Although we like the comfort of knowing that our programs have proven themselves somewhere else, implementing someone else's program frequently fails. Often there are unique aspects of one's organization that limit the effectiveness of programs developed by others. This means that every organization must craft a rewards strategy that reflects its own mission and character. This is the best way to extract the greatest value from compensation expenditures and create the competitive advantages needed to be successful in the marketplace. It is just that simple—and that important.

## What is a total rewards strategy?

To answer this question, let's examine each word in this phrase. *Rewards* are those things that people receive for doing something in their workplace that is meaningful and valuable to them. It could be as simple as showing up to work and getting a salary. The effort is to show up, and the salary is the reward. It could be working on a new-product design, seeing it become successful for the company, and receiving accolades, bonuses, stock awards, or celebrations commensurate with the achievement. This could include working hard to handle a particularly high level of work volume or projects and getting most things correct and in on time. You know what you have accomplished, your boss values these results, your customers appreciate what you have done, and your colleagues are glad you are on the team. You feel rewarded if you have received something that you value for accomplishing these things.

By *total*, we mean everything that is associated with the rewards. In most cases, the rewards have an extrinsic source—they are given to you for what you have done. They also may be felt internally (or intrinsically) because at some point in your work experience, someone truly appreciated what you did that was similar to what you just accomplished. You know that this work is good, and you know that others value what you did. These external sources could be a salary and an increase in pay; an incentive award; a commission payout; a promotion; a stock award; a trophy, plaque, or certificate; or public or private comments of appreciation by someone you respect. You may work for a company that provides benefits important to you. These benefits may share the costs of services (e.g., healthcare insurance), provide income protection (e.g., life and disability insurance), enable you to accumulate savings (e.g., 401(k) or deferred compensation), or take advantage of the company's services (e.g., discounts on company products or use of concierge services). Based on your performance, you could receive greater authority, a bigger budget, broader job responsibilities, a new job title, or increased stature within the organization. There are many types of rewards, and they come in a wide variety of forms, timing, and experiences. Thus, by *total rewards*, we mean those things that an individual may receive for doing the work that is needed by the organization.

A *strategy* is a plan, playbook, or conceptual framework that compels action. A business strategy serves to focus people on taking critical action that will accomplish a set of future goals or objectives. Strategies focus on adding value or meeting a need. Whatever the focus, its goal should be to create some type of competitive advantage. A strategy guides decisions and actions and helps to focus goal-setting, policies, practices, behaviors, and investments. Strategies help the organization to achieve what it needs to be successful.

In summary, a *total rewards strategy* is a meaningful statement that defines the purpose, requirements, and desired features of how an organization rewards its people for doing the things it needs to do to fulfill its mission and achieve its long-term objectives. A total rewards strategy should meet the following criteria:

- Reinforce the core mission, values (or culture), and critical success factors of the organization

- Define what are (or will be) the key elements needed to create a strong competitive advantage in the marketplace for talent

- Provide important clarity and guidance to decision makers so that they can assess the effectiveness of current programs and practices, determine what is needed to improve their effectiveness, and answer why a particular program is designed or functions in a particular manner

The words that create and communicate a total rewards strategy are only important if they influence decisions and actions and reflect a common framework for how employee pay is handled throughout the organization. The result of a successful total rewards strategy is the efficient allocation of employee pay to the people who help, and will help, the organization succeed.

# What does a rewards strategy include?

A rewards strategy is always linked to one or more of the components of the organization's business plan. These components include market, environment, and regulatory and other factors that have an impact, or will, on the organization. The following three elements of a rewards strategy statement must be tied to these components.

## 1. Establishing the Context

Establishing the context for a total rewards philosophy is the first step in developing one. A rewards context contains the organization's mission, key success factors and strategies, and core values. Here is an example from Google:

> Our employees, who have named themselves Googlers, are everything. Google is organized around the ability to attract and leverage the talent of exceptional technologists and business people.... In line with that philosophy, we have designed our compensation programs to support three main goals:
>
> - Attract and retain the world's best talent
>
> - Support Google's culture of innovation and performance
>
> - Align employees' and stockholders' interests
>
>   We pay Googlers competitively compared to other opportunities they might have in the market. We also offer competitive benefits that help Googlers and their families be healthy and happy and provide unique perks that make life and work more convenient, design compelling job opportunities aligned with our mission, and create a fun and energizing work environment. We have a deeply rooted belief in paying for performance.[1]

## 2. Stating the Total Rewards Philosophy

The context for the total rewards strategy is the input for the statement of total rewards philosophy. This statement connects the core mission, strategy, and values of the organization to the rewards programs and practices that influence organizational behavior. Although it might be helpful to see the statements of other organizations, a total rewards statement is best created by the organization itself. This is perhaps the most challenging element of a total rewards philosophy. The difficulty is not in expressing what needs to be done but in how to express something succinctly that is meaningful to employees.

The statement of philosophy becomes the basis of the strategy statement. It should define the overall objective desired from all the total rewards programs, with the realization that each program will focus on what it does best. Here is an example from Whole Foods Market:

> Our compensation and benefit programs reflect our philosophy of egalitarianism. While the programs and individual pay levels will always reflect differences in job responsibilities, geographies, and marketplace considerations, the overall structure of compensation and benefit programs should be broadly similar across the organization.
>
> The primary objective of our compensation programs, including our executive compensation program, is to attract and retain over the long term, qualified and energetic team members who are enthusiastic about our mission and culture,

providing them with sufficient income and other benefits to keep them focused on the Company as their employer. A further objective of our compensation programs is to reward each of our team members for their contribution to the Company. Finally, we endeavor to ensure that our compensation programs are perceived as fundamentally fair to all stakeholders.[2]

## 3. Define the Purpose of Each Reward Program

Once an organization has a total rewards philosophy, it can define, and develop, the purpose of each primary reward program. These programs include base salaries (both the salary levels and pay increases), variable pay plans (these include bonus plans, sales incentives, project or team incentives, management bonus plans, gain-sharing or goal-sharing plans, companywide profit-sharing plans, etc.), employee benefits programs (e.g., health insurance, life insurance, retirement programs, etc.), and recognition and development processes (e.g., performance and service recognition, promotions, spot awards, targeted training investment, etc.). The purpose statement can be developed by answering these three questions:

- Why does each program exist?
- Why is it meaningful to your employees?
- How does it give the organization a competitive advantage?

These questions should assist in forming the purpose statements for each major category of reward programs. Intuit provides a very good illustration of these purpose statements for its reward programs. Here are examples of the purpose statements for some of them:

### "Be Rewarded"
Our Total Rewards program is more than just a paycheck. It includes compensation and recognition programs designed to reward your performance, tools to help you plan your financial future, and benefits and services for your whole family. Our pay and recognition plans offer cash and other nice rewards.

### "Be Recognized"

*Base Salary*
We offer competitive salaries to attract, retain, and motivate you. We believe in rewarding you for excellent performance. Our merit-based system ties salary increases and promotion opportunities to the results you deliver that help Intuit grow.

*Incentive Pay*
You deserve rewards for exceptional performance, so we offer bonus and incentive programs at all levels of the organization. They include sales commissions, support and customer service incentives, and other programs.

*Spotlight Recognition*
Everyone appreciates being appreciated. To thank you for a job well done, our peer recognition tool allows us to recognize each other with cash and other awards. And if you stick around a while, we'll celebrate your milestone employment anniversaries with service awards.

### "Be Secure"

Planning for tomorrow is important. That's why we offer several tools and programs to help you plan your financial future.

#### *401(k) Investments in Your Future*

Intuit's 401(k) Plan allows eligible employees to save for their future by contributing on a pre-tax or post-tax (Roth) basis and receive a company match on a portion of the savings. Employees may choose from a broad range of investment funds, including funds designed for anticipated retirement date and self-directed options for their savings.

### "Be Well"

Your family's health, wellness, and security are a top priority. We offer excellent healthcare benefits plans, insurance, and more.

#### *Medical, Vision, and Dental Care*

There are several plans available, so you can choose the option that's right for you. Choose from three medical plans, a PPO, a consumer directed health plan, and a managed network plan.

#### *Life Event Program*

Our life event program provides a free resource and referral service to assist in life's everyday issues and even the bigger issues that come up. This includes things like parenting, childcare, elder care, adoption assistance, educational assistance, and work issues.

### "Be Balanced"

You've got a busy life outside of work, too. To help you balance it all, we offer several great programs, including time off, fitness incentives, and tons of on-site services.

#### *Vacation and Time Off*

Everyone needs a little time away. We offer paid vacations, personal holidays, and sick leave. Temporary, contract, flextime, and seasonal employees are not eligible for time off with pay.

#### *Parental Leave*

Having a child changes everything. New mothers and fathers can take up to two weeks of paid parental leave to welcome a newborn or newly adopted child.[3]

A total rewards strategy based on a defined philosophy and programs based on this philosophy outline why and how a company or organization spends its money on people.

## How to Develop the Right Strategy for the Organization

The total rewards strategy is built on the mission, strategy, and core values of the organization. This strategy must consider two other important factors:

1. What is the stage of development facing the organization?

2. What is important to the people who work for the organization?

The stage of development recognizes that the challenges and pressures facing an organization differ along a continuum of growth and maturity. Consider these different stages and the implications on how they would shape a total rewards strategy:

1. *Startup and emerging companies.* These companies are just forming, sparked by a new idea, a new service, or a new product. If they are successful, they are the disrupters in the marketplace. They are driven to determine the proof of concept and to build demand in the marketplace for their product or service. The implications for a rewards program are clear. The company probably does not have much money, but its founders are driven by passion, a belief, and a hope that someday they will be rich, famous, or both. Therefore, the type of compensation plans the company has usually involve a minimal salary and, if so structured, an equity stake in the long-term or ultimate growth and success of the business. People get as much from the experience as they receive monetarily, at least in the beginning and to a point.

2. *Investing and growing companies.* Organizations in this category have proven themselves and may have acquired capital to expand and grow. They start hiring people because the original founders can no longer do all the work needed to serve customers. The pressure is intense, and in many ways, they are making things up as they go. They need to figure out ways to proactively respond to the increasingly complex customer demands. In these organizations, people are hired who fit the organization's culture and immediate needs. Such organizations need people with some experience who can meet the demands of the company. Because people joining the firm are no longer founders, the company needs to pay salaries that are sufficient to attract and retain these people. Employee benefit plans become installed, if only at a basic level. Bonus plans may exist if the company has sufficient profitability to afford these expenditures. If not, there is more reliance on equity, with a more reliable promise for a future fortune. The firm is likely to have professional investors who reinforce this alignment of growth and future rewards. The wise use of cash is critical, and this is reflected in what compensation the company can and does pay.

3. *Formalized and professionalized companies.* Organizations at this stage have demonstrated their value to the market, they have hired a lot of people using the "let's make a deal" practice, and at times they are out of control. They need specialized help. At this stage, professional practices and consistent processes are needed to build the foundation for future growth. Issues are starting to arise about the internal fairness of the "deal." There is a growing need to align all the promises and expectations with a sensible and effective set of practices. If the company is successful, structures start to emerge in a number of areas, and people are hired who are specialized and highly experienced in doing the work needed to help the company grow. Some companies regard this as hiring "adult supervision." There are concerns about the dramatic change in the firm's culture and often a sense of loss from the earlier "wild west" adventure that may be romanticized by the long-service employees. Transition to this stage is essential if the firm continues to grow.

   The implications for a compensation program are profound. At this stage, the company starts to adopt different programs that are linked to the performance requirements, desired culture and practices, and needs or profiles of the employees. Organizations start to define career paths because people want to know if there is sufficient opportunity to remain with the firm. There are bonus plans that are both corporate and individually based. Equity plans, which may have been awarded to everyone, are now being limited to those who truly make a difference on the long-term value of the company. Benefit programs are instituted that meet the needs of a diverse workforce and based on what is most important to people. If the organization continues to be successful, it will grow, develop, and provide guidelines that inform and enable good decisions to be made regarding resources and expenditures.

4. *Diversifying and consolidating companies.* If the company continues to grow and prosper, it starts to be larger than can be managed in the original fashion. The company at this stage is more likely to be geographically diverse with offices and operations in multiple regions of the country or world. Companies start to establish free-standing divisions or subsidiaries that can be more responsive to the local markets. Product lines merge into sectors of a business, and companies acquire other firms, consolidate operations to gain economies of scale, and seek ways to balance the need both to delegate functions to lower levels and to ensure integration and collaboration across functional areas. It is moving in multiple directions.

Here the rewards systems often change and adapt to a changing business environment. Some programs remain centralized or retain a common foundation for (hopefully) good reasons—economies of scale, cost savings, cultural requirements, legal regulations, and to retain a connection with the parent company. But many programs are decentralized to better align how people are compensated for who they are and what they do. Diversity in programs and practices is encouraged. However, at times, a central theme or guiding principles are necessary to retain the sense that the employees are all part of the same organization. Bonus plans now have more emphasis on business-unit results than corporate results; companies use different pay plans that fit with different markets globally; and employee benefits are as diverse as the organization is, with different countries and legal or cultural requirements. One size does not fit all, and that is okay.

5. *Revitalizing and renewing companies.* There comes a time, and perhaps there were several times during the life span of the organization, that it needs to renew itself, reshape itself, and reconfigure itself into something that is better prepared to address the needs of a dynamic marketplace. Companies divest businesses that no longer fit their core mission or the performance requirements of the share- or stakeholders. Some firms will contract to focus on what they do very well, their core competencies; other firms will expand globally through acquisitions and investments that reshape who they are in the marketplace.

At this stage, it is difficult to describe the direction of the total rewards programs. It depends on the journey (and strategy) the company is pursuing. The firm will, if it is smart and successful, use some of the experiences with programs that worked for it in the past, as well as develop new ones needed for the new organizational model. It should use this knowledge and these principles to reshape the employment relationship.

Given this continuum of growth and development of an organization, one can easily see how a total rewards strategy will be very different across these stages. The implications are important. The differences reflect a combination of financial sources, diversity of staffing, and expertise requirements. Depending on the stage of development and, more important, on the transition of the firm to a next stage, the total rewards strategy needs to reflect this reality and the firm's unique requirements. But this is not all.

A sound rewards strategy considers the nature and wants of the workforce. Understanding the current needs and aspirations of the workforce is essential to the development of a set of programs and services that are meaningful to individuals. Consequently, the staffing plan and profile of the workforce should shape the design and communication of the rewards strategy. As stated earlier, a reward is something that one perceives as meaningful for doing something the organization wants. This means that the employee is the one who determines the value of the reward, not the executives or human resources program manager.

Understanding the needs of the workforce is similar to understanding customer segments in the marketing function. The marketing profession has many frameworks for researching and describing different segments of a marketplace. Every successful company knows the value of this understanding and then designs its products or services to be appealing to the desired market segments. So too, in the competitive landscape of human resources and talent management, the organization's leaders need to know what is important to their workforce so that they can effectively communicate and motivate them to optimal performance. There are many studies that describe the differences between the primary generations—traditionalists, baby boomers, generations X and Y, and the millennials. Further, there are differences in employee perceptions about what is valuable when you cross geographic boundaries. Describing these in detail is beyond the scope of this chapter, but it is important that both the content and the medium for communicating the total rewards strategy reflect these differences. New technology and communication tools are enabling rewards to be personalized to the requirements of the organization and, ultimately, to its people. Then the organization can form a stronger bond and engagement with each person who seeks to maximize his or her contributions to the organization's success.

## Conclusion

The strength of an effective rewards strategy will be in how it achieves the right connection between the strategic business requirements of the organization and what is meaningful to the individuals who make the organization successful. This process of strategy development, program and process assessment, and change implementation translates the vision of the firm's leaders into actions that people can use every day.

## Notes

1. Google's Founder IPO Letter, 2004.
2. Whole Foods Market, Inc., Proxy, Compensation Discussion and Analysis Section, 2013.
3. Intuit website: http://careers.intuit.com/professional/compensation-benefits.

# 4

# Winning Compensation Strategies for Organizational Sustainability

DOROTHY R. BERGER
*Lance A. Berger & Associates, Ltd.*

In sports, a winning team can never rest on its laurels and maintain consistent competitiveness. Teams must constantly develop bench strength and emerging players' skills while assessing the competition and changing rules and conditions within the sport. So it is with winning corporate teams. Relying on past and current success can only guarantee an uncertain future. Corporate giants must stay vigilant to changing business conditions. As with many dynasty teams, top companies of the not-so-distant past are mere shadows or memorials of their old selves in the wake of emerging technologies, improved and innovative products and services, and the inability to quickly and efficiently change course or business practices to meet the *current reality*. In 1980, the top 10 companies by market capitalization were IBM, AT&T, Exxon, Standard Oil of Indiana, Schlumberger, Shell Oil, Mobil Oil, Standard Oil of California, Atlantic Richfield, and General Electric. Interestingly, 6 of the top 10 were oil companies. Jumping forward to 2014, the top 10 companies list looks very different. Apple now tops the list, followed by Exxon (previously third), Google, Berkshire Hathaway, Walmart, General Electric (previously tenth), Microsoft, Chevron, IBM (previously first), and Johnson & Johnson. In 2014, 2 of the top 10 companies remained on this ever-changing list, with IBM going from topping the list to ninth and General Electric moving from tenth to sixth. Two oil companies are on the list. Many of the original 100 companies were absorbed, folded, or moved further down the financial scale and were replaced by newcomers. Apple, Google, Berkshire Hathaway, Walmart, and Johnson & Johnson vaulted into the top 10. Most of the top 100 companies no longer exist in their founding form or are extinct.

Most of the defunct organizations were unable to align themselves with changing business conditions for a variety of reasons. One lesson clearly emerges from these corporate fluctuations. The performance-management processes, including compensation practices, of the declining and defunct organizations were static and failed to sustain them. Successful organizations found ways to consistently reinvent themselves through expanding markets with new and/or improved products or services or expanding their customer base for existing products. For future viability, performance-management processes must be dynamic and focused on continual organization renewal.

This chapter will cover

- Winning compensation strategies for organizational sustainability
- Talent-management strategies that best align with each business strategy
- Alternative compensation strategies and salary administration processes to drive the talent-management strategies necessary to ensure competitive advantage

The critical key human resources issues addressed include

- Sustaining organizational performance
- Implementing total compensation programs that adapt to rapidly changing business and workforce scenarios
- Ensuring that compensation programs create competitive business advantage

## Business Drivers

Four business drivers determine the success of organizations going forward. Organizations must consider *target growth rate*, which is the determined long-term growth rate for successful continuance. Companies that do not grow, even at a small rate, are unsustainable. Second, organizations must consider *strategy*. Strategy is the investments currently made to achieve a targeted growth rate in the future. Next, a *risk profile* must be considered. This is the probability of achieving a targeted growth rate based on the strategic orientation. Ultimately, *culture* is the defining factor. A target culture must take into account the organization's risk orientation and the types of people needed to implement the strategy successfully.

### Targeted Growth Rate

Targeted growth rates both drive strategy and are the result of the strategy. Growth rates affect all aspects of an organization, including the structures and processes required to deliver competitive results and the numbers and types of people who will achieve those results. The faster an organization grows, the greater is the requirement for continual change and fluidity, and consequently, the higher is the ongoing risk of actions and inactions. Alternatives and options are necessary and required in strategy, culture, and compensation. Static organizations ultimately meet their demise. In this chapter, we are assuming growth and viability.

### Strategy

The strategic plan looks forward. The impact of today's strategic compensation decisions will be evidenced in future business performance. It results in the organization's ability to focus, reward, attract, and retain the types of people who will fulfill the strategy. It takes into account business, talent management, and compensation strategies, thereby establishing an operating framework for allocating current investments that will pay off in the future.

## Risk Profile

Winning business strategies are driven by the unique relationship between products/services and the market. When an organization's strategy is based on new markets and new products, the risks to success are at the highest level. Companies frequently operate with several strategies simultaneously. One strategy could be to expand current market revenues by improving on current products/services. Another strategy could be focused on the same customer base but with the objective of increasing revenues through broadening their purchases with new products/new services. A third strategy could be reaching out for new markets but with current products/services. Expanding even further, the strategy could be major growth through both new markets and new products/services. To win in an environment with multiple winning strategies, an organization needs different cultures and alternative rewards systems that align with each risk orientation. Organizations find this very uncomfortable and counter to their historic operating mode. A policy of one size fits all, that most companies adhere to, does not work when hiring, promoting, and rewarding the diverse cultures needed to stay competitive.

Every organization is made up of lots of different people. They are all part of the framework for a successful business. Each winning strategy, however, needs to have a dominant personality type that supports its strategies and risk level. When a company's strategy is growing current markets with current products/services, the main desired type of people could be described as *engineers*—those striving to make products/services better. These people have a low risk orientation. When reaching out to current markets with new products/services, the desired type could be described as *designers*—those with an enhanced orientation. These individuals have a slightly higher risk orientation than engineers. When new markets and current products/services are the strategy, *architects*—those with an enriched orientation—are the desired type. Here the ideal employees require a greater tendency for risk acceptance. However, when the risk orientation is at its greatest with a strategy of new markets and new products/services, the dominant people type necessary can be described as *innovators*—people with entrepreneurial leaning in accepting personal and business risk. When the organization's talent-management systems, including compensation, are not geared to building and/or sustaining one or more of these cultural orientations, winning becomes impossible. Things can be even worse when growth rates and strategies shift, and the organization's culture is unwilling or unable to adapt to a new risk profile. Before discussing alternative compensation strategies, an understanding of the target cultures associated with each risk profile is helpful.

## Culture

Culture is an organization's personality. It evolves from the shared knowledge, experience, emotions, beliefs, values, attitudes, meanings, and concepts that are developed, acquired, and transmitted by the people in the organization. Culture determines whether business strategies will be supported, at what risk level, and what rewards systems will work. Culture is shaped in three ways:

- Tacit covenants are the heart of culture. These include unwritten rules, taboos, organizational politics, and personal and group ethics that are felt but not observable.

- Recognizable reality includes behaviors; facilities; dress codes; people interactions; those hired, promoted, and terminated; and compensation practices.

- Explicit principles establish the way organizations control behavior and the tacit covenants. Examples are the mission, vision, institutional competencies, written and verbalized goals, procedures, policies, processes, and methods; credos are the basis for organizational conscience. Explicit principles establish the expectations that shape the culture. Talent-management systems are among the most important organizational guidelines, and compensation is one of the most important elements of talent management.

Only cultures that are aligned with a corresponding strategic orientation will drive business success. There is a different cultural context and an alternative compensation alignment for each business scenario.

*Target Cultures.* Different target cultures require different compensation strategies. The target culture aligns with the winning strategies and risk profiles mentioned earlier and described here (Figure 4.1). The hypothetical engineer is *risk accepting and change cautious*, highly pragmatic and efficient, flexible, and directive, participative, and collaborative. The designer has most of the characteristics of the engineer but is *risk oriented and change responsive* and less pragmatic and efficient. The architect is *risk and change seeking*, innovative, progressive, adaptive, and also participative and collaborative. The innovator is *risk craving and change driving* and creative, opportunistic, venturesome, highly adaptive, participative, and collaborative. The organization's talent-management system, and most important, its compensation component, needs to take a lead role in driving the creation and maintenance of the appropriate culture.

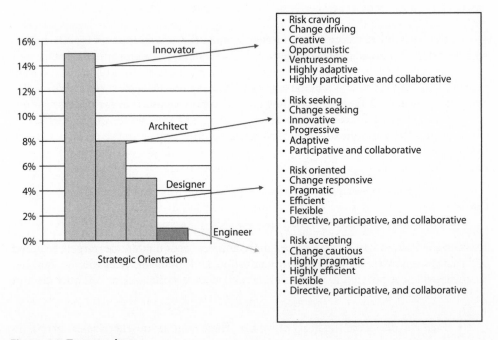

**Figure 4.1 Target cultures.**

*Talent Management.* Talent management shapes the target culture. It is the proactive management of all the processes needed to mold an organization culture that is aligned with its personality profile—the engineers, designers, architects, and innovators. Talent management consists of the following components:

- A *creed* is a statement of the organization's expectations—the explicit principles, institutional competencies, core values, and individual style for its employees—and it includes its pay approach. The creed is based on a strategic orientation and the organization's ethics and values. The creed tells people what to expect from an organization and what the organization expects from its people. The creed ultimately gets translated into a compensation policy.

- A strategy for hiring, developing, advancing, rewarding, and retaining people who fit the creed. The dictates of the creed are integrated into all assessment and implementation programs in the form of selection, promotion, development, and compensation processes.

- A system for implementing all processes needed to realize the strategy that includes investment in training, rewards, education, assignments, and development.

- A process for aligning compensation programs with the talent-management process.

Each culture personality must be translated into a talent strategy: people are assessed by that strategy, and investments are made in individuals who have the greatest value to the organization. The talent strategy is usually reflected in investments made in employees (including compensation) based on the following illustrative classifications:

- *Superkeepers.* These employees embody the creed and are the transmitters of the winning culture. They have achieved superior results and have developed others who also have achieved superior results. They are about 3 percent of the organization's employees. These employees should receive *a very high investment in compensation,* particularly in long-term compensation, rapid movement through the salary structure, and frequent assignment changes. Total pay should be targeted to the 75th percentile and above in the targeted pay market.

- *Key position keepers.* These are employees in critical positions who exceed expectations, have achievements that exceed expectations, and have developed others. These employees comprise about 15 percent of the talent base. They should receive *high investment in compensation,* special-achievement awards, recognition, and long-term incentives. Total pay should be targeted above the 50th percentile.

- *Solid citizens.* These employees meet the expectations for the targeted cultural requirements and performance and also show initiative in achieving expected results. They should receive *moderate compensation,* with total pay at about the 45th percentile.

The specific definitions of superkeeper, key position keeper, and solid citizen will be different in each of the four culture personas and within each organization's history and unique leadership style. A superkeeper could be an innovator, architect, designer, or engineer depending on the target culture.

## Compensation Strategy

A *compensation strategy* is the investment in employee remuneration needed to catalyze the talent-management strategy. The elements of the compensation component include

- *Affordability.* Every organization must determine the overall level of base pay, also considering benefits, that it can afford to pay in at least two successive years based on its current and projected growth level. From this, it can determine how much it can afford to move the entire pay structure in each of two years. Once base-salary midpoints (salary structure) are determined, the organization can establish the potential funding pools for annual salary increases for variable pay programs.

- *Pay markets.* The organization must determine which pay markets are most relevant to sources of hiring and potential turnover. In short, the organization needs to find surveys with the companies that it recruits from and that potentially pirate its employees. The organization then needs to account for selection and retention in these pay markets within affordable levels. Most likely, there will be multiple salary structures or accommodations in market pricing within a single grade structure for "hot-talent" markets.

- *Competitive level.* Once base-salary affordability and pay markets are assessed, the organization can determine at what levels it can compete in each pay market and what levels of performance-funded pay are necessary to improve overall competitive levels of total pay.

- *Mix.* Once base-pay affordability levels and funded performance pools are established, the entire compensation administration process is adjusted to reflect the mix of fixed to variable pay appropriate to the strategic orientation and targeted pay market.

- *Allocation based on employee classifications.* Within the affordable base-salary levels and funded variable performance pools, compensation is allocated based on the superkeepers, key position keepers, and solid citizens discussed previously. Furthermore, the pay strategies are delimited in terms of the organization's risk orientation, which is dictated by the growth strategy.

The components of pay strategy illustrate the changing mix of pay in each growth environment.

### Pay-Strategy Components

As indicated in Figure 4.2, base contribution to total pay increases as risk level decreases, and long-term incentives increase as a proportion of pay as growth and risk increase. An organization can have more than one pay strategy depending on how many winning business strategies it will be implementing. Within each strategy, pay is allotted to employees based on their contribution or performance level.

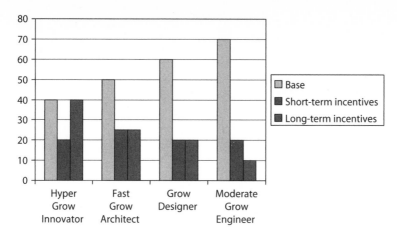

**Figure 4.2 Pay-strategy components.**

## *Keys to Compensation Strategies*

The keys to success for all strategies are affordability, annual funding, and long-term funding (Figure 4.3). Managing compensation alignment by strategic orientation is contingent on recognizing that affordability is the driving component of base pay and that short- and long-term funding (stock, cash, etc.) is grounded in financial achievements within the strategic measurements for each orientation (i.e., hypergrow, fast grow, grow, moderate grow). As long as compensation is affordable, funded by financial results, and driven by measures based on strategic orientation, the chances of success are high, and the risk of layoffs, pay freezes, and other drastic compensation actions is minimized.

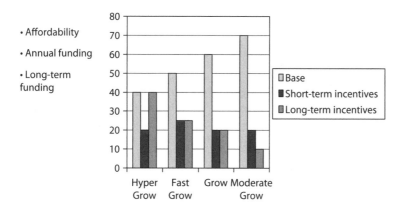

**Figure 4.3 Keys to compensation strategies.**

Significant problems could arise when an organization is forced to transition quickly from, say, a hypergrowth company to a moderate-growth company or, conversely, from a moderate-growth company to a hypergrowth company. Fast changes in risk level associated with quick changes in business priority usually will meet with culture resistance. This situation could be further exacerbated by shifting to a new compensation strategy that is not aligned with the existing culture.

*Variable Pay.* Variable pay does many good things. Since variable pay is distributed only when it is affordable, an organization is protected from making bad strategic decisions based on short-term swings in business situations, and employees are protected against sudden layoffs. It also focuses people on metric-based outcomes tied to funding and shareholder profit protection. Most positively, it molds a culture of achievement by establishing *stated rules* that govern organization personality based on measureable individual and group contributions to organization success.

Figure 4.4 identifies primary variable pay plans that can work in most business situations. The Xs indicate where we have found the stated incentives to work best in each of the cultures.

| Culture/Variable Pay | Innovator | Architect | Designer | Engineer |
|---|---|---|---|---|
| Profit sharing | | | X | X |
| Group incentives | | | X | X |
| Individual incentives | X | X | X | X |
| Long-term | X | X | X | |
| Combination | X | X | X | X |

**Figure 4.4 Variable pay: top culture-driving programs.**

*Merit Pay.* Historically, merit pay has been a permanent increase in an employee's base salary rooted in evaluated performance. It is individually driven and permanent and clearly distinguishable from annual and long-term incentives, which are variable. Moreover, it is not frozen into the employee's base pay and ideally is funded by a metric-based organization or individual achievement. The amount of merit increases and their timing typically consider the employee's performance and position in the salary range and, frequently, tenure in the organization. The idea is to move people differentially to a competitive-pay market position at a rate commensurate with their performance and acquisition of competitive competency levels. Simply, the better you demonstrate achievement, the quicker you reach the competitive rate. It is all contingent on the notion of internal and external equity, the ability to measure performance, the capacity to actually get good market data, and having a sound pay strategy in place. In the case of most merit increase programs, there is a gap between the goal and the reality of the implementation.

In reality, most people are dissatisfied with merit pay, but organizations continue to use it. There are multiple reasons, including

- *Poor performance standards and systems.* Typically, they are not well connected to the organization's strategy, annual plan, or even the boss's performance standards.

- *Inability to differentiate performance levels between people, particularly in staff positions.* It is difficult to assess the roughly 67 percent of employees in the middle of the bell curve.

- *Either unwillingness or inability of the boss to apply standards.* Bosses typically have little or no training in assessing people and are reluctant to "play God."

- *Low trust in both the organization and leadership.* Usually this is a result of poor use of merit programs.

- *Merit amounts are typically below the thresholds necessary to motivate.* Often they are too low to even be viewed as a financial reward.

## An Alternative to Merit Pay

We are proposing that there is an alternative to merit pay. We suggest separating the market pay adjustment from the performance adjustment and introducing achievement awards. In this approach, the compensation philosophy is to provide employees with a level and form of compensation that is fairly administered and equitable across the organization, recognizes at least solid citizenship, and is affordable. Everyone who at least meets performance expectations will get an affordable salary increase if they are below the strategic midpoint. Annual salary progressions are based on range position (see left box in Figure 4.5). Base salary increases are determined solely by position in the range, as reflected in the compa-ratio or the ratio of base pay to the market value determined by the pay strategy.

| | |
|---|---|
| • CR < 80% = 5.0%<br><br>• CR < 80% and < 90% = 3.0%<br><br>• CR > 90% and < 100% = 2.0%<br><br>• CR > 100% and <110% = 1.0%<br><br>• CR >110% = 0% | • All fixed salary increases based on "meeting expectations"<br><br>• Salary progressions based on range position<br><br>• Achievement pool reserved for "true" top 20%<br><br>• Meaningful achievement increases (10%) |

**Figure 4.5  Alternative to merit pay.**

Achievement pools are reserved for rewarding the "true" top 20 percent, with their achievements rationalized through peer and supervisory review boards and payment in a lump sum annually. Supervisors submit applications to support recommendations, and a fixed number of employees are selected for increase depending on the pool of available funds. A meaningful achievement increase of at least 10 percent should get an employee's attention.

*Recommendations*

- Construct a clear compensation strategy based on the organization's business and talent-management strategies.

- Determine the affordability level of fixed base salaries based on profit projections for at least the next two to three years.

- Contingent on affordability, determine the competitive level of base pay in your pay markets.

- Position compa-ratios for nonstrategic groups at 5 percent below affordable mid-points. This will create a suitably sized pool for achievement increases for super-keepers and keepers.

- Reward solid citizens based on compa-ratio.

- Eliminate fixed merit increases. Based on affordability, shift to variable lump-sum achievement awards for no more than 20 percent of the workforce.

- Introduce funded long-term incentives (e.g., stock, cash, etc.) that are performance driven to as many employees as possible. Again, affordable funding must be assessed.

Everything is contingent on aligning the right strategic risk profiles with the right processes. You will move from establishing risk profiles, to creating and implementing your strategic talent-management plan, to developing and implementing compensation strategies. The ultimate goal is to shape the culture that will drive a competitive strategy for the organization.

# Excelling as a Compensation Professional

Brian Moore
*WorldatWork*

Sue Holloway
*WorldatWork*

Compensation professionals must balance the organizational needs of today and in the future with the ways employees are and will be compensated for their contributions. Along with determining compensation, today's professionals also must consider the effects that their recommendations and decisions will have on attraction, motivation, engagement, and retention of their workforces. While this has never been an easy proposition, many factors make this more complicated today (see the sidebar entitled, "The Complicated Context of Compensation").

## The Complicated Context of Compensation

Many factors lend credence to the notion that connecting to the business is increasingly complicated for compensation professionals. The goals of the business have become a moving target, making it more difficult for compensation professionals to attract, motivate, and engage a workforce that now must be nimble enough to respond to rapidly changing priorities. The increasing pace of change in organizations is evident based on the rate of churn in lists of large companies, specifically those on the Standard and Poor's Index. From new competitors quickly becoming large corporations to mergers, acquisitions, and epic failures, this rate of churn is merely one indicator of growing business competition and complexity (Kaplan and Foster, 2001).

Additionally, both the nature of work itself and the composition of the workforce are changing. Specific to the nature of work, a growing share of all work involves activities that information workers perform that draw heavily on their creativity and judgment (tacit interactions). The growth in this type of work has particular implications for compensation professionals in terms of harder-to-monitor and harder-to-measure activities and longer-term objectives (Beardsley, Johnson, and Manyika, 2006).

Specific to the composition of the workforce, in the United States, the younger share of the workforce (generation Y or millennials) is larger than any other generation has been since the baby boomers started their careers. These younger workers make up a larger share of overall turnover in organizations. Based on this information, one may conclude that younger workers are less loyal and, further, that this is some sort of new generation Y phenomenon.

However, in investigating more deeply, the median job tenure for males aged 25 to 34 years is essentially flat.[*] The difference in the makeup of the workforce is that the larger share of *all workers* is in this lowest-tenured category. Also, the median job tenure for males aged 55 to 64 years is down considerably from its peak in 1983. These factors indicate the likely reality of a less-tenured workforce (Copeland, 2012). Also, growth in temporary and part-time employment[†] and the majority of job creation in the United States being at lower income levels both play a role in the ongoing challenge of attraction, motivation, and retention.

Add to this list the usual suspects of globalization, technology, legislation, and regulation, and it is evident that both the compensation profession and compensation professionals are facing broader challenges today than have been seen in the past.

[*] Comparison of long-term labor-force data for females is complicated by large increases in the rate of women participating in the labor force since the 1950s.
[†] In part, cyclic responses to the Great Recession but as of this writing showing signs of persisting as the "new normal."

The need for the compensation function to connect with the business is not necessarily more important today than it has been at any other time in the past. Most human resources (HR) professionals agree that human resources and employee rewards strategies should be based on the organization's business strategy. However, to be able to connect total rewards strategy and practice to business strategy, today's professionals must understand the business.

In fact, in 2013, this critical need for compensation professionals to understand the business was made clear when *business acumen* was resoundingly considered the top factor most valued when hiring new HR talent (Korn Ferry Institute, 2013). It also is true that experience in compensation and benefits is increasingly common among holders of top HR positions in Fortune 100 companies (up from about one-quarter to one-third between 1999 and 2009) (Cappelli and Yang, 2010).

Clearly, the compensation professional is a key connection between an increasingly complex business environment and the organizational outcomes driven by employee attraction, motivation, engagement, and retention. How are compensation professionals to progress toward this ideal role?

Technical competence not only remains an essential component for today's professionals, but it also has grown in breadth and depth itself (see the sidebar entitled, "The

## The Expanding Body of Knowledge in Compensation

Professional training and technical skill in compensation are essential building blocks for growth in the profession, and the idea of a common core of technical knowledge in compensation is, in fact, supported by a defined and widely accepted body of knowledge. The concepts, terms, and activities that comprise this body of knowledge for the compensation profession include such elements as

- Designing and administering base pay programs
- Designing and administering variable pay programs
- Integrating compensation programs with business strategy
- Complying with legal and regulatory requirements
- Communicating compensation information
- Designing and administering other total rewards programs

In recent years, the body of knowledge has expanded in response to increased specialization and complexity. The depth and breadth of the profession has changed and deepened over time, as evidenced by the specialities in sales compensation and executive compensation, both of which now have professional certifications offered through WorldatWork's Society of Certified Professionals.

Expanding Body of Knowledge in Compensation"). However, a broader view of what excellent contributors know and do at work will expedite the advancement of professionals.

## The Next-Generation Professional: Beyond Technical Knowledge

As compensation professionals continue to be challenged in areas such as legal complexity, growing research and understanding of human motivation, and navigating an increasingly complex and diverse workforce, HR and compensation leaders are constantly seeking to anticipate and identify the skills and knowledge that will take the profession into the future. In his book, *Average Is Over: Powering America Beyond the Age of the Great Stagnation*, economist Tyler Cowen (2013) wrote of an increasing share of the labor-income pie going to individuals whose skills are complementary to computers. Indeed, Cowen's findings align with a growing need for so-called soft skills among compensation practitioners. The idea of today's (and tomorrow's) compensation professionals being internal consultants who are able to answer the question of how their skills complement new and improved technological tools is among the key challenges of the day.

The "WorldatWork 2012 Total Rewards Professionals' Career Census" (WorldatWork, 2012b) of 2,300 human resources professionals in compensation, benefits, and work-life revealed eight key differentiators of top total rewards performers. These key focus areas were identified to move the profession forward and create a broad view of success factors for top performers in total rewards broadly. One of the eight differentiators is technical mastery of the skills and body of knowledge (see Figure 5.1). But fluent command of specialized skills to practice compensation is not a sufficient differentiator in and of itself. Technical mastery is considered to be table stakes, or the minimum requirement. It is the

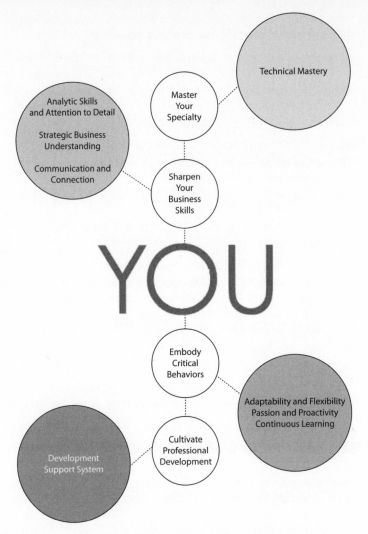

**Figure 5.1 WorldatWork career excellence model for total rewards professionals.**

*Source:* WorldatWork, 2012.

foundation, but seven other differentiators—the soft skills—are what propel a technically competent compensation professional to higher levels of performance.

### Differentiator 1: Strategic Business Understanding

Whereas having a total rewards strategy plus policies and programs that support the larger organizational or business strategy is implicit, there is a common refrain from compensation leaders that seems to get at something bigger: the expectation that the highest-performing employee will understand the business well enough to be a significant contributor to business success. This is about the issues the organization faces not only today but also in the future. In a nutshell, it is the ability to see the big picture.[1] This differentiator includes the need for high performers to successfully prioritize and to exercise the strategic use of resources in the context of what is most important to the business. The ideal state for professionals embodies business acumen that reflects

- Understanding of how the organization works financially
- Literacy in key accounting terms and financial statements
- Knowledge of the customer and client base
- Focus on key business objectives and performance measures
- Acute awareness of the local, regional, national, and global organizations that the business competes with for talent
- Connection of functional decisions with their effect on the business as a whole

### Differentiator 2: Analytical Skills and Attention to Detail

Top performers use experience and information to visualize, articulate, and analyze data, problems, and concepts. This ability results in making skillful decisions that guide future actions. Working beyond technical analysis, top performers

- Reframe problems across multiple perspectives and mental models to produce new insights and options
- Know what to measure and how
- Are able to simplify complex processes

With the vast amounts of employee and quantitative data that compensation professionals often analyze and the high stakes/difficult-to-undo implications of their work, a keen attention to detail is imperative.

### Differentiator 3: Communication and Connection

Connecting with other people is one part of building strong communication channels. Professionals must deal comfortably with individuals at all levels, including senior executives, to understand how they think and process in order to craft an appropriate and effective approach. In peer relationships, the goal is to be able to quickly find common ground, represent your own interests, and still be fair and cooperative.

The evolving professional must do more than just share technical information. He or she must be armed with the ability to tell the story in a way that is meaningful to the audience. In some situations, influence and persuasion might be paramount whereas, in other situations, *communicating* is as simple as being understood. Specific applications of communication and connection can vary substantially, but at the core is the notion that "it's not what you say, it's what they hear."

### Differentiator 4: Adaptability and Flexibility

Today's breakneck speed of changing business priorities is logically an important driver behind the acute need for a compensation professional to be adaptable and flexible. Adaptability is the ability to adjust to new or changing circumstances and implies versatility and resilience in the face of shifting situations and priorities. Flexibility is the ability to bend without breaking: be open to new ideas and situations and be able to adjust, but not be pliant to the point of being ineffectual.

Most jobs—and increasingly as one's career progresses to higher-level roles—require the ability to deal with ambiguity and easily shift gears, even without having all the information. It means being able to make decisions and act on them while remaining calm in the face of the unexpected. Composure is a hallmark of this behavior; humor is used to ease tense situations, and risk and uncertainty are accepted as the price of doing business.

### Differentiator 5: Passion and Proactivity

Passion for one's work implies an ability to sustain enthusiasm and reject cynicism. Top performers savor challenges and pursue new opportunities with energy and drive, even in the face of resistance or reversals.

Proactivity assumes an active role in accomplishing objectives. Top performers take the initiative rather than simply reacting to whatever happens. Personal responsibility for projects and decisions is a given; top performers like taking charge of problems or issues, and others count on them to persevere until the goal is accomplished. Setting priorities and strong planning skills help these performers to set objectives and goals as well as anticipate and adjust to problems and obstructions.

### Differentiator 6: Continuous Learning

Top performers are versatile and regularly expand their knowledge when it comes to learning. These professionals take advantage of any opportunity, enjoy the challenge of unfamiliar tasks, and are personally committed to continuously improving themselves. From an employer's perspective, mentoring and coaching relationships should be consciously cultivated and challenging assignments encouraged.

One of the most persuasive findings in Robert E. Kelley's (1999) business classic, *How to Be a Star at Work: 9 Breakthrough Strategies You Need to Succeed*, is that a key trait that sets high performers apart is how they leverage the opportunities they receive. Kelley addresses the ability to take advantage of learning opportunities with the idea that the stars at work are both prepared for and ready to excel in all activities presented—even those seemingly menial tasks. There are far more activities that *can be* leveraged into development opportunities than *actually are* leveraged. And stars at work find ways to get more out of each task or opportunity.[2]

### Differentiator 7: Development Support System

Relatedly, the most effective professionals are conscious of the need to build and cultivate a development support system. This reflects an initiative to create individual development plans as well as being adept at marshalling resources—whether people, funding, or support—to achieve development goals. Formal training, on-the-job opportunities, a mentor relationship, and peer relationships all offer opportunities for top performers to cultivate an environment in which ongoing development is the highest priority.

Management support and opportunities were mentioned prominently among study participants in the "WorldatWork 2012 Total Rewards Professionals' Career Census" (WorldatWork, 2012b). Some comments even implied that the opportunity to perform was all that was missing for some average performers to improve. Almost certainly true in some cases, it is important to understand that supervisors and senior leaders are putting their own reputations on the line when they provide opportunities for their employees to shine.[3]

Formal internal mentoring programs were mentioned infrequently by respondents, but it is important to recognize that mentors are not necessarily "assigned," nor must they work at the organization of the protégé to be helpful.

## Application of Key Differentiators

This book is full of powerful context and perspectives on the key challenges facing the compensation profession in the future by many of the most respected thought leaders in the field. However, not everyone is willing to put forth the extra effort it takes to turn to a tool like this volume to expand their horizons. For those who choose to make the effort, we hope and expect it to be a valuable journey.

And this journey begins with the understanding that, perhaps with the exception of passion and proactivity, the elements of the career excellence model have a contextual dimension that is obvious on its face but often is manifested as knowledge of how something is done in some *other* context. Professionals must be able to connect those dots in the current situation.

## Looking Ahead

The landscape in which organizations conduct business is more complicated and demanding than it has ever been. In that light, business leadership requires a consultative partnership from compensation professionals. The future is bright for professionals who become key partners in their organizations and are able to apply a broad toolkit to the most pressing problems.

## References

Beardsley, Scott C., Bradford C. Johnson, and James M. Manyika. May 2006. "Competitive Advantage from Better Interactions." *McKinsey Quarterly*.

Cappelli, Peter, and Yang Yang. 2010. "Who Gets the Top Job? Changes in Attributes of Human Resource Heads and Implications for the Future." PricewaterhouseCoopers, New York.

Copeland, Craig. 2012. "Employee Tenure Trends, 1983–2012." *Notes*. Employee Benefit Research Institute, Washington, DC.

Cowen, Tyler. 2013. *Average Is Over: Powering America Beyond the Age of the Great Stagnation*. Dutton Adult, New York.

Kaplan, Sarah, and Richard N. Foster. 2001. *Creative Destruction: Why Companies That Are Built to Last Underperform the Market—And How to Successfully Transform Them*. Currency/Doubleday, New York.

Kelley, Robert E. 1999. *How to Be a Star at Work: 9 Breakthrough Strategies You Need to Succeed*. Crown Business, New York.

Korn Ferry Institute. 2013. "2013 CHRO Pulse Survey." Los Angeles, CA.

Peters, Tom. 1999. *The Project 50 (Reinventing Work): Fifty Ways to Transform Every "Task" into a Project That Matters!* Knopf, New York.

WorldatWork. 2012a. "The Evolving Compensation Function." Scottsdale, AZ.

WorldatWork. 2012b. "WorldatWork 2012 Total Rewards Professionals' Career Census." Scottsdale, AZ. Available at: http://www.worldatwork.org/waw/Content/research/html/tr-professionals-census.html.

WorldatWork. 2012c. "WorldatWork Career Excellence Model for Total Rewards Professionals." Scottsdale, AZ. Available at: http://www.worldatwork.org/waw/careerexcellence/index.jsp.

WorldatWork and Mercer. 2012. "2012 Metrics and Analytics: Patterns of Use and Value." Scottsdale, AZ.

## Additional Resources

Boudreau, John W., and Peter M. Ramstad. 2007. *Beyond HR: The New Science of Human Capital*. Harvard Business Review Press, Boston.

Boudreau, John W., and Wayne F. Cascio. 2008. *Investing in People: Financial Impact of Human Resource Initiatives*. FT Press, Upper Saddle River, NJ.

Schirm, John, and Eric Schaffer. June 2011. Interview by Alison Avalos. "Using Statistical Research to Change Compensation Strategy at Google," Part 2. workspanTV, WorldatWork, Scottsdale, AZ.

Wagner, Frank H., and Monica Patel Davis. June 2011. Interview by Marcia Rhodes. "Using Statistical Research to Change Compensation Strategy at Google," Part 1. workspanTV, WorldatWork, Scottsdale, AZ.

## Notes

1. See also the discussion under the heading of "Differentiator 3: Communication and Connection" for more on how things like "knowing who knows" (as Robert E. Kelley typology refers to knowledge networks) factor into high performers' understanding of their organizations and where they can make the most impact.

2. In *The Project 50 (Reinventing Work): Fifty Ways to Transform Every "Task" into a Project That Matters!*, author Tom Peters (1999) made similar points, specifically calling for individuals to mentally transform their department at work into a professional service firm and approach all assigned projects with a specific eye toward learning. As Peters said, "[E]very project can be formulated to have an R&D component ... some intriguing hypothesis to be tested. ... Life is too short to suffer non-learning experiences."

3. In *How to Be a Star at Work: 9 Breakthrough Strategies You Need to Succeed*, Kelley (1999) asserts that nonstars frequently view being asked to present at an important meeting as what sets the stars apart—without much acknowledgment of all the things that might have happened along the way to make that particular employee the one chosen by senior leaders to present.

# Emerging Compensation Issues

JOSEPH J. MARTOCCHIO, PH.D.

*School of Labor and Employment Relations, University of Illinois at Urbana-Champaign*

*I felt like I was an arrow, pulled back and ready to be launched into something big.*

—A. B. SHEPHERD, LIFEBOAT[1]

Compensation professionals continually manage current challenges, and they anticipate how they will approach new ones. A. B. Shepherd's quote can be applied to the world of compensation professionals, in which they must stand ready to engage in understanding and take action. This chapter identifies three issues that define some of the challenges facing compensation professionals in a rapidly changing business environment:

- Ripple effects of the Great Recession
- Anticipation of possible changes to the Fair Labor Standards Act
- Influence of rising wages in China

The goal is to offer a brief discussion of each and to advance reasonable conjectures about how these issues may influence compensation practice.

## Ripple Effects of the Great Recession

The U.S. economy experienced an economic recession from December 2007 through June 2009. The term *Great Recession* is widely used to describe the significance of this recession. It was the longest recession since World War II, lasting 19 months. Although the recession ended a few years ago, its effects still remain evident in employment activity in general and compensation in particular. This section provides a brief review of the definition of an economic recession and its relevance to a pressing matter—the compensation–productivity gap.

## The Great Recession

*Economic recession* refers to a general slowdown in economic activity. Evidence of economic recessions include reduced gross domestic product (GDP) and increased unemployment rates. Multiple complex factors lead to recessions. Reduced consumer spending is among the primary causes of economic recessions. Consumers' demand for products and services, particularly big-ticket items such as automobiles and homes, declines. For example, automobile manufacturers, among them General Motors and Chrysler, respond to lower consumer demand for their products by cutting production levels in order to avoid excess inventory.

Recessionary forces create a domino effect that disrupts business activity and employment throughout an industry's supply chain. For example, in the automobile manufacturing industry, supply chains of vehicle components (e.g., dashboards, windshields, etc.) are disrupted because production slows down. Reduced production adversely affects other companies' operations. Hundreds of companies alone supply components to automobile makers. Layoffs occur in these companies as well as in the automobile manufacturing companies.

## The Compensation–Productivity Gap

The gap between real hourly compensation and labor productivity indicates whether workers' pay is keeping up with productivity. The pervasive concern is that real compensation falls short of productivity gains notwithstanding increases in nominal pay. Real hourly compensation measures the purchasing power of a dollar, whereas nominal hourly compensation is the face value of a dollar. Figure 6.1 shows this trend for the period 2007–2011, which straddles the period of the Great Recession. Increases in the costs of goods and services cause nominal pay to be less than real pay, which further complicates the problems discussed earlier. Quite simply, employees as consumers have less money to spend on essential items such as housing and discretionary items such as leisure and entertainment.

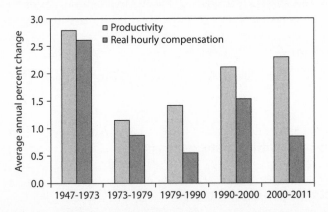

**Figure 6.1  Trends in productivity and real hourly compensation growth, 2007–2011.**

*Source:* U.S. Bureau of Labor Statistics.

Productivity growth promotes rising living standards in the following manner: increases in productivity growth indicate companies' investments in capital equipment and information technology. Examples of capital equipment include new manufacturing facilities, research and development (R&D) laboratories, and sales distribution centers. Examples of information technology (IT) include structured databases containing expert information to help end users make informed decisions in complex situations. For instance, physicians may access databases to help them diagnose health conditions based on patients' symptoms and health histories. Another example occurs in the marketing field, where information systems enable companies to identify customers for new products and services based on a variety of factors including household income and purchase history.

Since the 1970s, real hourly compensation has lagged behind labor productivity growth.[2] The growth of productivity and real hourly compensation in the nonfarm business sector (which accounts for three-fourths of output and employment in the total U.S. economy) was comparable until 1973. The annual change in productivity averaged 2.8 percent and real hourly compensation growth averaged 2.6 percent during the 1947–1973 period. In 1973–1979, the annual averages were at 1.1 and 0.9 percent, respectively. Real hourly compensation growth failed to keep pace with accelerating productivity growth over the past three decades, and the gap between productivity growth and compensation growth widened. During the 2000–2011 period, average annual growth in productivity and real compensation equaled 3.3 and 1.0 percent, respectively.

For the 18-month period following each recession after World War II, companies experienced increases in productivity each time, but the gain in real compensation was substantially less. Most noteworthy is the difference between increases in real compensation relative to increases in productivity since the end of the Great Recession, which is much more substantial than in any of the prior recessions.

There are two reasons that may explain the compensation–productivity gap. First, high unemployment following recessions leaves employees with relatively lower power to bargain for higher pay because the supply of individuals seeking work is greater than the companys' demand for new workers. Second, most companies experience profit losses during economic recessions, and then, profits generally increase following recessions. Companies promote profits, in part, by holding down employees' pay.

Often companies respond to lower demand through significant layoffs of employees. Among the economic reasons for extended mass layoffs, events related to seasonal factors accounted for 39 percent of related separations during the first quarter of 2013.[3] Over the year, the largest decrease in separations occurred in layoffs due to business-demand reasons such as in this example. The number of layoff events along with separations and initial claimants rose dramatically during the recession and began decreasing following the recession, although the numbers following the recession remain substantially higher than prior to the recession.[4]

## Anticipation of Possible Changes to the Fair Labor Standards Act

The Fair Labor Standards Act of 1938 contains three major provisions, including minimum wage, overtime pay, and child labor. In 2013 and 2014, the first two provisions were brought to the national stage, causing great consternation within companies, particularly in small companies.

### Minimum Wage

The amount of the minimum wage has changed several times since it was first introduced in 1938. Most recently, this wage was raised from $6.55 to $7.25 per hour in 2009. In 2013, President Barack Obama called for an increase in the hourly federal minimum wage from $7.25 to $10.10 by 2016, only to be struck down by the U.S. Senate in early 2014. Even though the federal and some state governments raise the minimum wage from time to time, President Obama has argued that most workers who earn the minimum wage find that it is insufficient for them to afford the basic necessities. In the summer of 2013, fast-food workers across the United States walked off their jobs to protest what they believe to be insufficient pay.

Nearly half the states plus the District of Columbia have enacted minimum-wage laws throughout the years, and several more states are debating the issue in their legislatures. Recently, some states have passed provisions to increase the minimum wage, including Maryland, Minnesota, Delaware, West Virginia, and Hawaii. Three of these states will make substantial increases to their minimum-wage rates. In 2015, Maryland's minimum wage was raised to $8.25 in increments until it reaches $10.10 by 2018. Minnesota's minimum wage is increasing to $9.50 by 2016, and beginning in 2018, the wage will be indexed to inflation. Until this change, Minnesota's minimum wage was set to the federal level. In Hawaii, legislators approved a four-step hike from the state's current wage floor of $7.25 to $10.10 by 2018.

Within some cities and states, pushes for higher local minimum-wage rates have taken hold. For example, in Los Angeles, unions are lobbying for a minimum-wage rate for hotel workers—the lowest paid in the city—to $15.37. If successful, concerns about layoffs could arise. However, one study found that municipalities with higher pay did not suffer job losses among low-wage restaurant workers.[5] This study also found that restaurants often instituted modest price increases to avoid layoffs. And higher wages often resulted in lower turnover, which can be attributed to higher wages.

Not all economists believe that raising the minimum wage will be harmless to the overall economy. Many argue that increasing the minimum wage will have negative ripple effects throughout the U.S. economy. These arguments are based on the economic principles of supply and demand. In this context, raising the minimum wage could lead to increases in the price of goods and services as companies try to offset some or all of higher labor costs. As the prices of goods and services increase, consumers are more likely to buy less. In turn, reduced demand for products and services stands to cut into profits, which may lead to cost reductions in the form of layoffs rather than further price increases.

Much scholarly research supports this conclusion. An exhaustive review of recent research concluded that approximately 85 percent of minimum-wage studies provide strong evidence of negative employment effects resulting from minimum-wage laws.[6] However, a recent study by the Congressional Budget Office indicates mixed outcomes. On the one hand, an increase in the minimum-wage rate to $10.10 likely would lead to the loss of 500,000 low-skilled jobs. On the other hand, raising the minimium would raise the pay of nearly 1 million workers to above the federal poverty levels.[7] Some of the loss in labor would be offset by lower-cost automation. In the fast-food industry, for example, labor-cost-saving alternatives include online ordering and touch-screen kiosks.

Notwithstanding these broader dyanmics, compensation professionals face the challenge of managing pay inequities between a company's employees who are distributed across municipality or state lines where minimum-wage rates differ. In addition, rising minimum-wage rates stand to compress pay structures that include minimum-wage jobs. Compression in this context occurs when a higher minimum-wage rate boosts the pay-range minimum rate. Unless all the pay rates are increased commensurately, the reduced pay differences effectively understate the relative value of higher-paying jobs, creating opportunities for more highly paid employees to feel pay inequity.

Compensation professionals also face the challenge of planning budgets. Dozens of states are considering possible increases to their minimum-wage rates. Political debates, business and labor lobbying efforts, and politicians' interest in boosting reelection chances create uncertainty about whether minimum-wage rates will increase and, if increased, by what amount.

Finally, increases in the minimum wage force companies to reconsider their total compensation offerings. Mandated higher wage costs are not necessarily accompanied by increased total compensation budgets. It is possible that compensation professionals will have to eliminate or reduce the level of some benefits offerings. For example, a company could choose to offset the cost of a higher minimum wage by eliminating a tuition reimbursement benefit.

### Overtime Pay Protections

In 2014, President Obama announced his intention to amend an element of the overtime pay regulations that pertains to the weekly pay or annual salary amount below which a salaried employee is entitled to receive overtime pay. In 2004, the U.S. Department of Labor fairpay rules set the amounts to $455 weekly (or $23,660 annually). To qualify for the white-collar exemption, employees must be paid at least $455 per week on a salary basis, and their job duties must meet specific tests. In general, their duties must include managing a part of the enterprise and supervising other employees or exercising independent judgment on significant matters or requiring advanced knowledge. Job titles do not determine whether employees are exempt from the overtime requirement.

Although the president did not specify a new threshold, widespread speculation suggests that the new salary criterion would approximately double to nearly $970 weekly (or $50,440 annually). It is believed that part of the reason for President Obama's request is pressure from California and New York, which already have salary threshholds that are higher than the federal level. California and New York State recently began raising the salary threshold for overtime exemption to $800 and $675 weekly, respectively, by 2016. If the federal rules were to change, it is expected that at least 10 million employees will benefit.[8]

In principle, raising the overtime pay threshold could create an economic advantage for employees and companies. If millions of additional workers qualify and earn overtime pay, perhaps discretionary incomes will rise, encouraging higher spending. In turn, some companies could benefit through higher revenue, assuming that any price increases put in place to compensate for higher overtime payroll costs are minimal.

However, it is possible that making more employees eligible for overtime pay may have an unintended consequence. Raising the threshold does not necessarily equate with a pay increase. Moving millions to qualify for overtime pay, however, may place these workers at a disadvantage. For example, it is possible that employers likely would require managers to schedule more cautiously to avoid higher payroll costs.

Another unintended consequence pertains to workplace culture. Higher overtime pay thresholds may undermine cultures characterized by trust. Employers may require that managers and supervisors increase monitoring of nonexempt employees through greater observation and review than usually would be the case.

In reality, it is difficult to predict how employers would respond to a higher federal threshold and how this increase might influence compensation practice. Nevertheless, some changes are within the realm of possibility. It is possible that employers will choose not to modify their hiring plans or not to backfill jobs that are subsequently vacated. Rather, compensation professionals could adjust (lower) base pay for newly hired employees in anticipation of bearing greater overtime pay expenses. Unless under a collective-bargaining agreement or an individual's employment contract, employers could choose to lower current employees' base pay. This choice does not come without risk. Well-qualified and high performers, who stand to have good job alternatives elsewhere, may leave. Alternatively, employers may adjust to higher thresholds through additional job creation. If planned and executed carefully, employers could avoid the need for employees to work on an overtime pay basis. Compensation professionals then would analyze patterns of past overtime work activity and the costs based on the current pay structure as well as the current and proposed overtime pay thresholds.

Finally, compensation professionals could identify which employees possess job duties that fit exemption criteria and whose base pay is within close proximity to the higher overtime pay threshold. To the extent that these employees generate substantial overtime pay costs, it may be worthwhile to consider pay increase awards that just exceed the higher threshold if and only if the cost savings are substantial.

Responding to overtime pay changes could create a competitive disadvantage, particularly where starting base pay is lowered, because not all employers will follow suit. In any circumstance, compensation professionals must take care not to propose policy changes that would lead to an adverse impact or to create grave pay inequities across the pay structure. Lowering base pay could be difficult for other reasons. As discussed earlier, President Obama is committed to raising the federal minimum-wage level, we have already seen upward movement at the state level, and many additional states are debating future increases. Lowering base pay today may pose a challenge in which such changes may inadvertently set base pay below newly instituted higher minimum-wage standards.

## Influence of Rising Wages in China

In recent decades, many U.S. companies relocated manufacturing facilities from the United States to other countries such as the People's Republic of China because the cost of labor was substantially lower there than in the United States. In recent years, the costs of labor in China have been increasing rapidly. Rising costs are quickly reducing the competitive advantage gained from closing manufacturing operations in the United States and reestablishing those operations in China.

Among developing Asian economies, China's average pay rate is highest (versus Indonesia, Philippines, Vietnam, and Bangladesh). In recent years, the Chinese central government has been substantially raising minimum-wage rates, creating pressure throughout the wage structure. Minimum-wage rates recently increased an average of 13 percent across the country's provinces.[9] Widespread news reports suggest that the Chinese government has been planning annual increases in minimum wages at least through 2015.

Chinese policy makers are supportive of increased wages for the following reason: in recent history, the growth in the Chinese economy has been based largely on a trade surplus. That is, the value of goods and services being shipped for sale outside the country exceeds the value of goods and services shipped from other countries to China. Encouraging higher wages promotes domestic consumption, that is, the purchase and use of goods and services within its national borders. Increased domestic consumption will decrease the country's reliance on exports to sustain growth. Reduced reliance on exports is particularly necessary as labor costs within China increase rapidly. As China's labor costs rise, so would the cost of its exports, making the country less competitive in the global economy.

Labor shortages also have contributed to wage increases in China. These shortages are due, in part, to the rapidly aging Chinese population after 30 years of its one-child policy.

This policy, still in effect, limits most couples to having one child only. The Chinese government implemented the policy to curb population growth in large cities. Economic growth is creating the need for new jobs, but the one-child policy has slowed population growth as intended, vastly reducing the number of young workforce entrants. As a result, this policy has inadvertently contributed to an aging population. The largest segment of the Chinese population is currently in the 35- to 44-year age range, and the 45- to 64-year age segment is expected to decrease by 11 percent through 2050, whereas the 65-year and over segment is expected to increase by 17 percent.[10]

Altogether these factors are contributing to the rise in "reshoring" activities and domestic sourcing. "Reshoring" occurs where previously outsourced personnel and services are being brought back to the United States, and domestic sourcing happens where firms move jobs to lower-cost regions of the United States instead of to other countries.[11] Advocates of "reshoring" believe that manufacturers should calculate the total impact of off-shoring because there are often hidden expenses such as higher costs for travel, packaging, shipping, and inventory.[12] Also, "reshoring" has become a part of recent labor agreements. For instance, a portion of the 2011 labor agreement between Ford Motor Company and the United Auto Workers involved Ford agreeing to "reshore" some work presently being done in Mexico, China, and Japan.

There are additional numerous examples of "reshoring" by American firms. General Electric (GE) is "reshoring" its appliance manufacturing with an investment of about $432 million in its facilities in Kentucky, Tennessee, Alabama, and Indiana. Some of the reasons cited include rising costs due to unfavorable currency exchange rates, transportation, and labor in countries that were once much less expensive.[13] A whole host of companies has chosen to move some or all of their manufacturing back to the United States. Wham-O, a company that makes inexpensive toys, recently announced that it was moving 50 percent of its Frisbee and Hula Hoop production back to the United States from China and Mexico, which will create hundreds of new American jobs.[14] Vaniman Manufacturing, a dental equipment producer that has been off-shoring most of its sheet metal fabrication to China since 2002, is now returning to the United States. NCR Corporation, which has been producing its ATMs in China, India, and Hungary, is returning all its production to a facility in Columbus, Georgia.[15]

On return to the United States, companies typically locate their manufacturing plants in right-to-work states. Twenty-three states, located primarily in the South and West, have adopted such laws. Right-to-work laws prohibit management and unions from entering into agreements requiring union membership as a condition of employment. These laws are state statutes or constitutional provisions that ban the practice of requiring union membership or financial support as a condition of employment. They establish the legal right of employees to decide for themselves whether to join or financially support a union.

U.S. Bureau of Labor Statistics data reveal that weekly wages in the private-sector construction industry (an industry that is highly unionized) are generally lower in right-to-work states. For example, the average weekly pay was $832 in Alabama and $782 in Florida. In Illinois and Massachusetts—non-right-to-work states—average weekly wages were $1,115 and $1,233, respectively.[16]

"Reshoring" activities do not come without challenges. Increasingly, employers recognize a skills gap that has created staffing challenges, in part, because of more complex manufacturing processes that require specialized knowledge and skill sets. Also, while ongoing debates continue about the value of vocational education and the practicality of college education, it is clear that companies must take on this challenge now by providing extensive training opportunities. Compensation professionals may have opportunities to develop skill-based pay programs to set starting base pay lower than the market average that will increase as employees complete essential job training.

## Summary

Compensation professionals face numerous challenges. The focus in this chapter was on the compensation-productivity gap, changes to the Fair Labor Standards Act or minimum-wage increases based on state and municipal laws, and rising wages in China. Each issue is a mix of complex economic, social equity, and demographic dynamics. Each of these challenges will require that compensation professionals anticipate policy and compensation system design features that will serve the interests of shareholders and employees.

## Notes

1. A. B. Shepard, *Lifeboat*. CreateSpace Independent Publishing Platform, June 25, 2013.
2. J. Glaser and S. Sprague, "The Compensation-Productivity Gap: A Visual Essay," *Monthly Labor Review* 134(1):57–69, 2011.
3. U.S. Bureau of Labor Statistics, *Extended Mass Layoffs—First Quarter 2013* (USDL 13-0926), 2013. Available at: www.bls.gov.
4. U.S. Bureau of Labor Statistics, *Mass Layoffs—February 2013* (USDL 13-0479), 2013. Available at: www.bls.gov.
5. A. Dube, T. W. Lester, and M. Reich, "Minimum Wage Effects across State Borders: Estimates Using Contiguous Counties," *Review of Economics and Statistics* 92(4):945–964, 2010.
6. D. Neumark and W. Wascher, "Minimum Wages and Employment: A Review of Evidence from the New Minimum Wage Research," *National Bureau of Economic Research Working Paper 12663*, Cambridge, MA, 2006.
7. Congressional Budget Office, "The Effects of a Minimum-Wage Increase on Employment and Family Income," Publication 4856. Congress of the United States, Washington, DC, 2014.
8. D. Cooper and D. Hall, "Raising the Federal Minimum Wage to $10.10 Would Give Working Families, and the Overall Economy, a Much Needed Boost," EPI Briefing Paper 357. Economic Policy Institute, Washington, DC, 2013.
9. Bloomberg News, "China Wages Seen Jumping in 2014 Amid Shift to Services," January 6, 2014. Available at: www.bloombergnews.com.
10. "China's Achilles Heel," *The Economist*, April 2, 2014. Available at: www.economist.com.
11. U.S. Bureau of Labor Statistics, U.S. Department of Labor, "Industrial Production Managers," *Occupational Outlook Handbook*, 2014–2015 edition. Available at: www.bls.gov/ooh/management/industrial-production-managers.htm.
12. J. Northam, "As Overseas Costs Rise, More U.S. Companies are 'Reshoring,'" *NPR*, January 27, 2014. Available at: www.npr.org.
13. C. Koepfer, "A Look at Total Cost Can Change the View," *Production Machining* 11:6, 2011.
14. B. Powell, "The End of Cheap Labor in China," *Time* 177:1–4, June 27, 2011.
15. "Off-Shoring Comes Full Circle," *Trends Magazine*, January 2012, pp. 25–28.
16. U.S. Bureau of Labor Statistics, *County Employment and Wages* (USDL 14-0433), 2014.

# PART II

# BASE SALARY

# Positioning Salary Structures within the Total Rewards Context

Andrew S. Rosen

*Buck Consultants*

A *salary structure* is the combination of job groupings and salary ranges that make up the foundation of an organization's pay system. On the one hand, it is perhaps the tool most commonly used (and most often taken for granted) for helping organizations build a human resources infrastructure. On the other hand, if crafted carefully and strategically, the salary structure can communicate clearly an organization's cultural values and priorities and serve as a primary building block of a compensation program. Seen in this latter context, the salary structure can be a strong ally in a company's efforts to attract, retain, and energize its workforce. "A 'structure' serves a useful purpose if it helps managers make rational pay decisions that are viewed as fair and competitive by employees, and if the company views it as useful in retaining and rewarding the right people."[1]

Building on this statement, the primary purposes of a salary structure are, in my view, to help ensure that

1. Jobs are positioned properly within the organization and in the context of the marketplace.

2. Individuals are paid fairly and competitively and in a manner consistent with the goals of the organization.

3. People managers and human resources business partners have the tools and the information they need to make effective pay decisions.

All these purposes are essential underpinnings to the effective management of people and their perceptions within organizations. Point 1 says that we think carefully about our jobs and how they are situated internally and relative to the market. Jobs are core building blocks of an organization and the work accomplished in that organization. Understanding (job analysis) and documenting (job descriptions) job content are essential ways to ensure that those building blocks are strong and visible. The structure is the ultimate framework

63

that holds those jobs and, if designed and administered effectively, helps to ensure that (1) jobs are positioned equitably, fairly, and in line with how they are designed (in the context of the work that needs to get done and how that work is configured in terms of job families, job levels, staffing levels/ratios) and (2) pay *opportunities* (not *actual* pay) are fair and competitive.

Points 2 and 3 are really talking about the delivery of pay. The purpose of this chapter is not to focus on salary administration processes such as merit increases, salary adjustments, performance management, and related pay-for-performance decision making but rather to show that a well-designed, clearly communicated structure supported by effective policies (meaning that they reflect the proper balance of ensuring financial controls and providing managers with the tools to reward their people appropriately) will, in fact, facilitate successful pay decision making.

In addition to the critical technical aspects of structure design, it may be helpful to consider the qualitative communication aspects of the design as well. Important organizational infrastructure elements such as job families or categories, career levels, salary grades, salary structures, and pay ranges do, in fact, communicate the values and priorities of the organization, often aside from the actual pay itself. That is, where an individual sits within the organization [e.g., line-job family (sales and operations) versus staff-job family (marketing, human resources), support/technical category versus professional or management, grade 5 versus grade 3, research structure that reflects an 8 percent bump versus core structure that is right at the market, etc.] can tell a very clear story about status of that individual.

We know that different people value different things: some say, "Call me what you want; just pay me the big bucks," whereas others—yes, it's true—would rather have that senior vice president or presidential fellow title or be at that higher career level than receive another $5,000 or $10,000 in pay. I am not suggesting changing designs based on possible responses from individuals or cadres of individuals, but I am suggesting that compensation designers need to fully understand the qualitative impact of new programs/structures before developing and implementing them and hence put in place carefully crafted educational and communication campaigns at all levels of the organization to ensure successful deployment.

The type of salary structure(s) selected must be consistent with the company's compensation strategy and fit within the context of the total compensation program. This choice will be determined within the context of a number of important program design and policy issues, such as the following:

- How much flexibility is needed for managers to be successful at managing, developing, and rewarding their key people? The need for flexibility should be balanced by how much variation the organization can tolerate and/or support in a salary structure.

- Should the organization plan to target pay for each job, job level, and/or employee at the same market level (e.g., at the market median)? To help answer this question, the organization must consider whether there are some areas (e.g., job families, locations) where it must pay at higher levels to recruit and retain higher-caliber employees and/or workers who are uniquely skilled, in high demand, or have considerable strategic impact.

- How many salary structures are needed to accommodate the dynamics of the labor markets and the organization's staffing and career-management plans? If multiple structures are required, the organization must consider whether all structures would be based on similar concepts and philosophies. As the organization becomes more of a truly global enterprise, it also must consider how to balance a global strategy with regional and/or local structures and practices.

- What form should the salary structure take to support career-management plans? For example, will career paths be hierarchical (i.e., based on sequential promotions), or will employees make more lateral-horizontal career moves? Or both? Will there be more advancement "by the numbers" or by described job content?

- How will performance be recognized and rewarded within the framework of the salary structure, and should the pay-for-performance philosophy be the same across the system?

To get to the bottom of things, let's start with the architecture (building blocks).

## Architecture

As discussed earlier, a salary structure is, at its most fundamental, the job groupings (sometimes referred to as *job clusters*) and salary ranges that reflect the hierarchy of jobs and the subsequent delivery of pay to individuals. It is one of the basic building blocks of a base compensation program and, in fact, often of total cash and direct compensation, in which case both short- and long-term incentive targets are defined and differentiated by job grouping or level.

The structure is built on a four-part framework:

1. *Job architecture.* The combination of job groupings, levels, and progressions that together help to define an organization's management and deployment of talent and the opportunities for individuals to advance in their careers, contribute more fully to the organization, and ultimately earn greater reward and recognition consistent with their advancement and increased contribution. "Job grades were once the sole purview of rewards teams, while an organization's overall HR [human resources] tool kit included an entirely different hierarchy of career ladders, competency models and progression criteria unrelated to compensation. Organizations can no longer afford to maintain such separate rewards and talent frameworks. The design of a job-leveling solution must satisfy both agendas. Today, the burning platform for a common leveling infrastructure is often first fueled by questions of how to consistently assess, develop and progress a global talent pipeline across the enterprise."[2]

2. *Job evaluation.* The relative ranking of jobs or roles according to an organization's internal valuing system. Methodologies range from point-based systems, to classification/leveling, to pure market pricing.

3. *Benchmarking.* The incorporation of external market values via the process of benchmarking (or market pricing).

4. *Salary ranges.* The clustering of jobs based on both internal ranking or equity and market pay levels. The result is, most often, a series of salary ranges that apply to each similarly leveled cluster of jobs. A salary range describes the minimum and

maximum an organization will pay for a particular job or job grouping based on the organization's compensation philosophy. Using a salary range as opposed to a single pay rate provides flexibility for managers to pay in a manner consistent with an individual's experience, performance, competency, and business impact, as well as with market pressures connected to a particular job or job family.

The salary structure emerges as salary ranges are assigned to job groupings, but positioning jobs within the structure often also determines the degree of participation in other programs, such as bonuses, stock awards, additional benefits (e.g., vacations), supplemental benefits (e.g., deferred compensation, supplemental life insurance, or disability benefits), and perquisites (e.g., financial counseling, medical examinations, or club memberships). Whereas giving greater reward opportunities to individuals in "bigger" jobs that have a greater impact on the success or failure of the organization is a rational approach, compensation program designers should keep in mind the following:

- A "have versus have not" culture may emerge if employees in the higher-level positions view increasingly "rich" reward opportunities simply as entitlements. On the flipside, people in lower-level jobs (often equated with nonexempt or hourly classifications) will often feel undervalued, especially if noncash offerings are tied to grade level or to broad employee groupings, which happens not infrequently. We all have seen circumstances in which higher-level positions have access to more generous vacation or severance policies and more typically to cash bonus or equity programs. Although there is nothing inherently wrong with such an approach (predicated on the assumption that reward types and levels should be aligned with the degree of impact people in certain jobs, levels, and functions actually can have), employers first have to determine the extent to which they want to have policies that support a culture of inclusion or one of competition or differentiation. Regardless, to avoid the challenges noted earlier, each organizational level must be clearly defined, the impact of its jobholders substantiated, and the rewards set accordingly.

- A not insignificant outcome of tying noncash offerings to grade level is the tendency for employees and their managers to push to be promoted into the next grade (regardless of the work requirements) and for them to experience possible dissatisfaction if promotions are not as forthcoming as anticipated. On a related topic, in these recent (now six years and counting) times of economic distress or at least caution, there has been an increasing tendency to push for promotions as a way of delivering greater increases than can be justified by the 2 percent (or so) merit budget. This is not a structure issue per se, but it is an issue of how managers use (read "misuse") the structure and related classification policies and of the impact on the compensation staff of having to respond to a flood of job evaluation/reclassification requests, resulting in a poor use of staff time and a bastardization of job descriptions and related policies. The more that total rewards packages at each level are appropriate to the jobs and their impact on the company and are communicated clearly, the less likely organizations will devolve into this state of affairs.

The following sections review four basic types of salary structure (i.e., traditional, flexible, career based, and global) and the advantages and disadvantages of each. Note that while each type is treated as distinct for the purpose of this discussion, in reality, the characteristics of each often overlap considerably.

# Traditional Structure

The structures considered most traditional are those that are highly layered and technically driven. Highly layered structures use many grades with relatively small distances between adjacent grades/ranges. In technically driven structures, grades are defined primarily by compensation levels, whether market based or internally focused, rather than by career or organizational levels described in terms of job content.

## Reasons for Adopting a Traditional Structure

The reasons for adopting (or maintaining) a traditional structure vary from organization to organization based on alignment with the organization's strategies. Several common reasons are as follows:

- Traditional structures place emphasis on promotion/career advancement through a hierarchical system; individuals can "see" their promotions in the form of moving from grade to grade, although sometimes what employees see is more of a black-box outcome than an intuitive result.

- Typically, these structures are predictable and easy to administer in that the reasons and timing for pay movement are clearly defined by the structure and associated pay delivery policies.

- A traditional structure typically has a strong technical, mathematically derived foundation, which may be viewed as more objective than a more flexible structure (see "Flexible Structure" below), recognizing, however, that in reality it may not actually be more objective.

- Traditional structures are the tried-and-true approach to building compensation programs and hence are relatively easy to explain and justify.

## Disadvantages

- Traditional programs are highly structured and may not always respond effectively to changing organizational or individual needs.

- They may create perceived or real barriers between or within functional work groups because of differences in perceived value or status as defined by grade levels and the lack of clarity regarding what those differences are based on.

- Managers may not participate actively in the pay decision-making process, instead following established procedure regarding pay delivery (i.e., promotional, top of range, new-hire guidelines).

## Examples

Following are two examples of traditional structures. More specifically, these examples illustrate different approaches regarding salary-range symmetry (i.e., midpoints versus control points) and the spacing between salary ranges.

Figure 7.1 illustrates a salary structure that reflects a number of characteristics commonly considered to be traditional. These characteristics include the use of midpoints, the 80-120 format, relatively small distances between grades (10 percent), and considerable overlap of salary ranges (a function of the small distances between grades as well as the relatively typical range size, 50 percent from minimum to maximum). Such a design is sometimes called a *box structure*, reflecting the fact that the ranges are all the same proportional size, as are, for the most part, the spreads between midpoints.

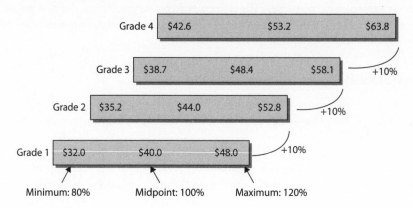

**Figure 7.1  Example 1: Traditional structure.**

*Midpoints.*  The midpoint value is often viewed as the pay level associated with fully competent performance in a job. Typically, the midpoint is the middle of each salary range and is tied to the market target consistent with the company's compensation strategy. This target represents the destination salary (or going rate) for jobs in a particular grade level. The actual value of the midpoint will depend on the organization's compensation philosophy (i.e., what to pay within the context of the organization's goals and the local, regional, or national markets) and its selection of pay survey sources.

One common method for determining how midpoints will be used to develop salary ranges is the *cluster analysis* (Figure 7.2). In this process, market rates for the clustered jobs are reviewed, and target pay levels are developed based on approximate average or median values (or other competitive levels depending, once again, on the organization's particular philosophy).

After creating the preliminary set of grades and ranges based on a market analysis, the compensation analyst places each position in a proposed grade (based primarily on the market findings and secondarily on internal relationships) and then compares the market values to the new midpoint. This preliminary slotting often is quite instructive because it may show jobs whose market values are farther away from the new midpoints than desired, suggesting a need for repositioning (see "Manager of Information Technology" in Figure 7.2), jobs with titles that sound different but are matched and priced similarly (see "Laboratory Associates I and II" in Figure 7.2), or the possible need for additional grades to fill in gaps.

Midpoints are not the only approach to calibrating ranges:

- Determination of the extent to which an individual's pay has progressed into the range, sometimes called *point-in-range* or *range penetration*. "Often range penetration is a preferred tool because it does not focus on one number alone, the midpoint. Instead it refers to how far into the range a particular individual's salary has penetrated."[3] Some view this as more intuitive than the midpoint.

| Benchmark Job Title | Target (P50) | Proposed Grade | Proposed Midpoint | % Midpoint Difference |
|---|---|---|---|---|
| Laboratory Associate I | $26,006 | 1 | $25,000 | −4% |
| Laboratory Associate II | $26,967 | 1 | $25,000 | −7% |
| Research Associate I | $30,275 | 1 | $25,000 | −17% |
| Accounting Assistant | $34,484 | 2 | $36,300 | 5% |
| Senior Research Associate I | $36,961 | 2 | $36,300 | −2% |
| Research Associate II | $37,628 | 2 | $36,300 | −4% |
| Administrative Assistant | $40,705 | 2 | $36,300 | −11% |
| Engineer Technician I | $42,501 | 3 | $45,400 | 7% |
| Senior Research Associate II | $45,039 | 3 | $45,400 | 1% |
| Human Resources Analyst | $49,866 | 3 | $45,400 | −9% |
| Payroll/Benefits Coordinator | $49,866 | 3 | $45,400 | −9% |
| Legal Administrator-Patents | $52,346 | 4 | $56,800 | 9% |
| Senior Research Associate III | $55,620 | 4 | $56,800 | 2% |
| Supervisor of Process Quality Management | $55,620 | 4 | $56,800 | 2% |
| Engineer I | $63,086 | 4 | $56,800 | −10% |
| Unix and Systems Administrator | $63,192 | 4 | $56,800 | −10% |
| Research Scientist | $72,306 | 5 | $73,800 | 2% |
| Lead Software Developer | $72,306 | 5 | $73,800 | 2% |
| Manager of Accounting | $73,412 | 5 | $73,800 | 1% |
| Manager of Human Resources | $76,275 | 5 | $73,800 | −3% |
| Project Leader | $79,822 | 5 | $73,800 | −8% |
| Senior Research Scientist | $92,121 | 6 | $95,900 | 4% |
| Manager of Information Technology | $85,035 | 6 | $95,900 | 13% |
| Patent Agent | $85,655 | 6 | $95,900 | 12% |
| Senior Software Engineer | $86,767 | 6 | $95,900 | 11% |
| Database Administrator | $93,442 | 6 | $95,900 | 3% |
| Senior Facilities Manager | $99,866 | 6 | $95,900 | −4% |
| Group Leader | $111,510 | 6 | $95,900 | −14% |

Figure 7.2 Cluster analysis method.

- The use of zones, sometimes overlapping, instead of specific points (see additional discussion on zones later). Often these are seen in quartiles or thirds, with the first zone reserved for new employees and/or those coming up the learning curve, the middle zone for those who are fully experienced and performing competently, and the highest zone reserved for individuals who perform at the highest levels, are typically highly experienced, and may be in high-demand jobs. Although zone approaches have a reasonable degree of structure, the use of overlapping range segments does allow for some flexibility on the part of managers and human resources to position pay appropriately.

*The 80-120 Format.* This is a method for establishing salary ranges in which the minimum of each range is set at 80 percent of the midpoint, whereas the maximum is set at 120 percent of the midpoint. The symmetry of this approach is appealing and relatively easy to understand, but it does not necessarily reflect the realities of the recruiting market. For example, the hiring rates for a particular job may not be at or near the 80 percent mark; they may be either higher or lower. Further, the rigid formula may not match the organization's performance philosophy regarding how much higher than a market target it is willing to pay for extraordinary performance within the boundaries of the job.

One approach to generally traditional range design is the use of *market reference ranges* (MRRs). These may (but not always) reflect a similar structure to those discussed earlier, but the differentiating factor is a more explicit use of the market in determining the mileposts in the range. In such instances, the midpoint continues to be targeted to the desired market positioning (which is, in most cases, the median value), but the minima and maxima are typically calibrated to either a representation of, say, the market 25th percentile (minimum) or 75th percentile (maximum) or the actual values of those market points. In the former case, the minimum and maximum values are often about ±15 percent from the midpoint. In the latter case, the values are derived more directly from the applicable market numbers, meaning that the range spreads generally will be less consistent from grade to grade than in mathematically derived ranges (e.g., 80-120, 85-115, 75-125, or the like).

Figure 7.3 is an example of a more directly derived MRR-type range. Note that because the range limits are market based, such ranges are more often than not asymmetrical in design (see discussion under "Asymmetry" below).

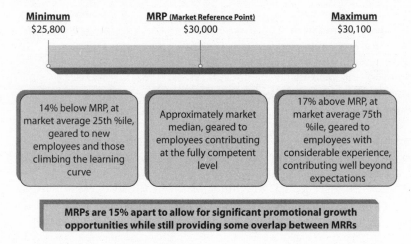

**Figure 7.3  Market reference range example.**

*Closely Nestled Ranges.*  Relatively closely nestled ranges ensure that promotions from one grade to the next will not be associated with "windfall" salary increases. This approach also ensures that promotions are viewed more as incremental progressions than significant leaps in responsibility.

Figure 7.4 illustrates a structure that looks similar to the structure in Figure 7.1, but the structure in this example was actually set up in a very different way. Key differences include a much greater interrange distance (19 to 22 percent versus 10 percent), progressively greater distance at higher grades (typically called a *fan structure*, reflecting the fact that the ranges spread out at higher grade levels), and ranges that are about the same overall size (about 50 percent from minimum to maximum) but that are asymmetrical in design.

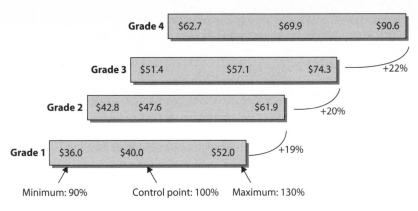

Figure 7.4  Example 2: Traditional structure.

*Asymmetry.*  In contrast to the 80-120 format used in Example 1, the range minimums in this example are set at 90 percent of the salary target, whereas the range maximums are set at 130 percent of the target. Some organizations prefer calling the salary targets in such a structure *control points* rather than midpoints because their purpose is less to bisect a range evenly and more to establish a framework for determining pay for individuals within that range.

There is no inherent rationale for establishing a symmetrical salary range. Although range symmetry may appeal to our sense of orderliness, it is more important that salary range frameworks accurately reflect hiring practices, development processes, compensation philosophy, and the degree of linkage between pay and performance. It also is important that employees and their managers understand how ranges work and how the structure affects current and future pay opportunities. Questions to answer in determining how low minimums should be and how high maximums should be include the following:

- *How much below target is the hiring rate for a job? Will the organization, in fact, expect to hire qualified but inexperienced people at the minimum or above it?* Another way of thinking about this is to ask how long it would take for a newly hired, inexperienced employee paid at the minimum to achieve competence, thereby arriving at market target pay. The longer the expected time period, the greater the distance should be between the minimum and the target. Of course, the answer may differ depending on the job level. For instance, a basic assembler may take weeks or months to get up to speed in the job, whereas a senior-level enterprise architect might take years to gain the technical and organizational knowledge needed to be able to contribute fully. This is why the distance from minimum to control point is smaller for nonexempt/hourly types of positions than for professional and/or management roles in many organizations.

- *How much is the organization willing to pay above a market-competitive rate for extraordinary performance and/or contribution within the same job?* To some extent, the answer to this question may be influenced by how quickly a company is growing. An organization that is expanding rapidly, both from a business and a staffing perspective, will tend to be much less concerned about this issue given the likelihood that many people, particularly top performers, will be promoted to the next level before they come close to the midpoint, much less the maximum. Nonetheless, it is important for the company to answer the question to its satisfaction.

- *What should be done when an individual reaches or exceeds the range maximum?* The reality of this situation is often hard to deal with, particularly in mature businesses where employees tend to be long tenured. In such circumstances, there is a greater likelihood of individuals maxing out in their ranges. Companies have to be very diligent in communicating their rationales for range caps, in providing alternative means of recognition and reward (e.g., lump-sum or incentive awards) to individuals at the top of their ranges who remain significant contributors, and in identifying and helping to forge a path to realizing true promotional or developmental opportunities that will expand work challenges and the possibilities of higher pay levels.

*Greater Distance between Ranges.* Greater distance between salary ranges tends to correlate with more expansive clustering of jobs. In a sense, this is self-evident given that the use of broader grades will result inevitably in fewer grades to hold the organization's populations of jobs. Although such a structure is not an actual broad band, it is moving in that direction. It is very likely that employees would spend more time in each grade in the structure shown in Figure 7.4 than they would in the structure shown in Figure 7.1. And given that there is less overlap between ranges, resulting in promotional increases that will tend to be more significant, it behooves management to make sure that its policies and programs around performance management, employee development, and promotion/advancement are well defined and clearly communicated.

## Flexible Structure

Let us now take a look at more flexible structures. In the last edition of this book, this chapter equated flexible structures with broadbands, noting that "[b]road bands are 'describable' clusters of jobs with broadly similar characteristics (e.g., impact, scope, career stage, function, level, etc.) that create a sense of group belonging and career opportunity.... Bands themselves are not compensation tools, although pay ranges, pay reference points, or pay opportunities may be (and almost always are) nestled within bands."[4]

While broadbands have not quite become extinct yet, they are definitely on the human resources list of endangered species! Why is this? Well, to some extent, employers tended to treat broadbanding as a silver bullet, which is, unfortunately, not unusual for compensation or "hot" human resources interventions. In many instances, broadbanding was viewed as *the* way for an employer to effect cultural and structural change without having to develop and implement the necessary changes in the supporting processes of development, communication, work process, or organization structure. Additionally, the company's view of broadbanding may have been that of "supergrades" associated with "superranges" of 100 to 200 to 300 percent in width. In these incarnations, the salary structure is viewed as endlessly flexible, giving managers adequate rope to make the desired pay decisions (or, more likely, hang themselves!) and as a way of breaking down all sorts of hierarchical barriers between employees who are in differently graded jobs.

The sad truth is that many such banding implementations did not work as expected. In fact, they cannot work unless managers have direct and ongoing access to robust external data on market levels by job and individual, as well as valid internal data on performance, experience, dates of hire/promotion, and so on. Short of such information, managers need guidelines on where jobs and people fit within the organizational and pay hierarchy and what types of salary increases or target salary levels are appropriate in various situations. On their own, the huge "superbands" just do not have the necessary degree of infrastructure to help managers make effective pay decisions for rewarding and holding onto their "superkeepers."

Historically speaking, broadbands might have made a good deal of sense in the days of what seemed to be an endlessly growing economy (the 1990s) because managers wanted more flexibility to reward their people and companies had the money to fund those rewards. Managers still want flexibility, given the ongoing globalization of labor markets and the continuing challenges of attracting and holding onto key talent, but in the context of financial conservatism that was born during the Great Recession and continues as economies still work on truly recovering, the flexibility inherent in broad bands would be viewed as a cruel joke: "So I can pay my artificial intelligence engineer anywhere from $90,000 to $210,000, but I have only a 2 percent budget to use for increases?"

If our discussion of flexible structures does not focus on broadbands, then what are we talking about? Well, we are talking about structures that

- Provide employees with the opportunity for personal growth and extensive performance recognition.
- Are more transparent and intuitive, thus providing managers and employees with more ammunition for considering and following through on advancement opportunities.
- Typically (but not always) have fewer ranges with larger spreads between adjacent midpoints, coupled with (often but not always) wider ranges than the standard 50 percent minimum-to-maximum width.
- Facilitate (and encourage) lateral job moves.
- Place more human resources decisions in the hands of managers.
- Reduce the administrative burden of job evaluation and often seemingly endless reclassifications.

An approach that often has many of these characteristics, coupled with a much closer integration between compensation and talent management, is the career-based structure.

## Career-Based Structure

One of the interesting characteristics of career ladder–type structures is how intuitive and commonsensical they are to both employees and their managers. Figure 7.5 illustrates a nonbroadband career-oriented structure.

The power of this type of framework starts with the approach to its development. An effective process typically includes considerable employee involvement, uses criteria for job families (i.e., Administrative Support, Finance) and levels (i.e., AS-1, AS-2, etc.) that are specific to the organization (step 1 on the following list), and allows for the development of levels within each job family (making it highly customized to each work area). Ultimately, this framework provides an integrated salary structure based largely on a formal evaluation of levels (step 4) and market analysis (step 6). Key steps typically include

1. Define job families and elements of accountability (compensable factors).
2. Create and validate job family frameworks using content experts from each job family.

| Job Family | Pay Grades/Job Levels | | | | | | | | |
|---|---|---|---|---|---|---|---|---|---|
| | Grade 18 | Grade 19 | Grade 20 | Grade 21 | Grade 22 | Grade 23 | Grade 24 | Grade 25 | Grade 26 |
| Administrative support | AS-1 | AS-2 | AS-3 | AS-4 | AS-5 | AS-6 | | | |
| Technical and research | | | TR-1 | TR-2 | TR-3 | TR-4 | | TR-5 | |
| Information technology and media | | | IT-1 | IT-2 | IT-3 | IT-4 | | IT-5 | IT-6 |
| Safety and facility services | | SF-1 | SF-2 | SF-3 | SF-4 | SF-5 | | | |
| Finance | | | F-1 | F-2 | F-3 | | F-4 | F-5 | F-6 |
| Marketing | | M-1 | M-2 | M-3 | M-4 | M-5 | | | |

**Figure 7.5 Career-based structure.**

3. Define each level of work in each job family described in terms of the compensable factors, again using content experts.

4. Evaluate each level within each job family to identify the relative hierarchy of work levels.

5. Map all jobs to the appropriate job family and defined level within the job family (using input from content experts).

6. Conduct competitive analysis on benchmark jobs.

7. Establish salary structure by aligning levels and market values.

An additional benefit is the transparency inherent in publishing the leveling matrix, such as the one shown in Figure 7.5. This more open communication approach allows employees and managers to see and understand the opportunities for growth, whether by advancing through levels within a family (e.g., from M-2 to M-3) or by moving from one family to another (e.g., from AS-3 to F-1) to shift functional areas and/or careers.

As long as this system is viewed as a tool for developing careers and promotional opportunities, as well as a guide to the compensation advances that inevitably come along with such development, it can be a powerful aid in engaging employees and improving organizational effectiveness. As with any career-based system, however, to the extent that it degenerates into an entitlement-based giveaway, it will lose credibility, add unnecessary labor costs, and may very well hurt morale, particularly among the high-performing or high-potential employees who see that performance and hard work are not necessarily required for advancement.

Another plus of a well-designed career-based structure is its potential connection to other core human resources processes. For instance, I know at least one organization that built its job descriptions on the foundation of the job family and work-level descriptions while allowing for department-specific clarifications/additions and tied its performance-management process to the requirements described in the leveling.

## Dual-Career Ladder

An interesting twist on career structures is the dual-career ladder, a framework that exists in many scientific, research, and technically oriented organizations. Similar to the job family structure, the value of such configurations is in the intersection of level of responsibility/impact, compensation, and recognition/status.

Figure 7.6 represents a sample dual-career ladder from a scientific organization. Dual-career ladders came into being and continue to be used as a way to recognize and reward individuals who make increasingly significant scientific contributions without requiring them to move into management roles, thus trying to avoid the downsides of the Peter Principle.

There are a number of reasons for companies to consider this structure. Some of the more common reasons are that dual-career ladders

- Encourage top scientists, engineers, or developers to continue to focus on their disciplines without requiring them to give up status or reward opportunities or to assume management positions where many of them may not excel.

- Facilitate the recruitment and retention of the best technical experts.

- Reinforce the organization's commitment to research or engineering excellence through consistent recognition, reward, and communication. This is particularly important if world-class discovery, research, and development are viewed as core to the business's strategy and market success.

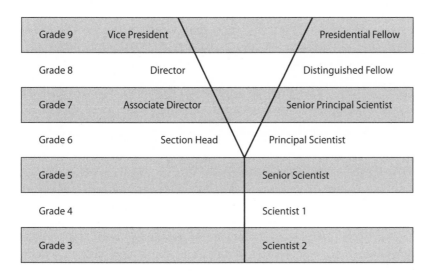

**Figure 7.6  Dual-career ladder.**

Each dual-career ladder must fit the culture, values, and hierarchy of a particular organization. (Figure 7.6, including the titles associated with it, is an illustration only.) Titles are particularly important in technical organizations as both internally and externally discernible indications of achievement and recognition and as a way of comparing status across the dual ladder. For instance, in Figure 7.6, if Vice President on the management side were equated with Executive Scientific Director (as opposed to Presidential Fellow), there could be a perception that management jobs are more highly valued than scientific ones.

The number of levels below and above the point where the ladder forks tend to be specific to each organization. Key determinants typically include

- The entry level (grade) for Ph.D. positions. In Figure 7.6, this is the level of the Senior Scientist. The Grade 3 and Grade 4 positions typically require undergraduate and/or "nonterminal" graduate degrees. The more positions suitable to non-Ph.D. workers an organization has, the more levels there typically will be prior to the start of the dual path.

- How layered the organization is and how many viable and necessary levels of work can be identified on the technical and/or management side.

As with any structure or compensation program, it is essential that the actions of the company be consistent with the intent of the dual ladders. For example, *compensation opportunities* (e.g., base salary, short-term incentives, stock awards) should be equivalent for employees in the same grades but on opposite sides of the dual-career path, *recognition opportunities* should be consistent with the company's business focus and values (e.g., mentions in newsletters, acknowledgments in ceremonies, placement on walls of fame, participation in key scientific initiatives, attendance at/presentation to important conferences, etc.), and *staffing* proportions (e.g., the balance between management staff and scientific staff at each grade) should be appropriate to business and human capital needs.

## Global or Multifaceted Structure

Another important consideration in today's business world is whether or not structures should be singular/centralized or decentralized/localized. The number (and type) of structures in an organization depends on many factors, including the following:

- Whether different lines of business are in separate industries and/or whether different functions require different skills.

- Whether various employee groups represent different labor markets and total compensation profiles (e.g., nonexempt, exempt, executive, sales).

- Whether there exist divergent cultures or work environments, which, for example, may range from a customer-service organization staffed by self-directed work teams (where a skill-based system might be appropriate) to a functionally organized manufacturing plant (in which a more layered, step-based system may be called for).

- The extent to which the organization wants to create a seamless "one-for-all" organization (single structure) versus decentralized, entrepreneurial operations (multiple structures).

Important considerations in determining the ideal number of structures include

- *The degree to which internal equity is valued.* For instance, how often do people transfer across business units or geographic sites? Are functional specialists located in many or most sites, or has the company established centers of excellence, which may require the "importing" of highly skilled staff from anywhere in the world? To the extent that an organization operates more often using the latter model, it will require a more common structure to ensure that people movement is not hindered by grades and ranges that are only applicable locally.

- *The ability of the organization to support and administer a complex array of structures effectively.* One would hope that an organization could create and maintain the pay framework it needs to support its human resource strategy and needs. In reality, however, sometimes companies do not have the information infrastructure (i.e., human resources information system, titles, job codes, etc.) that makes it easy to translate (and transfer) jobs and employees across geographic boundaries. An organization must make its list of the pluses of multiple structures and the minuses associated with infrastructure gaps before barreling down one path or the other. The sophistication and accessibility of many current human resources systems should make it easier to follow the multiple structure route if appropriate to the organization.

Even within a single country, the concept of localization can be relative based on job levels and the variability of employee location. For example, compensation and recruiting professionals typically look to the national labor market for leadership and management jobs and very often for workers in high demand or professionals with rare skills. For office support and basic production/blue-collar jobs, though, the "local" job market will be much more appropriate.

Given that companies with operations in many areas across the globe are beginning to act like truly global organizations, perhaps the more strategic question is whether or not these companies should adopt global salary structures. If so, what does this mean in terms of salary levels and currency valuation, as well as both cash and stock incentive awards?

Of course, an organization's degree of "globality" can be viewed on a continuum. On the low end of this continuum, we would find organizations in which each country or region or business unit handles its own compensation system in a fairly autonomous fashion. In such instances, while the quality of market data and the objectivity of decisions might be highly variable, more weight still would be given to independent decision making than to corporate control and/or quality assurance. This would be typical in more entrepreneurial organizations/units and/or where the circumstances in each country are unique and/or in flux.

On the other end of the continuum, we find companies that emphasize consistency of treatment and encourage and/or require the movement of employees across functional silos and sovereign borders. In such instances, a more consistent leveling of jobs is essential to ensure that, for example, a Principal Scientist at a Grade 6 in the United Kingdom does not find himself or herself in Grade 5 after being transferred to the same job in the company's operations in Japan. The issue may be less about pay and more about status and recognition (and possibly perquisites and supplemental benefits as well), which are typically matters of great importance in scientific/engineering/academic organizations, the very ones that often have dual-career ladders.

In companies that do use global structures, the typical approach is to establish consistent leveling (the Principal Scientist has the same grade, job description, and experience/education requirements everywhere), to provide pay opportunities in alignment with a common pay philosophy (e.g., 50th percentile target salaries and 75th percentile short-term incentive targets), and to ensure that the market data and currencies are localized.

## Application

A key element of a salary structure is how individual employees progress through it, both within ranges and between grades, and how managers make pay decisions within it. As I noted earlier in slightly different words, there is no point to having a structure if it does not facilitate pay decision making and job/pay advancement. Figure 7.7 shows a common approach to managing pay within a range, primarily using performance.

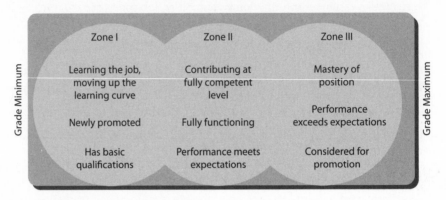

**Figure 7.7  Salary range with pay zones.**

The concepts behind this model include

- *Pay zones within the salary range.* The pay zones are not rigidly defined or mutually exclusive, but they do divide the range into practical segments that are tied to approximate levels of experience, performance, and promotability. This recognizes that pay determination is more an outcome of systematic, informed management judgment than of a scientific process and/or a mathematical formula.

- *A more flexible framework.* This allows companies to take into account market and individual factors. For example, if the market for financial analysts is very hot, it may be difficult or impossible to hire even new college graduates at the range minimum, in which case a zone (as opposed to a single point) at the beginning of the range will allow some individual discretion. If a pharmaceutical company needs to hire a world-class pharmacologist or an engineering company needs a top-notch, highly experienced aerospace engineer, the appropriate salary ranges for these jobs may be wide enough to handle their market-based pay requirements, but the hiring rate may need to be in the upper echelons of the range. As long as the new pay for these individuals does not unduly disrupt internal equity or create damaging compression, these higher rates may be justified.

- Performance-based pay. A pay-for-performance salary policy fits well with this model, whether it is applied via the more typical *merit matrix* for determining annual salary adjustments (Figure 7.8) or a more holistic but harder to implement *target pay* approach (Figure 7.9).

## Merit Matrix

In contrast to the salary range shown in Figure 7.7, the salary range depicted in Figure 7.8 is divided into four quartiles as opposed to three zones. Both methodologies are widely used and conceptually sound.

| Performance Rating | Position in Range | | | |
|---|---|---|---|---|
| | 4th Quartile | 3rd Quartile | 2nd Quartile | 1st Quartile |
| Exceeds | 3% to 5% | 5% to 7% | 7% to 9% | 9% to 12% |
| Fully Meets | 0% | 3% to 5% | 5% to 7% | 7% to 9% |
| Needs Improvement | 0% | 0% | 0% | 1% to 3% |

**Figure 7.8  Merit matrix.**

## Target Pay

In Figure 7.9, the midpoint is defined as a market reference point (MRP) (see "Midpoints," "Control Points," and "Market Reference Ranges" above). Whereas the range itself is fairly typical, the approach to pay determination focuses not on what kind of increase the employee should get in a given year but instead on an appropriate pay level based on his or her sustained performance/contribution, his or her experience, and perhaps his or her "rating" on other relevant criteria the organization may have identified.

The pros of the approach shown in Figure 7.9 are that it allows a company to take a coordinated look at the relationship between an individual's overall contribution to an organization and the amount of money he or she is receiving (establishing an explicit *quid pro quo*) as opposed to looking only at what amount of increase the individual should receive. In the example, Jane's current pay of $27,000 is well below her target pay range of $32,250 to $34,500, which is predicated on the fact that Jane has significant experience and a sustained track record of making exceptional contributions to the company. Limiting Jane's salary growth to an incremental increase each year may prolong the time it will take for her to reach her target range. The delay could result in Jane's feeling undervalued, possibly making her susceptible to offers from other organizations that are willing to pay her in a way that recognizes her value.

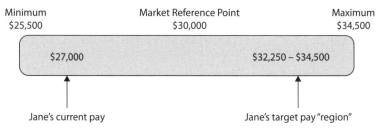

**Figure 7.9  Example: Jane's salary.**

The challenges of this approach are the need for company agreement on the key metrics, accurate and accessible data on an individual's contribution, and a confidence in management's ability to make decisions that often have significant cost implications for the company and personal impact on the employee being reviewed. In this example, Jane's manager needs to be able to quantify or at least justify the impact Jane is having on the company in light of how her pay compares with the market target and the significance of the expected increase. The combination of necessary criteria described here makes this a very difficult model to implement in most organizations.

## Summary

Salary structures, though often overlooked as high-impact tools, can be strong foundations for companies to communicate their priorities and develop total compensation programs that can help to recruit, retain, and develop key talent. To allow salary structures to live up to their considerable potential, employers need to

- Determine the design that will best suit their human resource strategies and cultural values and where on the spectrum they fall between rigid and flexible, between technically based and career based, between locally controlled and centrally controlled, and between singular and dual careers.

- Decide on the basis for their structures: market, internal values, or a combination.

- Agree on how to apply the structure to pay decision making: pay zones supported by a merit increase program, target pay levels, or other.

The bottom line is that salary structures work best when they are established and administered as living systems in support of the strategic people needs of an organization and not merely as technically correct frameworks for slotting jobs and adjusting pay.

## Notes

1. Andrew S. Rosen and David Turetsky, "Broadbanding: The Construction of a Career Management Framework." *WorldatWork Journal*, Fourth Quarter 2002, p. 46.
2. Sandra McLellan, "It's Not Just About Money, It's About Talent: 5 Principles for Creating the Right Global Job-Leveling Approach for Your Organization." Compensation Focus from WorldatWork, Scottsdale, AZ, February 2013.
3. *The WorldatWork Handbook of Compensation, Benefits and Total Rewards: A Comprehensive Guide for HR Professionals*. WorldatWork, Scottsdale, AZ, 2007.
4. Andrew S. Rosen and David Turetsky, "Broadbanding: The Construction of a Career Management Framework." *WorldatWork Journal*, Fourth Quarter 2002, p. 48.

# 8

# Selecting and Developing a Salary Structure

Michael Armstrong

*E-reward.co.uk*

Salary structures provide the framework for managing pay effectively. It is important to get them right because they support the achievement of business goals and sustained competitive advantage. They do this in four ways. First, they ensure that pay levels in the structure compare favorably with market rates and thus enable the organization to get and keep the talented people it needs. Second, any efforts made to achieve pay equity can create employee job satisfaction and therefore increase productivity. Third, salary structures can help to increase levels of employee motivation and engagement by providing scope for salary progression through performance pay. Finally, the grade structures underpinning salary structures can be used to define career opportunities and therefore contribute to the attainment of talent-management objectives.

This chapter is about the use and development of salary structures. The main learning points are

- The definition of salary structures

- The guiding principles that can be used to develop and maintain structures

- The different types of structures and their advantages and disadvantages

- The criteria for choosing a structure

- The basic steps required to design the chosen structure

## Definition of Salary Structures

Salary structures consist of pay ranges that are attached to each grade, band, or level in a grade structure. They are described in terms of their *range spread*—the span or width of the pay ranges attached to each grade. This provides for pay progression or the allocation of different rates to jobs placed in the grade and is usually measured as the difference between the lowest and the highest point in the range as a percentage of the lowest point.

The number of grades, bands, or levels they contain defines salary structures. A grade structure consists of a sequence or hierarchy of grades, bands, or levels. *Grades* contain groups of jobs that are broadly comparable in size or are paid within the same range of market rates. They are usually structured with a midpoint that facilitates the management of pay (midpoint management). *Bands* are broader grades (with wider range spreads) and may be unstructured, although bands can incorporate grades. *Levels* consist of a sequence of what are in effect grades but, as used by some organizations, are defined in terms of *decision-making accountability*. The job evaluation process of *leveling*, as described in Chapter 10, is used to allocate jobs to levels.

There may be a single structure that is defined by the number of grades, bands, or levels it contains. Alternatively, the structure may be divided into a number of job families consisting of groups of jobs where the essential nature and purpose of the work are similar, but the work is carried out at different levels.

Some organizations do not have a formal graded structure and rely entirely on *spot rates* that provide no scope for the progression of pay in the form of a pay range, although bonuses may be provided on top of the base rate. This is especially the case in smaller or loosely structured organizations and those that place a premium on flexibility and responsiveness to market pressures. A less frequently used method is to have *individual job grades*, which are, in effect, spot rates to which a defined pay range of, say, 20 percent on either side of the rate for the job[1] has been attached to provide scope for pay progression. Spot rates or individual ranges are common in the United Kingdom, where the Chartered Institute of Personnel and Development (CIPD) 2013 salary survey established that they were used by 49 percent of respondents. They enable businesses to keep pace with market rates, often by what is sometimes called *extreme market pricing*, which relies entirely on market rate information to establish pay levels and does not use any form of job evaluation.

## Guiding Principles for Salary Structures

There are no universal rules about which salary structures should be adopted and how they should be managed. However, the following guiding principles ought to be considered when evaluating the design of a new structure or the operation of an existing one. These state that salary structures should

- Be appropriate to the culture, characteristics, and needs of the organization
- Provide for competitive pay by taking account of market rates in determining rates of pay for jobs in accordance with the policy on the relationship between internal and external rates (market stance)
- Facilitate the management of relativities and the achievement of equity, fairness, consistency, and transparency in managing grades and pay
- Enable jobs to be graded appropriately and not be subject to grade drift (unjustified upgradings)
- Be flexible enough to adapt to pressures arising from market rate changes and skill shortages

- Facilitate operational flexibility and continuous development

- Provide scope as required for pay progression

- Clarify reward, lateral development, and career opportunities

- Be constructed logically and clearly so that the basis on which they operate can readily be communicated to employees

- Enable the organization to exercise control over costs and the implementation of pay policies and budgets

- Minimize the amount of administrative effort required to maintain the structure

- Achieve flexibility within a framework, the aim being to provide an appropriate balance between flexibility and control

## Types of Salary Structures

As described in this section, there are a number of different types of salary structures.

### Multigraded Structures

A multigraded, sometimes called a *narrow-graded* or *traditional*, structure consists of a sequence of job grades into which jobs of broadly equivalent value are placed. There may be 10 or more grades, and long-established structures, especially in government organizations, can have as many as 18 or even more. A range of job evaluation points may define grades so that any job for which the job evaluation score falls within the points bracket for a grade would be allocated to that grade. Alternatively, they may be defined by grade definitions or profiles that provide the information required to match jobs if analytical factor comparison or job classification is used as described in Chapter 10.

Pay ranges are attached to each grade to allow scope for pay progression. They are usually described in terms of their range spreads (the percentage by which the highest point exceeds the lowest point). This is usually between 20 and 50 percent (30 to 40 percent is typical). The center of the range is called the *midpoint*, and this can be aligned with market rates in accordance with pay policy.

Midpoint management techniques can help to control the structure. They use compa ratios, which express the actual rate of pay as a percentage of the midpoint when the latter is regarded as the policy rate of pay or the reference point. The analysis of compa ratios indicates what action may have to be taken to slow down or accelerate increases if compa ratios are too high or too low compared with the policy level. Compa ratios also can be used to measure where an individual is placed in a salary range and therefore provide information on the size of pay increases.

Differentials between pay ranges—the percentage by which the midpoint of a range is higher than the midpoint of the range below—are typically between 5 and 15 percent, but they can be as high as 25 percent. Too low a differential means that the scope for pay progression on upgrading is limited. Too high a differential means that a decision to upgrade may mean that the increase in pay is disproportionate to the increase in responsibility.

There is usually an overlap between ranges. This is the difference between the highest point of the range below and the lowest point of the range above. The argument in favor of overlaps is that they provide more flexibility by enabling recognition to be given to the fact that a highly experienced individual at the top of a range may be contributing more than someone who is still in the learning-curve portion of the next-higher grade. However, if overlaps are too high, they can cause confusion.

The advantages claimed for multigraded structures are that they provide a framework for managing relativities and for ensuring that jobs of equal value are paid equally. In theory, they are easy to manage because the large number of grades enables fine distinctions to be made between different levels of responsibility. Staff may favor them because they appear to offer plenty of opportunities for increasing pay by upgrading.

But there are major disadvantages. The main problem is that if there are too many grades, there will be constant pressure for upgrading, leading to *grade drift*. They may be aligned with a traditional extended hierarchy that no longer exists and can function rigidly, which is at odds with the requirement of flexibility in team and process-based organizations. They also reinforce the importance of promotion as a means of progression, which may run counter to the need for organizations to be more flexible and grow capability by moving people within grades to broaden their experience and competencies.

### Broadbanded Structures

In its original version as described by Leblanc[2] and Abosch,[3] a broadbanded structure contained no more than five or six bands, each with, typically, a span of 70 to 100 percent. Bands were unstructured, and pay was managed much more flexibly than in a conventional graded structure (no limits may be defined for progression), and much more attention was paid to market rates, which governed what were in effect the spot rates for jobs within bands. Progression in bands depended on competency and the assumption of wider role responsibilities. Bands were described verbally, not by reference to the results of analytical job evaluation. More authority was devolved to line managers to make pay decisions within a looser framework.

The original notion of unstructured broadbands is now no longer commonly practiced. It created expectations of the scope for progression that could not be met. This had to stop somewhere if costs were going to be controlled, and no rationale was available for deciding when and why to stop. Line managers felt adrift without adequate guidance, and staff members missed the structure they were used to.

Inevitably, therefore, structure crept in. It started with reference points aligned with market rates around which similar roles could be clustered. These were then extended into zones for individual jobs or groups of jobs. Reference points were frequently placed in zones so that they increasingly resembled conventional structure grades. Armstrong and Brown[4] established that in the United Kingdom, 80 percent of the organizations they surveyed had introduced some controls in the form of zones (43 percent) and zones with reference points (37 percent). Job evaluation was used not only to define the boundaries of the band but also to size jobs as a basis for deciding where reference points should be placed in conjunction with market pricing.

Progressively, therefore, the original concept of broadbanding was eroded as more structure was introduced and job evaluation became more prominent to define the structure and meet equal pay requirements. Zones within broadbands began to look very much like conventional grades, and so-called broadbanded structures became in effect broadgraded structures, as described later.

The main advantage originally claimed for broadbanding was that it appeared to provide for more flexibility by catering for broader roles rather than tightly defined jobs, by adopting less rigid approaches to the allocation of roles to bands and how people progress within them, and by being able to respond more quickly to market rate pressures. The advantages of doing without formal job evaluation and using market pricing also were powerful arguments in favor of broadbanding. Moreover, broadbanding was in accord with the drive for de-layering. The reduction in the number of grades meant that the pressure for upgrading was reduced, there was less likelihood of grade drift, and it was thought that grades would be easier to manage.

Two reservations that emerged from the experience of developing broadbands in the 1990s and early 2000s were (1) what's the point of unstructured broadbands if they simply consist of spot rates? and (2) what's the difference between, say, a 4-banded structure with three zones in each band and a 12-graded structure? The answer given by broadband devotees to the first question was that at least there was some overall structure within which spot rates could be managed. In reply to the second question, the usual answer was that as roles develop, movements between zones within bands could be dealt with more flexibly. Neither of these responses is particularly convincing.

Apart from such fundamental reservations, there are a number of other objections to broadbanding. In general, it has been found that broadbanded structures are harder to manage than narrower-graded structures despite the original claim that they would be easier—they make considerable demands on line managers as well as human resources. Pay can spin out of control unless steps are taken to prevent that happening. As a reward manager in an engineering company told Armstrong,[5] "Broadbands offer huge scope for flexibility but equally huge scope for getting it wrong."

Broadbanding can build employee expectations of significant pay opportunities, which are doomed in many cases if proper control of the system is maintained. It can be difficult to explain to people how broadbanding works and how they will be affected, and they may be concerned by the apparent lack of structure and precision. Decisions on movements within bands can be harder to justify objectively than in other types of grade and pay structures.

Broadbanded structures may be more costly to operate than more conventional structures because there is less control over pay progression. Research conducted by Fay et al.[6] in the United States found that both base pay and total cash compensation were significantly higher in the companies with broadbanded structures than in those with more conventional structures. They estimated that broadbanding increased payroll costs by more than 7 percent.

## Broad-Graded Structures

The aim of *broad-graded structures* is to achieve the better of the two worlds of multigraded and broadbanded structures. They do this by reducing the number of grades from the 12 or more in multigraded structures to 6 or 7 and, as established by the WorkatWork 2013 survey,[7] adopting wider-range spreads—30 to 80 percent compared with 20 to 40 percent. The grades and pay ranges in broad-graded structures are defined and managed in the same way as in multigraded structures except that wider pay spans mean that organizations sometimes introduce mechanisms to control progression in the grade so that staff members do not inevitably reach its upper pay limit. Close attention is paid to market rates in establishing pay ranges and fixing salary levels.

Broad-graded structures are used to overcome or at least alleviate the grade-drift problem that is endemic in multigraded structures. If the grades are defined, it is easier to differentiate them, and matching (comparing role profiles with grade definitions or profiles to find the best fit) becomes more accurate. But it may be difficult to control progression, and this would increase the costs of operating such systems, although these costs could be offset by better control of grade drift. They usually cost less to implement than multigraded structures because fewer people are likely to fall below the pay limits of a broader grade. They also overcome the main disadvantage of broadbands—which is that it is difficult to control progression and therefore cost.

WorldatWork describes broad-graded structures as market-based structures to emphasize the link to market rates. But, as defined by WorldatWork, a market-based structure exhibits the typical features of a broad-graded structure. WorldatWork's 2013 U.S. survey found that market-based structures were by far the most popular structure (64 percent compared with the 23 percent who had traditional or narrow-graded structures and with the mere 12 percent with broadbands).

### Job Family Structures

*Job families* consist of jobs in a function or occupation such as marketing, operations, and finance that are related through the activities carried out and the basic knowledge and skills required but in which the levels of responsibility, knowledge, skill, or competency needed differ. In a job family structure, the successive levels in each family are defined by reference to the key activities carried out and the knowledge and skills or competencies required to perform them effectively. They therefore define career paths—what people have to know and be able to do to advance their career within a family and to develop career opportunities in other families. Typically, job families have between six and eight levels, as in broad-graded structures. Some families may have more levels than others. The job families may be treated as market groups in which pay levels differ between families in accordance with market rate levels.

Job family structures provide the foundation for personal development planning by defining the knowledge, skills, and competencies required at higher levels or in different functions and by describing what needs to be learned through experience, education, or training. Level definitions in a family can be more accurate than in a conventional structure because they concentrate on roles within the family with common characteristics and do not attempt to cover a wide and in some ways unconnected set of skills across the whole organization. However, they can be more difficult to develop, explain, and manage than single-grade structures. They are popular in the United Kingdom, where the CIPD 2013 survey found that they were used by 30 percent of the respondents. They are not mentioned in the WorldatWork 2013 survey.

## Criteria for Choice

It is important to remember that with regard to salary structures, one size does not fit all. The choice of structure will depend on the type, needs, and values of the organization. They are summarized in Table 8.1.

## Developing Salary Structures

The process of developing a salary structure will, of course, depend on the type of structure adopted. In general, though, the steps required are as follows:

| Type of Structure | Criteria for Choice: The Structure May Be Considered More Appropriate When: |
|---|---|
| Multigraded | The organization is large and bureaucratic with well-defined and extended hierarchies. |
| | Pay progression is expected to occur in small but relatively frequent steps. |
| | The culture is one in which much significance is attached to status as indicated by grades. |
| | Some but not too much scope for pay progression is wanted. |
| | The values of the organization favor the achievement of internal equity as well as external competitiveness. |
| Broadbanded | Greater flexibility in pay determination and management is required. |
| | It is believed that job evaluation should no longer drive grading decisions. |
| | The focus is on rewarding people for lateral development. |
| | The organization has been de-layered. |
| | Pay policy in the organization is market driven. |
| Broad-graded | It is believed that if there are a relatively limited number of grades, it will be possible to define and therefore differentiate them more accurately as an aid to better precision when grading jobs. |
| | An existing multigraded structure is the main cause of grade drift. |
| | It is considered that pay progression through grades can be related to contribution and that it is possible to introduce effective control mechanisms. |
| | The values of the organization emphasize the need for pay to be competitive if necessary at the expense of internal equity. |
| Job family | There are distinct market groups that need to be rewarded differently. |
| | The range of responsibility and the basis on which levels exist vary between families. |
| | It is believed that career paths need to be defined in terms of competency requirements. |

**Table 8.1  Appropriate Salary Structures**

1. *Determine the number of grades, bands, or levels.* Point-factor job evaluation can be used first to produce a rank order of jobs according to their job evaluation scores and then to analyze the rank order to establish where jobs might be grouped into grades and how many grades emerge from this procedure. Alternatively, an a priori decision may be made on the number of grades, bands, or levels required based on an analysis of the value-adding tiers in the organization.

2. *Define the grades, bands, or levels.* This can be a range of job evaluation points for each grade or a verbal description. To enable job matching with grades, the latter

may refer to a number of factors such as problem solving, level of responsibility, and resource complexity.

3. *Conduct a market rate survey of benchmark jobs.* Use a typical job that represents the different occupations and levels of work in the organization and can be used as a point of reference with which other jobs can be compared and evaluated.

4. *Decide the policy on how the organization's pay levels should relate to market rates—its market stance.* This could be at the median or above the median if it is believed that pay levels should be more competitive.

5. *For a narrow or broad-graded structure, calculate the average market rates for the benchmark jobs in each grade according to market stance policy.* This produces the target rate for each grade that can act as the midpoint. In a broadbanded structure, the benchmark rates can be used to determine individual reference points or zones.

## Notes

1. Chartered Institute of Personnel and Development (CIPD), *Annual Reward Survey.* London, 2013.
2. Peter Leblanc, "Banding: The New Pay Structure for the Transformed Organization." *Journal of Compensation and Benefits*, January–February: 34–38, 1992.
3. Kenan Abosch, "The Promise of Broad-Banding." *Compensation & Benefits Review*, , February: 54–58, 1995.
4. Michael Armstrong and Duncan Brown, *New Dimensions in Pay Management.* CIPD, London, 2001.
5. Michael Armstrong, "Feel the Width." *People Management,* February: 34–38, 2000.
6. Charles Fay, Eric Schulz, Stephen Gross, and David Van De Voort, "Broad-Banding, Pay Ranges and Labor Costs: An Empirical Test." *Worldat Work Journal* 19(2):21–29, 2004.
7. Greg Stoskopf, Sheila Sever, Michelle Nguyen, and Warren Mueller, "The Evolution of Salary Structures over the Past 10 Years: Are Market-Based Salaries the New Normal?" *Worldat Work Journal*, First Quarter:29–39, 2013.

# 9

# Making Merit Pay and Bonuses Matter

Myrna Hellerman
*Sibson Consulting*

James Kochanski
*Sibson Consulting*

No organization has an unlimited pool for annual pay actions. So what can organizations do to convince their employees that superior job performance will result in superior pay opportunities? How can employers avoid the "one-size-fits-all" pay increases and bonuses that send the message that individual performance does not count? How can employers encourage pay for performance but discourage managers from "gaming the system" for their employees?

Making annual pay actions matter is not easy, but the bottom line is that it is well worth the effort. The key is to improve how an organization thinks and talks about performance. Organizations that *prove with pay* that performance matters create a culture that is good for people and good for the organization. This chapter discusses how to take pay actions that matter.

## The "Merits" of Differentiation

Although the one-size-fits-all approach to base salary increases and bonus awards certainly scores points for administrative ease and convenience, it also communicates a very powerful and negative message: "Individual performance does not matter here . . . or at least it doesn't matter enough for us to make the effort to differentiate and reward the top contributors to the company's success." This message is likely to cause good performers to disengage, thinking, "Why push myself if I'm going to get the same pay opportunity as everyone else?"

Or look at it this way: given a 3 to 4 percent merit increase (as little as $100 per month before taxes for a $40,000 per year employee) and a token $500 per employee bonus, a performance evaluation process may not seem worth the effort. However, consider an organization with 6,000 employees whose average pay is $40,000 per year. A 3.5 percent merit budget adds about $8.4 million to the cost base, and a $500 per employee bonus payment adds another $3 million. To that $11.4 million, add the costs associated with pay-related benefits (e.g., paid time off, 401(k) plan matches, and pension accruals). That is a lot of money to give away because the performance evaluation process does not seem worth the effort.

## Get More Bang for Your Annual Pay Actions

Putting merit back into annual pay actions requires tough decisions, and it may take several performance cycles to achieve. Nonetheless, meeting the challenge can be worthwhile. Studies show that the existence of pay consequences based on individual performance and impact promotes employee engagement in the success of the organization.

Here are several tested ideas from companies that are getting more bang for their buck in their base pay increase and bonus budgets:

- *Create set-asides to reward top performers accordingly.* A top performer set-aside pool (merit increase and/or bonus) ensures that the organization systematically identifies top performers and sees that they receive greater financial rewards than do individuals who perform at average/expected performance levels. The organization can carve the set-aside pool out of the merit increase and/or bonus pool.

   For instance, using the example given earlier: if an organization has 6,000 employees whose average pay is $40,000 per year, a 3.5 percent merit budget would produce a merit pool of about $8.4 million. A set-aside of $900,000 would provide an average additional $1,500 merit increase for the company's top 10 percent of performers and still allow for an average basic merit increase of $1,250 for all 6,000 employees.

   Companies that use a set-aside pool find that the allocation determination process is beneficial in itself. For instance, in order to tap into its top-performer set-aside pool, one multi-million-dollar service provider requires managers to "nominate" their top performers. Using a simple form with very specific criteria, managers provide "evidence" of superior performance. Both the manager and the nominee must sign the form. The divisional senior management team then reviews the nominations and allocates the top-performer set-aside pool among the most meritorious.

   The company introduced this approach because it wanted to return to a pure merit pay process. However, four years later, it still uses it because of four valuable benefits that have emerged:

   1. *The truly top performers hold their manager accountable for performance discussions and the nomination process.* Employees know that they are eligible for nothing more than the across-the-board increase unless their manager gives evidence of their superior performance through a top-performer nomination.

   2. *The design of the nomination form helps to frame what top performance looks like.* After the first year (when there was a flood of nominations), managers

developed a better understanding of what it takes to rate a merit increase from the top-performer set-aside pool.

3. *Allocating the pool requires silo-breaking cross-organization calibration.* It also involves thoughtful senior management discussions about performance expectations.

4. *Performance conversations at the senior management team level provide valuable insights into the organization's depth and quality of talent.* They now inform the company's evolving human capital planning process.

A variation on this approach was adopted by a large healthcare system with several thousand hourly and supervisory employees. For many years, the system's merit increase pool has been 0 to 1 percent, and the bonus pool (based on system financial performance) has hovered around 1 percent. Given the continued financial constraints, leadership decided not to make any further investments in the across-the-board wage increase and performance bonus pools. Instead, leaders took savings realized from a change in bonus plan eligibility, added another 0.25 percent of base, and thus created a high-performer award pool. This set-aside pool is distributed through a nomination and review process similar to that of the service provider described earlier. The fairness and recognition built into the pay program are considered strong reasons why this healthcare system continues to be considered as an employer of choice.

- *Clearly define performance expectations and communicate that the organization rewards top performers.* Employers who embrace this approach identify what they expect and what constitutes superior performance—and then reward accordingly through merit pay and incentive opportunities.

Take the case of a multi-billion-dollar retailer that had been teetering on the edge of bankruptcy for several years until a new CEO stepped in. Two years later, he was widely acclaimed by employees and investors alike for having saved the company. So it was a bit of a surprise when the CEO made the following statement at a town hall employee meeting: "To help you calibrate this year's performance evaluations and corresponding pay expectations, you should know I am a three (strong contributor) on the five-point performance evaluation scale used for merit increases. That's what the board has told me. In my career I have earned a higher rating only a few times."

This highly acclaimed CEO's candor about his performance rating served to recalibrate the performance standard for the entire company. "If he's a three after all he has done, how can I justify a four or five?" the employees reasoned. The pay-for-performance message received even more credibility when the board's decisions for CEO compensation were consistent with his performance rating.

In just one performance cycle, the ratings moved from their historic distribution of mostly fours and fives into an almost perfect bell curve. The company used its limited merit increase budget to recognize and reward key contributors at all organization levels. After three performance cycles, vibrancy and credibility were restored to the pay-for-performance linkage.

- *Create employee ownership of the performance outcomes that fund the base salary increase and bonus pools.* Ideally, employees who receive wage increases and year-end bonuses exhibit superior performance and skill building and make meaningful contributions to the organization's success. This, of course, assumes that they know what they must do to drive the desired business performance outcomes, which, in turn, fund the merit increases and bonus pools.

Some employers say, "Our employees won't understand and can't do anything about all this financial stuff. It's just easier to tell them that we didn't meet our targets and there isn't much money for base salary increases and bonuses." Others, however, see an opportunity to create an economic win-win situation for the company and its employees.

The leadership team of a meat-processing company realized that the continued viability of the company was at risk. The team analyzed the business's economics and developed sophisticated value trees that began with return on capital and flowed through each financial and nonfinancial measure that affected returns. The analysis suggested the need for severe belt tightening (including wage freezes) in order to ensure the business's survival. The senior vice president in charge of plant operations protested the ivory-tower corporate conclusions. "I bet if we can educate my guys on the slaughter floor about how we make money, [and] we can get improvements that will generate money for wage increases and bonuses."

The senior vice president set up a simple financial literacy program for his employee group. It included a discussion of how the company and its customers make money (and how the company can help its customers to make more money). After introducing them to a simplified version of the value trees, he asked his employees to work in teams to figure out what they could do in their day-to-day actions to improve the trees' financial outcomes. The "guys on the floor" took ownership of the performance outcomes and identified process improvements and individual skill-development opportunities that improved profitability and sustainability— and today consistently result in "meaty" merit budgets and bonus pools.

- *Aggregate merit budgets and annual bonus pools so that small departments can participate fully.* A growing number of employers combine their merit increase budgets for small departments with those for the next level or create merit budgets that cover at least 30 employees under three or more managers. In this way, the organization can address the concern that small departments with only a few employees cannot differentiate pay.

  As an added advantage, the managers of these small departments learn to talk about pay and performance. Through these peer discussions, they establish a clearer standard that differentiates top performance from expected performance. Further, groups of managers who the organization holds accountable for allocating a limited merit pool find a way to differentiate performance equitably.

  For example, a food-distribution company had a multitude of three- to four-employee teams each with its own manager. These teams, all located at headquarters, provided a specific support service to the field operations. Although the teams were accustomed to thinking of themselves as isolated units, when their merit increase budget was aggregated, the managers were forced to think about all their employees as part of a total service process. In their examination of the total process, it became very apparent which individuals and which teams were carrying more than their load in serving the field. The managers distributed the merit dollars accordingly and started to revamp the inefficient and ineffective aspects of the process.

- *Form groups of managers to calibrate performance ratings, merit increases, and bonus pool allocations to lessen manager-to-manager differences.* A frequently heard employee complaint is, "The system isn't fair because my manager rates tougher than your manager." One way to solve this problem is to convene a group of peer managers to calibrate performance ratings, merit increases, and bonus awards prior to finalization. Performance calibration is a method of having peer managers review each other's decisions before they are final in order to adopt common norms and adjust decisions so that they are fair and accurate.

Some organizations educate managers so that they understand why inflated performance ratings are bad for the organization and people. As a result, managers hold each other accountable for accurate ratings. A grid such as the example in Table 9.1 helps managers to understand that if they inflate ratings, there is less money to reward and recognize those designated as high performers.

| | Percent of Employees | | | |
|---|---|---|---|---|
| Designated high performer | 75 | 50 | 25 | 10 |
| Designated average performer | 25 | 50 | 75 | 90 |
| | Percent Increase | | | |
| Raise for high performer | 3.17 | 3.5 | 4.5 | 7.5 |
| Raise for average performer | 2.5 | 2.5 | 2.5 | 2.5 |
| Source: Sibson Consulting | | | | |

**Table 9.1  Ratings Differentiation Drives Pay Differentiation**

Another idea, taken from behavioral economics, is that performance rating is too complex to be done well on a consistent basis. A solution is to create a *default rating* that is in the middle of the scale. Managers only need to address individuals who do not meet the definition of average/expected performance. Without such a default, some organizations find that the default rating becomes a high rating, and in effect, almost everyone is rated high but paid as if they are average.

In a calibration meeting, managers bring a set of preliminary ratings and sometimes merit and bonus recommendations. Managers who have to justify their recommendations tend to be more responsible in their recommendations than those who can make such decisions on their own or with only a single signoff by their boss.

A large multinational manufacturer adopted the group calibration of ratings approach. After the first, very painful attempt at group calibration, there was (and continues to be) an increase in the number of hits on the relevant online learning modules and increased attendance at company-sponsored training sessions on performance management and calibration.

Calibration also increases employee confidence in the process. Employees who know that their performance is reviewed by managers in addition to their own have more trust in the fairness of the decisions.

- *Reposition the organization's mind-set so that it views merit increases and bonuses as investment spending.* The merit increase budget and annual bonus pools are long-term investments in talent that will drive the organization's sustainable success.

Investing in employees who have not demonstrated the level of performance and skill building that the company expects does not make financial sense.

Repositioning the organization's mind-set requires consistent and frequent communication with executives, managers, and employees. For example, a mid-sized financial services employer talks the language of its business to its employees. This firm positions all compensation discussions in terms of an investment. Employees understand that decisions with respect to individual merit increases reflect an evaluation of prior-year individual performance and applicable skill acquisition and the expectation of continued further "returns on [the merit increase] investment."

A large insurance company took the return-on-investment concept in a courageous direction. Its go-forward business strategy totally restructured the products offered and the markets served. As a result, the company's talent needs changed dramatically. Unfortunately, there was no increase in merit and bonus dollars to attract, engage, and retain the specialized talent needed to execute the go-forward business strategy.

To address the issue of financial resource constraints, the company segmented its talent by business-performance impact. The limited merit and bonus dollars were "invested" in the high performers in the roles that were critical to driving long-term sustainable business success—that is, the high performers in roles with the largest return-on-investment potential for the company. The company said no to any future base pay and bonus investments in talent segments where skills no longer were aligned with the company's needs.

- *Simplify the performance evaluation process—aim for less paperwork and conversation that is more meaningful.* Even when merit increase budgets and bonus pools are more robust, many employers still question the time and effort it takes to recognize and reward employees based on differentiated performance. In many cases, the protocols and processes are too complex—and sometimes too depersonalized and mechanical.

A global 25,000-employee engineering firm decided to automate its traditional, highly interactive approach to performance evaluation and pay action determination. An elegant 100 percent online solution replaced the performance-contracting dialog between managers and employees. All interactions were Internet based. It was a very efficient system: the firm met every payroll deadline associated with merit increases, the merit increase and bonus pools were exactly spent, and there were no tough, time-consuming face-to-face conversations. Everything was on time, on budget, and "on spec."

After several years with the online approach, the firm analyzed the outcomes. Among the findings, managers and employees alike had learned to game the system. There was little differentiation of performance (and thus pay increases); almost everyone was a four or five on a five-point rating system. The online forms were complicated and time-consuming to complete. Employees and managers saw the process as a burdensome "joke." Even more important for a firm that prided itself on high performance, its annual performance targets (strategic, operational, and financial) were achieved but not exceeded.

As a result, the firm made several important changes. While it preserved the document trail associated with the online system, it introduced simplified forms and restored face-to-face interactions between managers and employees. The updated approach requires specific manager-employee and manager-manager "conversations" as well as cross-unit managerial calibration of performance ratings, merit increases, and bonus determinations.

The most lauded aspect of the new approach is the beginning-of-cycle small group meetings where the firm's strategic, operational, and financial performance imperatives for the new year are reviewed. Employees and managers discuss the performance expectations required to deliver on those imperatives. The employees then use this information to develop their annual individual goals, which are used to inform future pay action decisions.

While the updated approach is still time-consuming, managers and employees agree that it takes the black box out of performance expectations and pay consequences and has reenergized the firm to deliver once again the superior performance that results in superior pay opportunities.

## Is Your Organization Ready for This?

Before an organization adopts any one (or a combination) of the approaches described in this chapter, it needs to evaluate how the approach fits its performance culture. It also should assess its leadership's capability and willingness to "put the organization's money where its mouth is" to show employees that their performance matters.

Some leaders want to add "making performance matter" to their successor's to-do list. For instance, the CEO of a midsized service business stated, "I'm only a few years from retirement. I want my legacy to be as a 'well-loved' leader. Why rock the boat? My successor can tackle this." Unfortunately for this CEO, the business suffered an economically catastrophic event. Many of the organization's top performers had already left because of a perceived unfairness in pay administration and the better opportunities for financial recognition elsewhere. The remaining employees had inadequate capabilities to fix the problems. The CEO was retired by the board but without the laurels he had anticipated.

Additionally, organizations must be ready to accept that limited pools for base pay increases and bonuses are no excuse for a one-size-fits-all approach to annual pay actions. Organizations in which annual pay actions are essentially the same for individual employees regardless of how they perform need to take steps to put performance back into their annual pay actions.

No matter how small they may seem, merit increases and bonuses can be made more meaningful if they are linked directly to superior individual performance, effective skill building, and contributions to the organization's success. Employers that clearly define performance expectations, communicate that top performers will be rewarded, and then take the necessary steps to make it happen can create an environment in which merit pay and bonuses truly matter.

# 10

# The Purpose and Nature of Job Evaluation

Michael Armstrong
*E-reward.co.uk*

Paul Thompson
*E-reward.co.uk*

This chapter is about the nature and use of job evaluation as a means of establishing how much jobs are worth. The main learning points are

- The purpose and nature of job evaluation
- The pros and cons of job evaluation
- How job evaluation works
- The main types of job evaluations
- The use of computer-aided job evaluation
- The criteria for choice

## The Purpose and Nature of Job Evaluation

*Job evaluation* is a systematic process for deciding on the relative worth or size of jobs within an organization. Gupta and Jenkins[1] stated that the basic premise of job evaluation is that certain jobs "contribute more to organizational effectiveness and success than others, are worth more than others, and should be paid more than others."

Job evaluation takes place in various forms. These consist of the traditional nonanalytical schemes such as ranking and job classification and the traditional analytical schemes such as point-factor rating. There are also the more recent developments of leveling and analytical job matching. These schemes deal with the assessment of internal relativities (comparable worth). However, the process of valuing jobs extends beyond these internal concerns to the analysis of external relativities, that is, market rates, through the process of market pricing (the analysis of data on market rates to provide a basis for fixing rates of pay).

A formal approach to evaluating comparable worth provides the basis for designing or amending a grade structure, and information on market rates enables pay ranges to be attached to the structure. Traditional job evaluation techniques or the newer methodologies of leveling and analytical job matching can be used to determine where a job is placed in the structure and therefore the rate or range of rates for that job. Alternatively, market pricing can be used directly to fix the rates of pay for jobs or individuals. The performance of individuals also affects their pay, but this is not a matter for job evaluation, which is concerned with valuing the jobs people carry out, not how well they perform their jobs.

Although many businesses rely entirely on an informal, indeed ad hoc, approach to valuing jobs, there is a good case for formal job evaluation. However, a strong case against traditional methods has been made.

## Arguments for and against Job Evaluation

A systematic approach to job evaluation enables organizations to make decisions on the true worth of their employees in relation to both their coworkers and the external labor market. It helps to ensure that the compensation arrangements are both internally equitable and externally competitive. It brings order and discipline to situations that can too easily become chaotic without the structure developed by job evaluation.

However, it can do more than that. In the resource-based view, as explained by Barney[2]:

> Creating sustained competitive advantage depends on the unique resources and capabilities that a firm brings to competition in its environment. To discover these resources and capabilities, managers must look inside their firm for valuable, rare and costly-to-imitate resources, and then exploit these resources through their organization.

Systematic job evaluation can provide crucial help in attracting and retaining the valuable and rare people the business needs by developing an employee value proposition that spells out that they will be rewarded according to the value they create, that rewards will be competitive, and that clarity and transparency are fundamental principles governing the reward system. The aim will be to incorporate the benefits of job evaluation into the employer brand so that the firm becomes an employer of choice.

The major criticism of traditional approaches to job evaluation is that they focus on internal relativities and ignore the importance of the external market. Nielsen[3] took exception to the fact that traditional job evaluation is not concerned with external relativities, which, he claims, are what really matter. But traditional methods of evaluation such as point-factor rating also have been criticized for being cumbersome, bureaucratic, inflexible, time-consuming, and inappropriate for the types of roles found in today's organizations.

However, things have moved on. It is now generally acknowledged that businesses must take account of market rates as a necessary part of the process of valuing jobs in order to be competitive in the external labor market. Market pricing, as described in the next section of this chapter, is by far the most common method of valuing jobs in the United States. Although formal job evaluation schemes, as also described in the next section, are still in use, there is much less reliance on the elaborate and time-consuming traditional versions that, when adopted, do no more than support the simpler processes of leveling and analytical matching.

## How Formal Job Evaluation Schemes Work

Formal job evaluation schemes use comparative, judgmental, structured, and analytical processes, as discussed next.

### Job Evaluation as a Comparative Process

Job evaluation deals with relationships, not absolutes. It does this in one of the following ways:

- *Job to job.* Jobs are compared with other jobs in order to decide whether their value is greater, lesser, or the same, as in ranking, whole-job matching, and market pricing.
- *Job to scale.* Jobs are compared with a scale, which could be a graduated scale of points attached to a set of factors, as in point-factor rating, or a defined hierarchy of job grades, as in job classification or leveling.
- *Factor to factor.* Jobs are analyzed into their elements or factors and compared factor by factor with grade or role profiles analyzed under the same factor headings, as in analytical matching.

### Job Evaluation as a Judgmental Process

Job evaluation requires the exercise of judgment in interpreting data on jobs and roles, comparing one job with another, and comparing jobs against scales or factor by factor. This approach can be described as a subjective process carried out within an objective framework, although Graeff Crystal[4] argued that "[e]ssentially, job evaluation boils down to organized rationalization."

### Job Evaluation as a Structured Process

A formal job evaluation scheme is structured in the sense that a framework is provided that aims to help evaluators make consistent and reasoned judgments. This framework consists of language and criteria used by all evaluators, although, because the criteria are always subject to interpretation, they do not guarantee that judgments will be either consistent or rational.

### Job Evaluation as an Analytical Process

Job evaluation is, or should be, based on a factual description of the characteristics of the jobs under consideration. This means that although judgmental, at least the judgments are informed. However, schemes may be described as analytical in the sense that jobs are analyzed and compared in terms of defined elements or factors or nonanalytical in the sense that "whole jobs" that have not been analyzed by factor are compared with one another. Properly designed and executed analytical schemes can help to ensure that judgments are structured and consistent.

## Types of Job Evaluations

The main types of job evaluations are

- *The traditional nonanalytical schemes.* Job ranking, job classification, and job matching.
- *The traditional analytical schemes.* Point-factor rating, factor comparison.
- *The most recently developed approaches.* Leveling and analytical job matching.
- *Market pricing.*

### Job Ranking

Whole-job ranking is the most primitive form of job evaluation and is little used on its own. The process involves comparing whole jobs with one another and arranging them in order of their perceived value to the organization. In a sense, all evaluation schemes are ranking exercises because they place jobs in a hierarchy.

### Job Classification

This approach is based on a definition of the number and characteristics of the levels or grades in a grade and pay structure into which jobs will be placed. The grade definitions may refer to such job characteristics as skill, decision making, and responsibility, but these are not analyzed separately. Evaluation takes place by a process of nonanalytical matching or job slotting. This involves comparing a "whole" job description, that is, one not analyzed into factors, with the grade definitions to establish the grade with which the job most closely corresponds. The difference between job classification and role-to-grade analytical matching as described earlier is that in the latter case, the grade profiles are defined analytically, that is, in terms of job evaluation factors, and analytically defined role profiles are matched with them factor by factor. However, the distinction between analytical and nonanalytical matching can be blurred when the comparison is made between formal job descriptions or role profiles that have been prepared in a standard format that includes common headings for such aspects of jobs as levels of responsibility or knowledge and skill requirements. These "factors" may not be compared specifically but will be taken into account when forming a judgment. This has been the most popular form of nonanalytical job evaluation, but in the United Kingdom it was used by only 5 percent of the respondents to the UK 2007 e-reward survey.[5]

### Point-Factor Evaluation

The basic methodology is to break down jobs into factors or key elements representing the demands made by the job on jobholders. It is assumed that each of the factors will contribute to the value of the job and is an aspect of all the jobs to be evaluated but to different degrees.

Each factor is divided into a hierarchy of levels. Definitions of these levels are produced to provide guidance on deciding the degree to which the factor applies in the job to be evaluated. Evaluators consult the role profile or job description, which ideally should analyze the role in terms of the scheme's factors. They then refer to the level definitions for each factor and decide which one best fits the job.

A maximum point score is allocated to each factor. The scores available may vary between different factors in accordance with beliefs about their relative significance. This is termed *explicit weighting*. If the number of levels varies between factors, this means that they are implicitly weighted because the range of scores available will be greater in the factors with more levels.

The total score for a factor is divided between the levels to produce the numerical factor scale. Progression may be arithmetic, for example, 50, 100, 150, 200, and so on, or geometric, for example, 50, 100, 175, 275, and so on. In the latter case, more scope is given to recognize the more senior jobs with higher scores.

The complete scheme consists of the factor and level definitions and the scoring system (the total score available for each factor and distributed to the factor levels). This comprises the *factor plan*.

Jobs are scored (i.e., allocated points) under each factor heading on the basis of the level of the factor in the job. This is done by comparing the features of the job with regard to that factor with the factor level definitions to find out which definition provides the best fit. The separate factor scores are then added together to give a total score that indicates the relative value for each job and can be used to place the jobs in rank order.

Point-factor rating is the most common form of traditional analytical job evaluation. In the United Kingdom, it was used by 70 percent of the respondents to the e-reward 2007 survey[6] who had job evaluation schemes. In the United States, though, the 2009 Worldat-Work survey[7] found that point-factor schemes were used by only 14 percent of respondents for senior managers, 18 percent for middle managers, and 19 percent for administrative staff.

### Factor Comparison

The original and now-obsolete factor comparison method compared jobs factor by factor using a scale of money values to provide a direct indication of the rate for the job. The only form of factor comparison now occasionally in use is graduated factor comparison, which compares jobs factor by factor with a graduated scale. The scale may have only three value levels, for example lower, equal, and higher, and no factor scores are used.

### Leveling

*Leveling* is a term often used by consultants to describe a process of identifying and defining the levels of work that exist in an organization. As a form of job classification, it may serve as the basis for a pay structure, but increasingly, leveling provides guidance on career mapping, organizational analysis, developing and describing international organization structures, and providing a link to an information technology (IT) system.

When it is used simply as a means of defining pay structures, leveling could be regarded as no more than a euphemism adopted by consultants who want to dissociate themselves from the negative connotations of traditional job evaluation schemes. However, it is more meaningful when the focus is on the career mapping and organizational and IT applications mentioned earlier. Defining an organization structure in levels may express the philosophy of a business about how it should be organized and the career steps that are available to its people.

In practice, leveling uses established job evaluation techniques such as analytical matching or job classification and may be underpinned by point-factor rating. It starts with a decision on the number of levels required, which could be based on a ranking exercise using either point-factor scheme scores or whole-job ranking. Alternatively, an a priori decision may be made on the number of levels required by a study of the organization structure, which may be supported by a role profiling exercise. This decision may be amended later after the level structure has been tested. Levels may be defined in terms of job evaluation factors or a selection of them. In cases where the focus is on career mapping as well as or instead of pay determination, the level definitions or profiles may be stated in ways that clearly establish the career ladder, often in a career or job family. The definition may express what people are expected to know and be able to do at each level (technical competencies), and/or they may refer to behavioral competencies. The aim is to produce a clear hierarchy of levels that will ease the process of allocating roles to levels and define career progression steps in and between families.

### Analytical Job Matching

Like point-factor job evaluation, analytical job matching is based on an analysis of a number of defined factors. Profiles of roles to be evaluated that have been analyzed and described in terms of job evaluation factors are compared with grade, band, or level profiles that have been analyzed and described in terms of the same job evaluation factors. The role profiles then are matched with the range of grade or level profiles to establish the best fit and thus grade the job.

Analytical matching can be used to grade jobs or place them in levels following the initial evaluation of a sufficiently large sample of benchmark jobs, that is, representative jobs that provide a valid basis for comparisons. This can happen in big organizations when it is believed that it is not necessary to go through the whole process of point-factor evaluation for every job, especially where "generic" roles are concerned. It takes much less time than using a point-factor scheme, and the results can be just as accurate. The 2007 UK e-reward survey[8] found that 12 percent of organizations with job evaluation schemes used this method. In 2004, it was used for over 1 million National Health Service staff in England in a massive job evaluation exercise.

### Market Pricing

What has been called *extreme market pricing* directly prices jobs within an organization by means of a systematic analysis of market rates (external relativities). Internal relativities reflect those present in the marketplace, and conventional job evaluation is not used. An organization that adopts this method is said to be *market driven*.

Advocates of market pricing assert that it obviates the need for spurious attempts to validate formal job evaluation. They claim that market rates are ascertainable facts not subject to the judgments present in traditional approaches. However, judgments still have to be made on the use of market-rate data, especially where it is difficult to match internal jobs with external ones. The accuracy of market pricing depends on the availability of robust market data and the quality of the job-to-job matching process, that is, comparing like with like.

In the United States, the 2009 WorldatWork survey found that market pricing schemes were used by respondents for 75 percent for senior managers, 70 percent for middle managers, and 67 percent for administrative staff, making this approach by far the most common. In contrast, in the United Kingdom, the 2013 Chartered Institute of Personnel and Development (CIPD) reward management survey[9] found that only 21 percent of the respondents used market pricing. The preference for analytical job evaluation schemes in the United Kingdom can be explained by the fact that in accordance with equal pay legislation, an equal pay claim can only be defended through an analytical scheme.

## Computer-Aided Job Evaluation

Computer-aided job evaluation uses computer software to convert information about jobs into a job evaluation score or grade. It is generally underpinned by a conventional point-factor scheme. Computers may be used simply to maintain a database that records evaluations and their rationale. The software used in a fully computer-aided scheme essentially replicates in digital form the thought processes followed by evaluators when conducting a manual evaluation. It is based on defined evaluation decision rules built into the system shell.

## Choice of Approach

In deciding on what to do about job evaluation, the three basic considerations are

1. Will the approach we adopt further the achievement of the organization's goals?
2. Is the approach consistent with our compensation philosophy?
3. Will it fit the context in which it will be used, that is, the organization structure and the jobs it will have to cover?

In the light of the answers to these three questions, the approach can be chosen by reference to the criteria set out in Table 10.1. These criteria are based on the experience of Michael Armstrong[10] as a practitioner and consultant in developing and/or installing 14 job evaluation schemes.

| Criteria | Job Ranking | Job Classification | Point-Factor Rating | Leveling | Analytical Job Matching | Market Pricing |
|---|---|---|---|---|---|---|
| | | | Score: 1 to 10 | | | |
| Achieve internal equity | 4 | 5 | 8 | 7 | 8 | 1 |
| Achieve external competitiveness | 1 | 1 | 1 | 1 | 1 | 10 |
| Accurate | 3 | 4 | 7 | 7 | 8 | 8 |
| Perceived as fair by employees | 5 | 5 | 8 | 7 | 8 | 4 |
| Ease of development and operation | 6 | 5 | 4 | 6 | 7 | 7 |
| Cost of development and operation | 6 | 6 | 4 | 6 | 5 | 7 |
| (higher score = lower cost) | | | | | | |

Table 10.1  Michael Armstrong's Criteria for Job Evaluation

# Bibliography

ACAS. 2005. *Job Evaluation: An Introduction*. London.

Armstrong, Michael, and Angela Baron. 1995. *The Job Evaluation Handbook*. Chartered Institute of Personnel and Development, London.

Armstrong, Michael, and Ann Cummins. 2008. *Valuing Roles*. Kogan Page, London.

Dive, Brian. 2004. *The Healthy Organization*. Kogan Page, London.

Egan, John. 2004. "Putting Job Evaluation to Work: Tips from the Front Line." *IRS Employment Review*, no. 792, January 23, pp. 8–15.

Eargle, Fred. 2013. *Job Evaluation: Traditional Approaches and Emerging Technology*. Lulu.com, Raleigh, NC.

Emerson, Sandra. 1991. "Job Evaluation: A Barrier to Excellence." *Compensation & Benefits Review*, January–February:4–17.

Heneman, Robert. 2001. "Work Evaluation: Current State of the Art and Future Prospects." *WorldatWork Journal* 10(3):65–70.

Elliott, Jaques E. 1961. *Equitable Payment*. Heineman, Oxford, UK.

Lawler, Ed. 1986. "What's Wrong with Point-Factor Job Evaluation?" *Compensation & Benefits Review*, March–April:20–28.

Paterson, Tom. 1972. *Job Evaluation: A New Method*. Business Books, London.

Pritchard, Derek, and Helen Murlis. 1992. *Jobs, Roles and People*. Nicholas Brealey, London.

Quaid, Maeve. 1993. *Job Evaluation: The Myth of Equitable Settlement*. University of Toronto Press, Toronto.

Risher, Howard. 1989. "Job Evaluation: Validity and Reliability." *Compensation & Benefits Review*, January–February:22–36.

Watson, Steve. 2005. "Is Job Evaluation Making a Comeback—or Did It Never Go Away?" *Benefits and Compensation International* 34(10):8–12, 14.

# Notes

1. N. Gupta and G. D. Jenkins, "Practical Problems in Using Job Evaluation to Determine Compensation." *Human Resource Management Review* 1(2):133–144, 1991.
2. Jay Barney, "Looking Inside for Competitive Advantage." *Academy of Management Executive* 9(4):49–61, 1995.
3. Niels Nielsen, "Job Content Evaluation Techniques Based on Marxian Economics." *WorldatWork Journal* 11(2):52–62, 2002.
4. Graeff Crystal, *Financial Motivation for Executives*. American Management Association, New York, 1970.
5. "Survey of Job Evaluation," 2007. Available at: e-reward.co.uk.
6. Ibid.
7. WorldatWork, "Job Evaluation and Market Pricing Practices Survey," Scottsdale, AZ, 2009.
8. "Survey of Job Evaluation," 2007. Available at e-reward.co.uk.
9. Chartered Institute of Personnel and Development, "Reward Management Survey," London, 2013.
10. Michael Armstrong, "Job Evaluation Factsheet," 2014. Available at: e-reward.co.uk.

# 11

# Optimizing the Use of Salary Surveys

Tim Brown

*Radford Surveys & Consulting*

This chapter will help readers to better understand and use the numerous sources of external market compensation data (from labor groups, industry groups, government entities, and commercial survey vendors). Our special focus is on a discussion of the role commercial third-party-vendor compensation surveys play as a resource for making pay decisions in organizations today, as well as the features companies should consider when determining which survey or surveys best meet their needs.

## Current Business Issues

Beyond this introductory scenario, companies around the world are facing an environment in which pay data are increasingly critical. The tools available today for gathering, storing, and analyzing data are increasing in adaptability and effectiveness. The emergence of "big data" creates an expectation that business decisions are increasingly based on facts and supported by analysis. Many human resources decisions remain subjective, and the "art" of compensation plan design is as important today as always. Yet the effective and sophisticated use of data is now the norm in a world where employment levels are recovering from the Great Recession, labor markets continue to expand globally, and demographic trends in some parts of the world point to an aging (and, in the long-term, contracting) workforce.

Organizations are also facing stricter regulations related to compensation. During the past several years, regulatory agencies and shareholder activist groups have stepped up scrutiny of executive pay, resulting in new requirements for greater disclosure of pay levels and pay practices for top executives. At the broad-based employee level, changes in the U.S. Fair Labor Standards Act and locally driven minimum-wage regulations have added complexity. In addition, tax rules often motivate a review of how compensation is delivered. These dynamics make awareness of the rules very important. As one example, accounting requirements for stock-option expensing contributed to the increased use of restricted stock among technology companies.

## Forms and Applications of Compensation Data

Fundamentally, compensation surveys provide information about how much people are paid to perform a given job. This data typically are broken down into types of compensation, such as base salary, allowances, bonuses and commissions, equity, and other rewards. The data reflect the surveyed labor market based on the types of companies that participate. It is important to remember that compensation surveys do not tell companies how much they should pay their employees. Rather, they reflect what other companies actually pay their employees in similar jobs (typically referred to in surveys as *benchmark jobs*). How the information is used remains the prerogative of the user.

Typical applications of survey data include

- Assessing external pay competitiveness for specific employees, groups of employees, or the whole organization

- Creating market-competitive salary ranges for benchmark jobs, thereby serving as the basis for building entire salary structures

- Capturing compensation plan characteristics useful for plan design or redesign considerations, including competitive pay mix (between fixed and variable pay, as well as between short- and long-term incentives)

- Reflecting what competitors are doing with respect to pay practices, for example, the frequency of bonus payouts, the vesting policies for equity, and the target mix of fixed and variable pay

- Understanding competitors' promotional increase policies, merit budget practices, salary range movement, and geographic pay differentials in various locations within a country

- Revealing trends in the labor market, for example, growth in demand for particular jobs, and the shift from stock options to restricted stock

- Providing the data necessary to effectively communicate a new compensation strategy by showing survey data on current and projected pay positions

- Establishing how much to offer a new hire to achieve a specifically targeted pay level or how much pay is needed to meet prevailing wage requirements for employees proposed for a work visa

- Justifying the assignment of a salary grade to a newly created position

## Types of Surveys

Compensation surveys are published by a variety of sources and take numerous forms. Almost all of them incorporate the concept of *benchmark jobs*—jobs that are defined in a certain way in the survey so that participating organizations can be consistent in reporting compensation data for their employees in roles that match the descriptions of the survey jobs. Benchmark jobs are often defined in terms of employee category (e.g., executive, management, professional individual contributor, support individual contributor), function (e.g., product development, operations, marketing, sales), and level (e.g., entry, career, advanced).

*Government Surveys.* The U.S. government, through the Bureau of Labor Statistics, publishes data for certain jobs and specific geographic areas. The time it takes to collect, analyze, and report such data often allows alternative surveys to better meet the needs of private companies.

*Subscription Surveys.* Subscription surveys are typically published by a third-party commercial survey publisher, which collects, analyzes, summarizes, and reports the compensation data. Participating companies (those providing data) pay a fee, and typically, results are only available to participants or those who agree to participate in a subsequent edition of the survey. Subscription surveys often produce both overall results and additional cuts of data (e.g., geographic, industry, company size, etc.). Participants frequently have the opportunity to supplement standard reports with custom data cuts (e.g., selecting specific companies to form a peer group–based report). These surveys typically are conducted on an annual basis and have a fairly consistent participant group. This stability contributes to meaningful year-over-year comparison of results. A variation on this model allows non-participants to obtain overall survey results for a much larger fee than that paid by participants.

*Custom Surveys.* Custom surveys are often conducted on behalf of a sponsoring company or organization to meet specific data needs. Similar to subscription surveys, custom surveys are often conducted by a third party. However, unlike subscription surveys, custom surveys are limited to a targeted small group of potential participants (e.g., a specific list of companies, industry niche, geographic area, etc.) and may be conducted on an infrequent basis. This type of survey may go by the name of a *club survey*, where the ability to join the survey is limited to those whose data are considered valuable to other survey participants.

*Online Self-Reported Surveys.* An emerging survey type is self-reported compensation data, often conducted online. As opposed to a typical subscription or custom survey, where employers report data for all employees performing specific roles, data from self-reported surveys come from individuals who directly provide their own pay information. There are several drawbacks to this type of survey:

- Participating employees are not as skilled as compensation professionals at assessing their own job levels and matching them appropriately, nor do they typically have access to the full scope of available tools and information to job match effectively.

- Data provided by employees cannot be easily verified and validated by the vendor.

- Employees typically provide their data on an ad hoc basis, resulting in a less-than-consistent database.

- There is an inherent question regarding whether self-reported data are representative of the market overall. It is impossible to know if it accurately or over- or understates the level of pay reportable by a more statistically valid sample.

*Practices Surveys.* These surveys typically focus on *how* companies compensate their employees rather than *how much*. Practices information details the ways in which companies structure and implement the various components of their compensation programs. Comprehensive surveys in this category cover incentive and equity plan types, participation levels, payout or vesting schedules, funding mechanics, equity burn rate, and many more plan design and administrative issues. These surveys also may cover compensation of the board of directors as well as company-wide pay practices, including salary increase budgets and actuals, salary structure adjustments, geographic differentials, new hire and retention bonus programs, car policies, and turnover. Pay-related topics such as new college graduate new hire guidelines, shift premium policies, and on-call pay programs may be conducted as practices surveys.

*Pulse or Flash Surveys.* *Pulse* and *flash* are generally terms for a topical survey that is meant to focus on a key area of concern facing organizations. These surveys, partially characterized by the speed with which they are produced, are meant to fill the need for intelligence on how the market is responding to particular events, such as regulatory or accounting changes, emerging practices, and/or demand for a particular skill or specialized job type. These surveys often focus on a single topic. Some hot topics or emerging trends become content for future ongoing surveys, but many topics are surveyed only once. The value of a flash survey is tied to the clarity with which the questions are defined because they often measure jobs or practices where standard practices do not exist.

## Survey Data: Input and Output

Surveys are designed to collect a varying level of detail depending on the question they aim to answer. For certain surveys, base salary data alone may be sufficient because other compensation components typically may not be included in the compensation package. For other surveys, a more comprehensive picture of the market is essential. In addition to base salary, these surveys cover incentives (both target incentives and actual payouts), equity and long-term incentives in various forms (e.g., stock options, restricted stock, performance shares, long-term performance bonuses), and potentially, allowances and perquisites.

In the most complete surveys, compensation elements will be reported in combination as well as individually. For example, total cash compensation (i.e., base salary plus incentives) is reported in addition to separate base salary and incentives figures. Because pay at the 50th percentile for base salary plus a 50th percentile incentive award does not necessarily equal 50th percentile total compensation, the total cash compensation figure should be calculated in the survey output separately. In this way, the survey user has a better picture of the market range of total cash compensation.

Surveys that collect complete short- and long-term incentive data also may report additional data combinations, such as total direct compensation, which combines base salary plus annual incentive plus equity/long-term incentive value. The most comprehensive value, total remuneration, adds the value of benefits to the equation.

## Survey Data Sample

There is an ongoing potential conflict between the size and selectivity of the data sample in surveys. Put another way, for a given survey job, is it better to have a larger number of incumbents for a more general cut of the data or a smaller sample that captures a more narrow market niche? Overall survey results are appropriate for many jobs, but companies often want to compare their compensation levels with those of companies with which they compete for talent. It is important to acknowledge that if the market is too narrowly defined, the size of the data sample may be too small to be reliable or may overweight a relatively small number of companies. In such cases, taking a somewhat broader view of the market renders more reliable and representative results.

Company demographics used to define the market sample can include one or more of the following elements:

- *Company size.* Data segmented by company revenue (or assets, market capitalization, or number of employees) are particularly useful for executive-level positions given the general correlation between company size and compensation at that level in the organization.

- *Geographic area.* In regions where pay is high, data from that local area are important to use. When talent is sourced primarily from the local pay markets (typical for lower-level positions), geography is a key component of the competitive frame of reference. By contrast, geography tends to be a less significant driver in professional, management, and executive compensation; in these cases, revenue and industry play a larger role than does geography where talent may be recruited with relocation in mind.

- *Industry.* Certain jobs are industry specific, making access to data from other companies with the same type of job in the same industry niche very important. The structure of compensation packages also may differ by industry; for example, the high-technology and life-sciences industries emphasize equity more than other industries. At the same time, industry segmentation (subindustry) may be less significant for more senior-level positions. A CEO may be equally effective coming from outside a specific industry segment. In this instance, company size is more important than industry.

- *Company type.* Companies can be independent corporations or subsidiaries, public or private, mature or emerging (and numerous combinations of these). The pay structure differentiations driven by company type are particularly relevant to senior executive positions. For example, compensation levels for general management and finance positions tend to be higher in independent corporations than in subsidiaries, and equity tends to play a bigger role for more senior-level jobs in emerging prepublic companies than in public entities.

## Survey Data Presentation

### Report Types

Surveys providing a variety of data-presentation approaches offer a distinct advantage for participating companies. As opposed to the traditional static paper output in a binder, surveys are now typically published online. Although many survey providers still publish paper or PDF reports, others augment those reports with spreadsheet output and online access to certain elements of the survey database. Each of these distribution vehicles has advantages and disadvantages. Paper (or PDF format) reports provide easy access to answers for specific questions in presentation-ready form. But they are difficult to update, may limit information sharing among multiple users, and require data entry into another form (such as a spreadsheet) when additional analysis is necessary. Spreadsheet output may interface directly with a company's human resources information system (HRIS), facilitating salary planning, competitive analysis, and aggregation with other survey databases. Spreadsheet limitations include the work needed to format data for presentation with senior management or other audiences. Online reports and data-access capabilities can be updated on a periodic basis as the database changes and also can generate downloadable data sets in camera-ready presentation formats. Multiple users in different locations also can access data more easily with online reporting.

## Calculation Considerations

*Mean or Average.* The mean is the average of a set of values calculated by adding all the numbers and dividing by the number of values. Contrary to the median, averages are more susceptible to the influence of outliers.

*Median.* The median (also known as the *50th percentile*) describes the midpoint of a range of numbers sorted from high to low; half the numbers in the range are above the median and half below. The median is used in working with compensation data to mitigate the impact of pay that is at the extreme highs and lows of the range. It is not unusual to see significant variability between the highs and lows of compensation data because actual pay can be affected by several factors, including length of service of the incumbent, variability in the responsibility or criticality of the role, and the company's pay approach.

*Percentile.* The percentile marks the percentage of the data falling beneath it. For example, if the base salary for a job is $50,000 at the 75th percentile of the market, this means that 75 percent of the incumbents in the data sample are paid less than $50,000 for the job. Compensation data are often displayed in quartile buckets using the 25th, 50th, and 75th percentiles; some surveys will include the 10th and 90th percentiles to provide a more complete picture of the range of data.

*Array of Data.* Most survey reports contain both averages and percentiles; some also will show the absolute high and low values of the data. It is important to analyze the data in a variety of ways. Although the average is an appropriate summation of the data for a particular element, it does not convey the range of practices and can be skewed when the data sample is small and there are significant outliers. Using the 50th percentile (median) rather than the average can offset skewing of the data. Percentiles also reflect the range of the data sample and allow users to more specifically target their competitive position. For example, a company can have a stated competitive position of being "5 percent above the average" without knowing where that places it against its competitors. However, if the targeted competitive position is stated in terms of a percentile (e.g., 60th percentile), the pay position philosophy is directly reflected in survey data.

*Diluted and Undiluted Data.* Assume a world with six people. Three receive a bonus of 10; the other three receive no bonus. What is the average bonus? If you say that the average is 10, you are defining the universe as "reporting employees." That is, only those who reported receipt of an incentive are included in the calculation. This also may be called an *undiluted* value. If you say that the average is 5, you are considering the fact that the total bonus (30) was given across a universe of six people. This calculation reflects "all employees" and may be called a *diluted* value. Different situations tied to the specific question being asked about the market data dictate when it is best to use the "reporting employees" versus the "all employees" view of the data.

For example, in the case of incentive data, "reporting employees" limits the database to employees for whom incentive amounts are actually reported. These data are the appropriate frame of reference when users position their employees receiving incentives against other employees receiving incentives. The "all employees" look at the market includes employees not eligible for or not receiving incentives and therefore reduces or dilutes the average incentive amount reported. This can be a useful way to look at typical incentive spend competitive practices across the entire pay market.

*Weighted and Simple Average.* The weighted average (sometimes also called the *employee average*) takes into account all incumbents in the data sample. Companies matching more employees to a survey job will have a greater impact on the employee-weighted average than companies reporting fewer employees. Weighted averages are used in compensation surveys to express the overall market rate for a particular job. However, a simple (or *company*) average weights the data for each company in the sample equally. It is essentially an average of each company's average for the data element. Simple averages can be useful when a small number of companies dominate the data sample.

*Equity.* This term applies to one of the more difficult compensation elements to survey. Whereas cash compensation such as base salaries and incentives uses a common language to describe amounts (e.g., dollars in the United States), there are various equity vehicles as well as different ways to quantify the size and/or value of equity grants. A complete discussion of this topic is beyond the scope of this chapter, but following is a brief discussion of the key issues.

## Types of Equity or Long-Term Incentive Vehicles

Plan types include stock options, restricted stock, performance shares, phantom stock, and cash long-term incentive plans, among others. Because not all equity grants are equal (see below), it is important for a survey to collect equity plan data by separate vehicle to ensure proper valuation. Combining different types of equity grants into a single value (in the results) can provide a more complete picture of the competitive market in long-term compensation, but certain assumptions need to be made regarding relative equivalencies, and such assumptions need to be clearly stated in the survey report.

*Types of Grants.* Equity grants include those made at or about the date of hire (*new-hire grants*), grants made periodically after hire (on an ongoing basis for some position levels, sometimes referred to as *ongoing grants*), and those made on an unscheduled basis or for special reasons, such as promotion grants, retention grants, grants in connection with a merger or acquisition, and so on. It is important that the survey present data on different types of grants separately so that survey users can evaluate the competitiveness of specific features of their own programs. For example, the size of new-hire grants is often a multiple of the size of ongoing grants. Combining these two types of grants would compromise the effectiveness of using the survey data for either situation.

Some surveys provide further detail on equity grant practices by reporting grant guidelines and actual grants. The former is the equity equivalent of *target incentives* and can be useful in developing a picture of typical equity practices in the market. However, not all companies have guidelines, and those that do have guidelines do not always follow them, so it is important that the survey capture and report equity grants that have actually been made.

*Equity Quantification Approaches.* There are various ways to quantify the size of an equity grant, ranging from number of shares or percentage of company outstanding shares (which do not attempt to value the grant), to starting value or face value (the number of shares multiplied by the stock price at the date of grant), to net present value (NPV) or Black-Scholes value, which includes the potential future value of the grant based on certain assumptions. Different types of equity vehicles lend themselves to one or more of these quantification approaches, and some more comprehensive surveys will report equity data using several different quantification methods. For example, stock option amounts are often reported in terms of NPV or Black-Scholes value, as well as face value or number of shares, whereas restricted stock amounts are typically reported in terms of face value or numbers of shares.

*Combining Equity Vehicles.*  Although it typically would not be appropriate to combine new-hire grants and ongoing grants (as noted earlier), it is useful to combine the types of equity vehicles commonly used in the market to provide a more complete picture of the overall value or amount of equity provided in a competitive environment. For example, in the wake of accounting rule changes requiring stock option expensing, the use of restricted stock became more widespread, used either in tandem with stock options or in lieu of options. A survey that presents data for options and restricted stock combined, as well as separately, provides a more complete view of the market. In reality, companies are using different vehicles for the same purpose, that is, as long-term incentives. When designing a competitive long-term incentive plan, it is more important to first consider the relative value of the overall package and then to determine the vehicle (or vehicles) that will be used to deliver that value. Said another way, competing on an options-for-options basis may miss the reality that some competitors also may be using restricted stock. Even if a survey reports the separate values, it is essential to consider the combined value to get the best overall view of the market.

Because the values of a stock option and a restricted share are not equal, certain assumptions need to be made when combining them together. For example, some surveys will combine the *calculated value* of options (using either NPV or Black-Scholes) with the *face value* of restricted stock to arrive at a combined value. Others may provide a combined number of shares that restates restricted stock in option equivalents based on certain conversion ratios. As long as the survey vendor clearly states the methodology and assumptions used, the survey user can apply the same methodology and assumptions to quantify his or her company's own equity grants to make an "apples-to-apples" comparison to the survey data.

## Evaluating Survey Data and Vendors

A number of factors should be taken into consideration when evaluating sources of compensation data, including cost, the time required to participate, validity and reliability of the data, survey methodology, confidentiality, and timeliness of the data. The following issues should be considered when evaluating surveys and survey vendors.

*Sample Size.*  The $N$, or number (sample size), is a significant consideration when determining whether or not a survey will meet your company's needs. The size of the sample should be representative of the group you are evaluating. In other words, if you are looking at pay at U.S. automobile manufacturers, the $N$ will necessarily be low; conversely, if you are evaluating pay practices at high-technology companies, you should expect a sample size that runs into hundreds of companies. The larger the sample size, generally speaking, the more valid the data will be. Also, surveys with a large participant base tend to have relatively stable participation by the same companies year after year. Large, stable samples result in a better basis of comparison when analyzing data from one year to the next. Some surveys (e.g., custom and pulse surveys) will inherently have a small sample size relative to large, established annual surveys. Determining whether a survey has a sufficient number of participants and employee data points is related to the compensation question being asked and the availability of surveys with larger data samples. For example, when looking at data for jobs that tend to be found in a given industry, it is generally preferable to use an industry-specific survey that may have a smaller data sample than a general-industry survey with a larger sample.

Each survey vendor has its own data sufficiency guidelines for publication (typically at least five companies must submit data for a given job), but users of market data may want even larger quantities of data to ensure that adequate data samples are used for compensation analysis. At a minimum, there must be enough data to maintain the confidentiality of participating companies such that antitrust violations are avoided.

*Peer Representation.* The sample size should be composed of companies that are considered pay market peers. Often these companies are competitors for customers as well as employees. Survey providers typically make the list of participating companies broadly available.

*The Age of the Data.* In general, the more recent the data, the more reliable they are. In markets that move quickly (whether with respect to aggressive salary increase budgets, dynamic pay elements such as incentives and equity, or a rapidly changing role such as Internet developer), it is preferable to use current data rather than rely on data older than 12 to 18 months. Older data can be used when there is no alternative with certain entry-level jobs or in certain services industries where pay may be less dynamic.

The age of the data should be clearly stated on survey reports. For point-in-time surveys, where data are collected from all participants at one time, generally the data-collection effective date is noted and should be used for aging purposes. Other surveys may be published on a rolling data-collection schedule, where data are collected from different participants at different times during the year, based on, for example, the timing of each company's salary increase cycle. These *evergreen* surveys often contain data with different individual data submission dates, but the publication date can be assumed as the effective date. Rolling surveys typically are published more frequently than annual surveys, so the publication date is closer to the effective date than it is during the latter portion of the year with a point-in-time survey (Figure 11.1). Irrespective of the age of the data, there are situations where companies elect to *age* the data in using the survey results or apply a premium that reflects either pay movement not captured between the data collection date and the date of the survey, or to project future compensation rates based on anticipated changes to current data because of expected salary increases.

Figure 11.1 is an illustration of the time lapses that occurred between changes in payroll and how those changes are reflected in quarterly versus annual survey reports. The chart assumes a universe where one-fourth of companies conduct pay administration at the start of each quarter and grant 5 percent increases to employees each year. These assumptions are not necessarily reflective of actual market practices but are used to illustrate the increasing separation that occurs over time between actual market practices and the data reported in a static survey published annually. Although there will always be a gap between actual and reported compensation, the gap between actual practice and reported results remains smaller and is more consistent in evergreen survey publications. With annual survey reports, the lag can be significant.

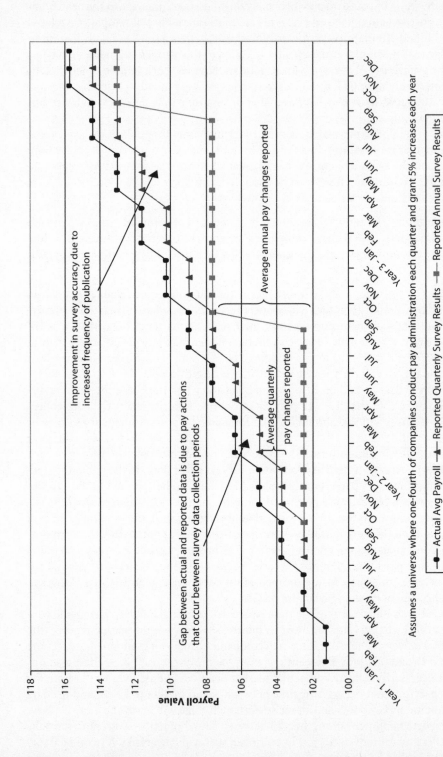

**Figure 11.1 Impact of a rolling-survey database on reported survey results versus actual average payroll.***

* Assumes a universe where one-fourth of companies conduct pay administration each quarter and grant 5% increases each year.

*Presentation.* It is important to ensure that the way the data are presented will be useful for your organization. For example, assume that your company's annual revenue is $1.1 billion and that the survey results have a company size cut that includes companies with revenue over $1 billion. To understand the usefulness of this data cut, you will want to know what proportion of the data is coming from companies close to your size. If, in this example, a substantial number of companies have annual revenue of $10 billion or more, the data may be less applicable to your company than if the typical company were between $1 and $2 billion in revenue. When the data sample is widely dispersed or varies substantially from your company's size, a customized peer-group analysis can offer a report that better reflects pay practices at companies that are closer to your current size.

*Source.* Evaluate the source of the data, which generally should be companies, not individual employees. As discussed earlier, employee-reported pay data may not be reliable or representative of the market. Similarly, some vendors offer aggregated data, which are data that come from numerous sources, potentially gathered at different times. Generally speaking, such data are difficult to validate and may be unreliable if the component surveys use different methodologies for leveling jobs, have different effective dates, and use inconsistent definitions for various forms of compensation.

*Job Matching.* Participate in job-matching sessions and discuss company matches with the survey vendor. Compensation data reported by job and level are only as good as the survey participants' common understanding of job definitions and leveling criteria. Clearly written job descriptions and leveling guidelines will increase every user's confidence in the survey results.

*Costs.* Generally speaking, the cost of purchasing or participating in surveys is a reasonable expense in relation to the financial stake a company has in ensuring that its compensation programs are competitive. Costs for compensation surveys can vary considerably and typically are driven by the size of the data set, the quality of the analysis, the uniqueness of the data, and the market demand. Participation in a large-scale annual benchmarking survey can cost several thousand dollars or more. Other, less complex surveys can be purchased for a few hundred dollars or less. Along these lines, when evaluating survey vendors, check to see how customer service and support are delivered to participants because service levels can vary among survey providers.

*Data Validation.* The steps a survey provider takes to ensure the quality of data can vary considerably, and it is important to have a clear understanding of how the provider "cleans" the data it receives from participants prior to creating reports. Some survey providers have built validation processes into their online submission systems; others manually examine the data and follow up with participants when there are questions about the data. Ideally, survey providers employ a combination of these approaches.

*Time.* The time commitment to participate in a compensation survey can be substantial, and as human resources departments are increasingly taxed, this has become a significant factor in the decision about which survey providers to choose. Complex organizations with many types of jobs that also use a variety of compensation vehicles likely will find that considerable time is required to gather the data needed for participation. Although it is important to understand how much time will be required for participation, ultimately, it is a balancing act; there is often a connection (or should be) between the time required for submitting data and the comprehensiveness and quality of the data provided in return. The value found in the results, their completeness, and their ease of use must be considered when evaluating participation costs.

*Advisory Groups and Participant Feedback.* Survey providers often seek out the advice of the market when making changes to survey questionnaires and the tools used to gather, analyze, and report data. Participating in this way with survey providers allows companies to have a say in the ongoing design considerations of a survey and its processes.

*Thought Leadership.* Survey providers also may help the participants understand the broader business context within which compensation data are relevant. Survey providers often analyze the data in their databases to produce regular update or trend reports, topical articles or white papers, and presentations for participants. This information not only adds to the breath of a user's knowledge, it is also a reflection of the thinking behind the survey vendor's design considerations for survey tools and reports.

*International Surveys.* Many companies have employees in more than one country and require data on local competitive practices. This can present a particular challenge when surveys cover different compensation elements across countries that have varying definitions of what is included in a given element and use different benchmark jobs and leveling schemes. Surveys in each country need to capture all the components of compensation, such as car allowances, housing, meal and transportation allowances, extra-months pay, holiday or festival bonuses, and so on. It is important to present the data in a consistent format suitable for both local and global users. As multinational companies move toward global job leveling, where job X is at the same level from country to country (although pay levels may be different), surveys with consistent global platforms are becoming essential tools for compensation planning.

*Use of Multiple Data Sources.* Companies commonly rely on more than one source of compensation data. This practice increases a company's assurance in the validity of the data sets it uses to ultimately establish pay levels; however, it is important to understand how different survey providers level the various jobs within a survey and how that process affects the data reported in the survey.

*Application of Big Data.* In contrast to the old-school collection of limited amounts of data for core benchmark positions from which companies could extrapolate findings for salary plan and design considerations, today's use of HRIS and spreadsheet tools offers the ability for surveys to collect and analyze greater quantities of data. This allows for new applications of survey results. One area that is growing as a result is the field of *survey analytics*. This aspect of data analysis allows survey users to consider organizational characteristics of other companies and consider whether or not a similar footprint would foster improved results for them. Areas for analysis consider the percentage of workers in various functional areas, the distribution of labor across job level or category, the ratio of workers in various countries, and so on. The collection of complete census data (rather than just the data for employees matched to benchmark jobs) makes this type of analysis possible.

## Summary

Salary survey data are always a snapshot of a moment in time. They reflect the levels of pay for the employees who were reported in the specific jobs surveyed at the specific time data were collected. Because employees are hired, fired, promoted, and relocated all the time, the data will never be 100 percent complete and accurate.

Some will criticize the completeness and accuracy of the survey data you provide to support your recommendations for pay levels or practices, but just as opinion surveys do not survey everyone but still give a general sense of public sentiment, a compensation survey that does not include every job, company, and employee still can offer a sufficient measure of pay markets for compensation professionals to use as a basis for effective opinions about pay plans.

Nonetheless, in the same way that some opinion surveys are better than others, some compensation surveys are better than others as well. From the descriptions provided in this chapter, you now know that the data elements, jobs, and scrutiny used in processing the data make a difference in the level of confidence you should have about a survey.

Because pay markets are constantly changing, the limits of even the best data should be well understood. The application of the data is still part art and part science. Good data lead to more great questions than simple answers. It is tempting to use salary data to find one number to the question of how or how much should we pay our employees. The dynamics of the market require that pay levels will always be defined as a range of values and not a discrete number. Determining the appropriate range—and choosing a value within that range as a specific recommendation—requires a combination of the science found in the calculated values and the art of using these figures in alignment with an organization's strategy and pay philosophy.

# 12

# Rationale for and Approaches to Benchmarking

Tom McMullen
*Hay Group*

Iain Fitzpatrick
*Hay Group*

The rewards strategies of most organizations can be summed up as "pay the right people the right amounts for doing the right things." But is it really this simple? Compensation benchmarking is a key component in addressing the middle part of this statement: the *right amounts*.

Using surveys for compensation benchmarking ensures that the compensation levels determined by the organization are not extraordinarily misaligned with market practice—that is, pay is not too low or too high. Determining the appropriate amount of compensation is a balancing act. No organization wants to waste its financial resources by paying too high relative to the market, and those that pay too low risk unwanted turnover from employees looking for a better deal elsewhere.

Benchmarking also provides valuable insights into compensation administration and pay delivery practices such as prevalence of practice in the use of different types of compensation, performance measures, performance results, benefits plan design, and compensation administration guidelines. Organizations also can benchmark total labor cost levels as well as the perceived effectiveness of their compensation programs with employees and managers. Although much of the focus of this chapter is on the foundational activities and processes related to benchmarking cash compensation levels, we will also cover these other core benchmarking applications later in the chapter.

## Compensation Benchmarking Environment

Frequently, an organization's compensation costs are the highest component of its total cost structure. As such, those in management positions are increasingly being scrutinized with regard to pay decisions and the level of human resources costs relative to the company's operating revenue (or total operating budget in the case of nonprofits).

Moreover, one-size-fits-all compensation policies are not always effective for managing compensation across various businesses, locations, and functions. Market data for jobs, functions, or locations can reflect fluctuating premiums and discounts as labor supply and demand vary. With the transparency and often publicly available compensation data sources accessible to the public (no matter how suspect they may appear to management), organizations face new challenges in communicating the credibility of their compensation programs and pay levels to employees.

As a result, managers are demanding better information and processes to validate specific market rates. Also, realize that some managers want to pay more or less for the value of their jobs relative to the reported value in the marketplace. Managers want better and more relevant information about the value of positions within their organizations. Better compensation information leads to better decisions, clearer messages, and defined expectations. Better information helps to better manage pay.

## Sources of Compensation Benchmarking Information

Organizations should use relevant, reliable, and credible market data in benchmarking their compensation programs. Key considerations for information sources include

- Coverage of comparator organizations (e.g., industry, company size, geography, etc.)
- Coverage of comparator jobs
- Timeliness of information
- Direct and indirect costs of acquisition (i.e., out-of-pocket costs and time)
- Measurement of all relevant components of the rewards opportunity (e.g., base cash, total cash, total direct cash, total remuneration)
- Reliable availability over time

The number of compensation survey providers is growing, and the following list provides some ideas as to where you may find sources of compensation information. This list is by no means exhaustive. Omission from the list does not impugn a survey's quality, nor does inclusion on the list endorse the quality. Consider this as a starting point in your search for compensation benchmarking information.

- Contact counterparts in your peer group. The surveys they participate in are probably the ones you also should join. Your own functional and line managers also may be aware of surveys covering their particular business or discipline.
- Many major compensation and/or human resources consulting firms conduct compensation surveys (i.e., domestic surveys as well as some international surveys).

- The U.S. government is a significant surveyor. Contact the Department of Labor, Bureau of Labor Statistics (BLS), Wage and Hour Division. Most major cities have BLS offices. Your state and local Chamber of Commerce also may produce surveys.

- Many regional and local human resources and compensation associations conduct surveys. Trade and professional organizations are often good sources as well.

Finally, several survey bibliographies (e.g., WorldatWork) are published periodically and include extensive lists of available pay surveys.

## Types of Compensation Surveys

Most often compensation surveys are conducted on a basis of one of the following methods.

*Job Title Matching.* Comparing jobs solely by job title, for example, recruitment advertisements, while simple, is highly subjective and can lead to the development of erroneous conclusions regarding competitiveness. This approach may have some use when there is a need for "ballpark" estimates in the absence of any other information but is not recommended for the development of compensation structures.

*Market Pricing (Job Title and Job Description Matching).* With this approach, benchmark (i.e., representative) job descriptions are used to match an organization's jobs to appropriate survey jobs. Although this is more accurate than relying on job title alone, comparisons are limited to matched jobs in similar industries and therefore are most effective when conducted among competitors within industry sectors.

To ensure the validity of comparisons in job-based surveys, it is essential that an organization have good job matches. As a general rule of thumb, if the jobholder spends 80 percent or more of his or her time on the listed major activities, then the job is typically a good match.

To provide the most useful information, benchmark jobs are ones that are typically well represented across the functions and businesses of the organization and span multiple levels or grades. As such, they are a *diagonal slice* of jobs.

*Job Evaluation (Typically a Point Range, Grade, or Factor Comparison System).* A large number of jobs cannot be matched to the marketplace. Research suggests that an organization is lucky to be able to have good matches on at least 60 percent of its roles.[1] Often it is the critical positions such as executive, management, and individual contributor roles that cannot be matched to market surveys. These also happen to be roles that might be uniquely designed to provide the organization with competitive advantage in the marketplace. It is important for an organization to have a robust process that ensures that the value of these roles is determined effectively. More often than not, some form of job evaluation is used to ensure that these jobs can be priced using appropriate internal values, which then can be priced in the marketplace.

This method places emphasis on understanding the content of surveyed jobs and so overcomes the comparability problems of job title or job description matching surveys. But this extra comparability comes with a requirement for additional inputs and resources. Also, job evaluation–based surveys can be restrictive if specific data are required about particular, unusual, or unique jobs. However, an effective job evaluation system will enable more accurate compensation comparisons, both internally and externally, across any market (e.g., industrial sector, geographic location).

## Compensation Survey Elements

Compensation surveys typically look to collect one, some combination, or all of the following compensation elements:

- *Base salary.* This is the sum of the basic cash amounts paid for work performed as stated in the employment contract plus all fixed payments that have been awarded to eligible jobholders automatically year over year irrespective of individual, unit, or company performance (e.g., fixed bonus, a.k.a. thirteenth-month bonus, holiday bonus, leave loading, vacation allowance).

- *Total cash.* This is the sum of base salary plus short-term variable payments, which are the annualized cash amounts paid that can vary year over year (most typically, these refer to incentive payments that are contingent on discretion, performance, or results achieved).

- *Total direct compensation.* The sum of total cash plus long-term incentive payments (LTIPs), where LTIPs are the economic value to the employee on the date of grant of each long-term incentive vehicle (the values are calculated using a long-term incentive valuation methodology and are annualized and reported as a cash equivalent).

- *Benefits.* Employee benefit programs are multifaceted and often are more detailed and complex surveys. Comparison of benefits programs typically requires specific functional expertise and is difficult to complete without a single common denominator on which all programs are measured. Benefits surveys typically compare programs in one of two ways:

  - *Cost basis.* The employer's cost of a named benefit or perquisite's provision.

  - *Value basis.* The perceived value of a benefit to an employee based on the level of benefit received.

Cost is clearly the most direct common denominator. However, an organization's cost for a benefits program is subject to numerous variables, such as group demographics, claim experience, geographic location, and even how it is funded or accounted for. Thus, programs with identical plan provisions and benefits can have widely differing costs from organization to organization or even from unit to unit within an organization.

Surveys deal with this inherent variation by gaining a sense of a given benefit program's value in order to help the organization understand where to direct its spending—how to get the best "bang for the buck." However, true value is calculated in the "eye of the beholder." For this reason, cash-equivalent values for benefits are based on standard assumptions. For benefits that are conditional on the occurrence of an event such as disability, retirement, or death, the cash equivalent is calculated based on the probability of receiving such items using appropriate actuarial assumptions. For perquisites such as cars, loans, and subsidized meals, which have an immediate value, the cash equivalent is calculated on the basis of average replacement cost.

## The Use of Peer Groups

Selecting an appropriate peer group (or a comparator group) is a key decision in how an organization compares and sets its pay levels relative to the external marketplace. Peer groups are typically used for external benchmark comparisons in terms of levels of compensation, compensation mix, administrative practices, and performance comparisons. Peer groups are helpful in grounding organization pay decisions.

Shareholder activist groups are increasingly scrutinizing comparator group selection in executive compensation circles. In broader employee groups, managing compensation toward the selection of an inappropriate peer group can have serious financial consequences as well as send the wrong messages concerning the intent of the organization's rewards programs. Selection of the peer group must make business sense and be credible to the organization. The following principles serve as a guide for determining an appropriate and defensible comparator group:

- *Select a relevant and current peer group.* Markets are dynamic and are constantly changing. As a result, an organization that was an appropriate peer last year may have changed strategy or lines of business, been acquired, divested an important business line, experienced a dramatic change in performance, or even gone out of business. For these and other reasons, a company may no longer truly be a peer to the employer. Accordingly, effort is needed to update the organizations included in any comparator group.

- *Peers should stem from a reasonably large sample.* The ideal peer group typically contains at least 10 organizations. Smaller sample sizes are susceptible to large year-to-year changes in data if a company changes in the sample.

- *Peers should be consistent in size and scope.* A peer should be reasonably aligned with the size and operating characteristics of your organization. The most common factors in selecting peer groups for professional, management, and executive jobs tend to be industry sector and organization size.

Although peer-group selection and benchmarking are foundations that steer decision making with regard to the establishment of pay practices, they are guidelines. The organization should take this benchmarking information as a reference point and establish a compensation peer group that meets the needs of the business rather than a mechanistic application of market data.

## Data Displays and Terminology

Surveys appear in a variety of forms and formats. Some reports extensively slice and dice the data provided; some provide minimal interpretation. Remember, though, that the underlying value of a survey is not in the numbers it presents but in the answers you are able to infer from its use.

Most survey data are presented in one of three fashions: tabular displays (numeric), graphic displays (visual), or regression analyses (containing formulas and chart lines that project compensation levels). Tabular displays (Figures 12.1 and 12.2) include statistical reference points, arrays, and frequency distributions.

*Arrays.* Arrays are high-to-low listings of all data collected in a given category (see Figure 12.1). Arrays allow the analyst to inspect each data point reported (often by company code) to see how the data distribute through the range.

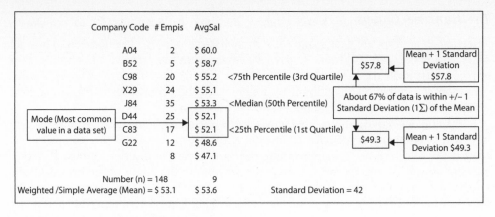

**Figure 12.1  Array with statistical reference points.**

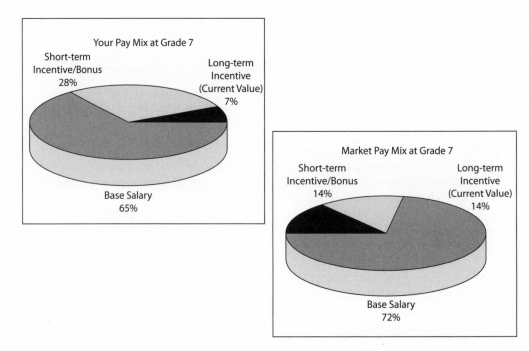

**Figure 12.2  Pie charts.**

*Statistical Reference Points.* Also called the *arithmetic mean* (or simply the *mean*), the average is typically one of the following:

- The *weighted average* is the sum of all salaries (or other compensation values) divided by the number of incumbents reported. [In Figure 12.1, the weighted average is $(2 \times \$60.0) + (5 \times \$58.7)$.] This is the best indicator of the real market for a given survey position; large organizations with many incumbents weigh heavily here.

- The *simple* (or *unweighted*) *average* is the sum of the averages for each company divided by the number of companies providing information. [In Figure 12.1, the simple average is $60.0, $58.7, etc. (a total of $482.2).] This number can be used to compare company policy, for example, on midpoint levels; small companies with few incumbents and large companies with many weigh evenly here.

- The *standard deviation* is a measure of how widely values are dispersed from the mean. The data within ±1 standard deviation cover approximately the middle two-thirds of the observations.

- The *median* (also the *50th percentile* or *second quartile*) is the middle of all the data points reported. This is commonly referred to as the *market rate*. Focus on the median when data are erratically distributed, especially when you have a small sample.

- The *percentiles* (also *quartiles*, *deciles*, etc.) refer to locations in an array below which a certain portion of the data lies. The 75th percentile is frequently viewed by high-paying companies; many analysts prefer to view data at the 25th, 50th, and 75th percentiles.

*Frequency Distributions.* These are often used in lieu of arrays if presenting individual data points strains the confidentiality concerns of the participants. Table 12.1 shows how many times a salary is reported within certain ranges of salaries; actual salaries or averages are not shown.

*Graphic Displays.* Graphic displays include many types of charts (e.g., line, pie, bar, and so forth) that can be used effectively in presenting data, especially to top management, when the big picture is more desirable than showing all the data detail (Figures 12.3 and 12.4).

| Range | Frequency |
|-------|-----------|
| $45.0–47.9 | 1 |
| $48.0–50.9 | 1 |
| $51.0–53.9 | 3 |
| $54.0–56.9 | 2 |
| $57.0–59.9 | 1 |
| $60.0–62.9 | 1 |

**Table 12.1  Frequency Distribution**

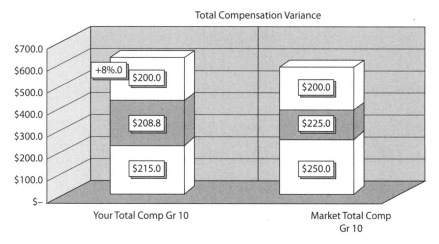

**Figure 12.3  Bar charts: Your company vs. market total compensation.**

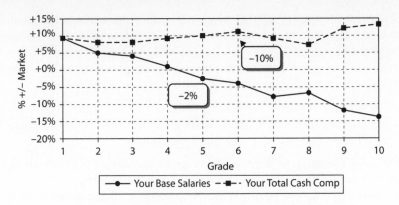

**Figure 12.4  Line charts: Your base salaries vs. your total cash compensation.**

*Regression Analysis.*  Regression analysis (Figure 12.5) is a powerful form of presentation that relates two or more data elements and shows, through formulas and charts, the central data relationship tendencies. Based on one or more measures (e.g., job level, company sales, or time in job), regressions forecast the value of the related measure (i.e., the dependent variable, such as total cash compensation). Regression analysis also correlates the reliability of the information with its dispersal around the line of central tendency. The closer the correlation coefficient is to 1, the greater reliance you can place on the forecast. Regression charts often use logarithms because the range of data covered can be so great and because the formulas often are more accurate when the data relationships are curvilinear.

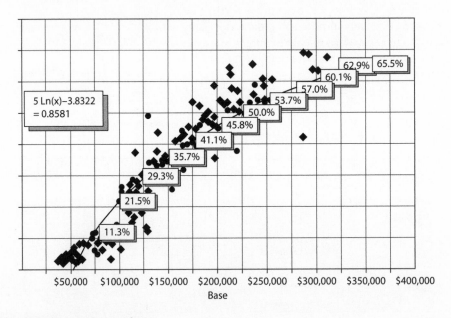

**Figure 12.5  Regression analysis.**

A few words of caution: regression analysis infers that if one condition exists, then the other also exists. In addition, when looking at a chart, the eye and mind can lead the untrained observer to conclusions that may or may not be valid. The assumption that you should provide a 35.7 percent incentive opportunity to a $150,000 employee based on the data in Figure 12.5 is no more valid than if you were to conclude that $150,000 is the right amount to pay that employee just because that is the peer-group average for the individual's position.

## Using a Compensation Survey

Competent compensation practitioners assess a survey's reliability and the usefulness of the data before incorporating the information into a spreadsheet or database to be analyzed. All survey data are not as meaningful as you would like them to be. Because organizations vary so widely in the way jobs are designed, data quality can vary markedly and should be checked before you decide to base one of your key management decisions on such data.

It is critical when you are in front of an executive team, asking team members to make key business decisions based on data you are presenting, that you are comfortable with the source of the information. The following tips[2] are provided to help you make the right compensation survey sourcing decisions:

*Input Processes*

- In our experience, there is no such thing as a perfect data submission. Be wary of survey publishers that have no questions after you provide your submission.

- Value a survey publisher more highly if it conducts job-matching meetings to ensure better job matching.

- Job matching should be completed by individuals familiar with the jobs; the quality of matches affects the validity of the data to your organization and the overall quality of the survey.

- Involve line managers in the job-matching process to ensure better results. They tend to have the best knowledge of what specific jobs actually do.

- Choose a survey publisher that employs more detailed job descriptions in order to provide more context for job matching.

- Confirm that data are submitted by participants and do not include publicly available data that you could obtain without charge.

- Be wary of placing your trust in survey publishers that do not identify survey participants.

*Analysis and Reporting Processes*

- Be a discerning consumer of survey data: ask survey publishers to summarize their processes for ensuring consistent and reliable data.

- Choose a survey publisher that collects individual incumbent data as opposed to averages by job to ensure representation of the full dispersion of pay for the population.

- Ensure that there are clear and consistent definitions of terms used (e.g., base salary, midpoint, variable cash, benefits values, total direct compensation, etc.)

- Verify that data are available to be analyzed via the core elements of interest to your organization. This might include analysis by function, industry, location, job group, and so on.

- Trends should be analyzed on the basis of comparing the same organizations on each survey date to establish the exact movement for each level of job size to establish each pay component.

- Ask your survey publisher about how it deals with missing data. If it interpolates data, request a clear explanation of the process the publisher uses. If the publisher is not clear or resorts to a "black-box" explanation, it is asking you to trust it without providing supporting data or rationale.

*Ongoing Survey User Processes*

- Consider becoming a member of a survey group to increase reliability and inclusion of relevant benchmark jobs.

- Organizations that band with others in the same industry or geographic survey group are often able to establish rules (or peer pressure) to ensure participation each year. The benefits of this are job coverage and, as a result of consistent participation, greater data consistency.

- Organizations should try to submit data to their selected surveys every year (even if they may not be purchasing the results); doing otherwise injects unwanted fluctuation into the survey results.

By becoming an informed consumer of survey information, you will be able to decide for yourself whether survey data are worthy of your trust and increase the value of surveys to your organization. Realize that survey costs represent only a small fraction of the human capital investment that benefits from the data they provide. In short, surveys can be one of the highest value-added investments you can make.

## Legal Concerns Associated with Sharing Compensation Information

Limited information sharing, such as discussing your company's average wages for a single position with a neighboring company's counterpart, may not seem like a big deal. However, sharing this information directly with competitors and making decisions based on those data can present some real problems. Using another company's specific compensation data to establish salary levels can be perceived as *wage setting*.

In some countries, businesses must be careful in obtaining compensation survey information. For example, U.S. courts and agencies, such as the Federal Trade Commission (FTC), advise organizations against conducting their own compensation benchmarking surveys because they could be considered anticompetitive under provisions of the Sherman Anti-Trust Act. These entities have issued opinions regarding the exchange of compensation data between organizations. While not legally binding for all organizations, these opinions can be considered as a best practice in how to use compensation surveys. For this reason, one of the safest and most efficient ways to obtain survey data is through a disinterested third party—such as a trade organization, consultant, or information survey company—thereby preserving the industrial participants' data confidentiality.

To ensure a successful survey benchmarking process, organizations would be well served by keeping the following points in mind when conducting their compensation studies:

- The survey should be managed by an independent third party (e.g., independent consultant, academic institution, government agency, or trade or professional association).

- Data provided by survey participants must be more than three months old.

- The survey must contain data from at least five survey participants, with no individual participant's data representing more than 25 percent of the weighted basis of a given statistic.

- Each company must report the results in a way that ensures that no recipient can determine specific participant data (the FTC does allow some exchange of information without a third party, depending on the use and the anticompetitive effect).

- When conducting a salary survey, companies should seek legal counsel throughout the planning process, execution, and reporting.

## Getting the Most Out of Your Benchmarking Efforts

If you are responsible for using compensation surveys to develop compensation programs in your organization, take the following ideas into consideration to get the most out of your survey investment:

- *Start by creating a survey library.* Set aside a shared network drive or some other common location where you and other authorized users can access all your organization's survey data. Alert others in your organization to forward all surveys and requests for survey participation to you so that you can respond to them most efficiently.

- *Be selective in responding to surveys.* Limited resources and unlimited day-to-day work requirements often preclude participation in every survey in which a company is asked to participate. You must balance your current and future needs and the ability to get what you want from others. Participate in the surveys that benefit your organization and your primary comparator groups the most. Most organizations report participating in between two and four compensation surveys per role.

- *Consolidate your data onto one spreadsheet or database.* Surveys are often consulted to respond to specific questions from a variety of constituencies. Try consolidating qualified position data from multiple survey sources onto a single electronic spreadsheet or database for more convenient consultation. By arranging your organization's position table alongside the survey data, you have a good tool for developing solid answers during your annual compensation planning and structure review.

- *Derive a single answer from each set of data presented in a survey.* If you consolidate data from multiple sources or have several views of the data presented in one source, you have a decision to make: of the data available, of the different numbers purporting to be "the market," what is the single number that best represents the market for your organization? Practitioners can take different approaches here:

- If you average data from multiple surveys, be careful not to average diverse values. Averaging $80,000 with $40,000 does not result in a "consensus" value of $60,000.

- Some simply aggregate all the data available from all sources, throw out odd data, and then assign "company weights" to each data point to replicate what it would cost to staff your company at market rates.

- Some analysts feel that certain survey sources are more reliable than others, so they might weight that source differently (say, 75 percent) from all other sources (say, 25 percent) as they aggregate and consolidate.

- Others rely on one or two primary surveys and weight those but have the others available as secondary sources if needed.

- *Answer all survey questions to the best of your ability.* Assume that all data requested in a survey have value in the quality of the results and that without certain data from you, the survey will be reduced in value to you and to others. This includes doing the best job you can on job matching and perhaps involving others such as human resources colleagues or line managers in verifying your job matches to the survey.

Whereas senior management is interested in knowing market levels of pay for jobs in the marketplace, this only tells part of the story management wants to hear. Specifically, executives want to know what the market pays for their jobs, which takes into consideration role complexity and accountability. They also want to understand what competitors pay for a mix of responsibilities—regardless of organization size or industry segment, that is, the variables making a job worth more (or less) than market rates and how to link market data to internal career paths. At the end of the day, executives have a limited budget for compensation surveys, and they want to spend it as effectively as possible.

Managers will say that they want market data that reflect what they would have to pay to hire a competent performer from the marketplace. They do not want market data that do not take into account the role and value of the job at their organization. What managers really want is information that allows them to assess pay for their team and assurance that people are paid appropriately given their role and value to the company. They also want an ability to manage retention, tools to support accelerated people development, and pay programs that encourage people to take on more.

Compensation decisions are like any other economic buy or sell decision—the more information there is, the sounder the decisions will be. To bring this issue home, consider the following example: if your boss asked you for market information to help him or her buy a new house in a new area, would you

- Provide the 10th through 90th percentiles of house price data for all houses in the city?

- Provide the 10th through 90th percentiles of house price data for all houses in the neighborhood area?

- Provide the percentile data for the neighborhood area but increase it by 10 or 20 percent to recognize that your boss is looking at houses that are a little better than the average in the community?

Or would you identify the boss's personal requirements and then consider the relative value of homes in different neighborhoods? Examine the selling prices of recently sold homes?

Determine the variables that drive value in the housing market? Use the combination of these factors to determine the fair price for that specific house?

At the end of the day, pay determination should apply the same rigor. Executives are interested in understanding not only various rates of market pay (e.g., percentiles of compensation) but also what drives the value of jobs. Your role as a compensation professional goes much beyond calculating and reporting statistics from compensation surveys. It needs to include acting as a trusted advisor who can help senior management to think through and act on assessing the value of work within your organization and getting the best return on your sizable investment in your human resources.

Although benchmarking is indeed a core process of the compensation function, realize that benchmarking should be viewed as a reference post for establishing a compensation structure—the going rate of jobs—and is not an end result in and of itself. Compensation professionals who blindly follow external market data without fully considering the design of the work as it relates to the marketplace or how the role relates to other jobs within the organization are providing a disservice to their organizations. If you are title and revenue matching, you are missing an opportunity for an important dialogue about jobs. Effectiveness requires both looking at the market and measuring work internally.

## The Changing Role of Managers

Over the past few years, many human resources and rewards departments have lost headcount and budget, with the ratio of their people to total employees steadily decreasing. At the same time, the work of human resources is not decreasing, and in most organizations, there is a need for human resources to be a stronger strategic business partner than ever before. The everyday work requests are also not decreasing. Human resources is often slowed down by the important everyday requests and queries for information and decision making from line managers. From a recent Hay Group study, two-thirds of human resources directors estimate that their teams spend 21 to 50 percent of their time dealing with such matters. Nearly half of organizations (43 percent) agree or strongly agree that this is too long and is preventing them from taking on more strategically important initiatives.[3]

Our research also found that almost half of line managers (United Kingdom: 48 percent; United States: 41 percent; China: 39 percent) feel that their internal human resources teams are slow to respond, and 39 percent (United Kingdom: 41 percent; United States: 29 percent; China: 47 percent) actually believe that Google is a better source of information than human resources, and a healthy minority of organizations (United Kingdom: 40 percent; United States: 23 percent; China: 26 percent) feel that human resources *actively obstructs* them from making these decisions themselves.

Human resources and line managers agree that the power to act decisively on people-management issues must be extended from the central human resources function down the line to managers. For this to work effectively, though, human resources needs to relinquish a degree of control and entrust line managers with tools, information, and governance processes to manage their people better while retaining its role as the steward over the organization's human capital asset. The way forward may be to actively engage line managers in having more accountability to act within the framework of the organization's operating model to make more empowered decisions in compensation-management matters including benchmarking. Given the means and the active support of human resources, properly empowered line managers can indeed breathe new life into compensation strategy and implementation, including benchmarking processes.

Human resources leaders have an opportunity to engage in more active partnerships with their line managers. They can help them to become more successful by supporting their individual development, ensuring that they fully understand the strategic intent of rewards programs and not just the technical details. They can ensure managers' involvement in the implementation and administration of compensation programs, including gathering input on job model-matching processes, specific job matches, and interpretation of compensation survey benchmarking and applications of the results. Managers, for their part, must accept a new level of accountability within a refined policy framework defined by human resources and, ultimately, the corporate strategy as a whole.

Developments in technology—and specifically in mobile technology—mean that there is an opportunity like never before to put in the hands of line managers what they need, when they need it to "activate" themselves and their employees. If human resources—as the "owner" of the policies—is willing to facilitate this process, it will not only free them up for more strategic activities but also will enable the line to do what it is willing and indeed wants to do.

## A Broader and More Holistic View of Compensation Benchmarking

Many organizations say that they do a good job of externally benchmarking their compensation programs, but for many of these companies, this simply means that they annually (or biannually) compare the compensation of a subset of their jobs with compensation paid in the market for comparable jobs using the processes described in this chapter. Benchmarking for these organizations is largely focused on the *efficiency* of their compensation programs (i.e., are we spending too little, too much, or the right amount) versus the *effectiveness* of their compensation programs (i.e., do compensation programs actually achieve what they should be achieving). Moreover, focusing solely on this type of efficiency benchmarking does not take into account the following:

- *The total cost of employment.* The vast majority of benchmarking surveys rely on a sample (i.e., subset) of jobs in the organization, and a typical organization reports that it can only match up to 50 to 60 percent of its jobs. We have often found organizations to be less than competitive relative to market compensation on a job-by-job basis only to have *total* employment costs exceeding the market because of above-norm staffing levels.

- *Return on investment/productivity.* This is a comparison of revenue, profit, or labor cost per employee, and it helps organizations to assess whether the combination of their staffing levels and total remuneration costs compares with that of their comparator group.

- *Perception of effectiveness.* The most fundamental evaluation of a compensation program is how it is perceived—both by program participants and by their managers. A common reaction, especially if employees do not understand a new program, is the belief that the organization may be trying to cheat them by demanding more work for less compensation. If employees feel that the compensation program is unfair, it will meet resistance. Managers who have a negative view of the compensation program will be unenthusiastic supporters and likely will not use the reward as intended. Perceptions of rewards programs typically are assessed by employee opinion surveys, focus groups, and interviews.

Given that compensation program expenditures are often the largest or second-largest controllable expense for an organization, it would seem that human resources and senior executives would undertake a formal return-on-investment (ROI) analysis of their remuneration costs—the annual base salaries, merit budgets, incentive plans, and value of health and welfare benefit programs and equity programs. But this is not the case. According to Hay Group research, most rewards professionals indicate that their organizations make little attempt to measure the ROI of their compensation programs. In addition, organizations that do measure ROI are split between doing this informally and using more structured, quantitative processes to evaluate the effectiveness of their rewards programs. We have found that only 20 percent of organizations consistently involve employees in the assessment of compensation program effectiveness.

Perhaps more interesting is that most human resources professionals believe that their rewards programs are either effective or highly effective. How can human resources professionals believe that their compensation programs are effective without knowing whether these programs provide a reasonable ROI? Do organizations really know if their compensation programs are working? Do they really care to know? As Jack Nicholson's character said in the film, *A Few Good Men*, can they "handle the truth?"

Compensation program benchmarking is not just an opportunity to collect information; it is also an opportunity to clarify and communicate compensation-management priorities and values and a willingness to listen to employee concerns. Building on the work by Kaplan and Norton in the balanced scorecard[4] and Kirkpatrick in human resources training and development program evaluation[5], an assessment of overall compensation program effectiveness can be made considering multiple assessment criteria to determine effectiveness.

If we are to improve the effectiveness of compensation programs, gaining a deeper understanding of employee and management perspectives, as well as employee and management involvement in the compensation program evaluation process, will foster considerable commitment to improving the compensation program. Compensation programs must change in the face of changes in the organization's business priorities and external competitive environments. Effectively changing rewards programs involves multiple and balanced perspectives and viewpoints, and it is essential to have a strategy for engaging these stakeholders and implementing change.

Evaluation of compensation program effectiveness requires careful thought and a commitment to using feedback to improve these programs. However, given the substantial investment organizations make in compensation programs and the impact they have on organizational effectiveness, comprehensive program evaluation makes good business sense. A systematic and balanced evaluation process can add significant value to compensation programs when one goes beyond relying solely on financially oriented ROI measures. As Figure 12.6 indicates, a robust evaluation process making use of financial, operational, and perception measures of success, as well as internal and external analyses, will provide the organization with a well-rounded assessment of rewards program effectiveness.

This approach reduces the dangers of overdependence on lagging financial indicators and considers employee perceptions, knowledge, and behaviors associated with pay programs, which form the basis for getting the desired results. An effective evaluation approach collects information on how employee opinions relate to external comparators as well. There are information sources that can provide external norms on employer branding and corporate reputation assessments (e.g., the Hay Group conducts *Fortune* magazine's "Most Admired Company" analysis) and that can provide external employee opinion survey norms. By undertaking this type of compensation effectiveness review, rewards

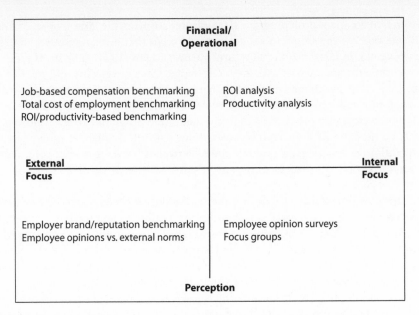

**Financial/
Operational**

| | |
|---|---|
| Job-based compensation benchmarking<br>Total cost of employment benchmarking<br>ROI/productivity-based benchmarking | ROI analysis<br>Productivity analysis |

**External
Focus**                                                                 **Internal
Focus**

| | |
|---|---|
| Employer brand/reputation benchmarking<br>Employee opinions vs. external norms | Employee opinion surveys<br>Focus groups |

**Perception**

**Figure 12.6  Balanced framework for assessing compensation effectiveness.**

*Source:* Hay Group.

professionals will be better prepared with answers and, more important, suggestions as to how compensation programs can be made more effective.

Despite some inherent challenges, evaluating compensation programs in terms of their effect on end results and their ultimate ROI is a worthy goal. This information allows management to make more informed comparisons and decisions relative to other investment needs and to get a better perspective on the value of compensation programs to their organizations. Again, it is not sufficient to only judge outcomes. The assessment must examine *how* those outcomes were achieved to provide a more robust evaluation and to provide the information needed to improve the rewards program.[6]

## Notes

1. Dow Scott, Thomas D. McMullen, and Richard S. Sperling, "Fiscal Management of Compensation Programs." *WorldatWork Journal* 14(3):13–25, 2005.
2. David E. Borrebach and Iain Fitzpatrick, "15 Ways to Be a Better Survey Consumer." WorldatWork, Scottsdale, AZ, July 2009, pp. 19–21.
3. Tom McMullen and Iain Fitzpatrick, "Activating the Line: How Management Tools Can Make Reward Programs Really Work." *Journal of Compensation and Benefits*, March–April: 34–42, 2014.
4. Robert S. Kaplan and David P. Norton, *The Balanced Scorecard*, Cambridge, MA: Harvard Business School Press, 1996.
5. Donald L. Kirkpatrick and James D. Kirkpatrick, *Evaluating Training Programs: The Four Levels*, 3rd ed. San Francisco: Berrett-Koehler Publishers, 2006.
6. Tom McMullen, "Reward Effectiveness: How Do You Know If Your Reward Programs Are Working?" *Journal of Compensation and Benefits*, March–April: 5–13, 2013.

# 13

# Paying for Skills, Knowledge, and Competencies

GERALD E. LEDFORD, JR.
*Center for Effective Organizations*

Implementation of skills, knowledge, and competency pay has become commonplace, and use gradually has increased in the last three decades. WorldatWork's 2012 "Compensation Programs and Practices Survey"[1] reported that 70 percent of private-sector firms (although fewer government or not-for-profit organizations) use skill acquisition as a base pay increase criterion. However, use of such pay systems is broad but not deep. Surveys consistently show that a relatively high percentage of firms use some form of pay for skills, knowledge, and competency, but typically with just a small percentage of the workforce. Two decades ago, various authors predicted that this form of compensation eventually would replace standard job-based pay systems. This clearly has not happened, nor does it appear likely to happen in the foreseeable future.

This chapter argues that pay for skills, knowledge, and competencies can take a variety of forms and that the most appropriate form for a given organization depends on the business context it must support. Overreliance on some forms and underuse of others have led to the misapplication of the concept of pay for skills, knowledge, and competencies. In particular, bonus-oriented systems are very underused as a way of addressing the fluid business needs of contemporary organizations. A better understanding of design options and their suitability to different conditions can lead to greater use of these pay plans and greater effectiveness of the plans adopted.

## Definitions

Pay for skills, knowledge, and competencies (referred to as *SKC pay* in this chapter) is a compensation system that rewards employees for formal certification of the acquisition and mastery of skills, knowledge, and/or competencies. *Skill* is observable expertise in performing tasks. *Knowledge* is acquired information used in performing tasks. *Competencies* are general skills or traits needed to perform tasks, often in multiple jobs or roles.

Oversimplifying somewhat, we can generalize about the emphasis of different versions of SKC pay for different populations. Systems that emphasize pay for skills tend to apply to nonexempt employee groups, such as factory workers and call-center employees. Knowledge-based pay systems can apply to any type of employee. Competency pay plans tend to apply to exempt employee groups, such as professionals and managers. The use of different terms for different groups often leads to a lack of appreciation of the commonalities of these approaches. Rewards professionals often fail to recognize that all these systems share basic characteristics that make them different from traditional job-based pay.

Key characteristics of SKC pay include the following:

1. Employees receive rewards only after demonstrating mastery of relevant skills, knowledge, or competencies. In traditional job-based pay systems, employees are paid for the job they hold, even if they cannot perform the job especially well.

2. There is a formal assessment of whether the employee has mastered the skills, knowledge, and competencies covered by the plan. This usually includes a formal certification of some kind. In conventional job-based systems, there is no need for certification; merely holding the job results in the pay for that job. Pay typically changes as soon as the employee changes jobs.

3. Most SKC pay plans provide greater pay opportunities than under job-based pay plans. The usual expectation is that not all employees will take advantage of the opportunities, but the opportunities are there for those who wish to pursue them.

## Four Types of Pay for Skill, Knowledge, and Competency

SKC pay systems can reward up to three dimensions of skill, knowledge, and competency. These are depth, breadth, and self-management SKCs. *Depth* involves gaining greater expertise in existing SKCs. Examples of depth-oriented pay systems include the dual-career ladder for technical personnel and the skilled-trades system for blue-collar workers. *Breadth* involves increasing the range of the employee's SKCs. Classic skill-based pay systems in factories encouraged breadth so that employees could competently perform all the tasks in a self-managed team. However, these systems also often had depth and self-management dimensions as well. *Self-management* involves workers associated with higher levels in the organization, such as planning, training, budgeting, and so on. Organizations that reward such SKCs, such as in classic skill-based pay plans in factories, typically attempt to eliminate the cost of first-line supervision by providing teams of employees with the necessary SKCs to take over management responsibilities.

SKC pay can be delivered in three ways: it can be an alternative base pay (salary or wage) plan, it can be part of a merit pay system, or it can be delivered as a bonus that does not affect base pay. Most SKC pay systems in use today are base pay systems designed from the ground up with SKC principles in mind. Nearly all the research and most of the writing that has been done on SKC pay systems have focused on such base pay systems. A second approach is to splice an SKC component into an existing merit pay system. In many merit pay systems, for example, performance assessments that determine pay increases are based on a combination of goal attainment and competencies demonstrated. The third approach is to pay bonuses for mastering SKCs. Bonuses offer the most flexibility and the least risk to the organization because the payments do not have the annuity feature of salary increases.

Combining the different dimensions that SKCs can reward and the different delivery methods of SKC rewards suggests four different types of SKC pay systems. Type 1, *career depth*, systems date to antiquity as a career path for employees to learn specialized skills. The apprenticeship approach for learning skilled trades is an archetypal example of this approach. The goals of this approach are to deepen employee expertise over a long period of time and to outline training and certification requirements clearly for the employee.

Type 2, *classic skill-based*, systems typically emphasize breadth of skill blended with some level of self-management skill and skill depth as well. These systems are very complex but often can be very effective in increasing organizational performance by leaner staffing and reduced managerial layers. The primary goals of these plans are to increase employee flexibility and to provide employees with a broad perspective on the production or service-delivery process so that they can help manage it.

Type 3, *merit pay*, systems often use competencies that are defined for the entire organization, although in some cases these can be customized for particular categories of employees or even individuals. The purpose is to reinforce competencies that management believes are especially relevant to organizational performance. However, the competencies most often used (e.g., teamwork and analytical thinking) can seem vague and may be difficult to assess.

Finally, type 4, *bonus pay*, systems permit the organization to make frequent changes based on immediate talent availability and needs and to attract and retain specialists who might otherwise consider the company's base pay system inadequate. The primary users of this approach today are the U.S. armed forces, where skill bonuses are used extensively for the attraction and retention of specialized talent (e.g., doctors, pilots, and Special Forces). Descriptions of the plan are limited to obscure federal publications.

A human resources group at the Pentagon monitors the degree to which the armed forces have been able to fill each of hundreds of occupational specialties. If they have difficulty attracting and retaining personnel, a temporary enlistment and/or reenlistment bonus is offered. This may be modest—most are less than $10,000—but it is possible to offer up to $40,000 for enlistment bonuses and $150,000 for reenlistment bonuses. (Reenlistment bonuses are higher because SKCs can be more readily assessed for existing troops.) Bonuses may be used for both officers (e.g., pilots and medical personnel) and enlisted personnel (e.g., Special Forces). The author's nephew, a Marine helicopter mechanic, was offered a $70,000 bonus to reenlist for two years at the height of the war in Iraq, which would have, in effect, doubled his cash compensation. Such bonuses are used sparingly and are offered only as needed; they disappear when staffing needs for a specialty are met. The specialties for which bonuses are paid and the amounts offered change so frequently that the military does not announce them.

Some teacher SKC pay systems also use bonuses rather than base pay increases for mastery of specific competency blocks (e.g., use of technology) or for certification by the National Board for Professional Teaching Standards. Use of bonuses rather than base pay increases is determined by state and local school board policy. Table 13.1 summarizes the discussion of the SKC dimensions required and the form of payment for each type. It also lists examples of each type.

Each type of pay plan fits some organizational conditions better than others. Type 1 systems work best when there is a long-term competitive demand for specialized expertise and long training cycles are required to build key skills. These conditions make the

| Plan Type | SKC Dimensions Rewarded | Form of Payment | Examples |
|---|---|---|---|
| 1. Career depth | Depth | Base pay | Dual-career ladder, skilled-trades system |
| 2. Classic skill-based | Multidimensional | Base pay | Skill-based pay in factories |
| 3. Merit pay | Multidimensional | Merit pay component | Competency pay, e.g., some teacher SKC pay |
| 4. Bonus pay | Mostly depth so far | Bonus | Military critical skills bonuses, some teacher competency pay |

Table 13.1  Types of Pay for SKCs: Where Does Each Type of SKC Pay Fit?

retention of specialists highly desirable because replacing such specialists is expensive. This provides a return on the significant investment required for a well-designed pay system, training programs, and certification testing. The system also provides incentives for employees to deepen technical skills as a way to increase salary and experience career progression rather than seeing progression through a management hierarchy as the only path for career progression. Type 1 plans are less successful if the SKCs represented by the plan are rapidly changing. This is sometimes an issue in dual-career ladders for scientists and engineers, as well as in plans for information technology (IT) professionals. The problem is that employees may be well paid for SKCs that have become obsolete. Moreover, changing these plans may be difficult because they build entrenched interests in maintaining the plan, whether or not it meets current conditions. Skilled-trades apprenticeship systems faced this problem during the past 15 years as companies have introduced multicrafting (which emphasizes skill breadth) to increase the flexibility of maintenance workers and other tradespeople and to reduce unnecessary staffing. Many employees who spent years on a depth-oriented system often found this change hard to accept and actively resisted it.

Type 2 systems are an excellent fit with high-involvement and lean organization designs that require employee versatility and/or a high degree of self-management. Procter & Gamble pioneered these plans in "greenfield" high-involvement plants starting in the 1960s. Research suggests that type 2 plans tend to work best in manufacturing settings, perhaps because it is easiest there to specify the skills required. These plans emphasize technical skill development and are tightly woven with training programs, job rotation plans, and formal certifications. They require a significant investment of design and development time. These plans are less successful if business needs, technology, and organization designs are rapidly changing. A study of eight long-term skill-based pay plans in high-involvement manufacturing plants (Ledford, 2008) found that plans that survived were redesigned periodically to keep up with new skill requirements. It may not be worthwhile to invest a year or more in redesign work if the rate of change is so high that redesign cannot keep up with business needs.

The most prominent failures of classic skill-based pay plans have been in the high-technology field (e.g., Motorola and Intel). This is probably because of the very rapid changes in technology and work processes in that industry. Rapid change in technology, products, and production techniques means that the organization is constantly reinventing itself on the fly. It is difficult for type 2 plans to keep up with this rate of change. In one case of failure in high tech, the plan was obsolete before it was implemented and was abandoned.

Type 2 plans also fail if the organization does not use job rotation and recertification policies that ensure that it is receiving value for the pay. If employees learn the skill once and do not rotate back to positions where they can use the skill, they tend to lose the skill over time and cannot perform the tasks for which they are paid if called on.

Type 3 systems require the existence of a merit pay plan to which the competency system can be added. Merit pay plans tend to be used primarily with professional and managerial employees, partly because many nonexempt wage plans do not receive merit pay. The competencies emphasized in these plans tend to apply to a wide range of positions and job families, and usually attempt to encourage development of competencies that reinforce strategic corporate directions, competencies that internal research has shown to contribute to organizational performance, and/or competencies that embody desired attributes of the organizational culture.

Merit plans demand a great deal of focus to be successful. For example, one successful plan by a food processing company based managers' salary increases on two traditional managerial competencies (leading for results and leveraging technical and business systems) and two competencies that reinforced major corporate initiatives (building workforce effectiveness and meeting customer needs). The company carefully defined and communicated each competency. The plan worked because it brought great focus to a limited number of SKCs that were the basis for the plan.

All too often, however, competency systems lack focus. Competencies may be one component of several in a performance appraisal. It is all too common to see appraisals based on the achievement of multiple goals, behavioral criteria, and several competencies chosen from a menu. In the era of 3 percent salary increases, the weight of each competency in assessing performance in such a system is so small as to be almost irrelevant. Also, companies tend to take the easy way out in choosing competencies to reinforce by allowing very diverse and numerous choices by those on the pay system, not providing well-designed behavioral anchors for competencies, and using generic competencies that are not relevant to their particular organizations. As a result, the entire exercise can appear "fluffy" and lacking in value.

Type 4 systems are very versatile. Because the pay delivered by bonus plans does not have the annuity characteristics of salary increases, the organization pays one time only for an SKC increase. If the SKCs that the organization needs change from one year to the next, that is not a problem; the list can change easily and quickly to meet changing needs. Also, because there is no annuity feature to bonuses, the cost of design errors is much smaller in bonus systems than in base pay systems. In addition, bonuses are very easy to add on top of any base pay system; they do not require the overhaul of the salary system, as is required in the other types (especially type 1 and type 2 systems).

The primary problem with bonus plans is that they can become too sloppy because they appear to be so forgiving. Management does not escape the need to think through the types of SKCs that it wishes to reinforce through the plan and how employees will be able to gain the skills. A certain level of rigor is required if the plan is to be credible and if employees are to understand why they need to acquire certain SKCs and what they must do to obtain those SKCs. A plan that seems arbitrary or capricious will not be motivating.

One type of problem is seen frequently in all types of SKC pay but especially in types 1 through 3: poor infrastructure for supporting the plan. Infrastructure includes good communication about the plan, training opportunities that permit employees to acquire SKCs the plan rewards, renewal systems to keep the plan current, and good implementation practices. Research suggests that infrastructure is more important than the actual design in determining success. [See Ledford and Heneman (2011) for a detailed discussion of this

However, bonus plans are somewhat more forgiving because the organization wipes the slate every year and to some degree can start over—as long as management has credibility with the workforce (Table 13.2).

| Plan Type | Conditions for Best Fit | Common Problems |
|---|---|---|
| 1. Career depth | Need for expertise | Obsolescence |
| | Multiyear training cycles for key skills | High rate of change in expertise required |
| | Expensive to replace talent | Poor infrastructure |
| 2. Classic skill-based | High-involvement and lean work systems | High rate of change in organizational conditions |
| | Well-defined competency system | Obsolescence |
| | | Poor infrastructure |
| 3. Merit pay | Prior use of merit pay | Appraisal too complex |
| | Succinct list of desired competencies | Competencies too numerous or vague |
| | | Poor infrastructure |
| 4. Bonus pay | Rapidly changing demand for SKCs | Overly sloppy implementation |
| | | Poor infrastructure |

Table 13.2 Types of Pay for SKCs: Best Fits and Common Problems—The Case for Greater Use of Type 4, SKC Bonuses

SKC pay in general is underused as a way to increase the development of employee capabilities in an era in which continual learning and development are needed. Even if pay for SKCs never fulfills the hopes many had for it to replace job-based pay systems, its use is likely to continue to expand in the future. Clearly, there are many areas of the economy where serious skill gaps exist despite high unemployment in the economy as a whole. Pay for skills can help to address such gaps and can help to prevent gaps in the first place by providing employees with incentives to build skills in emerging areas of need.

However, the preceding analysis suggests that the most common designs for SKC pay are part of the problem in increasing its usage. Types 1 and 2 are base pay forms of SKC pay that are increasingly difficult to develop and administer well. The conditions under which they experience difficulties are increasingly prevalent in today's economy. The rate of change in technology, work systems, organization designs, and business models is accelerating, and base pay SKC systems are difficult to design and maintain in such an environment. Indeed, SKC pay systems are more difficult to maintain than traditional pay systems in such conditions. SKC pay rewards skill redundancy, and everyone who is eligible to earn pay for a given skill, knowledge, or competency is affected every time that a relevant skill, knowledge, or competency changes. Thus the ramifications of organizational changes are greater in SKC pay systems.

In addition, SKC obsolescence is an increasing threat to SKC pay systems. These systems assume some level of stability in the learning content of the work. Without at least a reasonable level of stability, it is difficult to design a system for career advancement that involves career advancement over many years. Yet increasingly this requirement for stability cannot be met. Consider the new SKCs in IT and software engineering that did not exist only a few years ago—social media, mobile hardware, smart phones that are more powerful computers than the mainframes of 30 years ago, new programming languages, and so on. Any SKC pay system designed for IT as recently as seven years ago would be obsolete today.

Furthermore, SKC pay system success depends on good infrastructure—training, communication, renewal system, implementation, and so on. Unfortunately, infrastructure is a management weakness in far too many companies. Even if the original designers of the pay plan are dedicated to maintaining the infrastructure, conditions change. Manager advancement and turnover eventually lead to new players and new priorities, and maintaining the system of the prior leadership may not receive high priority. Ultimately, telling managers that they must maintain the infrastructure of the plan seems only a little more realistic than the demand that managers do performance appraisals well.

Bonus-based systems look increasingly attractive in a chaotic environment, and they deserve far greater use than they have received to date. Bonus systems never face the problem of obsolescence. The plan can be changed every year or discontinued at any time without doing violence to the base pay system. Changing organizational conditions become a reason to use this form of pay, not a hindrance. Indeed, a bonus system can be used to reinforce SKCs relevant to management's new goals and initiatives each year. The quality of the infrastructure can be good in some years and poor in others as managers change, and as long as it is not so bad as to lose the goodwill of the workforce, the damage will not be lasting. Managers wise enough to make good use of infrastructure will be more successful, but those who are not so wise will not necessarily make the system ineffective.

## Conclusion

This chapter has outlined four different approaches to paying for skills, knowledge, and competencies. It has indicated that each type fits a different set of conditions, and each tends to experience a different type of problem. The chapter concludes by arguing that there should be a far higher use of the least-common form of SKC pay, SKC bonuses. This type of plan is less susceptible to the problems that affect other forms of SKC pay, and indeed, it is most suited to the rapidly changing world of contemporary organizations.

## Note

1. http://www.worldatwork.org/waw/adimLink?id=65522.

## References

Ledford, Gerald E., Jr., and Herbert G. Heneman III. 2011. *Skill Based Pay*. SIOP Science Series. Society for Human Resource Management, Alexandria, VA.

Ledford, Gerald E., Jr. 2008. "Factors Affecting the Long-Term Success of Skill-Based Pay." *WorldatWork Journal* 17(1):6–17.

# 14

# Using Nonmonetary Awards to Support Behaviors that Drive Business Results

Melissa Van Dyke

*Incentive Research Foundation*

As the post–Great Recession American economy emerges, it is no secret that many organizations are conspicuously lean on traditional human capital reward levers, including raises, bonuses, and promotions. Coupled with a new capitalism heavily dependent on the knowledge worker who is often asked to wear many unrecognized hats (e.g., employee, innovator, trainer, project leader), it is understandable why executives have expanded their interest in optimizing nontraditional portions of their total rewards strategy. Specifically, the interest in nonmonetary rewards and recognition has continued to grow since WorldatWork introduced it as a key part of the total rewards model, with 74 percent of U.S. businesses now using noncash rewards to recognize key audiences in the form of incentive travel, merchandise, or gift cards.[1] These organizations understand the impact that nonmonetary rewards can have, with studies showing that the annual corporate revenues (measured year over year) for companies that use nonmonetary rewards and recognition are as much as 6 percent higher than those that did not.[2] Equally important, as shown in Table 14.1, businesses

|  | Cash | Travel | Merchandise | Prepaid Cards |
|---|---|---|---|---|
| Employees only | 37% | 27% | 48% | 67% |
| Channel only | 17% | 33% | 56% | 67% |
| Employees and channel | 25% | 57% | 65% | 61% |
| Use only this award | 6% | 8% | 10% | 26% |

Table 14.1  Typical Rewards Options Mix of Businesses Today

today leverage a broad mix of rewards options within both their total rewards strategy and their nonmonetary programs.

## Why Nonmonetary Awards Are Effective

When carefully deployed within the total rewards framework, nonmonetary awards can be more effective than cash in motivating specific behaviors toward major business goals. When asked what amount of award was most effective, human resources leaders noted that it took one to five times as much cash to motivate their various constituencies.[3] Dr. Scott Jeffrey, a professor at Monmouth University, in a paper entitled, "The Benefits of Tangible Non-Monetary Incentives," uncovered the following four psychological processes that, when used appropriately, allow noncash awards to create a greater overall impact on the recipient:

- *Separability.* Dr. Jeffrey's study[4] is one of many studies that have shown how non-monetary award recipients mentally account for noncash rewards differently than they do an equivalent cash award. Award recipients are more likely to mentally file noncash awards into discretionary (or "fun") mental accounts and to use non-monetary awards for this purpose; they are also consistently more likely to file cash awards into mental accounts reserved for bills and necessities. It is also significantly more probable that award recipients will *increase* the amounts available in their mental accounts when they receive a noncash award and *offset* the amount available when receiving cash. This process of raising the amount in mental fun accounts with nonmonetary awards but absorbing cash awards into stagnant bill accounts means that nonmonetary awards recipients often "feel" that they received more than the cash equivalent.[5]

- *Evaluability.* When awards are properly selected and presented, noncash award recipients tie positive emotion to the award and to the event in which they receive it. This causes the recipient to assign a higher mental value to the reward than its cash equivalent.

- *Justifiability.* Cash award recipients are often likely to feel that they should divert the gift toward daily necessities, such as bills or groceries. Because nonmonetary awards are separated from cash compensation, employees are more likely to feel as though they "deserve" the award and less likely to experience guilt when "splurging." Nonmonetary awards therefore offer a more pleasurable experience than cash because there is no guilt associated with diverting income into something special.

- *Social reinforcement.* In most cultures, it is not acceptable to publicly discuss the amount of cash compensation a person receives. Nonmonetary award recipients are therefore more able to promote their award to family and friends, making it a tool for bonding with the communities that matter to them. Discussing a firm-sponsored award in public with friends and family also creates greater alignment between the recipient and the organization. It is this attribution—relating how the organization recognized one's effort—that is natural with nonmonetary awards and rarely mentioned by recipients of cash payments.

For all of these reasons, noncash awards also maintain a halo effect, making them more memorable than cash awards, with recipients remembering why they earned and what they earned months, even years, after the event.

From a design perspective, however, it is important to know that these results also depend on the award being top of mind, contingent on some level of performance, and most important, personally valued by the recipient.[6] As with any award, cash or nonmonetary, an award perceived as insufficient for the effort or accomplishment will be ineffective. Always consider the recipient and the award value when selecting a nonmonetary award or offer a broad choice of awards of an appropriate value.

## Application for Nonmonetary Awards

As more organizations acknowledge the need for a broader reward offering by embracing the total rewards framework, there is an increased focus on nonmonetary awards. Some of the reasons organizations choose to use nonmonetary awards include

- *To recognize outstanding performance.* By far the most traditional approach to using nonmonetary awards is to recognize and reward outstanding sales or operational performance (e.g., top performer in sales, highest customer satisfaction, or best safety rates) with awards such as gift cards, merchandise, and travel.

- *To optimize their rewards mix.* Nonmonetary awards should never replace a fair compensation plan. When properly developed and targeted at key organizational outcomes (e.g., customer satisfaction, employee referral, etc.) and behaviors, though, research shows that it can take from one to five times less payout to motivate recipients with nonmonetary awards versus cash.[7]

- *To increase engagement.* With Gallup estimating that lost productivity from disengaged employees costs U.S. businesses over $450 billion a year,[8] developing and maintaining an engaged workforce have become key topics in most organizations. Although there remains a good deal of incongruity regarding the exact definition and precursors of engagement, most consultancies note that organizational reward and recognition play a strong role in the engagement equation. Nonmonetary awards help organizations to answer the question, "Engaged in what?" by offering the workforce fair reward and recognition for taking on critical job roles both inside and outside a worker's core job. Noncore job roles could include everything from being an innovator, a trainer, or even an investor in their own ongoing skills and education.[9]

- *To energize wellness programs.* Rising healthcare premiums and lost workforce productivity due to preventable diseases have made workforce wellness a key issue for most U.S. businesses. Savvy organizations have found great results in wellness initiatives, with comprehensive ongoing corporate wellness programs showing savings-to-cost ratios of more than $3 saved for each $1 invested. Nonmonetary awards play a key role in these efforts, with Johnson & Johnson, for example, finding that voluntary participation in its wellness program increased from 26 to 90 percent when noncash incentives were introduced.[10]

- *To ease the transition to a cash incentive plan.* Cash awards quickly become embedded in employees' expected compensation. Organizations therefore have found great success in using nonmonetary awards to test and refine a new incentive plan.

- *To enhance the employee value proposition.* The influx of multiple generations and redefined family constructs in the workplace has forced many organizations to differentiate and target their employee value proposition. Many now offer a mix of nonmonetary awards offerings such as mentoring, professional development, personal development, unique travel experiences, and so on. Because nonmonetary award recipients naturally attribute the award to their personal performance with halo effects to the organization, this attribution can be a powerful retention tool in today's competitive labor market.

- *To enhance organizational agility.* The Great Recession often brought on the death of five-year plans and the introduction of much shorter planning horizons. Shifting traditional compensation to help organizations focus employee performance toward rapidly changing goals (e.g., customer satisfaction or productivity) is often not optimal or even an option. Employees are generally suspicious of and cynical about changes in compensation and especially resistant to frequent changes. Nonmonetary rewards help companies to quickly refocus employees to ever-changing goals. Additionally, raising the cash sales commission for a particular product can have the effect of cannibalizing efforts put toward other products in the product line. The addition and deletion of nonmonetary awards can add emphasis without "tipping the scales" in either direction. Finally, if the organization has or is implementing a gain-sharing plan, nonmonetary awards are also a good way to differentiate between the productivity objective of the existing cash compensation plan and the other objectives.

- *To support peer-to-peer connections.* Organizations looking to support peer-to-peer connections as a result of either mergers, engagement issues, or a focus on core values have found success in allowing peers to reward and recognize each other with nonmonetary awards. These peer-to-peer programs also have the added benefit of helping the host organization to identify, catalog, and recognize front-line behaviors that are making a difference to the host organization.

## Types of Nonmonetary Awards

*Informal Recognition.* Informal recognition that can be used to raise morale may include a pat on the back, a simple "thank you," a show of respect, new training, a short written note, the opportunity to mentor, and so on. With the cost of these gestures being nothing to minimal, the return is limitless. Organizations should help managers to become more comfortable with this type of award by providing managerial education on the importance and practice of informal recognition.

*Awards Catalogs.* Awards catalogs in support of recognition and incentive programs are available from a variety of sources, including full-service performance-improvement agencies. The items included in an awards catalog have been specifically selected and promoted for their ability to create a memorable and rewarding experience called *trophy value.* Awards catalogs promote goal-setting in performance-improvement programs by allowing employees to focus on earning specific items they find highly motivational. Catalogs can be small booklets of 15 items grouped by value levels or comprehensive catalogs with over 2,000 high-quality items selected for their appeal to a broad range of tastes. Coffee table–type awards catalogs also have the advantage of being strong promotional vehicles that engage entire families when they are sent to employee homes. With the Internet, these catalogs can be online as well, but do not overlook the value of using a hardcopy catalog.

These catalogs are seen as unique because (1) they arrive in the home for the entire family to see, and (2) everything else is on the Internet, and as such, it can lose its uniqueness.

*Award Certificates.* Organizations using this option send award earners the appropriate denomination of merchandise certificate that can be redeemed at one or more retail locations or through a catalog. Certificates are normally easy to source and can be awarded "on the spot" to employees who are not connected to the Internet. The downside, however, includes the lack of fraud control, the need to source from many retailers to accommodate diverse tastes, and the inability to easily replace lost or stolen certificates. These problems make award certificates a challenge to use for sizable programs.

*Retail Award Cards.* Retail award cards have replaced a large percentage of programs that traditionally used certificates. These cards are normally easy to source and can be purchased with a set denomination directly from retailers. Depending on the retailer, these cards also may be offered at a bulk discount, branded with the company logo, or offered as a "virtual" (e-mailed code) option. Retail award cards can only be used in one retailer's stores or through that retailer's website and are sometimes called *closed-loop cards*. Award earners have the advantage of redeeming their points at competitive prices (including sales), and the sponsoring firm can have a great variety of award choices and redemption options (e.g., store, online, catalog). Retail cards can have limited fraud protection and often have state-mandated expiration-date restrictions and late usage fees.

*Stored-Value Cards.* There are two main types of stored-value cards: open or filtered. The open-ended stored-value card allows the participant to shop at any retailer that accepts the award-card supplier (e.g., American Express, MasterCard, Visa, Discover, etc.). The filtered card limits the award earner to the vendors selected but has the advantage of ensuring that the award is memorable and special and that it aligns with the organization's brand and values.

*Individual Travel.* Individual travel awards provide the award earner with the opportunity to enjoy a travel experience by himself or herself, with family, or with a significant other. From a recipient's point of view, this experience is similar to a personal vacation without all or at least a major portion of the expense. Although recipients miss out on the opportunity for organizational networking and events during a group travel experience, this award offers flexibility in scheduling and the ability to have individual experiences without conforming to a group schedule. Individual travel awards generally come in the form of travel certificates, travel vouchers, award points in an awards bank account, or stored-value award cards, all of which can be redeemed for travel. They generally cover only the major aspects of the trip (i.e., airfare, rental car, and hotel), or they can be all-inclusive to include meals, beverages, transfers, and activities. Travel awards can be obtained from local travel agencies, on the Internet, or through full-service incentive companies.

*Group Travel.* Group travel awards generally are used as top-performer awards for channel partners (e.g., resellers, distributors, retailers, agents, or dealers) and sales forces but have been expanded recently to also include nonsales personnel (e.g., service personnel, individual contributors, and/or special project teams).[11] Recipients have the opportunity to enjoy the destination, to network with peers and executives, and to enjoy the on-site travel activities with other top performers while being recognized by executive hosts. The organization has the opportunity to create unique and special events that are not easily replicated for individuals, making this award especially valuable and memorable. Learning and developmental opportunities also can be included with group travel by having workshops and/or bringing in experts to provide training.

*Symbolic Awards.* The use of symbolic or logoed awards is widespread, especially as recognition to acknowledge and express appreciation for participation in corporate projects and events. Many organizations have created unique representations of individual or organizational achievement and include logoed premium items as diverse as clothing, crystal, desk sets, and one-of-a-kind trophies. Symbolic awards can be personalized in terms of both the sponsoring company and the individual recipient. These awards are usually sourced online, through a catalog, or by symbolic award representatives. A number of organizations such as ad specialty, recognition award, and full-service performance-improvement agencies supply these types of nonmonetary awards.

*Earned Time Off.* An always-popular reward is paid time off. This reward has grown in preference over the past decade as the pace of business has accelerated and the hours spent at work by salaried employees have increased. There are several important considerations when time off is used as a reward, including

- The state and federal labor laws surrounding time off, including comp time for nonexempt employees

- How the time off will be tracked and calculated, its costs determined, and then reported

- Impact on team workload during the employee's absence and impact on company productivity

## Sourcing and Fulfillment of Awards

For any nonmonetary award program, there are two distinct sourcing and fulfillment options: a full-service performance-improvement agency and a fulfillment source. Full-service performance-improvement agencies offer research, training, communications, promotion, program rules structures, and reward systems design, in addition to supplying merchandise, travel, and symbolic awards. Fulfillment sources focus solely on supplying awards. For example, a *merchandise fulfillment source* might be the incentives division of a merchandise manufacturer, a *travel fulfillment source* might be a local travel agency, and a *symbolic award fulfillment source* might be a local advertising or promotional products provider. For a sample list of different provider types, go to the Incentive Marketing Association's website (http://www.incentivemarketing.org/).

The choice of whether or not to use a full-service agency or a fulfillment source depends on two factors: (1) the goals of the nonmonetary awards strategy and (2) the availability of internal staff to do administrative and technical support. Generally, as the scope of the nonmonetary awards strategy increases or as the availability of internal support decreases, the need for support from a full-service performance-improvement agency increases.

*Awards Catalog Administration.* Full-service performance-improvement agencies provide the online and offline catalogs (which display a value for each award listed in points or award credits) and deposit points into an electronic bank account based on the organization's or employee's performance. Once points or checks are issued, employees then can redeem them immediately or accumulate them for a larger award. The agency also handles all performance tracking, statements, tax reporting, management reporting, order entry, shipping, customer service, auditing, and billing. Employees naturally have high expectations in product quality, delivery, and customer service for earned awards. To ensure this level of service, a good full-service fulfillment agency will have the most requested items on hand and highly trained customer-service personnel to assist award earners. Full-service agencies have two billing methods: *bill on issuance*, where billing occurs when the points or checks are issued, and *bill on redemption*, where points or checks are billed only after they have been redeemed by an employee for an award. Billing on issuance allows the organization to account for all nonmonetary awards in the year for which they are budgeted; this transfers the liability for awards redeemed after year-end to the supplier company. Bill on redemption allows the organization to pay for only what it uses, but this means that the organization may be subject to a large outstanding liability that needs to be paid when outstanding points or checks are redeemed in subsequent time periods. Forecasting these redemptions can cause challenges to financial planning. Shipping and sales tax are either paid by the employee or billed directly to the organization. Some agencies also roll the fixed costs of project management, technology, and administration into the variable cost of the awards. When choosing an agency, organizations should be sure to identify where the agency accounts for these costs to ensure that they are accurately calculating their employees' buying power and the full cost of their nonmonetary awards program.

*Gift Card Administration.* Many retailers who offer awards cards or certificates can offer some degree of help with program tracking, promotion, and administration if the cards are purchased in bulk and these services are requested. Full-service performance-improvement agencies provide the gift cards and usually specialize in point issuance, record keeping, stop payments, tax reporting, and other important program administration tasks. Card administration services can vary from a do-it-yourself provider to a full-service agency that can handle all the details. Retail card and certificate suppliers provide a wide range in levels of customer service, which, good or bad, will reflect on the program and the sponsoring organization. Gift cards and certificates are billed on issuance and may include an additional processing fee when the awards are issued.

*Group Travel Administration.* As with the preceding options, full-service agencies go beyond sourcing the travel elements (e.g., air travel, hotel, meeting space, activities planning, etc.) for an incentive travel program and also provide expertise in overall program administration, return-on-investment (ROI) calculations, vendor negotiations, on-site staff, and participant surveys.

## Plan Design

The research paper, "Incentives, Motivation and Workplace Performance: Research and Best Practices,"[12] was the first to detail the performance improvement by incentives (PIBI) model. Based on extensive research, this model provides a guide to the design and implementation of nonmonetary awards programs. The eight steps (or "events") that an incentive program designer should follow in order to ensure a successful program are as follow:

- *Event 1: Identify unrealized work goals ("Determine if it's necessary").* Organizations should first assess the gaps between the organization's strategic or cultural goals and employees' current performance or behavior to identify the unrealized work goals that can be improved through an incentive program. Goals that are nonspecific, unclear, undesirable, lower in priority, or perceived as unchallenging often go unrealized by the workforce. If there is a gap in performance and it is due to motivation and not a lack of tools, a program is appropriate.

- *Event 2: Identify incentive system design ("Determine if it's appropriate").* Organizations then should identify the recipients, format, type, and time span of the improvement system. Although the details will greatly depend on the organization involved, successful performance-improvement plans tend to
  - Include tangible awards and intangible recognition.
  - Last for longer than a year.
  - Involve employees in the design.

- *Event 3: Establish task value ("Determine if it's worth it").* Individual employees will perform their own cost-benefit analysis to determine whether the communicated awards are worth the effort of changing or redirecting their behavior. If they believe that the award is worth the effort involved in accomplishing the new task or achieving the behavior, they will focus on the identified tasks.

- *Event 4: Establish efficacy ("Determine whether I/we can do it").* Once employees have established that the new task or behavior is worth the effort, they will evaluate their personal capabilities. The more employees have faith in their personal capabilities, the tools they are given, and the capabilities of their team, the more likely they are to commit to the new goal, task, or behavior.

- *Event 5: Establish agency ("Determine whether it will work").* Employee confidence in management's ability to fairly implement and manage the new reward system is paramount. Employees will evaluate immediately the organizational support of the program; the greater their level of confidence that the organization will provide the resources, support structures, and incentives necessary to achieve program success, the greater will be their willingness to ensure that the plan succeeds.

- *Event 6: Consider mood ("Determine whether it feels good enough").* The current emotional state of employees, both collectively and as individuals, will affect the organizational level of commitment to the program. Recent layoffs, pay freezes, or industry downturns will have a dramatic impact on a program's success.

- *Event 7: Active choice/persistence/effort ("Determine whether we've started, are persisting, and are getting smarter").* Once installed, organizations should gauge the success of the new system by evaluating whether employees actively started to do something differently than before (active choice), whether they are doing more of what is desired (persistence), and whether they are bringing more innovation to their work on the incentivized goal (mental effort).

- *Event 8: Performance improvement ("Determine that I/we did it and that it was worth the cost").* As a final event, organizations should evaluate whether the choice, persistence, and effort exhibited by employees have closed the necessary gaps in performance. If so, the organization should evaluate whether the benefits of the program outweigh the cost and whether the organization should evaluate both the goal and the program structure behind it.

## Taxes and Nonmonetary Awards

As a general rule, in the United States, most nonmonetary awards are taxable. It is therefore important to seek legal and tax advice before implementing any size or type of nonmonetary awards program. To ensure that employees do not incur the tax bill associated with their nonmonetary awards, most organizations choose to "gross up" the awards by adding the amount of applicable federal, state, local, and FICA taxes to the amount that is reported on the employee's W2 Form. As long as the nonmonetary awards do not push an employee into a higher tax bracket, grossing up awards ensures that there is little or no tax cost to the employee. Here is an example formula for gross-up calculations:

$$X = Y + wX + sX + lX + fX$$

where
$X$ = gross award value (in $)
$Y$ = new award value (in $)
$w$ = federal tax rate (%)
$s$ = state tax rate (%)
$l$ = local tax rate (%)
$f$ = FICA tax rate (individual %)

If the tax-rate estimates are 28 percent for federal, 3 percent for state, 1 percent for local, and 7.65 percent for FICA, then the calculation for a $100 award item is

$$X = \$100 + 0.28X + 0.03X + 0.01X + 0.0765X$$
$$= \$100 + 0.3965X$$

$$0.6035X = \$100$$

$$X = \$165.70$$

In this example, a nonmonetary award worth $100 has a gross award value of $165.70. To ensure that an employee receives the full buying power of the $100 award, the organization must fund $165.70.

There are two exceptions specifically addressed in the (current) U.S. Tax Code related to award taxation on certain length-of-service awards and safety-achievement awards that have tax advantages based on a number of parameters and restrictions. Some of these considerations are listed below, but consult your tax advisor for the specific application of these to your organization:

- The maximum amount an employer can deduct for a single employee in a single tax year for both service and safety awards is $400 for an unqualified plan and $1,600 under a qualified plan.

- A plan will be qualified if it is an established, written plan and if the average combined value of service and safety awards per employee in the given tax year does not exceed $400.

- The awards must be "tangible personal property." Award certificates, cards, or credits are not eligible unless they are redeemable only for tangible personal property.

- Length-of-service awards may be given tax-free to an employee only on a fifth anniversary and then only once every five years thereafter.

- Safety-achievement awards may be given tax-free to no more than 10 percent of eligible employees in any one year.

- Productivity awards are never eligible for tax benefits.

- Many other restrictions apply.[13]

In addition to taxation, heavily regulated and public companies should review all significant nonmonetary expenditures to ensure their compliance with the Sarbanes-Oxley Act of 2002.

## Trends in Nonmonetary Awards

For the last 10 years, the Incentive Research Foundation (IRF) has been tracking trends in nonmonetary rewards and recognition programs, reaching out to thousands of program owners twice a year. According the IRF's latest pulse study in late 2013, the following nine trends, listed in order of prevalence, were most widespread in nonmonetary award programs:

- *Points–based systems.* Highly pervasive, over 80 percent of respondents said that they were using some form of points-based system as a part of their nonmonetary reward and recognition program.

- *Measurement techniques.* Understating program impact remained a key topic in the postrecession economy, with 70 percent of program owners indicating that they use "results assessment (ROI, etc.)" to determine a program's success. More than half also used sales success, budget achievement, and/or participant feedback to measure their programs.

- *Social media.* Nearly two-thirds of respondents indicated that they used social media tools/techniques to enhance their incentive programs, including Facebook, LinkedIn, Twitter, and YouTube.

- *Procurement.* Over half of program owners agreed that procurement involvement in nonmonetary rewards programs will continue to rise over the next few years.

- *Corporate social responsibility.* Almost half the respondents indicated that they were including corporate social responsibility in their travel, gift card, and merchandise programs. This included everything from "give-back" team-building exercises in incentive travel programs to merchandise awards that provided donations back to a host charity.

- *Wellness.* Upward of 45 percent of incentive travel program owners were concerned about wellness and/or had included specific options for attendees, such as healthy menus, spa or gym access, and even FitBit contests and organized 5K races.

- *Gamification.* Almost 40 percent of program owners were adding game mechanics to their program, including such things as badges, leaderboards, levels, and automated notifications.

- *Merchandise electronics.* Electronics were the most popular nonmonetary merchandise award item selected by program owners, with 40 percent of programs using them. Jewelry (including watches), open-loop gift cards, and luggage were close behind, with a third or more of program planners adding these items into their programs.

- *Travel quality over quantity.* Although incentive travel program owners overall were making only very slight increases in the length or size of their programs, the research showed that many planners are continuing their investments in the additional nonmeal components of their programs, such as including all airline fees, offsite excursions, transfers, gifts, and so on. The nonmeal components portion was the only program area to have seen *both* an increasing number of planners investing and fewer planners cutting these elements in the last two years.

## Conclusion

In the new economy, organizational agility and workforce engagement will be paramount to ongoing success. As the rising need for workers to show up and do more than just the minimum job assigned continues, so will the need for organizations to deploy effective, targeted total rewards models complete with nonmonetary awards programs. Astute organizations are already deploying well-constructed nonmonetary awards programs to engage the hearts and minds of their workforce, meet rapidly changing employee expectations, and redirect workforce focus amid unending noise. Technological advances, increased options for program delivery, and ongoing research into the construction and measurement of nonmonetary awards programs will only contribute to the growth of this important workforce communication and motivation tool.

## Notes

1. See incentivefederation.org, "Incentive Market Study," October 2013. Available at: http://theirf.org/direct/user/site/0/files/Incentive percent20Marketplace percent20White percent20Paper percent2010132013.pdf.
2. See "Noncash Awards as a Vital Compensation Component." Available at: http://theirf.org/research/content/6085642/rewards-and-recognition-as-a-vital-compensation-component/.
3. See "The Use of Awards in Organizations." Available at: http://theirf.org/.6081797.html.
4. Scott Jeffrey, "The Benefits of Tangible Non-Monetary Incentives." Available at: http://theirf.org/direct/user/site/0/files/the%20benefits%20of%20tangible%20non%20monetary%20incentives.pdf. See also, for example, D. Kahneman and A. Tversky, "Choices, Values, and Frames," 1984. Available at: web.missouri.edu/~segerti/capstone/choicevalues; R. H. Thaler, "Mental Accounting and Consumer Choice." *Marketing Science* 4:199–214, 1985; and R. H. Thaler, "Mental Accounting Matters." *Journal of Behavior Decision Making* 12:183–206, 1999.
5. See Rebecca White, "Format Matters in the Mental Accounting of Funds: The Case of Gift Cards and Cash Gifts," November 30, 2006, University of Waterloo, Canada.
6. See R. Kanungo and J. Hartwick, "An Alternative to the Intrinsic-Extrinsic Dichotomy of Work Rewards." *Journal of Management* 13(4):751–766, 1987.
7. http://theirf.org/research/content/6081797/the-use-of-awards-in-organizations/.
8. See "How to Tackle U.S. Employees' Stagnating Engagement." *Gallup Journal*, June 2013. Available at: http://businessjournal.gallup.com/content/162953/tackle-employees-stagnating-engagement.aspx.
9. See Theresa Welbourne, "Engaged in What? Creating Connections to Performance with Rewards, Recognition, and Roles," Incentive Research Foundation, St. Louis, MO, 2014.
10. See "Energizing Workplace Wellness Programs: The Role of Incentives and Recognition," Incentive Research Foundation, St. Louis, MO, 2011. Available at: http://theirf.org/research/content/6078727/energizing-workplace-wellness-programs-the-role-of-incentives-and-recognition/.

11. See "Critical Findings for Recognition Travel Programs." Available at: http://theirf.org/research/content/6068361/critical-findings-for-recognition-travel-programs/.
12. Available at www.loyaltyworks.com/incentive-program-research-articles/ispifull.pdf.
13. IRS Circular 230 Disclosure: "To ensure compliance with requirements imposed by the IRS, we inform you that this written advice was not intended or written to be used, and cannot be used, for the purpose of avoiding penalties under the Internal Revenue Code."

# PART III

# VARIABLE COMPENSATION

# 15

# Choosing the Incentive Compensation Program that Best Promotes Performance

Linda E. Amuso

*Radford, an Aon Hewitt Company*

The importance of incentive compensation or variable pay in a company's total rewards program has continued to grow as companies aim to align pay with performance and manage expenses. Incentive compensation can take on different forms, but generally, it refers to the payment of variable compensation that rewards achievement of specified results, typically measured over a period of 12 months or less. As one component of a company's total rewards program (including base salary, short- and long-term incentives, equity, benefits, and learning and development), incentives can be the most effective form of compensation in building and maintaining a strong pay-for-performance culture. By placing pay at risk through the use of incentives, companies help to ensure that compensation dollars are used optimally to reward and motivate the results achieved and to align decisions and behaviors to optimize performance with the hope of building value for shareholders. The most well-designed incentive plans will directly link business performance with pay such that the total compensation expense will increase with strong performance and decrease with weaker company performance.

This chapter will assist practitioners in developing effective incentive programs by examining design considerations and best practices for designing programs. Incentive programs have taken on increased importance following the economic decline that occurred in late 2008 and into 2009 and as companies look to manage fixed costs to drive profitability during a time when the war for talent has increased. Further, shareholder activism is increasingly aimed at improving the alignment between executive compensation and company performance. Although there are numerous forms of incentive compensation, including spot awards, profit sharing, sales incentives, and others, this chapter will focus on incentive plans typically targeted at management and/or key employee populations as part of a formal program. Figure 15.1 provides a description of incentive plan types and

Rewards ←→ Incentives

| | Discretionary Award | Spot Award | Milestone Reward | Profit Sharing | Project/Milestone Incentive | Formal Short-Term Incentive Plan |
|---|---|---|---|---|---|---|
| **Reward/Incentive** | Reward | Reward | Reward | Reward or Incentive | Incentive | Incentive |
| **Eligibility and Participation** | Management and key employees | All employees except senior management | Teams and/or individuals | All employees | Teams and/or individuals | May be for all employees or more targeted based on company culture |
| **Frequency and Timing** | May occur at any time | At time of event throughout year | Payout after project milestone | Quarterly to annually | Payout after project milestone | Quarterly to annually |
| **Pros** | Easy to control | Recognizes exceptional efforts; immediacy of feedback | No goals are set; recognition provided after the fact | Recognizes all employees based on specific company-wide goals; easy to control | Drives toward specific results and timelines | Aligns behaviors with specific objectives at the company, BU and individual level |
| **Cons** | Does not drive specific behaviors | Managers may be reluctant to single out individuals | Payment is after the fact therefore does not drive behaviors | Based on company performance with no individual differentiation | Goals must be set in advance with expectation of achievement | Goal setting can be complex<br><br>Requires strong performance management culture for individual differentiation |
| **Company Examples** | Early-stage companies | Most technology companies | Project-based companies; companies with fluid goals and priorities | Established technology companies looking to provide additional cash incentive and not focus on individuals | Software developers; drug research companies; companies that have a stable goal-setting process | Most public companies irrespective of stage |

**Figure 15.1 Incentive plan characteristics.**

*Source:* Radford.

their characteristics. The figure outlines the characteristics of various incentive plan types, including plan features, plan participants, frequency of payout, and performance metrics. Management and key-employee incentives are an important component of total rewards systems at companies committed to building a strong pay-for-performance culture. The types of incentive plans that are typically deployed in an organization need to be specifically tied to the company's overall business and human resources strategy to be most effective.

Once limited to the executive suite, incentive compensation is being implemented throughout the organization by more companies to better align business results and priorities with company-wide pay programs. This shift is in part a reflection of the power of incentive compensation to direct specific behaviors (and their outcomes) and in part an effort to mitigate an employee mentality of entitlement for base salary increases—a form of compensation that does little to distinguish good from great performance and little to motivate specific behaviors required to drive organizational success. Incentive pay has increased in importance as a rewards tool to differentiate performance as companies have limited their merit increase budgets, particularly in the United States, to 2 to 3 percent of payroll, making it more challenging to make meaningful distinctions using base salary alone.

## Current Issues in Incentive Compensation

Pay-for-performance practices have been under intense scrutiny since the beginning of the decade, and that scrutiny shows no sign of abating as shareholders demand that boards of directors improve the link between company results and executive compensation. Shareholder activist groups such as Institutional Shareholder Services and Glass-Lewis and some large institutional funds cite pay for performance as a critical measure of a company's overall performance and of the performance of the compensation committee of the board of directors. Increasingly, shareholders are holding the board of directors accountable for ensuring that pay is aligned with company results and are issuing "no" votes for directors they deem out of synch with these ideals. With this increased scrutiny, board members, specifically compensation committee members, are focused on how to most effectively design incentive plans that ensure that rewards are based on company performance to improve their overall pay governance.

## Design Considerations

Incentive plans (as is the case with all compensation plans) invariably reflect an organization's culture. However, the extent to which an incentive plan supports the *desired* culture is determined within the plan design. In other words, incentive plan design is undertaken within the context of a company's human resources strategy and total rewards philosophy and must specifically support these tenants. Companies focusing on stable growth and long-term performance may place less emphasis on short-term incentives compared with companies seeking consistent near-term delivery of specific outcomes. Also, a company's cash resources will factor into the affordability of the plan and the role of cash compensation, particularly incentive compensation compared with forms of long-term compensation or equity incentives.

Successful plan design and implementation are predicated on a company's ability to identify its key business objectives and translate those goals into meaningful performance requirements at the business and individual employee level to affect decision making and behaviors. Plan participants also must believe that there will be a personal benefit to changing their behaviors or making investment tradeoffs from which they will benefit (e.g., increased pay, additional career opportunities, etc.). Determining the best-fit incentive plan or combination of plans is a key aspect of linking a company's human resources strategy to the overall rewards strategy. As indicated in Figure 15.2, most companies have a formal bonus plan within the technology sector as their primary incentive plan tool.

| Performance Metrics | Prevalence |
|---|---|
| Formal bonus | 84% |
| Discretionary bonus | 39% |
| Cash profit sharing | 12% |
| Other | <1% |
| **Plan Combinations** | |
| Formal bonus only | 54% |
| Formal bonus + discretionary bonus | 21% |
| Discretionary only | 13% |
| Formal bonus + cash profit sharing | 5% |
| Formal bonus + discretionary bonus + cash profit sharing | 4% |
| Cash profit sharing only | 2% |
| Discretionary bonus + cash profit sharing | 1% |

**Figure 15.2  Prevalence of performance metrics.**

*Source:* Radford's "Global Technology Survey Practices Report," April 2014.

Although there are various types of plans, the fundamental elements of plan design remain the same and include

- Funding and affordability
- Metrics
- Eligibility and participation in the plan
- Award opportunities frequency tied to the total rewards philosophy
- Administrative rules

## Plan Funding and Affordability

The financial considerations and implications of incentive plan design are aligned directly with a company's total rewards philosophy and the role of fixed pay (base salary) versus variable or at-risk incentives (cash and/or equity incentives). A company must consider the plan affordability to help inform the plan design. Typically, we see this being addressed from two perspectives: bottom up or top down.

When examining a *bottom-up approach,* companies must first determine their overall pay philosophy and where total rewards should be positioned in the market (e.g., 50th, 60th, or 75th percentile). With this framework, a company can apply a market-based model to determine the overall cost of a program (Figure 15.3). A market-based model implies that a company's staff will be paid consistent with peers, including base salary, incentive opportunities, and levels of participation. When this model is applied to a company's staffing model, the resulting plan cost is achieved.

**Figure 15.3  Market-based cost model.**

*Source:* Radford.

This bottom-up view may or may not be affordable at a company because of the need to deliver appropriate financial performance for shareholders. Therefore, the bottom-up approach must be compared with a *top-down perspective*, whereby in the strategic planning process or budget process a company establishes the overall cost envelop for employee pay (cash versus equity) to determine what percent of base salary, revenue, and/or profits should be allocated to plan participants. This approach implies that there is specific cost tolerance, assuming that the company achieves the stated business objectives.

Balancing both perspectives will yield an outcome that incorporates the competitive demand for talent while being sensitive to shareholder expectations. Because incentive compensation typically can account for approximately 8 percent of base payroll (ranging from 4 to 10 percent at the 25th and 75th percentiles, respectively) according to Radford's "Global Technology Survey Practices Report" (Table 15.1), a company must ensure that these assets are invested to drive the right performance.

| Plan Cost as a Percentage of: | 25th | 50th | 75th |
|---|---|---|---|
| Revenue | 0.7% | 1.7% | 3.0% |
| Payroll | 3.9% | 7.8% | 10.0% |
| Operating Income | 6.4% | 12.8% | 29.1% |
| *Source:* Radford's "Global Technology Survey Practices Report," April 2014. | | | |

**Table 15.1  Plan Cost as a Percenage of Competitive Level**

As part of the process of establishing the best-fit plan design, a company also must consider the level of financial performance that must be achieved to justify incentive compensation or pay beyond base salary. These hurdles are typically referred to as *thresholds*, which are considered a best practice for plan governance to protect the company from added expense in a challenging business environment. Plans also typically establish a *cap* or *maximum level* of performance and payout so as not to encourage excessive risk taking by business leaders and employees. These design features typically are referred to as *plan leverage*, defining the downside protection and upside opportunity provided based on company performance. It is common practice today in most industries to establish plan thresholds and caps for good plan governance following the economic crisis and the criticism of these plans for encouraging business leaders to take on excessive risk for personal gain.

To set threshold performance and payouts, a company must consider the question of affordability to establish the right level of performance and rewards at the company level. Most companies set a threshold level of performance between 80 and 90 percent of "budget or plan," with plan funding falling between 50 and 75 percent for this level of achievement. The same is true for stretch performance and overall affordability of the plan and at what point the plan should be capped, returning additional value to the business for added investments and/or to shareholders via dividends or other forms of capital distribution. Caps also can serve as a way of providing budget predictability in the funding process. Most companies cap the amount of award payouts at 150 to 200 percent of target plan funding, according to Radford's research.

## Performance Metrics

The measures a company selects to gauge performance under the plan are a critical factor in determining the success of the program. This is perhaps the most difficult aspect of plan design because companies must select metrics that are easily understandable and reportable and for which there are reliable data. Key considerations of metric selection include an understanding of the following:

- The company's business objectives and priorities and how each specific measure can be translated into a specific objective goal within the desired time frame

- The appropriate complement or number of metrics required to ensure that the plan focuses on the desired results and can align the necessary actions and decisions

  - Too many metrics can fragment the attention of plan participants and can be a challenge to administer.

  - Too few metrics can result in missed priorities and/or a lack of alignment across all plan participants operating in different businesses, geographies, and functions.

- The relative importance of each metric and thus the weighting of the measures and how this might change by different levels of authority and influence to drive behaviors

- What impact the short-term metric could have on longer-range corporate goals

- How the measures selected are affected by the employees to whom they apply

Line of sight is an important factor when considering metrics. Holding employees accountable for results they cannot influence likely will produce a situation in which goals are not met and employees are dissatisfied with the plan, not to mention that management misses out on having a key tool to align performance and pay. Ultimately, the measures chosen will help to drive certain behaviors, and companies need to be alert for the unintended consequences of plan design (e.g., overemphasis on expense management may motivate layoffs that otherwise could be avoided, a lack of investment in innovation might create a drive to hit short-term milestones that may erode long-term goals, etc.).

The process for setting performance metrics, as well as the performance levels chosen for the senior executive plan, has become an area of intense focus by shareholders and shareholder activist groups, as alluded to earlier in this chapter. In the wake of changes in the Securities and Exchange Commission's proxy filing requirements, companies are required to disclose in greater detail today than ever before the *what* and *how* for executives receiving compensation. This includes more detailed disclosure on plan metrics, the metric weighting, in addition to how executives performed against the specific objectives on which specific awards were based, whether at the company or individual level.

Companies also have had to adjust to increased involvement by the board compensation committee in the selection of measures used to determine the level of achievement required for plan funding as well as the leverage designed within the plan to motivate overachievement and protect against underachievement. As compensation committees assume a greater role in the policy decisions and design of these plans, they are taking a much more active role in selecting the metrics and ensuring that the performance goals associated with them are neither too low nor unrealistically aggressive. Figure 15.4 provides a range of corporate-level metrics that are typically used to align business performance with funding and/or awards under the plan.

| Performance Metrics | Prevalence |
|---|---|
| Sales/revenue or growth | 81% |
| Profit/income | 82% |
| Achievement of nonfinancial objectives | 54% |
| Customer satisfaction | 17% |
| New product introduction/development | 15% |
| Quality | 13% |

| Number of Metrics Used | Prevalence |
|---|---|
| 3 or more | 47% |
| 2 metrics | 37% |
| 1 metric | 16% |
| **Metric Combinations** | |
| Sales/revenue + profit/income + other measure(s) | 41% |
| Sales/revenue + profit/income | 26% |
| Profit/income only | 9% |
| Sales/revenue + measure(s) other than profit/income | 8% |
| Profit/income + measure(s) other than sales/revenue | 7% |
| Sales/revenue only | 6% |
| Measure(s) other than sales/revenue or profit/income only | 4% |

**Figure 15.4  Typical corporate performance metrics.**

*Source:* Radford's "Technology Survey Practices Report," April 2014.

## Eligibility

As incentive pay has increasingly been pushed down from the executive ranks to the broad employee population, eligibility most often was determined by base salary level or job grade or level. A company's culture plays a key role in determining eligibility in the incentive plan. For example, more entrepreneurial and/or egalitarian organizations may seek to make all employees eligible under the incentive plan, whereas other companies might elect to shield their employees from the economic risks inherent in these incentive arrangements and deliver substantially all compensation for most employees via base salary. These differences are often a by-product of a company's culture as well as the competitive pressure for talent.

While a company can designate a relatively large segment of the employee population as "plan eligible," typically not all these eligible employees ultimately will participate (e.g., receive an incentive award) during the course of the plan cycle. Figure 15.4 also shows the average percentage of employees that are eligible for a formal incentive plan within the technology sector. At small startup organizations, companies may allow all employees to be eligible for the plan, whereas larger, more established organizations may limit participation to middle management and above in order to concentrate the plan on decision makers in the company. Actual participation at the individual level typically factors performance against objectives, team contribution, and time with the company (e.g., hire date during the period).

For example, in Table 15.2, 89 percent of the companies indicated that the manager level is eligible for the incentive plan, which compares with 74 percent for professional individual contributors at the career level. This reflects the fact that in the overall market there are companies that support broad-participation cultures, whereas others are using these plans in a more targeted manner. Overall, we find that 80 to 90 percent of eligible participants actually receive some form of incentive payment in the technology sector.

| Job Level | Percent Eligible for Incentives |
|---|---|
| CEO | 100% |
| Executives (VP/SVP/EVP) | 99% |
| Directors | 96% |
| Managers | 89% |
| Supervisors | 76% |
| Professional (Principal/Expert) | 84% |
| Professional (Career/Advanced) | 74% |
| Professional (Entry/Developing) | 65% |
| Support | 57% |
| Overall Percentage Receiving (Median) | 82% |
| *Source:* Radford Technology Practices Report, 2014. | |

Table 15.2  Incentive Eligibility by Job Level

## Incentive Award Opportunities

The central questions in determining award opportunities include

- What is the company's target total cash (base salary plus cash incentives) pay position?
- How are total compensation levels and pay mix currently positioned against the market?
- How much can the company afford?

*Target Awards.* Award opportunities are generally based on the employee's level and the criticality of the position. Typically, award opportunities are expressed as a percentage of base salary, but determining the appropriate award opportunity across organizational levels is an art and is largely tied to what a company can afford, its pay philosophy, and its culture for inclusivity. That said, as a generality, lower-level employees have less at-risk pay, which means lower incentive opportunities as a percent of base salary, with targets generally between 5 and 10 percent of base salary; at the more senior levels, this increases to between 30 and 100 percent of base salary (Table 15.3). Market data from surveys reflecting labor market practices are typically taken into account when setting award opportunities.

| Job Level | Award as a Percentage of Salary |
|---|---|
| CEO | 75% to 100% |
| Executive (VP/SVP/EVP) | 30% to 60% |
| Directors | 20% to 30% |
| Managers | 12% to 15% |
| Supervisors | 8% to 10% |
| Professional (Principal/Expert) | 12% to 15% |
| Professional (Career/Advanced) | 7% to 10% |
| Professional (Entry/Developing) | 6% to 8% |
| Support | 5% to 7% |
| *Source:* Radford's "Technology Survey Practices Report," April 2014. | |

**Table 15.3  Target Award as a Percent of Salary by Job Level**

Once award opportunities are determined, companies often struggle with where to set the bar for performance; in other words, what, for example, constitutes the target (and thus threshold and maximum), and how are individual payout opportunities set relative to performance? Typically, some portion of a participant's award is tied to company performance, in addition to that person's business group and/or department, as well as individual contributions. Individual performance measurement faces many of the above-mentioned design challenges as companies seek to define the varying levels of individual performance required to receive payment. At a minimum, most companies require an employee to be in good performance standing to receive an award. Individual awards typically range from 0 to 150 or 200 percent of the target depending on the actual plan funding. Most companies manage the plan to a fixed pool; thus, for any participants receiving above-target awards, other participants must receive below-target awards in order to manage to the approved budget or pool funding.

## Award Frequency

The frequency of award payouts depends on several factors, but most important is the ability to set and measure performance at the company and individual levels if this is part of the payout formula. Some companies can set goals only one or two quarters in advance, therefore suggesting that awards should be issued quarterly or semiannually to best align pay and performance; other companies set annual goals tied to their business plan and financial objectives, therefore aligning payouts with the annual plan. How far a company can look into the future is determined by its business and product-development cycles and the features of its performance-management system to assess individual performance if in fact this is considered a factor in determining awards. The most common practice is to align payouts with the annual financial plan and the performance-management cycle (Table 15.4); this is particularly true at larger, more established companies. As a guideline, the tighter the time frame between goal achievement and award, the more power incentives can have in driving results, but this has to be evaluated against the administrative nature of goal setting and performance tracking, which involves intensive time by business managers and may mean tradeoffs in time between customers and innovation for plan administration.

| Frequency | Percentage of Companies |
|---|---|
| Annual | 69% |
| Semiannual | 15% |
| Quarterly | 15% |
| Other | 1% |
| *Source:* Radford's "Technology Survey Practices Report," April 2014. | |

Table 15.4  Frequency of Awards

## Administrative Rules

*Adjustments to the Plan.* Effective incentive plan design is predicated on management buy-in of the plan and on the company's commitment to use it to drive performance. Making midcourse adjustments to the plan undermines its effectiveness and can lead to an entitlement mentality if payouts are made and not warranted by performance. Changing the rules of the game also can insulate employees from negative events, again affecting their attitude toward the plan. This practice is generally met with skepticism by shareholders and others who monitor the link between executive pay and company performance. There are situations where adjustments are justifiable and advised, including during acquisitions and divestitures, in the wake of asset additions or disposals in capital-intensive markets, and in reaction to volatile foreign-exchange fluctuations. However, the best plans establish these rules at the beginning of the year, which assists with ensuring that the plan is perceived to be fair among employees and certainly creates a stronger governance structure for the plan.

*Communication.* Communication is an often-overlooked aspect of incentive plan implementation and can be one of the most critical aspects of ensuring plan effectiveness. As is the case with many aspects of design, how (or whether) a company communicates the plan details to participants reveals (and in part determines) a company's culture and view on transparent information sharing. The goals, processes, opportunities, and rationale of incentive compensation plans should be communicated clearly and frequently, whether it comes in the form of centralized communication, communication from line managers, or some combination of the two. The plan is best owned by line managers and not human resources. Companies rely on a number of forms of communications, including

- Summary plan descriptions
- Training and educational sessions
- Total compensation statements
- Individual performance-management feedback sessions
- Business updates to keep participants informed of goal alignment and performance

Prior to plan execution, participants should have a very strong understanding of what the company and they individually must do to achieve or exceed the plan and maximize their earnings potential. In addition to a sound outbound communication strategy for incentive plans, employees also should have the opportunity to communicate their perspectives on the plan via survey or some formal type of communication that creates data that management can use to improve program design from year to year.

## Summary

To determine if your plan is designed with market best practices, here is a top 10 list of common plan characteristics of high-performing companies:

1. The plan has demonstrated support from senior management in all aspects.
2. The plan has realistic and meaningful performance objectives that are tied to the business priorities outlined in the board-approved business plan.
3. Willingness exists within the company to differentiate performance by level, business, geography, and/or function. This has the effect of creating "winners and losers" where there is a fixed pool to allocate.
4. Above-market awards are granted to a limited population (10 percent) of high performers.
5. There is differentiation of incentive awards relative to other forms of awards [solid performance can earn cash incentives but not additional awards (e.g., mentoring, training, equity, access to senior management, autonomy, and other development opportunities)].
6. Performance-management ratings or talent distribution is managed to ensure that above-market awards can be provided to overachievers; if no performance distribution is used, managers are provided with discretion to differentiate awards to top talent.

7. Top performers are tracked more directly by cross-functional management to plan their futures and celebrate their contributions.

8. Companies establish a strong and dynamic link between the goal-setting process and the company's performance-management philosophy to provide feedback.

9. Companies understand and measure the return on investment of their incentive plan dollars.

10. There are clear plan rules at the start of the period to avoid surprises to participants when awards are issued.

# 16

# Designing and Implementing Effective Variable Pay Programs

Erin C. Packwood

*Mercer's Talent Business*

Human resource professionals are always looking for ways to ensure that employees are contributing to organizational success and that the right people are in the right roles doing the right things. To facilitate this, they are continually evaluating potential additions to their rewards toolkits in an overall effort to implement total compensation programs that adapt to rapidly changing business and workforce scenarios. When used effectively, each reward—whether a benefit program, a compensation plan, or other means of recognizing employee contribution—supports the achievement of an employer's business objective in some way and ensures that compensation programs create a competitive business advantage.

One of business's more versatile reward tools is variable pay. Although variable pay is not new, particularly among the executive ranks, it has become much more widespread in recent years as employers realize the impact it can have on employees throughout an organization and on how they perform their jobs.

## Variable Pay as an Attraction Tool

Even before an employee joins a company, variable pay can have an impact, especially if it is part of a thoughtfully developed compensation strategy derived from a broader human-capital approach that outlines the type of employee the company deems necessary to accomplish its business goals. This talent profile may have been defined for the company's entire population or for a particular segment of the workforce. However, the fact that the company includes variable pay in its mix of rewards is usually because leadership has concluded that employees who fit the desired profile will see value in the program and will be motivated to realize the full potential of the additional rewards available to them. The program then becomes part of the selection process by attracting employees who appreciate this particular type of reward. Depending on the nature of the program, variable pay can say a lot to an employee about the type of company he or she is joining. Is it an organization that openly shares financial success with its employees? Does the company value teamwork and/or individual contributions? If so, does it demonstrate this in a way that the prospective employee values?

*Variable pay* generally refers to all forms of ongoing cash compensation other than base pay that employees receive during their employment. These programs take various forms, as described later in this chapter. In a highly competitive market, the ongoing variable pay programs available to employees also can play a critical role in attracting talent by enhancing the competitiveness of the compensation package in relation to the packages offered by other potential employers. As mentioned earlier, although variable pay has long been a key component of compensation for senior management and executive employees, it is now used by most employers to reward employees at all organizational levels.

According to research conducted each year by Mercer, the percentage of U.S. employees eligible for variable pay has increased significantly since 2000, and the vast majority of organizations participating in Mercer's 2014–2015 "U.S. Compensation Planning Survey" of more than 1,500 companies in the major industry sectors have incentive plans in place for at least one segment of their employee population (Table 16.1). When compared with base pay increase trend data for the same period, there has been a notable rise in the prevalence of variable pay, coinciding with the first major decline in base pay increase budgets that the United States has seen in over 10 years. During this period, many researchers were inclined to attribute this trend to the economic downturn occurring at the time. Although this may partially explain the trend, it is just as clear that employers were beginning to face significant annual increases in the costs of their healthcare benefits. These two factors together, in fact, prompted employers to evaluate the affordability of all reward programs and to seek ways to ensure that their spending in each area was sustainable.

| Type of Incentive | Percent Organizations |
| --- | --- |
| Management incentives | 83 |
| Individual incentives for nonmanagement employees | 63 |
| Sales incentives | 54 |
| Spot cash awards | 41 |
| Broad-based equity (e.g., stock options) | 25 |
| Team/small group incentives | 15 |
| Project milestone incentives | 14 |
| Cash profit sharing | 14 |
| *Source:* Mercer, "2014–2015 U.S. Compensation Planning Survey." | |

Table 16.1  Organizations with Incentives

When looking for ways to better manage reward expenditures, variable pay programs emerge as one of the most controllable expenses. Unlike many other alternative reward investments, properly designed variable pay programs can contribute to business performance and profitability by linking employees' rewards to the activities expected of them. These are among the key reasons that variable pay programs have become so common since 2001. As variable pay eligibility increases and additional cash compensation opportunities become more popular, employees have taken notice and have begun to place greater importance on their availability. Thus variable pay has become an increasingly effective attraction tool in its perceived potential to provide highly competitive and attractive total cash compensation to employees who have confidence in their ability to succeed.

So what sort of variable pay opportunity is considered competitive? Mercer's research indicates that where variable pay programs are present, the expected individual award, or *target*, is at least the equivalent of one month's pay, or 8.3 percent of an employee's annual salary.

## Variable Pay as a Motivation Tool

Just as variable pay opportunities must be considered significant to be attractive to prospective employees, so must they be to have any motivational impact once new hires become active employees. In addition, the requirements that an employee must fulfill to receive the awards must be viewed as realistic and achievable. When employees view performance expectations as reasonable and the reward for such effort is perceived as material, they will strive to earn the additional rewards available to them.

What is considered material? In general, an amount equal to at least one month's pay is considered sufficient to be meaningful to an employee and sufficient to attract his or her attention. More than half the organizations in Mercer's survey use individual performance ratings as a factor in determining employee incentive payouts (Table 16.2).

| Performance Level | Executive | Management | Professional (Nonsales) | Professional (Sales) | Office, Clerical, Technician | Trades, Production, Service |
|---|---|---|---|---|---|---|
| Highest | 142% | 142% | 140% | 146% | 137% | 139% |
| Middle | 98% | 101% | 99% | 98% | 97% | 99% |
| Lowest | 48% | 43% | 40% | 43% | 32% | 38% |
| *Source:* Mercer, "2014–2015 U.S. Compensation Planning Survey." | | | | | | |

**Table 16.2  Differentiation by Performance Rating: Incentive Amount (Percent of Target) as a Function of Performance—Organizations with Three Performance Categories**

Managers and human resources professionals often struggle to find ways to maintain competitiveness in their pay programs and still provide meaningful rewards to employees for desired results through annual base pay increases. In some instances, the traditional annual pay adjustment seems too far off into the future to effectively motivate employees. However, when annual base pay adjustments can be combined with variable pay, total cash rewards can have a much greater impact.

Compensation professionals generally subscribe to the idea that you will get the behaviors and results you reward. Thus it is important that a variable pay plan be carefully designed so as to reinforce what is important to the company and to motivate the right things. If properly designed, a variable pay program can focus employees on business drivers that are within their control. The effectiveness of such a program depends on how the plan is designed and how it is communicated to employees.

## Variable Pay Plan versus Bonus Plan

When most people think of variable pay, they think of bonus plans, but bonus plans can take many forms. In fact, some people use the term *bonus* to refer only to purely discretionary awards that are not linked directly to performance. Variable pay plans that are clearly driven by performance are commonly called *incentive plans*. It is worth noting that bonuses generally award performance that is assessed after the fact, whereas incentive pay rewards performance objectives that are set in advance.

### Variable Pay Plan Design Elements

The ultimate form of bonus or incentive plan is determined by its unique design features. There are seven core features of a variable pay plan:

- *Eligibility*. Once the decision has been made to implement an incentive compensation plan and the objectives of the plan have been clearly defined, among the first criteria to address in designing the plan is eligibility. Which employees will participate in the plan? A common practice is to include everyone in the plan that contributes to achieving what have been defined as the objectives of the plan. In many cases, this may be every employee. In others, the objectives of the plan may suggest that eligibility should be limited to just a portion of the workforce, such as all employees with a certain level of managerial responsibility or all employees in a certain function or department.

- *Payout timing and frequency*. How often will awards be paid, and when? The frequency of the awards (e.g., monthly, quarterly, annually) can be influenced by many drivers, including how often the performance rewarded by the plan can be measured and how frequently such performance should be reinforced through rewards. These considerations also will drive the timing of the award payment.

- *Funding*. Funding incentive awards is an important design component because it determines the total amount available to be distributed to eligible employees. Will the incentive awards be funded based on a predefined financial formula (i.e., self-funding), or will they be budgeted using an assumed performance level that can be either financial or nonfinancial? Alternatively, the "pool" used to fund incentive awards may be determined on a purely discretionary basis at the end of the performance period. Depending on the objectives set out for the incentive plan, one approach may be more effective than the others.

- *Performance measurement*. Just as the eligibility and award timing will be driven by the objectives of the incentive compensation plan, the ways in which "success" will be measured, or performance measurement, will be dictated by the desired outcomes. Will performance be measured at the corporate level (e.g., year-over-year revenue growth, profitability, etc.), the department level (e.g., achieving a certain level of cost savings, completing a major project, etc.), or the individual level (e.g., fulfilling specific performance objectives, closing a particular number of transactions, etc.)? Selecting the right performance measures is a critical component in ensuring that the incentive plan is aligned with organizational objectives, driving the right behaviors, and thus achieving the highest return on the variable pay investment.

- *Performance mix.* The level at which performance is measured—and rewarded—can say something about an organization's culture and what the organization considers important. Many companies use incentive compensation to reinforce multiple types of performance by placing weight on a number of performance measures. The performance mix determines how much each metric will factor into the variable pay award. For example, corporate performance criteria may drive 50 percent of the award, whereas the achievement of departmental and individual goals may each contribute 25 percent. The decision as to the appropriate mix of performance measures used to determine the award typically is driven by the degree to which the eligible employee can influence each measure. Senior executives may have an incentive award based entirely on corporate results because they are the group held accountable for corporate performance, whereas staff employees may have incentive awards based primarily on their individual activities because they are among the furthest removed from the achievement of overall corporate objectives.

- *Award levels.* Award levels provided for in the incentive plan design specify the award opportunity each participant in the plan will have. We have already established that in order to be considered meaningful and to drive behavior, an individual award generally should be targeted to be at least 8 percent of the employee's annual base pay, or about one month's pay. However, the significance of the award also should increase with the level of accountability, which is generally why variable pay is more significant and award targets are higher for more senior roles (see Table 16.2). In addition to establishing target award levels, the incentive plan also should account for the amount of variable pay that is warranted in circumstances where objectives are only partially met but are still worthy of reward (also known as *threshold performance*) and in circumstances where objectives are significantly exceeded (also known as *superior performance*). In other words, how much should the targeted award be discounted in the case of threshold performance? And what is the maximum amount warranted in the event of superior performance?

- *Allocation.* The final element of an incentive plan is allocation, or how the incentive award pool will be distributed to individual participants once the size of the pool has been determined or funding has occurred. The allocation approach typically is linked to performance mix. However, depending on the funding approach outlined by the plan, individual awards may not be determined using a precise formula. Instead, a more subjective or modified approach to allocating incentive awards may be warranted, taking into account individual performance and targeted award levels. For example, and depending on the provisions of the plan, the incentive award pool may be divided among different groups (e.g., divisions, business units, etc.) disproportionately. In such instances, the plan also should indicate whether managers should allocate the funds using a formula that takes into account the variables that affect the size of the pool provided for their group or whether the funds should be allocated in another way.

## Types of Variable Pay Plans

Given the myriad possible design options, the type of plan that is appropriate for one organization may not be appropriate for another. Different approaches to variable pay have characteristics that often make them suitable for very different environments.

*Profit Sharing.* For instance, one form of variable pay plan, the *profit-sharing bonus*, emphasizes profitability—an overall company performance indicator—as a success measure. Typically, a profit-sharing bonus plan provides for a common award level, either a fixed amount or a percentage of base pay, that will be paid to all eligible employees on achieving a certain level of profitability. This basic framework makes profit-sharing bonus plans among the simplest to administer. Profit-sharing plans are used by many organizations in a wide variety of industries and often are credited with contributing to a low employee turnover rate. Although most profit-sharing plans are similar in the type of performance they are trying to reward and the measures considered most important, there are still some variations. For example, a profit-sharing bonus program at one high-tech company pays out a percentage of net income or pretax margin (whichever is greater) twice yearly. Another large manufacturing organization calls its profit-sharing plan a "wage dividend program." This plan reportedly provided payments that ranged from 2 to 8 percent of an employee's earnings each year over a five-year period.

By their design, these types of bonus plans also tend to communicate a strong emphasis on organizational performance rather than individual performance. As a result, profit-sharing bonus plans are considered to be less effective than other forms of variable pay in motivating specific individual behaviors because they have a less direct line of sight to results. For this reason, other forms of variable pay have become more popular in recent years.

*Gain Sharing.* Another form of variable pay plan that emphasizes group or organizational achievement is the *gain-sharing plan*. Gain-sharing plans are, as the name implies, intended to share the financial gains achieved above a certain threshold or benchmark level with employees who contribute to creating those gains. In their truest form, gain-sharing plans are self-funded: a percentage of the incremental operational or financial gains above a stated minimum measure are used to create the bonus pool. Gain-sharing plans can be effective in supporting the achievement of operating efficiencies and in engaging employees in controlling costs. In a typical gain-sharing environment, there is pressure within workgroups for each employee to do whatever he or she can to ensure a high level of productivity, to manage expenses, and to otherwise identify process improvements.

Gain-sharing plans are most common in production or production-oriented environments (e.g., logistics, manufacturing, call centers, etc.) and are used to similarly reward all employees in a group for achieving predefined benchmarks. For example, in 2007, a leading automotive manufacturer announced that it would pay bonuses to its salaried and hourly employees in the United States and Canada as a result of quality and cost-cutting improvements achieved in 2006. Nonmanagerial employees reportedly earned bonuses that ranged from $300 to $800 each. Other industries, such as retail, may use a gain-sharing bonus program to encourage warehouse workers to achieve certain productivity targets. When the productivity targets are achieved, employees' weekly wages can increase 5 to 10 percent.

Although some might argue that there is always room for more efficiency, gain-sharing plans can start to lose their motivational value as incremental gains over prior performance periods start to diminish. In fact, financially rewarding continued gains can come at other costs, such as neglecting to reinvest in the necessary maintenance of equipment or compromising quality as employees look for additional cost savings. Therefore, true gain-sharing plans are often most effective when viewed as a temporary incentive tool. Once optimal productivity levels and efficiencies are achieved, it may be appropriate to shift to another form of variable pay that can be more effective in focusing employees on maintaining the performance levels realized under the gain-sharing model. However, as technology and processes evolve and new production techniques come into play, gain sharing continues to be a useful variable pay tool.

*Group or Individual Incentives.* Depending on their specific design parameters, traditional incentive plans can take the form of either group (or team) incentives or individual incentives. The funding vehicle, performance mix, and allocation model of the plan will dictate whether variable pay should reward the performance of groups or teams within the organization or individuals rather than reward overall organizational success.

As organizations seek to improve the linkage between individual behaviors and their financial rewards, group incentives and individual incentives have become increasingly popular. Furthermore, when incentive awards are based on measures that employees feel are at least partially within their control, either as an individual contributor or as a member of a work group, then the opportunity to receive the award becomes a more effective motivational tool.

An example of a group incentive plan is the program implemented by a large aerospace organization in 2001 that ties performance to team goals. In this example, teams can range in size from 60 to 900 employees. Each team's performance is based on achieving an overall profit objective and a team *scorecard rating*, although specific scorecard criteria vary by unit (Table 16.3). If company profit objectives are not met, partial payouts may be awarded based on the team's scorecard rating. The incentive awards can be as much as $1,500 per year, with a preliminary midyear payout of up to $500 if the team is performing well.

| Employee Group | Average Impact | | | |
| --- | --- | --- | --- | --- |
| | Company Performance | Division Performance | Department Performance | Individual Performance |
| Executive | 62.8% | 13.4% | 2.8% | 20.9% |
| Management | 49.4% | 18.1% | 6.0% | 26.5% |
| Professional (nonsales) | 46.4% | 15.8% | 5.9% | 31.9% |
| Professional (sales) | 29.7% | 14.7% | 6.6% | 48.9% |
| Office, clerical, technician | 46.8% | 13.1% | 5.3% | 34.8% |
| Trades, production, service | 45.9% | 16.8% | 8.1% | 29.1% |

*Note:* Participating organizations were asked to identify the level of impact that different performance criteria or measures have on determining employee awards. This table provides the level of impact (or weighting) of each measure by employee group. As expected, performance measures for executives are heavily focused on company performance, whereas more emphasis is placed on individual performance for sales professionals.

*Source:* Mercer, "2014–2015 U.S. Compensation Planning Survey."

**Table 16.3  Performance Criteria**

Individual incentive plans are widely accepted today, and most of them contain provisions that encompass corporate and group objectives. But what makes them truly individual incentive plans is the fact that the actual awards to employees are differentiated based on individual performance criteria. For example, a global chemical company's performance award program is designed to share the company's financial success with employees. But individual employee awards are determined based on a combination of how the individual—his or her team, function, or business—and the company have performed relative to predefined performance objectives.

Similarly, a global financial services organization's annual incentive award program for management employees is based on individual and business performance, as well as the successful achievement of specific goals. Individual performance ratings, which reflect the extent to which an employee either meets or exceeds performance expectations, are used to determine an individual's incentive payout. At other companies, the individual incentive compensation program rewards employees in such areas as marketing, sales, and finance for their individual performance in support of the achievement of the company's goals.

Another form of individual cash incentive award is the *spot award*. Spot awards generally refer to one-time cash rewards that are awarded at any time rather than on completion of a predefined performance period. Spot award programs typically are funded by a budget that is set aside for recognizing employee contributions throughout the budget year. Among the primary benefits of such an approach is the fact that awards can be given promptly following the behavior or event that is being rewarded, thus increasing the perceived linkage between the reward and the activity. The amounts of such rewards also can vary depending on the significance of the activity.

## Multiple Incentive Plans Can Be Implemented

The different types of variable pay plans in use today have different strengths and weaknesses. Some might look at the strengths of each approach and see some benefits to all of them. As a result, it is not uncommon to see multiple types of incentive plans being used within a single organization. Tailoring the incentive approach to the unique needs of various segments of the workforce actually can improve the alignment of employee behaviors with organizational goals. For example, a leading U.S. bank's profit-sharing bonus plan includes only employees in certain roles whose salaries are less than $100,000 per year and who do not otherwise participate in a commission or other variable pay plan.

However, where multiple objectives are considered important to highlight, it is feasible that employees could participate in multiple incentive plans. For instance, where an organization desires to focus the efforts of an employee on the handful of specific activities they can control and that have been deemed to have an impact on organizational success, the employee may participate in an individual incentive plan. Meanwhile, in an effort to also signal to employees the need to collaborate with others in the achievement of their goals or the goals of the organization, they also may participate in a profit-sharing plan.

Where each incentive award opportunity is, by itself, considered significant, a layered approach such as the preceding example can help to focus the employee on multiple interrelated goals. It is important, however, not to overly diffuse the focus of the individual employee so that multiple performance objectives become too numerous and confusing. Ideally, the number of goals an employee should be tasked with achieving—both individual and organizational goals—should be limited to no more than five.

## Other Variable Pay Considerations

Aside from the design and administration issues that must be carefully considered to ensure that variable pay supports an organization's attraction and motivation objectives, sufficient planning is also required around communicating the plans to employees and monitoring their effectiveness over time. Experience has shown that for an incentive compensation plan to effectively motivate employee behaviors, employees must understand (1) how their actions affect the success of the organization and (2) how their performance will affect their rewards. Thus the communication strategy cannot be underestimated as a key to the success of a variable pay program.

For instance, in the previous example highlighting a firm's group incentive plan, it was mentioned that the incentive awards are based on a combination of achieving financial objectives along with team scorecard objectives. To maintain employee focus on these criteria, the company posts information indicating progress toward achieving the performance objectives in each work area for all employees to see. In addition, the team scorecards are available on the company's intranet.

Finally, it is important to continually evaluate the impact the variable pay plan is having on the organization's performance and its culture. Is it getting the expected results? Are there objectives that have been overly influenced or perhaps neglected as a result of the increased employee focus on specific measures? And has the emphasis on selected criteria resulted in unintended negative consequences in other areas considered important to the business? Periodic evaluation of the variable pay plan and the results to which it is contributing will help to ensure that the program is delivering the desired return on the financial investment in the plan.

## Summary

As illustrated in the various incentive plan examples described in this chapter, each plan has different elements or plan features that influence their effectiveness in supporting business objectives by attracting the desired talent and motivating employee behaviors. In choosing the type of variable pay plan that is appropriate, an organization should consider its compensation philosophy and strategy. What is the expected role of variable pay? What type of program is right for your business? Different approaches will support the fulfillment of an organization's efforts to attract and motivate talent in different ways, all in the service of implementing total compensation programs that adapt to today's rapidly changing business and workforce scenarios.

As an attraction tool, variable pay can assist in ensuring the competitiveness of the rewards an organization can offer to prospective employees. It can facilitate the attraction of high-quality talent by allowing for greater compensation in order to make the employment proposition more compelling than that of the average employer. And variable pay can facilitate the attraction of employees whose values are consistent with those of the employer.

As a motivational tool, variable pay can support the achievement of organizational goals by focusing employees on business drivers that are within their control and rewarding them for the desired behaviors and results. If their employer's performance expectations are considered realistic and attainable, they will take steps to earn the additional rewards available to them, thus contributing to organizational objectives.

Before closing this chapter, it is worth noting that in addition to being a widely used attraction and motivation tool, variable pay, when combined with other rewards programs, can help to reinforce just about anything that is considered important to the employer, including the desired corporate culture, and help to ensure that compensation programs create a competitive business advantage. Variable pay can communicate certain things about the organization's priorities, such as the importance placed on team or individual performance. Variable pay also can aid in the retention of highly valued employees by providing greater rewards to those who most demonstrate the desired behaviors or make significant contributions to the company's success. Finally, variable pay can effectively leverage an organization's compensation spending, creating greater rewards when business results are better and lower rewards when business results are below expectations.

# 17

# Aligning Sales Compensation Plan Design with Talent Retention Strategy

JEROME A. COLLETTI
*Colletti-Fiss, LLC*

MARY S. FISS
*Colletti-Fiss, LLC*

For most companies, the essence of business success is the ability to attract and retain customers. Because the sales force is a vital link between a company and its customers, it holds the key to business growth and profitability. A properly directed, motivated, and rewarded sales force will make a significant contribution to the achievement of these business measures. The sales compensation plan is one of a company's biggest investments in its sales organization and one of the most powerful tools available to help management achieve optimal sales force motivation and performance. This presumes, of course, that the company attracts and retains the right caliber of sales talent through its compensation plan.

Salespeople can and do make a difference when customers choose to buy from a company instead of from its competitors. This is particularly true in markets characterized by high product parity. In such markets, the major players offer equally high levels of product quality and customer service. When this is the situation, one advantage a company can leverage is the quality of the relationship between customer and salespeople. The results of a buyer study that focused on 700 business-to-business (B2B) purchases involving over $3.1 billion in sales reported that sales reps who won the deal educated the buyers with new ideas and solutions perspectives, on average, three times more frequently than the runner-up sales reps did.[1] The sales compensation plan—particularly the incentive component—can play a pivotal role in attracting and retaining the sales talent required to make the quality of relationship both a reality and a competitive advantage.

The overall objective of this chapter is to discuss how to align the design of a company's sales compensation plan with its sales talent retention strategy. A fundamental premise of this chapter is that high-caliber sales talent contributes to a unique competitive advantage in relationships with customers because those relationships enable a company's salespeople to outperform their peers in other companies.[2] Thus, incorporating a company's sales talent strategies into the compensation plan design process ultimately can contribute to high performance for a business.

## Why Sales Talent Retention Is a Top Priority

There are three reasons why using the compensation plan to attract and retain sales employees a company wants to keep is a critical issue. First, a recent Accenture survey reports that 41 percent of U.S. companies and 50 percent of global companies consider sales as the most important function in their organization.[3] Generally speaking, sales are responsible for top-line growth, and in many B2B markets, customers buy because of their relationship with a salesperson. Our own research shows that when a sales representative leaves a company, 20 to 80 percent of the business with his or her customers is at risk. Often this is not because the sales rep attempts to take business away but rather because the customer/buyer becomes more receptive to calls from competitors' salespeople.

Next, the HR Chally Group, experts in sales force selection, reports that salesperson effectiveness accounts for 39 percent of a customer's choice of a vendor.[4] According to HR Chally's research, salesperson effectiveness during interactions with customers/buyers is more important than price, quality, or the ability to provide a total solution. In many industries, we see sales reps as the glue between a company and its customers. When a sales rep leaves a company, the strength of that glue may be materially weakened, particularly if a replacement or interim sales rep is not immediately available to work with customers.

Finally, our research shows that the costs associated with replacing one sales rep, particularly a top performer, is 35 to 200 percent of annual total cash compensation. This is not because of high recruitment costs but rather because, as indicated earlier, when salespeople leave, customers turn over too. The most significant cost is lost business, particularly the profit contribution from those lost sales. Thus a clear sales talent retention strategy and supporting compensation elements that help companies to retain top talent are essential to business success.

## Make the Sales Talent Retention Strategy Explicit

The right place to start is with a defined, explicit sales talent retention strategy. This strategy should be developed and agreed to by key stakeholders prior to the time of compensation plan design. We find that shaping an appropriate strategy for a particular company requires answers to the following questions based on data analysis from the prior two or three years:

- Are the highest-paid reps the best performers relative to the one or two most important performance metrics associated with the plan?

- Are tenured/experienced reps rewarded proportionately more than other reps? Is this the intent or an unintended consequence of current plan(s) design?

- Is the magnitude of opportunity for performance gain among core performers (middle 60 percent of sales force) quantified, for example, reduction in turnovers and performance distribution shift to the right?

- What is the business impact of losing one rep—high performer (top 10 percent) versus core performer (middle 60 percent)?

- What are the employment costs related to replacing one rep and lost sales and margin dollars associated with that rep's territory?

The answers to these questions will help management to begin to crystallize a talent strategy for its sales organization in terms of employee retention goals and the level of financial investment the company can afford to make to keep them.

In summary, we often hear that a company's goal is to retain its sales staff at a rate greater than the industry average. To do so, it is essential to retain the most talented performers in the sales force. Knowing what the right compensation levers are and how to pull those levers to achieve the desired result are important to attaining this goal. Before moving on with specific initiatives focused on aligning the compensation plan with a talent retention strategy, it is useful to ensure that a solid foundation is in place for plan design and the decision-making process associated with how various compensation elements are used.

## Establishing the Ground Rules for Plan Design

Prior to the actual plan design process, it is critical to establish the basis for decisions about sales compensation plan elements that are critical to support a successful retention strategy. The two key areas that require management's attention are the company's philosophy of pay and the principles or rules that establish expectations for the program.

*Philosophy of Pay.* In order to develop an effective sales compensation plan, its design should be consistent with an organization's compensation philosophy. When the philosophy is informal, undocumented, or both, we suggest that plan designers discuss the topic with management and then document the company's compensation philosophy using the following list of key criteria:

- *Objectives.* Confirmation of the strategic purpose of compensation and its elements.

- *Pay market comparison.* Identification of relevant companies and job matches.

- *Competitive positioning.* Percentile standing for pay levels.

- *Salary–variable pay ratio.* Based on the company's philosophy of risk versus reward, competitive practice, and the influence of eligible job(s) in getting and keeping business with customers.

- *Base salary determination.* Factors and practices that will be used in setting and adjusting base salary.

- *Short-term incentives.* Eligibility and type of incentives considered appropriate.

- *Long-term incentives.* Eligibility and type of incentives considered appropriate.

- *Communication.* Roles and responsibilities.

Confirming this information is the first step to ensure that the sales compensation plan will be designed to be consistent with other compensation programs in the company and that the plan is aligned with the financial and motivational elements associated with retaining top performers.

*Compensation Principles.* Typically, the design of a sales compensation plan is influenced by the compensation philosophy and practices used throughout a company. In fact, in many companies, top managers ask human resources or the compensation function to ensure that the sales compensation plan is in alignment with the enterprise's programs because employees are moved in and out of the sales organization as part of a company-wide career-development initiative. With this background in mind, sales compensation plans should be grounded in core principles that are compatible with those that guide a company's overall compensation and rewards system. While there are many publications—including this *Handbook*—that provide details about the tenets of effective and appropriate compensation, the following list briefly summarizes essentials that a sales compensation plan designer should keep in mind:

- The compensation philosophy must actively reinforce the company's strategy and vision to achieve its objectives.

- Compensation programs must be consistent with legal and regulatory requirements.

- Compensation should be consistent with the financial requirements and administrative capabilities of the company.

- Compensation must be consistent with both internal equity and external requirements to attract, retain, and motivate talented employees.

- Compensation program details must be based on clearly defined jobs and their role within the buying and selling process.

In addition to these core principles, it is generally useful to establish other ground rules specific to a company's needs. Consideration should be given to the following topics:

- *Business objectives.* What objectives are critical for this year? What objectives must the plan reinforce?

- *Human resource objectives.* Have competitive practices changed? How can key plan elements ensure that top performers are motivated and retained?

- *Strategy.* What are the company's marketing and sales strategies?

- *Job definition.* What jobs will be required to achieve the company's strategies?

- *Performance measurement.* How should performance be defined and tracked over time? How should performance objectives be set? What level of achievement should be expected? What is the range of performance that can be used in sales compensation plan design?

- *Compensation plan.* Who should be involved in the design process? What mechanics are most appropriate to direct and motivate sales jobs?

- *Administration.* When should we credit performance for incentive purposes? What is our communication strategy? Who should be involved?

Once the ground rules have been established, an efficient six-step design process can be initiated.

## Six Essential Components of Plan Design

There are six essential components of sales compensation. Figure 17.1 illustrates the relationship of these components to business-management considerations addressed prior to plan design. The ideal design process, including the sequence of decisions required, is a derivative process. That is, the design of an effective and appropriate plan is based on the solid foundation provided by business-management decisions for the plan year.

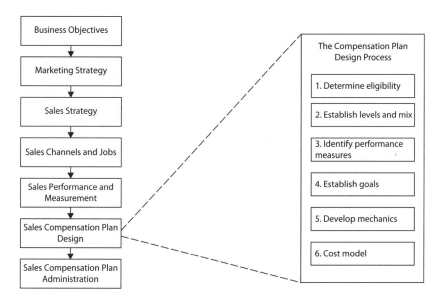

**Figure 17.1  Six essential components of sales compensation.**

The six essential components must be addressed through the design process as follows:

### Step 1: Confirm Jobs and Eligibility

*Key concept: Determine incentive eligibility based on the degree of impact in the buying decision and participation in the process to access/persuade customers and fulfill customer needs.* Typically, positions that initiate, persuade, and fulfill in the customer coverage process and those positions' line managers are eligible to participate in the sales compensation program. Corporate philosophy is also a key determinant in eligibility to participate in a sales compensation program. For example, team members may be eligible for sales compensation only as long as they are on a customer team.

### Step 2: Establish Pay Levels and Mix

*Key concept: Ensure that pay levels are externally competitive and internally equitable based on the roles and responsibilities of the job.* The total target cash compensation is the cash compensation (including base salary and variable incentive compensation) available for achieving expected results. Use of market data and application of the company's philosophy of pay result in a reference point for decisions about the level of compensation the company is willing to pay for each job. The total target cash compensation level for each job must be large enough to motivate and pay for performance to drive business results.

Determination of the pay level for each job serves as a foundation for decisions related to mix (ratio of base salary to incentive opportunity as a percentage of the total target compensation, expressed as two portions of 100 percent) and leverage (the amount of upside opportunity beyond total target compensation that outstanding performers are expected to earn). The mix is determined by defined criteria, including the type of sale, sales cycle duration, number of transactions in a year, and degree of influence the job has on the decision to buy. The sales compensation plan should provide upside opportunity (leverage) consistent with the job, the company's philosophy of pay, and labor-market realities. Outstanding pay generally should be available for excellent performers (i.e., the plan should provide increased dollars on the upside after target performance is achieved).

### Step 3: Identify Performance Measures

*Key concept: You get what you pay for. Three or fewer measures should be used based on the key objectives of the organization and the key accountabilities of the job.* This is perhaps the most critical design component to address effectively. Several decisions are required to ensure that the performance measures selected are aligned with the business and the job as follows:

- *Confirm business objectives affected by the job(s).* Examples include growth, profitability, productivity improvement, cost reduction, and customer loyalty and retention or some combination of these five.

- *Select the indicators that are associated with achievement of those objectives.* Ensure that systems or processes are in place for measurement. If a key indicator cannot be consistently tracked and achievement calculated, potential alternatives must be identified and examined.

- *Ensure that the measures are consistent with the job.* Measures used in the sales compensation plan should be influenced by reasonable effort and behavior. Measures must be based on job roles and the salesperson's ability to affect results.

- *Determine level of measurement.* The unit of aggregation of results (i.e., territory, accounts, team, etc.) for the purposes of sales compensation calculation should be based on the level at which results are affected by the job and the level to which company systems can accurately track, credit, and report results.

- *Confirm the relative importance of each measure.* The weight of each measure in the plan is based on the strategic importance of each to the achievement of business objectives. In addition, the relative weight among measures helps the sales force to understand how to deploy its time based on the plan message and its alignment with management requirements.

The sales function is primarily responsible for the maximization of top-line results. Therefore, a measure of total volume is generally the first consideration for any sales job. The design process determines the appropriate measure of overall volume that can be associated with a salesperson's performance. This may mean total sales dollar volume, sales volume from new business, new business and recurring sales dollar volume from regular customer ordering (a measure of retention), revenue derived from volume, or number of units sold. In most plans, one measure should be a volume measure that rewards growth.

Additional criteria should complement the volume measure, communicating what type of volume is best, where the volume should come from, or how it should be achieved. Additional categories to consider include profitability (financial measures), sales productivity (may include both financial and nonfinancial measures), and strategic planning (generally nonfinancial measures).

## Step 4: Set Goals

*Key concept: Assign expectations for key performance measures based on job influence and a uniform process.* Once performance measures have been selected, many companies assign goals to the sales force for one or all of the selected measures. Particularly for volume- or profitability-focused measures, these goals are frequently referred to as a *quota*. In the past, companies used primarily financial measures of performance in the sales compensation plan, and perhaps 50 percent of all companies established quotas. Many companies simply assigned a uniform percent or dollar increase across the sales force based on the growth objectives for the plan year.

In today's competitive environment, many more companies are establishing performance expectations for both financial and nonfinancial measures. The process to arrive at goals varies widely across industries, companies, and types of measures. Regardless of practices, many firms find goal (quota) setting to be difficult and express frustration at both the process and the outcomes. However, giving proper attention to setting goals is essential to the success of the sales compensation plan. Properly assigning goals provides the opportunity to manage for results, allows for maximum flexibility, and visibly aligns the success of field resources with corporate resources.

Once goals are established, attention should be paid to the performance standards or the performance range associated with incentive payout. The sales compensation plan has varying degrees of payout depending on performance levels. Below a certain level of performance, no payout may occur. A threshold level of performance is used to communicate the minimum standard of performance. Above a certain level of performance, many companies provide higher amounts. While a ceiling or cap is used in cases where it is difficult or impossible to set realistic ranges, an uncapped plan generally is desirable. However, earnings above an excellence level should become increasingly difficult to achieve. Some statistical rules of thumb for the performance range are based on an optimal performance distribution (e.g., 90 percent achieve threshold, 60 to 70 percent achieve or exceed goal, and 10 to 15 percent reach or exceed excellence).

## Step 5: Develop Incentive Mechanics

*Key concept: Select plan mechanics based on the desired relationship between pay and performance.* Sales compensation in its broadest sense includes all elements of remuneration for sales and sales-management positions. Although base-salary-only plans are appropriate for nonpersuasive selling environments, many companies are moving to putting some percent of pay at risk even for nonselling jobs in customer-coverage organizations. Therefore, in this penultimate component of plan design, all previous components are aligned through the plan mechanics associated with the incentive (or variable) element of total cash compensation. *Mechanics* refers to the type of plan, plan formula, and the ways in which incentive elements interact to calculate payment.

*Plan Type.* There are two primary plan types: commission plans and bonus plans. Either type may be used in conjunction with base salary, or both may be used. In addition, either a bonus or commission may use a quota or goal. Bonus plans always use some type of goal, whereas commissions may or may not use a goal or quota as one element in the calculation.

A commission plan provides a percent share or dollar amount tied to gross dollar sales, product unit sales, or gross profit dollars. Commission programs support absolute measurement systems—the more of a product or service sold, the greater is the incentive paid. Commission may be capped or uncapped. This type of plan is used most commonly in new-market selling situations, where individual persuasion skills and short sales cycles are key differentiators. Organizations use commission programs to reward individual effort and drive results with payout tied directly to sales results. In some industries, commissions typically have been used to push new products and gain market share with specialized sales forces.

Bonuses are a percent of base pay or a fixed dollar amount for accomplishing objectives. They are used most appropriately in more complex sales environments and are always goal based, whether the goal is financial (i.e., volume, profitability, productivity) or nonfinancial. These programs support a relative measurement system—payout depends on performance against individual goals. They may be capped or uncapped. A salary plus bonus plan manages the amount of incentive payout to a preferred market rate while accommodating goal-based measurement.

*Plan Formula.* Plan formulas may be linked or unlinked.

- An *unlinked* formula is a series of additive payouts.

- A *linked* formula means that payout for one measure depends on achievement of another. Linking measures together in the formula ensures a clear message that two performance measures must receive the salesperson's attention. There are three ways to accomplish a linkage:

  - *Gate (or hurdle).* Hurdles are the minimum performance levels a salesperson must achieve in one plan component to be eligible for variable pay in a different component.

  - *Multiplier.* Multipliers or modifiers *increase* or *decrease* the salesperson's earnings in that plan component based on his or her performance in another measure.

  - *Matrix.* The matrix design is used when there are two competing measures against which the salesperson must perform. The salesperson has to manage performance between two measures.

### Step 6: Cost Model

*Key concept: The final design is based on the results of both aggregate costing (effect on the company) and individual plan modeling (effect on individuals).* This step may be completed by finance and human resources working with sales or sales operations. The results are critical to finalize such plan elements as the performance range (threshold and excellence), the upside available at excellence, and the relative weight of each measure. Until this step is complete, the plan cannot be considered final.

## Six Design Areas that Support Sales Talent Retention

With this foundation in mind, there are six options to choose from when a company's goal is to strengthen the retention value of its investment in a sales force. Each design topic is identified as follows:

1. *Job levels.* As companies grow and diversify in both products offered and customers they sell to, it becomes necessary to consider more than one level of the principal sales jobs. This is so because the range of variability in the size and types of business transactions require commensurate sales skills and experience. Multiple levels of a sales role provide career progression associated with larger and more diverse responsibilities. Also, target compensation (both salary and incentive pay) can be calibrated to the level of the job (e.g., entry level versus senior level). Because careered salespeople often prefer moving up the selling ladder to taking a supervisory assignment, introducing and using job levels within a sales organization can be a valuable retention tool.

2. *Salary as the incentive multiplier.* Generally speaking, two prevalent techniques are used to set the incentive opportunity for a sales job after the target cash compensation level and mix ratio have been determined. The first approach is to express the incentive opportunity as a percent of salary-range midpoint, and the other approach is to express it as a percent of the salesperson's salary. The second technique may be more attractive as a retention tool for two reasons: it is easier to communicate the incentive opportunity to sales people in this manner, and using salary as the incentive multiplier favors individuals with higher base salaries. Often those salespeople are longer-tenured employees, and thus, if a company's goal is to communicate to salespeople that it values retention, then it is an appropriate technique to use in the plan.

3. *Merit pay treatment.* The performance-appraisal program is another tool that a company can use in its sales force retention effort. Research shows that 91 percent of surveyed companies have a formal performance-management program and that the top goal in two-thirds of such companies is to differentiate rewards based on individual performance.[5] Generally speaking, a company's performance-appraisal program extends to its sales force, and the results of appraisal are an important consideration in making decisions about merit pay treatment. If management is confident that the company's performance-appraisal program and its results validly differentiate merit ratings, using it as another tool in sales force retention is wise.

   For the merit process to be effective, the company should identify through the appraisal process the talented salespeople it must keep and ensure that for those individuals there is merit pay treatment commensurate with their contributions. The outcome of appraisal and its related merit pay treatment should be well communicated to those talented sales employees so that they know that their contributions are valued.

4. *Performance threshold.* It is quite common, particularly in sales incentive/bonus plans, to set a performance threshold below which no incentive is paid. The reason for this practice is to establish a minimum level of performance that a sales employee must achieve before the company pays an incentive. In industries where it is common practice to compensate salespeople through high salary/relative low incentive opportunities (e.g., 75 percent salary/25 percent incentive), thresholds make a great deal of sense because of the requirement to cover the cost of the company's sales investment. However, in industries where business is largely transactional (e.g., insurance, financial services, brokerage), the salary/incentive ratio is at the other end of the spectrum (25 percent salary/75 percent salary, assuming that there is salary), and in such cases, the incentive is paid "from dollar one." Although top performers are unlikely to fall below a performance threshold, low threshold (or no threshold) may not be consistent with the company's requirements for a high-performance sales organization.

5. *Incentive pay opportunity for overachieving performance goals.* Whereas the upside on target incentive opportunity is available to all sales employees who overachieve assigned performance goals (e.g., 100 percent of quota), the opportunity (and related incentive rates) is often carefully scrutinized by the top performers. Typically, the top performers represent the top 5 to 10 percent of the sales force, and they are often among the most tenured employees in the sales force. For these individuals, the key question they ask when looking at the overachievement incentive opportunity is this: "Is it financially worthwhile to overachieve the performance goal?"

   The reason why they ask themselves this question is for those who do overachieve, the overachievement performance results are often reflected in next year's quota. To make overachievement financially worthwhile, it is a best practice to identify the overachievement performance point at which the company is willing to pay a significant upside (e.g., two to three times the target incentive opportunity). In addition to considering competitive incentive pay practice for performance overachievement, which is typically reported in the leading sales compensation surveys, management should review the results of internal analysis on the cost of lost business when top performers leave the company. The conclusion may be that the company could reduce the risk of losing top performers as a result of increasing the overachievement incentive opportunity two to two and a half times, and the cost of doing so is relatively insignificant compared with the cost of lost customer business—both revenue and margin contributions.

6. *Long-term performance plans.* Many companies deploy strategic or major account salespeople to sell to and manage relationships with critically important customers. The Strategic Account Management Association (SAMA) reports that companies in 28 industries use that sales role in their businesses.[6] The prevalence of strategic account sellers and the importance of the customers with whom they interact pose a particularly challenging retention problem for companies. Knowing that when salespeople leave customers who become more receptive to competitors' sellers is only half the problem. The other half is that building the business with strategic accounts often occurs over several years. It is not uncommon to find that early sales efforts with a strategic or major account may not develop into significantly large revenue and profit until two or three years down the road.

When business success in a strategic or major account role requires a balance between short- and long-term efforts and the company is committed to rewarding and retaining sellers for doing so, then management should explore the feasibility of using long-term cash incentive plans. A recent Aon Hewitt survey reports that 74 percent of companies base participation in long-term incentives (LTIs) on a sales role rather than grade level, position title, or some other criterion. Typical awards in such a program vary between 5 and 25 percent of total annual compensation, thus making LTIs a financially attractive proposition for the participants.[7]

The goals of the long-term incentive plan for strategic sellers are to (a) reward performance accomplishments over multiple years and (b) encourage high-performing sellers to stay with the organization in their role over a longer period of time than might be the case without such plan.

## Summary

Companies and their leaders—both sales and human resources executives—should focus on designing sales compensation plans that reflect an explicit retention philosophy and specific annual objectives for the sales organization. The plan should be built on a foundation of sound principles and practices as described in this chapter. Careful consideration should be given to the six design features that we indicated are typically associated with a sales force retention strategy. Doing so increases the likelihood that the company's business strategy and sales goals—in both the short and long terms—will be achieved because management is clearly signaling that it values and wishes to retain talented salespeople. Our goal in this chapter has been to encourage plan designers, particularly human resources/compensation professionals who participate in the design process, to take the initiative in helping their companies to use the sales compensation plan as a competitive tool in the war for sales talent retention.

## Notes

1.  Mike Schult and John E. Doerr, *Insight Selling: Surprising Research on What Sales Winners Do Differently*. Wiley, Hoboken, NJ, 2014.
2.  Jerome A. Colletti and Mary S. Fiss, "Designing Sales Incentive Pay for Competitive Advantage," in Dow Scott (ed.), *Incentive Pay: Creating a Competitive Advantage*. WorldatWork, Scottsdale, AZ, 2007, pp. 43–56.
3.  Accenture, "High Performance Workforce Study," San Francisco, 2010. Available at: www.accenture.com/us-en/Pages/insight-workforce-study-2010-usa-findings-summary.aspx.
4.  Howard Stevens, *The Future of Selling: The End of Sales as We Know It*. HR Chally Group, Dayton, OH, 2014.
5.  WorldatWork/Sibson, "2010 Study of the State of Performance Management," Scottsdale, AZ, 2010.
6.  Strategic Account Management Association (SAMA), "Survey on Current Trends and Practices in Strategic Account Management," Chicago, 2012. Available at: http://strategicaccounts.org/resources/current-trends-and-practices.aspx.
7.  Aon Hewitt, "Long-Term Incentive and Recognition Practices for Sales Roles," Lincolnshire, IL, June 2012 ($n$ =111 U.S. companies).

# 18

# Developing and Applying a Return-on-Investment Methodology to Drive Sales Force Performance

REBECCA SANDBERG
*SalesGlobe*

CARRIE WARD
*SalesGlobe*

Return on investment (ROI) pertains only to financial transactions such as acquisitions or product purchases, right? And it is really just a calculation that finance professionals use, right? Wrong. ROI is important in every type of investment. We will focus here on sales compensation. This approach focuses on creating and maintaining a culture of performance in the sales force based on a customized application of ROI.

Why is ROI important in sales compensation? Most C-level executives want to know the answer to two questions:

1. What are we getting out of our sales compensation plan?
2. How much does it cost us?

ROI has many definitions depending on the type of investment. The most common definition for sales compensation is productivity value divided by the resource costs that were committed:

Sales compensation ROI = Productivity value ÷ Resource costs

This sounds like a simple concept, but similar to ideas, such as *strategy* and *change management*, sales compensation ROI is a gray area and not a simple task. Productivity value is a measure of a specific value or set of values derived from the compensation plan. These measures include many things beyond just financial metrics. For example, productivity value could include such areas as customer satisfaction, employee satisfaction, and product success in the marketplace. Resource costs are a measure of the financial costs invested in the compensation plan. These costs primarily include what sales professionals are paid. However, other important measures include investments made in processes (e.g., approval and crediting processes), talent acquisition in sales and support personnel, and tools and technology.

There are many ways to develop your company's sales compensation ROI equation. Your end result will depend on what is most important to your company. In this chapter, we will illustrate a proven process that will help you to develop your own ROI definition. Once you develop yours and put it into use, you will take a critical step toward

- Competitive compensation plan design that will help to sustain and/or improve performance levels

- Compensation programs that are easily and quickly changed to respond to changing strategy

- Increased employee engagement because of clarity and success of the compensation program

Figure 18.1 illustrates the key drivers to developing your ROI definition: the seven essential sales compensation questions. This figure shows an iterative process that starts with, and always comes back to, the overall company strategy.

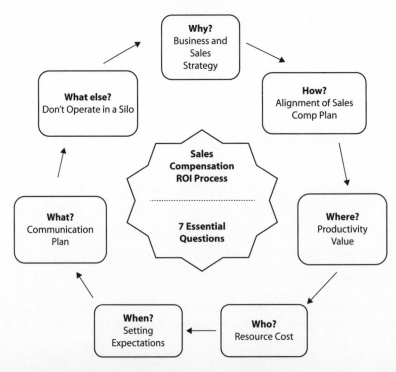

**Figure 18.1  The seven essential sales compensation questions.**

## Step 1: Why? Define the Strategy and Business Objectives

In simple terms, the strategy and business objectives are the company's action plan to achieve its long-term goals. The strategy is critical because it drives decisions on product focus, customers, and the go-to-market plan. Knowing and understanding this strategy will determine how your ROI definition is developed. For example, your company may be interested in growing revenue in a certain area of the business or focusing on a new product set. Metrics associated with the return on those facets of the business will drive how you develop what is important in your ROI definition. Your strategy may dictate that you need to invest more in an emerging market or technology that is new or different from your traditional business. In that case, you could calculate a separate ROI on those business lines or products in order to understand that specific return. Setting a company's strategy is a collaborative exercise that evaluates goals broken out by customer, product, coverage, financials, and talent[1] and is clearly communicated throughout the sales and sales support organization. It is from this point that you can start to develop critical elements for your sales compensation plan.

## Step 2: How? Sales Compensation Plan Alignment to the Strategy

The movie *Moneyball* told the story of how Billy Beane, manager of the Oakland A's, achieved one of the longest winning streaks in history with one of the smallest budgets in baseball. He did this by focusing on the numbers alone—no one else was doing this. He invested in people and processes that supported new metrics as a recruiting and training strategy (on-base percentage and minimizing outs). Billy Beane's strategy was clearly defined, and the metrics heavily influenced the desired outcome. This *Moneyball* concept can be leveraged when aligning your sales compensation plan to your company strategy. Placing specific, identifiable elements in the plan that drive toward the overall strategy is critical to meeting your company's objectives.

This seems simple, but we have found many instances of the sales compensation plans not aligning and often misaligning with the company's strategy. For example, a company we have previously worked with had a strategy of driving long-term revenue growth. However, one of the largest and most lucrative components in its sales compensation plan was a one-time payment for the sale of products that encouraged the opposite—short-term revenue growth. This product represented a revenue line in the profit and loss statement that was not sustainable in long-term growth. This is a great example of a misalignment between the stated company strategy and the compensation plan. It is a well-known fact that the sales compensation plan will drive sales behavior. To ensure that the company is driving the right behavior, it is imperative that the sales compensation plan and ROI definition align with the strategy. The following are critical elements to consider when building your sales compensation plan around your strategy:

- *Roles and coverage.* Sales personnel in appropriate roles covering strategic territories and customers.

- *Market pay.* Competitive total compensation for a specific job.

- *Pay mix.* The proportion of fixed versus variable costs. This will vary by role, sales strategy, and the sales process.

- *Upside and thresholds.* The performance level required for payment under the plan and the multiples of target pay when quotas are exceeded. One common test of a good compensation plan is whether the Reverse Robin Hood Principle is in place: taking from the underperformers to pay the overperformers.

- *Measures.* Components that align with the company's strategy and business objectives. Keep it simple—stick to the rule of three or fewer components, and keep the message clear.

- *Mechanics.* How compensation is calculated. It is important to ensure that there is a connection between performance and pay; that is, better performance equals even better pay. Although it is tempting to jump to this section first to manipulate ROI by adjusting pay, the strategy, roles, and measures must be addressed first.

- *Quota setting.* Setting goals and objectives for expected performance to earn target pay. Quotas set too high can be de-motivating. Quotas set too low can cause complacency. Hitting the sweet spot is critical for your ROI.

The next two steps will walk through ideas on how to redefine the traditional value of productivity and resource cost.

## Step 3: Where? Define Productivity Value—The Numerator

At SalesGlobe, we go beyond the basic definitions of ROI. The concept of moving deeper requires innovative thinking from finance and compensation leaders beyond traditional means. Traditionally, when we ask finance leaders how they would measure sales force effectiveness and productivity (i.e., the numerator of the equation), it would be the top line of all financial statements: revenue. Instead, ask: what does revenue mean?

- *Overall revenue.* The true top-line number impact.

- *Retention revenue.* Repeat revenue from existing customers. This revenue is a result of strong account management in key accounts focusing on customer satisfaction.

- *Penetration revenue.* New revenue from existing customers. This revenue is the result of a salesperson focusing on developing new relationships or new products in a current account.

- *New revenue.* New revenue from a new customer. This revenue is the result of a salesperson's efforts with relationships, acquisitions, and new opportunities outside the current accounts.

These different revenue components demonstrate innovative ways to redefine productivity value in terms of revenue. Company strategy will dictate which revenue component is most critical. There may be multiple ROI calculations if multiple revenue components are critical. For example, if new revenue is a focus, the ROI calculation would take new revenue divided by the resource cost specifically focused on new customer acquisition. Here is an example calculation:

New revenue ROI = New revenue ÷ (New product marketing cost
+ New business sales rep comp + CRM enhancements for new product)

In addition, penetration revenue may be important for an account manager role. A separate ROI calculation could be used for this plan that divides penetration revenue for these accounts by account manager resource costs. Here is an example calculation of penetration revenue ROI:

$$\text{Penetration Revenue ROI} = \text{Penetration Revenue} \div (\text{Account Manager Comp} + \text{Relationship Management System Build Out})$$

Over the past few years, trends have moved away from revenue to profit or margin, specifically in the software industry. A former software client explained that in a software company, license sales have very little direct cost to deliver, and services sometimes have a lot of costs to deliver. So management definitely wants to look at margins. If sales professionals have latitude over pricing and have some level of control over costs, profit or margin may be an appropriate measure of success. Focusing on margin will help to ensure that sales professionals bring revenue to the company with consideration for costs, thus creating profitable accounts.

Regardless of the financial measure, companies should consider categories that align with their strategy. For example, it may be important to segregate by product type, accounts, geographies, or target markets. Whether it is specific type of revenue, operating income, profit/margins, volume of widgets sold, or net present value of customers, the productivity value should tie back to the strategy and be a major component of the sales compensation plan. It is recommended that the measures be quantifiable financial measures. However, there are other important considerations for productivity value outside more traditional financial measures. While sometimes difficult to measure in relation to a sales compensation plan impact, these measures include brand awareness, customer satisfaction, net promoter scores (NPS), low turnover, and employee satisfaction. In fact, customer satisfaction measures can be broken down into categories related specifically to sales that will provide quantifiable value. For example, surveys can be administered to customers to determine their satisfaction with the sales professionals—their knowledge of the product, confidence, ability to understand the customer's needs, and so on. This feedback ties directly back to the sales professionals' motivation, happiness, and understanding of how they are paid. Another measure of a good compensation plan is essentially an NPS among sales professionals. Would your sales professionals recommend your company to other sales professionals in the market? This, too, can create brand awareness in the marketplace.

## Step 4: The Who? Determine the Resource Cost—The Denominator

To keep it simple, companies have defined their resource costs as base salary plus incentive pay excluding benefits or actual total compensation. At SalesGlobe, we call this the *surface-level ROI* because it fails to understand the influence of other elements necessary in the overall sales compensation program. This is the biggest moving piece in ROI calculations across companies. Through our client work and interviews, we find that most companies use the surface-level ROI to define their resource cost in one of three ways:

- *Bottom up.* Total actual cost of sales compensation (base salary plus incentive excluding benefits).
- *Top-down amount.* A flat dollar amount based on history or projected analytics.
- *Top-down ratio.* Percent of projected sales.

These are all valid approaches to determining the resource cost used in the ROI calculation. However, we propose two additional categories of investment to surpass the surface-level ROI. The first category is to align specific resources with a specific growth objective. For example, if the objective is to retain revenue from the top 20 customers, the company may align resource costs such as account managers, reporting, and tools that specifically help to achieve that objective. An ROI would be measured on that specific breakout of resource costs and productivity value. The second category comprises the non-compensation factors that allow sales personnel to optimize their productivity, thus making it easier to sell. This would include

- Training and development programs and resources
- Sales leadership resources
- Recruiting/talent-acquisition resources and processes
- Sales operations resources
- Crediting, approval, and quota-setting processes
- Real-time reporting tools such as performance analytics and pay estimators
- Customer relationship management and compensation administration systems
- Territory management

These costs can have a direct correlation with the productivity value in your ROI calculation.

## Step 5: When? Setting Expectations

In the preceding steps, we walked through the framework and considerations for the productivity value (numerator) and the resource cost (denominator). Now that the measurement is defined, the next step is to determine when we will define it, over what time period, and how often. In addition, expectations should be set regarding the look of the reporting, the distribution, and definitions of success.

A CFO from a conferencing software client measured the ROI of a new sales professional over a 12-month period. The ROI calculation was the individual's annual revenue divided by his or her total compensation excluding benefits. Instead of calculating as a percent, the company used an absolute-dollar-value comparison. The expectation was that the sales professional should be paying for himself or herself within that 12-month period. However, these guidelines do change based on the sales professional type (small accounts versus major accounts), level within the organization, and annual revenue responsibility. This definition has been consistent for several years and is simple, such that all sales employees can calculate their own ROI. Compensation plan changes can affect a sales professional's behavior quickly, so it is important to have a process in place to measure the appropriate ROI early and often.

## Step 6: What? Communication Plan: Speak the Same Language

Many stakeholders are involved in defining and creating a sales compensation ROI—sales, sales operations, human resources, finance, and so on. Getting all stakeholders to speak the same sales compensation ROI language is an iterative and ongoing process. This is one of the more challenging tasks during sales compensation design. In general, the sales or sales operations teams will own the design. However, finance manages the budget and plays a significant part in the process. In order to capture full engagement of the sales team, everyone should have a full understanding of the strategy, sales compensation plans, and ROI components. We often conduct field interviews for our market studies and receive responses such as, "I don't know what I will earn until the check appears through my direct deposit" or, with regard to strategy, "We have one, but I do not know what it is."

Success of the sales compensation plan and its ROI comes from full understanding by the sales team. To achieve success, company leaders need to reinforce the strategy message outside the compensation plan through frequent feedback loops such as forecast reviews, frequent questioning of results, metrics, dashboarding, and coaching. All stakeholders must be in sync with the strategy and compensation message to accomplish this. To ensure that the ROI process and results are communicated effectively, the audience should be able to answer three questions:

- How do we measure success or the effectiveness of our resources?

- How much is the sales compensation plan going to cost us?

- Have we achieved success based on our results?

Clarity of the preceding ensures that the company has alignment between optimal sales resources and organizational priorities, which can lead to maximizing returns and sustaining organizational and individual performance. In simpler terms, everyone wins.

## Step 7: What Else? Don't Operate in a Silo

A part of your ROI success or failure will come from factors that are outside the control of the sales compensation plan. No matter how well you define your strategy, design your sales compensation plan, and determine your ROI measures, other influences will be there. Your success also may be a result of marketing efforts, new products, change in the competitive landscape, or customer satisfaction levels. Companies must analyze the whole picture, not just the sales compensation plan in a silo—you must analyze product, market, and customer readiness as well to ensure success. A great sales compensation plan without these readiness factors risks failure from an ROI perspective. Although the sales compensation plan is a huge factor in driving productivity, it does not predict everything. When selling a strategic product, the sales compensation plan can motivate sales professionals to sell it, but there are other factors, such as product availability, the right markets, the right sales messages and process, and the appropriate sales personnel, that contribute to that product's success. Attributing success to the sales compensation plan because it helped achieve certain objectives often comes with the understanding that sales compensation was just one piece of it.

Sales compensation is one of the single largest expenses a company incurs. Maximizing the impact of the investment is critical to gaining a competitive advantage. We find it very useful to move focus away from the number. Take the focus—and the argument—away from the number alone and break down the components driving that number. Then the conversation is a lot more productive. The key points to remember from this chapter are

- *Strategy and ROI go hand-in-hand.* The strategy needs an ROI to ensure success, and an ROI needs the strategy to provide direction as to what should be measured. If one area changes, then the other one needs to change as well.

- *Take the time to define your ROI.* Take some time in your compensation planning process to determine your best objective definition of ROI, and stick to it as long as it continues to align with your strategy. Include all stakeholders to research, build, communicate, and sustain it. You will see the benefits.

- *Look beyond traditional measures of ROI.* Push your thinking to incorporate elements of productivity value and resource cost outside the simplest measures. Many factors contribute to the success of your sales compensation plan. Consider them in your ROI so that you can adapt them to your benefit.

- *Numbers can lie.* To ensure that the ROI is credible, it is imperative that the framework and components are broken down into simple, nonfinancial verbiage. The process should be consistent from period to period to maintain objectivity and consistency in the message.

- *Conflict will exist.* The framework we outlined cannot be done in a silo. In general, sales, sales operations, finance, and human resources are the key players at the table. Each function has its own priorities, challenges, and opinions. It is vital to consider the perspective of each party. For example, finance wants better results with less money, whereas sales wants to attract and retain the best talent without a price tag. Human resources can help by providing external benchmarks that minimize this conflict. Sales operations can provide reporting with objective evidence of a particular issue at hand.

- *ROI is not one size fits all.* The metrics for ROI will vary by sales strategy, customer type, product mix, role type, contract length, and revenue type. Also, several ROI calculations may be needed depending on the structure of your sales team and strategy components.

- *ROI is not one and done.* Whereas financial statements are issued annually, the sales compensation ROI is an ongoing process. The framework of the productivity value and resource cost may not change from period to period, but the components need to adapt to rapidly changing business needs and strategy. Keep it simple so that you can adapt quickly.

## Note

1. Mark Donnolo, *What Your CEO Needs to Know about Sales Compensation*. AMACOM, New York, 2013.

# 19

# Creating a Culture of Collaboration, Innovation, and Performance through Team-Based Incentives

Luis R. Gomez-Mejia
*Mendoza College of Business, University of Notre Dame*

Monica Franco-Santos
*Cranfield School of Management, Cranfield University*

A growing number of organizations are moving away from the long-held belief that individual achievement and success, often through internal competition, are to be encouraged and reinforced. Research indicates that the use of teams can bring about a number of benefits: it greatly improves productivity,[1] induces employees to set challenging and spontaneous group goals,[2] facilitates communication across organizational barriers,[3] improves financial performance,[4] and engenders a social climate that promotes the exchange and combination of knowledge, enhancing new-product and new-service development.[5]

For firms using team structures, the adoption of team-based incentives is perceived to be a core mechanism for enhancing team performance. A *team-based incentive* is a compensation program that links payments to the achievement of team performance goals.[6] The underlying logic for using team-based incentives is that they are believed "to promote trust, cohesiveness and mutually supportive behaviors among team members."[7] A meta-analysis published in 2003 of 45[8] studies using team incentives found that overall, the use of incentives tied to the achievement of team goals resulted in a 22 percent increase in performance. Despite this encouraging result, the use of team-based incentives may have potential drawbacks. For instance, there is evidence suggesting that employees (in certain cultures) tend to prefer rewards based on individual achievements rather than on team achievements, that team-based incentives are prone to unfavorable sorting effects (i.e., they may discourage high-productive applicants and employees), that when team size increases the effect of team incentives decreases due to "line of sight" issues (i.e., it is difficult for individuals to see a clear link between their effort and their rewards), and that using team incentives creates free-riding problems (i.e., poor performers benefit from the efforts of high performers).[9] Given these issues, organizations must be cautious when designing and implementing team incentives. As with any other management tool, team-based incentives do not function in a vacuum. They need the support of other management practices to work well, and they need to fit the organization's idiosyncratic characteristics.

In this chapter, we review the reasons for choosing team-based incentives, their different structures, their main advantages and disadvantages, and the key factors that organizations need to consider to make the most out of team incentives. The chapter concludes with a checklist for managers with key suggestions for making team-based incentives successful.

## Reasons for Choosing Team Incentives

Rewards based on team performance are likely to affect an organization's ability to attract, retain, and motivate employees and shape the culture of the organization. Team-based incentive plans should be chosen when they are consistent with both the nature of the team's work and the goals to be accomplished.

### Nature of Work: High Interdependence

Recent efforts to redesign jobs have focused on enhancing cooperative work relationships among employees to attain desired outcomes, such as improved innovation and creativity, enhanced quality and quantity, and lower costs. A cooperative work environment can be defined as one in which "the objectives of individual employees are mingled together in such a way that there is a positive correlation among the group members' goal attainment."[10] In other words, no one individual can achieve success without the willingness of coworkers to contribute to the desired group performance outcome. Under these conditions, work is said to be interdependent as opposed to independent. When there is high interdependence among employees' work, it is often difficult to separate the contributions and performance of individuals. Thus performance can be assessed more accurately at the level of the team rather than at the level of the individual, and compensation programs contingent on team performance might be more appropriate.[11]

When work is highly interdependent, the use of individual incentives is likely to be dysfunctional. An often-cited example of failing to match the nature of work with the type of rewards offered can be found in traditional sales commission plans. A sales representative is commonly paid strictly for units sold (or sales volume), representing an individual contract between the salesperson and the employer. Unfortunately, the contract only delineates the amount of money the sales representative receives based on the quantity of goods sold rather than on the value the customer derives from the products sold or the quality of service delivered to the customer. This may create problems with customer satisfaction that are only revealed after the sale. The customer-service and technical teams can become frustrated because of the salesperson's disinterest in and inability to effectively provide a quality service to the customer and to enhance loyalty for the long-term benefit of the headquarters office. Because the employment contract between the salesperson and the firm is focused on the salesperson's individual outcomes, he or she is not concerned with cooperating with the customer-service group, back office, or technical field representatives. By narrowly defining the jobs and not acknowledging the degree of interdependencies within the function, the firm's overall goal of achieving effective sales and customer service is not realized. When certain types of jobs are intrinsically team oriented, team rewards could assist in realizing the organization's true goals with both volume and quality.

### Nature of Performance Goals

There is abundant research suggesting that the use of specific and difficult goals leads to improved performance.[12] Most of the studies have focused on individual goal setting and resulting individual performance. Few studies have considered the issue of team goals and subsequent team performance. In general, it appears that team goal setting leads to improved team performance when team members accept the team goals.[13] The goals should be difficult, providing a challenge for team members, but not unattainable.[14] It also has been suggested that team goal-setting processes persuade individuals within the team who have not accepted the team's goals to personalize such goals.[15]

Research has found that linking team rewards to the achievement of team goals has a positive effect on performance.[16] When the achievement of team goals is linked to rewards, the team goal-setting process becomes more effective. Effective goal setting has a positive long-term effect on team performance.[17]

Compensation programs provide an essential feedback link for the goal-setting process. Pay related to the goals set by the team signifies that the organization is committed to the program, and the performance feedback provides employees with positive reinforcement in addition to an incentive to continue pursuing the team goals.

It is important to note that the types of goals an organization emphasizes may influence the degree to which team incentives work. For instance, research has shown that when an organization focuses attention on accuracy (or quality goals), then team incentives that encourage cooperation, cohesion, and information sharing will generate better results; however, when an organization focuses attention on speed (or quantity goals), then team incentives may be less effective than individual incentives because they are likely to slow down task completion by the team.[18]

A recent study has found that teams working with a team reward structure perform better on the convergent aspects of creativity (e.g., generating feasible ideas), whereas teams working with individual rewards tend to perform better on the divergent aspects of creativity (e.g., generating original ideas).[19]

It is also critical to highlight that the existing knowledge on the application of goal setting to individuals does not always apply to teams. Managers need to be aware of this difference and tailor their practices accordingly.[20]

## Structure of Team-Based Incentives

Team incentives are contingent on team goals, and their achievement is assessed according to the results of team-based performance measures. Incentive payments can be made in cash, corporate stock, and through noncash items such as trips, time off, and luxury items. The structure of the incentives is often explained according to the way in which payments are distributed. The literature often focuses on two key distribution structures: equality based and equity based.[21] In an *equality-based incentive*, all members receive the same pay regardless of how much they contribute to the team performance. In an *equity-based incentive*, pay is distributed according to individual contributions to the team. The general consensus is that equality-based incentives are more appropriate when the work is highly interdependent and it is difficult to differentiate team members' individual performance. This type of incentive structure is easy to administer, cost-effective, and likely to increase perceived harmony, cohesion, and solidarity within the team; however, it also entails the risk of motivational losses as a result of free-riding problems.[22] Equity-based incentives are more costly and difficult to administer but may be useful when teams have fairness and trust concerns and when individual performance can be accurately assessed.[23]

Team incentives also can differ regarding the type of performance measures used. Team performance can be assessed according to process or outcome measures of performance. *Process measures* refer to the means of achieving desired outcomes (e.g., behaviors, procedures, etc.) and are evaluated when the team tasks are being executed. *Outcome measures* refer to the ultimate results expected and are assessed after team tasks have been completed. Research on the consequences of these two types of team incentives is limited. Currently, there is some evidence regarding project teams suggesting that when projects are long and complex, process-based incentives may be less effective than outcome-based incentives. However, if the projects are performed under high-risk and competitive conditions, then outcome-based incentives are also deficient and can be detrimental in terms of quality.[24]

Team incentives can be combined with individual, business-unit, and organizational reward programs. The key to success in integrating all these compensation methods is that they are consistent with the strategy of the organization. If they are not designed to be consistent with the business strategy, then each individual method of payment can conflict with others or with the organization's objectives. This misalignment will communicate mixed messages to employees about what is critical for the organization. When team incentives are implemented and individuals continue to possess personal goals in addition to their incorporated team goals, the rewards system can be effective in ensuring that individual and team goals are consistent rather than in conflict with each other.

## Factors that Influence the Effectiveness of Team Incentives

Existing research suggests that there are four sets of factors that may influence the effectiveness of team incentives. These factors are individual factors, team factors, organizational factors, and reward structure factors.[25]

### *Individual Factors*

The characteristics of the individual members of a team in which the team incentive is applied will influence its effectiveness. When designers of team incentives review the characteristics of team members, they should pay special attention to three individual factors.[26] First, high-*ability* team members are more likely to perform well and thus be more supportive of incentives. Second, team incentives applied to team members with a high individual *need for achievement*, are less likely to be effective than in cases where members are more group oriented. Third, teams that have a large number of members whose *preferences are for individualism over collectivism*, will have difficulty in impelementing team incentives.

Two other factors that influence the degree of effectiveness of team incentives are also often mentioned. One is the *personality* of team members (the greater the number of extroverts and agreeable people on the team, the more likely team rewards are to be effective, and vice versa with introverts and disagreeable people).[27] The other factor is the gender composition (teams with a high number of women are more likely to make team incentives effective).[28]

## Team Factors

The idiosyncratic characteristics of the work team are also believed to affect the extent to which team incentives enhance team performance. Research[29] has found that the higher the degree of intragroup task interdependence, the higher the degree of between-group independence, the smaller the team, the higher the measurability of team goals, and the more stable or long-term oriented a team is, the more effective the team incentives will be. In addition, the degree of heterogeneity on teams will have mixed effects because high heterogeneity will be positively related to team performance in terms of higher creativity and better decision making. It will be negatively related, however, to performance tasks such as those found in production and service work because it generates greater feelings of inequity. Furthermore, the degree to which the team incentive design fits with the stage of development of the team also will influence team incentives effectiveness. More recently, experimental research has found that prevention-oriented teams (i.e., teams with goals that focus on avoiding negative consequences such as safety, reduction of product defects, etc.) are more likely to find benefits in team incentives because this reward structure generates social support. Promotion-focus teams are less influenced by the reward structure applied to them.[30]

## Organizational Factors

The conditions under which the organization operates are also determinants of team incentives effectiveness. Organizational culture, the congruence among organizational subsystems, and the organizational structural characteristics can influence the extent to which team incentives will enhance performance. Regarding the culture of the organization, research suggests that there are cultural values that are more supportive of team incentives. Organizations that emphasize values such as communication, information sharing, collaboration, and employee engagement are more likely to benefit from the implementation and success of team incentives.[31]

Another factor that influences the effectiveness of team incentives is the extent to which they are congruent with the strategy of the organization, its structure (teams), and other control systems (e.g., performance measures, performance reviews, and additional reward systems). The greater the fit, the more effective the team incentives will be. When incongruence exists, teams and individuals will experience tensions and conflicts that will be detrimental to team performance.[32]

## Reward Structure Factors

The design elements of the team incentives are also critical for their effectiveness. These elements are the incentive size, the frequency of payout, the type of payout (monetary, nonmonetary, or mixed), and the reward distribution procedure (equality versus equity). There is very little research for guiding managers in the selection of the appropriate size, frequency, or type of payout. It is widely accepted that the greater the size of the incentive, the greater is the attention that team members will dedicate to accomplishing team goals. This increased attention may or may not be optimal. It will be optimal if performance is accurately measured and teams know how to achieve it; however, if performance is difficult to measure or performance measures used are ill defined and the team does not necessarily know how to achieve the expected performance, then the greater the size of the incentive, the more it can generate dysfunctional behaviors. It is widely known in psychology research that rewards should be distributed to team members as frequently as possible to reinforce the expected behaviors. Nevertheless, it is often the case that team rewards are provided on an annual basis, normally owing to administrative and cost-effective reasons. The type of team incentive payouts can be monetary and nonmonetary, but to our knowledge, there is limited research in this area. Thus, robust conclusions are difficult to draw. Despite the scarce research in these three aspects of the reward structures, there is a considerable amount of research on the conditions under which equality- or equity-based incentives are more beneficial. This has already been described in this chapter (see the "Structure of Team-Based Incentives" section).

## Advantages and Disadvantages of Using Team-Based Incentives

As with any other management practice, the use of team incentives has its pros and cons. There is general agreement in the literature that the advantages of team-based incentives outweigh problems. Nevertheless, it is important to be aware of potential pitfalls so that they can be avoided. To summarize, key advantages of team-based incentives include the following[33]:

- Reinforcing norms of collegiality and cooperation within groups

- Helping to reduce disciplinary and background diversity barriers in cross-functional work teams

- Helping teams to focus on the achievement of project goals and objectives

- Allowing firms to differentially reward teams and groups that are most strategically important

However, there are potential disadvantages associated with the use of team-based incentives. These need to be managed to ensure that the advantages noted earlier are forthcoming. Potential downsides with the use of team-based incentives include the following[34]:

- Free riding; that is, some team members may receive the incentive even if they have made little contribution to the achievement of group goals. This may occur because of a lack of effort or perhaps because some team members have much lower ability levels or skills than other team members. To counteract this potential problem, one option is to use peer rating to assess the contributions of individual team members. Research looking at free riding in information-related groups also has found that penalizing the worst free riders may be a good strategy because it reduces their tendency to free ride and avoids the rest of the group regressing to free-riding behavior over time.[35]

- While team decisions enjoy greater acceptability among team members and generate greater commitment to the achievement of group goals, it is possible that the most talented individuals within the team may come up with better solutions to problems facing the team. To counteract this potential problem, team members need to be trained so that the opinions of individual team members are carefully weighed and the team avoids rushing to reach a decision.

- It is difficult to carve out independent groups for reward purposes because of interdependence. To the extent that the performance of a group depends on the performance of other groups, team-based incentives may be problematic because it is not possible to isolate and reward the performance of each group. One approach to deal with this issue is to amplify the size of the team being rewarded, perhaps including all teams that are interdependent with each other.

- Incompatible cultural values; that is, as noted later, some countries are characterized by an individualistic culture so that excessively pursuing team-based incentives may provoke a negative reaction among employees who believe they should be rewarded for their own personal contributions. One approach to deal with this issue is to offer a combination of individual and team-based rewards, soliciting the opinions of team members as to the perceived appropriate mix.

- Entrepreneurship may suffer if group rewards are pushed too far. Entrepreneurs are often individuals who work independently with their own personalities. They tend to be driven by their own personal desire for success and the recognition of personal achievement by others. These people may play a critical role in many organizations and often do not work well in teams over a sustained period of time. Thus, even when team-based incentives are in place, allowance needs to be made for employees who exhibit a strong entrepreneurial orientation.

## Individualism as a Cultural Value

Although many organizations are moving to the team concept, relatively little attention has been paid to the nature of the American worker in a team environment, which is foreign to the basic culture from which the employee has emerged. Hofstede[36] in a comprehensive study employing a database with over 116,000 questionnaire responses, found that the United States ranked number one on a construct that he called "individualism." High-individualism countries are characterized as places where the culture emphasizes the individual rather than the group. Each individual is expected to care for himself or herself. The organization is not committed to care for individuals on a long-term basis. Pay policies within these countries tend to emphasize individual rather than group performance.

An employee's ability to demonstrate his or her successful individual achievements to others is important and evidenced by the accumulation of rewards for performance, such as salary, company cars, job title, number of subordinates, and other rewards found in traditional compensation systems. As team concepts are employed, one must ask how the mentality of individualism, which is typical of the American worker, can survive in this atmosphere. The compensation program can be one tool for satisfying both individual and group needs.

Awards for outstanding individual performance cannot be ignored in a society so insistent on individual accomplishment, but they must be carefully incorporated within an organizational environment whose survival depends on team rather than individual effort. Turnover should be carefully monitored when a business moves from individual to team programs. This will provide feedback on the types of personnel who are challenged by the team concept and those who are not satisfied with the environment. This information will be essential for future recruitment efforts, succession planning, and program evaluation.

Creative compensation management, in which pay is tailored to the needs of the organization, the nature of work, and the characteristics of the workforce, is playing an important strategic role in the organization. The team concept is rapidly gaining popularity because of the positive outcomes that many organizations have experienced after implementing such programs. Team-based, rather than individual, criteria for pay should be used when the goals of the business are to strengthen the team's performance, not only the individual employee's performance within the team. In a culture so dominated by individual goals and objectives, organizations must strive to be creative in their deployment of effective team incentive programs that communicate to the worker that group, rather than individual, performance is critical for success.

## What If Incentives are Not Necessary after All?

Most managers wanting to increase collaboration, innovation, and team cohesion often turn to incentives as a quick solution to bring about change and enhanced team achievements. The power of incentives is well documented for influencing behavior and decision making; however, more and more scholars are raising concerns about the perils of incentives and their potential long-term detrimental effects, especially in environments where outcome performance is extremely difficult to assess, such as in healthcare,[37] defense,[38] and education.[39] In these environments, other mechanisms are being proposed for enhancing the delivery of outcomes (e.g., high-control recruitment, socialization, exploratory use of performance measures, self-monitoring, shared leadership and awards) that are worth considering as an alternative to any type of performance-related incentives.[40]

## Closing Note: A Checklist for Making Team-Based Incentives Successful

Compensation is an important aspect of the success of team-based work designs, as discussed in this chapter. Table 19.1 provides a checklist of key things to consider when linking pay to team performance. We have created this list based on our own consulting experience and the literature. One important caveat is that effective compensation design is only one aspect that contributes to improved team performance. The firm also needs to consider other important issues in tandem. Additional practices in conjunction with team-based incentives that can enhance team performance are noted in Table 19.2.

---

- Never forget that you get what you measure and reward!

- The best way to reduce free riding is through peer pressure (peer pressure increases through cohesion; cohesion increases by providing group rewards; rewards should go to the entire team and not be associated with one person, e.g., "Walter's shop") or by penalizing the worst free riders.

- Evaluation and rewards must take into account the difficulty of the assignment and the probability of failure. People will not take risks if they are penalized for taking on difficult assignments, especially if there are easier ways to be recognized.

- Space out rewards so that they are linked to different stages of projects to reinforce short-term accomplishments without losing sight of long-term objectives—for example, from key intermediate landmarks, through patenting of innovations, through commercialization of a project.

---

**Table 19.1  Key Issues and Best Practices When Designing Team-Based Incentives**

- If an employee works for multiple teams, use all available inputs for measuring team performance and allocating rewards.

- Identify internal and external customers of each group, and measure their expectations and assessment of teams.

- Reduce hierarchies (e.g., Technician I, II, III, etc.) as a way of promoting and rewarding people. Hierarchies create status and power differentials that are dysfunctional in a team environment.

- Use broadbanding as a flexible way to provide rewards without creating tall career-grade structures.

- Reward teams through lump-sum payments for landmark accomplishments. These are more noticeable and less contaminated with other factors, such as cost of living.

- Identify and reward key contributors through group nomination, using cross-functional groups for the evaluation of nominees.

- Be creative in providing nonfinancial rewards that promote team spirit, such as trips, a picture of the team in the company newspaper, and company events such as banquets or picnics.

- Use peer appraisals with the supervisors consolidating and integrating this feedback so that it is provided to the employee in a manner that is useful.

**Table 19.1  Key Issues and Best Practices When Designing Team-Based Incentives (*continued*)**

- Ensure that each team has an effective facilitator.

- Each individual should have a loosely specified role within the team; thus team composition needs to be carefully thought out, considering both personality and technical issues.

- Recognize major challenges to innovation: being able to work with people and technical expertise are often at odds with each other. Mavericks need to be protected because they are crucial for innovation.

**Table 19.2  Key Issues and Best Practices for an Internal Team Organization**

## Notes

1. C. Ichinowski and K. Shaw, "Beyond Incentive Pay: Insiders' Estimates of the Value of Complementary Human Resource Management Practice." *Journal of Economic Perspectives* 17(1):155–180, 2003; G. Hertel, U. Konradt, and B. Orlikowski, "Managing Distance by Interdependence: Goal Setting, Task Interdependence, and Team-Based Rewards in Virtual Teams." *European Journal of Work and Organizational Psychology* 13(1):1–28, 2004; and F. Roman, "An Analysis of Changes to a Team-Based Incentive Plan and Its Effects on Productivity, Product Quality, and Absenteeism." *Accounting, Organization, and Society* 34:589–618, 2009.
2. J. P. Guthrie and E. C. Hollensbe, "Group Incentives and Performance: A Spontaneous Goal Setting, Goal Choice Commitment." *Journal of Management* 30(2):263–284, 2004.
3. C. Harbring, "The Effects of Communication in Incentive Systems: An Experimental Study." *Managerial and Decision Economics* 27(5):33–53, 2006.

4. J. Devaro, "Teams, Autonomy, and the Financial Performance of Firms." *Industrial Relations* 45(2):217, 2006.

5. C. J. Collins and K. G. Smith, "Knowledge Exchange and Combination: The Role of Human Resource Practices in the Performance of High-Technology Firms." *Academy of Management Journal* 49(3):544–560, 2006.

6. J. S. DeMatteo, L. T. Eby, and E. Sundstrom, "Team-Based Rewards: Current Empirical Evidence and Directions for Future Research." *Research in Organizational Behavior* 20:141–183, 1998.

7. B. Beersma, J. R. Hollenbeck, S. E. Humphrey, H. Moon, D. E. Conlon, and D. R. Ilgen, "Cooperation, Competition and Group Performance: Towards a Contingency Approach." *Academy of Management Journal* 46:572–590, 2003.

8. S. T. Condly, R. E. Clark, and H. D. Stolovitch, "The Effects of Incentives on Workplace Performance: A Meta-Analytic Review of Research Studies." *Performance Improvement Quarterly* 16(3): 46–63, 2003.

9. B. Gerhart, S. L. Rynes, and I. Smithey Fulmer, "Pay and Performance: Individuals, Groups, and Executives." *Academy of Management Annals* 3(1):251–315, 2009.

10. M. Deutsch, "A Theory of Cooperation and Competition." *Human Relations* :129–152, 1949.

11. B. Beersma, J. R. Hollenbeck, S. E. Humphrey, H. Moon, D. E. Conlon, and D. R. Ilgen, "Cooperation, Competition and Group Performance: Towards a Contingency Approach." *Academy of Management Journal* 46:572–590, 2003.

12. G. P. Latham, *Work Motivation: History, Theory, Research, and Practice.* Sage Publications, Thousand Oaks, CA, 2007; and G. P. Latham and E. A. Locke, "New Developments in and Directions for Goal-Setting Research." *European Psychologist* 12:290–300, 2007.

13. C. R. Gowen, "Managing Work Group Performance by Individual Goals and Group Goals for Interdependent Group Tasks." *Journal of Organizational Behavior Management* 7(3):5–27, 1985.

14. J. Forward and A. Zander, "Choice of Unattainable Goals and Effects on Performance." *Organization Behavior and Human Performance* 6:184–199, 1971.

15. J. T. Austin and P. Bobko, "Goal Setting Theory: Unexplored Areas and Future Research Needs." *Journal of Occupational Psychology* 58:289–308, 1985.

16. R. D. Pritchard and M. Curtis, "The Influence of Goal Setting and Financial Incentives on Task Performance." *Organization Behavior and Human Performance* 10:175–183, 1973.

17. J. T. Austin and P. Bobko, "Goal Setting Theory: Unexplored Areas and Future Research Needs." *Journal of Occupational Psychology* 58:289–308, 1985.

18. B. Beersma, J. R. Hollenbeck, S. E. Humphrey, H. Moon, D. E. Conlon, and D. R. Ilgen, "Cooperation, Competition and Group Performance: Towards a Contingency Approach." *Academy of Management Journal* 46:572–590, 2003.

19. B. Beersma and C. K. W. De Dreu, "The Aftermath of Group Negotiation: How Social Motives Affect Distal Group Functioning and Performance," working paper, University of Amsterdam, 2003.

20. J. D. Nahrgang, D. S. DeRue, J. R. Hollenbeck et al., "Goal Setting in Teams: The Impact of Learning and Performance Goals on Process and Performance." *Organizational Behavior and Human Decision Processes* 122:12–21, 2013.

21. B. Gerhart, S. L. Rynes, and I. Smithey Fulmer, "Pay and Performance: Individuals, Groups, and Executives." *Academy of Management Annals* 3(1):251–315, 2009; and S. Sharin and V. Mahajan, "The Effect of Reward Structures on the Performance of Cross-Functional Product Development Teams." *Journal of Marketing* 65(2):35–53, 1988.

22. O. Rack, T. Ellwart, G. Hertel, and U. Konradt, "Team-Based Rewards in Computer-Mediated Groups." *Journal of Managerial Psychology* 26(5):419–438, 2011.

23. K. K. Merriman, "On the Folly of Rewarding Team Performance While Hoping for Teamwork." *Compensation & Benefits Review* 41:61–66, 2009.

24. S. Sarin and V. Mahajan, "The Effect of Reward Structures on the Performance of Cross-Functional Product Development Teams." *Journal of Marketing* 65(2):35–53, 2001.

25. J. S. DeMatteo, L. T. Eby, and E. Sundstrom, "Team-Based Rewards: Current Empirical Evidence and Directions for Future Research." *Research in Organizational Behavior* 20:141–183, 1998; and Y. Garbers and U. Konradt, "The Effect of Financial Incentives on Performance: A Quantitative Review of Individual and Team-Based Financial Incentives." *Journal of Occupational and Organizational Psychology* 87:102–137, 2014.

26. J. S. DeMatteo, L. T. Eby, and E. Sundstrom, "Team-Based Rewards: Current Empirical Evidence and Directions for Future Research." *Research in Organizational Behavior* 20:141–183, 1998.

27. B. Beersma, J. R. Hollenbeck, S. E. Humphrey, H. Moon, D. E. Conlon, and D. R. Ilgen, "Cooperation, Competition and Group Performance: Towards a Contingency Approach." *Academy of Management Journal* 46:572–590, 2003.

28. Y. Garbers and U. Konradt, "The Effect of Financial Incentives on Performance: A Quantitative Review of Individual and Team-Based Financial Incentives." *Journal of Occupational and Organizational Psychology* 87:102–137, 2014.

29. J. S. DeMatteo, L. T. Eby, and E. Sundstrom, "Team-Based Rewards: Current Empirical Evidence and Directions for Future Research." *Research in Organizational Behavior* 20:141–183, 1998.

30. B. Beersma, A. C. Homan, G. A. Van Kleef, and C. K. W. De Dreu, "Outcome Interdependence Shapes the Effects of Prevention Focus on Team Processes and Performance." *Organizational Behavior and Human Decision Processes* 121:194–203, 2013.

31. J. E. Nickel and S. O'Neal, "Small Group Incentives: Gainsharing in the Microcosm." *Compensation & Benefits Review* 22(2):22–29, 1990.

32. L. Gomez-Mejia, P. Berrone, and M. Franco-Santos, *Compensation and Organizational Performance: Theory, Research, and Practice.* M. E. Sharpe, Armonk, NY, 2010.

33. L. R. Gomez-Mejia, D. Balkin, and R. Cardy, *Managing Human Resources.* Englewood Cliffs, NJ: Prentice Hall, 2007.

34. Ibid.

35. M. Hashim and J. C. Bockstedt, "Overcoming Free-Riding in Information Goods: Sanctions or Rewards?" Presented at the 48th Hawaii International Conference on System Sciences, 2014. Available at: http://ssrn.com/abstract=2463453.

36. G. Hofstede, *Culture's Consequences: International Differences in Work-Related Values.* Sage Publications, Beverly Hills, CA, 1980.

37. B. Frey, F. Homberg, and M. Osterloh, "Organizational Control Systems and Pay-for-Performance in the Public Service." *Organization Studies* 24(7):949, 2013.

38. M. Chwastiak, "Rationality, Performance Measures and Representations of Reality: Planning, Programming and Budgeting and the Vietnam War." *Critical Perspectives on Accounting* 17(1):29–55, 2006.

39. D. Marsden, "Pay-for-Performance in English Schools," Centre for Economic Performance, London School of Economics, 2014.

40. B. Frey, F. Homberg, and M. Osterloh, "Organizational Control Systems and Pay-for-Performance in the Public Service." *Organization Studies* 24(7):949, 2013; and L. Segel and M. Lehrer, "The Institutionalization of Stewardship: Theory, Propositions, and Insights from Change in the Edmonton Public Schools." *Organization Studies* 33(2):169–201, 2012.

# 20

# Revolutionizing Workplace Culture through Scanlon Gain Sharing

Dow Scott
*Loyola University, Chicago*

Paul Davis
*EPIC-Organizations.com*

## Scanlon Gain Sharing: Where the Best Ideas Come Together

In the novel, *Moby Dick*, Ishmael signed on for "the three hundredth lay." Provided that he survived the three years at sea, he would receive 1/300th of "the clear net proceeds of the voyage." His friend Queequeg was a master harpooner, so he signed on for a nineteenth lay, or 1/19th of the net proceeds. These nineteenth-century whalers were engaged in gain sharing, a concept as old as human history.

Gain sharing has stood the test of time because it meets a fundamental human need for fairness and combines a primal understanding of group dynamics with the realities of a business enterprise; that is, *as we work together, we should all benefit according to what we have contributed. Unless we work together to create a "gain" or something of value, there will be nothing to share.* The nineteenth-century whalers were motivated. They faced hardships together, and when successful, they shared in the rewards that resulted from both their individual talent and group effort.

Multiple studies by Jerry McAdams and Elizabeth Hawk conducted by the Consortium for Alternative Reward Strategies Research have shown that gain sharing is a powerful tool for creating high-performance workplaces.[1] Gain sharing, on average, produces a 3 percent increase in pay for employees and a 134 percent return for the company while fostering teamwork, enhanced communication, and improved morale. In *The Ultimate Advantage*, Edward Lawler notes, "[T]he most important thing we know about gainsharing plans is that they work."[2]

Research conducted by Gallup worldwide shows that 70 percent of employees are not "engaged" in their work (Gallup, 2013). They are waiting to jump ship, to find more rewarding work.[3] With the retirement of the baby-boomer generation, reduced immigration, and lower birth rates, the competition for talent will increase. Attraction and retention of talent will become even more critical.

Compensation is important for attracting and retaining talent, but alone it is at best a blunt tool. For decades, surveys have shown that pay is just one of the many reasons that employees stay with an organization (e.g., Hausknecht, Rodda, and Howard, 2009). Gain sharing provides increased pay, but it also can provide the psychological rewards that research shows people want and a method for aligning organizational goals with employee efforts.

As competition increases, organizations are faced with two critical areas that must be managed for survival. First, they must maximize efficiency and productivity by reducing all forms of waste in systems and processes. Traditionally the domain of production area industrial engineers, Lean methods are becoming a job requirement in all areas of manufacturing, including the office. Lean methods are now rapidly spreading to healthcare and other areas of the economy. The second area that must be managed is innovation. New products and services were once the domain of product-development departments. Today, the most successful companies tap all employees, asking them to constantly scan the environment for new products and services that can increase the "top line" of the organization and to devise more efficient methods for producing those products and services. The idea is to tap into employee knowledge of the business and bring innovation more quickly to fruition by engaging employees in the development of products and improvement in processes.

Gain sharing is a group, operation, or facility-wide reward system that can improve productivity, efficiency, and innovation by developing and better using human capital. Gain sharing—in particular, Scanlon plans—has been studied extensively (e.g., Gerhart, Rynes, and Fulmer, 2009; Ledford and Allen, 2012; Schuster, 1984) and has proven itself in a wide variety of industries, including manufacturing, retail, nonprofit, government, distribution, telecommunications, financial services, hospitality, and healthcare. Gain sharing is successful in union as well as in nonunion environments and has proven successful in various cultures around the world.

The goal of this chapter is to help compensation professionals understand how to create and maintain work cultures of innovation, engagement, leadership, and performance through Scanlon gain sharing.

## The Crow and the Cormorant

In this classic Japanese fable, a starving crow watches as a cormorant fills its belly with fish. The cormorant, like the crow, is a black bird, but it is able to swim and dive underwater to catch its prey. The crow, reasoning that he too is a black bird, dives into the water only to drown. The moral of the story is: *pay attention to what is truly important, and do not get distracted by what isn't important.* In the crow's case, the ability to swim was more important than the color of his feathers.

Compensation practitioners would be wise to consider this fable as they explore various gain-sharing systems. Gain-sharing systems that seem similar at first glance reveal critical differences in philosophy, scope, and results on closer inspection. Gain-sharing systems are often classified by the nature of the bonuses they use. Just like the crow, focusing on the wrong thing—the formula—can result in missing what is really important. Years of research have shown that the magic of gain sharing has less to do with the type of formula (i.e., single ratio, operational measures, profit sharing, etc.) than with the way in which the system creates gains, the leadership of the unit doing gain sharing, and the method by which the plan is installed (e.g., Scott, Davis, and Cockburn, 2007; Scott et al., 2002; Shivers and Scott, 2003).

The Consortium for Alternative Reward Strategies Research Study IV found that

1. Differences in plan implementation and support drive effectiveness twice as much as differences in plan design.

2. The strongest driver of the culture that supports gain sharing is the plant manager.

3. The clearest element that separates effective from ineffective gain-sharing plans is employee understanding of measurement details and how to implement them.

4. A key indicator of effectiveness is how much people think about the plan.

5. Companies are missing the boat on providing the recognition that employees want from their gain-sharing plans.[4]

## The Scanlon Plan: Setting the Record Straight

Any student of gain sharing will eventually read about the Scanlon plan. It is one of the longest lasting and most researched approaches to gain sharing. It is also the only classical approach that is neither trademarked nor copyrighted. And while there are over 400 books in print that cite the Scanlon approach to gain sharing, much of the information published is misleading or simply wrong. Like the crow, these works focus on the wrong elements of the Scanlon plan and miss the most important ones.

We have spent a major part of our careers—a combined total of over 60 years—studying and implementing Scanlon plans. It is our hope that this chapter will set the record straight so that compensation professionals will know what aspects of gain-sharing plans truly drive organizational performance and employee engagement.

Carl Frost, who spent a lifetime researching and developing Scanlon plans, stated

> The Scanlon Plan is an innovative management process for total organization development. It consists of a set of assumptions about human motivation and behavior, general principles for the management of organizations based on these assumptions, and specific procedures for implementing these principles.[5]

Scanlon plans are named for Joseph N. Scanlon, a prizefighter, steelworker, cost accountant, researcher, and lecturer at the Massachusetts Institute of Technology (MIT) who lived from 1899 to 1956. Articles in *Fortune*, *Life*, and *Time* magazines made this modest man "the most sought after consultant in America."[6] Joe's radical idea was that the average worker has value and knows his or her own job better than anyone else in the company. Scanlon believed that most companies did not tap into the creativity and talent of the majority of workers. He resisted the notion of "the economic man." In other words, he believed that people are motivated by much more than money. He recognized that people want to do good work, enjoy being part of a team, and have many ideas for reducing waste and improving the efficiency and effectiveness of organizations. Scanlon believed that lack of business literacy and skills development severely limits the contribution employees can make. He felt that there was too much external competition to encourage internal competition in organizations. Scanlon found that many human resources practices and systems designed to increase productivity actually prevented people from cooperating and resulted in decreased productivity and efficiency. They often pitted one group against another to the detriment of the organization.

Based on these beliefs, Scanlon developed one of the most successful models for labor-management cooperation just prior to the entrance of the United States into World War II. The war years proved that labor and management could work together cooperatively to increase productivity and improve quality. By the end of the war, Scanlon's faction within the Steelworkers Union that advocated cooperation found itself pushed out as the unions and management returned to their traditional adversarial relations. Scanlon was invited by Dr. Douglas McGregor to join the faculty of MIT as a lecturer, where he continued the work that today is known as the *Scanlon plan*. At MIT, Scanlon joined Paul Pigors, Charles A. Myers, Douglas McGregor, Paul Samuelson, Walter W. Rostow, George P. Schultz, Robert M. Solow, Charles P. Kindleberger, Fredrick Lesieur, and Carl Frost. This interdisciplinary group of scholars engaged in pioneering work in industrial relations.

Dr. Frost continued to evolve and test Scanlon's ideas in organizations such as Herman Miller, Donnelly, Motorola, Bridgestone-Firestone, and Beth Israel Hospital, eventually developing the four basic principles/processes and a participative implementation strategy that are the basis for designing and successfully implementing Scanlon plans today.[7]

## Scanlon Principles

The following four principles are the critical elements of the Scanlon plan—this gain-sharing program is definitely not just another bonus formula.

*Identity/Education.* In order to make a meaningful contribution and to take ownership of business challenges and opportunities, every employee must understand the reality the organization confronts in its business environment. In addition to financial information about the business, employees need fundamental knowledge of the wants and needs of customers, the strengths and weaknesses of competitors, and the contribution that investors make to the organization's success. As a result, companies committed to the Scanlon principles were practicing open-book management long before it became a popular management strategy. Management is challenged to create a compelling mission and vision for the organization that all employees understand and embrace.

*Participation/Responsibility.* The Scanlon plan is based on the premise that most improvements or gains come from "working smarter, not harder." As a result, to increase productivity, employees must have the opportunity and feel the responsibility to provide input and influence decisions. Scanlon companies are high-involvement organizations, and Scanlon leaders use a variety of techniques, such as formal suggestions programs, team meetings, kaizen events, and special task forces to encourage participation. Key to meaningful employee involvement is a disciplined and rigorous process in which employees trust that their input will be heard and that their ideas that can contribute to the business will be quickly implemented. In fact, employees in Scanlon companies are expected to contribute their ideas for improvement; it is part of their jobs.

*Equity/Accountability.* Systems must be developed that ensure accountability to the multiple stakeholders in every organization; these stakeholders include investors, customers, and employees. Scanlon companies use gain-sharing, goal-sharing, or profit-sharing formulas to help employees focus on the critical needs of these stakeholders. Bonuses are often distributed monthly so that employees can fully appreciate the connection between their efforts and the success of the organization. The formula rewards the contribution of investors and offers discounts in prices or rewards for customers. However, for employees, pay is not put "at risk." Employees are paid competitive wages within their industry and labor markets. Equity formulas reward excellence, defined as performance beyond what normally could be expected by the company or within the industry. To build trust and transparency, employees are often involved in calculating the bonus payouts. In some companies, the concept of equity includes dispute-resolution systems should disagreements occur. As is evident, the equity formula is not just about cash bonuses for employees but also about recognizing and rewarding the contributions of important stakeholders. Even if the bonus is very small, bonus checks are still paid because they provide a clear message regarding the success of employee and management efforts that month.

*Competence/Commitment.* Everyone must commit to continually improving on personal, professional, and organizational levels. Scanlon organizations have learned that employee development is an important investment, especially in a participative work environment where the scope of employee job duties is broader and where employees are expected to offer innovative suggestions for improving organization effectiveness and efficiency. Leaders of companies where Scanlon plans have been implemented often state that higher levels of competence are required than in traditionally managed companies. The Scanlon mantra is "Continuous improvement requires continuous learning." Scanlon organizations invest heavily in the training and development of employees; they follow the basic principles of what are often termed *learning organizations*.

Scanlon principles are believed to be universal. They can be applied in any organization in any culture or country. Processes or applications are flexible and can be changed to meet the unique needs of each organization. For example, the identity principle requires that everyone understand the reality of their organization and business environment. However, the process of education is multidimensional, and companies employ a variety of methods to help employees become business literate. These methods include face-to-face meetings with management, published financial statements, business games, and posting performance results on bulletin boards and company intranets. As another example, equity is established through a variety of formulas that include labor cost savings, goal sharing, economic value added, and profit sharing. The combination of universal principles combined with flexible processes has allowed Scanlon plans to create a competitive advantage for over 75 years.

## Implementation Strategy for Installing Scanlon Plans

Carl Frost and subsequent generations of academicians and consultants have developed a specific process or road map for successfully installing Scanlon gain-sharing programs. The road map mirrors the high involvement/informed culture the Scanlon plan is designed to create. Scanlon gain-sharing plans are created by the people who will be affected by the plan. They are not generic programs created by consultant or compensation professionals and then "sold" to the organization, as are many traditional gain-sharing plans.

Implementation of a Scanlon gain-sharing program begins with the top leader(s) developing a mandate. A *mandate* is a statement that describes what the organization must do to survive and prosper. Just as the Declaration of Independence outlined why the United States sought independence and change, a mandate outlines why an organization must change. Beginning with the top leadership team, the mandate is discussed and debated. In some organizations, a secret ballot is taken among the senior management team. Is the mandate compelling? Is there a critical need to change? Is the leadership team on board and unanimous in the need for change? Is the leadership team convinced that Scanlon principles and implementation strategy offer the best means for responding to the mandate? If the leadership team is not convinced that the plan is going to drive organizational performance, then it is time to go back and build a compelling reason for implementing the plan.

Assuming that the leadership team is committed, the process of building commitment continues throughout the various management levels and down to the front-line supervisors. Where a union exists, the mandate is shared with the union leadership. This part of the Scanlon implementation process is designed to build commitment and vision for the future.

Eventually, the mandate is shared with all the employees, who are asked if they are willing to participate in a design team, representing a cross section of employees, to develop a Scanlon gain-sharing program to respond to the mandate for change. Management may ask employees to formally indicate their commitment to building a Scanlon gain-sharing plan. An employee vote forces the leadership and management team to explain the reason that change is needed and their commitment to this change in language that the average employee can understand. Often the front-line employees know that change is needed but do not believe that management is serious, focused, and willing to work with them to improve the organization. This phase of the road map requires honest communication, a willingness to admit past mistakes, and trust in team building. If most employees do not vote to proceed, management must take this as a sign that employees are not convinced, and other changes may have to be made before employees are willing to commit themselves to the Scanlon plan.

The next step is to create a design team charged with leading the efforts to create a Scanlon plan adapted specifically for their organization. The design team consists of both elected and appointed members and is chaired by the senior manager of the organization unit for which the program will be installed (e.g., CEO or plant/facility manager). Top leader involvement sends a strong message that the Scanlon initiative is an important priority. The design team has four subcommittees charged with designing the best system(s) to practice the four Scanlon principles of identity/education, participation/responsibility, equity/accountability, and competence/commitment. These are described in detail next.

The *identity/education subcommittee* wrestles with the problem of how to make sure that everyone knows the critical issues or realities that are important to the organization. Who are the organization's customers? Who are the investors? Who are the competitors? How will information about the organization and the program be shared? This subcommittee is charged with helping employees to understand the business. If employees do not have this fundamental business literacy, their ability to contribute to the effectiveness and efficiency of the company will be limited.

The *participation/responsibility subcommittee* has one of the toughest jobs—how to tap into the creativity and improvement ideas of all employees. Participation is key to creating the gains that later will be shared through the financial formula. Research conducted by Daniel Dennison (1990) at the University of Michigan showed that participative organizations have a three times greater return on investment (ROI) than do traditionally managed organizations. *Identity* creates knowledge about the organization. *Participation* puts the knowledge to use to make improvements.

Because Scanlon gain sharing is based on the idea of "working smarter, not harder," employees must have the opportunity to provide input and influence decisions. The traditional Scanlon plan has a suggestion system that drives organizational improvement. All ideas are recorded and tracked so that no idea falls through the cracks. Employees share their ideas with their immediate work team. If the team likes the idea, it can be quickly implemented. If the idea needs the support of other teams or departments, or if it requires more money to implement than the team is authorized to spend, the suggestion goes to a screening team. The screening team is made up of representatives from all the work teams and the top leader. The screening team has the authority and resources to act, allowing improvement ideas to be debated and implemented quickly. Ideas that require additional research are assigned to the necessary resource (e.g., industrial engineering, human resources, or finance) and are tracked. Because everyone shares in the reward for increased productivity or profits, other employees, supervisors, or managers are motivated to make sure that good ideas are clearly articulated and quickly implemented.

This classic approach resulted in over 10,000 suggestions at National Manufacturing, resulting in millions of dollars in savings (Davis, 2000). This approach continues to be used successfully in organizations such as the ELGA Credit Union and was used by Watermark Credit Union to become one of the "50 best places to work" in the state of Washington (Scott, Davis, and Cockburn, 2007).

Scanlon companies have experimented with all forms of participation and employee involvement. Donnelly (now Magna) was one of the first organizations to be totally organized into teams. Self-directed, cross-functional, and Six Sigma teams, Lean cells, and *kaizan* events are all used in Scanlon organizations to mine the ideas of employees, to improve productivity, and to reduce waste. In 1991, the average employee in a Scanlon organization contributed over $2,200 per year in cost-saving suggestions (McAdams, 1993). Scanlon high-involvement systems are not limited to cost-saving ideas. Employees are also encouraged to submit innovation ideas for new businesses or products, and this input has resulted in the creation of new billion-dollar industries and services—a direct result of their Scanlon involvement systems.

The *equity/accountability subcommittee* is charged with designing the performance measurement and reward system(s) to make sure that the organization is accountable to key stakeholders. Accountability to Scanlon practitioners means balancing the needs of all organizational stakeholders, building *valid and reliable measures* of organizational performance, and taking responsibility for that organizational performance.

The idea that companies must focus on multiple stakeholders instead of just the stockholders is still not universally accepted. One business writer wrote about "stakeholder folly" when describing a public Scanlon company's efforts to balance the needs of multiple stakeholders. His view, shared by many business writers, was that a company does best when it focuses exclusively on the needs of the stockholders. Yet this is a simplistic view of business. It begins with employees who care about their company and the work they do. This drives employees to meet the needs of customers. Customers shop where their needs are met. When satisfied customers buy products and services, the investor makes more money.

Kotter and Heskett (1992, p. 11) contend that

> Corporate Culture can have a significant impact on a firm's long-term economic performance. . . . cultures that emphasized all the key managerial constituencies (customers, stockholders, and employees) and leadership from managers at all levels outperformed firms that did not have those cultural traits by a huge margin. Over an eleven year period, the former increased revenues by an average of 682 percent versus 166 percent for the latter, expanded their work forces by 282 percent versus 36 percent, grew their stock prices by 901 percent versus 74 percent and improved their net incomes by 756 percent versus 1 percent.

The research is clear: investors who wish to maximize their investment must support employees so that employees can create products or services of value for customers.

When organizations are performing and customer and investor needs are being met, employees naturally expect to be treated fairly and to share in the gains (i.e., gain-sharing formula). Financial and compensation professionals are usually appointed to serve on the equity team, along with a cross section of elected employees, to make sure that the system is fair, economically viable, and meets the requirements of all wage and hour laws.

Early Scanlon plans often used a ratio of labor costs to sales as a measure of gains. As the cost of labor was reduced below a historical baseline, gains were shared between the employees and the company. Joe Scanlon used this approach not because he believed that it was the only approach, but because it was easy for the average employee to understand and implement.

The labor-to-sales formula stuck, and today this remains the most misunderstood part of the Scanlon plan, with many authors claiming that the formula *is* the Scanlon plan. Like the crow, they have made a serious mistake. Scanlon plans are created with every type of formula imaginable. Profit sharing and economic value added (EVA) are popular financial formulas. Scrap reduction, safety, and quality measures are popular operational measures. The formula is limited only by the equity team's imagination and creativity. The key to a successful formula is twofold: employees must be able to understand how it will enable them to increase performance (as measured by the formula), and they must believe in its intrinsic fairness.

There are countless books and articles available for the compensation professional on how to design bonus systems, but very little has been written about why they should create an equity system instead. Incentive systems focus on the dollars employees can earn, whereas an equity system focuses of the relationship among investors, customers, and employees. Each of these important stakeholders must benefit from the program.

The identity principle requires that Scanlon organizations share both good and bad information. Scanlon employees understand that in order to survive, their companies need customers and investors. They understand that sometimes in the life of an organization everyone may be called on to make sacrifices. Scanlon organizations have had to lay off employees, eliminate bonuses, require transfers, outsource, and so on to meet the needs of their customers and investors. More often than not, these sacrifices are made participatively and cooperatively because Scanlon employees know why the sacrifices are needed (identity), are involved in creating solutions to the problems (participation), and trust that they will be treated fairly (equity).

During a time when Beth Israel Hospital was struggling economically, employees participated by donating their own blood. Each donation helped the hospital save $200. The aggregate savings prevented layoffs. Employees at Spring Engineering gave up their bonuses so that they could save two jobs during a downturn in their business. Faced with huge deficits during a business downturn, Scanlon employees at Herman Miller offered millions of dollars of cost-saving suggestions. Donnelly Mirror (Magna) employees found ways to save a million dollars during a business downturn through their active involvement in the job elimination process, and their acceptance of the suspension of bonus payments.

The *competence/commitment subcommittee* is responsible for ensuring that all employees have the means for improving personally, professionally, and organizationally. In smaller organizations, the task may be as simple as designating core training competencies and documenting how to obtain them. In larger organizations, it could be as complicated as creating a corporate university. Most often the task requires identifying available training resources and encouraging employees to use them. It also may involve developing a system to provide accurate and timely feedback to enhance what employees have learned from the work experience.

Scanlon practitioners believe that increasing personal competency ultimately benefits their organizations. Atlantic Automotive found that among its minority employees, very few were homeowners (Scott, Shivers, Bishop, and Cerra, 2004). The controller provided free classes after work on personal financial management. He then helped the employees complete mortgage applications with the local bank. The increased understanding of business realities (i.e., investors) had a sizable side benefit of dramatically increasing home ownership among hourly employees.

Minutes from subcommittee meetings are shared throughout the organization while the design team works to create the plan. The organization follows the debates as the plan takes form. This part of the Scanlon implementation process requires communication, facilitation, and leadership skills.

Once the draft plan is completed, it is taken back to the organization, where a secret ballot determines if employees are agreeable to a one to two trial implementation period. The trial period allows those with doubts to test the system before granting their full support. It also allows the design team to test their systems to discover what works and what does not. At the end of the trial period, the design team makes any necessary changes, and the plan is submitted for a final vote. In most Scanlon companies, the Scanlon plan then becomes a way of life, and the plan is not subjected to additional votes. Some Scanlon organizations will continue to vote and renew their plans when major changes occur or after a certain number of years have passed.

Although this implementation process seems long and complex, experience demonstrates that long-term success of the plan is enhanced with this process. Furthermore, productivity improvement begins to appear during the development of the plan as employees better understand how the business operates and become more engaged.

## Scanlon Servant Leadership

It takes an unusual leader to practice the Scanlon principles and processes. These leaders must be dedicated to developing others. They must be willing to share information and power. They must trust others. Douglas McGregor identified them as "theory Y" leaders. The great Scanlon leader and best-selling author Max DePree wrote in *Leadership as an Art* that "[t]he first responsibility of a leader is to define reality. The last is to say thank you. In between the two, the leader must become a servant and a debtor."[8]

Today many leaders inspire to be "servant leaders," as popularized by Max DePree, Robert Greenleaf, and Larry Spears. The Scanlon plan provides a proven method for servant leaders seeking to create high-performance cultures. In sum, one might say that Scanlon considers human resources an investment to optimize not a cost to minimize.

## Resources and Support

Anyone can use the Scanlon name, principles, and implementation process without paying royalties or seeking permission. A tremendous amount of Scanlon-related information is available at no cost at www.EPIC-Organizations.com. The site contains links to videos and podcasts. It also contains free downloadable articles and essays. *Scanlon EPIC Leadership: Where the Best Ideas Come Together* (Davis and Speers, 2014) is the best anthology of modern Scanlon practice. Dr. Frost's book (1996), *Changing Forever: The Well-Kept Secret of America's Leading Companies*, remains a definitive book on the Scanlon principles and road map process.

## Notes

1. J. McAdams and E. Hawk. *Organizational Performance and Rewards: 663 Experiences in Making the Link.* American Compensation Association and Maritz, Inc., Scottsdale, AZ, 1994; and J. J. McAdams. "Research from the Trenches: Making Incentives Work." Presentation at the Scanlon Plan Associates Incentive Systems for Effective Organizations Conference, Chicago, October 6–7, 1998.
2. Edward Lawler. *The Ultimate Advantage.* Jossey-Bass, New York, 1992.
3. Gallup, "State of American Workplace: Employee Engagement Insights for U.S. Business Leaders," Washington, DC, 2013.
4. Jerry McAdams. "Consortium for Alternative Reward Strategies Research Study IV," 1997. A synopsis is available at http://compforce.typepad.com/compensation_force/2007/05/lessons_from_ca.html
5. Carl Frost, personal correspondence, 2013.
6. "The Scanlon Plan," *Time*, September 26, 1955.
7. P. Davis and L. Spears (eds.), *Scanlon EPIC Leadership: Where the Best Ideas Come Together.* Scanlon Foundation, Houston, TX, 2008.
8. Max De Pree, *Leadership as an Art*, revised ed., Crown Publishing, New York, 2004.

## References

Anonymous. 1955. "The Scanlon Plan." *Time*, September 26, 1955, pp. 88–90.

Branham, L. 2005. *The 7 Hidden Reasons Employees Leave.* AMACOM, New York.

Davis, P., and L. Spears, eds. 2014. *Scanlon EPIC Leadership: Where the Best Ideas Come Together.* Scanlon Foundation, Houston, TX.

Davis, P. 2000. *Exploring Scanlon Handout.* Scanlon Leadership Network, East Lansing, MI.

Dennison, D. 1990. *Corporate Culture and Organizational Effectiveness.* Wiley, New York.

Frost, C. F. 1996. *Changing Forever: The Well-Kept Secret of America's Leading Companies.* Michigan State University Press, Lansing, MI.

Frost, C. F., J. H. Wakely, and R. A. Ruh. 1974. *The Scanlon Plan for Organizational Development: Identity, Participation and Equity.* Michigan State University Press, Lansing, MI.

Gallup. 2013. "State of American Workplace: Employee Engagement Insights for U.S. Business Leaders," Washington, DC.

Gerhardt, B., S. L. Rynes, and I. S. Fulmer. 2009. "Pay and Performance: Individuals, Groups, and Executives." *Academy of Management Annals* 3(1):207–271.

Hausknecht, J. P., J. Rodda, and M. J. Howard. 2009. "Targeted Employee Retention: Performance-Based and Job-Related Difference in Reported Reasons for Staying." *Human Resource Management* 48(2):269–288.

Kotter, J., and J. Heskett. 1992. *Corporate Culture and Performance.* Free Press, New York.

Lawler, E. 1992. *The Ultimate Advantage.* Jossey-Bass, San Francisco.

Ledford, G. E., and J. L. Allen. 2012. "Managing Unit Incentives from the Corporate Level." *WorldatWork Journal* 21(2):8–21.

Lewis, D. 1992. At Beth Israel, Workers' Ideas Count for Plenty." *Boston Sunday Globe*, March 1, 1992.

McAdams, J. 1993. "Scanlon Leadership Network Equity Forum." Grand Rapids, MI.

McAdams, J., and E. Hawk. 1994. *Organizational Performance and Rewards: 663 Experiences in Making the Link*. American Compensation Association and Maritz, Inc., Madison, WI.

McAdams, J. 1998. "Research from the Trenches: Making Incentives Work." Presentation at the Scanlon Plan Associates Incentive Systems for Effective Organizations Conference, Chicago, IL, October 6–7, 1998.

McGregor, Douglas. 1960. *The Human Side of Enterprise.* McGraw-Hill, New York.

Scanlon, Joseph. 1941–1945. *The Joseph Scanlon Papers.* United Steelworkers of America, Rolls 1550 and 1551, Pennsylvania State University Historical Collection and Labor Archives, University Park, PA.

Schuster, M. H. 1984. *Union-Management Cooperation: Structure, Process and Impact.* Upjohn Institute for Employment Research, Kalamazoo, MI.

Scott, D., P. Davis, and C. Cockburn. 2007. "Scanlon Principles and Processes: Building Excellence at Watermark Credit Union." *WorldatWork Journal* 16(1):29–37.

Scott, K. D., J. Floyd, J. W. Bishop, and P. G. Benson. 2002. "The Impact of the Scanlon Plan on Retail Store Performance." *WorldatWork Journal* 11(3):25–31.

Scott, K. D., G. Shivers, J. W. Bishop, and V. A. Cerra. 2004. Building a Company Culture that Drives Performance: A Case Study." *WorldatWork Journal* 13(1):46–54.

Shivers, G., and K. D. Scott. 2003. "Gainsharing and EVA: The United States Postal Service Experience." *WorldatWork Journal* 12(1):21–30.

# PART IV

# EXECUTIVE COMPENSATION

# 21

# Formulating and Implementing an Executive Compensation Strategy

TED BUYNISKI

*Radford, an Aon Hewitt Company*

The last five years have brought significant changes in the way companies structure their executive compensation strategies. Although some of these changes have been positive, they have been driven largely by external influences that do not necessarily support company performance, which should be the overarching objective of a compensation strategy.

The external influences exerting pressure on executive compensation include

- The regularity of changing policies from the institutional investor advisors

- The degree to which institutional investors have outsourced research for their proxy voting to advisors such as Institutional Shareholder Services (ISS) and Glass Lewis, encouraging a "punch list" approach to executive compensation

- The continuing impact of the Dodd-Frank Act on the increasing density of proxy disclosures

- The focus on "say on pay," including the "unimplemented" portions (CEO pay ratio, clawbacks, etc.)

- The "usual suspects" in the media who fan the flames of the inequality debate

For example, on average, more than a third of companies' proxy disclosures are devoted to reviewing the compensation of a mere handful of employees. Half of Intel's 2014 proxy disclosure is devoted to reviewing the compensation of seven employees. For General Electric, 22 pages of the 55-page proxy disclosure are devoted to executive compensation review.

As a result, we are increasingly seeing the compensation equivalent of "teaching to the test." Companies are increasingly standardizing both the structure and metrics of their compensation programs to address these influences on pay. The near death of stock options (despite the fact that they are a highly efficient and effective means of linking employee and shareholder interests in the appropriate circumstances), the diminished ability of boards to account for unusual circumstances, and the limited range of solutions companies can use to address their business cycles are all outcomes of the move toward compensation structures in an effort to juggle the pressures of an increasingly complex and unbalanced executive compensation landscape.

At its best, executive compensation strategy should establish goals for executives that specifically drive performance and reflect the company-specific definition of *winning* and use the most effective compensation tools to achieve that goal. Given the mix of external factors and the heightened scrutiny of executive pay, it is more critical than ever that companies give clear, concise context to their executive compensation programs.

- *What* are we paying executives to do?
- *How* do we determine which compensation vehicles will be used?
- *What* will be the right mix of compensation across the defined vehicles?
- *How much* will we pay them?
- *What* will the impact be for different levels of performance?
- *When* will we pay them?
- *Who* is an executive?

This chapter will address each of these key issues in turn.

As we know, executive compensation design takes place not in isolation but surrounded by a ring of competing interest groups, each with different though sometimes overlapping agendas. *Executives* focus on whether the strategy provides them with the opportunity to build their wealth and careers better than competing offers. *Shareholders* are concerned with whether they are getting sufficient "bang for the buck" in terms of pay for performance, how much their executives are costing them, and ultimately, their return on investment (ROI). *Regulators* from the Securities and Exchange Commission (SEC) to the stock exchanges are increasingly requiring additional procedural safeguards and disclosures. Finally, *boards of directors* have to balance the needs of all these parties.

Within this context, the *compensation committee* is charged with developing an executive compensation strategy that meets the company's needs *and* satisfies all the other constituencies. So how should a compensation committee go about establishing a company's executive compensation strategy?

## Step 1. Know the Goal

The first question the compensation committee must answer is "How do we know we're winning?" The company's *business strategy* must drive its executive compensation strategy. There will be significant differences in what a company will want to measure and reward depending on the goals of the organization. Figure 21.1 matches company business objectives with a variety of performance metrics and their importance.

The choice of company goals must also reflect the stage of the company's life cycle. Is it a fledgling pre-IPO biotech company focused on raising money and pushing a new drug through the FDA approval process, or is it a heavy equipment company in a mature

| Business Objective | Cash Flow | TSR | Row/ROI | ROIC | ROA | Stock Price | EPS | Net Income/Earnings | Op Income | Revenue |
|---|---|---|---|---|---|---|---|---|---|---|
| Increase revenues/sales | ○ | ○ | ○ | ○ | ○ | ○ | ○ | ◐ | ● | ● |
| Manage cash outflow | ● | ○ | ○ | ○ | ○ | ○ | ○ | ● | ◐ | ○ |
| Generate cash | ● | ○ | ○ | ○ | ○ | ○ | ○ | ● | ◐ | ◐ |
| Increase income/earnings | ● | ○ | ◐ | ◐ | ● | ○ | ● | ● | ● | ◐ |
| Increase margins/control costs | ● | ○ | ◐ | ◐ | ● | ○ | ○ | ● | ● | ○ |
| Increase stock price | ○ | ● | ○ | ○ | ○ | ● | ● | ◐ | ○ | ○ |
| Increase shareholder return | ◐ | ● | ◐ | ○ | ○ | ● | ● | ○ | ○ | ○ |
| Promote new business investment | ◐ | ○ | ● | ● | ● | ○ | ○ | ◐ | ○ | ◐ |
| Utilize assets efficiently | ○ | ○ | ● | ● | ● | ○ | ○ | ○ | ○ | ○ |
|  | ● | ◐ | ○ | ● | ● | ● | ○ | ○ | ○ | ○ |

Figure 21.1  Business objectives and performance metrics.

industry focused on maximizing its cash flow? These are key questions for determining company goals and driving toward a fitting business strategy.

As we discussed earlier in this chapter, companies still have to be mindful of the outside influences as well. Under the constraints of Dodd-Frank, companies are required to disclose their performance targets and their performance against those targets. The institutional advisor community also imposes constraints on companies, wanting to see multiple metrics without duplication between annual and longer-term performance.

## Step 2. Know the Tools

Different elements of executive compensation become more or less attractive at any given time due to changes in taxes, accounting rules, institutional concerns, or all of the above. Things like the decline in deferred compensation post-409A, the expensing of stock options post-FAS123R, the elimination of pensions for directors, and the almost complete disappearance of perquisites from public companies in the past decade create issues for companies as they navigate the governance environment and solidify their compensation practices. But even with these additional factors acting on executive pay, the tools companies can apply have remained constant: salaries, short-term cash incentives, long-term cash and equity incentives, benefits, and perquisites. Each of these compensation tools has advantages and drawbacks from the perspective of how they affect the executive. Furthermore, they differ in how they affect the company from the standpoint of cash flow, tax and accounting consequences, and perhaps even more so from the perceptions of shareholders, the public, and the executives themselves.

Figure 21.2 lists each compensation vehicle and its effectiveness in achieving basic human resources goals.

| Compensation Vehicle | Attract | Motivate | Retain |
|---|---|---|---|
| Salary | | | |
| Annual Bonus | | | |
| Long-Term Cash | | | |
| Options | | | |
| Restricted Stock | | | |
| Performance Shares | | | |
| Qualified Benefits | | | |
| Executive Benefits | | | |
| Perquisites | | | |

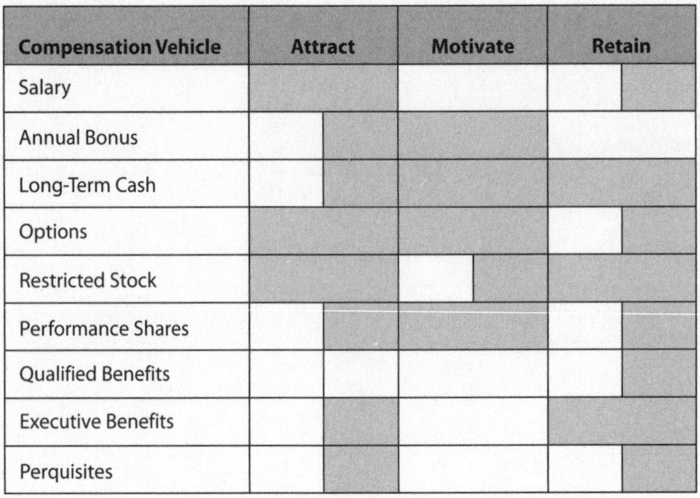

**Figure 21.2  Effectiveness of compensation vehicles in achieving basic human resources goals.**

Organizations typically apply compensation vehicles based on their  their stage of institutional life cycle. Table 21.1 describes the importance of each pay element in each life cycle stage.

| Pay Element | Life Cycle Stage | | | |
|---|---|---|---|---|
| | Startup | Growth | Mature | Declining |
| **Salary** | Low | Competitive | Competitive/ High | High |
| **Annual Bonus** | Low | Competitive/ High | Competitive | Low |
| **Long-Term Incentives** | High | Competitive/ High | Competitive | Low |
| **Form of LTI** | Options | Options/Performance Shares | Performance Shares/ Restricted Stock/Cash | Restricted Stock/ Cash |
| **Qualified Benefits** | Low | Competitive | Competitive | High |
| **Executive Benefits** | None | Low | Competitive | High |
| **Perquisites** | None | Low | Competitive | High |
| Source: Radford. | | | | |

**Table 21.1   Importance of Pay Element by Stage of Life Cycle**

It should be noted these are general tendencies reflecting competitive market practices rather than "must follow" rules. For example, a startup that is throwing off significant cash flow might have competitive bonuses, while a declining company may, as part of a turnaround strategy, look at cutting fixed compensation (salary, benefits, perquisites) to fuel the turnaround.

## Step 3. Know the Market

"Knowing the market" really means three things. First, you have to know who your "market" is from several perspectives. Who do we compete with for talent? Who do we compete with for business? Who is our peer group for proxy purposes? Although these groups may well overlap, they are by no means identical. Second, you need to know where to position your pay relative to the market—not only how much the company will pay, but how to balance the compensation vehicles relative to those peers. Finally, you need to know the actual dollar values paid to peer executives in the market. Once you have the numbers, then you can begin the real work of determining how much to actually pay your executives.

> *Choosing a peer group.* Choosing a peer group is one of the most contentious discussions taking place in compensation committee meetings today. Historically, management would come to the compensation committee with a list of companies that loosely consisted of those companies management recruited from, lost people to, or competed with on product. Usually, though not always, the companies on that list would be roughly similar in size. Now, with the advent of the new proxy disclosure rules, companies are applying significantly more rigor to identifying their proposed peers. Additionally, with the institutional investor advisors now creating their own notions of who the company should have as a peer group, companies have to apply multiple screens to the peer-selection process, including:

- Similar size—For better or worse, the strongest correlation in the marketplace remains between revenue and salary. However, it is going beyond revenue, with companies needing to consider number of employees, market capitalization, profitability, assets, and other metrics.

- Similar business—As the markets have evolved, there are markedly different pay structures for some industries (e.g., high technology, financial services, regulated utilities).

- Similar economics—Looking at performance, the analysis might include a review of margins, multiyear revenue growth and even the underlying strategy and value proposition (e.g., value-added reseller vs. fully integrated manufacturer).

- Staff sourcing—From where does the company recruit and to whom does the company lose executive talent? This factor must be used cautiously, however. It is too easy to say "we recruit from substantially larger companies," even though the company is *not* recruiting laterally (e.g., a company with $200 million in revenue may recruit a #2 financial person from a $2 billion company to be their CFO, but they will not be recruiting the $2 billion company's CFO to be their own).

- Additional factors—When the institutional advisors opine, they also give heavy weight to such factors as GICS code (rather than doing the deeper dive to base the group on the specifics of a company's business and economics) and whom the company's peers identify as their peers.

Naturally, there are tradeoffs to be made. For many companies, it is not possible to find a sufficient number of companies of the same size, in the same business, with the same strategy to create a meaningful 15–20 company peer group. Then judgment must be applied to determine the criticality of each of the criteria, and whether finding a meaningful number of companies take the "market" too far away from its core.

*Positioning.* The media has made much of the "Lake Woebegone Syndrome" of executive pay, decrying the use of competitive market data for determining pay. However, the alternative is to shoot in the dark and try and make compensation decisions without any information. The issue isn't the market data, but how companies choose to apply it—companies still need to determine where, in aggregate and in component, they will pay their executives relative to the market. Generally, there are strategic and market pressures that may suggest paying above or below the prevailing pay market for executives, just as for any other employee. Table 21.2 outlines rationales for determining an executive pay market level.

| Positioning | Rationales |
|---|---|
| Below Market | • Affordability—Company has insufficient cash/equity to pay at the market |
| | • Company tends to be smaller than most of its peers |
| | • Company is using other means of attracting and retaining employees (e.g., location, working conditions, corporate mission, etc.) |
| | • Other pay elements are targeted above market so that total is in line with the market |
| | • Lack of competition for employees |
| | • Low turnover, so compensation isn't an issue |
| | • Local market conditions (e.g., exceptionally low cost of living, or depressed conditions making employer the "best game in town") |
| | • Low performance expectations |
| Above Market | • Need to attract/retain executives in a competitive market |
| | • Company tends to be larger than its peers |
| | • Pay is the primary motivator in the company's philosophy (e.g., a "no frills" environment) |
| | • Difficult market conditions (e.g., turnaround) |
| | • High turnover |
| | • Compensates for other elements of pay that are positioned below market |
| | • High performance expectations |
| Source: Radford. | |

Table 21.2  Rationales for the Selection of Pay Market Level

The key is that compensation committees should not simply default to paying "market median." If all companies were alike, everyone could simply set their targets at median and be done. The potential flaw against which compensation committees must steel themselves is the notion that we must set *target pay at least* at market levels. This leads to a natural escalation in compensation, generally outstripping the natural inflation we see in wages overall.

*Data.* Finally, once the company determines whom the peers are and where to pay against those peers, only then is the actual data discussion relevant. The key becomes finding the "best" data, of which there are essentially two sets of sources:

- **Public Data.** Sources that essentially trace back to companies' public filings with the SEC or other regulatory bodies. This includes proxy filings as well as companies that collect and disseminate publicly available information. With the new proxy disclosure rules, public data has become a much richer source of information, both in terms of the quality of the compensation data and the company practices that generate pay. However, there are three critical limits to using only public data. First, it is generally available only for the "top 5" executives. Second, while some jobs are relatively standardized (i.e., comparing Chief Executive Officers across companies will be relatively straightforward), other jobs may not be so easy to compare (i.e., is a "Senior Vice President, Global Solutions Marketing Officer" equivalent to a "President Sales, Marketing and Institutional Business Development"?). Finally, proxy data is always retrospective—it looks at what was done for the last year, not what is being done in the current year.

- **Survey Data.** Sources that collect confidential data from participants and then analyze and package that data for the use of the participants (and sometimes others who can buy the data). These sources address the drawbacks of public data. First, depending on the survey, many more positions are reviewed than are available in public data. Second, because most surveys include job descriptions, and means of adjusting data for jobs that do not specifically fit the descriptions, they can provide a better "apples to apples" comparison for most jobs. Finally, since the data in many surveys is collected more frequently, it is generally "fresher." Despite these advantages, companies need to exercise caution in using survey data. Not all surveys are created equal. Care needs to be taken to ensure that the companies in the survey reflect the peers, or potential peers, of the company. Second, there needs to be processes in place to ensure that the survey results accurately reflect the market. There must be enough companies involved for the data to be robust, and some "data scrubbing" must be done to make sure the data submitted is accurate and meaningful. This can be especially troubling with some of the online survey engines, where there is no quality control of data entered by individuals accessing the website. Third, and related, is the question of the objectivity of the survey: does the sponsor of the survey have an agenda that might color the results? Another potential issue with survey data is availability—some surveys are available only to participants, and even participation is on an "invitation only" basis ("club surveys").

Nonetheless, a judicious use of *both* sources of data is important to ensure that the compensation committee has a well-rounded view of the competitive market. This analysis will provide a baseline. The committee can then determine, based on the relevant market and desired positioning versus that market, where they wish to position target pay for target performance. The next step is to determine the opportunities when performance doesn't exactly match plan.

Ultimately, though, the committee must also remember that the numbers—the peer group, the positioning, and the compensation data—are only the *beginning* of the discussion, not the end.

## Step 4. Planning for Contingencies

A crucial part of executive compensation strategy is planning for what *could* happen, either outperforming or underperforming expectations, or something completely unexpected happening in the company, the industry, or the economy as a whole.

In terms of executive compensation strategy this means that programs must be able to address not just the expected scenarios, but *all* scenarios. For example, one increasingly common means of providing long-term incentives is to make performance-based share grants, with the performance measure based on how a company performs relative to its peers. In the "down" leg of a cyclic market, this can incentivize executives to perform superior "damage control," minimizing the impact of the negative part of the cycle. However, if plans are not properly structured, it can lead to counterintuitive results that reflect poorly on the company. For example, one company in the semiconductor space based its annual bonus solely on performance versus peers. In one year, due to strong inventory management and cost cutting, they saw their performance rise to above the 75th percentile versus their peers, which generated a payout of almost 200 percent of target. From the perspective of the primary objective—getting executives to focus on "damage control"—the plan worked. However, at the same time, the company was losing money, laying off more than 10 percent of its workforce and suffering a 50 percent decline in its stock price. This created a public relations conundrum that resulted in the compensation committee deferring part of the bonuses and converting them to restricted stock, both to minimize the economic impact and defuse employee and shareholder criticism.

Ideally, planning for contingencies needs to take into account a number of factors, including:

- The likelihood of *not* hitting target—How good is the management at setting goals? How much of a company's performance is subject to the control of management and how much to the vagaries of the marketplace?

- How much of the business has a "tail"—is the company fulfilling multiyear agreements, or is it more akin to starting each year at step 1?

- At what point do results, either good or bad, move from the realm of good (or bad) execution to "luck" or "Act of God"?

Essentially, these answers will facilitate both the leverage of plans (e.g., thresholds and maximums) and the vehicles selected (e.g., stock options are more volatile than restricted stock, which, in turn, are more volatile than long-term cash). Finally, the committee, in its planning, must always build in contingency plans to take into account unexpected events like acquisitions or changes in laws and regulations.

Historically, compensation committees had broad discretion in these matters. If the actual performance were outside the bounds of expectations and planning, the committee could adjust compensation down if the company scored a "bluebird" or up if the economy tanked but management did an exceptional job of controlling the decline. Now, taking these actions, which may be appropriate in the context of the business, are subject to limits, and positive discretion for the senior-most executives could cost the company tax deductions under IRC 162(m), as well as potential shareholder kickback (for example, ISS looks on positive discretion built into compensation plans as a poor pay practice).

## Step 5: How Does Pay Relate to Performance?

Ultimately, all the planning comes together here: defining performance, choosing among the different executive compensation tools, examining the market, and planning for a range of performance.

In an ideal world, the results will be that pay and performance align, whether for good or bad. See Figure 21.3.

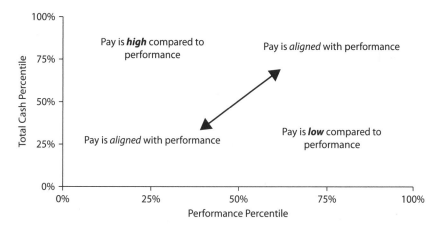

**Figure 21.3  Total cash versus performance.**

The reality, of course, is often different because of what we noted earlier: winning is subject to definition, and different companies may have different notions of what constitutes winning. To make matters more complex, the institutional shareholder advisors tend to have a simplistic view where all that matters is year-to-year or, at most, three-year stock performance, either relative to others or in absolute terms. While stock price appreciation should be the long-term goal of the company, it is not necessarily something that is directly in the control of executives. In many cases, this has caused companies to replace long-term *incentive* plans, where the payment of awards is contingent on predefined internal, controllable goals, with long-term *bonus* plans, where there is not a predefined level of performance, but rather an after-the-fact reward based on a *post hoc* review of performance. While this is not necessarily a problem, in many instances it requires a reeducation of executives with regard to their performance goals and what they are paid for.

## Step 6: How Long Is the Performance Period?

In addition to determining the needed *level* of performance, companies also need to determine over what period of time performance is measured. Performance can be measured annually, multiyearly, or less than once a year. The performance period needs to reflect three different factors. First, what is the business cycle for the measurement? Is it tied to annual budgeting, a shorter sales cycle, or a longer strategic planning period? Second, how does the opportunity link to the attraction, retention, and motivation goals noted earlier? Finally, as always, there are the external factors. Institutions want to see multiyear performance periods for stock-based plans that look at more than one-year *performance,* regardless of multiyear *vesting.*

## Step 7: Who Is an Executive?

The last element of the strategy is to determine who is an executive for purposes of inclusion in the executive compensation plans. For the top, it is a relatively easy decision. Obviously the CEO, CFO, or anyone with a "CxO" designation is classified as an executive, but ultimately, there is a boundary where the compensation committee's scope of authority fades and where the employees' role turns from planning to executing the plans of others. Some companies draw this line between "Directors" and "Vice Presidents." Others may draw the distinction between different types of Vice Presidents (especially those with large, client-facing sales forces), and still others between Vice Presidents and Senior Vice Presidents. Regardless of where the line is drawn, there are a number of issues that are highlighted by this differentiation, for example:

- Participation in compensation plans—Many companies will provide different annual or long-term incentives for executives.

- Benefit and perquisite participation—Generally participation in "executive" benefits and receipt of perks (or different levels of perks) hinges on being an "executive."

- Ownership requirements—With many companies requiring executives to own stock equal to one, two, or more times their salaries, there are downsides and benefits to being considered an executive. After all, in addition to requiring that the executive hold some multiple of shares, all the executive's *unvested* equity is contingent on company performance, as well as their underlying job.

## Conclusions

Ultimately, despite the pressures toward uniformity in plan design and strategy, one size does *not* fit all. There is no single answer, no silver bullet to implement an executive compensation strategy. Rather companies need to focus on the business drivers:

- The metrics that reflect the success of the business at any given point in its life cycle

- The market for executive talent

- The level of risk tolerance of both the company and the executive

- The timing and level of performance

- The company's ultimate performance

At the end of the process, if the compensation committee can say they have addressed all these issues and are comfortable with the outcomes, they've done their job and discharged their duties.

# 22

# Designing and Executing Long-Term Incentive Plans

Ben Burney

*Exequity, LLP*

Bill Gentry

*Grant Thornton LLP*

This chapter will help readers design and execute long-term incentive plans. It covers six areas of critical information that will enable them to accomplish this task. The six areas are:

- Types of long-term incentives

- Deriving the intrinsic value of the most common long-term incentives

- Introduction to approaches to awarding long-term incentives

- Overview of performance plans and their most common structures

- Overview of the most prevalent performance plan metric—relative total shareholder return

- Key questions when considering alternatives for long-term incentive design

Long-term incentive compensation (LTI compensation) serves as the backbone of contemporary incentive design and retention strategy. In its most basic form, LTI compensation provides recipients with the opportunity to earn additional compensation based on the attainment of predefined multiyear service and/or performance conditions. The primary objectives of LTI compensation are to align the interests of employees with those of shareholders, to promote employee retention, and to offer long-term prospects for wealth accumulation based on company performance. Each of these objectives serves the interests of the company by rewarding employees for service and performance intended as well as the employee for contributing to long-term company performance and shareholder value creation.

## Origins

The phenomenon of LTI compensation is long standing. Various forms of LTI compensation opportunities were awarded to executives through multiyear profit-sharing arrangements and periodic awards of stock and stock options throughout the post–World War II period up to 1970s, with values increasing modestly over each successive decade. In the early 1980s and coinciding with a long-term bull market, the frequency with which LTI compensation opportunities were afforded to executives increased so as to become less periodic rather than an annual part of the compensation process.

Over the 1980s and 1990s, stock options continued to gain in popularity as companies found various advantages to deliver pay through equity vehicles over cash. By the mid-2000s, it became much more common than not for senior executives to receive a significant portion of their annual compensation in the form of LTI compensation. Today, practices reflect a balanced approach, typically consisting of multiple LTI compensation vehicles delivered annually. Use of multiple vehicles reflects the complexity of the objectives that LTI compensation is intended to solve and the recognition that no single LTI compensation vehicle addresses all objectives.

The rise of LTI compensation as the primary component of compensation for senior executives from the 1980s until today may have roots in the early 1970s because the downstream implications of the doctrine espoused by Nobel Prize–winning economist and professor Milton Friedman make a strong case for LTI compensation. In a seminal—and controversial—*New York Times* article published in September 1970 entitled, "The Social Responsibility of Business Is to Increase Its Profits," Dr. Friedman stated that the responsibility of the corporate executive as "employee[s] of the owners of the business" is "to conduct the business in accordance with [the owners'] desires, which generally will be to make as much money as possible." In other words, the corporate executive is an *agent* of the owner (in other settings, such as discussions of principal/agent theory, the owner may be referred to as the principal). The owner is motivated to hire agents who will increase profits and therefore increase the value of the business, which benefits the owner. In the absence of LTI compensation, the agent may seek short-term gains (which also may incentivize excessive short-term risk taking). On the agent's receipt of an equity interest via LTI compensation, the agent's interests become more aligned with the owner's because both have the same goal: an increase in enterprise value by way of an increase in corporate profits. LTI compensation aligns the interests of owners and agents by rewarding value creation in a meaningful way.

## Types of Long-Term Incentives

LTI compensation is typically delivered in cash and/or equity-based vehicles that are usually described in three ways: share-appreciation vehicles, full-value-share vehicles, and performance-plan vehicles. Share-appreciation vehicles are denominated in share options (i.e., stock options, a type of equity derivative). Full-value-share vehicles are denominated in shares (or share units linked to share price) such as restricted stock. Performance-plan vehicles are often denominated in shares (i.e., linked to share price) but also may be denominated in cash units (i.e., not linked to company share price).

# Key Characteristics of LTI Compensation Vehicles

## Share-Appreciation Vehicles

- Most common share-appreciation vehicles are stock options or stock appreciation rights.

- They focus recipients on stock price by allowing option holders to purchase employer shares at a predetermined (exercise) price for a specified period of time (often as long as 10 years from the grant date).

- They generate value (ordinary income) for the option holder only if the employer's price per share of the underlying stock exceeds the exercise price if the option is exercised.

- They allow recipients to control the timing of exercise after the lapse of vesting requirements.

- They introduce market risk as an influencing factor in award outcomes because stock price performance reflects a broad array of considerations that might be unrelated to managerial effectiveness.

- They are structured as either a tax-advantaged incentive stock option (for the option holder if certain conditions are met) or as a nonqualified stock option (proceeds are fully taxable to the option holder at exercise; the employer receives a deduction equal to the option holder's ordinary gain).

- They result in a nonreversible accounting expense that is recognized over the option vesting period using an option pricing model (i.e., Black-Scholes) or other approved methodology.

- Stock-appreciation rights (SARs) serve as an alternative to stock options, allowing for cash or stock settlement and, if settled in cash, avoiding the dilution that results when stock options are exercised.

## Full-Value-Share Vehicles

- Most common full-value-share vehicles are restricted stock and restricted stock units (RSUs).

- They focus recipients on stock price because the award is valued in terms of the employer's stock.

- Restricted stock awards convey ownership at the grant date, providing voting and dividend rights.

- RSU awards convey ownership on the vesting date (no voting or dividend rights until restrictions lapse, but dividend-equivalent rights can be granted to replicate dividends).

- They prevent the sale or transfer of shares until lapse of the vesting restrictions.

- They allow for inclusion of performance-enhancing features, such as a reduction in or outright cancelation of the award arising from failure to achieve a predetermined performance goal at the end of the vesting period.

- They create ordinary income for the recipient on lapse of the vesting requirements and a corresponding tax deduction for the employer.

- They provide an opportunity for recipients to receive capital gains treatment on vested shares when the shares are eventually sold.

- They result in an expense based on the award's grant-date fair market value.

### Performance Plans

- They focus recipients on key financial, operating, or market-based goals over multi-year periods.

- They measure performance against absolute or relative performance standards.

- Performance-plan awards may be denominated in cash, shares, or stock options (often referred to as *performance units*, *performance shares*, and *performance stock options/SARs*, respectively), although most companies using performance plans chose share-based awards.

- Share-based performance plans typically are referred to as performance shares.

- They include other characteristics as discussed under "Performance Plans in Focus" below.

### Other LTI Compensation Vehicles

- *Restricted or long-term cash* provides companies with a retention mechanism during periods of share price uncertainty or other constraints. Except when used in a performance plan, long-term cash is rarely used by publicly traded U.S. companies.

- *Formula value shares* provide private companies and the divisions of larger parent organizations with an LTI compensation vehicle that rewards value creation defined using revenues, earnings, cash flow, or other valuation methodologies.

- *Phantom shares* are much like formula value shares except that the basis for valuation can be actual market value, allowing employers to grant LTI compensation when shares are unavailable or when ownership dilution is not feasible or desired. Common applications include LTI compensation awards and as a deferred compensation vehicle where the rate of return during the deferral period is determined by changes in employer stock price and, if applicable, dividend-equivalent payments.

## Calculating the Value of LTI Compensation Awards at Grant

Companies often determine the number of stock options, restricted shares, or performance-plan awards to grant based on a target value ascribed to each LTI compensation vehicle. The value may be determined based on the estimated accounting expense for each vehicle or other methodology with alternative valuation assumptions. The value-based approach simplifies the messaging to award recipients, who then may understand that the LTI compensation value delivered and mix of vehicles reflects the company's compensation philosophy and business goals. Alternatives include fixed-share guidelines, a percentage of company shares outstanding, or stock-incentive-plan shares available for future grant.

# Calculating the Value of LTI Compensation Awards at Settlement

- *Share-appreciation vehicles.* The difference between the exercise price (i.e., stock price at exercise) and the strike price (i.e., usually the stock price on date of grant) multiplied by number of stock options or SARs awarded.

- *Full-value-share vehicles.* The number of shares awarded multiplied by the stock price on vesting date.

- *Cash-based vehicles.* The per-unit value multiplied by the number of units.

Table 22.1 shows the value of three LTI compensation vehicles at differing share prices. In each case, we assume that a recipient is awarded $100 of LTI compensation value in either a share-appreciation vehicle (i.e., stock options), a full-value-share vehicle (i.e., restricted stock), or a long-term cash vehicle (i.e., restricted cash or the target value of a performance plan denominated in cash). Assuming poor stock price performance, the cash and full-value-share vehicles are preferable to stock options. Assuming strong stock price performance, the stock options may be advantageous. In this example, we first assume that four stock options are equivalent in value to one share of stock. In other words, the Black-Scholes (or other) stock option valuation is 25 percent of face such that to award the participant in stock options the equivalent value of one share of stock, the company would need to award four times the number of stock options. In the second scenario, we assume that two options are equivalent to one share of stock (50 percent of face). Depending on a company's market characteristics, the Black-Scholes formula will return differing stock option values. In general, "risky" (volatile) stocks are valued at higher percentages of face than less risky (less volatile) stocks because the Black-Scholes model ascribes a higher likelihood that the risky stocks will appreciate more than the less risky stocks. In this table, the "25 percent of face" example represents the less risky stock and the "50 percent of face" the "more risky" stock. The issue of market risk does not affect full-value-share vehicles or long-term cash vehicles because in each case their intrinsic values are not derived solely from price appreciation because both have tangible values at grant.

| Vehicle | Award Value | Grant Date Stock Price | Value per Option, Share, Unit | Options/ Shares/ Units Awarded (No.) | Intrinsic Value of LTI Award at Share Price of | | | | |
|---|---|---|---|---|---|---|---|---|---|
| | | | | | $5 | $10 | $15 | $20 | $40 |
| Share appreciation (less risky stock) | $100 | $10 | $2.5/option (25% of face) | 40 options | $0 | $0 | $200 | $400 | $1,200 |
| Share appreciation (more risky stock) | $100 | $10 | $5/option (50% of face) | 20 options | $0 | $0 | $100 | $200 | $600 |
| Full-value share | $100 | $10 | $10/share | 10 shares | $50 | $100 | $150 | $200 | $400 |
| Long-term cash | $100 | N/A | $1/unit | 100 units | $100 | $100 | $100 | $100 | $100 |

Table 22.1 Compensation Vehicles at Different Share Prices

## Approaches to Awarding LTI Compensation

Today's LTI compensation approaches are dominated by stock options, restricted stock, and performance shares. In each case, a strong majority of actively traded U.S. companies relies on one or more of these award types, reflecting a clear preference for a combination or portfolio of different LTI compensation awards working in tandem to address business and compensation objectives. In general, regardless of the type of LTI compensation award, vesting restrictions lapse over one to five years based on service or performance conditions. The heavy reliance on these vehicles ensures a strong linkage between LTI compensation outcomes and the market results of the employer's shares, which stock settlement further reinforces.

Performance shares are emerging as the LTI compensation vehicle of choice, with stock options and/or restricted stock continuing to play a supporting role given the unique attributes of each award type. For a company seeking to align financial or operating results more directly with employee pay, most LTI compensation value may be delivered in performance shares, with stock options or restricted stock of lesser value granted to provide additional stock-price leverage or holding power, respectively. Alternatively, a company seeking to align pay primarily with stock-price appreciation might choose to deliver the majority of the LTI compensation value in stock options. Restricted stock could be added to the mix to ensure that the new LTI compensation grant provides holding power. Finally, an employer might choose to emphasize restricted stock to retain and motivate talent during periods when establishing realistic multiyear performance goals is impractical, market conditions are highly unpredictable, or when confronted with corporate uncertainty.

Companies determine the mix of LTI compensation based on numerous factors, including business goals, long- and short-term growth prospects, and dilution concerns (among numerous others). Some companies choose to grant LTI compensation in a single vehicle, although in recent years a portfolio approach has become more common. Even when multiple LTI compensation vehicles are used, however, companies are often willing to demonstrate a preference for a specific LTI compensation vehicle, providing clarity of purpose, prioritization of performance goals, and the expectations of shareholders and proxy advisory firms. Today companies that change the mix of LTI compensation tend to prefer increases to the value devoted to performance plans over stock options and restricted stock.

To fully appreciate the role of performance plans, consider the CEOs of Standard and Poor's 500 Index (S&P 500) companies: more than half receive at least 50 percent of their total LTI compensation value in the form of performance plans, and more than 80 percent receive performance-plan awards (source: Exequity analysis of S&P 500 CEO compensation). Because performance plans often serve as the gateway to enhanced pay for performance, it is critical for practitioners to understand the basic tenants of common—and sound—performance-plan design.

## Performance Plans in Focus

Performance plans directly link compensation to achievement of multiyear financial and/ or market goals set by the company. These arrangements often rely on a range of performance outcomes to determine the extent that a target award is earned at the end of a predefined performance period. Since the award is typically settled in shares, the value to be realized by the recipient is a function of business and market results. Cash settlement provides a means to decouple award outcomes from market performance, conserve shares, and prevent dilution of ownership. Given the increasing emphasis of performance plans within LTI compensation strategies, most companies choose stock-settled awards to ensure that award outcomes reflect market results.

The ability to create an incentive that considers business and market results is a key and differentiating feature of performance plans. Shareholders benefit from all that superior corporate performance provides, with market results serving as the final arbiter of performance. Effective performance plans ensure that recipients benefit only to the extent that business and market results are positive. Misalignment between these two performance outcomes creates offsetting forces intended to ensure that the value ultimately realized is appropriate.

As mentioned earlier, performance-plan awards are typically denominated in shares, known as *performance shares* (or *performance-share units*), but they also may be denominated in *cash-based units*, sometimes referred to as *performance cash*, *long-term incentive plan cash*, or *performance units* (we will refer to dollar-denominated awards as *performance units* where one unit is equivalent to one dollar). Assuming target performance, the value of one performance share will follow the company's stock price, whereas the value of one dollar of performance units will remain constant.

The structure of the pay versus performance relationship in performance plans is similar to some annual bonus plans. Typically, performance-plan recipients are awarded a target value for future achievement of specified target goals. Performance achievements above target may result in enhanced awards, often with a payout multiple of up to (or in exceptional cases exceeding) 200 percent of the target number of shares or units. Poor performance may result in partial or total forfeiture of the award. Payouts for performance achievements falling in between specified levels are determined by linear interpolation. Performance levels below threshold generally result in total forfeiture of the award; there are no further award enhancements for performance levels above maximum (Table 22.2).

| Performance Level | Payout |
|---|---|
| Below threshold percent | 0% |
| Threshold | 50% |
| Target | 100% |
| Maximum percent | 200% |

**Table 22.2  Payouts and Performance Thresholds**

Annual grant cycles dominate the frequency at which new performance-plan opportunities are provided to recipients. Annual grant cycles mean that at any point in time multiple awards are outstanding. The resulting overlap of performance periods provides companies with an opportunity to align the goals embedded in each new award with goals reflective of corporate expectations or industry cycles, but goals rarely change after the awards are granted. The cumulative effect of overlapping cycles provides strong holding power and some degree of connectivity between different grant cycles, but it also introduces unwanted complexity if measures or goals change significantly from year to year. Most companies grant new performance plan awards with performance periods that coincide with the first year of the performance period for which the award applies.

When performance shares form the basis for the award, the intrinsic value of the performance-plan award will fluctuate based on both the achievement of the goal(s) as well as the company's share price. When awarded as performance units, the unit value does not fluctuate with the company's share price, only performance achievement. (Note that one hybrid design is denominated in cash units but is settled in stock at payout; another hybrid is denominated in shares but settled in cash. In either case, the performance share value will fluctuate with stock price and performance achievement regardless of settlement, and the performance unit will fluctuate based on achievement only.) Performance shares therefore offer recipients more leverage than performance units. Table 22.3 shows two performance-plan awards, one in performance shares and the other in performance units. Assuming payout at maximum, the share-based award offers additional upside at maximum performance based on share price. As share price decreases, so too does the potential award value, even at maximum performance.

| Performance-Plan Vehicle | Award Value | Share/Unit Value | Shares/Units Awarded (No.) | Maximum Value (200%) | | |
|---|---|---|---|---|---|---|
| | | | | $5/Share | $10/Share | $20/Share |
| Performance shares | $100 | $10/share | 10 shares | $100 | $200 | $400 |
| Performance units | $100 | $1/unit | 100 units | $200 | $200 | $200 |

Table 22.3   Comparison of Awards Under Performance Shares and Performance Units Plans

The performance metrics used in performance plans are generally financial or market measures. Common financial-plan metrics used in performance plans are profitability or growth measures (e.g., revenue growth, operating/net/other income growth, earnings per share) or return measures (e.g., return on invested capital). Company stock price also may be used as a performance hurdle. The process for selecting financial metrics and determining associated performance hurdles depends on a variety of factors, including business strategy and key financial metrics communicated to investors and Wall Street, among numerous other factors and considerations. However, many companies in a variety of industries may have difficulty determining reasonable long-term forecasts for a range of factors. Out of this uncertainty grew the rise of both relative financial performance measurement and relative market performance measurement.

The growing reliance on relative performance measures represents one of the most important developments in incentive design in the past 20 years. The challenge of setting realistic long-term goals was an early impetus for relative metrics. A second impetus that rapidly gained in importance and now dominates executive compensation discussions is the need for companies to clearly demonstrate that their pay is fully reflective of performance compared with a benchmark community of competing firms. Absolute performance measures—based purely on a company's performance in relation to budget or shareholder return—reflect one dimension of pay for performance. By incorporating relative performance features—those measuring and adjusting award outcomes based on performance relative to a benchmark community of peers or an index—into performance plans, awards can reflect a balanced view of performance so often preferred by shareholders.

Implementation of relative performance measures is a decision that companies should never take lightly. Any missteps or design flaws are difficult to reverse given the high appeal of relative performance measures to shareholders. The design decision process needs to consider the advantages and disadvantages of absolute and relative performance measures and their application to a company's unique circumstances (Tables 22.4 and 22.5).

| Advantages | Disadvantages |
| --- | --- |
| • Closely aligned with the business strategy | • Can be difficult to set goals |
| • Provides flexibility in measurement selection and goal targeting | • Easily manipulated |
| • Emphasizes business objectives during strategic transition or large, one-time goals | • No consideration of relative performance |
| • Provides line of sight | • Subject to criticism if excessive windfall or shortfall |

**Table 22.4 Advantages and Disadvantages of Using Absolute Performance Measures**

| Advantages | Disadvantages |
| --- | --- |
| • No goals to set | • No accountability for operating plans |
| • Minimizes ability to manipulate results | • May encourage complacency as long as at or above median of relative peer group |
| • Provides more objective standard of comparison | • May generate payouts even if internal performance goals are unmet |
| • Reasonability of future payouts as long as performance exceeds bottom-quartile results | • Performance is highly dependent on who is in the peer group |
| • Effectively measures success in both good and poor economies | • Plan participants have no idea of their impact on award achievement |
| • Easy to administer and communicate and readily measurable at any time | |

**Table 22.5 Advantages and Disadvantages of Using Relative Performance Measures**

The growing number of companies implementing performance plans with relative performance features has raised the profile of relative *total shareholder return* (TSR). Today, relative TSR often serves as a key input in the determination of award outcomes rather than providing context for the value of earned awards. The next section discusses one of the most commonly used market-based and relative measures, *relative TSR*, and explores methods of incorporating it into incentive plans.

## Relative TSR Design Considerations

*Total shareholder return* is defined as the change in a company's stock price plus dividends over a defined period of time. For example, the TSR for a non-dividend-paying stock with a price of \$10 at $t_0$ (the measurement-period start at time zero) and \$11 at $t_1$ (the measurement-period end) would be 10 percent [i.e., $(t_1/t_0) - 1 = $ TSR; ($11/$10) $- 1 = 10\%$]. If the stock pays an annual dividend of \$1 (reinvested at \$11 per share), under the same scenario, the TSR would be 20 percent, and if the dividend were reinvested at \$10 per share, the TSR would be slightly higher (21 percent). Current common practice is to reinvest dividends quarterly, monthly, or on the ex-dividend date. [Often TSR is described in annualized terms, but it also may be expressed in cumulative terms. For example, the *cumulative* three-year TSR of a stock with a price of \$10 per share at $t_0$ and \$20 at $t_3$ would be 100 percent, that is, $(t_3/t_0) - 1 = $ cumulative TSR; ($20/$10) $- 1 = 100$ percent. The *annualized* TSR would be 26 percent, that is, $(t_3/t_0)^{1/t} - 1 = $ annualized TSR; ($20/$10)$^{1/3} - 1 = 26$ percent. Proxy disclosure advisory firms tend to report TSR in *annualized* terms.]

When incorporated into an incentive program, TSR is most often measured relative to the TSRs of a peer group of companies—*relative* TSR. Note that when referencing a peer group in this section, we refer to the group of companies used to measure relative TSR, which may or may not be the same as the company's peer group used for compensation benchmarking purposes. [An increasing number of companies use absolute TSR in addition to relative TSR by requiring a specified level of TSR to achieve an above-target payout (e.g., if company TSR is negative, a relative TSR award cannot pay out above target.]

### Metric versus Modifier

Relative TSR generally is employed primarily as a discrete metric within a performance plan or as a method to modify awards. At the time of this writing, most companies employing relative TSR include it as a discrete metric in performance-share/unit plans, either as the sole metric or as one of multiple metrics.

When relative TSR is used as a metric, the payout schedule often mirrors that used for other performance measures. (Most performance-share plans offer payouts ranging from 0 to 150 or 200 percent.) In recent years, the *TSR modifier approach* has gained prevalence as companies seek to focus primarily on internal financial performance but also align payouts with relative returns—although with less market risk versus the discrete metric approach. Typically, when the modifier approach is used, relative TSR modifies a performance-share/unit plan in which financial measures serve as the basis of the award (Table 22.6). A typical approach offers an upside of 20 to 25 percent based on superior relative TSR results or a downside of –20 to –25 percent for inferior results. Thus, if the financial performance metric pays out at 100 percent and company TSR is superior to that of its peers, the payout may be 120 percent. Similarly, if TSR is relatively poor, the payout may be 80 percent (assuming a ±20 percent relative TSR modifier).

| Percentile Rank versus Peer Group | Payout Percent of Target |
| --- | --- |
| 0% | 0% |
| 25% | 50% |
| 50% | 100% |
| 75% | 200% |

Table 22.6  TSR and Financial Metrics

## Relative TSR Performance and Payout

The most commonly used method for measuring relative TSR is the *rank method:* company TSR is ranked against the TSRs of peer-group companies (Table 22.7). Two common methods for measuring rank are as follows: percentile rank (e.g., the Microsoft Excel function PERCENTRANK) or a numerical rank (e.g., tenth highest among 12 peers). In each case, rank determines payout levels according to a predetermined pay-performance schedule. Performance within specified levels under the percentile rank method relies on interpolation to determine payout as a percentage of target. Higher company TSR rank relative to the companies in the peer group results in a higher payout, and vice versa.

| Numerical Rank versus Peer Group | Payout Percent of Target |
|---|---|
| 11 | 0% |
| 10 | 0% |
| 9 | 40% |
| 8 | 60% |
| 7 | 80% |
| 6 | 100% |
| 5 | 120% |
| 4 | 140% |
| 3 | 160% |
| 2 | 180% |
| 1 | 200% |

Table 22.7   TSR and a Ranking Method

The peer group used to benchmark a company's relative TSR will depend on a variety of factors, including, but not limited to, the company's long-term relative performance goals, the competitors for investment capital, and the availability of reasonable industry competitors by way of industry classifications (e.g., Global Industry Classification Standard, commonly known as GICS, which is maintained by Standard and Poor's). Increasingly, companies also incorporate rigorous statistical and financial analyses measuring the market comparability of the company relative to others. The traditional users of relative TSR are energy and utilities companies, which tend to benchmark relative TSR to their compensation peers, a custom performance peer group, or a predefined sector index such as the S&P 1500 Utilities. Across all industries, companies benchmark relative TSR to one of the following types of peer groups:

- *Custom compensation peer groups.* The same group of companies used to benchmark compensation.

- *Custom performance peer groups.* A hand-selected group of industry competitors.

- *Industry index peer groups.* A predefined list of companies set by an independent organization, such as Standard and Poor's (e.g., S&P 1500 Utilities).

- *Multisector index peer groups.* A predefined list of companies across multiple industries maintained by an independent organization such as Standard and Poor's (e.g., S&P 500 or S&P 500 excluding energy and utilities).

An alternative method for measuring relative TSR involves the use of an index composite. Performance is not measured against the index *constituents* but rather against the TSR of the composite index (Table 22.8). In this context, specified performance levels above and below that of the selected index composite result in varying payout levels.

| Performance versus Index | Payout Percent of Target |
| --- | --- |
| Index −2% | 0% |
| Index +0% | 50% |
| Index +2% | 100% |
| Index +10% | 150% |

Table 22.8   TSR and a Composite Index

## Valuation

The Financial Accounting Standards Board (FASB) Accounting Standards Codification Topic 718 (commonly referred to as FASB ASC Topic 718) governs the accounting for stock-based compensation as well as compensation subject to market-based vesting requirements, such as a performance based on incorporating relative TSR. ASC Topic 718 requires vehicles with market-based measures to be valued differently from vehicles with time-based requirements (e.g., restricted stock) or performance incentives with financial metrics (e.g., a non-market-based measure such as revenue growth). The rules specify a Monte Carlo simulation as one technique that satisfies the valuation requirement, and this is how most, if not all, vehicles using relative TSR are valued. It is not unusual for the accounting expense for performance-plan awards to exceed the face value of the underlying stock on the grant date. This occurs given the asymmetrical relationship between share-price upside, which is unlimited, and downside, which is limited to −100 percent.

## Conclusion

LTI compensation vehicle selection requires careful consideration of multiple factors that can validate past decisions or serve as the business case for change. Those who design or oversee a company's LTI compensation program must consider a wide range of factors to ensure that their design recommendations support the needs and objectives of the company, the LTI compensation plan participants, and the company's shareholders, ideally within a representative range of market-share use levels and reflective of the accompanying regulatory and technical considerations. The decision to incorporate, expand, modify, or fine-tune performance plans is ongoing. The reliance on performance plans that incorporate relative performance standards has reshaped how companies pay their executives.

The migration to performance plans reflects a strong desire to provide incentives that focus recipients on business and market results, providing a balanced view of performance that other LTI compensation vehicles lack. Relative TSR plans represent the dominant performance-plan design employed by large companies today. Given the nuances of relative TSR plans, it is likely that at any point the number of companies taking a positive or negative view of their plans will be mixed, whereas shareholders likely will take a positive view. For this reason, the decision to implement a relative TSR performance plan or one that incorporates a relative TSR design feature should be made only after careful consideration of the company's objectives for the plan and its situation.

## Design Stage Questions

1. How should our approach to LTI compensation support and reflect business needs, talent objectives, shareholder expectations, and risk considerations? Does our approach align with our compensation philosophy?

2. What message do we want our LTI compensation strategy to convey to our employees and our owners/shareholders?

3. Does our LTI compensation strategy complement incentive opportunities provided by our short-term incentive plans? Should it?

4. Does our LTI compensation strategy encourage appropriate levels of risk taking?

5. Should our LTI compensation strategy reflect business results, market results, or both?

6. What LTI compensation vehicles and performance metrics do our peers use? How do we compare? Note that although market intelligence is important, it should not be the driving factor in determining the most appropriate approach in designing your program.

7. What approaches did we use in the past? What was our experience? How did participants and owners/shareholders react?

8. What performance metrics are best managed in the time period being considered?

9. Is absolute, relative, or a balanced approach the best way to determine performance-plan outcomes? What is the basis of benchmarking performance?

10. What are the technical implications (accounting, tax, legal, and share utilization)?

## Post–Implementation Stage Questions

1. Do the LTI compensation opportunities we provide appropriately reflect our absolute and relative performance?

2. Are the performance parameters over which awards are earned appropriate and defensible?

3. Do we provide sufficient levels of stock compensation in relation to other forms of compensation and our compensation peers?

4. Is our benchmark community for relative performance assessments appropriate and defensible?

5. Does our LTI compensation program facilitate acceptable executive stock ownership levels? How soon?

# 23

# Regulating Executive Compensation

FRANK P. VANDERPLOEG
*Dentons US, LLP*

Recent years have seen growing public and shareholder attention to executive compensation and increased government regulation in response to these concerns. As a result, the people involved in structuring and administering stock-option plans and other forms of executive compensation—human resources managers, boards of directors, and/or compensation committees and their advisors—must take into account a rapidly changing and increasingly intricate set of laws and regulations to sustain organizational performance and maintain competitive advantage.

This brief chapter cannot describe all the legal and regulatory structures that may impinge on executive compensation, nor can it review the tax treatment of executive compensation generally. Instead, it will focus on generally applicable laws and regulations that particularly affect the design and implementation of executive compensation arrangements and that therefore need to be considered at the outset in establishing such arrangements.

Compensation in some industries—particularly finance and health—may be regulated in some detail by industry-specific laws. Compensation planners in those industries must consult the specific regulations of their regulators, a review of which is beyond the scope of this chapter.

This chapter will tell you

- How to meet management's obligations to the board and shareholders
- What compensation in public companies is open to public disclosure
- How the Fair Labor Standards Act applies to compensation
- How to avoid the most dangerous tax pitfalls
- Best practices for the process of setting executive compensation

# Background

The start of the millennium saw substantial compensation, option gains, and perquisites paid to executives of companies that went bankrupt or paid to executives facing criminal prosecution for bilking public companies through excessive or unauthorized compensation arrangements. Hardly had the dust settled on these developments when a new wave of stock-option backdating scandals erupted. Even as these developments were being litigated, a market implosion lead to the near collapse of the U.S. financial system, exacerbated, many believed, by executive compensation practices that encouraged excessive risk taking and failed to hold executives responsible through their pay for dismal corporate performance.

Outcry over these developments feeds two somewhat different pressures on executive compensation. One source of pressure—perhaps the one felt most keenly in the boardroom—is intensifying activism by public-company shareholders, particularly institutional shareholders, attacking weaknesses in corporate governance that permit such excesses, especially when executive pay is not, in the shareholders' eyes, justified by corporate performance.

A second source of pressure—perhaps the one felt most keenly in Congress—is the broader public dismay at the levels of executive compensation generally. CEO pay is reported to have increased from 20 times average employee pay in 1960 to more than 383 times average worker pay in 2000, remaining at 273 times average pay as of 2012. The fact that many companies reporting significant executive compensation simultaneously hold the line on rank-and-file wages, restructure their operations, and lay off employees adds to the public controversy.

Governmental response has been vigorous but so far without radical changes to the regulatory structure for executive compensation. These are mainly securities disclosure requirements for public companies and special disincentives in the tax law for all companies. The most significant development since the last edition of this *Handbook* is the Dodd-Frank Wall Street Reform and Consumer Protection Act of 2010. Under the Dodd-Frank Act, shareholder "say-on-pay" is now a reality for public companies, and regulations have been proposed under the Act for disclosing the pay ratio of CEO compensation to median employee compensation. More notably, the Dodd-Frank Act moves toward substantive regulation of executive compensation by leveraging the Securities and Exchange Commission's (SEC's) authority over the exchanges on which public-company stock is traded. Listing requirements of those exchanges now (or soon will, when regulations are issued) strengthen the independence of compensation committees and mandate the clawback of unwarranted excessive compensation.

The enhanced disclosure requirements and indirect regulation through the tax laws, together with the Fair Labor Standards Act, set the parameters within which innovation must operate. Most important, the increasing visibility and potential for controversy respecting executive compensation puts a premium on following best practices to design, implement, and set benefit levels for executive pay. This is especially vital now because best practices today can become standard practices tomorrow and minimum legal requirements the following day.

# Shareholder Rights and Director Obligations

## *Role of the Board, Compensation Committee, and Management*

Corporate law generally provides that the business and affairs of a corporation are managed by or under the direction of the board of directors. The directors, in turn, hire the officers to actually run the corporation. However, there is an obvious conflict of interest in letting those officers set their own compensation. Accordingly, although the board can seek management's recommendations on compensation, the actual decision on executive compensation is a direct responsibility of the board of directors. In large companies, this responsibility will be assigned to a compensation committee of the board that will be composed of independent directors for a public company (in light of various requirements of the SEC, the tax laws, and the exchanges on which shares are listed for trading). The Dodd-Frank Act strengthened the independence of compensation committees by mandating (through exchange listing requirements) that their members meet stipulated criteria for independence and must similarly evaluate the independence of consultants, counsel, and other advisors they select.

Corporate directors owe the corporation and its stockholders fiduciary duties of care and loyalty. (Law in some states adds a separate duty of good faith.) Director business decisions complying with those standards are entitled to the protection of the *business judgment rule*. This is a presumption that in making a business decision, the directors of a corporation act on an informed basis, in good faith, and in the honest belief that the action taken is in the best interests of the company. Acting on an informed basis, in turn, requires that the directors have investigated (and understood) all material information reasonably available to them, which may include reports and recommendations from outside consultants (as well as management).

The duty of care emphasizes the procedures that board members use to inform themselves about the decision before them. Failure to follow appropriate procedures, especially in a case involving the payment of large benefits to an executive, may prevent a finding that directors acted in good faith. It is thus naturally important for the record behind any decision on executive compensation to demonstrate that the members of the board, and particularly the members of the compensation committee, have fulfilled their duty of care. Practices that may contribute to this are set out at the end of this chapter.

### Role of the Shareholders

Shareholders may set overall corporate policy but typically have no direct role in managing the corporation (except, of course, that they can refuse to reelect directors or sometimes remove directors if the shareholders are unhappy with board decisions). The major exception to this principle for executive compensation is that shareholders usually must approve stock-option plans (or restricted stock or similar equity compensation). Some state corporate laws require shareholder approval of option plans. Even where not required, shareholder approval may be necessary in practice to obtain favorable accounting or tax treatment for incentive stock options if those will be granted. A public company also will find shareholder approval of equity compensation plans necessary to comply with the stock exchange listing requirements, to obtain the benefit of exemptions from the insider trading laws, or to avoid the $1 million limitation on tax deductions under Section 162(m) of the Internal Revenue Code.

Shareholders take a keen interest in equity compensation plans that they are being asked to approve. Firms such as Institutional Shareholder Services (ISS) review public companies' proxy disclosure statements in light of their own criteria for plan features and *burn rate* (the amount of stock that can be issued under option or other awards) and make voting recommendations to their institutional shareholder clients.

Under the Dodd-Frank Act, shareholders of public companies now must be given the opportunity to cast a nonbinding say-on-pay vote to approve executive compensation every one, two, or three years. In addition, the Dodd-Frank Act requires a shareholder advisory vote to approve certain "golden parachute" arrangements in business combination proxy disclosure statements. The company must report to the shareholders how the compensation committee took the results of the last say-on-pay vote into account in making subsequent compensation decisions. This response naturally becomes most sensitive in the relatively few cases where the shareholders disapprove of the executive compensation package or fail to approve it by a significant margin.

## SEC Disclosure Rules

The public and shareholder concerns just outlined drive demands for increased disclosure (and regulation), and disclosure of executive compensation, in turn, drives increasing public and shareholder concerns. A major round on the disclosure side of this endless feedback loop resulted in the SEC 2006 final rules for disclosure of executive officer compensation in proxy disclosure statements and annual Form 10-K reports of publicly traded companies (the SEC Disclosure Rules).

The SEC Disclosure Rules require extensive disclosure of all types of compensation for named executive officers (NEOs) and directors at publicly traded companies. NEOs are generally anyone who served during the year as principal executive officer or principal financial officer and the three (generally) most highly compensated executive officers (other than the principal executive and financial officers) serving as executive officers at the end of the last fiscal year.

Disclosure begins with a narrative discussion in nonboilerplate, plain English called the *compensation discussion and analysis* (CD&A). This disclosure is followed by a summary compensation table that assigns all current and deferred compensation (including equity) to one of seven specified columns for covered executive offices. Other tables and related discussion then must report in more detail on equity-based compensation, retirement benefits, and other actual or potential postemployment compensation. The Dodd-Frank Act adds that annual meeting materials must show the relationship between executive compensation actually paid and the financial performance of the issuer.

### Compensation Discussion and Analysis

The CD&A is a principles-based narrative overview of the material factors underlying a company's compensation policies and decisions. Under the regulations, it must describe the company's compensation program objectives, the method by which the program incentivizes certain behaviors, each element of compensation, the reason the company chooses to pay each such element, the amount of (or formula for) each such element, and the manner in which each element helps to achieve the company's compensation objectives.

According to the regulations, the CD&A should include, among other things, the rationale behind immediate versus long-term compensation and cash versus other compensation, specific items of corporate performance that are relevant, the factors used to determine a material increase or decrease in compensation, the benchmarking undertaken by a company in establishing compensation programs, and the role of executive officers in the compensation process. Unsurprisingly, considering the stock-option backdating concerns at the time, the CD&A also must include an extensive discussion regarding equity grants.

### The Summary Compensation Table

After the narrative CD&A, a summary compensation table will disclose the compensation of the NEOs for the last three fiscal years. Compensation, generally in the amounts determined for financial statement reporting purposes, is disclosed in a stipulated columnar format:

- Salary (both cash and noncash) earned by the NEO during the fiscal year

- Discretionary bonuses (both cash and noncash) earned by the NEO during the fiscal year

- Stock awards, including restricted stock and phantom stock

- Stock-option awards, including options and stock appreciation rights

- Nonequity incentive plan compensation, which includes formula-based annual bonuses as well as long-term nonequity performance awards

- The dollar value of the annual change in the actuarial value of all qualified and nonqualified defined-benefit pension plans and arrangements, including the incremental value of any above-market or preferential earnings on nonqualified defined-contribution plans

- All other compensation, such as compensation costs for certain discount stock purchases, tax "gross-ups," termination or change-in-control payments, company contributions and other allocations to all defined-contribution plans (vested or unvested), company-paid premiums for life insurance, dividends, or other earnings paid on stock or option awards, and perquisites and other personal benefits

- The dollar value of total compensation for the fiscal year

### Other Tables

The summary compensation table is supplemented by other tables (and discussion) for particular forms of compensation depending on the types of compensation actually paid. These include grants of plan-based awards, outstanding equity awards at fiscal year end, option exercises and stock vested, postemployment compensation, pension benefits, and nonqualified deferred compensation.

Instructions for the tables require additional discussion of some items, particularly payments in connection with the resignation, severance, retirement, or other termination of an NEO or a change in control of the company. Finally, the regulations require a director compensation table.

### New and Enhanced Disclosures

In addition to compliance with the SEC Disclosure Rules on an annual basis, as discussed earlier, a public company undergoing a business combination transaction must disclose all elements of the compensation arrangements and understandings in connection with that transaction (golden parachutes) in narrative and tabular form in the proxy disclosure statement seeking shareholder approval of the combination. These arrangements are also subject to a nonbinding shareholder advisory vote.

The Dodd-Frank Act further requires disclosure of whether a public-company employee or member of the board may purchase financial instruments designed to hedge or offset any decrease in the market value of equity securities forming part of the individual's compensation. Covered financial institutions (whether or not public companies) also must reveal whether their incentive-based compensation structures provide excessive compensation, as determined by the financial regulators, or could lead to material financial loss to the institution.

The most recent addition to the growing list of required public company disclosures is the CEO pay ratio mandated by the Dodd-Frank Act, to be implemented by regulations proposed by the SEC in 2013. This must cover the median of the annual total compensation of all employees of the company (other than the CEO), the total compensation of the CEO, and the ratio of the all-employee median to the CEO pay. How this information will benefit shareholders is unclear, but it is sure to increase awareness and drive criticism of the level of executive pay in public companies.

### Moving Toward Substantive Regulation

Within what is fundamentally a disclosure regime for public companies, the federal government is inching toward substantive regulation of their executive compensation. The Sarbanes-Oxley Act of 2002 outlaws public-company loans to directors and executive officers. That act and the Dodd-Frank Act now nudge the SEC to use its regulatory authority over stock exchanges to require the exchanges to enact listing standards that, in turn, impose substantive regulation on compensation, at least for public companies. Listing standards issued in 2003 mandate shareholder approval of most equity compensation plans, an area hitherto governed mainly by state corporate law. The Dodd-Frank Act calls for forthcoming SEC regulations to require listed companies to adopt an executive incentive pay "clawback" policy to recoup performance-based compensation when there is a restatement of the financial statements on which the compensation was based.

### Impact

The SEC Disclosure Rules and similar requirements must be considered in designing executive compensation programs not only because of the impact of disclosure but also because companies may want to amend or design their compensation programs to avoid unpleasant or complicated disclosures. For example, companies may want to simplify disclosures by eliminating multiple option grants throughout the fiscal year that lengthen the tables or by ensuring that compensation arrangements fall clearly into one or another regulatory pigeonhole in order to avoid ambiguities and reduce the need for lengthy, technical, and nuanced narrative explanations. Companies also may reconsider benefits and perquisites where disclosure creates a potential for controversy that outweighs their intrinsic value. All these factors gained enhanced force with the advent of the shareholder say-on-pay vote because these disclosures are the basis for shareholder decisions on how to cast their votes. Needless to say, the time to consider the impact of disclosure is when the compensation program is first considered.

## The Fair Labor Standards Act

The Fair Labor Standards Act (FLSA), originally enacted in 1937, is still a cornerstone of federal regulation of employment and compensation. The FLSA addresses four areas: minimum-wage requirements, overtime-pay requirements, restrictions on child labor, and equal pay. Minimum-wage and child-labor restrictions do not typically affect executive compensation (although the minimum-wage requirements should at least be considered when employees of a startup company volunteer or are recruited to work for nothing or for vague promises of future compensation or stock options). A discussion of equal pay and other federal nondiscrimination laws is beyond the scope of this chapter.

It might be thought that overtime requirements also have little application in the executive suite, but FLSA has some subtleties in this area that cannot be ignored in designing executive pay arrangements. Properly classifying employees as covered by or exempt from the overtime requirements of FLSA is crucial. There are many FLSA exceptions to the overtime requirements, most applicable to specified occupational groups, but the broadest one, which is generally thought of as applying to most management employees, is for individuals employed in "bona fide executive, administrative, or professional capacity," as defined by regulations of the Department of Labor.

Those regulations provide several alternative tests for exempt status, but almost all require that employees be paid on a salaried basis for the exemption to apply. Under FLSA, an individual is salaried if he or she receives a predetermined amount each pay period, and the amount is not subject to variation because of quantity or quality of work. The salary requirement means that an individual (other than an attorney) paid on an hourly basis almost never can be exempt. For some companies, particularly in professional or consulting fields, many highly paid employees whose time is charged to clients by the hour are also paid by the hour, and these individuals are subject to FLSA overtime protection.

For all nonexempt employees, the regular hourly rate from which overtime is determined must be calculated. One of the issues arising in this calculation is the treatment of bonuses or other incentive or equity-type compensation. Generally, discretionary bonuses are excluded, whereas nondiscretionary bonuses are included. In addition, under the 2000 amendments to FLSA, stock purchase plan, stock-option, and stock-appreciation right benefits are excluded on certain conditions. Compliance with these exceptions (or the increased overtime cost if they are not complied with) must be considered when bonus and equity plans are extended to nonexempt employees.

Additional requirements apply for the actual exemption of salaried employees. These include an executive exemption, which covers individuals paid more than $250 per week in salary and whose primary duties are the supervision of two or more other employees or paid at least $155 per week in salary and whose primary duties are management of a business or department and who have authority to hire and fire, regularly exercise discretionary authority, and spend more than 80 percent of their time in the preceding duties. Other sets of requirements in the same vein delineate the statutory exemptions for administrative and professional employees, and further exemptions cover very highly compensated employees, computer systems analysts and programmers, motor-carrier employees, commission salespeople, and the like.

There are two major limitations on benefits that employers may derive from these exemptions. First, they typically involve not just an objective salary component but also a more subjective component that evaluates the particular job duties of the person involved. For instance, whether a lower-level executive regularly exercises discretionary authority is something about which two people can sometimes disagree.

More significantly, these are federal exemptions only. Most states have their own FLSA-equivalent laws governing overtime requirements, which may state their exemptions in different terms or not have comparable exemptions at all. State laws that give enhanced protection (require overtime) beyond the federal requirements are *not* superseded by federal law. Since state laws (like the federal FLSA) allow employees to recover unpaid overtime (and usually interest, penalties, and attorneys fees) and the borderline cases where treatment is unclear generally involve relatively high-paid categories of employees, the potential employer liability for misclassifying employees can be severe.

FLSA (and its state counterparts) cover only "employees" and not "independent contractors." This is one of the myriad areas where proper classification of workers as employees or independent contractors is essential. Because the distinction is also important to whether federal or state tax-withholding rules apply, government revenue authorities also take a deep interest in proper worker classification. Both workers and governments have become increasingly aggressive in pursuing proper classification and collecting damages (or taxes) for misclassification.

Employers therefore must be aware of state requirements, exemptions, and limitations on exemptions (as well as their federal counterparts) in the states where they do business and are wise to periodically review the employee or independent contractor classification of their workers and the exempt or nonexempt classification of employees, particularly in the borderline situations, for new job classifications, or for jobs whose functional description has changed since the last review.

## Indirect Regulation Through the Tax Laws

A full discussion of the tax treatment of executive compensation is beyond the scope of this chapter. Instead, this section will focus on four tax rules that affect the design of executive compensation arrangements or procedures for adopting them. Even here, this chapter cannot discuss these provisions in depth. Actual compliance (avoidance of tax penalties) requires careful attention to voluminous details in lengthy regulations. This section can only briefly describe these provisions with some comments on their broader implications for stock-option plans and other forms of executive compensation.

### Section 162(m): Compensation Exceeding $1 Million ($500,000 in Some Cases)

Internal Revenue Code Section 162(m) in its basic and original form generally denies a deduction for compensation in excess of $1 million in a taxable year paid to the CEO or any of the three other most highly compensated executive officers other than the CFO of a public company unless the compensation is "performance based." As a result, compensation arrangements that are capable of being performance based are generally designed to meet the requirements of the statute and regulations.

Base salary and time-vested restricted stock will not qualify as performance based. However, bonus and most other incentive compensation generally can be designed to be performance based. To be performance based, the compensation must be paid only on attainment of a predetermined objective performance goal, which is established by a compensation committee composed solely of independent directors and the material terms of which are approved by shareholders.

Under the regulations, to be preestablished, the performance goal must be established not later than 90 days after the start of the period of service to which the compensation relates, must be stated in terms of objective business criteria (i.e., stock price, earnings, or the like), and must be part of an objective formula that lets the ultimate compensation be computed based on the performance results. After the end of the period, the compensation committee must certify the level of attainment of the performance goal. In other words, discretion generally is precluded. But the regulations allow the compensation committee to apply "negative discretion" to reduce the resulting formula compensation downward (but not upward). A consequence of this feature is that bonus plans can comply with the letter of IRC Section 162(m) but violate its spirit by providing an objective formula that creates a high bonus based on soft performance targets, with the compensation committee then using "negative discretion" to reduce the bonus to what it really wants to pay.

Under a special rule, stock options and stock-appreciation rights (SARs) are considered performance based if the plan states the maximum number of shares for which options or SARs may be granted in a specified period to any employee and the option price (or SAR strike price) is not more than the fair market value of the stock when the option or SAR is granted. The regulations also describe in excruciating detail when directors are "independent" for purposes of Section 162(m).

In light of IRC Section 162(m), compensation committees administering bonus or incentive plans under the regulations usually will meet within the first 90 days of the performance period to select the performance criteria from among those in the shareholder-approved plan; establish the threshold, target, and maximum goals for the eligible employees; and certify the degree to which goals for the prior year have been attained and the resulting bonuses payable. Because of the limitations on flexibility under IRC Section 162(m), some companies will have one Section 162(m)–compliant bonus plan solely for the covered executives whose compensation is (or may be) subject to IRC Section 162(m) and a separate (and more discretionary and more subjective) bonus plan for other managers. The relative ease of establishing an arrangement as performance based (if the technicalities are observed), coupled with the negative-discretion feature, means that public companies generally can avoid the basic deduction limit of IRC Section 162(m) except for base compensation and other non-performance-based (i.e., time-vested) compensation.

The idea of a dollar limit on deductions for executive compensation, at least for some purposes, has proved politically popular, and Section 162(m) has been expanded into two new areas. The Emergency Economic Stabilization Act of 2008 added Section 162(m)(5) to limit deductions by companies that sell assets to the Treasury under the Troubled Assets Relief Program (TARP) to $500,000 per individual per year for any year when an obligation arising from the receipt of financial assistance under TARP is outstanding. It applies to the CEO, the CFO, and the highest-paid three other executives of both private and public companies (that have received over $300 million in financial assistance). There are no exceptions for performance-based compensation, and once an executive is covered, his or her compensation is always subject to the limit for all future years that the TARP obligation is outstanding.

More recently, the Patient Protection and Affordable Care Act of 2010 (PPACA) added Section 162(m)(6) to limit the deduction for compensation paid to employees and independent contractors by "covered health insurance providers"—these are basically companies offering the minimum essential health insurance coverage that PPACA requires individuals to obtain—to $500,000 per individual per year. In contrast to other limitations on compensation deductions imposed by Section 162(m), this limit applies to all compensation paid to all employees, officers, and directors of the covered health insurance provider and all members of the provider's controlled business group. There is no exception for performance-based compensation and no safe-harbor exceptions.

It remains to be seen whether these provisions actually will induce the targeted employers to limit the compensation they pay to their executives or other employees or be viewed merely as an additional income tax levied, via the deduction limitation, on employers particularly favored by controversial government largesse.

## Section 280G: Golden Parachutes

IRC Section 280G was enacted in 1984 to restrict "golden parachute" benefits. It denies a deduction for "excess parachute payments" paid to a "disqualified individual" as a result of a corporate change of control. A companion provision (IRC Section 4999) imposes a 20 percent excise tax on the individual receiving "excess parachute payments." Unlike IRC Section 162(m), these provisions apply to many private companies as well as public companies.

Generally, a *parachute payment* is any payment of compensation that is contingent on a change of control (as defined in the statute and regulations). This can encompass not only traditional parachute benefits but also sale or retention bonuses and similar arrangements. "Disqualified individuals" are 1 percent or more of shareholders, officers, or highly compensated individuals, all as more specifically defined (with some exceptions) in the regulations.

IRC Section 280G contains a complicating leveraging feature. The tax penalties apply if (and only if) "excess parachute payments" exceed three times the individual's "base amount." *Base amount* is essentially the individual's average annual taxable income from the company over the five-year period preceding the change of control. However, if the parachute penalties are triggered, they then apply to all parachute payments in excess of *one* times the base amount. Thus a small excess above the three-times-base-amount-trigger can cause a substantial and disproportionate adverse tax impact.

Responses by companies and executives subject to the parachute tax are varied. One response is for the plan or contract to limit potential parachute payments to 299 percent of the base amount. However, this can have arbitrary and counterintuitive results. Another approach is for the company to "gross up" the payment to neutralize the parachute excise tax. But gross-ups can become very expensive (particularly if the marginal tax rate of federal and state income and 20 percent excise tax exceeds 50 percent) and are a sensitive topic with shareholders. Alternatively, the company can just let the tax fall where it falls. More sophisticated formulas apply a gross-up or forego the 299 percent limit only if the resulting after-tax benefit to the executive is, say, 10 percent more than the executive would receive if cut back to three times the base amount.

The parachute penalties apply to all public companies and their "disqualified individual" executives. Privately held corporations may benefit from one of two exemptions. First, "small-business corporations," those eligible to be taxed as "S-Corporations" under IRC subchapter S, are automatically exempt (whether or not they have actually elected to be taxed as S-Corporations). Second, other nonpublic companies are exempt if the payment is approved by 75 percent of the shareholders (as determined immediately before the change in control) after adequate disclosure (as specified in the regulations) of all the material facts concerning the payments. Complying with the conditions for this exemption at the time of the initial contract may be difficult. The usual solution for private companies about to undergo a change in control is *parachute cleansing*. Executives waive their existing parachute benefits, and the shareholders reapprove them (normally) after the requisite disclosures.

### Section 409A: Requirements for Deferred Compensation

Another foray into regulation by taxation is IRC Section 409A, effective in 2005, with voluminous technical regulations generally effective in 2008. The basic requirements of Section 409A are deceptively simple and fairly easy to apply to what we commonly think of as deferred compensation.

- The deferred compensation must be payable only on death, disability, separation from service, change in control, or unforeseeable emergency or pursuant to a fixed schedule.

- Payments on separation from service to a "specified employee" (key employee) of a public company must be delayed until at least six months after separation.

- The initial decision to defer compensation for a year must be made before the beginning of the year in which the services for which the compensation is earned are performed (with exceptions for the first year of eligibility and elections under a performance-based bonus plan).

- Further changes in the initial deferral decision are restricted, and acceleration of deferred compensation is prohibited.

If a deferred compensation arrangement violates these restrictions, the deferred compensation is included in income at the time deferred (or when it becomes vested and non-forfeitable, if later)—that is, the deferral does not work to defer tax—*and* is subject to an additional 20 percent income tax (over and above the individual's regular tax rate), *and* is subject to interest from the time of deferral (or vesting) at the IRC tax underpayment interest rate plus 1 percent. These taxes are imposed on the employee (or independent contractor), not the company. But the employer is required to withhold these taxes. This tax treatment is sufficiently severe that it is not practicable to provide deferred compensation other than in accordance with the new Section 409A rules.

The complicating problem is that the final regulations define deferred compensation extremely broadly. It can include anything that gives an employee or independent contractor a legally binding right (even though contingent or not yet vested) to compensation that might be paid in a later year, including stock options and SARs, separation payments (including postemployment reimbursements), nonqualified supplemental executive retirement plans (SERPs), and certain taxable welfare benefits. Even ordinary bonus arrangements may be deferred compensation.

The breadth of the statutory definition focuses attention on the exceptions. Qualified retirement plans and benefits that would be tax free under general rules are generally exempt. Other exceptions may apply to executive compensation arrangements. One of these exempts property transfers that are already subject to IRC Section 83. This would cover most restricted stock arrangements (awards of shares to employees that become vested based on performance or time).

Stock-option and SAR arrangements are exempt provided that the underlying stock is stock of the employer and the option or SAR price can never be less than fair market value on the date of grant. For public companies, grant-date fair market value is readily determined from the market (if the options are not backdated!). For closely held companies, the regulations prescribe safe-harbor valuation methods, generally requiring either an appraisal or formula value that is applied for all corporate purposes, although the appraisal requirement is relaxed for an illiquid startup corporation.

A "short-term deferral" exception states that compensation paid within two and a half months of the end of the calendar year in which it becomes vested is not deferred compensation. Restricted stock unit arrangements (where the award is to transfer shares in the future when vesting requirements have been met), and most bonus arrangements can be designed to fit within this exception if they have no other deferral features.

Another exception covers severance benefits paid on an involuntary termination of employment (or participation in a window program). The regulations allow a limited number of "good reason" termination events consistent with the involuntary termination. The amount covered by the exception may not exceed two times the individual's annual compensation [or two times the limit on compensation that may be taken into account for qualified pension and 401(k) plan purposes, if less], and payment must be completed within two years. Under the regulations, the exception applies to otherwise qualifying severance pay up to the amount limits even if the total amount paid will exceed the amount limits. One significant benefit of this exception is that the six-month delay rule for specified employees of a public company does not apply to involuntary termination payments within the limits of this exception.

The regulations cover in detail these and other exceptions and provide many special rules. They require all deferred compensation arrangements to be in writing and by their terms comply with the requirements of Section 409A. Therefore, the technical requirements of the regulations must be consulted and observed in drafting any deferred compensation arrangement either to comply with the standards or to ensure that it is exempt from them.

### IRC Section 4958: Intermediate-Sanction Standards for Tax-Exempt Organizations

Tax regulations governing compensation paid by tax-exempt charitable and educational organizations are naturally of paramount importance to those tax-exempt employers. But inasmuch as they require for those tax-exempt organizations the practices and procedures that the regulators see as standard (if not "best") practices in the for-profit sector, they are significant in revealing the regulators' view of what those practices are (or should be).

Section 4958 of the IRC imposes so-called intermediate-sanction excise taxes on "disqualified persons" (insiders) and "organization managers" (board members or comparable persons) of tax-exempt public charities (and civic leagues and social welfare organizations) whenever an impermissible "excess-benefit transaction" occurs between the organization and a disqualified person. An excess-benefit transaction includes unreasonable compensation paid to a disqualified person. However, the regulations describe the circumstances in which compensation will be presumed to be reasonable.

Under the regulations, an exempt organization has the benefit of the presumption if the board approving the compensation

- Was composed entirely of individuals who are independent and do not have a conflict of interest

- Obtained and made its determination based on proper comparability data

- Adequately documented the basis for its compensation decision concurrently with such determination

Comparability data for the second requirement are considered appropriate when, given the knowledge and expertise of the board members, they offer sufficient information for board members to determine that the compensation arrangement is reasonable. The board members must take into account the aggregate amount of all compensation and benefits to an individual, including compensation paid by or through related organizations.

Relevant information (for organizations with annual gross receipts of more than $1 million) to consider in determining whether compensation is reasonable includes compensation levels paid by similarly situated organizations, both taxable and tax-exempt, for a functionally comparable position, the availability of similar services in the geographic area of the organization, current compensation surveys compiled by independent firms, and actual written offers by similar organizations competing for the services of a particular individual. Boards also must ensure that any intention to treat benefits provided to executives is contemporaneously acknowledged or treated as compensation.

Documentation is the third element of the presumption, usually in the board's or committee's minutes. Specifically, the minutes must indicate the terms of the transaction that was approved and the date of its approval, the members of the board or committee who were present during the debate or discussion of the transaction that was approved and who voted on the proposal, the comparability data obtained and relied on and how the data were obtained, and any actions taken with respect to the transaction by any member of the board who had a conflict of interest with respect to the transaction.

Further, if the board determines to pay compensation that is either higher or lower than indicated by the range of comparability data, a record of that fact and the board's or committee's reasons must be part of the minutes. Factors that may be documented (where they exist) in support of above-average pay may include the ratio of the proposed compensation to the organization's revenues and expenses, the executive's track record, competing offers, the difficulty and costs of replacing the executive, or special circumstances for the organization that require the executive's special qualifications and talents.

## Best Practices

### Regular Schedule

Boards and compensation committees should have regular schedules and procedures for making compensation decisions. Because of IRC Section 162(m) considerations discussed earlier, the determination of performance bonus goals and targets and approval of bonuses to be paid already follow (or should follow, at least in public companies) a regular annual schedule. The same should apply to options and other equity awards. Ad hoc grants should be avoided (except where compelling business reasons require otherwise, such as the need to make a special grant for a newly hired or newly promoted executive). The timing of grants should be controlled by the board or compensation committee and not left up to management's discretion.

At least once a year, the board or committee should comprehensively review total compensation, postemployment compensation, and benefits payable under all foreseeable scenarios. The SEC Disclosure Regulations essentially mandate that a public company calculate and update these potential payments for disclosure on an annual basis.

### Tally Sheets for Compensation

Corporate management (or consultants) must ensure that the board or compensation committee has comprehensive tally sheets when any significant compensation decisions are made (including approval of employment contracts) or for the annual review recommended earlier. For employment contracts or other arrangements providing retirement or severance benefits or the annual review, a spreadsheet should show what the employee will receive under each circumstance that might potentially arise (e.g., death, disability, involuntary or good-reason termination, voluntary quit, or discharge for cause). The spreadsheet should place a dollar value on all forms of compensation (including pensions, deferred compensation, and postretirement perquisites, including the tax cost of nondeductible compensation). Where those amounts vary depending on other events (e.g., a change in control) or the company's stock value, the tally should include those alternatives.

Where only certain elements of compensation are up for decision (e.g., base salary review, bonus, equity awards), the tally sheet still should show all the elements of the affected individual's compensation. This allows the elements being considered to be evaluated in the context of total compensation. It also can identify areas where one element of compensation will swing because of changes in another. For example, a relatively modest increase in base salary may significantly increase SERP benefits or the company's obligation for a parachute tax "gross-up" in the event of a change of control.

Of course, these data have to be organized and presented in useful form, without information overload. A good place to start is with the format of the tables forming part of the compensation discussion and analysis under the SEC Disclosure Rules. For one thing, this will give a public company a head start on preparing those disclosures. It also will identify problematic issues or practices that might invite criticism and allow them to be addressed in a timely fashion in making the compensation decisions. Some revisions to plans or awards may avoid potentially undesirable disclosures. This may be especially true for severance plans, change-in-control agreements, retirement plans, and perquisites. Preparing pro-forma disclosure tables at the time of the compensation decisions also ensures that the board or compensation committee will not be surprised when it reviews the ultimate disclosures as part of the company's draft proxy disclosure statement or annual report.

## Consultants

Outside compensation consultants are an integral part of this process for companies of any size. The compensation consultant can provide information to benchmark executive officer compensation and prepare the tally sheets described earlier. However, outside consultants' reports and recommendations are an aid to board or compensation committee decision making, not a substitute for it. Directors should have a clear understanding of their company's executive compensation strategy and the various metrics and other standards that underpin it.

Compensation consultants should be truly independent. In larger companies where the amounts and stakes justify the duplication, the board or compensation committee may retain their own advisors or consultants independent of management's or the company's consultants. Where one consulting firm reports to both management and the board, it should at least have the ability to meet with the board or compensation committee outside the presence of management so that the directors have the opportunity to ask any questions about its report and recommendations on management compensation. If the consultants have other relationships with the company, this must be disclosed to the board or compensation committee so that those bodies can evaluate the independence of the consultant, and such relationships must be disclosed in the proxy disclosure statements of public companies. It is particularly important for the board or compensation committee to have independent consultant (and legal) counsel when renegotiating the employment contract or compensation package for an existing chief executive officer or other senior executive. Executive compensation is almost invariably set in light of (or at least after considering) data on the compensation for similar executive positions at similar companies. Care must be taken in selecting peer companies for this comparison. Adjustments to raw comparator data may be needed for the size of the company and the relative experience of the company's executives versus those of the comparator companies. If the comparison is to have any objectivity, the list of comparator companies needs to be developed in advance and stuck with, not adjusted to justify a decision on compensation levels already reached for other reasons.

## Stock-Option Grant Practices

Companies that have not already done so should review their equity compensation plans and stock-option grant practices. Granting options on a regular schedule at the same time each year, as recommended earlier, will help to ensure the integrity of the grant date, and providing tally-sheet estimates of the dollar value of awards (and other compensation) for the individuals being considered, also noted earlier, will help to ensure that the board or committee has appropriate information. The approval of the grant should cover not only the number of shares and exercise price but also the form of stock-option or other award agreement. Optionees should get prompt notice of the award (and a copy of the agreement). Reallocations or adjustments afterward should not be permitted. Where management recommends stock-option (or other equity) awards, the reasons for the recommendations (as well as the recommended number of shares) should be in writing and included with the committee minutes.

### Conduct of the Meetings

The records of the board or compensation committee should reflect that it has followed best practices as outlined earlier. Action should be taken at a meeting rather than by written consent to allow for member interaction. Where particularly significant or potentially controversial decisions are to be taken, consider presenting the arrangement for discussion at one meeting and postponing a vote until a later meeting. Tally-sheet and other documentation should be circulated well in advance to allow time at the meeting for thorough analysis and discussion. Management and compensation consultants should be available to discuss and explain the recommendations, and as noted earlier, the consultants should have the opportunity to do this outside the presence of management.

If one or two members of the board or committee have taken the lead in the matters being considered, the information and studies they developed or on which they relied, not just their conclusions, should be shared with the full board or committee membership. The board minutes must reflect consideration of the matter and the decision taken, including the reports of consultants and/or management giving support for the decision, and should be prepared promptly after the conclusion of the meeting.

## Conclusion

Most important, the compensation-setting process must be viewed as a vital corporate activity. It is key to reaching the decisions to best drive organizational performance, not just a matter of jumping through government-mandated hoops. A basic reason for much of the regulation discussed in this chapter is to help ensure that the company gets the most actual value for each compensation dollar spent. Even without the government, this should be the ultimate business goal of those responsible for the corporate compensation function.

## Bibliography

Bickley, J. M., and G. Shorter. 2007. "Stock Options: The Backdating Issue." *CRS Report*, March 15.
IRC Section 162(m) Regulations: 26 C.F.R. § 1.162-27.
IRC Section 208G Regulations: 26 C.F.R. § 1.280G-1-4.
IRC Section 409A Regulations: 26 C.F.R. § 1.409A-1-4.
IRC Section 4958 Regulations: 26 C.F.R. § 53.4958-6.
Kraus, H. 2007. *Executive Stock Options and Stock Appreciation Rights*. Law Journal Press, New York.

Mishel, L., and N. Sabadish. 2013. "CEO Pay in 2012 Was Extraordinarily High Relative to Typical Workers and Other High Earners." Economic Policy Institute Issue Brief 367, June 26.

SEC Disclosure Rules: 17 C.F.R. § 229.402.

SEC Say-on-Pay Rules: 17 C.F.R. § 240.14a-21.

SEC Proposed Pay Ratio Rules: Release Nos. 33-9452, 34-70443, 78 Fed. Reg. 60560 (Oct. 1, 2013).

Seitzinger, M. 2010. "The Dodd-Frank Wall Street Reform and Consumer Protection Act: Executive Compensation." *CRS Report*, July 21.

Shorter, G., and M. Labonte. 2007. "The Economics of Corporate Executive Pay." *CRS Report*, May 8.

# 24

# Formulating Executive Employment Agreements

ANDREA S. RATTNER

*Proskauer Rose LLP*

Although the demise of the executive employment agreement has been advocated and debated by and among various constituencies, the executive employment agreement continues to be alive and well, especially with respect to CEOs. This does not mean, however, that these agreements continue to take the same form that they did in prior years. Over recent years, the increased focus on corporate governance and "best practices" has caused certain provisions in employment agreements to fall out of favor, whereas other new provisions have emerged as part of the present-day executive employment agreement.

This "new normal" for executive employment agreements has not resulted from a single event or factor but rather has evolved out of a multitude of events and factors, including increased legislation and regulation, enhanced scrutiny of public companies from proxy advisory firms such as Institutional Shareholder Services (ISS) and Glass Lewis, increased shareholder activism, and public outrage over and media coverage of high-profile executive contracts that have been characterized as excessive or as paying for failure. With respect to the increased legislation and regulation, the adoption of Section 409A of the Internal Revenue Code regarding nonqualified deferred compensation has triggered the rethinking and potential restructuring of virtually every form of compensation other than the current payment of base salary. This has naturally affected the drafting of executive employment agreements. Further, adoption of the Dodd-Frank Wall Street Reform and Consumer Protection Act of 2010 (Dodd-Frank) and, in particular, the mandated say-on-pay shareholder advisory vote on the compensation of named executive officers have had some impact on the executive compensation practices of public companies and, accordingly, on the terms and conditions of executive employment agreements. However, because virtually all say-on-pay proposals were approved by shareholders since 2011, the first year of a mandated say-on-pay vote under Dodd-Frank,[1] it is difficult to determine whether this impact has been truly meaningful. Nonetheless, many companies seek to balance these legal and corporate governance considerations against their business priorities, including the need to develop and implement compensation packages that attract, retain, and motivate key talent and that adapt to rapidly changing business and workforce scenarios.

This chapter summarizes the key provisions that are often addressed and negotiated between a company and a senior executive when entering into a new employment agreement or amending an existing employment agreement in the context of this recent era of increased scrutiny and corporate governance; it does not purport to address every feature or aspect that may come up in the course of negotiations. Of course, every negotiation is affected by the specific facts and circumstances surrounding the company, and the executive and the ultimate terms and conditions of a negotiated employment agreement may deviate from the various features discussed in the summary at the end of this chapter. Further, depending on the circumstances, there may be situations in which no employment agreement is offered or provided to the executive. In such situations, however, there may be general uniform severance policies or plans in place for specified groups of employees as well as separate restrictive covenant agreements containing provisions on confidentiality, noncompetition, nonsolicitation of employees and customers/clients, and the like.

## Term-of-Employment Agreement

Many employment agreements for senior executives contain a fixed term during which the company commits to employ the executive and the executive commits to work for the company. The duration of the fixed term is typically subject to each of the parties' right to terminate the contract or the executive's employment for various articulated reasons at a time that is earlier than the scheduled expiration date of the term. Although once popular, it is now much less common to prohibit the employee from voluntarily terminating employment during the term (and if the employee did voluntarily terminate, the company could sue for damages). Similarly, it is less common to provide that if the company terminates the executive's employment (often for any reason other than "cause"), the employee would receive all payments and benefits that otherwise would have been paid or provided by the company under the contract had the employee continued in employment throughout the entire term. However, sometimes the remainder of the term is used as the basis to calculate the amount of severance to be paid to the executive on certain terminations, although this is not overly common because contracts today tend to specify a fixed severance amount on certain termination events without any reference to the term. An example of using the term in the calculation of severance occurs when the severance payable to an executive on a termination by the company without cause may equal the greater of a fixed amount (e.g., one year of base salary) and the base salary that otherwise would be paid to the executive had he or she continued to be employed for the reminder of the term.

The main issue that often arises today in connection with the term is whether the term is fixed (e.g., over a three-year period from the date of hire), is subject to renewal on certain notice (not particularly common), or is subject to automatic renewal unless notice of nonrenewal is given. If the employment agreement provides for automatic renewal, it will need to specify how the renewal operates (e.g., after the initial term, the contract is renewed for a single year, successive single years, multiyear periods, or rolling days or other periods). Although many executives have automatic renewal provisions, ISS and others generally view fixed contracts as a better practice than contracts with automatic renewal because a fixed contract gives the parties an opportunity to take a fresh look at the contract toward the end of the term and avoids the "grandfathering" and continuation of provisions that occur with automatic renewals, which may no longer be appropriate. By contrast, executives have significantly greater comfort with the automatic renewal approach. A related consideration described later in the section "Termination Events and Severance" is whether severance is payable on the company's nonrenewal of the term.

Unlike executive employment agreements, it is unusual to have a term of employment or of the agreement in offer letters and similar employment letters. Rather, these letters typically contain affirmative statements that the employment is "at will" and that the company may terminate the employee at any time for any reason.

## Title/Position, Duties, and Reporting

Most senior executives expect their employment agreements to specify their titles, duties, and reporting relationship in order to give them greater comfort with respect to their place within the employing organization. At the same time, companies want flexibility in running their businesses without fear of inadvertently triggering an executive's rights under an employment agreement (e.g., payment of severance on a termination for "good reason" due to a material reduction in title, duties, or reporting relationship).

Whereas it is typically straightforward to specify a senior executive's title in the employment agreement, specifying the duties and reporting relationship may raise certain considerations. Often the details of the duties are not specified in the agreement, but rather, the agreement states that the executive will have such duties that are commensurate with his or her position; sometimes executives seek to have this determined by reference to similarly situated executives at comparably sized companies, which is often difficult to determine. Care should be taken to ensure that the duties and authorities given to an executive do not extend into the realm of the authority granted to the board of directors pursuant to a company's bylaws. For example, while not often addressed in employment agreements, it may be appropriate to give a CEO certain rights with respect to the hiring and firing of executives; however, such rights should be subject to the company's bylaws or limited to making recommendations to the board (rather than giving the CEO ultimate authority).

From the company's perspective, it may be appropriate to state that the executive will use his or her best efforts to promote the interests of the company and to perform his or her duties and that he or she will use all or substantially all of his or her time (which is sometimes stated as "business time") to the business of the company, sometimes with very limited carve-outs. From the executive's perspective, he or she may agree in the contract to the company's request to dedicate substantially all of his or her time to the business, but only subject to the company's recognition that the executive may engage in some permitted outside activities that do not directly relate to his or her performance of duties for the company. A company may allow an executive to engage in certain permitted outside activities under the theory that at least some of those activities may provide the company with an incidental benefit beyond simply accommodating the executive's request and fostering trust between the parties. Permitted outside activities may include serving as a director of a not-for-profit organization or engaging in some other charitable activity, serving as a director of a for-profit entity, participating in industry or trade events (including writing opportunities and speaking engagements), and managing one's personal and family's financial affairs and investments. However, the company often will seek to limit these activities by providing in the employment agreement that these activities are only permitted as long as they do not materially interfere with the executive's responsibilities to the company or create a conflict of interest. Sometimes this standard is tougher with respect to for-profit boards (as opposed to any other activity, including activity on non-for-profit boards), and any such activities may be subject to prior approval of the board of directors.

Executives often want comfort in knowing the title of the person to whom they will report. For the CEO, this is typically the board of directors, although if there is a separate chairman of the board, the CEO also may report to the chairman. Senior executive officers (other than the CEO) typically look for a provision that provides for direct reporting to the CEO, although sometimes companies provide that they report to the CEO or his or her delegate. With respect to the CFO, an issue may arise as to whether he or she will report not only to the CEO but also to the audit committee of the company's board of directors (or the chairman of such committee). For executives below the most senior levels, the reporting relationship may not be specified, or if it is specified, flexibility is often built into the relevant provision.

## Compensation

The compensation section of any executive employment agreement is typically the heart of the agreement because it gives the executive the comfort that he or she will receive the benefit of the bargain that was negotiated between the parties (i.e., the executive agrees to perform services for the company and in return expects a certain level of compensation and benefits coupled with opportunities to earn additional compensation). Certain contracts specify the most basic components of the compensation package, such as a starting salary, a potential discretionary bonus opportunity, and benefits provided by the company subject to the applicable plans, terms, and conditions (including the right to amend or terminate such plans); other contracts detail every aspect of the current compensation package and establish rights to receive additional future compensation (e.g., specifying future rights to scheduled salary increases or future equity grants). Many contracts take a balanced approach and provide for some detail as to each component of the initial compensation package with locked-in salary and bonus opportunities for the term of the contract; often the company retains flexibility with respect to future increases to compensation, grants of equity awards, and other potential forms of compensation.

*Base Salary.* Virtually all employment agreements specify a minimum level of base salary that will be paid to the executive, which typically is set for the term of the employment agreement (other than in the case of offer letters, which may set an initial base salary for the first year of employment only). The employment agreement may state that the compensation committee of the board shall or may review the base salary annually and increase the base salary as it determines in its sole discretion. Although less common, the employment agreement may provide for increases to base salary that will occur at specified times during the term of the agreement, which may be based on negotiated amounts or on designated cost-of-living adjustments. Many executive employment agreements provide that once base salary is increased, it may not be decreased; accordingly, where severance amounts are calculated by reference to base salary (e.g., one times base salary), those severance amounts will increase as the base salary amount increases.

Corporations whose stock is publicly traded should be mindful that any amount of annual base salary that exceeds $1 million and is payable to the CEO and certain named executive officers listed in the proxy disclosure statement will not be tax deductible to the corporation under Section 162(m) of the Internal Revenue Code. Although a significant number of public companies limit CEO compensation to $1 million per year, many companies pay base salary that exceeds this threshold owing to various business considerations.

*Annual Incentives/Bonus.* Many executive employment agreements specify the annual bonus opportunity available to the executive. Although there are contracts that provide for discretionary bonuses, the growing trend is to provide for performance-based bonuses. The employment agreement may spell out the specific performance metrics and goals that apply to the bonus or may state that the compensation committee will set the performance metrics and goals in its sole discretion or in consultation with the executive. Often the amount of the bonus opportunity is expressed as a specified percentage of base salary in order to earn a target bonus (meaning a bonus that is payable on achievement of targeted performance metrics). Sometimes the agreement may specify the percentages that apply at threshold (minimum) performance as well as at maximum levels of performance (e.g., a bonus cap of 200 percent of base salary for top performance). Specifying the maximum possible bonus payout is viewed as a "best practice" because of its potential risk-mitigating impact—having no limit on what could be earned may be seen as encouraging excessive risk taking by the executive in order to achieve a very high bonus.

In light of the deferred-compensation rules under Internal Revenue Code Section 409A, employment agreements should clearly state the timing of payment of the bonus in order to establish whether the bonus is exempt under or compliant with Section 409A. Further, the agreement should be clear as to whether the executive must be employed on the bonus payment date or the last day of the company's fiscal year in order to receive the bonus.

The impact of different termination-of-employment events on the amount of bonus payable to the executive, if any, also should be considered and addressed in the agreement. For example, the contract may provide for the payment of a pro rata bonus (based on actual achievement of performance goals) on death, a termination due to disability, or a termination of the executive by the company without cause. For corporations whose stock is publicly traded, any payment of a pro rata bonus incentive that is based on target performance (rather than actual performance) with respect to certain terminations (generally, termination by the company without cause and by the executive for good reason) will jeopardize the performance-based status of the bonus in any situation under the $1 million tax-deductibility rules under Section 162(m) of the Internal Revenue Code. Further, the clawback or recoupment of an annual bonus incentive payment also should be considered, as more fully explained later in the section "Clawback Provisions."

For corporations with publicly traded stock, the bonus may be designed to constitute "performance-based compensation" for purposes of Section 162(m) of the Internal Revenue Code in order to preserve the tax deductibility of the bonus; because of technicalities under Section 162(m), special provisions may be added to the employment agreement to bolster this treatment (e.g., by making reference to the shareholder-approved plan under which the bonus will be awarded or by conditioning the bonus on shareholder approval of the specific arrangement or of a plan that will cover the bonus and be adopted in the future).

Note that employment agreements for new hires may have additional provisions that address the possibility of a sign-on or other special bonus that is designed to attract the candidate to the job and sometimes provide for a "make-whole" of compensation lost by the executive as a result of his or her departure from the prior employer. Guaranteed bonuses, especially those with multiyear commitments, are disfavored by institutional investors and proxy advisory firms such as ISS.

*Equity Awards.* Although there are executive employment agreements that are silent with respect to the grant of equity awards, many agreements address equity awards in some fashion. From the company's perspective, a general statement that the executive will be eligible to receive equity awards as determined in its sole discretion may suffice and provide the company with significant flexibility. However, such an approach may be ineffective because the executive likely will be seeking some comfort with respect to equity awards. This may take various forms—for example, the executive may be content with a commitment that the company will treat the executive in a manner consistent with other similarly situated executives. In many cases, however, in order to attract a prospective candidate (in particular, a CEO candidate), it may be necessary for the company to commit to make a specific equity award (often simultaneous with execution of the employment agreement) or to commit to recommend to the compensation committee of the board a specific equity award. This often involves providing in the executive employment agreement the amount of the equity award (e.g., by specifying the number of shares subject to the equity award or the amount in terms of a dollar value or percentage of base salary and the methodology by which it is converted into a share-based award) and the nature of the equity award (e.g., stock options, restricted stock, restricted stock units, or performance shares or units). Proxy disclosure statement advisory firms (such as ISS) and institutional investors will focus on the size and nature of the equity award and, in particular, whether the award is performance based.

The employment agreement also may specify that the company's normal terms and conditions under an identified stock-based plan will govern the equity awards; sometimes the employment agreement will specify certain key terms and conditions that will be applied to the specific equity award (e.g., term of award, vesting and exercisability, impact of certain termination events, and clawback or restrictive covenant provisions). Typically, these key terms and conditions apply to the equity award being made at the time that the employment agreement is entered into and not to all future grants because that approach has a significant impact on a company's ability to assess what may be appropriate in the future based on a multitude of factors, including the performance of the executive, developments relating to the company, and general market conditions. However, depending on the circumstances, it may be appropriate to set forth in the employment agreement the terms and conditions that will apply to equity grants (or regular grants) made during the term of the employment agreement.

Further, for public companies, care should be taken to ensure that the promise made with respect to the equity award comports with the terms and conditions of the shareholder-approved equity plan. One key feature to consider relates to share limits under the equity-based plan—the company should confirm whether the shareholder-approved equity plan has sufficient shares of common stock available for the anticipated equity grant and whether the size of the equity grant falls within the plan's individual share limits (or other applicable limits) that are designed to comply with Internal Revenue Code Section 162(m). In instances where the shares are not available, the employment agreement may provide for an equity award that is (1) conditioned on shareholder approval of an amendment to an equity plan to increase the amount of available shares, (2) not made unless and until appropriate shareholder approval is obtained, or (3) made outside the company's shareholder-approved equity plan as a "material inducement" equity grant for a new executive hire, subject to the various requirements of New York Stock Exchange (NYSE) and Nasdaq. There are many factors for companies subject to these exchange requirements to consider if they wish to use the material inducement grant exemption from the shareholder approval rules for equity plans. One consequence includes the likely loss of the tax deduction relating to the equity award under Internal Revenue Code Section 162(m).

*Benefits, Perquisites, and Fringe Benefits.* It is common to provide in an employment agreement that the executive will be eligible to participate in the company's benefit plans and programs subject to their terms and conditions. Sometimes executives seek to provide in their agreements that such eligibility will be for plans and programs that apply to similarly situated executives or seek to identify specific executive-level benefits that they want to receive [e.g., enhanced disability or life insurance benefits or certain nonqualified deferred-compensation or supplemental executive retirement plan (SERP) benefits]. Depending on the circumstances, certain executive "perks" and fringe benefits may be provided in the employment agreement, such as car allowances, financial planning and tax preparation services, and relocation expenses. However, as a result of the required proxy disclosure and ISS and institutional investor views concerning "egregious" pension and SERP payments and "excessive" perquisites, these arrangements have been largely eliminated. Any determination to give perquisites or fringe benefits should be carefully considered against this backdrop.

*Vacation.* Many executive employment agreements provide that the executive will be entitled to the vacation specified in the company's policy, although many agreements provide for a minimum number of weeks that apply to the executive. It may be appropriate to clearly specify in the employment agreement that the company's policy applies, including the company's policy on the treatment of vacation carryover.

## Termination Events and Severance

Provisions relating to termination and severance are significant aspects of the executive employment agreement and are often the provisions that are the most heavily negotiated between a company and an executive. However, as noted earlier under the discussion regarding the term, older-styled contracts sometimes did not have elaborate termination or severance provisions and, instead, provided for the continuation of the parties' respective obligations if the executive terminated employment or the company terminated the executive, in each case, before the end of the term. Depending on the terms of the agreement regarding the right to terminate, the terminating party may have breached the contract during the term, thereby giving the other party the right to sue the breaching party and seek damages. Where the company was the breaching party (i.e., terminating the executive prior to the end of the term), the executive typically would assert the right to receive the compensation and benefits that otherwise would have been paid under the contract had the company not terminated him or her.

By contrast, present-day contracts typically provide for termination-of-employment events that cut the term of the agreement short before its scheduled end date. The executive's termination of employment and the corresponding termination of the term of the employment agreement result in most (but not all) of the obligations under the agreement to cease. For example, the company's obligation to provide current compensation and benefits ceases, but its obligation to pay severance to the executive on certain types of terminations or to provide indemnification protection to the executive may continue. From the executive's perspective, he or she will no longer have any obligation to perform services for the company, but he or she may have continuing obligations to comply with restrictive covenants and may be subject to certain conditions, such as potential recoupment by the company of incentive compensation or the signing of a release in order to receive severance.

The termination events that are often addressed in an executive employment agreement include death, disability, the company's termination of the executive with or without cause (generally, bad acts on the part of the executive), the executive's termination with or without good reason (generally, adverse actions on the part of the employer that are tantamount to the constructive termination of the executive), and nonrenewal of the agreement (by the company or the executive). Not all contracts address all termination events; typically, good reason is not a trigger event in contracts other than those at the highest levels within an organization (C-suite executives).

Although not particularly common, in some contracts, there may be specific rights that apply in the event of an executive's retirement (often defined as the attainment of a specific age and the completion of a certain number of years of service or a combination of age plus service hitting a specified number such as the *rule of 75*). In the occasional instance where retirement issues arise, the treatment of compensation, benefits, and other rights tends to be evaluated on a case-by-case basis.

Although all these events may terminate the agreement and the employment relationship, they all do not create an entitlement to severance. Severance is typically payable on a company's termination of the executive without cause; if the contract has good reason rights, the same amount of severance that would be paid in a termination-without-cause situation would be payable as a result of the executive's termination due to good reason. In the case of a termination due to the company's nonrenewal of the agreement, practice varies as to whether it is treated as a without-cause or good-reason termination, where severance would be paid. When the term of the agreement is fixed without renewal provisions, it is less common to provide for severance under the theory that each party received the benefit of the bargain if the term was completed. In the case of death or disability, there have been occasions where severance has been provided (when given, it is usually at reduced levels), but many, if not most, companies do not provide severance on death or disability and instead rely on life and disability insurance policies to provide protection to the executive in the event of his or her death or disability. In the case of a termination by the executive (without good reason for the executive's possessing good-reason rights), it is highly unusual to see payment of any severance (including the pro rata bonus for the year of termination), although an executive's retirement may give rise to certain rights under equity arrangements (e.g., longer exercise periods for stock options, which would normally be addressed in the applicable award agreement and not necessarily in the employment agreement). In the case of a termination of the executive by the company for cause, nothing is provided, and in fact, vested benefits are typically forfeited.

*Death.* Although there is no need to define death for purposes of an employment agreement, care should be taken to ensure that the contract addresses to whom payment should be made in the event of the executive's death. Typically, most contracts contemplate that any payments (such as accrued salary) and benefits (such as vesting in certain benefits and rights to exercise stock options) would be made or provided to the executive's estate, although it is possible to set forth in the contract an ordering of beneficiaries or allow the executive to make a beneficiary designation (which, depending on how this is handled, may create potential ambiguities with the company's benefit plans and may create administrative issues). Some agreements solely pay accrued amounts on death and provide for life insurance that becomes payable on death. Other agreements take a step further and provide for certain benefits and rights on death, such as full or pro rata accelerated vesting and payment of equity or other benefits (such as a SERP) and payment of pro rata bonus on death (at target or based on actual performance).

*Disability.* Because employment agreements typically provide that a company may terminate an executive as a result of disability and not pay any severance, disability is usually defined in the agreement and, from the executive's perspective, should not be easy for the company to trigger. Often disability is defined by reference to the company's long-term disability plan, a set number of days (sometimes consecutive) over a specified period of time during which the executive cannot perform his or her duties (sometimes determined by a physician designated by the company or mutually agreed to by the parties), and/or "disability" as defined under Internal Revenue Code Section 409A. Under Section 409A, "disability" generally means the executive's inability to engage in any "substantial gainful activity" because of a medically determinable physical or mental impairment that can be expected to result in death or to last for a continuous period of at least 12 months or the executive's receipt of income-replacement benefits for at least three months under a company's accident and health plan as a result of a medically determinable physical or mental impairment that can be expected to result in death or to last for a continuous period of at least 12 months. Generally, if the employment agreement terminates as a result of a termination due to disability, a disability definition other than the Section 409A definition often applies; for Section 409A purposes, the trigger for the relevant payment is a termination of employment (which must constitute a "separation from service" under Section 409A) rather than disability. See the section "Section 409A."

*Cause.* The purpose of the cause definition is to define the executive's bad acts where the executive is terminated without any entitlement to severance or other benefits or where certain vested rights may be forfeited or amounts may be subject to recoupment. Cause usually includes some level of criminal activity (e.g., felonies and misdemeanors, sometimes with carve-outs for traffic offenses and sometimes with qualifiers with respect to the type of misdemeanor) that is triggered at commission, indictment, or commission of the crime and typically includes pleas of guilty or *nolo contendre* (i.e., no contest) to any such crime. Cause also includes an array of other bad acts, including, for example, the executive's fraud, embezzlement, or dishonesty; negligence (sometimes gross negligence) or willful misconduct; breach of the company's policies and procedures; failure to follow the directions of the company's board of directors; breach of the employment agreement (or other contracts); and failure to perform duties. Each bad act that potentially could constitute cause is typically subject to robust negotiation as to whether any such act must be "willful," result in "material harm" to the company and its reputation, or contain other qualifiers. Whether cause includes any failure by the executive to perform his or her duties is often hotly debated; most executives will want any performance component to be eliminated from the definition of cause, or at a minimum, they would want to qualify such definition with "willful" and "materially" standards or failures to "attempt to" perform. Sometimes the definition includes the executive's ability to cure any deficiencies within a specified period of time following the company's discovery of the cause event(s) to the extent that such an event is curable. Executives often seek to incorporate some procedural rights in the contract with respect to the company's cause determination (e.g., that a certain percentage of the board must determine that cause exists).

*Good Reason.* The purpose of the good-reason definition is to define situations in which the employer has made significant adverse changes to key aspects of the executive's compensation package or employment conditions. These changes are viewed as tantamount to a constructive discharge of the executive, and any severance that may become payable typically equals the severance that would be payable on a termination of the executive by the company without cause. The good-reason definition coupled with the cause definition typically are the most hotly debated terms in an employment agreement because these definitions establish the parameters regarding whether severance is or is not paid and whether other benefits and rights are extinguished or provided. *Good reason* usually includes any reduction (or material reduction) to base salary and/or other forms of compensation and benefits; diminution (or material diminution) in title, duties, authorities, and responsibilities; adverse change in the reporting relationship; certain relocations of the principal place of business; breach of the employer's obligations under the employment agreement; failure to be nominated to the board of directors (CEO only); and other adverse changes. Sometimes materiality qualifiers and other carve-outs are incorporated into the definition, such as the company's ability to reduce the executive's salary or benefits as long as it is done as part of an across-the-board reduction in salary and/or benefits applicable to all employees or similarly situated employees. Similar to the cause scenario, the good-reason definition often includes the company's right to cure any deficiencies; this is designed to allow an employer to correct any action or omission (often inadvertent) that may trigger good reason. Also, given the changing nature of businesses, many good-reason definitions contemplate that the executive's written consent to any adverse change will not trigger good reason.

It is significant that the definition of good reason plays into whether the severance or other forms of payment that are tied to a good-reason event may constitute "deferred compensation" subject to the rules under Internal Revenue Code Section 409A. If an employment agreement includes the Section 409A "safe harbor" definition of good reason (generally, material adverse changes to key aspects of the contract or employment relationship), the severance likely will not constitute deferred compensation, and therefore, it could be paid following a "separation from service." If, however, the definition does not conform to the safe-harbor definition or otherwise does not meet the IRS "facts and circumstances" standard, it is likely that the payment of severance would have to be delayed for six months following separation from service for "specified employees" of public companies [very generally, a 5 percent owner, a 1 percent owner with annual compensation in excess of $150,000, or any officer with annual compensation of more than $170,000 (for 2014 and as subsequently adjusted by the IRS), limited to the lesser of (1) 50 employees or (2) the greater of three employees or 10 percent of the employees].

The safe-harbor definition of good reason under Section 409A provides that the separation from service must occur during a predetermined limited period not to exceed two years following the initial existence of any of the following conditions: (1) material diminution in base compensation, (2) material diminution in the executive's authority, duties, or responsibilities, (3) material diminution in the authority, duties, or responsibilities of the supervisor to whom the executive is required to report (including a requirement that an executive report to a corporate officer or employee instead of the board of directors or similar body), (4) material diminution in the budget over which the executive retains authority, (5) material change in geographic location at which the executive must perform services, and (6) any other action or inaction that constitutes a material breach by the employer of the agreement under which the executive provides services (i.e., the employment agreement). It is interesting to note that the safe-harbor definition does not reference a material diminution in title or position; for certain executives, such as the CEO, consideration should be given to whether any such diminution would be covered under the material breach prong (assuming that the employment agreement sets forth the title/position). The safe-harbor definition also provides that the payment on a good-reason termination needs to be substantially identical to the amount, time, and form of payment due on an actual involuntary termination (assuming that such right exists). Lastly, the safe-harbor definition provides that the executive must provide notice to the employer within a period not to exceed 90 days of the initial existence of the condition, with the company having at least 30 days to cure.

# Severance

*Calculation of Severance.* The amount of cash severance that becomes payable on a termination without cause or for good reason is a business point subject to negotiation between the parties. For senior executive-level employment agreements, the severance amount is often expressed as a multiple of base salary and, in certain cases, of base salary plus bonus (which could be based on target or an average earned over a number of specified years). As noted earlier, severance could equal the salary (or the salary and bonus) that otherwise would be payable over the remaining term of the contract. Sometimes severance is articulated as the greater of the multiple of compensation approach and the remaining-term approach. Further, severance also may include a pro rata portion of the bonus that otherwise would be payable for the year of the executive's termination. In recent years, the bonus typically is tied to actual performance and is paid when paid to other executives, although there are instances where it may be based on a target. For corporations whose stock is publicly traded, the payment of a pro rata bonus at target on a CEO's (or, generally, a named executive officer's) termination without cause or for good reason jeopardizes the performance-based status of the bonus for purposes of the $1 million tax-deduction limit under Internal Revenue Code Section 162(m).

Although the amount of the severance is a key negotiated business term, institutional investors, proxy disclosure statement advisory firms, and others have been vocal about executive employment agreements that are viewed as providing for excessive severance amounts and/or easy triggers for the payment of severance. ISS cites, among other things, excessive payments on an executive's termination in connection with performance failure as a potentially problematic feature that it reviews on a case-by-case basis in connection with its say-on-pay vote. As described further later, executive employment agreements that provide for enhanced severance protection in the event of a change in control of the company are subject to intense scrutiny from ISS and others.

*Form of Severance.* The employment agreement must specify the payment form of any severance to be paid to the executive. Typically, companies prefer to pay severance in installments over time so that they could cease severance payments in the event that an executive breaches any of the restrictive covenants in the agreement. By contrast, the executive often prefers a lump-sum severance payment in order to ensure full payment without risk of cessation of the payments. In the change-in-control context, the executive's desire for a lump-sum severance payment is sometimes increased because the executive may also be concerned about the buyer's creditworthiness (particularly in highly leveraged transactions) and desire to pay. Elections by the executive or the company to pay in installments or a lump sum raise various tax issues under the constructive-receipt doctrine and Internal Revenue Code Section 409A and therefore generally are inadvisable.

*Other Severance Benefits and Rights.* Sometimes an executive employment agreement provides for additional benefits and rights beyond cash severance amounts that are payable in the event of a termination by the company without cause or by the executive for good reason (or potentially on a company nonrenewal of the contract, if so provided). These benefits and rights may include, for example, full or partial vesting of equity awards, extending the period of time to exercise stock options, full or partial vesting of nonqualified deferred compensation or SERP benefits, outplacement, continuation of life insurance, or continuation of health insurance under COBRA, with the terminated executive paying the applicable active employee rate and the company subsidizing its portion of the rate. Care should be taken not to provide continued benefits that may violate applicable law if provided after termination [e.g., generally 401(k) and other qualified retirement plan benefits]. In many cases, especially for public companies, providing a laundry list of fringe benefits and executive perquisites that apply following the executive's termination must be closely evaluated because it is generally not a favored practice. ISS has stated that perquisites for former or retired executives, such as lifetime benefits, car allowances, personal use of aircraft, or other "inappropriate" arrangements, are considered problematic and may result in a withhold or against recommendation on the say-on-pay vote on a case-by-case basis.

*Release Requirement.* It is typical to provide that the executive will be required to execute and not revoke a release of claims in favor of the company, its affiliates, and other related parties in order to receive payment of severance and the other benefits and rights triggered on a termination by the company without cause or termination by the executive for good reason (and potentially on a company's nonrenewal, if so provided). Depending on the surrounding circumstances, although the release is typically drafted very broadly to address every type of claim imaginable, there are some carve-outs that may be incorporated into the release. These carve-outs include, for example, the executive's right to receive the severance benefits (subject to any conditions specified in the release), rights to indemnification from the company to the extent provided under the bylaws or, if applicable, under the employment agreement, rights to directors' and officers' (D&O) insurance, and rights to vested accrued benefits under a pension plan [such as a 401(k) plan].

Sometimes the employment agreement specifies that the company's customary form will be used (with changes as determined by the company to reflect changes in applicable law); in other cases, the form of release is negotiated between the parties and attached to the employment agreement. Sometimes the employment agreement and/or the release contain a variety of other obligations that apply if the executive is entitled to receive severance. For example, a return-of-property clause or a cooperation clause obligating the executive to cooperate with the company in the event of a legal proceeding or investigation may be included in the release. In order to address Internal Revenue Code Section 409A, the release timing provisions in the employment agreement should be precise and define the time period during which the executive may consider, sign, and not revoke the release; it also should specify the payment date following termination (e.g., payable on the sixtieth day following the executive's separation from service, subject to the six-month delay to the extent applicable).

## Change in Control

Executives are particularly concerned about their fate when faced with a change in control of the company, and as a result, they typically seek to obtain extra protections under their employment agreements in the event of a change in control. Often the amount of cash severance payable and the benefits and rights provided in connection with certain terminations surrounding a change in control are enhanced. In this regard, although the change-in-control cash severance amount may increase compared with the regular cash severance amount, it is unusual for the severance to exceed a multiple of three (whether three times base salary and/or base salary and bonus).

In addition to negotiating the amount and nature of the cash severance and the other benefits and rights, the parties typically will negotiate the triggers for payment. In many cases, these payments are made and benefits are provided only on the occurrence of a *double trigger*, meaning the company's termination of the executive without cause or the executive's termination for good reason occurring on or within a designated period following a change in control (such as 12 or 24 months). Sometimes the executive will seek pre–change-in-control protection in order to avoid the situation in which the executive is terminated in anticipation of a change in control. Sometimes this type of protection is structured so that the executive will receive additional severance on the change in control if the change happens within a designated period following termination of the executive without cause or for good reason (e.g., 90 days). To avoid Internal Revenue Code Section 409A issues with this structure, the definition of change in control should be drafted so as to conform to the definition of a change-in-control event set forth in the Section 409A regulations.

Sometimes change-in-control severance is paid on almost any termination (but not on a cause termination) occurring within a designated period commencing on a change in control. This is typically referred to as a *walk-away right, trigger and a half,* or a *modified single trigger.* Sometimes the walk-away right is limited to certain window periods following the change in control. In certain other instances, the vesting of equity may occur on a change in control even if severance requires a termination of employment to occur; such vesting is commonly referred to as a *single trigger.*

As noted earlier, in the change-in-control context, the scrutiny of the severance amounts and payment triggers increases. The current policy of ISS states that certain change-in-control severance practices carry significant weight in its evaluation of a company's pay practices and will result in an adverse-vote recommendation on say on pay. These practices include change-in-control severance amounts that exceed three times base salary and average/target/most recent bonus and severance payments that are triggered without involuntary job loss or substantial diminution of duties (such as *single* or *modified single triggers*). Single trigger of equity vesting is not favored, although the practice continues to be somewhat varied.

Because these change-in-control-related payments may trigger golden parachute tax concerns under Internal Revenue Code Sections 280G and 4999, the treatment of any golden parachutes is often addressed in executive employment agreements, particularly those entered into with public corporations. In the event that the parachute payments exceed a certain threshold, the executive may be subject to a 20 percent excise tax on "excess parachute payments," and the company may lose the corresponding tax deduction on "excess parachute payments." Although tax gross-ups for the golden parachute excise tax were once customary (especially at the CEO level), they are now disfavored and are often replaced with either a *cutback provision* (which gives the executive an amount that is cut back to the maximum amount that could be paid without triggering the excise tax) or a *contingent-cutback provision* (which gives the executive the greater of the amount cut back so that the excise tax is not triggered and the amount subject to the excise tax, whichever gives the executive the greater net after-tax amount). ISS has included excise tax gross-ups on its list of problematic pay practices that likely will result in adverse-vote recommendations.

## Restrictive Covenants

From the company's perspective, a critical aspect of the executive employment agreement is the inclusion of various restrictive covenants in the agreement, such as clauses addressing confidentiality, noncompetition, nonsolicitation of employees, and nonsolicitation of clients and customers. Restrictive covenants protect the employer from a current or former executive's competition and other detrimental activity and typically apply while the executive is employed and for a designated period following the executive's termination of employment (e.g., 12 months, 24 months). Sometimes, but not always, the restrictive-covenant period matches the period on which the severance is based (e.g., 12 months of severance will equate to a 12-month posttermination restricted covenant period).

In structuring the restrictive covenants, there are a number of key issues to consider. These include the scope of the restrictions (i.e., what restraints should be imposed), the duration of the restrictions (i.e., for how long should they be imposed), the geographic location of the restrictions (i.e., where should they be imposed), and the remedies if the executive breaches the restrictions.

The key issue relating to restrictive covenants from the company's perspective is the enforceability of the provisions—this largely depends on the scope and breadth of the restrictive covenant. For employers that do business throughout the United States (and beyond), this is particularly challenging because state law governs and differs throughout the United States. What is reasonable and appropriate in one state may not be appropriate in another state. For example, in California, noncompetition covenants in the employment context are largely unenforceable. By contrast, some states have passed statutes governing the enforceability of the restrictive covenants, but certain states, such as New York, do not have any such restrictive-covenant statutes and generally take the view that restrictive covenants will only be enforced to the extent that they are reasonable and necessary to protect valid business interests (although New York also recognizes the *employee-choice doctrine*, where the employee may choose to compete and, accordingly, forfeit the benefit or, alternatively, keep the benefit and not compete). In many instances, to evaluate enforceability, a case-by-case analysis of the applicable facts and circumstances needs to be done. This may include a review of the type of industry involved, the nature of the executive's services, and the executive's position with the company.

If a restrictive covenant is held to be unenforceable, courts do not necessarily void the entire covenant. Instead, in certain states, courts may "blue pencil" or remove the provisions that are considered unreasonable and enforce the remaining portion of the covenant. To bolster this possibility, it is customary to include a blue-pencil provision in the restrictive-covenant section of an executive employment agreement subject to an analysis under applicable state law regarding whether the blue-pencil doctrine is recognized. There are many legal and business nuances and considerations that apply to restrictive covenants, much of which are beyond the scope of this chapter.

## Section 409A

As noted earlier, there are many features of the executive employment agreement that are affected by application of the nonqualified deferred compensation rules under Internal Revenue Code Section 409A. Whenever designing any aspect of the executive's compensation under an employment agreement (perhaps other than with respect to base salary that is paid on a current basis and not deferred), an analysis needs to be done regarding whether the feature is or is not subject to Section 409A, and if it is subject to Section 409A, the agreement should be structured to comply with the applicable rules (in order to avoid the imposition of an additional 20 percent tax and additional penalties and interest on the executive). This includes, for example, providing for the timely election of deferrals and the timing of the payment of the deferred compensation (e.g., certain forms of severance) on a permissible payment event under Section 409A (e.g., on death, a fixed payment date, a change in control, or a "separation from service as defined under Section 409A, subject to a six-month delay for certain specified employees of public companies). As noted earlier, there are special definitions of certain terms such as *disability*, *good reason*, and *change in control* under Section 409A for payments of deferred compensation made on any such date. Because Section 409A and the regulations therein are very technical in nature and the impact of Section 409A is pervasive and potentially punitive on the executive, extreme care should be taken when drafting an employment agreement and structuring the payment of compensation.

## Clawback Provisions

In light of Dodd-Frank and general trends, certain executive employment agreements include *clawback provisions* (also known as *compensation recoupment* or *recovery provisions*) that enable an employer to recover compensation paid to an executive on the occurrence of a certain event or a certain action by the executive. The triggers for the recoupment of compensation are varied and may include

- Material financial restatements (with or without misconduct)
- Material inaccuracies in the calculation of incentive compensation
- Acts or omissions by an employee that constitute cause (or that would have given rise to a cause termination if such acts or omissions were known prior to an employee's termination)
- Breaches of restrictive covenants (e.g., noncompetition and nonsolicitation agreements)
- Ethical or other violations

The executive employment agreement itself may contractually provide for a clawback of compensation, may require the executive to acknowledge that he or she is subject to and bound by the company's clawback policy, or may require the executive to acknowledge that he or she will be subject to a clawback policy to be adopted by the company that is designed to comply with Dodd-Frank or applicable law.

Section 954 of Dodd-Frank generally requires that the SEC issue rules requiring companies to recoup incentive-based compensation paid to current or former executive officers if the company is required to restate its accounting statements as a result of material noncompliance with applicable financial reporting requirements. Because the SEC has not yet issued such rules, there are open questions as to the interpretation and application of the Dodd-Frank clawback rules. Nonetheless, although some companies have taken a wait-and-see approach, others have adopted clawback policies that they wish to apply to incentive compensation that is set forth in an employment agreement.

There are numerous other miscellaneous provisions that may be included in executive employment agreements such as provisions regarding no mitigation/no offset, the company's indemnification of the executive, dispute resolution, governing law (very standard), and reimbursement of legal fees. Whereas certain provisions and approaches in executive employment agreements may continue to be somewhat standard, it is also clear that the protections and obligations set forth in executive employment agreements will continue to depend on the particular facts and circumstances that apply to the company and the executive and likely will be subject to negotiation, especially at the CEO level. Further, the practices governing executive employment agreements and the related compensation arrangements will continue to evolve and reflect the ever-changing legal and business environment.

## Note

1. According to Semler Brossy's report entitled, "Say on Pay Results Russell 3000 (July 16, 2014)," approximately 1.4 percent of the companies in the Russell 3000 failed in 2011, 2.6 percent failed in 2012, and 2.5 percent failed in 2013. As of July 16, 2014, 2.4 percent have failed. Of 1,642 companies that held annual say-on-pay votes in 2011–2014, 1,511 (92 percent) passed in all four years, and all but 22 percent (98.6 percent) passed in at least three of the four years. See http://www.semlerbrossy.com/sayonpay.

# 25

# Cracking the Secret Code of Long-Term Incentives in Private Companies

MYRNA HELLERMAN
*Sibson Consulting*

YELENA STILES
*Sibson Consulting*

Private-company long-term incentive (LTI) plans are unhampered by the scrutiny and commentary of regulators, investors, and the media. They do not need to rigorously conform to accepted practices and standard designs. Instead, LTI plans at private companies unabashedly reflect the owner's unique decisions about the sharing of long-term economic success. Many owners view their LTI plan as the secret code to company success and closely guard its design and deployment as a private matter between the owner and the participants.

Although private companies run the gamut in size, complexity, and ownership, Sibson Consulting has found that its approach to LTI plans fits one of six pay models, which this chapter describes. No model is exclusive to a specific type or size of company. Further, the design elements and execution of a specific model differ widely among employers. As a result, the pay model adopted by a private company artfully reflects the owner's distinctive mind-set about rewarding executives for their contribution to the company's long-term economic success.

In this chapter, you will learn about six models that will improve organization performance by helping crack the secret code of long-term incentives in private companies.

## Cracking the Secret Code

Six models are described below (and in Table 25.1) that explain different approaches taken by private companies. The variations among these six models create an infinite number of possibilities that are in use in private companies and are constantly evolving. Rather than seeking to force fit one of these six models, designers of plans for private companies are encouraged to consider which aspects of each plan are a best fit for the individual company, its owners, its goals, and its ability to execute.

| Pay Model | Base | Annual Incentive | Cash LTI | Staking Grant | Comments |
|---|---|---|---|---|---|
| *Hired hand*<br><br>Pay opportunity is limited to base pay (frequently targeted significantly above market) | ✓ | | | | • Upfront reward for the accomplishment of specific outcomes that may result in long-term economic success<br><br>• The owner assumes all the economic risk and reaps all the potential reward |
| *Annual settle-up*<br><br>Pay opportunity is based on competitive total cash compensation (TCC) (TCC = base + annual incentive opportunity) | ✓ | ✓ | | | • Rewards annual achievement of enterprise goals<br><br>• Assumes there is a cumulative long-term effect of the annual achievement of enterprise goals |
| *The big event*<br><br>Significant pay opportunity is contingent primarily on the consummation of a big event (typically retirement, an IPO, or a sale) | ✓ | | | ✓ | • Defers compensation costs and creates significant executive focus on building enterprise value to enhance personal payout at the big event<br><br>• The value of the staking grant not realized until the big event is consummated |
| *Some now/a lot later*<br><br>Pay opportunity is targeted on a TCC basis and supplemented by an expected significant payout at the time of an event | ✓ | ✓ | | ✓ | • Intended to balance short-term business decisions and the creation of long-term value<br><br>• The value of the staking grant not realized until the "big event" is consummated |

Table 25.1 Six Private-Company Pay Models

| Pay Model | Base | Annual Incentive | Cash LTI | Staking Grant | Comments |
|---|:---:|:---:|:---:|:---:|---|
| *Classic*<br><br>Pay opportunity is targeted based on a competitive total direct compensation (TDC) basis (TDC = base + annual and long-term incentive opportunities) | ✓ | ✓ | ✓ | | • Balances the focus on short- and long-term goals<br><br>• Recognizes contributions to long-term success; realizable independent of a big event |
| *Classic plus*<br><br>Pay opportunity is targeted on a TDC basis and supplemented by a staking grant for select executives | ✓ | ✓ | ✓ | ✓ | • Creates a balance among each compensation element<br><br>• Recognizes contributions to long-term success; realizable independent of a big event<br><br>• Rewards consummation of a big event if and when it occurs |

*Source:* Sibson Consulting.

**Table 25.1  Six Private-Company Pay Models (*continued*)**

*Hired Hand.*  The founder of a large consumer products company considered himself the rightful beneficiary of all long-term rewards resulting from his vision and strategy. As the company began to expand exponentially, he decided to hire a seasoned chief operating officer (COO) to execute his vision and strategy on a day-to-day basis. The COO role was to be a three- to five-year appointment—the owner believed that his son would be ready to step into the position by the term's end, and the "hired hand" would move on.

The founder chose this model because he could prepay for the accomplishment of specific outcomes without a commitment to share in the future value created for the enterprise. To understand what would constitute a compelling pay level for the seasoned COO he sought, he commissioned a market-pricing study. The new COO's agreement fixed the annual rate of base salary at slightly above the market-competitive total direct compensation level (base + annual incentive + LTI opportunity). "I've taken pay out of future discussions," the founder explained. "I'm okay with paying my COO a lot of money to execute against my plan. I'm not particularly interested in his input on my long-term strategy."

The first COO lasted less than a year. "He thought he knew better about how to successfully grow this company," the founder complained. "He wanted to make sure that he was getting a fair cut of our future economic success. What he didn't understand is that I take the risk, I get the rewards. My current COO gets it."

*Annual Settle-Up.*  Owners that adopt this popular approach prefer to "pay-as-they-go" for the annual achievement of enterprise goals that lead to long-term financial success. There is no intent to share any value that is created—the indebtedness is settled at the end of each year. To accomplish this pay model, owners must make three basic decisions:

- How will the total cash compensation be competitively positioned against the market?

- What will be the mix between base pay and annual incentive?

- Will the annual incentive be discretionary or formulaic?

These decisions lead to a plethora of design possibilities. At one end of the spectrum is the owner of a midsized high-tech company, who said, "I can't use performance-based incentive plans because I don't want to broadcast my performance expectations. If my strategy and expected outcomes leak to competitors, I will lose my competitive edge." This owner pays her team base salaries close to the 75th percentile and "tops up" the compensation at the end of the year with a flat-dollar discretionary bonus that reflects her evaluation of progress toward long-term value creation.

At the other end of the spectrum is a privately owned retailer that embraces a more typical annual settle-up model—total cash targeted at the median and a performance-based annual incentive design. However, in recognition of his executives' desire to participate in the long-term fortunes of the company, the owner mandates the deferral of above-target annual incentive awards and allows the two most senior executives to defer a specified percentage of the incentive to be earned in the coming year. The deferred amounts are credited at a rate that reflects the annual increase in the company's appraised value. The credited amounts on each year's deferrals vest over an extended period. In keeping with the annual settle-up mind-set, the owner retains the right to discontinue the deferral opportunity and stop future crediting on existing deferred amounts.

*The Big Event.* This model combines an above-median base salary with a significant future pay opportunity that is contingent on the consummation of a big event, such as retirement after long service, company achievement of a financial goal, an initial public offering (IPO), or sale of the company. The intent is to eliminate mixed messaging about performance expectations. The executive is adequately rewarded for the day-to-day responsibilities but is expected to focus on and will be rewarded for building long-term value.

The big event pay model is the granddaddy of private-company LTI plans. In its earliest form, the owner would pay key long-service employees base salaries combined with an implied commitment that at retirement there would be a significant payout if the company were "doing well." In recent years, these staking-grant payouts tied to a big event have become more explicitly defined. For instance, a Midwest financial services company provides select legacy contributors with a staking grant worth up to $500,000 depending on the enterprise value when they retire.

The big event pay model is frequently deployed in portfolio companies of private equity firms. The owners' handpicked executives are paid base salaries and receive a significant staking grant in the successful execution of an IPO, merger, or sale. The higher the enterprise value realized by the owner at the transaction, the greater is the payout.

*Some Now/A Lot Later.* This pay model, a blend of the big event and the annual settle-up models, is typically adopted when a big event has become illusive. The situation at a chemical company owned by a private equity firm is illustrative. "Although we thought we could IPO in three to five years, we've been in this investment for seven years," the CEO commented. "There's so much to fix before we can sell and cash out at our price point, it gets discouraging. To keep our key executives' minds in the game, we give them an annual progress award, in addition to base salary. The award is commensurate with the progress the company has made that year toward our long-term objective, a successful IPO."

*Classic.* This is the preferred approach for private companies whose owners want their executives to take "ownership" of the ongoing success of the business. The owners of these companies seek profitable growth and value creation, not an IPO or sale. Thus this pay model focuses on short- and long-term goals and recognizes that contributions to long-term success can be realizable without a big event. Most adopters of the classic pay model migrated from the annual settle-up model as their businesses matured. The design of the LTI plan requires the owner to make difficult decisions, which include the following:

- Who should be included? Whose contribution will affect our long-term sustainable success? What should be the messaging to legacy executives who are excluded from participation?

- How big should the payout opportunity be? What can the company afford? What should be the tradeoff between higher payout opportunities for a select group of executives and lower payouts to a larger group?

- How frequently should awards be made? Periodically? On a regular annual basis?

- Should the award be earned based on performance or service? If earned based on performance, how long should the performance measurement period be? What performance should be measured?

- How long should it take to fully vest in the awards? Should there be other restrictions on payouts?

- Should awards be denominated in cash or (phantom) equity?

The decisions of a recent classic pay model adopter are illustrated in Figure 25.1. The owner selected eight executives to participate in the plan, which was based on the achievement of cumulative net income targets during a two-year period (rather than a typical three- to five-year period). New grants are made each year. These decisions reflect the owner's desire to make the plan more responsive to the economic dynamics of his business's market. "If the market suddenly changes and I set the targets wrong, my executives could be stuck with a grant that will never pay out," he noted. "That can be very de-motivating. It's better to have frequent smaller opportunities that have a higher likelihood of being earned."

The award amount earned is determined at the end of the two-year performance period. The earned award vests over three years—one-quarter, one-quarter, and one-half—and is payable in cash on vesting. "I want this plan to result in a positive collaboration to build long-term value," said the owner. "Thus I'm not choosing the more punitive options like seven- to ten-year vesting schedules and mandated deferrals. I want the company to win, so I have to make sure the executives believe they can win."

Although the owner chose to denominate the awards in cash, other employers denominate them in cash-settled "equity units." This creates a tighter alignment between the executive and the long-term value growth of the enterprise. The value of the units typically is set at $100 at grant (e.g., a $50,000 grant would be denominated as 5,000 "equity units").

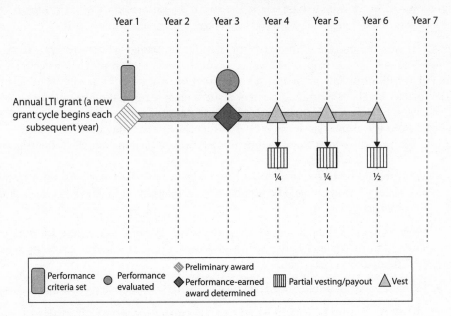

**Figure 25.1  Classic LTI plan framework.**

*Source:* Sibson Consulting.

At payment, the units are cashed out at a rate that reflects the annual increase/decrease in the company's book value between grant date and payout date.

*Classic Plus.* This pay model typically is an outgrowth of a private company's existing classic pay model. An owner decides to monetize the value created in the company through a sale, merger, or IPO. A very small group of executives (e.g., the CEO and CFO) is provided a staking grant whose payout value is linked directly to the value realized by the owner in the big event.

## The Real Secret Code

The six pay models used at private companies help to categorize how base salary and incentive arrangements respond to owners' specific mind-sets toward sharing long-term economic success. However, a successful LTI plan for one company may fail when an exact copy is applied at another. The real secret code for successful LTI design at private companies rests with the owners' ability to reject a generic solution and seek a unique fit for the company and the executives to be rewarded for long-term value creation.

# COMPENSATION AND THE BOARD

# 26

# The Compensation Committee and Executive Pay

Seymour Burchman
*Semler Brossy Consulting Group, LLC*

Blair Jones
*Semler Brossy Consulting Group, LLC*

Board compensation committees today are required to take a much more active role in managing executive pay. If you are a compensation committee member, you have seen the trend firsthand. At every meeting, you are being called on to be more of a partner in the development and implementation of executive compensation programs. This means that you play a key role in leveraging the compensation programs to communicate business priorities, reinforce strategic actions, and reward results that reflect competitive advantage.

This job has become more challenging in light of ongoing business forces, such as globalization, rapid industry change, and falling barriers to entry in your markets. Globalization has increased the number of competitors competing not only for your business but also for your talent. Change has accelerated in scope and scale as data and the ability to process them lead to frequent disruptive technologies. Industry convergence has led former collaborators—Apple and Google, for example—to become fierce competitors. Barriers to entry have fallen as companies that are flush with capital buy sophisticated technology to leap competitive hurdles. These forces influence a company's strategic choices, key success factors, and goals.

Adding to the challenge, the compensation committee also now has increased accountability for complying with a multitude of regulatory requirements and expanding governance expectations. The increased expectations stem from an ever-more-diverse set of constituencies entering the executive compensation debate—many with distinct agendas. The constituencies include proxy advisory firms, institutional investors, large pension funds, activist investors, union groups, legislators, and the public.

These constituencies are emboldened and empowered by today's level of transparency and disclosure and the "say-on-pay" vote. They are using the wealth of available information to scrutinize every compensation decision and hold compensation committee members' feet to the fire, lobbying companies to rethink what they see as questionable compensation designs. They or the government even may bring litigation over the issues.

The proxy disclosure statement's compensation discussion and analysis (CD&A) opens a big window on internal decision making. The proxy compensation tables do the same. The board's complete "story line" for executive pay is now in the proxy disclosure statement—and it must be aligned with company performance and strategic priorities in a rational and defensible way, clearly explaining how the pay program will contribute to corporate success. All these forces make your job as a compensation committee member bigger, more complex, more visible, and more crucial.

For better or worse, the executive compensation program has become one litmus test for good governance, placing the compensation committee in the spotlight. Recent experience shows that committees will be well served to partner with management to ensure that the executive pay program drives strategic execution and, in turn, supports the company in achieving competitive advantage. To do this, three related compensation committee responsibilities deserve utmost attention:

1. *Maintaining the pay program's foundations.* For this task, focus on establishing a sound pay philosophy and testing the pay program design to be sure that it supports the philosophy.

2. *Aligning the pay program with strategy.* Ensure that the pay program reflects the company's business situation, model, and strategy in compensation design. Also spend concerted effort reviewing and approving measures that gauge performance, as well as goals for increasing shareholder value and executing and sustaining strategy.

3. *Establishing the processes and structures for pay program execution.* Confirm that the right processes are in place to run the program. Also clarify decision rights and accountabilities, stand ready to correct program breakdowns, and continually update yourself on trends, legislation, regulatory actions, and other issues.

## Maintaining the Pay Program's Foundations

Traditionally, the compensation committee has been responsible for oversight of the compensation and benefits programs for all senior executives and directors of a company. As a committee member, you have authority to establish and interpret the terms of the company's executive salary and incentive plans, benefits and perquisites programs and policies, and other key terms of employment such as contracts and severance policies. You also have the responsibility to ensure regulatory compliance.

Most critical in setting up and maintaining the integrity of a compensation program are two accountabilities: (1) establishing a pay philosophy that becomes the underpinning for the executive compensation program and (2) periodically testing the program's effectiveness in linking pay to performance and attracting and retaining top talent. These two steps can help you to both design the compensation program and keep the program relevant in serving the interests of all stakeholders (Table 26.1).

The advantage of an objective framework is that it can minimize a lot of the awkwardness that arises when people's emotional reactions to compensation get ahead of the facts.

| Accountabilities | Issues to Probe |
|---|---|
| Establish a sound pay philosophy that becomes the framework for the program and the basis for the CD&A disclosure | Does the philosophy reflect the company's business characteristics and talent needs? |
| | Does it address the key principles of compensation? |
| | Does it support the company's unique positioning in its market? |
| | How does it help to attract and retain talent versus the competition? |
| Build and continually test the design to ensure that the design is aligned with the philosophy | Does the design support the philosophy and business and talent needs? |
| | How is the program supporting the desired pay/performance relationship? |
| | Does the program support attraction and help with retention? |

**Table 26.1 Key Accountabilities of the Compensation Committee**

When sensitive issues raise hackles, you can use the philosophy and related guiding principles to bring the discussion back to reasonable common ground. As a member of the compensation committee, you can then focus on the real issues: does the program operate as designed, delivering results expected for the company, the executives, and shareholders?

## Establishing the Pay Philosophy

The pay philosophy should express the company's beliefs about compensation. It also should explain how rewards would support the vision, mission, business strategy, and financial priorities of the company. To develop the philosophy, first define guiding principles for establishing compensation programs, including how prominent compensation should be in driving executive actions and decisions, where the emphasis in the pay program should be placed, the types of metrics to consider, and how goals will be set.

The guiding principles, in turn, can serve as a yardstick for later evaluation. They also can provide a framework for plan administration and future design. Avoid principles that amount to lofty statements that do not provide adequate direction. Instead, pay attention to design elements crucial to the company's efforts to drive strategy and the company's talent needs (Table 26.2). Beware a pay philosophy that sounds all the right notes but ultimately rings hollow. Shareholders want more than promises in the CD&A disclosure in the proxy. They want proof that the program advances company priorities and drives results.

As a part of the development of pay philosophy, be sure to ask senior managers to help you to understand how the company's philosophy, program design, and pay levels evolved. An historical pay audit, breaking out pay components, can show what factors influenced changes in pay over time and how the design has evolved to attract, motivate, and retain key executives. Figure 26.1 shows an actual example of one company over a 10-year period. Note how pay mix and stock-ownership practices held steady, but performance measures and standards changed.

Compensation philosophies cannot stay fixed forever. They need periodic tweaking—and even overhauls—to drive strategy and financial results. Changes in the market

| Principle | Definition |
|---|---|
| Pay prominence | The visibility and impact of pay relative to other programs that influence behavior. Prominence is influenced by pay variability, executives' influence over performance results, and the explicitness of communication about the pay/performance relationship. |
| Emphasis | The role of pay in influencing behavior, i.e., the primary goal of pay (attraction, motivation, or retention). Typically each component of the compensation program has its own focus. |
| Comparative framework | The companies used for pay and performance comparison. This involves establishing a peer group of industries or organizations to compare pay practices and performance. |
| Pay positioning | Targeting pay levels relative to companies in the comparative framework for different levels of performance (e.g., fiftieth percentile vs. the fortieth or sixtieth percentile. |
| Pay mix | Addresses the proportion of fixed and variable compensation components, e.g., what percentage of pay will be delivered in salary vs. incentives? What percentage will be based on annual vs. long-term results? What is the optimal equity proportion? |
| Business unit differentiation | The extent to which designs and pay levels might vary based on differences in business unit characteristics. |
| External/internal balance | The relative influence placed on external market competitiveness in determining pay levels vs. internal factors, such as the strategic importance of jobs to the company. |
| Performance measurement | The measures, standards, and time frames for evaluating performance. Some companies also define the process and criteria for CEO evaluation, and the desired nature and scope of communication. |
| Stock ownership | Expected guidelines for holding company stock. |

**Table 26.2   Illustrative Design Principles in an Executive Pay Philosophy**

(e.g., customer preferences and competitor actions) may require a new strategy and new business imperatives and demand different talent. To keep up to date, you should review the philosophy each year and expect to make adjustments every few years as strategy evolves. Always consider your company's unique business and talent requirements and how they should influence program design.

In one consumer durables company, the global financial crisis forced executives to face the equivalent of a turnaround situation. The company sought to aggressively restructure to operate profitably in a world with tougher legacy markets, growth in China and other emerging markets, and the imperative to operate with a leaner product line. This required repairing the balance sheet, financing new-product development, and working better as a team globally. To match these strategic imperatives, the compensation committee pursued a philosophy to emphasize pay for team play, higher quality, and developing global

| Compensation Philosophy Element | Plan Year | | | | | | | | | | |
|---|---|---|---|---|---|---|---|---|---|---|---|
| | 2004 | 2005 | 2006 | 2007 | 2008 | 2009 | 2010 | 2011 | 2012 | 2013 | 2014 |
| Pay Mix | Incentives represent a significant portion (50% or more) of the total pay opportunity for top executives; actual mix fluctuates from year to year with performance; total pay opportunity cannot exceed utility industry median if incentive targets are not hit. | | | | | | | | | | |
| Performance Measures and Standards | Focus primarily on measurable results. Balance of company, team, and individual performance measures. Generally, goals set to require maintenance of or improvement over prior year's results | | | | | | | | | | |
| | **Base Salary:** Individual performance rating based on role contributions (salary increase matrix anchored by competitive merit budget increase) | | | | | | | | | | |
| | **AIP:** Both operational and financial measures | | | | | | **AIP:** Increased emphasis on EBIT and EPS, to better align measures with the measures used in other competitive industries and further enhance the linkage between executive and shareholder interests | | | | **AIP:** Cash flow for top two executives; return to operational measures for all others because their primary focus is excellent operation of the utility |
| | **LTI:** ROE relative to RRA companies through 1998; relative ROE and TRS starting in 1999, to enhance the linkage between executive and shareholder interests | | | | | | **LTI:** Absolute TRS (stock options); relative TRS (2003 long-term cash incentive) | | | | **LTI:** relative TRS vs. S&P utilities |
| Ownership | LTI programs intended to build ownership over time and historically have done so | | | | | | | | | | |

Figure 26.1  Evolution of compensation philosophy principles.

products that also responded to local tastes. The metrics for executives included global profit and cash flow but also cost, market share, and quality performance. Even at the business-unit level, executives earned incentive pay for meeting global team objectives.

Table 26.3 illustrates the characteristics that committees should consider in developing a pay philosophy or assessing the fit of an existing philosophy to the company. Too often compensation programs mirror popular designs or practices of competitors. Such programs may not contribute to better performance; in fact, they can motivate behaviors that hurt results.

| Key business imperatives | Current performance and prospects for future performance |
|---|---|
| | Strategy and anticipated shifts in strategy |
| | Business stage and growth |
| | Business unit autonomy |
| Market factors | Total return to shareholders (TRS) allocation strategy |
| | (share price appreciation vs. dividend) |
| | Level of stock volatility |
| | Influence of macroeconomic factors |
| | Sector cyclicality |

Table 26.3  Business and Talent Needs Influence Pay Philosophy

| Organizational characteristics | Ability to develop financial goals |
| --- | --- |
| | Ability to develop peer groups |
| | Planning time horizon |
| | Role of equity and incentives generally in employee value proposition |
| | Employee impact on stock price |
| | Resource sharing and employee mobility |
| Talent needs and characteristics | Risk of turnover |
| | Diversification preferences |
| | Need to attract or retain talent |
| | Employee risk and reward profile |
| | Level of employee motivation |
| | Desire to change behaviors |

**Table 26.3   Business and Talent Needs Influence Pay Philosophy (*continued*)**

Among the business issues that can influence program design are the business cycle and industry cyclicality and volatility. A company's stage in the business cycle, for example, can influence the degree of leverage suitable for the program. A startup company would be more likely to rely on a highly leveraged option program to provide the most significant portion of compensation; in contrast, a mature company would tend to rely on a performance-vested restricted stock program to align with key business priorities and reinforce sustained shareholder value creation. The cyclicality or volatility of the business sector can suggest the need for indexing or other mechanisms to control for factors beyond the influence of executives. One company in the highly volatile semiconductor industry indexed its earning goals to the rate of growth of the overall semiconductor market.

The company's emphasis on stock-price appreciation and dividends will help to determine the focus for equity vehicles, that is, stock-price appreciation alone or the inclusion of dividends too. Talent requirements can dictate the type of vehicle as well as vesting provisions: if retention is critical, you may want to go with full-value shares that vest over an extended period. Alternatively, you could structure the awards to vest with performance, for example, vesting when executives hit revenue or earnings targets.

Once crafted, the pay philosophy becomes your blueprint for designing the compensation program. Consider the case of a mature average-performing business whose margins had been eroding while battling for ever-declining market share. Executives decided to pursue a strategy aimed at more sharply differentiating their products through innovation and new supporting services. As a first step, the board approved more entrepreneurial compensation vehicles, raising the proportion of variable pay and building in higher leverage. The board also approved prescriptive metrics aligned with the new strategy, which encouraged new growth through differentiated products. Finally, they broadened the comparative framework to gauge performance against both industry competitors of similar maturity and companies with comparable growth trajectories. The goal was to drive executive behaviors associated with the desired strategic shift.

In another case, a company in turnaround needed executives to change behavior to improve customer responsiveness without undermining executive team unity. The board approved a modified pay program to focus on earnings growth, phasing in more aggressive goals over time. It also introduced nonfinancial metrics to hit hard on improved customer service. The company had annual plan rewards for target and stretch performance but also increased the proportion of long-term equity with extended vesting in anticipation of a multiyear turnaround.

In many cases, the pay philosophy also must foster business-unit success because, in businesses organized around business units, this is where the battle for competitive advantage is won or lost. However, you cannot ignore the importance of understanding interrelationships between businesses. Assume, for example, that you are the director of a highly decentralized company that requires strong coordination among its units. In the annual plan, you could stress business-unit results, using separate peer groups as performance benchmarks for each business unit. In the long-term incentive, you could reward people based 100 percent on corporate measures to encourage teamwork and collaboration.

## Test the Compensation Program

Testing the program requires qualitative and quantitative analysis of whether the pay program reflects the philosophy and meets objectives. If retention is the goal, you might assess turnover statistics or study executive commitment. If you want to bring in new talent, check the caliber of executive the organization has attracted. Gauge qualitative success by interviewing key executives and evaluating behavior and results. Gauge quantitative success by analyzing programs retrospectively and prospectively for pay/performance correlation, value sharing, and peer alignment. Here are three key tests:

1. *Is executive pay well correlated with company performance and shareholder returns?* Evaluate how much pay varies with different performance scenarios. Pay and company performance should correlate strongly.[1] Test for the correlation by comparing the relationship between changes in total cash compensation (TCC)[2] and company financial results such as earnings and cash flows over time. Or compare gains in long-term incentives (LTIs) and total direct compensation (TDC)[3] over time with changes in total return to shareholders (TRS).

2. *Are pay and performance well aligned given company and peer performance?* When performance has exceeded the median, has pay exceeded the median as well? Alignment between relative pay and relative performance is the goal. In addition, determine whether the relative positioning of pay levels for the CEO and the other top five executives corresponds to the relative performance positioning in the company's peer group.

   Historical tests on actual cumulative pay and performance can identify the degree of alignment in the pay programs compared with peers. Total compensation should be the sum of actual cumulative compensation earned during the period using "paper gains" for equity vehicles. If pay and performance are out of alignment, investigate further to find the cause, and consider solutions.

   Your investigation should include a calculation of realizable or realized pay, which provides an additional way to value pay outcomes. *Realizable pay* is the value of compensation an executive could potentially earn over a specific time period, taking into account actual performance to date. *Realized pay* is the amount actually earned and reported on the executive's W-2 Form. Although these metrics have their drawbacks, because you cannot easily compare them among companies, shareholders are increasingly looking for this additional information and how the tally links to performance.

3. *Are executives paid a reasonable percentage of both company and shareholder gains?* Assess whether there is a "fair sharing of the pie." Executives should get an appropriate amount of the value they create. You can view sharing from three perspectives: (a) the percentage of total value created (i.e., earnings and shareholder return) that will be allocated to the top five executives, (b) changes to that percentage given time and circumstances, and (c) the value-sharing percentage at your company compared with others.

   The "right" value sharing is a matter of figuring out the appropriate split between executives and shareholders. The split depends on the company's business circumstances, talent needs, and performance and rewards strategy. Figure 26.2 presents a sampling of factors to consider.

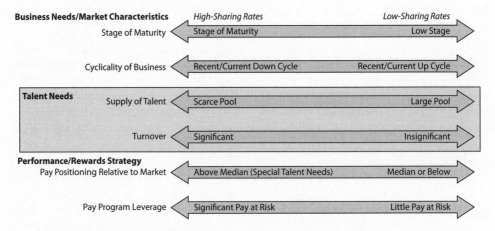

**Figure 26.2  Types of factors that could influence value-sharing rates.**

With this framework as a guide, you can gauge whether your sharing rates should fall closer to the higher or lower end of the competitive range. If your rates are high compared with competitors, you may have several problems: poor goal setting, a mix of total pay biased to salary rather than variable incentives, inappropriate leverage in incentive plans, the use of equity vehicles that vary less with performance, unjustified pay positioning versus the market, or incentive plans relying on the wrong performance measures.

## Aligning the Pay Program with Strategy

If pay is to contribute to driving strategy and competitive advantage, you should aim to leverage the program in three ways: to communicate priorities and reinforce strategy execution, to help attract and retain the top talent needed to create and execute the strategy, and to reward executives for developing skills and capabilities needed for executing the strategy. These three tasks often will follow naturally from the board's discussion of strategy and the measures of success that emerge from the financial and long-range planning processes.

If the strategy is to gain advantage through operational excellence, for example, you can structure the pay program to reward executives not just for profits but also for driving up a key operational metric such as quality. This added measure clearly communicates your strategic priorities. As a way to attract and retain executives, you can pay at the high end of the market for talent with the critical skills needed to execute the strategy. On top of that, you can compensate development-minded high-potential leaders who drive the operational excellence strategy with adequately differentiated pay, meaningful awards to recognize special achievements, promotions accompanied by meaningful pay increases, and retention awards to avoid losing the most capable people.

The compensation program should be carefully tailored to meet the company's strategic goals. Beware of simply following compensation "best practices" as a means to please proxy advisors and institutional shareholders. An off-the-shelf approach creates the risk of sending signals that fit neither your philosophy nor your strategy. This outcome is unlikely to happen if the board remains immersed in company strategy and resists pressure to conform to general rules that might create unintended consequences.

The process of aligning compensation with philosophy, value creation, and the company's strategy can proceed in four steps: identifying key drivers of value, operational success, and strategy; selecting metrics that have the greatest impact on each of these; setting goals for the chosen metrics; and linking the goals to incentives.

### Identifying the Key Drivers of Value, Operational Success, and Strategy

Although the ultimate goal of any company is to generate total shareholder returns (TSR), TSR provides little guidance in creating value, achieving operational excellence, and executing strategy. For this task, management should identify the key financial, strategic, and operational factors that contribute to TSR, starting with the highest-level drivers and working all the way down to the most specific. Again, this should be a normal outgrowth of financial planning and board strategy sessions, supplemented by discussions with analysts.

The top-tier measures normally include financial measures addressing profitability, cash flow, and returns. Under these are key supporting financial measures (e.g., sales growth, margins, working capital utilization) and nonfinancial measures addressing strategic and operational success.

As part of its oversight duties and to ensure clarity and completeness of the drivers, the compensation committee will want to monitor management's work on measures. A useful tool for management to perform its due diligence analysis is a *value tree*. Figure 26.3 is an example of a value tree for an insurer. The tree reflects the company's business model. It "unbundles" the key drivers of TSR, focusing first on the financial metrics that are the key determinants of economic value and then driving ever more deeply to the key operational and strategic factors needed for financial success.

Beyond the typical financial measures, you should look to see that the drivers of TSR cover all core aspects of the business that will have a significant impact on operational excellence and successful strategy execution. These drivers normally fall into one of four categories: customer value/cost tradeoffs—including total customer experience and price relative to competitors; internal operations and processes—including productivity, process quality, and timeliness; technical and human capabilities—including work systems, technology, and supplier relationships; and the ability to sustain performance—including measures of such things as innovation, flexibility, and adaptability. It is important to note that shareholders cast a skeptical eye on nonfinancial measures. Therefore, it remains imperative to create quantitative measures that cannot be criticized as soft. The best measures are objective and evaluate factors with significant impact on financial outcomes.

**Figure 26.3  Value tree for an insurer.**

## Select Metrics That Have the Greatest Impact

With the drivers clarified, management and the compensation committee will need to isolate the handful of drivers with the most leverage to improve performance. To ensure that the most critical operational and strategic drivers are chosen, take care to focus on those that matter most to customers and help the company outcompete competitors. If the metrics do neither, they are not worth the investment in measuring or tracking. If you have doubt about the handful of operational and strategic metrics chosen, you can use a simple test to verify that you have made the right selection (Figure 26.4).

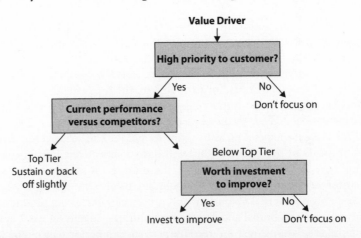

**Figure 26.4  How to prioritize the choice of operational and strategic measures.**

Regarding the metrics chosen, several points are worth highlighting. One is the necessity of choosing the right metrics, especially when the appropriate ones are nonfinancial indicators that gauge progress toward hitting softer goals, such as customer satisfaction. Another is choosing the right level at which to measure—company-wide, business unit, team, or individual—to avoid distortions of the kind suffered by the company that demotivated high-performing executives. A third is choosing the right time frame—do you measure quarterly, annually, or longer?

## Setting Goals for Chosen Metrics

With an accurate set of value drivers and high-leverage metrics, you can set goals. To start, does the company have the systems in place for timely measurement of each chosen metric? If not, this is an issue that needs tackling. Next, by what means should you choose the goals? What is the right standard, or benchmark, for comparison? Should it be a percentage above previous performance, against a budget, against a fixed standard, or against peer performance? In a race for competitive advantage, the right goal is probably one that ensures that you beat competitors.

Plan to set goals for three to five metrics that position the company on the right trajectory but also offer realistic targets. Consider combining a top-down and bottom-up approach. From the top down, ask, what must the company achieve to deliver acceptable returns to shareholders, taking into account performance versus peers and market expectations? From the bottom up, ask, what can the company do with its current (and future) business model, given the available improvement opportunities? Figure 26.5 offers an example. A fact-based analysis will yield achievable goals that contribute to competitive advantage.

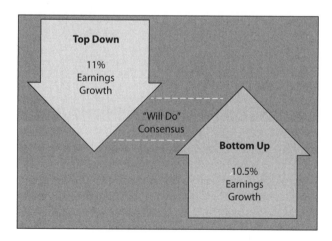

**Figure 26.5  An example of reconciling top-down and bottom-up goals.**

## Link Measured Goals to Incentives to Drive Strategy

Measurement and goal setting are the heart of making an incentive plan that drives and sustains competitive advantage. Although long-term performance awards may depend on top-level measures such as TSR, annual incentive awards should depend on measures derived from value drivers. Plan to choose three to five metrics derived from the highest-leverage drivers to link directly to incentives. As for the amount of incentive, executives who deliver on stretch goals—or even superstretch goals—should earn two to four times their target award. Executives who deliver on relatively certain goals should earn less, from 0.5 to 1.5 times target. Table 26.4 offers guidance. Presumably, executives will hit the superstretch goals only once or twice every decade but target goals six or seven years out of ten.

| Degree of Difficulty of Goal | Anticipated Frequency of Occurrence | Payout as Multiple of Target | Desired Effect |
|---|---|---|---|
| Superstretch achievement | 1–2 out of 10 | 2.0x–4.0x | Drive and reward extraordinary performance |
| Stretch achievement | 3–5 out of 10 | 1.5x–2.0x | Provide significant payout for superb performance |
| Target | 6–7 out of 10 | 1x | Provide somewhat consistent payouts with moderate upside |
| Reliable | 7–8 out of 10 | 0.5x–1x | Reliable compensation with limited upside |
| Near certainty | 9 out of 10 | 0.25x–0.5x | Provide reliable but rigid compensation |

**Table 26.4  Appropriate Payouts at Each Performance Level**

How tough should the goals be? If the goals are harder than at peer companies, then the pay targets and upside potential should be greater. If performance targets correspond to the 65th percentile, for example, so should pay targets. If not, the structure of the pay program could frustrate those who have worked hard to excel and do not get rewards commensurate with their performance.

Payouts should reflect the volatility of results. Evaluate historical volatility, and if the year-to-year volatility is great, make the range from threshold to maximum broad—70 to 130 percent of target, for example, instead of 90 to 110 percent.

Be careful not to set goals and measures that backfire as an incentive mechanism. For example, one company wanted to encourage teamwork among divisions, so it measured everything at the corporate level. One division performed so poorly that it dragged down everyone else, and nobody earned a full incentive payout. Executives in the better-performing units felt shortchanged. The lesson is that you have to make sure that well-intended measures do not act as a disincentive to performance.

The value of the compensation plan as an incentive system varies with the company and situation. When should the compensation plan play the biggest role in driving strategy? In three cases: when strategy execution is suboptimal, when management initiates a major strategy shift, and when the CEO or senior leaders change. You and management can work together to ensure that compensation is right for the business and aids in lasting company success.

## Establishing Processes and Structures for Pay Program Execution

In fulfilling your role on the compensation committee, you will want to lay the best groundwork possible, stay on top of issues, and remain capable of carrying on a robust discussion with other directors and managers. This requires taking responsibility for a number of factors. Here we highlight four: clarifying expectations and accountabilities, managing an annual calendar of events to aid planning and decision making, correcting program breakdowns, and studying executive pay practices and trends that influence future action.

## Set Expectations and Accountabilities

Today's executive compensation climate can complicate the relationship between the committee and management. Previously amicable relationships can fray when the committee tackles issues management once considered its own or when members feel that management is holding back information. To avoid conflicts, nurture a committee-management relationship that fosters conversation and transparency.

From the outset, both parties need to agree on what decisions must be made and how the decision-making process will work. One good idea is to have a candid conversation about expectations when a new committee chair comes on board. Another good time for a conversation is after the committee's annual self-assessment, which normally spurs discussion about areas for improvement. Management may choose to have individual conversations with directors first and then aggregate themes for full committee discussion. Alternatively, a third party might facilitate this process. In any case, plan to discuss how management and the committee can best work together to fulfill the committee's charter. Focus on questions such as those listed in Table 26.5.

| Issues for Discussion | |
| --- | --- |
| Committee charter | What elements of their charter do the compensation committee members consider most important? |
| | Is the charter still appropriate? |
| | Does it require modification? |
| | How well has the committee adhered to its charter? |
| | Specifically, what has it done well? |
| | Where does it need to improve? |
| | What are the reasons for any shortfalls? |
| Working relationship with management | How can management best help the committee fulfill its charter? |
| | To what extent has management been doing this already? |
| | What is working well? |
| | What areas could be improved? |
| | How can the committee help management deliver to the committee's expectations? |
| Briefings and skill building | Do the committee members feel they are getting the right information in a timely manner in order to fulfill their fiduciary obligations? |
| Decision making | How do the committee members want to be involved in the making of critical decisions? |

Table 26.5  Setting Expectations about the Compensation Committee Charter

Periodic discussions can lead to greater clarity on decision rights. The relevant rights include accountability for specific actions and decisions related to compensation, benefits, and perquisites. Clarifying these rights guarantees that policies and practices are in place to ensure the development of management talent, effective corporate governance, and the establishment of competitive and effective management compensation. Table 26.6 outlines typical decision rights, showing governance items (e.g., director compensation, CEO compensation, etc.), specific actions (e.g., initiate, develop, review, approve), and each party's accountability. The decision rights also should specify how often various reviews take place.

One decision right that has gained prominence is choosing the compensation consultant and "owning" the consulting relationship. Compensation consultants were once hired by and reported to management, but that practice has changed. Compensation committees now hire an independent consultant to support the board, typically with management assisting in screening and credentialing. In some cases, a single consultant serves both management and the committee. In others, particularly when a second opinion is sought or when the compensation program has come under scrutiny, separate consultants work for each party.

When you work with a consultant, establish rules of engagement or protocols that the consultant will follow in providing independent advice and counsel. Set expectations for operating procedures, and create an effective relationship that complies with corporate governance standards. Your protocols should stipulate reporting relationships and the responsibility for selecting an advisor, including the authority to retain, terminate, and approve fees.

As part of the rules of engagement, clarify the consultant's access to the committee and management. Although the committee may have hired the consultant, the work will require access to and collaboration with management. Be sure to identify with whom the consultant can engage and the purpose of the relationship. Also arrange for periodic assessment of and feedback on the consultant's effectiveness. A discussion of decision rights conducted in this way helps to start the conversation about critical governance items, ensures that people are comfortable with the protocols, and establishes parameters for discussion and decision making.

### Establish a Calendar

Structuring meetings appropriately, including executive sessions, will ensure that committee members' time is well used and that critical topics are covered. Expect to follow a routine annual process detailed in an annual committee calendar (Figure 26.6). Consider setting aside one meeting to examine trends and how they affect the company's business and talent needs. Assess at the same time how well the compensation program is meeting business needs. Obtain from management full information about the impact of executive pay decisions and a periodic report card on how the program is working. The timing of the meeting hinges on the company's fiscal year—Figure 26.6 shows the meeting in July–August. In any case, schedule the meeting when you are not facing significant decisions about payouts, plan changes, or proxy disclosure.

Depending on the topic, the right support, including the consultant, human resources, and legal should be available at the meeting. Schedule executive sessions either at each meeting or separately for longer sessions. This allows committee members to "ask the consultant" or legal advisor about issues without management present. Make sure that the agenda for each meeting outlines expected outcomes. Clarify what items are up for discussion and which require decisions. Important design issues should come before the

Ensure policies and practices are in place to ensure development of management talent, effective corporate governance, and competitive management compensation.

| Governance Item | Description | Decision Roles | | | Frequency |
| --- | --- | --- | --- | --- | --- |
| | | Management | Compensation Committee | Corporate Board | |
| Director Compensation | The compensation benefits and perquisites provided to directors (policy) | Initiate, develop | Review, recommend | Review, approve | Annually |
| CEO Qualifications | The skills and experience required of the CEO | Initiate, develop | Review, approve | Review, approve | Annually (review) as needed (recommend, approve qualifications) |
| CEO Compensation and Performance Evaluation | The compensation, benefits, and perquisites provided to the CEO; performance standards and evaluation process | Provide input and tools | Initiate, develop, recommend | Review, approve | Annually |
| CEO Succession Planning | Succession process under various scenarios | Develop | Initiate, review, recommend | Review, approve | Annually (review process) as needed (develop process) |
| Officer Compensation | The compensation, benefits, and perquisites | As to compensation: initiate, develop as to . . . etc. | As to compensation, etc.: review, recommend | Review, approve | Annually |

Table 26.6  Principal Duties and Responsibilities

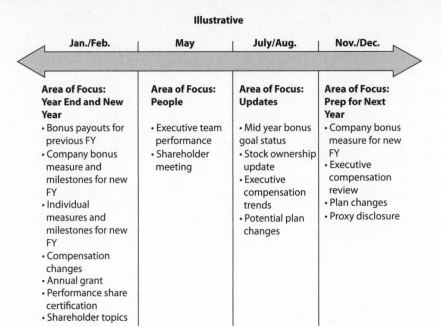

| Jan./Feb. | May | July/Aug. | Nov./Dec. |
|---|---|---|---|
| **Area of Focus: Year End and New Year** | **Area of Focus: People** | **Area of Focus: Updates** | **Area of Focus: Prep for Next Year** |
| • Bonus payouts for previous FY<br>• Company bonus measure and milestones for new FY<br>• Individual measures and milestones for new FY<br>• Compensation changes<br>• Annual grant<br>• Performance share certification<br>• Shareholder topics | • Executive team performance<br>• Shareholder meeting | • Mid year bonus goal status<br>• Stock ownership update<br>• Executive compensation trends<br>• Potential plan changes | • Company bonus measure for new FY<br>• Executive compensation review<br>• Plan changes<br>• Proxy disclosure |

**Figure 26.6  Annual committee calendar.**

committee at least two times. A clear chart or agenda can keep the meeting on track. Remember to provide the right amount of information well in advance of the meeting.

The role of the committee chair in preparing for meetings varies. In some cases, the chair manages the process, taking accountability for much of the prework and even decisions. In other cases, the chair takes a less active role, asking for a briefing of issues in advance but deferring discussion and decisions to the whole committee. The optimal model depends on the composition of the committee and people's expertise. The better informed and more knowledgeable the members, the more confident people feel thinking through the issues, and ultimately, the stronger the compensation program becomes as a driver of company competitive advantage.

### Are There Any Breakdowns in the Design or Execution?

Pay programs frequently break down in driving strategy either because the metrics underlying them are not tracking the right results or the goals simply are not tough enough. Breakdowns also may come from inappropriate vehicles, leverage, or pay mix. The biggest concern is that measures over time drift from their original connection to the drivers of TRS. In turn, they fail to represent high priorities in company strategy, and they cease to be appropriate targets to motivate improvement toward delivering competitive advantage.

You need to stay alert to this drift. To do so, check again for key links between strategy, measures, goals, and performance. You can ask some specific questions to help you decide if you are using the right measures, if some of your program components have become outdated, whether goals have enough stretch, and whether you have the right mix of variable pay, short- to long-term pay, and different long-term incentive vehicles.

*Do the Measures Drive TSR?*  Check to be sure that the financial, strategic, and operational measures reinforce the short- and intermediate-term results that contribute to TSR performance. You should look at both absolute TSR performance and relative performance in your industry. If needed, incorporate additional measures into annual incentives to create "line of sight" and aid people's understanding of the plan and the goals. Additional measures can foster collaboration at operational levels.

*Do Measures Represent High Priorities?* Ensure that the measures you choose have the greatest impact on TSR. Sensitivity analyses (i.e., percentage change in economic value, profits, returns associated with a 1 percent change in the measure) plus the review of key analyst metrics and business strategies can point to better drivers. Seek measures that gauge progress in improving success with customers and, most important, against competitors.

*Are the Goals Appropriate?* When it comes to goal setting, make sure that goals reconcile top-down and bottom-up perspectives. A top-down perspective reflects the company's obligations to shareholders—what a company should do to justify its continued independence and management's continued stewardship. A bottom-up view identifies what the company is capable of doing based on the current business model. Reconciliation of the two, given today's volatile environment, is one of the board's most difficult responsibilities. The challenge is to provide a balanced approach to goals that are achievable and yet have stretch.

*Are Thresholds and Maximums Realistic?* Set and approve thresholds and maximums by taking into account the company's planning processes, the likely effects of macroeconomic and other external factors, and the toughness of the goals themselves. Also consider the proportion of incremental value created for the company being shared, performance versus historical results, and peer performance. Some leeway in the performance range will ensure that executives are neither de-motivated when they perform only moderately well nor rewarded for unsatisfactory results.

With today's detailed disclosure of performance goals in the CD&A, goal setting has become ever more visible. You should aim to approve measures that truly drive performance and goals that represent tough hurdles. In so doing, shareholders will have the proof that the program furthers their interests.

### Keep Current on Executive Pay Issues

In recent years, the regulatory and governance environment has evolved continuously, requiring compensation committees to spend considerable time staying up to date. Even former CEOs may not have the familiarity with current regulations, proxy advisor guidelines, and institutional investor requirements and their implications for compensation design and reporting. You should expect to learn about new trends in compensation while operating and assessing the current program. It is helpful to have members who collectively have the following skills:

- A desire to keep current on trends and issues affecting executive compensation
- An ability to learn quickly and understand the implications of governance rules and regulations
- Strong financial and strategic acumen
- Deep industry knowledge
- Human resources expertise—a former human resources executive who has strong business background is an asset

Companies can help to some extent with the education of directors, but directors' colleges and similar curricula are also useful. Annual offsite meetings that cover trends and issues offer a good opportunity for committee members to get up to speed without the weight of decision making. The board secretary or human resources staff should circulate relevant articles and press briefings. They also should ensure that various advisors keep the committee informed of changes in executive compensation practices with implications for the company.

Committee members also should ask management to brief them each year on where the company stands in the eyes of constituencies, such as ISS and Glass-Lewis, major institutional shareholders, unions, and regulators. For this and other information, committee members should consider scheduling one-on-one meetings with people from human resources, legal, and finance, affording time to probe issues outside the formal meeting atmosphere.

## Summary

Making decisions about executive pay can seem daunting. Management and outside advisors play an important role in ensuring that all committee members are well equipped for the task. Yet committee members have an equal responsibility to build their own knowledge and prepare themselves for the decisions at hand. The best committee members create a strong relationship with management. They ensure that the pay program rests on a solid philosophical foundation. And they focus analyses and discussion on how well the measures, goals, and rewards address value creation, the company's strategy and talent needs, and alignment of pay with performance.

Committee members also have a responsibility to take corrective action when aspects of the program break down. At the same time, they need to constantly reinforce good relations through ongoing communication, clear expectations, and unambiguous decision rights. With all these responsibilities handled, compensation committees will have done their job in ensuring that compensation is right for the business, exhibits effective governance, yields sound pay/performance relationships, and aids in the company's ability to produce and reproduce competitive advantage.

## Notes

1. A correlation is a number between −1 and +1 that indicates the strength of a relationship between two variables. A +1 correlation indicates a perfect correlation (ideal for pay programs), and a −1 indicates a perfect inverse correlation.
2. Total cash compensation (TCC): base salary + annual incentives.
3. Total direct compensation (TDC): base salary + annual incentives + gain on long-term incentives.

# 27

# Dynamics of CEO Pay

DAVID SWINFORD
*Pearl Meyer & Partners*

JANE PARK
*Pearl Meyer & Partners*

Companies have found that effective communication of executive compensation and the board's rationale for setting pay levels to shareholders is critical. With all these outside pressures, companies are challenged to ensure that compensation programs effectively align with the business strategy, deliver value to shareholders, retain and attract the best high-level talent, and support succession planning.

An ongoing shift in the roles played by managements, boards, and outside forces over the past decade has transformed the process by which executive compensation programs are developed, administered, evaluated, and communicated. Indeed, it is the outside forces in recent years that have increased the scrutiny of executive compensation programs and, in turn, influenced the decision-making process of boards of directors. Securities and Exchange Commission (SEC) compensation disclosure rules have increased the transparency of compensation programs as well as the length of filings. The Dodd-Frank Wall Street Reform and Consumer Protection Act (the Dodd-Frank Act) required, among other things, "say on pay," giving public-company shareholders a nonbinding vote to approve or disapprove of their companies' executive compensation programs. The rising influence of outside proxy advisory firms and populist critiques of growing income inequality also have increased scrutiny on compensation programs and especially on CEO compensation.

These developments have prompted compensation committees to reassess virtually every aspect of how they discharge their duties. They are holding up long-time pay practices for examination not only in terms of compliance with the letter and spirit of new technical rules but also in terms of how well they align with heightened good governance standards and drive meaningful long-term shareholder value. Among the areas of concern are

- Creating programs to more effectively nurture an internal pool of executive talent
- Aligning the interests of the CEO and shareholders through meaningful equity programs without exceeding reasonable and appropriate standards of compensation

- Ensuring that pay opportunity levels are appropriately competitive by more closely targeting the organization's actual labor market and considering peers' relative performance

- Better defining and calibrating multiple aspects of executive and organizational performance to ensure proportional rewards for direct and measureable results that support the business and its overall strategy

- Addressing the need to have a clear, defensible rationale for how compensation programs are structured

- Balancing compliance with proxy advisory firms' opinions of "best practices" with overseeing effective compensation programs that effectively reward and retain management and deliver value for shareholders

## New Regulatory Considerations

The Dodd-Frank Act was signed into law in 2010 and was developed in response to the financial crisis beginning in 2007. The Dodd-Frank Act includes a number of executive compensation and corporate governance reforms, several of which directly affect CEO pay, including

- *Say on pay/say on frequency.* Shareholders get a nonbinding vote on executive compensation at least every three years, and investment managers are required to report how they voted. Shareholders also get a vote on whether the say-on-pay vote will occur every one, two, or three years. To date, most companies hold annual say-on-pay votes.

- *Say on golden parachutes.* Shareholders get a nonbinding vote on all executive change-in-control arrangements in the context of a transaction-related meeting.

- *Additional compensation policy and governance disclosures.* The rationale for choosing a combined or separate CEO/COB role. Other policies that have not yet been finalized by the SEC as of the date of this publication include (1) disclosure of the relationship between pay and performance, (2) disclosure of the ratio of median employee pay to CEO pay disclosure, and (3) policies on the hedging of company securities.

- *Mandatory clawback policies.* Companies must implement and report policies for recouping payments to current and former executive officers based on financial statements that are subsequently restated. This is an expansion of the Sarbanes-Oxley Act clawback provisions. As of the date of this publication, the SEC has not established a final rule on this policy.

Despite the absence of final SEC rules, many companies have voluntarily established hedging policies and general disclosures demonstrating a pay-for-performance relationship in compensation programs. Many companies also have voluntarily established and disclosed clawback policies and a commitment to adjust such policies to comply with the SEC's final rules.

The SEC adopted proposed rules on the disclosure of the ratio of employee pay to CEO pay in 2013. However, final rules have not been implemented as of the date of this publication. The proposed rule would require disclosure of annual total compensation of the median employee and the CEO, the ratio of the two amounts, and the methodology, material assumptions, and estimates used in the calculations. In its current form, the proposed rule is somewhat flexible and will allow companies to establish the most appropriate means for determining median employee pay. Unfortunately, no exclusion was offered for companies with international, seasonal, or part-time employees, and as a result, large companies with large workforces and international operations will be tasked with an administratively difficult calculation. Furthermore, all companies will be subject to heightened media and shareholder scrutiny of a ratio that could be misleading and unnecessarily inflammatory without meaningful benefit to shareholders to assess a company's compensation program. The evolution of the pay-ratio rules signals that the published ratios will be a significant political issue and potentially a public relations nightmare for some companies.

Although most companies oppose the proposed pay-ratio rules, some are tracking the ratio of the CEO's total compensation to that of his or her direct reports or comparing the ratio of the CEO's pay to that of the other named executive officers as disclosed in proxy disclosure statements. The concept is that a larger than typical ratio may indicate that the CEO is too dominant or too important within the organization. A high ratio also could signal to the market that the company has not identified a potential succession candidate in-house. Both issues could be negative signals to the market.

Say on pay has been in place for three full years. It has expanded transparency of compensation programs and communication efforts, transitioned the compensation discussion and analysis (CD&A) in the proxy disclosure statement to an active marketing tool, and established investor outreach as part of the normal annual process.

## Ensuring a Talent-Rich Organization

As the pool of premium executive talent shrinks, companies are recognizing the need to groom future leadership through programs that attract and retain senior managers with the abilities, integrity, and drive to advance strategic priorities. Numerous boards in recent years have been forced by investor pressure to quickly replace corporate leaders on performance or ethics grounds and have had to provide premium pay and special deals to lure outside talent into the organization. These highly publicized crises drove it home that succession planning is a vital board-level function that requires directors to put in place a formal planned succession process to enable a smooth transition of leadership under any termination scenario.

Historically, the succession-management process encouraged retention by increasing equity-based compensation as part of a broader-based strategic policy rather than on an individual basis. However, because succession-management needs differ by organization, these days companies are at least as likely to need a top executive to remain with the company longer as they are to want one to leave early. The impact of these considerations has been to reduce the focus on the compensation of the CEO and to put more focus on the pay of the rest of the leadership team. While there are still some "superstar" CEOs paid many multiples of the pay of subordinates, today it is more common to see a leadership pay hierarchy that progresses in a logical way as executives advance to the CEO position.

There is also a growing move to subject top leadership, including CEOs, to a formal evaluation process similar to that of other employees. Along with assessing specific financial goals, reviews are more likely to cover "soft" areas of executive performance, such as leadership, industry relations, ethics, and customer satisfaction that have an impact on internal morale and the organization's image. Such a frank performance review not only reinforces the board's preeminent oversight of all managers, including the CEO, but also sends a strong message to employees and shareholders that everyone in the organization will be held to account. It also may inspire CEOs to institute a more rigorous performance review process for their own direct reports.

Compensation planning is also being influenced by recognition of the critical need for organizations to maintain a leadership perspective beyond the current CEO's tenure. Faced with investor pressure to quickly replace corporate leaders who are underperforming or face ethics questions, boards are recognizing that their ability to protect and maximize long-term value for shareholders and to control compensation costs is jeopardized by the necessity to engage in time-pressured negotiations with outside candidates. Toward that end, more organizations are instituting a long-term succession-planning process that is based on recruiting, identifying, nurturing, and promoting future leadership from *within* the organization. Many consider General Electric a model of how to identify the organization's key long-term goals and the types of management skills that will be needed to achieve them and providing promising managers with the coaching, regular feedback, and regular opportunities to hone those skills.

At most organizations, oversight of talent development has fallen to the compensation committee as a way to make certain that the issue receives focused attention, just as nominating committees have assumed new governance-related responsibilities to which the full board cannot devote the needed time and effort. Equally important, having the compensation committee responsible for both functions helps to ensure that long-range talent-development issues are integrated into—and ultimately enhance—its decisions on compensation issues.

## Dealing with the Changing Labor Market

One of the most common but controversial tools in executive compensation design is the use of data from a selected group of corporate peers as a yardstick for setting pay levels. Although the proxy disclosure statement reporting rules do not specifically require the naming of peer companies or why they were chosen, the SEC does require that companies disclose any information "material to the decision-making process." As such, compensation committees are taking a proactive approach to identifying appropriate peer companies by size, by comparability of business, and as a potential market for executive talent.

Peer groups are almost universally used by directors in the decision-making process. The most frequent question asked today concerns how to use peer-group benchmark data. Companies should use peer-group data to inform market compensation for the CEO position but use their judgment to pay the CEO based on his or her tenure with the company, skills, experience, and performance. Furthermore, because proxy advisory firms and other shareholders may refer to other market data sources, compensation committees are better informed by reviewing market data from multiple sources.

Many companies are faced with using market data in determining pay for a newly promoted or newly hired CEO. Although a company's compensation philosophy may target the 50th percentile of the peer group, the compensation committee should evaluate the individual CEO to determine pay levels relative to the market. For example, a new CEO initially may receive target total compensation that is below the 25th percentile of CEOs in the peer group. A pay program that begins at the lower end of the market range is appropriate given the executive's newness to the role. However, the compensation committee should determine the amount of time that it believes the individual CEO should take to achieve median peer-group pay levels (e.g., three to five years). In practice, the compensation committee should assess the CEO's performance and skills each year and refer to the market data to determine the appropriate pay opportunity. Increases in the compensation package to recognize growth in the position should take into account the need for the executive to accumulate an ownership position that meets and then exceeds the stock ownership guideline for the job in order to demonstrate "skin in the game" to key shareholders.

There is a slight trend in the United States toward separating the CEO and board chair positions, a position advocated by many outsiders and common in Europe. We have not seen discernible differences in pay for CEOs in the separate versus combined positions. Board chairs, however, generally make more money than lead directors, typically resulting in modestly higher compensation expense for companies separating the positions.

## Getting the Right Performance from Executive Pay Programs

In recent years, pay elements linked to performance have increased as part of the overall pay mix. Such performance awards define the level of performance required to earn cash or equity awards over short- and longer-term periods (typically one to three years). Because the use of discretion has been maligned in recent years, boards have embraced such formula-based awards to decrease the need to exercise discretion in determining payouts. For example, boards are less willing to pay out for missed targets on the basis of unfavorable external circumstances on the grounds that executives should share at least some of the same risks as shareholders. Boards also have become more sensitive to payouts stemming from performance-based pay elements relative to the particular organization or individual, such as historic company pay trends or the executive's own expectations. For example, a payout in a record year should be reasonably consistent with how outstanding performance was recognized in the past.

Furthermore, the use of performance criteria in long-term equity awards has increased in prevalence. As companies moved more equity value into full-value shares, in line with governance concerns that the overuse of stock options tended to focus executives excessively on short-term price movement, there was outside pressure to incorporate performance considerations into the grants. For example, in 2000, the prevalence of performance-contingent awards to CEOs from the largest 200 companies (the "top 200") was only 30 percent. Stock options with a fair market value strike price and time-vesting-restricted stock comprised most of the remaining long-term incentive mix. In 2012, the prevalence of performance-contingent long-term incentive awards increased to 77 percent. The increase in performance-based pay largely has been the result of the policies of proxy advisory firms that require that at least 50 percent of total compensation be performance based (and they do not consider stock options to be performance based if they are time-vested and priced at fair market value). Economic growth in the United States has been relatively slow over the past several years, with boards searching for both good strategies to achieve more traditional growth rates and the best measures of progress along the way. These are the measures that compensation committees consider for their long-term performance plans. In addition, the design of performance-based pay elements has been influenced by proxy advisory firm policies: many proxy advisory firms measure long-term performance over three-year periods and based on relative total shareholder returns (TSR).

Proxy advisory firms' definitions of pay and performance alignment have challenged companies to establish pay programs that are appropriately aligned with business strategy and investment cycles. For example, proxy advisory firms may recommend against a company's say-on-pay vote if relative one- or three-year TSR performance is below the 50th percentile of the industry group. Under this relative TSR approach, all companies eventually will be faced with a negative say-on-pay recommendation regardless of whether the compensation program is aligned with the intended compensation philosophy and the business strategy over a longer time period. For example, a capital-intensive company may design the compensation program to be tied to appropriately achieving positive return on invested capital over a five- to ten-year period. In the current environment, that same company is pressured to establish a three-year performance award plan that pays out based on relative TSR performance only. For a capital-intensive business, a three-year period may be too short term, and relative TSR, as a lag measure, does not necessarily give information to the shareholders about the company's priorities and may not motivate executives to invest capital appropriately and build shareholder value over time. Relative TSR can be a useful metric for certain companies, but it should be balanced appropriately with other measures.

## Communicating Pay Programs

Transparency in compensation programs and the compensation committee's decision-making process increased almost immediately after the new SEC proxy disclosure rules were finalized in 2007. With the advent of say on pay, transparency is more important than ever. In fact, the CD&A in proxy disclosure statements has become longer and includes more graphic and tabular depictions of compensation programs. Proxy voting advisors and institutional investors focus on the pay of the CEO when determining how to vote on the say-on-pay resolution. As a result, many companies take great care in structuring the CEO's pay package and in determining how generously to reward current performance.

Specifically, companies have included graphic depictions linking compensation payout levels to key financial performance metrics as a means to demonstrate a pay-for-performance linkage. Companies also have added alternative tables in the CD&A that compare SEC-mandated summary compensation table grant values of pay with realized pay, approximating amounts the executives took home each year, or realizable pay opportunities that demonstrate the current values of equity compensation, which can be higher or lower than the grant-date value reported in the summary compensation table. Although not yet majority practice, the use of alternative compensation disclosures increases each year. Most expect that the SEC's rules on pay-for-performance disclosure will at least allow some compensation definition other than the summary compensation table in showing how pay has varied with performance. Also, as the CD&A has become the primary "marketing tool" for companies, many have incorporated executive summaries highlighting the key points of the executive compensation programs and corporate governance policies, key financial and other performance accomplishments, and the manner in which compensation and governance programs served to drive positive performance outcomes.

Three years of say on pay has taught companies that ongoing investor relations are critical; outreach to institutional shareholders a month before the say-on-pay vote is not always effective. Although a negative recommendation from proxy advisory firms can yield a sizable decrease in say-on-pay voting support, it is not fatal. Given that relative TSR performance is a major consideration of proxy advisory firms, it is likely that all companies eventually will face a negative voting recommendation. However, a well-written CD&A, an effective shareholder outreach program that links incentive programs with an effective business strategy, and reasons that the compensation committee's oversight of executive compensation is sound and thoughtful can achieve majority support for say on pay despite the negative recommendation.

## Conclusion

In public companies, CEO compensation is an activity carried out in the full light of day because of disclosure requirements and the number of outside parties who publicize disclosed results, especially when they disagree with what was done. In addition to the traditional audience of shareholders, interested parties include other employees, business partners, organized labor, the media, and Congress. The say-on-pay vote has reinforced the backbones of compensation committees, who now rarely compromise on rigorous performance standards or grant special awards in sympathy with executive teams who failed to achieve their goals under difficult circumstances. The overwhelming external emphasis on the CEO's pay has dampened board interest in special deals or benefits, and many CEOs have sacrificed pay to set an example either externally or internally when results have not met expectations.

# 28

# Board Compensation

Nora McCord

*Steven Hall & Partners*

Directors today operate in a landscape dramatically different from the one they have occupied historically. The recent economic collapse, high-profile failures in risk oversight, annual elections of directors, regular say-on-pay votes, and the advent of activist investors using director elections to agitate for immediate results have all contributed to this new reality. Far more time and effort are demanded, greater expertise is needed, and the risks of board service are higher. Directors are also subject to greater oversight by shareholders, voting advisory services, special-interest groups, and a critical media, all of whom scrutinize board decisions. This redefinition of the director role has resulted in a fundamental redesign of director pay.

## Role of the Director

In the earliest days of corporate America, directors were founders and investors in the companies on whose boards they served. With the shift to the representative director, a certain gentility, "clubbiness," and prestige, along with nominal payment, accompanied "rubber stamp" board service. Today, however, serving as an independent director means standing in the line of fire. Although directors have always been accountable to shareholders, the advent of the "withhold" vote, in which shareholders withhold their vote for a particular director (articles of incorporation at most U.S. companies preclude "against" votes), carries real reputational risk. Additionally, directors must conduct their affairs in the full glare of a public spotlight focused by shareholders, the media, the general public, corporate governance activists, voting advisory services, legislators, regulators, and unions on an increasingly broad array of financial, operational, and strategic initiatives. The responsibilities, risks, and performance expectations associated with independent directorship have risen exponentially in recent years.

This new, more perilous landscape has had a meaningful impact on the way in which directors do their jobs. No longer merely "rubber stamps," today's boards are actively involved in corporate strategy and the oversight of risk in all of its varied forms, in addition to supervision of more traditional areas of purview such as succession planning, executive compensation, and audit.

Board composition has evolved to support this expanded role. Whereas critiques that boards were comprised solely of the CEO's golfing partners may once have had merit, today's directors are most likely to have been identified and recruited by outside search firms engaged specifically to assist in the selection of qualified and engaged professionals capable of providing meaningful contributions to the board's overarching mission. Furthermore, it is not unusual for directors to be recruited to provide a specific talent or expertise to a board, such as manufacturing or logistics, social media, or certain key foreign markets.

The increasing importance of the skills and expertise of each individual director has reinforced the need for competitive compensation packages. Although most directors accept board positions for reasons completely unrelated to pay, it can be an important differentiator when directors are deciding between two otherwise equally attractive posts. Given the limited pool of qualified candidates and a marked preference for candidates who are also currently CEOs with limited ability to accept outside board positions, competitive pay opportunities are a must.

## Capitalism and the Role of Corporate Governance

American capitalism originated with small-business owners who worked hard and reaped the direct financial results of their labors. Equity was in their hands and their hands alone. However, as successful small operations grew into larger enterprises financed by external capital and staffed by multiple layers, the owner/manager disappeared. Chief executives were employees, and the clear correlation between performance and reward eroded. In an endeavor to restore this linkage, a portion of compensation formerly paid entirely in cash was shifted into equity.

In the 1950s and 1960s, stock options designed to tie executive compensation to the fortunes of the company and its investors comprised a mere 10 percent of CEO total pay. With the rise of the pay-for-performance movement, a major cash-to-equity shift was initiated at the senior executive level, causing corporations to move a growing portion of management as well as employee remuneration into company stock to motivate and reward the creation of shareholder value. In 2013, long-term incentive vehicles accounted for just over 60 percent of the present value of CEO total remuneration among the top 100 U.S. corporations. Full-value performance shares are now the dominant component of a typical CEO long-term incentive package (representing about 50 percent of the total), coupled with restricted stock (21 percent of the total) and options (29 percent of the total). With the added boost garnered from significant share ownership guidelines and holding requirements, the terms *CEO* and *stockholder* have again become virtually synonymous.

Once equity became firmly entrenched in the executive suite, governance activists turned their attention to outside directors. At the time, director compensation consisted of a rich mix of pay and benefits, including pensions, healthcare, and other perquisites. Thus began the initial stages of a similar movement to align director remuneration directly with long-term stock performance and the interests of shareholders. Director compensation has come full circle, with restoration of this all-important ownership stake at the board level.

## Corporate Governance and the Drive for Equity

Directors and their compensation—once beyond reproach—first came under attack in the early 1990s from institutional shareholders and activists. The issue was not *how much* directors were being paid, but rather *how* they were being paid. Bolstered by studies touting the direct linkage between meaningful equity ownership on the part of managers and directors and higher total returns to shareholders, aggressive corporate governance initiatives propelled equity to a position of indisputable prominence in compensating the outside director for board service.

In December 1994, the proactive establishment by the National Association of Corporate Directors (NACD) of a blue-ribbon commission to study board pay provided the catalyst needed to set change in motion. The commission's findings, and most important, its recommendations, resulted in sweeping alterations in how directors were paid. Director compensation transitioned from a predominantly cash-based payment system to one with a sizable equity component. Pensions were replaced initially with options, which then were supplanted by full-value restricted stock awards, and vesting schedules, once aligned with those of executives, have evolved so that awards are vested either at grant or on the first anniversary of the date of grant.

Today, the commission's recommendation that at least 50 percent of director pay be delivered in equity remains a best practice in director compensation, and its adoption has been nearly universal. Among the top 200 largest publicly traded U.S. companies, equity compensation comprised 55 percent of total compensation in 2012. This focus on equity compensation addresses shareholder concerns by reinforcing the alignment between the interests of the directors and those of the shareholders, on whose behalf directors are elected to serve.

## Elements of Director Compensation

Compensation for independent directors is comprised of a number of different elements. The largest component is typically the retainer for board service. Analogous to salaries for executives, board retainers generally are divided into a cash and equity component. In addition to retainers, directors may receive a smaller fee for each board meeting attended, although this practice is declining steeply in prevalence. Directors also may receive additional compensation for service on a board committee, which may include a retainer and/or a fee for attendance at each meeting, both of which are typically delivered in cash (Figure 28.1).

On an overall basis, consistent with the best practice established by the 1994 NACD blue-ribbon commission, today's directors typically receive just over half their total pay in cash (Figure 28.2).

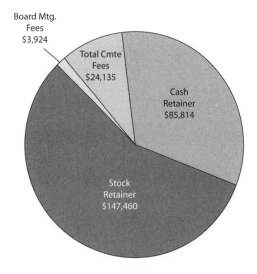

Figure 28.1  Average director compensation: top 200 U.S. companies, 2012.

| Equity 55% | Cash 45% |
| --- | --- |

Figure 28.2  Average director pay mix: top 200 U.S. companies, 2012.

## Total Compensation

As the responsibilities, workloads, and reputational risks associated with director service have risen, so too has director compensation. For directors serving at the 200 largest U.S. companies, total fees in 2012 were just above $260,000. After several years of little or no growth in director compensation, as directors eschewed pay raises in a show of solidarity with rank-and-file employees and executives facing steep reductions in pay associated with the economic downturn and the resulting uncertainty, director compensation has again begun to increase. In 2012, total remuneration increased 5 percent over 2011 levels compared with an increase of 4 percent in each of the two prior years and an aggregate increase of 15 percent over the past five years.

## Total Compensation by Role

Over the past five years, we have observed the greatest increases in compensation paid to compensation committee chairs (Figure 28.3); these increases are reflective of the greater

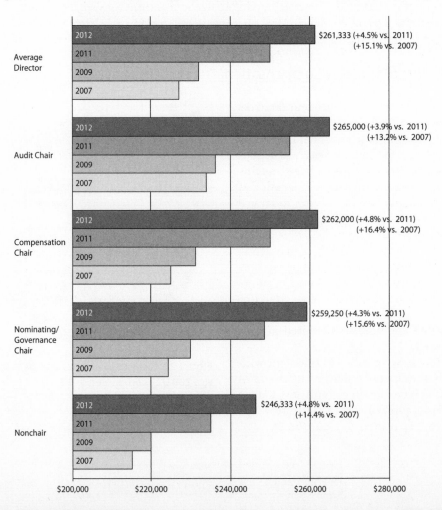

Figure 28.3  Median total board compensation values: top 200 U.S. companies, 2007–2012.

responsibilities imposed on this position by the recent Dodd-Frank legislation, which introduced a whole host of new compensation- and governance-related requirements for public companies. The most important of these new requirements, the say-on-pay vote, which gives shareholders a nonbinding vote on the company's compensation program, has heightened the reputational risks for directors serving as chairs of compensation committees because failures to address deficiencies in the pay program, whether real or perceived, often result in "withhold" vote campaigns against these chairs. Although significant withhold votes are not usually sufficient to prompt directors to lose their board seats, they are viewed as a black mark against individual directors, many of whom are reluctant to tarnish otherwise stellar reputations, particularly in the latter part of their careers.

## Equity Vehicles Used

Whereas equity was previously delivered predominantly in options, option use has steadily declined in practice. Today, most director compensation programs have shifted to full-value grants, either of restricted stock or the outright award of shares. From a governance perspective, full-value grants are deemed the more appropriate vehicle for board remuneration. Unlike options, full-value grants place directors in a position of immediate ownership with both upside opportunity and downside risk, as well as full voting and dividend rights on a par with stockholders. Among the 200 largest U.S. companies, 88 percent grant full-value awards only, 9 percent grant both options and full-value awards, and just 3 percent grant options only (Figure 28.4).

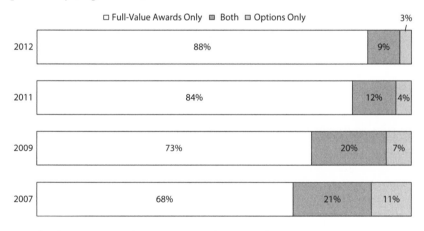

**Figure 28.4  Equity grant practices: top 200 U.S. companies, 2007–2012.**

From a governance perspective, full-value grants are deemed to be the more appropriate vehicle for board remuneration. Unlike options, grants place directors in a position of immediate ownership, with both upside opportunity and downside risk, as well as full voting and dividend rights on a par with stockholders.

## Vesting

Governance concerns also have had an impact on the vesting terms associated with director equity awards. In response to governance concerns that extended vesting periods and the resulting value of unvested equity might discourage a director from leaving a board when warranted, thus compromising director independence and responsible board oversight, vesting periods for director awards have declined steadily. Today, over two-thirds of equity awards granted to directors in the 200 largest U.S. companies vest either immediately or within one year of grant. Among companies with multiyear vesting schedules, step vesting (in which the award vests ratably over time) is the predominant practice (Figure 28.5).

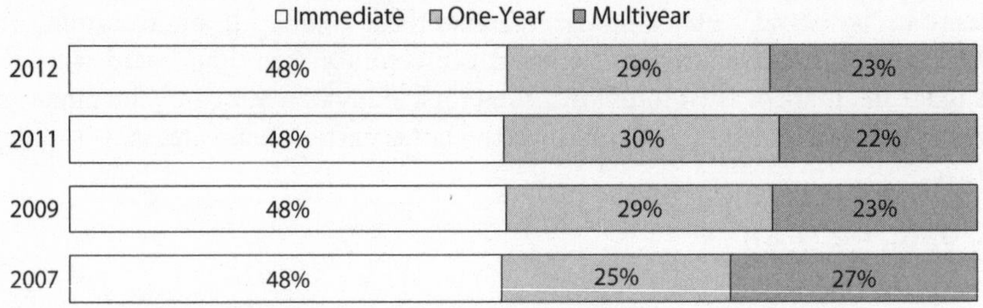

Figure 28.5  Equity vesting schedule prevalence: top 200 U.S. companies, 2007–2012.

## Performance-Based Compensation

It is also in the equity component of board pay that some have tried to insert a more explicit performance element. Although there have been several high-profile attempts to incorporate performance-based pay into director compensation programs, the practice has never caught on. The use of more performance-based pay for directors, such as performance-contingent vesting of long-term incentive awards, has been criticized for a variety of reasons. If both the board and management are paid in the same manner and rewarded for the same behavior, the system of checks and balances inherent in an independent board is largely abrogated. Who, the argument runs, will mind the store for the long-term shareholders if both managers and directors are incentivized to achieve predefined relatively short-term goals? The key to preserving director independence is recognition of the fundamental difference between the duties of a public corporation's board and its management and the need to reflect those different roles in the design of their compensation. A program that subjects nonemployee directors to the same pay-for-performance standards and pressures as management threatens to undermine outside board members' capacity to act in a truly disinterested manner, especially in setting such standards.

## Ownership Guidelines

Over the past 15 years, share ownership guidelines for directors have become nearly universal practice. Among the largest 200 U.S companies, 91 percent have guidelines requiring directors to own a specific level of stock. These requirements reflect widespread consensus that direct ownership of a meaningful number of shares is the most appropriate and effective way to align the interests of directors with those of the shareholders they are elected to represent.

The guidelines most typically require directors to hold a number of shares with a value equal to a specified multiple of the annual cash board retainer, although a sizable minority of companies (just over 15 percent) defines the guideline as a fixed number of shares. In response to concerns raised by shareholder advisory firms, the size of the ownership requirement has been steadily increasing, and just over half of large U.S. companies

(59 percent) require directors to hold shares valued at five times or greater the cash retainer, whereas 35 percent require directors to hold between three and five times the cash retainer, and just 6 percent require holdings of less than three times the cash retainer. The median value of required ownership was $375,000 in 2012.

Directors generally have five years to acquire the required ownership stake, although an increasing number of companies are eliminating this requirement in favor of a requirement that directors hold a specified percentage (often 50 percent) of net, after-tax shares received as payment for board service until the guideline is met. Such a modification ensures that directors are always in compliance with the guideline and eliminates potentially embarrassing disclosure in SEC filings of directors who have failed to achieve the guideline in the allotted time.

## Retreat from Board Meeting Fees

Over the past several years, there has been a pronounced shift away from the payment of board meeting fees. Payment of these meeting fees has not been a majority practice of the 200 largest U.S. companies since 2005, when just over half paid them, and rates have continued to decline steadily. Today, just over one-quarter of companies pay them (27 percent). Among companies that do pay such fees, meeting fees have held steady at a median of $2,000 for the past five years.

Many companies value the administrative advantages of not having to track and pay for attendance at meetings or, even more fundamentally in some instances, to define what constitutes a meeting. Additionally, it is relatively easy to incorporate amounts previously paid as meeting fees into cash and equity retainers, resulting in higher pay for board service but relatively similar total pay packages. However, this approach is not practical for all companies. Particularly in instances where companies are unable to establish a "typical" number of meetings, payment of meeting fees may continue to make good sense. One alternative for companies preferring to eliminate fees but facing unpredictable future workloads is to establish the number of meetings required for a typical workload and then pay for meetings in excess of that number on a per-meeting basis. This approach has the advantage of eliminating meeting fees during the ordinary course but provides important flexibility to ensure that directors are appropriately compensated when unusual circumstances cause workloads to increase significantly (Figure 28.6).

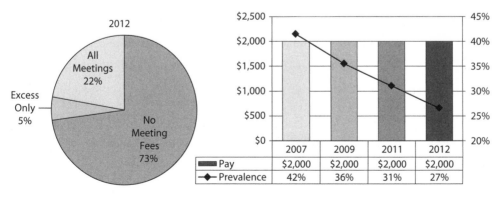

Figure 28.6  Board meeting fees, median values and prevalence: top 200 U.S. companies, 2007–2012.

## Fees for Committee Service

The committee has become the workhorse of the board, with committee chairs assuming leadership roles with respect to specific areas of board responsibility. In recognition of the heavy burden placed on committee chairs, payment of additional fees for this service is nearly universal. Fees generally include an additional retainer, and chairs also may receive additional fees for meeting attendance.

Audit chairs receive the highest additional fee in recognition of the work associated with the regular oversight of the company's financials. Median fees for audit committee chairs have held steady at $25,000 and are paid by 99 percent of the top 200 companies. However, fees for compensation committee chairs have been increasing in both prevalence and amount; with the advent of shareholder say-on-pay votes and intense public scrutiny of pay issues generally, these chairs are now in the hot seat and particularly vulnerable to shareholder criticism. Compensation committee chairs now receive a median of $20,000 in additional fees and are paid by 97 percent of the top 200 U.S. companies. Although fees for nominating and governance chairs are lower, $15,000 at median, the prevalence of these fees is rising, to 94 percent in 2012, in recognition of the increasing importance of this committee in today's environment (Figure 28.7).

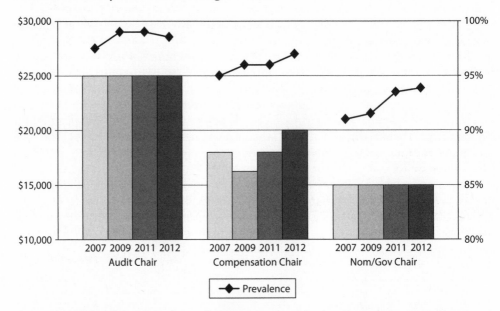

**Figure 28.7 Committee chair additional fees, median values and prevalence: top 200 U.S. companies, 2007–2012.**

Committee members among the top 200 U.S. companies are less likely than committee chairs to receive additional fees for their service on a committee. This distinction is attributable largely to the fact that many companies have eliminated additional fees for committee meeting attendance, which, for many companies, historically had been the way in which committee members were compensated. Today, only audit committee members are more likely than not to receive additional fees for committee service. Elimination of fees for service as a member of a board committee is often accompanied by a one-time increase in cash or equity retainers for board service and a confirmation that the burdens of committee service are distributed equally among the directors (Figure 28.8).

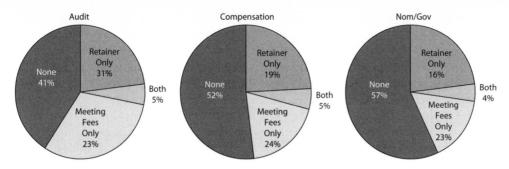

**Figure 28.8 Form of additional fees for committee members: top 200 U.S. companies.**

In instances where directors are compensated for service as a committee member, the median total additional compensation was $15,000 for audit committee members, $10,000 for compensation committee members, and $8,000 for nominating/governance committee members (Figure 28.9).

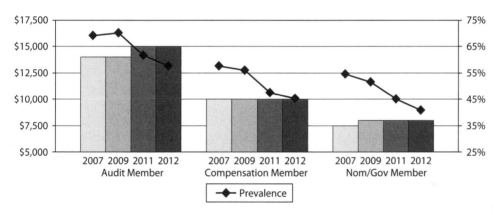

**Figure 28.9 Committee member additional fees, median values and prevalence: top 200 U.S. companies, 2007–2012.**

## The Future of Board Pay

Historically, director compensation was not on the radar screens of most corporate observers. Directors were widely respected for the role they played, which, combined with relatively low compensation amounts, caused many commentators to dub them the "best buy in corporate America." Those days are gone. Today, discontent with high and rising executive compensation levels, a growing public belief that pay should be linked to performance, and a sense that at least some directors were asleep at the switch and therefore failed to take steps needed to avert the recent financial crisis all have contributed to enhanced scrutiny of board pay. Questions such as, "What are we paying directors for?" and "Should directors be paid based upon performance?" have crept into the public discourse on director pay.

Shareholder advisory firms, responding to concerns of their institutional investor client base and influenced by a growing focus on director issues, including independence and diversity, in the European corporate governance arena, also have waded into the debate.

In addition to assessing director governance issues, they also have begun to compare compensation paid to directors with that paid to the company's comparators on a per-director basis.

This shift has had a meaningful impact on how corporations manage director pay. Already an evaluation of the market competitiveness of director compensation levels has become an annual event rather than something reviewed every two or three years. Increased scrutiny is also likely to result in greater conformity in both amounts paid and the way in which that pay is delivered. Finally, descriptions of how directors are paid and why, already included in SEC filings, are likely to become more robust as companies seek to "sell" shareholders on the idea that money spent on securing qualified and engaged directors with critical areas of expertise remains in their best interests.

# 29

# Structuring Board and Executive Pay

BRUCE R. ELLIG
*Noted Compensation Specialist and Author*

The challenge to the board of directors and its compensation committee is to ensure that executive compensation programs create a competitive business advantage within a rapidly changing business environment and meet stakeholders' expectations. This will be examined in this chapter by reviewing the following 10 areas:

1. Role of the board of directors
2. Stakeholder impact on board actions
3. Composition of the board
4. Board performance and compensation
5. Committees of the board
6. Compensation committee
7. Executive compensation philosophy
8. Reasonable versus excessive executive pay
9. Use of compensation consultants
10. Major issues facing the compensation committee and the board

## Role of the Board of Directors

The board of directors is elected by company shareholders and is expected to act as an agent in their best interests. The board's primary responsibility is to hire (and, if necessary, fire) the company's CEO. It is also expected to act (and interact with its shareholders) serving the shareholders' interests and complying not simply with the letter of the laws and regulations but also with the spirit of such requirements. It is expected to develop a corporate code of ethics along with action-guiding principles.

The board is expected not only to approve the mission and supporting objectives but also to measure how the company in general and the CEO in particular are performing. Based on said performance, it is responsible for setting the pay of the CEO and the other top executive officers. This should be within the framework of an approved compensation philosophy.

Directors are responsible for ensuring compliance with all legal requirements. Their fiduciary responsibilities include the *duty of care* (diligent in understanding business issues and the alternatives) and the *duty of loyalty* (placing shareholders' interests above all others). Corporate governance also requires directors to *exercise prudent judgment* in all actions and avoid a conflict of interest. The *business judgment rule* stipulates that if directors have acted in good faith and the best interest of the company and exercised prudent judgment, they cannot be held liable for poor decisions or mistakes.

It is common for boards to have a *lead director*, where the chair and CEO positions are combined. Among the responsibilities are chairing board meetings when the chair/CEO is not present (both planned and unplanned) and facilitating discussions between and among independent directors.

## Stakeholder Impact on Board Actions

Those having an interest in board actions (because they are affected by actions) are called *stakeholders*. They are community, customers, executives, other employees, and shareholders.

What do they want?

- The *community* where the company is located wants a significant number of good-paying jobs and no damage to the environment. The first improves the tax base and removes unemployment costs. The second means that there is no community expense to make improvements.

- *Customers* want quality products/services at a low price with good service.

- *Executives* want top pay for good performance and job security.

- *Other employees* want good pay and job security also.

- *Shareholders* want a good return on their investment in the form of dividends and increased stock prices.

Why is it important that the stakeholders' wants are significant to the board of directors? They are because sometimes it will be necessary to choose an action that may be unfavorable to one because it is more important to be favorable to another. An example would be deciding whether or not to recall all products because of contamination to several. The cost of doing so would affect earnings and probably stock price, but not doing so would damage the company's reputation with its customers. Because it is typically important to act quickly on issues such as this, it is important to have decided earlier the priority of the stakeholders.

A good case could be made for putting *employees* first. Without them, there is no company. And their output and interactions with customers have a major impact on *customers*, who would come second. Without customer purchases, there is no company. The *community* is an important third because their actions on taxes and other issues have a significant impact on the company. Then we have the *executives*, who are the beneficiaries of the named stakeholders in the form of level of pay and job tenure. And last but not least are the *shareholders*. The outcomes of the other stakeholders definitely will affect earnings and stock price. Some people believe that the shareholder should be number one, but that would add credence to actions that might be favorable in the short run but questionable longer term.

## Composition of the Board

Directors fall into two categories: those working for the company (and identified as *inside* directors) and those who do not work for the company (and identified as *outside* or *independent* directors). Some people identify *affiliated* as a third category. This includes retired executives of the company and those representing companies that do a significant amount of business with the company.

Historically, boards consisted only of insiders because companies started as private companies and only later "went public," selling their stock to others on a listed stock exchange. With that action, the Securities and Exchange Commission (SEC) entered and initially required that at least one outsider be on the board and sit on the audit committee. Over the years, the composition has shifted so that now many companies have only the CEO sitting as an insider and all others as outsiders. This makes it easy to staff board committees with disinterested persons.

Although it is important that the board reflect needed experience, the most typical director is either an active or retired CEO of another company. Given the need for experienced executives, the need exceeds the pool of CEOs, and companies are looking to those one level below the CEO category. This is especially helpful in addressing diversity and ethnicity objectives. Because of the need for financial experience, CFOs are a logical second category, although those with a technical background appropriate for the board also would be logical. Celebrity or trophy directors with star names are sometimes included, but this should occur only if the other needs are met. It is critical that directors identify and focus on the key issues, acting as owners and not simply as stewards of the company.

It is very easy for qualified persons to be on more boards than appropriate to meet their primary responsibility of serving as the CEO of their own companies. Those sitting on multiple boards are often identified as *boarded up*, being on too many boards.

Typically, the chairman of the board is also the CEO of the company, but this is changing. It is argued that because the board is responsible for hiring, compensating, and, if necessary, firing the CEO, it is a conflict of interest to have the combined role.

Many people believe that when a CEO retires, he or she should leave the board because the new CEO may want to make changes not approved by his or her predecessor. Others believe that having the retired CEO remain on the board adds to the experience in addition to providing a historical perspective for previous actions.

It has been argued that individual directors are part-timers who often lack the needed expertise for issues facing the company and depend on management for information. Just as auditing services come from an independent company approved by the board of directors, perhaps a board service company (BSC) should take on the role of corporate governance. It would reduce the previously noted weakness of the current system. Such an action would require careful consideration, meeting obstacles from the SEC and elsewhere. But such a bold step may be the answer to ensure that stakeholder issues are properly considered. Laws and regulations restricting the company continue to proliferate. Compliance is becoming more and more burdensome, and there is no indication that it will abate. Within this environment, the board of directors must meet its corporate governance responsibility. Who is better equipped to do this—a part-time director or a full-time service company?

## Board Performance and Compensation

If the mantra for executive compensation is "pay for performance," should not the same be true for board members? Conceptually, this is logical, at least for the board as a whole, but not for individual members for several reasons: (1) it is very time-consuming, (2) it is potentially disruptive, antagonizing members who are sensitive to being criticized, and (3) low-key suggestions for improvement from the chair may be more helpful in improving performance than a formal written appraisal. That said, how should the board be compensated?

Typically, directors are paid a retainer and a meeting fee both for the full board and for each board committee. The first reflects an ongoing responsibility. The second recognizes the need to attend meetings in order to meet ongoing responsibilities. Some boards pay only a retainer regardless of attendance, believing that board member attendance is not the critical factor. A few boards pay only for attendance, emphasizing the need to be present to discharge obligations.

There are a number of surveys that are helpful to boards to set an appropriate pay package. This includes pay for the board chair and lead director when such positions are used. In addition to determining the type and size of the pay package, it is important to decide who will approve the program. Historically, the inside (or management) directors approved the pay package. This was not an issue when the outside (nonmanagement) directors were in the minority. But now, with many boards, the majority consists of outside directors. Is it appropriate that they approve their own pay program? The company executives do not approve their own pay actions. Why should the directors? Some people believe that shareholders should approve directors' pay program. At the least, it should be put to the same nonbinding say-on-pay vote as executive compensation.

## Committees of the Board

Typically, boards have at least three committees: audit, compensation, and governance. The *audit committee* is responsible for recommending a specific audit firm to represent the company and meeting with that audit firm. The action typically is approved by the shareholders. The *compensation committee* is responsible for proposing changes in compensation and related programs for the CEO and other named executive officers, typically at least those listed in the company proxy statement. The *governance committee* proposes candidates for the board, as well as those who serve as officers of the company. It is also responsible for reviewing board performance and director pay.

Other board committees might include an *executive committee* (acting on behalf of the full board), a *finance committee* (reviewing capital budgets and dividend actions), a *pension committee* (approving fund managers and reviewing performance), a *public policy committee* (identifying and recommending action on issues affecting the company), and a *strategic planning committee* (proposing plans and assessing results).

Some boards believe that it is appropriate to ensure that all directors serve on each committee over a period of time. Doing so would rotate one director off a committee each year. With three or more directors on a committee, this would mean that there would always be at least two experienced directors on a committee.

## Compensation Committee

The role of the compensation committee is to take direct responsibility for determining the appropriate level and composition of pay for the CEO and other named senior executives consistent with approved compensation philosophy, competitive position, and appraised performance. The committee is typically responsible for drafting the contents of the compensation discussion and analysis (CD&A) section of the company proxy disclosure statement.

Committee actions are reviewed and approved by the board unless otherwise prescribed by law, regulation, or security listing requirement. An example of such a limitation is imposed by Section 162(m) of Internal Revenue Code, which stipulates the pay deductions for proxy-named executives that exceed $1 million must be linked to performance and approved by a compensation committee of disinterested persons.

The committee typically consists of independent board directors preferably with some knowledge of executive compensation and finance. It is important to avoid interlocking relationships, namely, where CEOs sit on each other's compensation committees.

The committee elects a chair to set the agenda and preside at the meetings, in addition to setting a timetable for the year that identifies what actions are to be taken at each meeting. A secretary is also elected. Rather than put the responsibility on a committee member, it may be appropriate to name either the human resources head or someone from the general counsel staff (e.g., the person responsible for SEC matters).

## Compensation Philosophy

The compensation committee and the board of directors are responsible for developing an executive compensation philosophy. It consists of three parts: significance of market stage; importance of attract, retain, and motivate; and degree of risk to be built into the system.

### Market-Stage Significance

The five *pay elements* are salary, employee benefits, executive benefits (i.e., perquisites), short-term incentives, and long-term incentives. The type of incentive is determined by the period of measurement. Short-term incentives are one year or less; long-term incentives are longer than one year, ranging from two to ten years.

The *market stages* are threshold (or startup), growth, maturity, and decline. It is important that the board determine the company's market-stage position in deciding what forms of executive pay to emphasize. It is also important to realize that different parts of the business may be in different market stages and therefore that customization is necessary.

- *Threshold.* Because of the shortage of cash, the emphasis is on long-term incentives, more specifically stock options.

- *Growth.* With improvement in both revenue and income, the company makes moderate change in salary, employee benefits, and short-term incentives. Long-term incentives still emphasize stock options, but various types of stock awards (especially performance based) are introduced.

- *Maturity.* With revenue flattening out, market-based incentives are pared back, but continued improvement in profits places high emphasis on short-term incentives, probably in cash form. Salary also has moved to a higher level of focus.

- *Decline.* With revenue and profit shrinking, the emphasis has shifted to salary and benefits, although short-term incentives that focus on reducing costs also will be important.

### Importance of Attract, Retain, and Motivate

It is important that the board review the significance of each of the three design objectives in structuring the executive compensation plan.

- *Attract.* Salary and short-term incentives will be emphasized to attract needed executive talent.

- *Retain.* Salary and long-term incentives will be the focus of retaining executive talent.

- *Motivate.* Short-term incentives based on individual performance will be the main focus of motivating.

### Degree of Acceptable Risk

This is a major consideration in the design of an executive compensation program. It is virtually impossible for management to succeed without undertaking some risk. Typically, the greater the risk, the greater are the rewards in the short- and long-term incentive plan.

Essentially, there are three *levels of risk:* virtually none, reasonable, and severe. Where there is little or no risk, the pay package should emphasize the salary component. Reasonable risk should be the basis for the incentive plans. No plans should reward severe or excessive risk because it could destroy the company or even affect the entire economy, such as happened several years ago with the subordinate-of-debt issue.

Having identified the level of risk, the next step is to identify the *probability* of occurrence, namely, none, moderate, or high. Again, salary plans are used for no probability of occurrence and incentive plans for both moderate and high probabilities, with greater incentive emphasis on the latter.

## Reasonable versus Excessive Pay

Boards and their compensation committees are expected to ensure that executive pay is *reasonable*, that is, that it is appropriate given the level of performance of the executive (typically the CEO) and the company (in terms of earnings and stock performance). It is important to understand and include in discussions and disclosures the difference between *realized pay* (compensation actually paid), *realizable pay* (potential pay opportunity), and *company cost* (as defined in the proxy summary compensation tables). To best understand and illustrate the differences is to include the summary compensation table headers for the named executive officers with one table reporting realized pay, the second reporting realizable pay, and the third the company cost. Only in showing this information can one understand the facets of executive pay actions.

Excessive or unreasonable pay is in the eye of the beholder. This would include the business press, shareholder advisory services, shareholders, and the Internal Revenue Service (IRS). The business press is focused on selling print, the advisory services are intent on receiving revenue for their advice, shareholders are concerned with stock price and dividends, and the IRS is looking to see if the tax deduction is appropriate (pay viewed as excessive is not allowed a tax deduction). Lacking abuse of fiduciary trust or good faith or outright fraud, the courts have been reluctant to override the judgment of boards of directors or their compensation committees. The reasonable issue is typically viewed in light of the degree of risk built into the plan. The severity and probability of risk are critical factors because they could send the company into bankruptcy.

Generally speaking, charges of excessive or unreasonable pay are significantly less than five years ago. One reason is the enactment of the 2010 Dodd-Frank Wall Street Reform and Consumer Protection Act, which requires that shareholders must be given a vote on a nonbinding approval (or not) of executive pay. To the surprise of many, the results typically endorsed the executive pay program of the company. Given such results, it would not be surprising for Congress to mandate the results of shareholder voting—after all, it seems that there is not much of an issue, so why should management object?

## Use of Compensation Consultants

The board of directors and its compensation committee typically make use of consultants in the design and administrative structure of the executive compensation plans. These consultants are either internal to the company or external stand-alone organizations. The *internal consultants* are executive compensation experts, SEC and general legal counsel, corporate finance representatives (from accounting and the treasurer's staff), and management information systems staff. The team is typically chaired by the head of corporate human resources. Each team member is an expert in his or her own area, and after a rough design of the plan is developed by the compensation expert, the other team members examine the plan to overcome obstacles and optimize design success. Typically, the internal consultant team would report to the CEO, who, on approving a proposal, would have it submitted to the compensation committee and perhaps to the board of directors directly.

The *external consultants* have evolved from external auditing companies to stand-alone organizations. The reason for the separation has been to establish independence from the company in general and the CEO in particular because compensation consulting fees are only a small portion of total auditing company bills. Good corporate governance means that the company cannot put pressure on the audit company for the type of compensation plan the CEO wants with the threat of switching to a different audit firm.

In considering the extent of independence of the provider, it is necessary to identify what other services are provided to the company and what the annual dollar relationship is versus the compensation consulting. Additionally, are there any personal relationships between the firm and management, including the amount of company stock owned?

## Major Issues Facing the Compensation Committee and the Board

- Shareholders and advisory groups will continue to put pressure to reduce, if not eliminate completely, executive benefits (pay for position) and severance pay (pay for failure).

- It is necessary to ensure that the risks built into the incentives are reasonable and do not lead to excessive risk and excessive pay.

- The CEO and other proxy-named executives should retain an appropriate amount of company stock acquired through the stock plans. An acquisition-cost model (retaining stock left after paying acquisition cost) or something similar should be employed and closely monitored.

- The interaction and relative roles and responsibilities of the board, the compensation committee, and employed consultants should be reviewed and evaluated continuously.

- Changes in executive compensation design elsewhere must be closely monitored for possible consideration.

- Performance of peer companies must be continuously aligned with the company's own performance and executive pay.

- Possible changes in legislation (e.g., taxes and other laws affecting the company), as well as the Financial Accounting Standards Board (FASB) and the SEC, must be closely monitored, and when appropriate, changes should be made to company executive compensation plans.

## Summary

Although there has been little abatement about the levels of executive pay, it appears to be less of an overall issue than in recent years. The supporting votes for executive pay by shareholders in the say-on-pay meeting are a good indicator. That said, boards and their compensation committees need to be ever vigilant to ensure that excessive pay does not become a topic with their stakeholders. This includes being very wary of possible intervening actions by the legislative and regulatory branches of government. Executives also need to be aware that pay packages whose numbers look like telephone numbers (complete with area code) are difficult to defend regardless of company and stock performance.

# 30

# Compensation Committee of the Board

ROBERT H. ROCK
*MLR Holdings LLC*

## Compensation Committee Composition

The compensation committee is a standing committee of the board of directors. Most companies have three standing committees. In addition to the compensation committee, there is an audit committee and a nominating/governance committee, and together they constitute the three core oversight committees. Each member of these committees is *independent*, as defined for members of the respective committee in the listing standards of the New York Stock Exchange (NYSE) or Nasdaq, as well as the company's corporate governance guidelines.

Compensation committee members must meet the definitional requirements of "outside director" under Internal Revenue Code (IRC) Section 162(m) and the definitional requirements of "nonemployee director" under Rule 16b-3 of the Securities Exchange Act. Independence generally means that a director has never been an officer or employee of the company and has not had any material interest in a transaction or a business relationship with the company. In addition to excluding from the committee current employees and anyone receiving fees from the company for any professional services (e.g., bankers, outside counsel, and management consultants), it also excludes former officers of the company as well as any former employees receiving compensation for prior services (except statutory benefit plans). Moreover, for compensation committee members, there can be no "director interlocks"; that is, a committee member cannot be an officer of another member's company or a director of another member's compensation committee. In general, three to five independent directors serve on the compensation committee, enabling an adequate forum for a useful discourse and a healthy debate.

## Chair of the Compensation Committee

In today's political landscape, the compensation committee chair may be the most difficult role on the board, superseding the audit committee chair. In the wake of the Sarbanes-Oxley, Dodd-Frank, and Consumer Protection Acts and in the crosshairs of shareholder activists and shareholder services firms such as Institutional Shareholder Services (ISS) and Glass Lewis, the compensation committee, and in particular its chair, is being more closely scrutinized for its determination of executive pay. Whereas the audit committee can refer to detailed though sometimes ambiguous formal rules and regulations, the compensation committee has no equivalent set of generally accepted compensation principles. In terms of executive compensation, there is no "right" way—only a general road map and some broad guideposts such as pay for performance. The Public Company Accounting Oversight Board and the Securities and Exchange Commission (SEC) oversee the work of the audit committee; no oversight board or agency has the legal responsibility to oversee the work of the compensation committee or its advisors. However, some professional associations and some accounting firms have recommended sets of principles.

The chair of the committee is generally elected by the board based on the recommendation of the governance committee, which also recommends the members who serve on the committee. The chair typically works closely with the CEO and the head of human resources, as well as with outside advisors, in determining the most appropriate and effective compensation design. The chair prepares the agenda for each meeting, presides at each meeting, and ensures the appropriate follow-up actions. The chair sets up an annual timetable that delineates when compensation actions are to be taken, including approval of salary changes, establishment of incentive targets, and approval of proxy disclosure materials. Preparing such a timetable requires the identification of what needs to be done, when, and by whom. The head of human resources generally provides administrative support to the committee, including the preparation of meeting minutes, and helps to ensure that information and reports are prepared and distributed in a timely fashion to committee members.

## Role

The compensation committee is charged with designing and implementing a compensation process that effectively rewards management for the achievement of business objectives. The compensation committee tries to ensure that executive compensation programs reward performance and are competitive with pay markets in order to attract, retain, and motivate high-performance executives with the requisite skill sets and performance focus.

The full board of directors is responsible for developing and assigning specific annual and long-term goals for the CEO and working with the compensation committee for measuring the degree of successful attainment of these goals. The compensation committee translates these goals into pay packages for the CEO and other top executives. In particular, the committee is responsible for developing and overseeing the executive compensation programs, including identifying performance expectations, delineating specific performance measurements, setting appropriate levels of compensation, and determining the proper mix of compensation elements and incentives such as base pay, performance bonuses, equity grants, retirement benefits, welfare benefits, perquisites, and other benefits. The compensation committee determines appropriate pay that reinforces business strategy; consequently, it needs to know how to design and manage compensation policies and practices that provide a foundation for business success.

The compensation committee is the steward of the shareholders' money; its job is not to please management. The committee must be willing and able to challenge the assumptions underlying compensation plans and to delve into their details, which requires them to be aware of important regulations such as Sections 162(m), 409A, and 280G of the IRC. The committee must be aware of tax and accounting issues related to the treatment of long-term incentive vehicles and other compensation arrangements. For example, committee members must fully understand the CEO's employment contract, including such details as the change-in-control provisions, so that they can identify the goals the pay package is designed to encourage and understand the potential costs of the package in a variety of scenarios such as a sale.

As fiduciaries for the shareholders, the committee can find itself in a difficult tug-of-war with top management regarding pay matters. The committee is trying to get the best management and the best business results at a reasonable and appropriate compensation cost. What constitutes reasonable and appropriate is the challenge for the committee. The committee often leans to the lower side; management, often to the higher. This back-and-forth negotiation can lead to some intense and sometimes stressful compensation committee meetings.

## Duties and Responsibilities

Compensation committees are required to have a written charter that is typically one or two pages outlining the committee's authority, responsibilities, and specific powers. The basic role of the committee is to provide the forum for the review and analysis of the company's executive compensation philosophy and programs, which entails balancing the interests of shareholders with those of management.

The duties and responsibilities of the committee are delineated in its charter. These include establishing the company's compensation philosophy, strategy, and policies; approving annual performance objectives for the CEO, evaluating the CEO's performance against these objectives, and making a recommendation to the board regarding the CEO's base salary and incentive payments; reviewing performance evaluations and approving annual salaries for all executive officers other than the CEO; approving annual and long-term incentive award opportunities (in cash, stock, and/or stock options) for all executive officers, including the CEO; administering the company's annual and long-term incentive plans; reviewing and approving certain benefit items (in particular, those delineated in the company's proxy disclosure statement); approving contractual arrangements with management, including employment and severance agreements; determining stock ownership guidelines for both executive officers and corporate directors; and making, along with management, disclosures in the compensation discussion and analysis (CD&A) section of the proxy disclosure statement and making recommendations to the board for inclusion of the CD&A section in the proxy disclosure statement and Form 10-K.

To meet these responsibilities, the committee is responsible for establishing a timetable of meeting dates and agenda items as well as for an annual evaluation of its own performance. A typical calendar would focus on the following agenda topics for four scheduled meetings. At the January meeting, the committee, for all executive officers (except the CEO), (1) evaluates the prior year's performance and determines the corresponding annual bonus and long-term incentive payouts and (2) sets the annual bonus and long-term incentive opportunities and their corresponding performance criteria for the upcoming year. At the February meeting, in preparation for its recommendation to the full board of directors, the committee (1) reviews the CEO's performance against the prior year's preestablished performance objectives and determines his or her base salary and annual bonus award, (2) reviews the CEO's performance objectives for the upcoming year and determines their corresponding incentive payout opportunities, and (3) reviews and discusses with management the company's disclosures under the CD&A. At the July meeting, the committee, with the aid of its outside advisor, (1) reviews current market trends in executive pay, (2) monitors stock ownership versus the guidelines established for the various levels of management, and (3) reviews management-development programs and the succession-planning process if these are within its purview. At the November meeting, the committee, with benchmarking data provided by its outside compensation consultant, (1) evaluates the competitiveness of the company's compensation policies and plans, (2) determines base salaries for the executive officers, and (3) reviews employment agreements, retirement plans, and other benefit programs.

Sometimes the compensation committee is charged with additional duties, including compensation for board directors. However, this duty is more often embedded in the charter of the governance committee. The compensation committee is often charged with overseeing the processes associated with management development, inclusion/diversity, and succession planning. With these additional duties, the committee is often called the *compensation and management-development committee* or the *human resources committee* with the responsibility for monitoring these processes.

## Outside Consultants

To help guide their decision making, compensation committees access ideas and opinions from outside consultants. These consultants monitor compensation trends and benchmark compensation levels, and they help in the development and evaluation of policies, plans, and programs related to remuneration of the company's executive officers. In the performance of its duties, the compensation committee, in its sole discretion, can hire and fire outside advisors, in particular compensation consultants who work directly for the compensation committee and provide impartial advice and analysis, free of undue influence from management. Thus the committee has the sole authority to approve the consultant's fees and other engagement terms.

The chair monitors communications between the outside consultant and management to ensure that the former retains its independent viewpoint and judgment. The committee works closely with members of management, in particular, the human resources department, in fulfilling its duties. Management provides the necessary information and coordinates with the committee's outside consultants, when appropriate, to ensure that the committee is sufficiently informed when taking action or recommending action on compensation matters. In conjunction, the compensation committee, management, and the outside consultants work to develop executive pay structures that are externally competitive, internally equitable, and performance oriented.

## Benchmarking Data

Every year the committee examines whether the compensation levels of the top executives are reasonable, both from an external perspective and from an internal one. To help in the development of the first perspective, the committee engages an independent advisor to conduct an executive compensation study that provides benchmarking data relevant to the company's external pay market. Generally, the only service this advisor provides to the company is data, analysis, and counsel regarding executive compensation matters. (Sometimes the advisor provides advice and counsel on director compensation, but this service is typically provided to the governance committee for its review and determination.) Accordingly, the committee's retention of an outside advisor creates no conflict of interest between the advisor and the company or any of its board committees.

Selecting a peer group that is appropriate to use in defining market compensation for a specific company's executive officers is not easy. Given the size, complexity, and diversity of businesses, this selection often requires a blend of compensation data from the advisor's proprietary databases, from other available compensation surveys, and from publicly filed documents such as proxy disclosure statements and Form 10-Ks. With the aid of the outside advisor, the committee selects a peer group that can approximate the nature of its businesses and thereby represent the "market" for compensation comparisons. Taking into consideration the counsel of the independent advisor, the committee and management agree on the composition of the peer group. To enable an adequate comparison that avoids anomalies or outliers, the peer group should include at least 10 peer companies, preferably 15 to 20. Some companies use peer groups of 50 or more. For example, a specialty chemical manufacturer may include in its database 20 or so publicly traded firms in the chemicals industry that are similar in size and composition. Compensation data from these peer-group companies provide a context for evaluating the external competitiveness of the company's executive pay levels.

After the data are collected and scrubbed, they are placed into a model that typically exhibits quartiles and the percentile levels that apply to each of the company's senior executives. The committee sets the target-level performance for total compensation against the peer-group data, which provide so-called market comparables. A committee may set total compensation for target-level performance at the 50th percentile of the comparative group and at the 75th percentile for maximum-level performance.

Most, if not all, compensation philosophies vary pay outcomes with performance. Pay for performance has become top-of-mind for almost all compensation committees. Committees are increasingly examining pay outcomes compared with market for the CEO and the other named executives against performance outcomes for the company. This examination enables the committee to understand and thus better align pay outcomes and performance results.

The benchmarking data also provide evidence of proportionality, that is, the balance or mix among salary, annual bonus, and long-term incentives. For example, CEO pay generally is weighted heavily in terms of its opportunity for long-term incentive compensation. The target mix may be 25 percent base salary, 30 percent annual bonus, and 45 percent long-term incentive. Above target, the ratio of long-term incentive increases, reinforcing the emphasis on sustained excellence. As a general philosophy, the higher the position in management, the more compensation is incentive based, and the more the incentive is long-term oriented, thereby aligning senior level pay with the long-term success of the company.

Although the benchmarking data are helpful, they offer only a broad context for decision making. A committee uses the benchmark data as a starting point and, when determining compensation for an individual executive, takes into consideration individual contributions and performance, as well as other factors, including experience, breadth of responsibilities, tenure in position, and internal equity.

Over the past decade, benchmarking has been challenged, most notably in research conducted under the auspices of Charles Elson at the University of Delaware. Dr. Elson's analysis indicates that the widespread use of benchmarking has led to the continual ratcheting up of CEO pay. Rather than relying on benchmarking, he proposes a value-added approach to setting CEO pay.

## Pay Philosophy

The compensation committee develops and submits the pay philosophy to the board for approval. This philosophy spells out the overarching purpose of the executive compensation policies, plans, and practices. For example, many companies set up their executive compensation plans so that salary range midpoints, annual incentive targets, and long-term incentive awards are at the median of the peer group of companies reported in the proxy disclosure statement. The maximum is sometimes set at twice the target for the annual incentive and four times the target for long-term plans. The threshold may be equal to 25 percent of the target for both the annual and long-term plans. This philosophy results in the company expecting to pay less than competitive rates in underperforming years and more than competitive rates in overperforming ones.

This pay-for-performance objective requires a clear definition of the target performance, which requires a budgeting process that ensures a sufficient degree of stretch in the setting of objectives. The budget that is reviewed and approved by the board is often considered "expected" performance and thus sets target performance. In terms of its degree of stretch, target performance is within the company's reach but not within its grasp. Thus target reflects a reasonable, not excessive, degree of stretch.

## Committee Deliberations

Typically, the CEO and the head of human resources, and sometimes the general counsel and the director of compensation and benefits, attend the compensation committee meetings. Making informed decisions takes time, information, and deliberation. Consequently, compensation committees are meeting more frequently, deliberating longer, and getting more objective outside advice.

Compensation committees need to be independent and to act independently. When discussing compensation issues, the committee members need to challenge management as well as their own fellow directors and their outside consultants. They need to bring to the boardroom heightened skepticism and increased scrutiny, enabling them to delve deep to understand the implications of the compensation decisions. Committee members have the obligation to get all the information necessary to provide good corporate governance, and they need to ask penetrating questions. Bringing to the boardroom their wisdom, experience, character, and judgment, these directors should be both confident and competent in engendering open debate that challenges both management and the outside consultants. Every compensation meeting should have an executive session in which committee members can freely offer their candid opinions and where the committee can debate compensation matters in private.

## Compensation Plans

Each year, the committee reviews and discusses the base salaries of the executive officers. Its final determination of salary increases depends on a number of factors, including market data provided by its outside advisor, specific position responsibilities, experience, tenure, job performance, and the company's overall financial results. For foreign-based executive officers, salary increases may reflect legal mandates of a particular country. The committee submits its recommendations for salary increases for the CEO and the other named executive officers to the board for approval.

In designing the annual and long-term incentive plans, the committee, in consultation with the CEO, takes the board-approved corporate goals and determines the performance/reward relationship for varying levels of performance achievement. Annual plans generally incorporate financial objectives, typically some form of earnings such as net income or earnings before interest, taxes, depreciation, and amortization (EBITDA), and individual objectives, both quantitative and qualitative, such as succession planning. The financial objectives are often weighted more heavily than the individual ones. Corporate financial standards typically are based on the budget, with the target bonus set at or near budgeted net income and targeted bonus payout set at approximately half the maximum award. The actual bonus varies depending on the level of performance against the preestablished standards.

The committee tries to align the compensation of the CEO and the other executive officers with both the short- and long-term performance objectives of the company. Payouts for annual performance generally are paid in cash; for longer-term performance, in stock options and performance shares. Corporate performance for the annual bonus plan is often measured in absolute terms, for example, growth in net income, sales, and return on equity. Corporate performance for the long-term incentive plan is often measured in relative terms, for example, total shareholder return (TSR) or return on capital (ROC) relative to a relevant peer group. Targets are set to reward performance that foster degrees of stretch; for example, threshold performance might be set at the prior year's net income; target, at budget; and maximum, at 10 to 15 percent above target. Relative TSR and ROC may be compared with a specific competitive peer group or a broad-comparative group such as the Russell 1000 Index.

Under a long-term incentive plan (LTIP), stock options, restricted stock (time and/or performance based), and long-term cash payments are based on the achievement of long-term performance, often measured in overlapping three-year performance periods. These overlapping periods enable LTIP payments to be earned each year. Equity-based performance compensation arrangements help to align the interests of management with those of shareholders. Long-term incentives generally are based on meeting financial objectives, such as total return to shareholders. Such measures enable comparison against a relevant competitive group. For example, a $750 million specialty chemicals company can gauge its TSR against that of the Standard and Poor's (S&P) SmallCap 600 (Materials Group) Index over a rolling three-year period. Its relative TSR determines its LTIP payouts.

In designing both annual bonus and long-term incentive plans, the committee needs to determine the payout not only at target performance but also at the prescribed threshold and maximum performance levels. Care must be taken not to set targets and associated rewards that encourage undue, excessive risk. In addition, the committee needs to determine the relationship of each component to salary and the percentage all three pay components constitute of total compensation. At target, these three components may be roughly equal, but at maximum, annual and long-term payouts can be two and four times salary, respectively, which places significantly more emphasis on the long term. Below threshold, no incentive is paid.

Annual bonuses typically are paid in cash, whereas long-term incentives typically are paid in stock or a combination of cash and stock. For many years, stock options were much "less visible" than stock awards, but today, present-value calculations and exercise gains receive significant attention. Consequently, stock options have become somewhat less prevalent in executive pay packages. Most companies are moving to a *portfolio approach* to equity pay that includes options, restricted stock units, and other stock vehicles that better align the varied goals of long-term incentive plans.

In general, the most effective pay strategies and structures are simple in design, straightforward in application, and easy to explain to management and investors.

## Compensation Discussion and Analysis

Each year, the compensation committee, in conjunction with its outside advisors, legal counsel, and management human resources staff, issues a *compensation discussion and analysis* (CD&A). As required by Item 402(b) of Regulation S-K, the committee reviews and discusses the CD&A with management and, based on such review and discussions, recommends to the board that the CD&A be included in the proxy statement and in the company's Form 10-K filed annually with the SEC. All committee members must sign off on the issuance of the CD&A. The CD&A provides a window into the company's compensation philosophy as well as a means for investors to assess whether and how closely pay is related to performance.

The purpose of the CD&A section of the proxy statement is to explain to shareholders how and why compensation decisions are made for the five highest-paid executives, the so-called named executive officers, which include the CEO. The committee presents its compensation philosophy, which most often includes providing opportunities for highly competitive levels of total compensation when merited by performance; creating incentives to perform over a multiyear period, usually three to five years; and aligning the interests of the management team with those of shareholders. The committee compensates its executive officers through a total compensation package that consists of a mix of base salary, an annual cash bonus, long-term incentives comprising both equity awards and cash payments, and a competitive benefits package consisting of medical, life, disability, and retirement using both qualified and nonqualified programs.

In general, compensation committees and their advisors are trying to make the CD&A more understandable by adding executive summaries and incorporating charts, tables, and graphics. Nevertheless, many CD&A reports are difficult to read and hard to interpret.

## Enhanced Scrutiny

In today's heightened scrutiny from Congress, shareholder advocates, and the mainstream media, the compensation committee is in the hot seat. In response to the financial meltdown of 2008, Congress enacted the Dodd-Frank Act of 2010, which codified say-on-pay (SOP) voting. Since 2011, U.S. public companies have held nonbinding say-on-pay votes, and compensation committees, compensation advisors, and financial regulators have seen the clout of ISS increase in the executive compensation arena. ISS is supposedly advocating for the policies and preferences of major institutional investors, and its recommendations on SOP votes have had a noticeable impact on the level of shareholder support for these proposals. Research has indicated that ISS opposition to an SOP vote has significantly reduced companies' shareholder support, typically in the 20 to 25 percent range.

The Dodd-Frank Act also instituted clawback, hedging, and pledging policies; required compensation committee independence; and recommended a CEO-to-employee pay-ratio disclosure. The latter has gotten a lot of attention as Fortune 500 CEO pay has risen to about 400 times that of the average worker. In addition, the act placed heightened attention on ensuring that both annual and long-term plans do not encourage excessive risk taking, as may have happened during the exuberance preceding the 2008 stock market collapse. Thus compensation committees need to formulate incentive plans with reasonable, not excessive, degrees of risk incorporated in their performance objectives and standards.

A host of public and private oversight bodies, including the SEC, the National Association of Corporate Directors (NACD), the FASB, and ISS, has weighed in on issues of executive compensation and the role of the compensation committee. In addition, many companies have been providing leadership in the development and oversight of executive pay. Although there is no "right" model that fits all, there has been an evolving set of best practices that provides guidance for compensation committees.

Over the past decade, there have been several notable reports on executive compensation by prominent organizations such as the NACD, TIAA-CREF, and The Conference Board that have specified better governance for the compensation committee. Their recommendations have included the absolute independence of the committee, greater emphasis on performance-based compensation, the need for a long-term focus, and clear and transparent disclosure. Most of their recommendations have been adopted and incorporated into best practices.

## Conclusion

The fundamental role of the compensation committee is to translate board-approved corporate goals and objectives into a pay delivery system that rewards top executives in proportion to the level of performance attainment. Thus the work of the compensation committee is critical to business success. In the wake of corporate governance transgressions, a wave of reforms and regulations has been instituted by government agencies and adopted by corporations. Compensation committees are working hard to ensure that executive pay rewards management for stretch performance. Keeping up with the accounting rules, tax changes, and securities legislation that affect executive pay has been challenging, but most committees have been up to the challenge and have embraced their increased responsibilities.

# 31

# Creating an Effective CEO Succession-Planning Process

JAMES F. REDA
*Arthur J. Gallagher & Company's Human Resources and Compensation Consulting Practice*

MOLLY A. KYLE
*Arthur J. Gallagher & Company's Human Resources and Compensation Consulting Practice*

The board of directors should make leadership and succession planning a high priority, with meaningful compensation opportunities, especially for the CEO. A strong succession-planning process helps to prepare the entire organization to handle senior executive departures when they inevitably occur. Thoughtful and proactive executive compensation policies and programs are important to CEO succession. A balance in CEO–senior executive compensation is important, and vigilance in ensuring that senior executives are paid appropriately for their ongoing contributions to the company's success is equally important. Long-term incentive awards should have meaningful performance goals but also have a subsequent vesting period, thus providing an incentive for executives to stay while the succession process unfolds.

In October 2009,[1] the U.S. Securities and Exchange Commission (SEC) issued Bulletin 14E, which provides that CEO succession planning is not "routine business." Thus, the SEC strongly recommends that boards of directors provide comprehensive succession plans to shareholders. The SEC bulletin provided three core criteria that directors should examine when weighing how to meet this new responsibility. Viewing these criteria in light of best practices for succession planning gives corporate directors a head start on an effective response to SEC Bulletin 14E.

The SEC acknowledged that poor CEO succession planning constitutes a significant business risk and is an indication of poor governance of the corporation that transcends the day-to-day business of managing the workforce. Shareholder proposals generally request that companies adopt and disclose written and detailed CEO succession-planning policies with specific features, including that the board develop criteria for the CEO position, identify and develop internal candidates, and use a formal assessment process to evaluate candidates. Prior to October 2009, these proposals were deemed routine and thus were excluded from being presented to shareholders because they were considered to be routine and part of ordinary business in terms of the hiring, promotion, and termination of employees.

Surprisingly, in 2011, 57 percent[2] of CEO transitions were planned, with the other 43 percent resulting in the CEO being fired, resigning, dying, or becoming disabled. This underscores the importance of being prepared by naming an emergency CEO, which may be a board member (typically acting or temporary) or a senior manager.

Although the decision of CEO selection should be based primarily on the company's strategic direction and circumstances, new data have surfaced recently showing the unseen burdens that external hires bear. According to Paul Hodgson, principal at BHJ Partners, "Hiring an outside CEO costs between three and five times the amount it does to promote an existing manager, so boards are failing in their fiduciary duty and wasting shareholders' money by not having a properly functioning succession plan in place."

Given the large size of pay packages for outside recruits, they are often more publicized and scrutinized than internal candidates. Outside candidates must be paid more for forfeiting prior stock awards and to compensate for the increased risk of jumping to another company.

The best scenario is when an internal candidate is selected for CEO following a planned departure of the outgoing CEO. Table 31.1 provides a summary of possible outcomes of a CEO succession process.

| Outgoing CEO | New CEO | |
| --- | --- | --- |
| | Internal Candidate | External Candidate |
| **Planned Departure (CEO retires)** | *Best Scenario* <br><br> • Presents the lowest risk, and can even have a positive impact on stock prices at the time of the announcement <br><br> • Allows time to identify and develop internal candidates, and use a formal assessment process to evaluate candidates <br><br> • Least costly | *Advantages* <br><br> • Come with new ideas <br><br> • Are more objective <br><br> *Disadvantages* <br><br> • Cost more than an internal candidate |
| **Emergency Departure (CEO becomes disabled, dies, is terminated , or resigns )** | *Advantages* <br><br> • Internal candidates understand the company's culture, and are aware of the specific internal needs of the company <br><br> *Disadvantages* <br><br> • In many cases, there are no viable candidates lined up <br><br> • Could result in interim CEO (in many cases a board member will take over for the interim) | *Worst scenario* <br><br> • Most value at risk: with greater surprise, comes with greater risk <br><br> • More publicized/ scrutinized |

Table 31.1 Outgoing CEO Circumstances: Internal versus External Candidates

## Relationship between Pay and Succession Planning

Although executive pay may not be the primary factor in an orderly and successful change of leadership, there are aspects of pay philosophy and policy that are important considerations in the CEO succession-planning process, including

- The level of the CEO–named executive officer (NEO) pay ratio, which may be an indicator of unbalanced leadership and concentrated roles and responsibilities or an "imperial CEO"
- Amount and makeup of the internal CEO candidate(s) before and after succession

The ratio of CEO pay to average worker pay (a component of the Dodd-Frank Act but not yet proposed by the SEC) does not inform investors of anything useful in part because of the difficulty of comparing companies with different business models, geographies, use of contractors, labor forces, product-line mixes, and so on. However, investors may be interested in the ratio of CEO pay to other NEO pay (which information is presently available in proxy disclosure statements but rarely specified directly) or, for larger companies, the ratio of CEO pay to that of some broader set of top executives (which typically is not disclosed)—collectively referred to as the *CEO:NEO pay ratio*. One benefit to investors of these ratios is that they may provide some insight into the internal CEO succession-planning process.

There has been a lot of discussion among shareholder advisors about the appropriate ratio of CEO pay to that of (1) the average worker, (2) the number two executive, (3) the other NEOs, and (d) tiers of senior management. The concept put forth is that when CEO pay is substantially above that of the rest of the executive team, it leads to dysfunction and inefficiency at shareholder expense. These groups further maintain that a disproportionate pay relationship among corporate leaders is unfair and a likely symptom of poor corporate governance. Whereas certain factions such as the labor unions would like CEO pay to come down and average worker pay to go up, there is some relevance to these ratios to CEO succession.

Unfortunately, there is no bright line test for the CEO:NEO pay ratio. Whereas a ratio of 2.75 to 3.0 times has been mentioned by rating agencies such as Moody's and shareholder advisory firms such as Institutional Shareholder Services (ISS), the appropriate ratio depends on a variety of factors including (1) the industry, (2) the tenure and roles of responsibilities of the executives, and (3) the ownership structure of the company.

The pay gap between the CEO and other executives varies by industry and other related circumstances. For example, high-performing CEOs may have justifiably higher CEO:NEO pay ratios. Moreover, CEOs of media and entertainment companies typically have total pay packages that may be three to four times higher than that of executives of financial services companies, and other executives engaged in strategic transactions also may have very high CEO:NEO pay ratios.

Higher CEO:NEO pay ratios may occur because the CEO is paid well above market levels or because the other executives are paid well below market levels or a combination of both. When the other NEOs are paid below market, the board is enabling the CEO to run the company without strong support from key operational and functional decision making normally vested in other senior executives that may have been usurped by the CEO.

A high CEO:NEO pay ratio is an indicator of many potential problems, which include the following:

- *An unbalanced leadership model.* A strong or imperial CEO who surrounds himself or herself with weaker senior executives and effectively usurps responsibility.

- *The likelihood of an internal candidate succeeding the CEO is lower.* In general, it will be difficult for any other senior executive to function at the level of the highly controlling CEO or to reassure external stakeholders that company stewardship will be transferred with minor disruption.

- *Higher cost of replacing the CEO.* The board may give further deference to the incumbent CEO as board members realize that the CEO is too valuable given the overall management team and exacerbate the situation by maintaining or even increasing the CEO:NEO pay ratio.

Along with the negative impact of a higher CEO:NEO pay ratio on the readiness of internal candidates, promoting a "tournament" approach to executive succession may hurt retention of top candidates because their career success is increasingly defined by the pursuit of the CEO's title. Not becoming a CEO may be seen as a failure or at least a critical juncture in their career progression. Worthy candidates are more likely to pursue outside job opportunities.

Pay dissatisfaction is rarely the primary reason that senior executives leave a company—it may be just symptomatic of other issues. When executives believe that their value is truly recognized (not just with compensation but with increasing board interaction, new leadership responsibilities, etc.), they are less likely to view getting the CEO's job as the only worthwhile step in their career.

Paying an exorbitant amount to a CEO runner-up will be quite costly and ultimately will not improve the likelihood of long-term retention under new leadership. In fact, this action may just delay the executive's departure and be more costly to the company in the interim and potentially create a difficult CEO transition.

Companies can increase the likelihood of holding key talent through a leadership transition by taking a proactive approach to executive compensation, including the following actions:

- *Make leadership and succession planning an explicit element of senior executive evaluation, especially for the CEO.* Directors should make clear that CEO performance is not just measured by stock price, earnings growth, and other such measures but requires performance in key leadership areas, such as putting into place a detailed and robust succession plan. This kind of qualitative performance issue too often gets cursory consideration in pay decisions. However, when the consequences of a disjointed succession become clear, the need for the succession plan as part of annual goals also becomes clear. As for other executives, emphasizing the importance of their own succession reinforces the prospect of other roles, such as promotions and lateral assignments that enhance their executive experience. Table 31.2 presents an overview of performance goals.

- *Pay top executives slightly above market levels.* Ensure that senior executives are paid not only appropriately against the market but also consistently with internal equity considerations. In other words, the company should generously compensate long-tenured executives who have proven that they are truly exceptional in their roles or are key "utility" players who ably fill varied roles as needed. During a period of stable CEO leadership and low executive turnover, boards may assume that these executives really do not need to be paid so well. However, taking a proactive approach that calls for fair and not just required compensation can make a big difference in the response of an internal CEO candidate who ends up a runner-up.

| | Quantitative | Qualitative |
|---|---|---|
| Financial | • EPS growth<br>• ROIC<br>• TSR | • Better understanding of company strategy in investment community<br>• Achievement of IPO/spin-off/restructuring<br>• Creation and implementation of financial strategy |
| Nonfinancial | • HR: employee turnover, diversity, employee satisfaction<br>• Market share<br>• New product development<br>• Quality | • Reputation<br>• CEO succession plan<br>• Leadership skills<br>• Communication effectiveness with board |

**Table 31.2  Quantitative versus Qualitative Performance Goals**

- *Impose a high penalty for voluntary separation.* This can be done by tying up more of total executive compensation in long-term incentives with extended vesting requirements (e.g., four or five years). Additionally, ensure that long-term incentive cycles overlap, keeping a perpetual payout opportunity just "over the horizon."

Once it is clear which internal candidates will not be getting the top job, act proactively—before the succession decision is made public—and consider providing special recognition grants of equity with long-term vesting to runners-up.

It should be noted that these actions assume that it is in the company's interest to retain the CEO candidates. Naturally, any good succession plan must contemplate leadership dynamics and operational needs. If a high-performing executive is passed over and the board does not believe that this executive could effectively perform under the new CEO, the board should not be afraid to effectuate an orderly and amicable departure.

Although disclosure on the CEO planning process is not required by the SEC, neither in the compensation, discussion, and analysis (CD&A) nor as part of the committee and board charters, it is required by part of the corporate governance guidelines (as required by Section 303A.09 of the New York Stock Exchange disclosure rules and available on each company's website) to include "Management succession. Succession planning should include policies and principles for CEO selection and performance review, as well as policies regarding succession in the event of an emergency or the retirement of the CEO." The Nasdaq does not require this disclosure, but most large Nasdaq companies follow the practice anyway.

## CEO Succession: Prepare for the Future

The cardinal responsibilities for a board of directors are the evaluation of the CEO and succession planning, including developing new leaders who may assume the role of CEO. CEO succession planning is vital if the CEO becomes disabled, deceased, terminated, or resigns. Accordingly, proper and timely CEO evaluations are essential for the company and its shareholders.

The CEO is and will always be closely related to the image of a company and has a significant effect on investors' perceptions. Investors and major stakeholders can react harshly to a CEO change, especially if abrupt or unplanned. Recently, Burger King has been flipping not only burgers but CEOs as well. Fred LeFranc, a founding partner at restaurant consulting firm Results Thru Strategy believes that the CEO turnover, as well as Burger King's continuous switching of corporate ownership, has caused unclear brand imaging for the fast-food giant.

Boards always should be prepared for CEO succession, even as a new CEO is beginning to settle in. In the event of an unexpected departure of the CEO, succession provisions will ensure that the company avoids potential damage from a lack of leadership. In addition, leadership development should be encouraged throughout the organization. There are a number of reasons for creating or improving these processes, but the most significant is preparing for the long-term success of an organization. Leadership development not only promotes hard work and increases performance but also builds a loyal and well-established group of employees.

## Back to the Basics

In *Corporate Governance Best Practices: A Blueprint for the Post-Enron Era*, released in 2003, The Conference Board stated that a successful succession-planning process should

- Be a continuous process
- Be driven and controlled by the board
- Involve CEO input
- Be easily executed in the event of a crisis
- Consider succession requirements based on corporate strategy
- Be geared toward finding the right leader at the right time
- Develop talent pools at lower levels
- Avoid a "horse race" mentality that may lead to the loss of key deputies when the new CEO is chosen

Understandably, this list should serve as a guide; there is no standard one-size-fits-all succession plan. Instead, each board must construct and produce its own specific plan to diagnose internal company needs. Generally, this will involve developing the existing executive talent pool, using executive recruiting firms, directors' personal contacts, and an overall ear-to-the-ground approach.

However, a 2010 survey on corporate governance showed that

- Over 50 percent of boards had no successor aligned in the event of an unexpected CEO departure.
- 39 percent of firms had no viable internal candidates lined up for possible succession.
- 50 percent of firms had no written policy on succession planning.
- On average, two hours were spent each year in board meetings on succession management.

This information, coupled with the fact that CEO succession is a critical risk factor, is a cause for concern. So how can boards prepare for the future if they are not even discussing succession planning in the present?

## The Succession-Planning Process

There comes an essential point when a decision has to be made as to the CEO successor. The succession-planning process aims to groom candidates over an extended period of time, although logically there is a more in-depth focus during the last 24 months of a CEO's tenure (Figure 31.1).

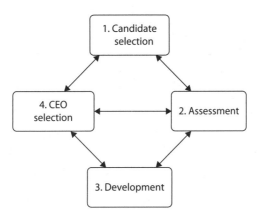

**Figure 31.1  CEO succession-planning steps.**

Via execution of an effective succession plan, there should be confidence in the candidates, with the successor being promoted to the number two slot prior to departure of the CEO. Following is a six-step process for selecting the CEO successor:

1. *Responsible committee.* The first step in planning for CEO succession is building a committee from the board. This committee may be either the compensation, nominating, or an ad hoc committee selected for the task of recommending to the board the CEO selection process (referred to as the *responsible committee*). The responsible committee has the obligation of keeping the board apprised of the process. Involving the board will enhance the attribute diversity of the incoming CEO, benefiting the future of the organization.

2. *Responsible committee leader.* Although not mandatory, it is recommended that the leader of the responsible committee have prior experience as a CEO. This approach will ensure that the demands of the position are fully understood by both parties. Additionally, an important factor in choosing the leader of the responsible committee is not his or her current role on the board but rather his or her understanding of the company's strategy and future outlook.

3. *Strategy.* Succession plans should relate directly to strategic initiatives for the company. The responsible committee, as well as the board, should reassess succession plans as corporate strategy shifts over time to meet long-term goals, ensuring continuous preparation for expected and unexpected departures.

4. *Candidate selection.* Candidates for the CEO position can be sourced from inside or outside the company. Internal candidates understand the company's culture and are aware of the specific internal needs of the company. However, external candidates can come in with new ideas and objectivity.

5. *Assessment.* When evaluating potential CEO candidates, it is crucial that each candidate be completely assessed. Although some characteristics may be subjective and prone to judgment, it is important that the responsible committee provide a comprehensive assessment of each candidate. This assessment should capture the attributes related to the agreed-on strategic direction of the company. The use of a systematic process, such as cumulative score evaluations, is beneficial for accuracy and comparing candidates.

6. *Decision.* The last step in succession planning is the decision. At this point, the board should be actively involved in assessing the remaining candidates. The requirement of the responsible committee to report to the board on a regular basis will ensure the most comprehensive assessment of each candidate and allow the board to select a successor based on the qualities and skill set deemed necessary for the position of CEO.

The date of the announcement for succession may differ for organizations based on their internal needs. In some cases, the successor is announced 18 to 24 months before a planned CEO retirement. In 2012, Marriott announced its CEO transition just three months before it occurred, yet it is regarded as a very successful CEO succession.

## Expect the Unexpected

Unfortunately, abrupt CEO change is seemingly the most common, even if the causes for transition are out of the CEO's control. Carnival's Mickey Arison was replaced by Arnold Donald in June 2013, after holding the position of CEO for over 34 years. Under Arison's watch, Carnival grew from owning 3 ships and $44 million in revenue in 1979 to 102 ships and over $15 billion in revenue by 2013. However, recent engine trouble and electricity issues on the ships have paved the way for reform.

In addition, confidentiality must be a priority. Today's global interconnectivity allows for a wealth of information to travel quickly. Although this is good for economic growth and development, it can make the CEO position a fragile one. A prime example of this is the plummeting stock of Abercrombie and Fitch (A&F). A 2006 interview with A&F CEO Mike Jeffries has surfaced again recently and has the public up in arms. In the interview, Jeffries defends the exclusivity of the brand, including that the company markets to "cool, good-looking people." This type of narrow-minded remark has resulted in a lot of negative brand imaging for A&F and a shrinking customer base.

## Final Thoughts

First, time is of the essence when negotiations are happening between a candidate and the board. Given the risks of the candidate pursuing other opportunities or losing interest in the position because of slow progress by an organization, it is critical that constant, progressive talks take place between the candidate and the board.

Second, the departing CEO's legacy includes not only his or her performance while in charge but also his or her ability to assist the new CEO. A positive relationship between the incoming and outgoing CEOs in the transition period is conducive to stronger investor confidence, company performance, and overall morale. Therefore, it is in the best interests of the new and departing CEOs to work together for the benefit of the organization.

Finally, whether it happens this year or in the distant future, your current CEO will need to be replaced. By following the six steps outlined in this chapter and adhering to your own organizational needs, the succession-planning process can be a swift and effective one. To maintain success, it is imperative that CEO succession be articulated and planned for. A well-planned succession can be the crucial element for an organization's longevity and without it can result in a chaotic mess. It is for good reason that the SEC recognizes CEO succession as a critical risk factor. Remember, a business can only proceed forward when it has a captain to lead it.

## Notes

1. Before October 2009, the division has permitted the omission under Rule 14a-8(i)(7) of shareholder proposals requesting that companies adopt and disclose written CEO succession policies that, among other things, provide for extensive board involvement in the development and application of a formal assessment process. In taking the position that CEO succession-planning proposals could be omitted, the Securities and Exchange Commission (SEC) relied on a statement set forth in the 1998 release adopting amendments to Rule 14a-8—that the management of the workforce, such as the hiring, promotion, and termination of employees, constituted ordinary business. The division now believes that matters pertaining to CEO succession "raised a significant policy issue regarding the governance of the corporation that transcends the day-to-day business matter of managing the workforce."

2. FTI Consulting, "Communicating Critical Events: CEO Transitions and the Risk to Enterprise Value," Washington, DC, 2011. Based on CEO transitions of companies in excess of $10 billion between July 1, 1997 and June 30, 2010, In all, the study evaluated 263 CEO transitions across companies based in 35 countries.

# PERFORMANCE AND COMPENSATION

# 32

# A Framework for Designing a
# Performance-Management Process

Charles H. Fay

*Rutgers, the State University of New Jersey*

Although performance management has replaced performance appraisal in the professional literature, many companies and managers still do not seem to get it. A common theme heard from employees is that the first time they saw an appraisal instrument was when they received their annual appraisal feedback; a common theme heard from managers is that they are far too busy with "real" work to spend time on performance management and that employees know what they need to do anyhow. Both managers and their direct reports resent the system because it hurts the relationship between them, it has no real value, and there are no meaningful outcomes. Management manipulates the system to help friends and to cut costs.

For many years, the solutions to these problems focused on the performance-appraisal process. The emphasis was on getting the most accurate appraisal format and training managers to rate employees using that format. Most research, whether by scholars or by professionals, was on rating formats, rater error, and the training of raters. The assumption was that if the correct format could be developed and managers were trained, the resulting ratings would be accurate. A reality check suggests that this emphasis on the appraisal was misplaced and that a different approach was needed.

During the 1980s, professionals and some scholars became interested in a different goal: improving performance (Banks and May, 1999; Bernardin et al., 1998). This led to thinking about the whole performance process, and attention shifted to performance management (PM). The PM process consists of three parts: (1) performance planning, (2) observing performance and providing positive and corrective feedback, and (3) developing periodic performance summaries to serve as a basis for performance planning for the next period while providing data for a variety of human resources decisions, including rewards, staffing, training, and other decisions affecting the employee's relationship with the organization. The main goal, however, is to improve employee performance, and the data that come from the process, while important, are ancillary to performance improvement.

Given the widespread mistrust and dislike of appraisal and performance-management systems by both managers and direct reports, why do organizations (and especially human resources departments) persist in the use of these systems? Quality expert W. Edwards Deming even called for abolition of the annual review (Deming, 1986). The reason for performance management's continuing use? Human resources scholars make a good case for the linkage between performance management and firm-level performance (e.g., DeNisi and Smith, 2014).

This chapter begins with a description of the performance-management process. It then considers some prerequisites that must be in place before a performance-management system can be established and then certain design-element requirements. Finally, a discussion of forced distribution in performance management is provided. The emphasis is on performance management for compensation purposes. The learning points covered include

- The difference between performance appraisal and performance management
- The process of performance management and its principal parts
- How performance planning links organizational strategy and individual performance
- The importance of performance feedback
- Prerequisites and design requirements for a good performance-management system
- The critical difference between stretch goals and performance standards
- Forced distribution performance management and its problems

## The Performance-Management Process

Performance management consists of five parts that occur in a continuing cycle: *performance planning*, culminating in a performance contract; *performance observation*; *reinforcement of good performance*; *corrective feedback, coaching, and counseling of poor performance*; and a *summary appraisal*. This summary appraisal, which is equivalent to the performance appraisal when there is no performance-management system, is the kickoff to planning for the next performance cycle.

### Performance Planning

Performance planning, like most management processes, must be constructed in such a way that any manager can do it regardless of management style or skills. Better managers involve the employee collaboratively in all phases of the PM process, but the system is designed so that even directive managers can follow the process. This discussion assumes that the manager is more directive than collaborative.

The manager first must define what performance means in the case of a specific direct report. At the broadest level, this refers to what the manager would have to do if the direct report were terminated and a replacement could not be hired. Ideally, this definition is based on a cascade of goals beginning with the organizational mission, strategy to achieve that mission, and the operating plan, with the immediate source being what the manager is expected to accomplish during the period and ending with the direct report's expected part of that accomplishment (Evans, 2001). This part of the process is what ties individual performance to corporate strategy; without it, performance metrics are largely meaningless.

The manager then must move from the general to the specific, usually expressed in terms of desired outcomes. This constitutes the performance dimensions for the direct report. (PM systems tend to speak in terms of managers and direct reports rather than managers and subordinates. While this may be, in part, window dressing, it is also an attempt to remove hierarchy from the PM process: an employee does something not because he or she is told to but because of awareness that high performance benefits the organization and the employee.)

Where outcomes are difficult to observe or measure, behaviors that are expected to lead to desired outcomes are added. For each performance dimension, the manager must develop specific outcomes and behaviors that will be used to measure the direct report's performance. For a performance dimension of budget management, an outcome might be "Stays close to budget for each budget category." A behavior on the same dimension might be "Checks expenditures against budget." After the measures are determined, the manager must set appropriate standards for each measure. The standard for "Checks expenditures against budget" might be "Checks expenditures against budget weekly." After defining standard performance, "Exceeds standards" and "Fails to meet standards" would be defined. The "Exceeds standards" level for "Checks expenditures against budget" might be "Checks expenditures against budget weekly; where discrepancies exceed 2 percent, checks those categories daily until discrepancies disappear." The "Fails to meet standards" level might be "Misses weekly check of expenditures against budget; allows discrepancies to continue without any follow-up." It should be noted that performance dimensions, measures, and standards are unique to each position, although attempts should be made to develop common standards for employees with identical job titles. In implementing a PM system, this calibration does not usually take place until several performance cycles have passed.

When performance dimensions, measures, and standards have been developed, the manager must communicate them to the direct report. The manager must make certain that the direct report understands measures and standards. The manager then gets the direct report to set goals for performance for the coming year. Note that goals and standards are not the same thing. The *standard* is what is expected of a fully job-knowledgeable employee who exerts normal effort. One purpose of PM is to get employees to set stretch goals—to be better than the standard. At the end of the goal-setting discussion, the direct report has agreed on some performance level as a *goal*. The set of performance measures, with standards and goals, becomes the performance *contract* for the period. It is subject to change as external contexts and company strategy and needs change, but such changes need to be discussed with the direct report as they occur.

*Formats.* Most organizations use performance instruments tailored to the type or level of the employee. For example, a nonmanagement or clerical position may have a relatively standard set of criteria that require little or no change year over year. However, management employees tend to be rated using a format that combines both behaviors and outcomes together. Most of the scholarly literature indicates that the format used in the rating is much less important than the process surrounding it and the training of managers and direct reports to use the system.

*Performance Period.* During the performance period, the manager uses the performance contract as a benchmark for observing the direct report. When performance above standard is observed, the standard becomes the basis for positive feedback. A typical positive-feedback incident would include (1) what the manager has observed, (2) how it relates to the performance contract, (3) the level of performance observed in the eyes of the manager, and (4) likely outcomes for the organization and the employee if this level of performance is continued. Clearly, a manager will not go through this process every time high performance is observed, but to do so is reinforcing the performance for the direct report. In fact, positive feedback is one of the most powerful reinforcers available to managers; it is an important management tool and should follow the general reinforcement rules. It should occur immediately after the high performance is observed, and a variable ratio schedule should be followed. A variable ratio reinforcement schedule is one in which reinforcement is given not every time or every fifth time (for example) but rather whenever reinforcement occurs, which happens on average every fifth time. This schedule has been shown to be the most powerful in the continuance of the behavior being reinforced.

When performance is below standard or below the goal set by the direct report, corrective feedback is used, again relying on the standard and on the goal set as the benchmarks for the performance observed. When discussion about performance is couched in terms of known measures, standards, and goals, performance feedback can be much more objective, and it is less likely to be seen as criticism of character. The direct report is not bad per se but is simply not performing at the agreed-on level on one or more measures.

### Periodic Performance Summary

At some point, a summary of performance during the period is provided to the direct report. In most organizations, this is an annual event, but some organizations have quarterly or semiannual performance summaries. At this point, the manager provides a summary of how the direct report has done on each performance measure and whether standards have been met. Consequences of achieving various performance levels are communicated, and planning for the next period's performance begins. If PM has been done correctly, the summary appraisal should have no surprises for the direct report.

One of the more important outputs of the PM process is an *individual development plan* (IDP) that is used to document any steps necessary to improve employee performance. Each employee should have an IDP. There are two parts to the IDP. The first part speaks to performance improvement in the current job. The second part speaks to development needed for the next job in the direct report's career path. Even though the incumbent is an exceptionally high performer in his or her current job, a promotion will entail new roles and responsibilities that do not exist in the current job and for which the direct report needs to be prepared.

The outcomes of the PM process from a compensation perspective include input to both merit pay and short- and long-term incentives. For merit-pay purposes, the PM system must output a single number summarizing an employee's performance at his or her job. These numbers should be equivalent for all performers—that is, a 5 junior accountant should be as excellent as a 5 market researcher. This may sound easy, but calibration across jobs is conceptually difficult and practically even more difficult. For incentive program purposes, the outputs of PM need to consist of specific outcome and behavior measures that capture what is being incented.

## Prerequisites for a PM System

The first prerequisite for a PM system is an organizational culture that values every employee's performance. Although this may seem obvious, there are many cultures that value performance far less than such factors as social networks within the organization (the "old boys' club," for example) and others that value only the performance of certain functions or certain layers of management. If senior management sees the PM system as a "human resources thing," it will not work.

Part of this is because managers have to be held accountable for doing PM, just as they are held accountable for their other responsibilities. Companies hold managers accountable in two ways. First, they enforce PM timelines. A manager may not be eligible for a bonus or an increase until the appraisals of all his or her direct reports have been turned in. Although this may get things done, it provides no guarantee that they will be done well. The second, and more useful enforcement occurs when a senior manager looks at the PM performance of every manager reporting to him or her and rates managers on how well their unit performs and how well the managers' direct reports are developing.

For both merit pay and incentive purposes, the organization must have appropriate measures. In most cases, this requires a good managerial (rather than financial) accounting system. Although a lot of organizations (and business schools) talk about metrics and analytics, there is less evidence that systems are in place that meet PM needs.

## Design Requirements for a PM System

### Alignment

The PM system needs to be aligned with other human resources programs. The link with rewards strategies and practices is obvious, but similar alignment needs to be achieved with staffing and training and development. If promotions, layoffs, firings, and other staffing decisions are not performance based (and the PM system is unable to support these systems), PM has failed. Similarly, if the PM system does not provide useful input to training and development, neither PM nor training and development are likely to be successful.

Alignment between different rewards systems is also critical. An employee who receives a relatively low merit increase but gets a large bonus based on a narrowly targeted incentive program will be receiving mixed messages about his or her performance, as will an employee who receives several recognition awards but a negligible merit increase. The impact of place in range in most merit pay systems means that a top performer who has a high compa-ratio may receive a merit increase that is lower than that of the peers he or she outperforms.

### Observation and Evaluation

Many people may be in a position to observe the performance of an employee: the employee himself or herself, the employee's manager, higher-level managers, peers, clients, vendors, and sometimes the public at large. Some employers even hire professional observers; local transit companies, for example, may hire people to observe whether a driver stops for handicapped riders and how closely the driver sticks to schedule. The literature suggests that employees are likely to behave differently when their manager is present than they do when he or she is absent. The literature also suggests that each class of observer (as well as individual observers) is likely to bring unique biases to the observations. Frequently, only the manager of the employee and the employee himself or herself know the performance criteria and standards that apply to the position.

Getting observational information from many sources seems appropriate if performance evaluations are to mirror actual performance. An example of a formal system doing this is the 360-degree performance appraisal (Morgeson, Mumford, and Campion, 2005). A less-formal system is described in Mosley's *The Crowd Sourced Performance Review*

(Mosley, 2013). Although many sources may report their observations, the actual evaluation typically is made by the manager.

### Goal Setting and Standards

Goal setting (Locke and Latham, 1990) is a powerful motivational tool that needs to be built into the performance-planning stage of the system. However, a distinction needs to be made between rating against standards and goal achievement. Briefly, goal-setting theory posits that employees who have high, specific, accepted goals will perform better than they would without goals meeting these standards. Stretch goals are an important part of increased performance. By definition, stretch goals often will not be met. When rewards systems focus on goal achievement rather than ratings of performance against standards, the only incentive to employees is to set the lowest goals they can get away with to be sure that they receive bonuses or merit increases. Management by objective (MBO), founded on goal achievement, has a short shelf life in organizations because employees who set stretch goals find themselves punished and observe that those who set lower, easy goals are rewarded. For some reason, organizations find this difficult to understand.

### System Evaluation

When designing a PM system, human resources needs to build in evaluation rules. Some near-term evaluation measures include whether the various parts of the system, when implemented, are actually carried out as designed. Concurrent with this is whether managers and direct reports understand the system, know how to carry out their assigned parts, and accept it as fair. Intermediate measures include whether the system outputs the measures needed for rewards, staffing, and training and development. The critical measure, of course, is whether employee performance gets better.

## Team Performance

The PM process described in the first part of this chapter applies to PM at the individual level. Yet most employees today work as an integrated part of one or more teams. The PM process does not change significantly for a team. It is usually easier to get outcome performance measures for a team than for an individual, and it is more difficult to get individual performance measures for a team member (Bing, 2004). Some organizations have elected to use team output as the primary outcome measure of performance for all team members and then develop a *team citizenship measure* for each team member. From a rewards perspective, it is important to align the organizational levels of performance and rewards. Performance that occurs at the organizational level should, in general, be awarded at the organizational level. (Executive rewards are an exception.) Similarly, performance that occurs at the team or group level should be rewarded at the team or group level. That is, all members of a team or group responsible for the performance should share in the reward.

## Forced Distribution Performance Management

A common approach used by a significant minority of organizations is forcing a specific distribution of results on performance measures (Stewart, Gruys, and Storm, 2010). In some cases, employees are compared with each other rather than rated against standards. In other cases, ratings against standards are done with the constraint that results follow some prespecified distribution, and if the organization (or some unit) does not achieve this distribution, ratings must be adjusted until the preferred distribution is achieved.

The goal of forcing a distribution on performance is several-fold: the system forces managers to make hard choices and select those who contribute least for dismissal from the organization, merit pay increases (and other rewards) are controlled, and getting rid of the poorest performers allows for their replacement with better performers. The forced distribution system does not reflect a number of realities.

1. Forced distribution systems operate on the assumption that performance capacity for any job is normally distributed in the population. Recent work by O'Boyle and Aguinis (2012) suggests that this is not the case. Instead, they find that performance follows a Paretian distribution, with the great bulk of cases far to the left of the mean of a normal distribution.

2. Even if performance were distributed normally (or approximately normally) in the population, organizations do not draw a random sample of employees from that population. If staffing procedures are even marginally effective, those with the lowest capacity for performance should be screened out and never enter the organization. If onboarding, training, and development are at all effective, incumbents should improve their capacity to perform at high levels. Similarly, if rewards programs are at all effective, employees should be motivated to perform at high levels. A true normal distribution of performance in an organization would be a sweeping indictment of the ineffectiveness of the human resources department and its efforts.

3. One of the oddest things done by organizations is to require a normal distribution of performance results not only for the organization as a whole but also at department levels. Even if sampling from a normal distribution, the sample is not likely to assume normality until it reaches about 30. In a department of 10 people, a normal distribution of performance would be very unlikely.

4. Philosophically, a forced ranking based on person-to-person comparison has problems because it lacks an anchor. That is, everyone in the group being ranked may be high performers, or they all may be very low performers. Without rating against performance standards and then ranking those results, there is not enough information to know whether anyone is any good.

5. There is a fundamental flaw in the "rank and yank" logic. Getting rid of the bottom 10 percent of employees might sound like a good way of upgrading the workforce. Given that the dismissed employees are replaced and that staffing has better results than it did when those bottom 10 percent were hired, at some point the unsatisfactory performers will have all been dismissed. If the organization continues to get rid of the bottom 10 percent, it will be getting rid of satisfactory employees.

These are all reasons to avoid forced ranking systems. More important, such systems ignore the management of performance except through dismissal. Dismissal and associated replacement costs are likely to be more expensive to the organization than improving the performance of substandard employees.

# References

Banks, C. G., and K. E. May. 1999. "Performance Management: The Real Glue in Organizations." In A. I. Kraut and A. K. Korman (eds.), *Evolving Practices in Human Resource Management: Responses to a Changing World of Work*. Jossey-Bass, San Francisco, pp. 118–145.

Bernardin, H. J., C. M. Hagan, J. S. Kane, and P. Villanova. 1998. "Effective Performance Management: A Focus on Precision, Customers, and Situational Constraints." In J. W. Smither (ed.), *Performance Appraisal: State of the Art in Practice*. Jossey-Bass, San Francisco, pp. 3–48.

Bing, J. W. 2004. "Metrics for Assessing Human Process on Work Teams." *IHRIM Journal* 8(6):26–31.

Deming, W. E. 1986. *Out of the Crisis*. Massachusetts Institute of Technology, Center for Advanced Engineering Study, Cambridge, MA, pp. 3–48.

DeNisi, A., and C. E. Smith. 2014. "Performance Appraisal, Performance Management, and Firm-Level Performance." *Academy of Management Annals* 8(1):127–179.

Evans, E. M. 2001. "Internet-Age Performance Management: Lessons from High-Performing Organizations." In A. J. Walker (ed.), *Web-Based Human Resources: The Technologies and Trends that Are Transforming HR*. McGraw-Hill, New York, pp. 65–82.

Locke, E. A., and G. P. Latham. 1990. *A Theory of Goal Setting and Task Performance*. Prentice Hall, Englewood Cliffs, NJ.

Morgeson, F. P., T. V. Mumford, and M. A. Campion. 2005. "Coming Full Circle Using Research and Practice to Answer 27 Questions about 360-Degree Feedback Programs." *Consulting Psychology Journal: Practice & Research* 57(2):196–209.

Mosley, E. 2013. *The Crowd Sourced Performance Review*. McGraw-Hill, New York.

O'Boyle, E., and H. Aguinis. 2012. "The Best and the Rest: Revisiting the Norm of Normality of Individual Performance." *Personnel Psychology* 65(1):79–119.

Stewart, S. M., M. L. Gruys, and M. Storm. 2010. "Forced Distribution Performance Evaluation Systems: Advantages, Disadvantages and Keys to Implementation." *Journal of Management & Organization* 16(1):168–179.

# 33

# Choosing a Performance-Appraisal System

Martin G. Wolf

Selection of the right performance-appraisal system to become part of your compensation program is critical to achieving your organization's business goals. Some organizations may require multiple appraisal systems. Over time, they may have to change their systems. Each type of performance-appraisal system represents an alternative way to

- Create and maintain a culture of performance, innovation, engagement, and leadership

- Retain talent and develop mission-critical skills

- Create competitive advantage

The goal of this chapter is to help readers select and implement the type of measurement system that will best connect to their compensation system and have the most positive impact on their organization's performance. The chapter is drawn from material presented in Chapter 9 of the second edition of *The Talent Management Handbook* (McGraw-Hill, 2011).

It is important to recognize that a performance-management (PM) system has two primary parts: (1) performance appraisal (the process of measuring performance) and (2) performance review (the process of communicating the results of the performance appraisal to the person whose performance was measured). This chapter focuses on performance appraisal—what to measure and how and when to measure it.

## Choice of Appraisal System

Appraisal systems can be categorized by what they assume and on what they focus measurement. When traits, behaviors, skills, and knowledge are linked to organization success expectations, they are sometimes called *competencies*.

- *Trait based.* Assumption that certain traits drive performance; measures personal characteristics of the position incumbent.

- *Behavior based.* Assumption that certain behaviors drive performance; measures what the position incumbent does.

- *Knowledge/skills based.* Assumption that certain knowledge/skills drive performance; measures what the position incumbent knows/applies.

- *Results based.* Assumption that achievement of objectives equals performance; measures what the position incumbent achieves.

Determining what type of appraisal system best fits your organizational and business needs depends primarily on your objectives; that is, what you are trying to accomplish with the system. Is your priority increased job understanding on the part of the incumbent, individual growth and development, or performance planning and control?

Following are other important factors to be considered:

- Business environment

- Strategy and objectives of the business

- Organization's size and the management levels considered

- Corporate climate

- Values and style of the senior management group

- Resources available

Further, not all appraisal systems can be used effectively with all types of employees. Appraisal systems are best suited to employee types as follows:

- *Trait based.* All employees.

- *Behavior based.* Supervisors and below.

- *Knowledge/skills based.* Production workers, clerical workers, and some professionals.

- *Results based.* Administrators/managers, most professionals, and executives.

Table 33.1 presents a comparison of the general characteristics, advantages, and disadvantages of the four systems.

Table 33.2 presents a different type of comparison of the four types of performance-appraisal systems, focusing on the utility of each for different performance-appraisal program objectives. In the table, an X in a box indicates that that type of measurement has utility for that objective. Two Xs in a box indicates a high degree of utility for that objective, whereas a blank box indicates that that type of measurement lacks utility for that objective.

| System Type | Characteristics | Strengths | Weaknesses |
|---|---|---|---|
| Trait-based | Assumption that certain traits drive performance<br><br>• Emphasis is on personality/style/values<br>• Traits are generic and may apply to all employees/groups<br>• Evaluation based on perception<br>• Rating tied to degree/frequency trait is exhibited | • Simple to conduct evaluation<br>• Can apply to different employee groups<br>• Communicates important traits up front | • Generic, not job-specific<br>• Tends to be subjective<br>• Tenuous link between traits and accomplishments |
| Behavior-based | Assumption that certain behaviors drive performance<br><br>• Behaviors are specific to the work environment<br>• Tailored to different jobs/groups<br>• Evaluation based on demonstrated actions<br>• Rating tied to degree/frequency behavior is exhibited | • Can be tailored to specific jobs<br>• Helps employees understand specifically how job is to be done<br>• Behaviors help reinforce culture/values | • Time-consuming to develop and evaluate<br>• Must be able to observe and measure discrete behaviors<br>• Behaviors may not produce desired results |
| Knowledge- or skills-based | Assumption that certain knowledge/skills drive performance<br><br>• Emphasis on employee capabilities<br>• Tailored to each knowledge/skill area<br>• Evaluation based on acquisition of knowledge/skills<br>• Rating tied to degree/diversity of knowledge/skill achieved<br>• Knowledge/skill tied to organizational objectives | • Competency required on each job<br>• Reinforces cross-training and flexibility<br>• Direct link to pay system<br>• Strategic view. Pay for competencies required in the future | • Assumes link between knowledge/skills and results<br>• Employee may not use certain knowledge/skills<br>• Difficult to measure diverse skills |

Table 33.1  Comparison of Performance Measurement Systems

| System Type | Characteristics | Strengths | Weaknesses |
|---|---|---|---|
| Results-based | Assumption that achievement of objectives drives performance<br><br>• Objectives tied to job or organization goals<br>• Develop objectives specific to individual/group by which performance is measured<br>• Evaluation based on results achieved<br>• Rating tied to degree of achievement | • Tailored to specific jobs/organization<br>• Emphasizes results<br>• Encourages dialogue and employee buy-in if goals are jointly established | • Time-consuming to develop and evaluate<br>• Limited to work where specific objectives can be established and measured<br>• Debate between short-term and long-term emphasis |

Table 33.1  Comparison of Performance Measurement Systems (*continued*)

| | Type of Measurement | | | |
|---|---|---|---|---|
| Program Objective | Trait-Based | Behavior-Based | KN/Skills-Based | Results-Based |
| Increased job understanding | | X | X | XX |
| Remedial performance improvement | X | XX | XX | XX |
| Career development | XX | X | XX | X |
| Focusing employee's efforts on specific tasks | X | XX | X | X |
| Increasing output | X | X | X | XX |
| Human resources planning | XX | X | X | X |
| Linking pay and performance | | X | X | XX |
| Improving teamwork | X | X | X | X |

Table 33.2  Utility of Different Performance Measurement Systems for Different Objectives

## Designing a Performance-Appraisal Program

Appendix 33A presents a detailed checklist of the many issues to be considered and the decisions to be made when designing a PM program. Most are straightforward and need no discussion. A discussion of two key issues that are not so straightforward follows.

## Choice of Rater

The person chosen as the rater must have the opportunity to observe the employee's performance on an ongoing basis. The most obvious choice as the rater is the employee's immediate superior (EIS). One problem with the EIS as a rater is that he or she may not have the opportunity to observe the employee during the most important aspects of performance. Strengths and weaknesses of various types of raters are summarized in Table 33.3.

For example, maintenance supervisors may have infrequent contact with maintenance personnel when they are performing repairs at various locations. Systems analysts may spend much of their time with users, far from where the EIS is working. Sales reps may be several states away from the EIS most of the time. In such cases, evaluation by the EIS alone is inadequate. Additional inputs are required to fully and fairly evaluate the employee. Several solutions are possible:

- Peer ratings
- Evaluation by subordinates
- Client/customer/supplier ratings
- Use of outside experts
- Some combination of these raters

| Rater | Strengths | Weaknesses |
|---|---|---|
| Peers | • Excellent opportunity to observe performance<br>• Good knowledge of job requirements | • Low rating may create resentment<br>• Possibility of collusion (everyone gets rated high)<br>• May weaken group cohesion/group trust |
| Subordinates | • Excellent opportunity to observe performance<br>• Good knowledge of job requirements | • They may distort ratings to curry favor—or to get even<br>• They may be afraid to be negative when it is deserved<br>• May weaken the supervisory relationship |
| Clients/ customers/ suppliers | • May observe the most critical aspects of performance | • May not see some important aspects of performance<br>• May distort the proper business relationship<br>• Possibility of collusion (employee does favors for rater in return for high rating) |
| Outside experts | • May possess excellent appraisal skills<br>• High degree of objectivity due to lack of personal relationship with appraisee | • Limited opportunity to observe performance<br>• May not understand all aspects of the job<br>• Can be expensive |

Table 33.3  Choice of Raters

The so-called 360-degree multirater feedback, using the first two or three of the preceding groups, has been widely used. Careful consideration must be given to the advantages and disadvantages of each alternative in each specific instance where the EIS needs assistance. Particularly in the case of peer ratings or evaluation by subordinates, care must be taken to keep the focus on performance and to avoid a "popularity contest."

It is particularly difficult to ensure that performance, as defined by these groups, is consistent with the organization's definition. For example, subordinates may rate their supervisor high on a dimension such as "Understands my job and helps me to perform it better" if the supervisor bends policy to facilitate the subordinate's performance of specific subtasks. Customers may rate a sales rep high on a dimension such as "Understands my business needs and supports me in accomplishing my objectives" if he or she violates policy and clues them in to upcoming price increases in advance of their public announcement.

## Method of Measurement

Each of the following sections presents detailed information on the design of one of the four types of PM. Although each of the four is different in various ways, there is some commonality.

Each trait, behavior, skill, or result constitutes a dimension of performance for that job. Dimensions communicate what traits, behaviors, skills, or results the organization considers to be important. Not all dimensions are created equal—some clearly are more important than others. Each dimension of performance must be assigned a weighting factor specifically for the job at hand. This weighting factor reflects the relative importance of the traits, behaviors, skills, or results to one another and to the job; it is simply an indication of time spent by the incumbent in these areas.

When assigning percentage weighting factors, apply the following rules:

1. No single trait, behavior, skill, or result can be weighted more than 20 percent. If a trait, behavior, skill, or result warrants more than 20 percent, this indicates that it is complex enough to be broken into more specific aspects. For example, if making sales is felt to be 70 to 80 percent of the performance of a sales rep, then sales should be broken into four or more aspects. These might be as follows: repeat sales of existing products to old accounts, sales of existing products to new accounts, sales of new products to existing accounts, sales of new products to new accounts, and average margin on sales.

2. No single trait, behavior, skill, or result can be weighted less than 5 percent. If a trait, behavior, skill, or result is less than 5 percent, then it should be incorporated as a subpart of another trait, behavior, skill, or result.

3. Avoid using fractions of a percent. It is impossible to determine such small differences. Many organizations prefer to stick to three or four weights—5, 10, 15, and 20 percent, for example. These then would correspond to important, quite important, extremely important, and critically important.

4. The total of all percentages must equal at least 95 percent and must not exceed 100 percent. (The use of less than 100 percent is allowed to indicate that there are other small but important elements to the job.)

Then, for each dimension, one or more measures must be established. Measures communicate how the organization will assess that dimension. The term *measure* refers to an index against which the dimension can be assessed; it does not specify the desired level (i.e., how much is "good," how much is "excellent," etc.). Finally, for each measure, standards, the definition of the levels of that dimension, must be developed. Measures are always meaningless unless a standard is developed, and this is where the subjectivity enters in. How much is marginal, good, or excellent? Basically, there are only three sources from which one can develop standards: the individual's history, peers, or management's wish based on hopes or pressures.

The latter is all too common but not worthy of further comment here. It is necessary to extrapolate from either of the first two to develop the projections that will form the coming year's standards. These projections must consider both internal limitations (i.e., financial and human resources, capacity, etc.) and external forces (i.e., macroeconomic conditions, competitive activity, technological changes, market trends, etc.). This process of extrapolation is the most critical part of the PM process.

If the individual's history is used as the basis for standards, care must be taken to recognize not just the period-to-period change, if any, but also the baseline level of the prior period(s). The author once won the "Most Improved Average" award in a bowling league by going from double digits to the still abysmal low 100s! However, it is unrealistic to expect continued improvement from someone who is already a top performer.

Similarly, when using peer performance as the basis for standards, care must be taken to recognize the group's overall level. All astronauts were well above the general population average mentally, physically, and educationally. However, as astronauts, some did not measure up and never received a mission, whereas others made multiple flights. Rank ordering, paired comparisons, forced distribution, and other peer-to-peer scales that lack external criteria are inherently flawed.

## Trait-Based Performance-Appraisal Process

As noted previously, a trait-based appraisal process rests on the assumption that certain traits drive performance, so it measures certain personal characteristics of the position incumbent. Therefore, the first step in developing a trait-based appraisal process is identifying the traits to be measured. There are two possible approaches. One is to select different traits for different jobs from a "pool" based on the characteristics that are considered to be important for that job. The other is to use a common set of traits for all positions, weighting them differently for each position based on their relative importance to each position.

The former approach allows for the best fit between the selected traits and the job requirements. However, it is time-consuming to develop. The latter approach not only is quicker and easier to develop, but it also has the advantage in human resources planning because it allows any employee to be compared with any job.

The following are illustrative traits:

- *Relationships with others.* Works in cooperation with others to achieve result.
- *Communication.* Transfers ideas and thoughts by speech and writing.
- *Planning/organizing tasks.* Develops and arranges activity to achieve a result.
- *Judgment.* Evaluates job situation to arrive at sound decisions.
- *Autonomy.* Works with minimal supervision required by job.
- *Work accuracy.* Works within error standards.
- *Work quantity.* Meets work volume required within designated time frames.

Sometimes the lines between traits, behaviors, skills, and results are blurred. Are communication, planning/organizing tasks, and judgment traits, or are they skills? Are work accuracy and work quantity traits, or are they really behaviors? Results?

## Behavior-Based Performance-Appraisal Process

As noted previously, a behavior-based performance-appraisal process rests on the assumption that certain behaviors drive performance, so it measures what the position incumbent does. Therefore, the first step in developing a behavior-based appraisal process is to identify the behaviors to be measured, selecting different behaviors for different jobs from a "pool" based on the characteristics considered to be important for that job.

One of the main problems with all performance-appraisal ratings is *rating inflation*. It is not only in Lake Woebegone that everyone is above average. Behavior-based scales attempt to reduce this type of creep by providing specific definitions of the levels of performance. Table 33.4 illustrates one type of behavioral anchoring. Selected points on the scale are explicitly defined, and in-between points on the scale are defined by implication. Other approaches to behavioral anchoring explicitly define every point on the scale (see Table 33.5).

| 5. High | Accurately identifies employees' strengths, weaknesses, and potential; makes some job assignments based on experience needed for promotability; ensures that development plans consider correcting performance deficiencies as well as building proficiencies; communicates expectations; keeps direct reports appraised of their performance; immediately confronts problems; deliberately lets subordinates wrestle with solutions rather than making decisions for them. |
| --- | --- |
| 4. | |
| 3. Medium | Recognizes individuals' strengths; may be unaware of developmental needs or hidden potential; appropriately places individuals in positions compatible with qualifications; may neglect to challenge good performers sufficiently; identifies and informs others of unsatisfactory performance, requests improvement but may not offer suggestions for change; at times, neglects to offer deserved praise. |
| 2. | |
| 1. Low | Inability to recognize or evaluate strengths and weaknesses of individuals; places subordinates in positions incommensurate with qualifications and experience; fails to view others as possessing unique talent and potential; stifles growth by confining people to predetermined roles; subordinates are confused about what is expected; sets up subordinates for failure; allows problem performance to continue unabated; fills job vacancies on personality alone. |

**Table 33.4  People Development**

The use of behaviorally anchored rating scales offers several options as to the number of rating levels and as to whether or not a middle point is available (i.e., an odd or even number of levels). Typically, four to seven levels are used. Many behaviorists feel that seven to nine levels represent the maximum number of distinctions that can be reliably made, but it is not unknown for some organizations to use a 100-point scale.

| | | | |
|---|---|---|---|
| 7 | [ ] | Excellent | Develops a comprehensive project plan, documents it well, obtains required approval, and distributes the plan to all concerned. |
| 6 | [ ] | Very Good | Plans, communicates, and observes milestones; states week by week where the project stands relative to plans. Maintains up-to-date charts of project accomplishments and backlogs and uses these to optimize any schedule modifications required.<br><br>Experiences occasional minor operational problems but communicates effectively. |
| 5 | [ ] | Good | Lays out all the parts of a job and schedules each part; seeks to beat schedule and will allow for slack.<br><br>Satisfies customers' time constraints; time and cost overruns occur infrequently. |
| 4 | [ ] | Average | Makes a list of due dates and revises them as the project progresses, usually adding unforeseen events; investigates frequent customer complaints.<br><br>May have a sound plan but does not keep track of milestones; does not report slippage in schedule or other problems as they occur. |
| 3 | [ ] | Below Average | Plans are poorly defined; unrealistic time schedules are common.<br><br>Cannot plan more than a day or two ahead; has no concept of a realistic project due date. |
| 2 | [ ] | Very Poor | Has no plan or schedule of work segments to be performed.<br><br>Does little or no planning for project assignments. |
| 1 | [ ] | Unacceptable | Seldom, if ever, completes project because of lack of planning and does not seem to care.<br><br>Fails consistently due to lack of planning and does not inquire about how to improve. |

**Table 33.5  Planning, Organizing, and Scheduling Project Assignments and Due Dates**

## Knowledge/Skills-Based Performance-Appraisal Process

As noted earlier, a knowledge/skills-based process rests on the assumption that certain knowledge/skills drive performance, so it measures what the position incumbent knows/applies.

Therefore, the first step in developing a knowledge/skills-based process is to identify the knowledge/skills to be measured, selecting different knowledge/skills for different jobs from a "pool" based on those considered to be important for that job.

The first challenge is to define the level of specificity to be used when defining knowledge/skills. Is leadership the skill to be measured, or is it to be broken down into more specific skills? The following list of leadership skills presents one approach to defining the component skills involved in leadership.

## Leadership Skills

1. **Creates Shared Vision.** Defines, communicates, and reinforces a common sense of purpose and set of values that are adopted by subordinate employees.

2. **Motivates and Empowers Others.** Influences, convinces, directs, and persuades others to accomplish specific objectives; provides sufficient latitude to allow subordinates to achieve specific objectives.

3. **Credibility.** Engenders the respect and confidence of others based on personal influence and reliability or organizational authority.

4. **Integrity.** Demonstrates consistency in beliefs, words, and behaviors.

5. **Sensitivity.** Alert to the motivations, attitudes, and feelings of subordinates and uses this knowledge positively to direct behavior and achieve desired results.

6. **Develops People.** Identifies and addresses principal developmental needs of subordinates; provides frequent, effective feedback about accomplishments, strengths, and development needs.

7. **Group Skills.** Plans, conducts, and participates in meetings in which the collective resources of the group are used efficiently.

The positive value of such a breakdown is that it allows for a much more exact assessment of leadership than is possible if it is measured as a single skill. For example, a given individual may have average leadership skill if it is evaluated as a single entity. However, if evaluated on the components of leadership, the individual may be excellent in some and deficient in other entities.

This more precise assessment has obviously greater utility for performance enhancement and career development. The problem with such a breakdown is that leadership is but one of a number of skill areas necessary for job performance. If each is broken into its component parts, the total will easily exceed 20 entities and even may exceed 30 entities depending on the position and the fineness of the breakdown. It is impossible to work effectively with that many elements of performance both for administrative purposes (developing an overall rating) and for performance review (How do you focus the interview when you have 20+ ratings to discuss?).

Even assuming that the proper number and fineness of knowledge/skills have been identified, there is still the question of how to measure them. The link between possessing a certain knowledge/skill and its application to performance is at issue here. If you define possession of a skill by its application on the job, you are essentially measuring results, not the skill per se. If you define possession of a skill other than by its application on the job, you are getting into complex, technically difficult measurements. Depending on the skill involved, this may require special skill tests or even getting into the individual's psyche.

For example, look at sensitivity, one of the components of leadership. An individual may appear to be "alert to the motivations, attitudes, and feelings of subordinates," but it is impossible to know if he or she really is "alert" except by actions that demonstrate this ("using this knowledge positively to direct behavior and achieve desired results"). Even if one treats leadership as a unitary skill, how do you assess it except by either its application (which is behavior) or its outcome (which is results)?

# Results-Based Performance-Appraisal Process

In any sound management system, an important element is some procedure, preferably quantitative, to determine the degree to which results are being achieved. For example, a budget is a plan for spending money over a period of time. Periodic review of actual against planned expenditures provides an important check to control and correct negative variances or permit reallocation of resources in the event of an unpredictable event.

The measurement of results is what most people think of when they think of performance appraisal. Indeed, most people equate performance with results: good performance is that which leads to desired results; poor performance is that which does not. The author has met thousands of managers over a 30+-year career as a management consultant, every one of whom believed that they could easily recognize good performance when they saw it. Yet few of them could appraise performance effectively. Their failure was rooted in the lack of proper definition of what constituted good performance.

The first step in results-based performance appraisal is to determine the dimensions of performance for that job. Dimensions may be permanent aspects of the position (e.g., making sales), specific one-time objectives (e.g., introducing a new product to the XYZ company), or a mixture of the two. Organizations that use a management-by-objectives (MBO) approach can fit these objectives into the performance-appraisal process as dimensions if they so choose. Some may prefer to keep the annually developed MBO dimensions separate, perhaps tied in to a bonus program, and use the permanent dimensions for a performance-appraisal program that is tied to base salary administration (pay for performance) and/or for development purposes. Then, for each dimension, one or more measures must be established.

## Measurement of Results

It must be recognized that all PM is subjective; there is no such thing as objective PM. What many people call *objective measurement* (e.g., sales volume, number of units produced, percent of products meeting quality standards, etc.) is just as subjective as what those same people would call *subjective measurement* (e.g., customer relationships, communication, product knowledge, etc.). The differences between the two categories are in the degree of quantification and when the subjective judgments are made.

So-called objective measurements are those that are highly quantifiable and that allow for putting the subjectivity at the beginning of the measurement period rather than at the end of it. For example, sales volume generally is considered to be an objective measure of sales performance.

Suppose that sales rep A sells $1,003,234.65 in a year, whereas sales rep B sells $1,534,201.32. What is A's level of performance—marginal, good, or excellent? What is B's? Clearly, B has sold more dollars' worth of product than A, but has B performed at a higher level than A? Not necessarily, depending on such factors as the products that each were selling (if A sells specialty items and B sells commodity items, A may represent a higher level of performance than B) and the territory in which they were selling (B may be in an established territory with little competition, whereas A may be in a new territory with well-established competition). Relative sales volume alone is meaningless for comparing performance. Measures are always meaningless unless a standard is developed. How much is marginal, good, or excellent? In which territories, for which products? Why is $X good? Why not 20 percent less or 20 percent more?

It is necessary to develop standards for every measure. These are usually developed at several levels—acceptable (just enough to get by), good (target or expected), very good (clearly better than expected), and outstanding. (Feel free to pick your favorite term for each of these four conceptual levels of performance.)

The development of the standards for each measure in advance of the performance period is critical to performance enhancement. As the saying goes, "If you don't know where you are going, you will never know when you get there." Many otherwise excellent performance-appraisal programs fail because standards were not properly developed and communicated in advance of the performance period.

## Comparison of Types of Results Measures

When thinking about the results-measurement process, there are a number of important points to keep in mind. First, in establishing indicators, we need to direct our efforts toward finding the most quantifiable measures of performance. As we do this, we increase the chances that regardless of who makes a performance assessment, the judgment will be the same. That is, there will be a high agreement among independent observers or evaluators.

In situations where measures must be less quantifiable (and these are common), it is possible to increase accuracy by using either more than one measure or more than one observer or evaluator. Because the use of multiple observers is limited, multiple measures are often used. As a rule of thumb, no more than four indicators should be used to measure achievement against any one dimension of performance. More than this tends to confuse people. The following list indicates the basic types of results measures, from least quantifiable to most quantifiable.

### Types of Results Measures

*Least Quantifiable*

1. **General Descriptions.** Judgments used to indicate end results, achievement. For example:

   • Satisfaction expressed by supervisor

   • Satisfaction expressed by customers

   • Favorable publicity

   • Quality of report or analysis

2. **Judgmental Scales.** Measurement based on rating of results on a scale, say of 1 to 7, with 1 representing worst results and 7 representing best. For example:

   • Perceived value of data processing services, low to high on 1 to 7 scale

   • Level of personnel support, low to high on 1 to 7 scale

   • Adequacy of drafting services, highly inadequate to highly adequate on 1 to 7 scale.

3. **Ratios.** These use quantified, numerical results; they match actual performance to available opportunities. For example:

- Employee turnover ratio

- Labor hours per unit of production

- Market share

4. **Direct Counts.** These are completely objective and quantified measures dealing with physical objects, specific occurrences, and other objective data. For example:

- Dollars of sales

- Cost of goods purchased

- Cost of operations

- Number of units produced or sold

5. Sometimes it is easier to count the exceptions than to count the normal occurrences. For example:

- Number of errors

- Number of complaints

### Most Quantifiable

Given our preference for quantification, we may find certain highly quantifiable measures that we cannot use. Why? They may be quantifiable but irrelevant—of marginal importance to the measurement process or even downright trivial. Quantification should be valued, but not at the cost of relevance, practicality, and common sense.

Finally, there is the problem of the appropriate *cost-benefit ratio* for any specific measure. We may believe that we can develop an unusually sound and highly quantifiable performance measure, but further analysis may show that the cost of developing the measure (e.g., time, energy, money) is so high that the benefit (i.e., relevance, practicality, objectivity) is not worth it. We may achieve a tour-de-force by developing and using the measure, but it surely is not good business practice. It is better to use a couple of rough-and-ready measures that are useful and inexpensive.

### Developing Results Measures

In some cases, measures are suggested directly by the dimension of performance, and they are fairly easily specified and quantified. In cases where this is not so, it is often helpful to ask two basic types of questions about the job:

1. *What are the concrete signs of outstanding performance on this dimension?* Often it is not too difficult to come up with the hallmarks of the real standout performance, and these signs should lead to measures of end results.

2. *What are the concrete signs of poor performance on this dimension?* It is often easier to bring to mind the things that represent an unsatisfactory performance. These, too, can be helpful in deriving useful measures.

The task is to identify the possible measures and narrow the choice to a few that capture most directly the nature of any end result that the position is to achieve.

The selected measures should meet the following criteria:

- *Relevant.* They should relate directly to the major results rather than to activities or less important results. Measures should focus on, rather than divert attention from, the result.

- *Specific.* They should accurately reflect performance the employee can control or directly affect with his or her job or organizational unit. For example, a manager of manufacturing might be measured on production costs or value added but not on profit because he or she has no control over the material costs or the selling price per unit, both of which also have a direct effect on profit.

- *Obtainable.* Wherever possible, use measures that now are or can easily become available; avoid the need for major new and/or complex tracking mechanisms.

- *Practical.* In most performance areas, many measures are already in use as a common means of setting goals, controlling operations, and reporting results. Use these whenever possible because they represent the organization's business focus.

- *Reliable.* Other raters will come to the same conclusions about level of performance from the measurement data.

- *Timely.* Data must be available soon enough after the end of the performance period to affect most of the following performance period.

Appendix 33B presents some sample measures for line and staff jobs. This list is not all-inclusive, but it should provide further clarification of the types of measures that can be used to assess performance.

### The Performance-Appraisal Process

Once the dimensions are identified and weighted and the associated measures and standards are developed, results-based performance appraisal is simple. Performance is defined as the attainment of the specified results as defined by the standards. Performance appraisal is simply the comparison of the results achieved versus these specified results. Appendix 33C presents an illustrative results-based performance appraisal form.

In summary, if the dimensions are well stated, and if realistic measures and standards of performance are formulated, there will be little question what has been accomplished. Although many of the measures may be qualitative, the process will be reliable in that any evaluator who knew the relevant facts would give the same rating to the employee.

| Appraisal Issue | Diagnostic Issues | Decision Choices |
| --- | --- | --- |
| Philosophy | What is the primary need to evaluate? | A. Accountability |
| | | B. Improvement/maintenance |
| | | C. Support of other systems (e.g., rewards, values) |
| Objectives | What specifically do we want to achieve? | A. Detailed evaluation |
| | | B. Summary evaluation |
| | | C. Combination |
| Types of criteria | What makes employees/teams effective? | A. Knowledge- or skill-oriented criteria |
| | | B. Process-oriented criteria |
| | | C. Output-oriented criteria |
| | | D. Combination |
| Type of measurement | How can we actually tell whether the employee/team is effective? | A. Trait based |
| | | B. Behavior based |
| | | C. Knowledge/skills based |
| | | D. Results based |
| | | E. Combination |
| Data for measurement | What type of information is available for assessing effectiveness? | A. Quantitative |
| | | B. Qualitative |
| Choice of appraiser | Who should evaluate performance? | A. Supervisors |
| | | B. Peers |
| | | C. Subordinates |
| | | D. Clients/customers/suppliers |
| | | E. Outside experts |
| | | F. Combination |
| | How many people should evaluate performance? | A. Single appraiser |
| | | B. Multiple appraisers |
| Choice of appraisal instruments | What kind of documents should be used? | A. Checklists |
| | | B. Narratives |
| | | C. Rating scales |
| | | D. Goal-oriented instruments |

**Appendix 33A   Performance-Appraisal Diagnostic**

| Appraisal Issue | Diagnostic Issues | Decision Choices |
|---|---|---|
| Appraisal interviews | How should information be fed back to the employee/team? | A. Interviews<br>B. Other (e.g., written document) |
| Appraisal training | How should training in the conduct of the appraisal be provided? | A. Internal staff<br>B. Consultants<br>C. Combination<br>D. Other (e.g., self-paced) |
| Assessment period and timing | Should timing be fixed or based on need? | A. Scheduled appraisals<br>B. Appraisal in response to problems<br>C. Both |
| | Is evaluation a continuous or discontinuous process? | A. Day-to-day data collection<br>B. Periodic data collection<br>C. Varies |
| Alignment of outcomes with objectives | Is appraisal going to do what we wanted to achieve? | A. Quality<br>B. Timeliness<br>C. Credibility<br>D. Cost<br>E. Accountability |
| Interactive appraisal design | Should the subordinates' appraisals be linked to the supervisor's appraisal and others in the value chain? | A. Separate appraisal systems<br>B. Linked appraisal |

**Appendix 33A  Performance-Appraisal Diagnostic (*continued*)**

**Sample Measures for Line Jobs**

Cost-effectiveness

    Actual/budget (by category and/or time period)

    Net income/net sales

    Forecasted/actual (by month/quarter)

    Gross margin or gross operating profit (by profit center, product line, etc.)

    Return on capital/risk

    Breakeven point as a percent of capacity

    Average collection period

    Return on investment

    Return on assets

    Earnings before taxes

Productivity

    Dollar cost/unit of product or service provided

    Actual/standard cost (by category)

    Currency of human resources planning

    Currency of work methods

    Bottlenecks in workflow

    Downtime of equipment

    Absenteeism

    Length of time for employees to meet performance standards

    Turnover of above-average performers

Relationships

    Promptness of problem notification to others

    Understanding of other functions' objectives and plans

    Minority employees' percent/percent in available workforce

    Grievances (employee, community)

    Agreement on schedules

    Adherence to schedules

    Peers' and superior's reactions

**Appendix 33B  Sample Measures of Performance**

Staff and organizational development

   Use of objectives by staff

   Completion and application of job-related study

   Number and type of decisions delegated

   Number of conflicting objectives

   Number of conflicting action plans

   Results of career discussions

   Job sequencing plans

   Job enrichment plans

   Results of attitude surveys

Quality

   Internal reject percent

   Complaints from customers

   Results of internal/external audits

   Employee commitment to standards

   Actual/standard (errors, reject rate)

   Warranty costs

   Accuracy (production reports)

   Raw material quality

   Results of work sampling

Marketing

   Knowledge of end-user requirements

   Number of new products (programs) developed

   Actual/forecast (sales, operating expenses)

   Market penetration (share)

   Percent net income in research and development (R&D)

   Results of market research and advertising (public information) programs

   Timeliness of forecast submissions

**Appendix 33B   Sample Measures of Performance (*continued*)**

Cost control

    Actual/standard (by cost category)

    Actual/forecast (by cost category)

    Workers' compensation costs

    Unemployment compensation costs

    Lost work hours due to absenteeism, accidents, tardiness, etc.

    Direct/indirect labor ratio

    Use of electric power

    Cost of telephone service

    Travel and per-diem expense

**Sample Measures for Staff Jobs**

Some performance dimensions, such as those found in certain staff positions, are difficult to review. In some cases, it is best to use a measure that indicates what has not occurred rather than what has. For example, "unscheduled downtime" might be the most reliable indication of the incumbent's performance on a dimension involving the effective use of EDP equipment. The reviewer can assume that the most likely thing is for the end result (effective use of equipment) to occur. Thus, rather than counting or describing what has happened, he or she focuses effort by considering only the times when the desired result was not accomplished. This amounts to keeping track of "unscheduled downtime."

Measures for staff positions must deal with end results that are to be accomplished by the staff unit. The vital question is: "What is the output of the position?" Some common measurements are

- Number of occasions on which schedules were missed.

- Number of proposals implemented per number of proposals made.

- Quality of service as rated or described by client or user.

- Number of complaints (or commendations) regarding services provided.

- Audits of effectiveness of services provided (internal or external).

- Number of exceptions found by outside sources—e.g., customer complaints, outside audit.

- Number of person-hours (or budget) spent per service area versus plan.

- Number of units of output per employee.

- Descriptions of kinds of service provided relative to kinds of service requested.

- The organization's record in an area (e.g., accident frequency, EEO data, workers' compensation rates) compared with industry average.

- Descriptions or ratings of the relevance and quality of innovations or new services developed.

**Appendix 33B  Sample Measures of Performance (*continued*)**

Name: _____ Date: _____

Position: _____ Dept.: _____

Performance period: From: _____ To: _____

I. Period Performance

Dimension: Weight: _____ percent

Measure(s) and standards: _____

Description of performance: _____

Dimension: Weight: _____ percent

Measure(s) and standards: _____

Description of performance: _____

Dimension: Weight: _____ percent

Measure(s) and standards: _____

Description of performance: _____

II. Other Comments (Optional)

Use this space (and attach additional sheets if desired) to make any statement that you feel will further explain and clarify this employee's performance.

_____

_____

III. Improvement Activities for the Next Period

This section should contain an improvement plan to correct any difficulties noted in Sections I and II. These should be spelled out as to who will do what, by when, and with specific behavioral objectives to be achieved.

IV. Overall Evaluation of Performance

_____

_____

V. Performance Plan for the Next Performance Period

From: _____ To: _____

Establish the dimensions, measures, and standards for the next performance-rating period.

Dimension: _____ Weight: _____ percent

Measure(s) and standards: _____

Dimension: _____ Weight: _____ percent

Measure(s) and standards: _____

Dimension: _____ Weight: _____ percent

Measure(s) and standards: _____

**Appendix 33C   Illustrative Results-Based Performance-Enhancement Program**

# 34

# Linking Compensation to Competitive Business Value

Mark Graham Brown
*Mark Graham Brown & Associates*

The foundation of any successful compensation plan is that it serves to drive the right employee behavior and that it is linked to strategy and operational success. The most important part of the system is the metrics or measures on which compensation is based. Selecting the wrong measures can result in rewarding undesirable behavior and decision making. Achieving or maintaining a competitive advantage in any field requires constant review and updating of plans and strategies. The days of a strategic plan and compensation that are good for three years are gone. Leading organizations today use real-time data to monitor performance in internal measures and external factors daily and make adjustments to plans as needed. What most organizations do not do, however, is also adjust the compensation plan. A good compensation system is flexible and adaptable as opposed to rigid and requiring approval of six layers of management to change anything. What gets measured gets done, but what you incentivize gets done even better. Much care needs to be taken in selecting and assigning importance to the measures used for incentive compensation.

We have all heard horror stories of how the wrong measures and incentives can lead to disaster. Sears's auto mechanics were incentivized to make the dollars on each repair orders as high as possible, so some recommended unnecessary work to customers. Dominos' pizza delivery people were taking risks and getting into car accidents to meet the 30-minute free-delivery guarantee the company once offered. IBM salespeople used to focus on selling hardware because it was more expensive than software and compensation was tied to revenue, not margin. All these companies have learned that what you measure and incentivize sometimes can drive undesirable behavior and company results. This chapter reviews some guidelines on ensuring that your compensation system drives the right behaviors and that those behaviors lead to greater organizational success.

Following are 10 rules for creating effective performance measures that can then be linked to bonuses or compensation.

## Rule 1: Select Measures that Link to Key Outcomes Employees Can Influence

*Process* is currently a big word. Organizations are implementing approaches such as Lean and Six Sigma to analyze and improve the processes used to get day-to-day work accomplished. Measures are often created around processes and improvements that are based on human behavior. A good scorecard or set of performance measures should include a balance of leading and lagging or process and outcome measures. However, compensation should be based on outcome metrics, not process measures. Outcomes such as sales, customer referrals, profits, projects completed successfully, and new products introduced on time are easily measured and important to the overall success of the organization. The problem with process measures is that they often do not predict success of outcome measures. This is especially true of processes that include a lot of human behavior. If a process is highly automated, such as manufacturing aluminum, process measures and standards are based on solid research and linked directly to key product outcome measures. Most processes in today's organizations involve a great deal of human behavior and are not an exact science. For example, building a relationship with a customer is not a formula, and what works with one customer may alienate another. Achieving most outcomes in an organization is a joint effort of a number of departments or units. The way to use these outcome metrics for compensation is to assign a percentage weight to each group that contributes to the outcome measure based on the group's level of influence. For example, a measure such as sales of new products might be on the scorecard of research and development (R&D), sales, marketing, and manufacturing. Each of these four functions has some degree of influence on the measure, but some have more control than others. The weights of each of these groups might look like the following example: R&D 50 percent, marketing 20 percent, sales 20 percent, and manufacturing 10 percent. Bonuses for R&D personnel might include other measures over which they have greater control, such as patents, products in the pipeline, or project milestones met, but the heavier weight should be on the outcome metrics, even though R&D personnel must work with others to achieve good performance.

## Rule 2: Avoid Linking Compensation to Overall Company Performance Except for Senior Leaders

A common practice is to link employee bonuses to overall measures of company performance, such as hitting sales or profit targets, stock price, or other high-level financial measures of company success. Although this is a good practice for compensating executives, it is not productive for most employees. The flawed logic is that everyone will work harder to help the company stock price rise or achieve some financial goal if their pay is tied to it. The reality is that the vast majority of employees see absolutely no connection between their own job performance and overall company performance. A sales manager might have his or her best year ever and beat his or her growth target by 15 percent yet receive no bonus because the company had a big R&D project fail, eating up all potential profits.

An individual employee in a call center was rated number three in the entire company for her customer-service performance but sadly received no bonus because the company did not hit its customer-satisfaction targets. Compensation should be linked to metrics for individual job performance, not company performance. The more control an individual has over performing well on certain measures, the more powerful the compensation based on those measures will be in driving desirable behavior.

## Rule 3: Avoid Basing Compensation on Metrics that Are Easy to Manipulate

It is currently common to link performance-based pay to measures of customer satisfaction. This is a good idea. The problem with this in many organizations is that there is only one measure of customer satisfaction—the dreaded survey. Whether it is comprised of 1 question (a recent trend called *net promoter score*) or 50 questions, survey data are easy to manipulate. A national real estate company I worked with counted on agents to hand out customer surveys at the end of a transaction to get buyers and sellers to rate their performance. When the agents knew that the transaction had not gone well and they were likely to get a bad score, they forgot to hand out the survey and ended up getting all high ratings. Car dealers are notorious for calling customers before a survey goes out and offering free detailing or other services in exchange for high ratings. I recently got a letter from my dealer after leasing a new car suggesting that I call the service manager first if I planned on marking anything less than the highest ratings regarding the sales process.

When you start linking pay to performance, people get very creative in coming up with ways of making the numbers look good without doing the work that the measure was intended to reward. Cheating on performance measures is not limited to surveys. All kinds of measures and data-collection methods are subject to manipulation. Using an outside company to collect the data helps to ensure the integrity of the data, but even that can be manipulated. A hotel I stayed in uses J. D. Power to do its customer-satisfaction surveys. A letter in the room from the hotel manager informed me of the upcoming survey, asking for my feedback, and suggesting that if there was anything I was not 100 percent satisfied with, I should call guest services to get it remedied before I checked out. The behavior that the survey might drive from some guests is to complain about something and get a fruit basket or room upgrade. I caution clients to test new metrics for a year before linking pay to them to ensure that the data cannot be manipulated. Measurement alone gives people an incentive to cheat, but metrics tied to compensation make it even more tempting. Make sure that the metrics and the methods used to gather data have integrity.

## Rule 4: Avoid Overly Complicated Compensation Formulas

To avoid driving behavior that is counterproductive by basing compensation on a single measure of performance such as sales or units produced, some organizations link compensation to indices or analytics that are a summary of several aspects of performance. This makes a lot more sense than trying to measure a complex dimension of performance with a singular measure. My most recent book (*Killer Analytics—Top 20 Metrics Missing from Your Balance Sheet*, Wiley/SAS, 2013) presents a number of examples from business and government of some of these index measures. The idea is that an overall measure of something such as R&D might include some leading or process metrics such as new products in the pipeline and patents and project-management metrics such as milestones along with lagging measures such as industry firsts, sales, and profits from new products. Each of the subfactors in the analytic is assigned a percentage weight based on factors such as its importance, data integrity, and other factors. The summary gauge or analytic then displays performance on typically a 0–100 scale. This approach allows you to combine unlike units of measurement such as number of patents, percentage of milestones met, and revenue in sales from new products into a single metric.

Although these analytic metrics are an excellent way for senior management to measure various aspects of performance, these summary analytics or indices are often too complicated to use for determining compensation for all employees. Employees should be able to track through the year how they are doing at earning a bonus. If bonuses are paid frequently (e.g., monthly), this is less of a problem, but it is still important that employees see a connection between their own job performance and the payout they are going to receive. If employees are mostly in the dark regarding how much bonus they are likely to receive or cannot explain the formula used to compute bonuses, you need to modify the metric to make it easier to understand.

## Rule 5: Set Realistic and Achievable Targets

It is hard enough to come up with valid performance measures that are likely to drive the right behavior from employees. It is even more difficult to set realistic targets or objectives for those metrics. It becomes very frustrating to be given a target that is linked to your pay and is unrealistically high. Leaders often think that setting ridiculously high targets will motivate people to stretch and work as hard as they can to get the payout. What happens more often is that they become disgruntled and frustrated.

When setting targets for any metric, it is important to consider past performance averages, best past performance, competitor performance, industry averages or typical performance, customer and/or resource constraints (e.g., time, dollar headcount, technical capabilities), and links to other metrics. Targets should be set high enough so that the organization achieves high levels of performance but should be realistic as well. A hospital I worked with had a target of 50 percent patient satisfaction, which sounds like a ridiculously low objective, but not when you consider that past performance was in the 30 percent range and current performance was 42 percent patient satisfaction. For some metrics, it becomes difficult to set a target that is less than perfection. For example, an airline would not set a target of 95 percent safe landings. A manufacturing organization would not set a target of having only 10 serious injuries or accidents this year. Achieving high levels of performance on one metric might result in poor performance on other related metrics, so that needs to be considered. For example, a corporate law department I worked with dramatically reduced its cycle time for processing company documents. However, as a result of rushing through each task, several mistakes were made that cost millions in lawsuits. Targets and metrics need to be balanced so as not to put too much focus on a single aspect of performance.

To ensure that compensation links to competitive business success, it is often important to adjust targets as needed to drive success. For example, R&D may have a target 14 months in the future for issuing a prototype new product. This target might be moved up by 6 months if you get wind that a competitor is going to release a similar product much sooner. I know that people hate it when you change targets because they rarely become easier, but this is necessary to ensure that you stay competitive. The thing to avoid is to change targets just because you see in the first quarter that you are not going to make them. However, even this is necessary sometimes. I recall working with a major homebuilder in Phoenix right before the housing crash in 2008, and the company had to go into survival mode and change from sales-growth targets to a focus on cost cutting and completing houses it had already started.

## Rule 6: Measure Performance as Often as Possible

Whatever you decide to measure to assess the performance of your employees, try to select dimensions that can be measured on a daily, weekly, or at least monthly basis. The best scorecard measures are those that are tracked on a daily basis. With daily feedback, people can monitor and adjust their performance on an ongoing basis. You would not find any business that only measures financial performance once a year. Even the smallest of businesses tends to measure some aspects of financial performance daily and at least once a month looks at factors such as costs and profit and loss. Yet some of the largest and most sophisticated organizations worldwide measure important things such as employee satisfaction and engagement or relationships with customers via an annual survey. Annual metrics are close to worthless. If the last data point shows poor performance, you have to wait 11 more months to get another data point to see if any improvement strategies are working.

One of the best compensation systems I have seen is the piece-rate system still being used in many clothing manufacturing facilities. Workers get paid a set amount for each good-quality component they produce. Quality inspectors check each piece or component for errors and return pieces to workers when rework is needed. The workers get paid more if they produce more, but only good-quality products count, so they also must focus on quality. The system often creates some tension between the workers and inspectors, but some organizations put the inspectors on incentive-based pay as well to encourage a more cooperative approach. The workers like the daily feedback, and the compensation system ensures that the best performers can earn more money than their average-performing peers. Seniority and experience are also rewarded because the workers with the highest pay and productivity tend to be more experienced.

## Rule 7: Make Individual and Team Performance the Basis of Compensation

Older compensation plans such as piece rate in the garment industry or commission for salespeople are based 100 percent on individual performance. The benefit of such approaches is that each individual has a great deal of influence over his or her own compensation and does not need to depend on anyone else. Individual compensation plans such as this tend to separate the best performers from their more mediocre peers. Systems such as this work best in organizations where individual contributors are completely on their own and do not need other employees or departments to achieve their goals. However, most organizations are not set up this way. In many jobs, performance is dependent on peers, bosses, other departments, and contractors or vendors. In a situation such as this, 100 percent individual performance-based pay systems tend to fail. Another problem with basing pay solely on individual performance is that these systems often create a culture of unfriendly competitiveness. The experienced worker will never help to train a new worker or share tips for performing better with peers. Everyone is out for himself or herself, and there are no rewards for cooperating and helping others do well.

A popular alternative compensation approach is not much better. Linking compensation to team performance sounds like a more valid approach for encouraging teamwork and a spirit of working together for common goals. What really happens is that some employees work to capacity or beyond, and others slack off and everyone gets the same bonus. On any team, there are some players who play better than others. With a team compensation system, there is no differentiation in pay for the good versus average or poor performers. The good performers end up angry because they were better contributors than others and received the same pay. The poor performers are encouraged to slack off continuously because they are rewarded with a healthy team bonus.

The best compensation systems are a mix of individual and team performance. A good combination is 60 percent individual performance and 40 percent team performance. This rewards the individuals who perform much better than their peers but also puts a strong weight on helping their peers to achieve high levels of team or unit performance.

## Rule 8: Provide Employees with an Easy Way to Track Performance throughout the Year

A common way to report performance data is to use spreadsheets for reports and graphic presentations for monthly review meetings. Neither of these methods is very effective for performance feedback. Spreadsheets are often very hard to read, with difficulty in spotting important statistics or problem areas. I sit next to executives on airplanes often and watch them squint trying to read the hundreds of tiny figures in their spreadsheet reports. I have sat in countless monthly meetings as well where managers were droning on with their impossible-to-read visuals that present data in charts and graphs that can be impossible to decipher. A better approach is to give everyone access to scorecard software linked to various types of important performance data. This allows managers and employees to view performance in more useful ways. Scorecard software extracts data from spreadsheets and other databases and coverts them to easy-to-understand graphics. The disadvantage of this simple software is that it does not allow any data analysis; it is strictly a presentation tool. Larger organizations may use more sophisticated software that has more extensive analytic capabilities but is also easy to use.

The advantage of using analytic software is that it can provide feedback to employees so that they can track how they are doing on a daily basis at their own desks, without attending meetings. Controls can be put in place to restrict access to sensitive data, and each employee can customize his or her own "briefing book" to look at his or her own performance measures in a format that he or she most prefers. Software such as this also eliminates the need to prepare charts for monthly review meetings. Someone brings a laptop to the meeting, hooks it up to the company database where the software resides, and sets out real-time performance data for review and analysis. This software is not inexpensive, but it can pay for itself in the first year because personnel no longer have to work overtime each month preparing charts and reports for meetings. Another benefit of these software tools is that employees at all levels can review their performance on a personal phone and/or other smart device.

## Rule 9: Beware of Strategy Maps to Define Metrics

A popular approach for identifying metrics linked to key outcomes such as profit or growth is to create strategy maps. These diagrams, typically constructed on flipcharts or white boards in small group meetings, are based on sound logic, but they are most often flawed. The idea is to begin by identifying some important outcome and then work backward by identifying important factors and measures that lead to that outcome. For example, a company might identify increasing sales by 15 percent as an important outcome goal (metric: percentage increase in sales from last year). The main strategy for improving sales is to increase loyalty from the best customers (metric: dollars spent per customer account compared with previous years). In order to get customers to spend more money, account managers need to get more face time with key players at each customer account (metric: hours spent per month in contact with customers). The strategy for spending time on the right activities with customers is implementation of a new customer relationship management (CRM) strategy (metric: milestones met on CRM implementation plan). The key to making the new CRM system successful is proper training of account managers and other sales support personnel (metric: percent of staff who have attended all required CRM training).

The big problem with this logic chain and the resulting metrics is that the links are all based on a string of assumptions and opinions. Every one of these links needs to be evaluated and tested to determine whether an improvement in one factor leads to a concomitant improvement in the later measure. For example, there might be an inverse relationship between face time with your account managers and an increase in spending by customers. It could be that the more time your account manager spends with customers, the more disgruntled they become and the more likely they are to switch their business over to another supplier that does not bother them as much. Another flaw in the logic chain might be that the new CRM software actually will make account managers more successful at account management. Most salespeople I know view the CRM software as a time-wasting distraction that encourages sales managers to second-guess all their decisions and micromanage them.

A compensation system that is based on process or activity measures developed using strategy maps is very dangerous. Unless all the assumptions in the various links of the strategy map are tested, you may be paying for employee activity that does nothing to contribute to positive performance. One guaranteed benefit of strategy maps is that they increase the billable hours of the consultants running the meetings to create them. Whether or not the circles and arrows allow you to define valid performance measures is a big risk. Strategy maps can be a good approach for identifying links between leading and lagging measures as long as research is done to prove that those links are more than just theory or hope.

## Rule 10: Eliminate "Chicken Efficiency" Measures

When I started my own consulting practice, my second client was a company in the fast-food business that sold fried chicken. At one time, the company was one of only a handful of international chains that had a menu based on fried chicken. Its market share eroded as more and more companies entered the business. The company asked me to conduct a study of its best-performing restaurants to determine what the managers did to make the restaurants so successful. The company was then going to give my findings to the training department to develop a workshop to teach the best practices to all of its restaurant managers.

After sitting in my first restaurant outside of Knoxville for half a day, I did not have many notes. After the lunch crowd came and went, I spoke with Roy, the manager. I asked him what the secret to his success was because the company had identified him as one of the best managers in the country. He explained: "The secret to success in this business is something we call 'chicken efficiency.'" Roy took me in the back room to show me his poster-sized graph of chicken efficiency. There was a little chicken sticker pasted on each day for his performance, which was often 99 to 100 percent so far that month. Now I was starting to see why he was selected as a great performer, but I was not sure what "chicken efficiency" was. Roy explained: "At the end of every day, I calculate my chicken efficiency percentage on these worksheets they give me, and I peel off one of these chicken stickers and mash it on the chart for my performance for the day."

Still confused, I asked him what factors went into calculating "chicken efficiency," and he explained: "You take how much chicken you cook, subtract how many pieces you sell, and you get a percentage which shows you how much chicken you throw away or how much scrap we have. The bean counters tell me that this number directly links to a store's profits, so I try to make sure I sell every piece of chicken I cook. We also have tough quality standards for how long it can sit under the heat lights before I have to throw it away."

When I asked Roy how he got nearly perfect performance and sold practically every piece of chicken he cooked, he explained that he never cooked chicken and put it under the heat lights after 6:30 p.m. Customers who came in after 6:30 had to wait 15 to 20 minutes for Roy's staff to custom cook a bucket of chicken for them. That is a long time to wait with six hungry eight-year-old girls in the minivan after a soccer game, so Roy explained that most of the people who came in after 6:30 p.m. were not willing to wait, and they left. The problem was that the company did not measure that, but it did measure "chicken efficiency" every day. The company only measured customer satisfaction once a year, so that did not drive employee performance. Employees got promoted for having good "chicken efficiency" scores as well as receiving other forms of recognition. Because of the focus on this performance measure, employees and managers were purposely not cooking chicken and subsequently were making customers angry in order to make this short-term financial metric look positive.

It may be hard to see how a major corporation could miss the most important point, but I have seen "chicken efficiency" measures in many large businesses and government organizations. In fact, it is rare to find a scorecard or set of performance measures that does not include a few of these "chicken efficiencies."

## Summary

The key to any successful compensation plan is that it is based on solid performance metrics. The metrics should be few, 1–6 versus 20–30; linked to individual and team performance; changed as often as necessary to link to strategy and changing business conditions; tracked frequently (at least monthly); balanced to address the needs of key stakeholders such as customers, shareholders, employees, and partners; and understandable to the employees being judged on them.

Despite how much care you put into defining the right measures that serve as the foundation of your pay-for-performance plan, you will need to continually fine-tune them. As soon as you think that you have the ideal systems that drive the right behavior, your situation will change, driving the need for new metrics and priorities.

# 35

# Using Financial Rewards to Drive Productivity

CHRISTIAN M. ELLIS

*Management Consultant and University Educator*

It is an empirical economic fact that along with innovation, productivity is the primary differentiating factor over the long term that determines the wealth of nations, societies, and organizations. Drawing from decades of research, we know that if the productivity of an enterprise is greater than that of its competitors over a sustained period of time, it has a much better chance of survival because of increased competitiveness, financial health, and overall value creation.

In our complex and global economy, where knowledge and specialization are increasingly important and where labor investment often exceeds capital investment, the productivity of people is a highly critical ingredient for success. With this in mind, it is shocking how little attention is paid to true workforce and enterprise productivity, especially in knowledge-work environments such as financial institutions, research and development organizations, professional services firms, Internet companies, and public-policy agencies, to name a few. Today firms spend vast amounts of time and resources on implementing new technologies to lower costs and increase efficiencies but often are unable to answer the most basic question of whether productivity actually improved as a result.

The definition of productivity and the metrics used to support it vary by business model, nature of work performed, and employee segment. Just as there is no single way to define productivity, there is no single way to measure it either. In the broadest sense, productivity reflects how well a system uses its resources to achieve its goals. Productivity is not the simple sum of the productivity of individuals or groups. Rather, it involves the systemic interdependence and integration of information, processes, networks, technologies, people, and other resources. The behavior of people, how they interact in groups and networks, how they exchange information, and how they make decisions all have profound effects on productivity.

Highly productive organizations have a culture of productivity and recognize it as the foundation of value creation. Regardless of what an organization produces—a service, a product, a piece of information, a unit of wealth, or a psychological experience—its productivity in doing so ultimately determines the degree to which it can create value for customers over the long term. Developing a culture of productivity requires a shared definition of productivity, an understanding of the drivers of productivity, and an application of the right mix of investments in those drivers in an integrated manner over a sustained period of time.

This begins with examining the current state of productivity in the enterprise. Consider the following questions:

- How does the organization define productivity today? How does it measure it? How does it link productivity to value creation?

- What are the organization's beliefs, assumptions, hypotheses, and facts regarding its current productivity levels?

- How competitive is the productivity of the organization with respect to its competitors? Does this matter?

- To what extent are productivity metrics used in managing and improving the performance of the enterprise?

- To what extent does the organization understand what drives productivity improvement today and what will drive it in the future?

- How are investments in people, such as compensation, benefits, and development, linked to productivity improvement?

The characteristics of highly productive organizations are as well understood as they are consistent. In productive organizations, there is a high degree of goal and role clarity, people are engaged in their work, there is open communication and cross-boundary information sharing, bureaucratic structure is despised, and there is zero tolerance for waste. Productive companies avoid layoffs that lead to superficial short-term efficiencies. They invest heavily in hiring, onboarding, and developing the right people. They are relentlessly committed to continuous process improvement. They are agile in adapting to the changing competitive environment and flexible in their ability to shift focus based on immediate operational needs. And they understand that competitive advantage lies in their disciplined capability to efficiently make hard decisions and rigorously execute their strategies and plans.

Although these characteristics of productive organizations are common, each enterprise has a unique set of productivity drivers that require a subsequent unique set of investments to support, reinforce, and sustain them. For every enterprise, there is an optimal combination of investments in the areas of process, people, capability, structure, and technology—the main driver categories. But what about rewards? Financial rewards are often overlooked or ignored when it comes to productivity, especially with respect to professional and managerial employee segments.

In economic circles, there is clear consensus that real wages are equal to the marginal productivity of labor. The standard of living of a society or the overall level of wages of an enterprise thus depends on the productivity of people. But something strange has happened over the past 20 or so years in our country. Wages have not tracked with productivity gains. The value of these gains has been disproportionately distributed. One study suggests that if the minimum wage had tracked with productivity, from a macroeconomic perspective, it would be over $20 per hour today. This chapter does not address this unfortunate gap, but it does offer insights into how organizations should and can do a better job of rewarding for productivity across different employee and job segments.

For decades, companies have used compensation to reward productivity improvement in production and service environments through gain sharing, goal sharing, profit sharing, and other group-based incentive programs. The approaches are often self-funding where productivity is (relatively) easily measured because of the nature of work involved, and there is a clear return on investment. The research on these programs shows that they are highly effective when both operational and financial metrics are used and should be continued. But a broader and deeper examination is required when considering using financial rewards—ranging from base pay to variable pay to wealth pay—to more effectively drive improvements in productivity across the whole enterprise. Consider these principles:

- *Base (fixed) compensation.* This is best used to reward for the value of work performed and the individual's behaviors and competencies demonstrated in how that work gets done. Because base pay delivers compensation going forward, it can be linked to the potential to contribute to productivity improvement in the future.

- *Variable (incentive) compensation.* This is best used to reward for the work that has already been done: the achievement of results. Because incentive pay delivers compensation based on the past, it can be linked to the attainment of short-term (annual or less) productivity-based outcomes.

- *Wealth (accumulating) compensation.* This is best used to reward for the value creation of the enterprise over the long term through the continuous achievement of productivity gains that build over time to create competitive advantage. Stock, forms of equity, or cash can deliver compensation based on year-over-year productivity increases.

The design attributes of effective base pay, incentive pay, and wealth pay programs are well documented and, of course, vary based on industry, company, and employee segment–specific variables. The main challenge in using these strategies to reward for productivity is determining the right measures, starting with a good definition of productivity that is specific to the organization.

Let's return to our original definition of productivity: how well a system uses its resources to achieve its goals. Although this is a helpful starting point, it is not sufficient for developing and implementing productivity-based rewards programs. How might an organization further define and refine its definition(s) of productivity? An in-house economist might define productivity involving an index of multiple factors that contribute to the overall valuation of the firm. An accounting executive might suggest that productivity reflects margin or profit as a function of capital and labor used to produce it. An industrial engineer might describe productivity using input and output ratios based on production processes. In summary, the major categories of productivity-oriented metrics include

- *Conversion.* Outputs relative to inputs involving capital, labor, and other resources.

- *Return on investment.* Revenue and/or profit and/or production per employee, per employee labor cost, or per compensation cost.

- *Value creation.* Growth in what the enterprise is worth relative to a baseline or expectation or growth in value relative to assets or equity.

- *Cycle and lead times.* The speed and efficiency involved in producing a product, delivering a service, completing a deliverable, or achieving an outcome.

- *Employee ratios.* Internal ratios involving employee absenteeism, turnover, spans of control, and talent or competency portfolios.

It is clear that definitions and metrics of productivity often vary not only by enterprise but also by employee segment. An organization can reward for productivity at the organization level by linking financial rewards to broad conversion, return on investment, value creation, time, and workforce metrics as just outlined, but an organization also can develop programs that link financial rewards to productivity metrics and drivers that are more specific to key employee segments. Consider the following applications:

- *Sales professionals.* Link variable pay to sales productivity reflecting inputs involved in generating sales and also to the economic value of sales achieved.

- *Healthcare professionals.* Link base pay to demonstrating competencies that drive productive activity and variable pay to the achievement of greater productivity in conversion—serving patients effectively.

- *Research and development professionals.* Link base pay to competencies that drive productive activity and variable and wealth pay to pipeline value creation.

- *Operations professionals.* Link base pay to competencies that drive productive activity and variable pay to the conversion and cycle/lead times involved in the sourcing, procuring, producing, and delivering products and services.

- *Financial and consulting professionals.* Link elements of base, variable, and wealth pay to key metrics and drivers of productivity in both the short and long term, with emphasis on conversion—serving clients effectively and value creation of the firm.

- *General managers.* Link elements of base, variable, and wealth pay to competencies that drive productive activity and results that reflect productive outcomes, such as conversion, value creation, and cycle and lead times.

- *Executives.* Link elements of base, variable, and wealth pay to key metrics and drivers of productivity in both the short and long term, with emphasis on value creation, return on investment in people, capital and assets, and overall employee ratios.

Productivity is one of the most critical drivers of the long-term success of an enterprise. Although some organizations mistakenly believe that technology is the primary tool for improving productivity, others have created a culture of productivity that involves a more optimal and balanced mix of investments that contribute to continuous productivity improvement. An often ignored or underused driver of productivity is compensation. Fixed compensation can reinforce the demonstration of key capabilities that are critical to reinforcing productivity. Variable compensation can motivate and reinforce the achievement of short-term productivity-based results. Wealth accumulating compensation can reward for long-term trends in productivity improvement.

In using financial rewards to drive productivity, it is vitally important to understand that productivity is not the same thing as performance. Productivity is more objective and is almost always defined in some way as relative to inputs and investments, whereas performance is more subjective and is often defined as relative to expectations. Achieving performance goals may or may not affect the productivity of an individual, group, or enterprise. Also, productivity should not be confused with efficiency, which typically involves a focus on quality and waste as key factors.

With this in mind, using financial rewards to unleash greater productivity requires a clear and specific definition of productivity, an understanding of the ingredients and capabilities that drive it, and a clear definition of the metrics and baselines that reinforce it. The effort to build a productive culture—supported by the financial reward system—takes time, commitment, and rigor, but the high return on investment will make it worthwhile.

# 36

# New Developments and Issues in Pay for Performance

MARK D. CANNON

*Peabody College, Vanderbilt University*

Intense competitive pressures and the need for continual improvement have increasingly led organizations to turn to financial incentives to boost employee performance. As a result, the use of various types of pay-for-performance programs and the interest in understanding how to make these programs most effective are at a record high. Pay-for-performance programs are designed to accurately measure employee performance while aligning pay such that it rises and falls in accordance with variations in performance. More corporations have adopted pay-for-performance programs now than at any other time in history, and these plans involve a greater percentage of workers than ever before. Even more dramatic has been the growth of pay-for-performance programs in new areas of application. In particular, pay-for-performance programs have expanded into healthcare and schools. However, the enthusiasm for pay for performance has not always been paralleled by the achievement of desired results from such programs (Beer and Cannon, 2004). This has led to an increasing recognition of the need to better evaluate and understand the complex dynamics of these programs in order to make them more effective.

In this chapter, we first examine the recent developments in pay for performance with a focus on the growth of programs in new areas of application. As key learning points for this chapter, first, we call attention to the surprising variability in outcomes of pay-for-performance programs. Second, we note that managers commonly make the error of being overly optimistic and insufficiently thoughtful when approaching pay for performance. Third, we identify a number of challenges that organizations must meet to maximize the benefits of these programs. Specifically, we examine and explore the challenges associated with learning from experience and identifying the best practices, design, implementation, and adoption of a strategic perspective. We also provide suggestions for meeting these challenges successfully.

# Current Trends in the Use of Pay for Performance

A 2014 survey of public companies found that 99 percent reported using some kind of pay-for-performance program (WorldatWork, 2014). This compares with only 51 percent of companies in 1991 (Kanter and MacKenzie, 2007). Not only does research show more companies using pay for performance than ever before, but it also shows that these plans are reaching a larger proportion of the employees within the companies (Lemieux, MacLeod, and Parent, 2007). This reflects a general trend away from providing across-the-board raises and toward performance-related bonuses. By focusing on bonuses, corporations hope to motivate workers, lower fixed costs, and reduce the sense of entitlement among the workforce.

In recent years, concerns about both cost and effectiveness of healthcare and public education have led to a significant shift toward adoption of a variety of pay-for-performance systems in healthcare and schools. A distinctive aspect of pay for performance in healthcare and schools is that it is being applied not only to the providers of services (i.e., healthcare workers and teachers) but also to directly influence the behavior of the patients and students that healthcare workers and teachers serve. The next sections describe some of the pay-for-performance methods that have been implemented and the preliminary results.

## Pay for Performance for Healthcare Providers

The United States spends more on healthcare per person than any other country, yet the quality and outcomes of care often fall short of where they should be given the expense (Berwick and Hackbarth, 2012). The extensive cost of healthcare and the desire for better quality have resulted in an increased use of pay for performance in the healthcare industry. Research estimates that adoption of pay-for-performance programs in the healthcare sector almost quadrupled during 2002–2007 (Robeznieks, 2007), with over half of health maintenance organizations (HMOs) adopting such programs (Rosenthal et al. 2005).

Healthcare systems can be complex and multifaceted with numerous roles and responsibilities. Thus a wide range of variables has been selected as measures of performance to provide a basis for pay for performance. For example, the United Kingdom developed 146 indicators to be used for pay-for-performance programs in family medical practices. These are grouped into broad categories of addressing specific medical conditions, the structure of practice, and the patient experience (Doran et al., 2006). As an illustration of addressing a specific medical condition, one measure is what percentage of asthma patients have had a review of their condition in the last 15 months. An indicator for cancer patients is the percentage whose condition had been reviewed within six months of diagnosis. For serious mental health patients, an indicator includes the percentage of patients reviewed within the last 15 months but also stipulates that prescriptions were checked for accuracy and that coordination arrangements with secondary care were reviewed.

Other indicators include more specific targets for patient results. For example, incentives are provided for the percentage of diabetes patients whose blood pressure is 145/85 mmHg or less. An indicator for stroke patients is whether their total serum cholesterol level was maintained at 193 mg/dl or less. In addition to indicators that address particular conditions, a number of indicators also address the structure of the practice and patient satisfaction. These are just a few of examples of a wide range of indicators that has been used in healthcare pay for performance across various healthcare settings.

Numerous studies have been conducted to assess the impact of pay for performance in healthcare (Greene and Nash, 2009). One theme that has emerged is that the outcomes have been highly variable (Van Herck et al., 2010). There are multiple examples of outcomes that could be considered successes, failures, having negligible impact, and inconclusive. In an effort to distill some useful conclusions to guide future action, a group of researchers conducted a "systematic review of systematic reviews" (Eijkenaar et al., 2013). After critical analysis of numerous studies, they determined that pay for performance has potential but that it is too soon to come to firm conclusions. One complication in drawing conclusions from these studies is the considerable variation in the quality of research designs. Often it was difficult to disentangle the impact of pay-for-performance programs from other interventions that were implemented at the same time. Although the researchers noted a number of successes, the stronger successes tended to be associated with the weaker research designs, making conclusions somewhat questionable.

A related issue and complication are that the healthcare worker behaviors that are measured and rewarded may be only indirectly associated with the primary intent of improving patient outcomes. Although pay-for-performance programs may influence the measured behaviors, there is less evidence thus far that they are successfully affecting the desired patient outcomes (Ryan and Werner, 2013).

## Pay for Performance for Healthcare Consumers

In contrast to offering financial incentives to influence the behavior of healthcare providers, many organizations are now offering financial incentives directly to customers or employees for managing their own health. In a 2013 survey by Fidelity Investments and the National Business Group on Health, 86 percent of respondents indicated that they are offering wellness-based incentives. The spending per employee has more than doubled from $260 in 2009 to $521. Such programs are offered not only by companies to their employees but also by insurance companies directly to their customers.

Healthways has made a business of helping organizations manage healthcare costs by coaching individual employees with health risks and providing them with financial incentives to mitigate their risks. Healthways monitors and regularly feeds back to employees their scores on 11 lifestyle biomarkers such as nicotine levels, blood pressure, body fat, and cholesterol, each of which is associated with chronic disease and financial strain on the healthcare system (Healthways, 2006). Employees who keep these markers within desired ranges are eligible for financial incentives such as reductions in health care premiums or contributions to health savings accounts.

Organizational wellness programs may offer a variety of incentives such as premium discounts, cash rewards, and gym memberships. Many also offer incentives for participation in general wellness programs, taking health risk assessments, on-site flu shots, and more targeted programs such as those for smoking cessation, weight loss, and diabetes management.

Increasingly, efforts are being made to measure the impact of these incentives. For example, a randomized, controlled experiment in a multinational company offered $100 for attending a smoking-cessation program, $250 for being smoke-free up to six months, and $400 for being smoke-free for an additional six months after the initial six-month cessation period (Volpp et al., 2009). In an experiment on obesity and weight loss, participants were provided with incentives of up to $252 a month depending on how much weight they lost (Loewenstein et al., 2011). In both these experiments, incentivized employees had better results than those who did not have incentives. However, the impact tended to wane over time once the incentives were removed. A 2013 Rand study analyzed incentives within wellness programs and concluded that although there was a statistically significant relationship between incentives and some target behaviors, the impact was fairly modest, at least at incentive levels of up to $200. Larger incentives may have potential to encourage higher levels of change, but larger incentives are also associated with other potential complications and controversies (Mattke et al., 2013).

## Pay for Performance for Teachers

Compared with those in other industrialized countries, students in the United States score poorly on reading and toward the bottom of standardized tests on mathematics and science. Ironically, the United States is in first place among industrialized countries in annual spending on education at over $11,000 per elementary student and over $12,000 per high school (OECD, 2013). Between 1960 and 1995, per-pupil spending in the United States increased 212 percent in real (inflation-adjusted) dollars (Bennett, 1999). This dilemma may provide fertile ground for pay-for-performance programs in the field of education.

Teacher pay in the United States is most commonly determined by years of experience and degrees held, as opposed to any parameters of quality teaching or student achievement. Under current systems, the worst teacher in a system can be paid exactly the same as the best teacher. Consequently, many have looked to financial incentives as a way to encourage better teaching and improved educational results.

A number of states have made significant investment into experimenting with pay for performance for teachers and schools. Florida, Minnesota, and Texas have allocated a combined annual funding of $550 million to provide performance incentives for high-quality educators. The federal government also has made $99 million available to states to fund pay-for-performance programs to enhance education. Chicago, for example, was the recipient of a $28 million federal grant to improve its at-risk schools. Chicago schools were authorized to receive $500,000 to $750,000 per year to provide annual performance bonuses to teachers in amounts ranging from $1,000 to $8,000.

Results thus far have been disappointing for advocates of paying teachers for performance. Studies of the large-scale experiments in Chicago, New York, and Texas failed to show a relationship between teacher pay for performance and the primary variable of interest, which was student achievement. However, some modest but positive effects were found on teacher absenteeism and retention (Podgursky and Springer, 2011). Despite the lack of promising results in these highly publicized programs, a number of researchers have argued that it is premature to conclude that pay for performance is not advisable for schools. For example, questions have been raised as to whether the incentive amounts were sufficient, whether the teachers had a clear enough understanding of the system, and how effective implementation was (Fryer, 2013). Others have argued that there may be some longer-term impacts of incentives, such as attracting stronger teachers to the profession over time (Podgursky and Springer, 2011).

## Pay for Performance for Students

As an alternative approach to enhancing educational outcomes, some policy makers have advocated providing pay for performance directly to students. Studies in Dallas, New York, and Chicago schools examined the impact of compensating students for reading books, performance on interim assessments, and student grades, respectively. Dallas schools offered an incentive of $2 per book read by second grade students. In order to qualify for the reward, students also needed to pass a short quiz to assess whether they had read the book. New York City provided incentive for performance on a battery of their regular assessments. In Chicago schools, ninth grade students were compensated every five weeks for grades in five different courses.

Results of these experiments also were disappointing for pay-for-performance advocates. In the final analysis, none of these interventions had a statistically significant impact on the targeted outcomes (Fryer, 2011). Another study in elementary schools showed no impact of incentives on reading, science, and social science test scores but did show some in math, especially for struggling students (Bettinger, 2010). However, researchers note that these are only a few of many possibilities for using pay for performance for students and that other interventions might conceivably prove more effective (Fryer, 2011).

## Realizing the Potential of Pay for Performance

Many leaders initiated pay-for-performance programs with high hopes about the benefits they might bring to healthcare and education. However, the results have been mixed and often disappointing. At this point, leaders in these areas arguably have been left with more questions than answers. Critics of pay for performance have argued against using incentives except under a narrow set of conditions (Pink, 2009).

Similarly, concerns have been raised in the popular press about incentives. In a survey of banks sponsored by the Institute of International Finance, 98 percent of banks responding agreed that incentives were a factor underlying the financial crisis (Fidler, 2009). As a notable example, Richard Fuld, who headed Lehman Brothers until its bankruptcy, was one of the top 25 highest-paid executives each year for the eight years prior to its collapse. He netted over $466 million during that eight-year period while he was overseeing the company's downfall (Carpenter, 2013). A 2013 survey of compensation and performance over the last 20 years concluded that 40 percent of the executives who had been among the top 25 most highly paid executives eventually were fired, arrested, or bailed out (Anderson, Klinger, and Pizzigati, 2013). More broadly, executive compensation has been under criticism for some time given that it is only loosely associated with organizational performance (Dalton et al., 2007).

Popular author Daniel Pink makes an impassioned critique of incentives in his 2009 book, *Drive: The Surprising Truth about What Motivates Us*, and in his 2009 TED Talk, "The Puzzle of Motivation." As of 2013, his TED Talk was one of the top 10 most watched talks. He argued that incentives as they are practiced in organizations today usually do not work and often do harm. He provided a number of illustrations from experiments with incentives. For example, in a task requiring creative problem solving, incentivized participants performed worse than those with no incentive. He called attention to an experiment sponsored by the Federal Reserve that assessed the impact of incentives on performance in a set of puzzles and games that required motor skills, concentration, or creativity (Ariely et al., 2005). Surprisingly, the most highly incentivized participants performed the worst on eight of the nine tasks.

More recently, incentives were blamed as a contributor to problems at the Veteran's Administration. In particular, it was argued that employees were pressured to falsify data in order for managers to achieve their bonuses. These actions covered up the actual delays in making medical services available to qualified veterans.

As another example, when Hewlett-Packard executives decided to discontinue an experiment with pay for performance, the employees threw a party to celebrate (Beer and

Cannon, 2004). The program had been seen as a nuisance, and maintaining the program took time away from tasks that employees perceived as more valuable. Although there is tremendous interest in pay for performance in business, healthcare, and education, it is important to note the variability in outcomes (Cascio, 2013). A broad examination of the research concluded that variable pay plans enhance performance only two-thirds of the time (Gerhart and Rynes, 2003). This figure suggests that in approximately a third of cases, the time and effort put into developing such plans either do not pay off or perhaps may even be damaging in some cases. Thus there appears to be room for improvement. One key problem is that when managers conceive of pay-for-performance programs (like other new initiatives), they are vulnerable to unreasonable optimism and thus may overestimate the likely benefits and underestimate the effort required to build and maintain an effective program. In addition, they are often not sufficiently thoughtful about what circumstances are more or less conducive to benefiting from pay-for-performance programs.

Some have argued that healthcare organizations, educational institutions, and a number of businesses are still scaling the learning curve and that results will improve as organizations learn from experience (Eijkenaar et al., 2013; Podgursky and Springer, 2011). The ability of our society to make the most constructive use of financial incentives depends on our ability to understand and meet a distinct set of challenges that create vulnerabilities for pay-for-performance programs (Nyberg, Pieper, and Trevor, 2013). Next, we identify and explore these challenges and what can be done to overcome them.

## The Challenge of Learning from Experience and Identifying Best Practices

Despite decades of interest in study on financial incentives, we lack specific, definitive conclusions about the conditions under which different kinds of financial incentives are most effective and what their impact will be. Reports on the efficacy of financial incentives are often anecdotal and lacking in scientific rigor. There is insufficient longitudinal research and not enough rigorously designed experiments (Eijkenaar et al., 2013). Current research has not done an adequate job of assessing the impact of different types of pay-for-performance programs that are used in combination with each other (Gerhart and Rynes, 2003). Researchers also have done a poor job of assessing the costs versus the benefits of pay-for-performance programs and how they compare with other types of interventions that are designed to enhance performance, such as coaching, mentoring, and other types of professional development (Beer and Cannon, 2004).

As the popularity of pay for performance grows, the need to learn from experience and identify best practices increases in importance. Meeting the challenge of learning from experience and identifying best practices means understanding and taking advantage of what we currently know from research on pay-for-performance practices. It also means tracking pay-for-performance programs as they are implemented and sustained in order to understand their impact and learn what is or is not working well so that the organization can make adjustments as needed. With more sophisticated methodological and analytic tools available than ever before, our ability to answer questions about the effectiveness of assorted pay-for-performance arrangements will be determined by whether we invest the effort to gather appropriate data.

A potentially favorable development for learning from experience and identifying best practices is the trend toward using "big data" and "evidence-based management" (McKinsey Global Institute, 2011). Organizations are becoming more oriented toward making decisions based on data and are becoming increasingly sophisticated with respect to capturing, analyzing, sharing, and using data for making decisions and monitoring results. This orientation and capability should better enable organizations to make informed decisions about where and how they could use pay for performance most effectively. The next section will address the challenges of designing effective pay-for-performance programs.

## The Challenge of Design

The challenges associated with effectively designing pay-for-performance programs can be enormous. Plans with flawed designs fail to capture the potential benefits of pay for performance and may cause damage if they inadvertently reward counterproductive behavior or produce divisive relationships when cooperation is necessary. Practitioners tend to underestimate the challenges associated with designing effective plans and the intensity of employee reaction to the need to periodically adjust plans. Common design challenges include difficulties in measuring performance, setting payouts at the correct level, managing factors outside the control of individuals being paid for performance, discomfort that managers and peers have with rating employees differentially, limited funding for payouts, resistance to adjusting payout levels as technology or market conditions change, and avoiding perceptions of unfairness (Rosenthal and Dudley, 2007). As one example of the challenge of setting payouts at the correct level, British policy makers thought that they had set physician pay-for-performance standards at the right level. However, they underestimated how quickly physicians would reach certain levels of performance, and they ended up owing physicians approximately $700 million more than they had budgeted for the program (Galvin, 2006).

Managers also need to balance how simple versus complex to make the programs. Overly simple programs appear to either lack important nuances of performance or encourage employees to focus on just one measure at the expense of others that are also important to organizational performance. By contrast, if plans are too complex, they risk becoming a source of confusion and frustration rather than a source of motivation.

Ineffective design of executive pay for performance is at the heart of much of the recent criticism. O'Bryne and Young (2006) concluded from their study of pay packages from 702 publicly traded companies that there was a clear lack of sensitivity between the measures determining executive pay and those contributing to shareholder wealth. They also noted that alternative designs that would correct this lack of sensitivity are available.

Pay at the highest managerial levels has it own unique complications that may be difficult to resolve. Fortunately, many of the other potential design problems described earlier can be managed if designers are realistic and thoughtful about the challenges associated with effective design, involve a variety of employees in the design process, and make time to pilot test and make adjustments prior to full-scale implementation.

## The Challenge of Implementation

Design is only part of the problem because the efficacy of a program also depends on the quality of implementation, and managers often underestimate the challenges associated with execution. One continuing challenge has to do with communication about how the program works and what is required to achieve rewards. One survey found that only 29 percent of respondents reported having clarity about the connection between their performance and rewards (Stiffler, 2006). Similarly, an examination of pay-for-performance initiatives in Florida schools found that fewer than half the teachers had a clear understanding of what they would need to do to achieve rewards (Jacob and Springer, 2007). In reflecting on her experience with pay for performance, one human resources executive shared her perception that employees in various companies lack a clear understanding of how their pay-for-performance compensation was determined, leading to suspicion and cynicism rather than motivation. When KeySpan Corporation (a New York gas and electricity company with about 9,700 employees) first initiated a pay-for-performance program, workers were "demoralized" by it (White, 2006). KeySpan had not taken the time to communicate and help employees understand the reasons for the program and how it was designed to work. Subsequently, KeySpan managers made the effort to explain and were able to change perceptions of the program.

Another problem that often receives insufficient attention is the match between current management skills and the skills necessary to implement a pay-for-performance program effectively (Helgason and Klareskov, 2006). Programs often require that managers rate employees and deliver critical feedback. Often employees are also asked to rate each other and sometimes to provide feedback. Managers and employees are often uncomfortable with the interpersonal tensions associated with the roles of evaluator and feedback giver and lack the skills necessary to carry out these roles effectively (Cannon and Witherspoon, 2005). Organizations often fail to assess what new skills will be needed and to provide appropriate training prior to implementing pay-for-performance programs. This was another reason that KeySpan employees were demoralized by the company's new pay-for-performance program. Supervisors were suddenly required to give critical feedback and manage performance in ways previously not expected, and many were unprepared to do so. Thus there was a rough implementation, and KeySpan had to take corrective action after the fact (White, 2006).

## The Challenge of Adopting a Strategic Perspective

The drive to use pay for performance comes from a simple desire to motivate more constructive behavior. However, compensation is a complex and multifaceted phenomenon that can affect organizational effectiveness in a variety of ways. Leaders need to be clear on the organization's purpose, strategy, and core competencies and consider how these might be affected by different types of compensation programs. Pay-for-performance programs should be designed to be consistent with and supportive of the organization's purpose, strategy, and core competencies. What might be good for one individual, group, or department might not be fitting for the organization as a whole.

Managers should consider the fit of pay-for-performance initiatives with their organization's culture and preferred management tools. Baron (2004) observed that organizations tend to either cluster around "harder" management tools (i.e., "incentive systems, standardized processes, and use of metrics") or "softer" management tools (i.e., "enculturation, personal networks, and corporate strategy statements"). Introducing harder management tools into a culture that is dominated by the use of softer tools may prove to be a poor fit and produce undesirable results (Baron, 2004).

The issue of fit may have particular relevance to the areas of healthcare and education and potentially to public-sector organizations and nonprofits (Ryan and Werner, 2013). More specifically, many employees in these areas are committed to the work because they are intrinsically motivated to make a meaningful contribution to the lives and development of others and to society. A historical critique of pay for performance relates its potential to decrease intrinsic motivation (Deci, Koestner, and Ryan, 1999). As one empirical example, research assessed the impact of providing incentives for donating blood and found that some participants were significantly less inclined to give blood when doing so was associated with a financial incentive than when there was no financial incentive at all (Mellström and Johannesson, 2008). Depending on the organizational context, some have argued that alternative interventions designed to enable workers to do their jobs more effectively might be as good as or better than incentives. For example, after reviewing a variety of incentive programs in healthcare, some researchers have questioned whether developing better feedback systems alone might be as valuable to performance improvement as the incentives (Eijkenaar et al., 2013).

In addition to considering the impact of pay for performance on motivation, managers are also advised to consider the impact on longer-term selection effects. Compensation systems influence not only motivation but also the types of prospective employees who are attracted to an organization and the types of employees who are likely to stay versus leave employment in a particular organization (Gerhart, Rynes, and Fulmer, 2009). This also should be a factor in determining the appropriate compensation system for an organization.

## Rocky Flats Illustration

When the challenges just listed are managed effectively, organizations can use financial incentives to achieve incredible feats. Consider the impressive results achieved at Rocky Flats (one of the nation's toughest nuclear cleanup sites). Initial estimates were that it would take 70 years and $36 billion to clean the site (McGregor, 2004). However, Kaiser-Hill set a goal for cleaning of roughly 10 years and less than $7 billion. In addition to the aggressive time frame, the leaders faced an additional challenge: the workers would be working themselves out of their jobs, so they would have a natural incentive to work slowly in order to prolong their employment. Thus leaders at Kaiser-Hill had to determine how to motivate workers to accelerate the pace at which they would work themselves out of their jobs. Despite the aggressive goal and significant labor obstacles, Kaiser-Hill completed the project within the self-set deadline and at a cost of just over $6 billion (Cameron and Lavine, 2006).

How did Kaiser-Hill achieve this feat? Leaders at the company adopted a visionary, strategic perspective that relied heavily on financial incentives while also integrating a number of other changes that all were designed to work in concert with each other. This included interventions designed to change the culture and build a supportive, collaborative working environment with the appropriate balance of structure and freedom. Thus the company encouraged initiative and innovation. Leaders also applied a number of organizational best practices and were continually adaptive to challenges that unfolded as they journeyed through their task [see Cameron and Lavine (2006) for a detailed account]. The incentives themselves were thoughtfully designed to reward the key strategic outcomes necessary for success—speed, quality, safety, and innovation. In total, $90 million was offered in bonuses. And while this may seem like an extremely large bonus pool, one senior executive commented that the incentives more than paid for themselves through their immense impact on worker productivity (Cameron and Lavine, 2006). According to this executive, Kaiser-Hill's eventual profit was far higher than it would have been without the incentives, despite the considerable expense.

In conclusion, the use of pay-for-performance programs has grown tremendously both within the traditional arena of the corporation and in new areas of application such as healthcare and schools. In considering whether to implement a pay-for-performance program, managers often have made the error of being overly optimistic and insufficiently thoughtful in their approach. Pay-for-performance programs will be most effective when they successfully address the challenges associated with learning from experience and identifying the best practices, design, implementation, and adopting a strategic perspective. Kaiser-Hill provides an example of the results that are possible when an organization effectively manages each of these challenges.

## References

Anderson, S., S. Klinger, and S. Pizzigati. 2013. "Executive Excess 2013: Bailed Out, Booted, and Busted." IPS. Available at: www.ips-dc.org/reports/executive-excess-2013 (accessed June 19, 2014).

Ariely, D., U. Gneezy, G. Loewenstein, and N. Mazar. 2005. "Large Stakes and Big Mistakes," Working Paper No. 05-11, Federal Reserve Bank of Boston. Available at: http://ideas.repec.org/p/fip/fedbwp/05-11.html.

Baron, I. N. 2004. "Commentary on 'Promise and Peril in Implementing Pay-for-Performance.'" *Human Resource Management* 43(1).

Beer, M., and M. D. Cannon. 2004. "Promise and Peril in Implementing Pay-for-Performance." *Human Resource Management* 43(1):3–48.

Bennett, W. J. 1999. "OECD Calls for Broader Access to Post-School Education and Training." *School Reform News*. Heartland Institute, Chicago.

Berwick, D. M., and A. D. Hackbarth. 2012. "Eliminating Waste in US Health Care." *Journal of the American Medical Association* 307(14):1513–1516.

Bettinger, E. P. 2010. "Paying to Learn: The Effect of Financial Incentives on Elementary School Test Scores," Working Paper No. 16333. National Bureau of Economic Research, Cambridge, MA. Available at: www.nber.org/papers/w16333.

Cameron, K. S., and M. Lavine. 2006. *Making the Impossible Possible: Leading Extraordinary Performance—The Rocky Flats Story*. Berrett-Koehler, San Francisco.

Cannon, M. D., and R. Witherspoon. 2005. "Actionable Feedback: Unlocking the Power of Learning and Development." *Academy of Management Executive* 19:120–134.

Carpenter, Z. 2013. "Paying CEOs Top Dollar for Poor Performance." *The Nation*. Available at: www.thenation.com/blog/175950/paying-ceos-top-dollar-poor-performance.

Cascio, W. F. 2013. *Managing Human Resources: Productivity, Quality of Work Life, Profits*, 9th ed. McGraw-Hill/Irwin, New York.

Dalton, D. R., M. A. Hitt, S. T. Certo, and C. M. Dalton. 2007. "The Fundamental Agency Problem and Its Mitigation: Independence, Equity, and the Market for Corporate Control." *Academy of Management Annals* 1:1–64.

Deci, E. L., R. Koestner, and R. M. Ryan. 1999. "A Meta-Analytic Review of Experiments Examining the Effects of Extrinsic Rewards on Intrinsic Motivation." *Psychological Bulletin* 125(6):627–668; discussion 692–700.

Doran, T., C. Fullwood, H. Gravelle, D. Reeves, E. Kontopantelis, U. Hiroeh, and M. Roland. 2006. "Pay-for-Performance Programs in Family Practices in the United Kingdom." *New England Journal of Medicine* 355(4):375–384.

Dudley, R. A. 2005. "Pay-for-Performance Research." *Journal of the American Medical Association* 294(14):1821–1823.

Eijkenaar, F., M. Emmert, M. Scheppach, and O. Schöffski. 2013. "Effects of Pay for Performance in Health Care: A Systematic Review of Systematic Reviews." *Health Policy (Amsterdam)* 110(2–3):115–130.

Epstein, A. M. 2006. "Paying for Performance in the United States and Abroad." *New England Journal of Medicine* 355(4):406–408.

Fidelity. 2013. "New Health Care Survey Finds Spending on Wellness Incentives Has Doubled in the Last Four Years." New York. Available at: www.fidelity.com/inside-fidelity/employer-services/fidelity-nbgh-wellness-survey.

Fidler, S. 2009. "Survey Finds Banks Aware of Pay Flaws." *Wall Street Journal.* Available at: http://online.wsj.com/news/article_email/SB123837870249668339-lMyQjAxMTI0MzE4NTMxNzU4Wj (accessed May 15, 2014).

Fryer, R. 2013. "Teacher Incentives and Student Achievement: Evidence from New York City Public Schools." *Journal of Labor Economics* 31(2):373–427.

Fryer, Jr., R. G. 2011. "Financial Incentives and Student Achievement: Evidence from Randomized Trials," Working Paper No. 15898. National Bureau of Economic Research, Cambridge, MA. Available at: www.nber.org/papers/w15898.

Galvin, R. 2006. "Pay-for-Performance: Too Much of a Good Thing? A Conversation with Martin Roland." *Health Affairs* 25(5):w412–w419.

Gerhart, B. A., and S. Rynes. 2003. *Compensation: Theory, Evidence, and Strategic Implications.* Sage, Thousand Oaks, CA.

Gerhart, B., S. L. Rynes, and I. S. Fulmer. 2009. "Pay and Performance: Individuals, Groups, and Executives." *Academy of Management Annals* 3(1):251–315.

Greene, S. E., and D. B. Nash. 2009. "Pay for Performance: An Overview of the Literature." *American Journal of Medical Quality* 24(2):140–163.

Healthways Center for Health Research. 2006. "Measuring the Success of the Healthways myhealthIQ Program." Nashville, TN.

Helgason, K. S., and V. Klareskov. 2005. "When the Halo Wears Off." *Public Manager* 34(4):42.

Jacob, B., and M. G. Springer. 2007. "Teacher Attitudes on Pay for Performance: A Pilot Study." National Center on Performance Incentives, Nashville, TN.

John, L. K., G. Loewenstein, A. B. Troxel, L. Norton, J. E. Fassbender, and K. G. Volpp. 2011. "Financial Incentives for Extended Weight Loss: A Randomized, Controlled Trial." *Journal of General Internal Medicine* 26(6):621–626.

Kanter, M., and M. MacKenzie. 2007. "Hewitt Study: While Salary Increases in 2008 Remain Modest, Variable Pay Awards Reach Record High." London.

Lemieux, T., D. Parent, and W. B. MacLeod. 2007. "Performance Pay and Wage Inequality," Working Paper No. 13128, National Bureau of Economic Research, Cambridge, MA.

Loewenstein, G. et al. 2011. "Financial Incentives for Extended Weight Loss: A Randomized Control Trial," *J. Intern. Med.* June 2011 26(6): 621–626.

Mattke, S., H. Liu, J. Caloyeras, C. Y. Huang, K. R. Van Busum, D. Khodyakov, and V. Shier. 2013. "Workplace Wellness Programs Study: Product Page." RAND Corporation, Santa Monica, CA. Available at: www.rand.org/pubs/research_reports/RR254.html (accessed June 23, 2014).

McGregor, J. 2004. "Rocky Mountain High." *Business Source Premier* 84.

McKinsey Global Institute. 2011. "Big Data: The Next Frontier for Innovation, Competition, and Productivity." Lexington, KY.

Mellström, C., and M. Johannesson. 2008. "Crowding Out in Blood Donation: Was Titmuss Right?" *Journal of the European Economic Association* 6(4):845–863.

Nyberg, A. J., J. R. Pieper, and C. O. Trevor. 2013. "Pay-for-Performance's Effect on Future Employee Performance Integrating Psychological and Economic Principles toward a Contingency Perspective." *Journal of Management.*

O'Byrne, S. F., and S. D. Young. 2006. "Why Executive Pay Is Falling." *Harvard Business Review* 84(6):28–28.

Organization for Economic Cooperation and Development (OECD). 2013. "Education at a Glance 2013: OECD Indicators." Paris. Available at: www.oecd.org/edu/eag2013 percent20 percent 28eng percent29—FINAL percent2020 percent20June percent202013.pdf.

Pink, D. H. 2009. *Drive: The Surprising Truth about What Motivates Us*. Riverhead Books, New York.

Podgursky, M. J., and M. G. Springer. 2007. "Teacher Performance Pay: A Review." *Journal of Policy Analysis and Management* 26(4):909–950.

Podgursky, M. J., and M. G. Springer. 2011. "Teacher Compensation Systems in the United States K–12 Public School System." *National Tax Journal* 64(1):165–192.

PricewaterhouseCoopers' Health Research Institute. 2007. "Keeping Score: A Comparison of Pay-for-Performance Programs among Commercial Insurers." New York.

Robeznieks, A. 2007. "P4P Programs Quadruple." *Modern Healthcare* 37(35):10.

Rosenthal, M. B., and R. A. Dudley. 2007. "Pay-for-Performance: Will the Latest Payment Trend Improve Care?" *Journal of American Medical Association* 292(7):740–744.

Rosenthal, M. B., R. G. Frank et al. 2005. "Early Experience with Pay-for-Performance." *Journal of the American Medical Association* 294(14):1788–1793.

Ryan, A. M., and R. M. Werner. 2013. "Doubts About Pay-for-Performance in Health Care." *Harvard Business Review*, October 13. Available at: http://blogs.hbr.org/2013/10/doubts-about-pay-for-performance-in-health-care/ (accessed May 16, 2014).

Stiffler, M. A. 2006. "Incentive Compensation Management: Making Pay-for-Performance a Reality." *Performance Improvement* 45(1):25–30.

Van Herck, P., D. De Smedt, L. Annemans, R. Remmen, M. B. Rosenthal, and W. Sermeus. 2010. "Systematic Review: Effects, Design Choices, and Context of Pay-for-Performance in Health Care." WHO, Brussels. Available at: www.who.int/workforcealliance/knowledge/resources/pay_for_performance/en/ (accessed May 16, 2014).

Volpp, K. G., A. B. Troxel, M. V. Pauly, H. A. Glick, A. Puig, D. A. Asch, and J. Audrain-McGovern. 2009. "A Randomized, Controlled Trial of Financial Incentives for Smoking Cessation." *New England Journal of Medicine* 360(7):699–709.

White, E. 2006. "Theory and Practice: Employers Increasingly Favor Bonuses to Raises; Companies Aim to Motivate Workers, Lower Fixed Costs; Losing 'Entitlement' Notion." *Wall Street Journal*, B.3.

WorldatWork and Deloitte Consulting, LLP. 2014. "Incentive Pay Practices Survey: Publicly Traded Companies (Survey)." Scottsdale, AZ. Available at: www.worldatwork.org/waw/adimLink?id=74763.

# 37

# Making Calibration an Integral Part of a Performance-Appraisal System

Dick Grote

*Grote Consulting Corporation*

In most organizations, the performance-appraisal rating is a major factor in determining the amount of an individual's salary increase. Appraisal ratings must be accurate. But are they?

We all remember from our school days that some teachers were hard graders and others were easier. So how do we eliminate this "tough grader/easy grader" phenomenon in the workplace and make sure that all appraisal ratings really are accurate? How do we make sure that regardless of the supervisor rating, a 3 is a 3 is a 3?

## The Problem

Performance appraisal affects almost everyone who works for an organization. There is probably no business practice that is more universally used than the annual performance evaluation. And there is probably no business practice that generates more discomfort.

A great part of this discomfort results from the belief that a manager's evaluation of the performance of a subordinate, and specifically the appraisal rating, may not be correct. People in organizations take for granted that it is appropriate to measure and evaluate the quality of the goods and services they produce, as well as the goods and services they receive. But their anxiety increases dramatically when they are asked to evaluate the quality of the employees in the organization and to reduce that assessment of the individual's performance to a number on a five-level rating scale. Complaints of unfairness abound. Both assessors and those assessed are uncomfortable.

From our school days, we learned that we had to work far harder to get a B from Professor Smith than we did to get an A from Professor Jones. And while we may accept the easy grader/hard grader phenomenon as an inescapable fact of life in school, we are extremely uncomfortable when the same phenomenon shows up in our company's performance-appraisal system and our annual rating.

This discomfort about inaccurate performance assessments is understandable. Ratings affect all areas of organizational life. A high rating generates a bigger pay increase. It increases the chance that we will be the one picked for a plum assignment. With a high rating, we will be more likely to be assigned to a fast-track development program and to be the one chosen for an advantageous promotion.

And a low rating—even if undeserved—likely will result in fewer career opportunities and smaller raises. We will face a greater probability of being passed over when promotional opportunities arise and sadly finding our name heading the list when a reduction in force is necessary.

It is vital that performance appraisals accurately reflect the quality of an individual's performance. So what do we do to ensure that the judgments of managers, reflected in the performance-appraisal ratings they assign their subordinates, are accurate? How can a company eliminate the tough grader/easy grader problem and address the fact that its managers are applying similar standards when the time for formal evaluation rolls around? How can line and human resources executives be sure that a rating of 3 in accounting represents the same quality of performance as a rating of 3 in marketing, manufacturing, or sales?

## The Solution: Calibration

About 10 years ago, a small number of companies starting using a process for ensuring accuracy and consistency in performance appraisal. They called the new procedure *calibration*, *leveling*, *rater reliability*, or some other term. But whatever the name, the process was essentially the same.

The growth of these calibration systems in large organizations is remarkable—from just a handful of companies 10 years ago to most of the Fortune 500 (and their international equivalents) today. However, although calibration now has become an accepted and standard practice in almost every organization, line managers and human resources professionals are nervous about it. The procedure seems almost *too* simple—put a bunch of supervisors together in a room, have them review the performance-appraisal ratings they are planning to give each of their subordinates, adjust up or down any that are inappropriate, and go on with business as usual. But there are an enormous number of practical, operational, and emotional questions that must be resolved for this deceptively simple system to work right.

A new step was added to the conventional appraisal cycle of setting goals at the start of the year, providing ongoing coaching and feedback throughout the year, and writing performance appraisals and discussing them with employees at the end of the year. This new step involves scheduling a meeting with a group of managers, all of whom supervise employees in reasonably comparable jobs. The meeting is held after the managers have written their performance appraisals but before they discuss those appraisals with their subordinates and the appraisals become official.

These calibration meetings typically begin with the managers posting the names of each of their subordinates on the wall, along with the appraisal rating they are planning to give that employee. When all names are posted and everyone has looked over the planned appraisal ratings, the calibration discussion begins.

"You're proposing to rate Sam a 5," one manager might say to another. "I know Sam. He's a nice guy. I've worked with him on a couple of projects. But I sure don't see him as a 5. How did you come up with that rating?"

Sam's manager responds. She explains the standards she used to determine her rating. She provides specific examples to support why Sam's performance is worthy of a 5 and to justify her planned appraisal rating. Other managers chime in, either giving additional examples to further support Sam's top-of-the-scale rating or questioning whether the top rating is really appropriate based on the quality of Sam's work that they have observed themselves over the course of the year.

During the meeting, the planned rating of every employee under review is discussed. Every rating is either confirmed or revised. Some ratings go up when managers—the tough graders—discover that they have set the performance bar far higher than their colleagues have. Other managers lower their planned rating of an individual when the feedback from their peer managers gives them information about a subordinate's performance that they were unaware of. The meeting closes when everyone agrees that they have applied uniform standards and that the performance-appraisal rating for everyone whose performance has been reviewed during the meeting is correct. Calibration works. It drives the truth into performance management.

## Making Calibration Work for You and Your Company

Although the concept of calibration is simplicity itself, execution of the process can be daunting. Hundreds of questions arise. Exactly how should a calibration meeting be conducted? What should participants in a calibration session be told about what they are expected to do? What do employees need to be told—if anything—about why people outside their chain of command are discussing their performance appraisals? How should the room be set up? What should the facilitator do when a recalcitrant manager insists that all his or her people are stars and worthy of the 5 ratings he or she gave each of them and will not budge when others object?

This chapter will answer these questions. First, I'll provide my recommendations about the procedures for implementing and conducting calibration sessions that have worked in dozens of companies. I will tell you step by step exactly how to run an effective session. Then I will provide a set of guidelines for the session facilitator. Next, I will go over the "ground rules" that make a session effective. Make a copy of these ground rules and hand them out to participants in advance of each session. Finally, I will provide a list of the factors that should be considered—as well as those that should *not* be considered—in making calibration decisions. I will assume that you are using a five-point rating scale, by far the most common rating scale used in performance-appraisal processes. If you are using a different scale, it is easy to make the appropriate adjustments.

## Calibration Sessions: Recommended Procedures

The best way to structure calibration sessions is to use a sticky-note and flipchart paper approach. Software programs can be used, but even high-tech firms find that the low-tech approach is better. If an individual's name and rating are going to be moved from one rating category to another, there is far more emotional and human impact in having the manager stand up, walk to the flipchart labeled 3, take Jane's sticky-note off that chart, and put it on the one labeled 2 than there is in just clicking a mouse to indicate the change. In this section, I'll assume that you are using the low-tech approach.

## Prework

All participants in the performance-calibration meetings need to come to the meeting having made a preliminary decision about the most appropriate performance-appraisal rating for each of their direct reports. Participants also should have all available data that support the recommended rating. Participants should come prepared to discuss the reasons for the recommendation, including specific examples to support either particularly high or particularly low ratings.

In setting up calibration pools (the employees to be reviewed in a calibration session), their managers in the performance-calibration sessions should have a reasonable familiarity with both the jobs being assessed and the employees holding these positions. Those participants who are not familiar with a specific individual being reviewed nevertheless must remain engaged with the process, paying particular attention to whether the rationale proposed by the person's supervisor justifies the rating recommended.

In addition, participants in calibration sessions who are not familiar with all the individuals under review should use the discussions in the calibration session as a means for gaining a richer understanding of the depth and location of the organization's talent pool.

All discussions that take place during performance-calibration meetings are confidential. Disclosing any comments made by oneself or by others about individuals whose performance is reviewed in a performance-calibration session is a serious breach of ethical behavior.

## Time Frame

About a half day should be provided per session, assuming that there are four to six raters per session and that each rater has four to six subordinates to be reviewed. If the number is smaller, the sessions will be shorter. If the number is much larger, consider dividing a session into two separate sessions. However, the actual time for each session may vary significantly depending on the depth and intensity of the discussions. About 5 to 10 minutes should be allowed for the discussion of each individual under review.

## Room Setup

The sessions should be conducted in a conference room that comfortably seats the number of participants and the facilitator and is sufficiently large to allow people to get up and move around easily. There should be a wall with enough blank space for several flipchart pages to be taped on it. A supply of 4 × 6 sticky-notes and the usual conference room supplies (i.e., water, markers, pens, pads, etc.) should be provided.

Five blank flipchart pages should be attached to the wall. At the top of each page, one of the five performance-appraisal ratings should be written (e.g., unsatisfactory, needs improvement, fully successful, superior, and distinguished) starting with the lowest rating at the left and moving up to the right. And, if you are using the calibration session, to ensure that your company's distribution guidelines are being met, write the distribution at the top of each chart.

At the end of the performance-calibration session, the following outcomes are expected:

1. The performance of each individual under assessment will have been thoroughly reviewed and discussed with inputs from all session participants who are familiar with the individual's performance.

2. The performance-appraisal rating assigned by the individual's manager will have been reviewed, discussed, and either confirmed or revised to a higher or lower rating.

3. The overall distribution of ratings of all individuals under consideration in the meeting will follow the company's guidelines.

## Ground Rules

All session participants must observe the following ground rules:

1. When an individual is under review, participants in the session who are directly knowledgeable of that employee's performance will actively participate in the discussion, providing examples to confirm or question the performance-appraisal rating recommended by the individual's manager.

2. When an individual is under review, participants in the session who are not directly knowledgeable of that employee's performance will remain engaged in the discussion, listening and asking questions to ensure that similar standards of performance are being applied by different managers.

3. In determining the appropriateness of the specific performance-appraisal rating to be assigned, participants will restrict themselves to discussing only the quality of the individual's performance during the appraisal period against the key job responsibilities, competencies, goals, and other performance-appraisal elements. Other issues, such as long-term potential, unique skills, previous successes or failures, job criticality, and other factors that are not directly related to the specific quality of performance, will not be considered.

4. When appropriate, participants will discuss their perceptions of the individual's unique strengths, needs for improvement, and suggestions for development. These factors, however, will not be considered in determining the appropriate performance-appraisal rating.

5. Confidentiality will be maintained by all participants. No disclosure of any comments made by oneself or others about individuals whose performance is reviewed in a performance-calibration session is permitted.

## Calibration Session Step by Step

1. The session facilitator will ask for and answer any questions about the organization's performance-management practices, compensation policies, and other issues.

2. The facilitator then asks participants to write the name of each of their direct reports on a 4 × 6 sticky-note, along with the performance rating recommended.

3. As a group, participants/raters post their notes on a wall or piece of flipchart paper. It is common for raters to put some of their sticky-notes toward the far left or right side of the flipchart paper to indicate that the individual is "almost a 4" or "just barely a 3." There is nothing wrong with their doing this, and in fact, doing so may help to identify people whose ratings need to be adjusted to meet the distribution requirements. It is also useful to ask each rater to use a different colored marker to write the names and recommended ratings on the sticky-notes so that there is easy visual identification of which rater provided which ratings.

4. Participants look over all the posted information. One by one, each of the managers describes to the group how he or she went about making the assessments, the criteria that were used, and any special circumstances taken into account. It is useful to begin the process by discussing the people whose ratings (high and low) are at the extremes. This will provide a benchmark for what a "distinguished" or an "unsatisfactory" performer looks like so that others under review can be appropriately compared.

5. Participants are asked to discuss with each other their reactions to the posted ratings. They should look for any ratings that surprised them or ones that, based on their necessarily limited knowledge of the individuals working for other raters, they feel might be either positively or negatively skewed. Raters who do not have a sufficient familiarity with the individual under consideration to engage in the discussion should nevertheless listen to the discussion to make sure that the organization's policies and expectations are being appropriately applied. If there are any cases where the facilitator feels a rating might be inappropriate based on the content of the appraiser's presentation, the facilitator should raise this concern with the rater and the group.

6. Discussions continue until there is agreement among the participants that the ratings assigned to each individual under review are appropriate and that the targeted distribution of performance appraisal ratings has been achieved.

7. Managers are then asked whether they anticipate any surprises (positive or negative) or pushback when they announce the ratings to their direct reports. The facilitator and other participants then coach them on how to deal with these issues.

8. The facilitator reviews the steps that the managers are to take after the meeting. (These steps include rewriting and revising the performance appraisal for each direct report to take into account the information and decisions resulting from the calibration meeting, reviewing the appraisal with the manager's immediate supervisor for approval, and discussing the appraisal with the individual.)

## Calibration: Guidelines for the Session Facilitator

### Before the Meeting

1. Make sure that you have all the supplies required (i.e., flipchart pages, masking tape, markers, sticky-notes, handouts, and participant name tents).

2. Make sure that the room arrangement allows people to talk face to face.

3. Post the flipchart pages on the wall, and write the performance-appraisal ratings on the top of each page.

4. [*If your company uses distribution guidelines*] On each flipchart page, just below the names and the performance-appraisal ratings, write the targeted distribution percentage for that rating. For example:

1. Unsatisfactory          Maximum of $X$ percent

2. Needs improvement       Maximum of $X$ percent

3. Fully successful        $X$ percent

4. Superior                Minimum of $X$ percent

5. Distinguished           Minimum of $X$ percent

5. Make sure that you have the list of managers and supervisors who are scheduled to attend the meeting and the list of individuals who are to be reviewed.

6. Calculate the number of people who must be designated for each rating category by applying the percentages to the total number of people being reviewed.

7. Make up and post a flipchart labeled "Parking Lot" in case any issues arise that need to be deferred for later discussion.

8. Make sure that the room allows privacy and that no one walking by will be able to see anyone in the room or anything on display.

9. Make sure that you have the calibration factors and ground rules documents for distribution to the group during the kickoff.

### Kickoff

1. Welcome the group.

2. Explain the basic purpose of the performance-calibration meeting.

   - To make sure that similar standards are being applied by all managers in creating performance appraisals so that employees are evaluated equitably throughout the company.

   - To make sure that all performance-appraisal ratings are accurate and consistent.

   - To make sure that the company's performance-distribution guidelines for appraisal ratings are adhered to.

3. Explain the time frame for the meeting. It probably will run about two to three hours unless the group under review is particularly small (<12 people) or large (>12 people).

4. Hand out the ground rules documents included later in this chapter and point out those that you feel are particularly worthy of note, such as participation, engagement, oversight, and openness. Briefly cover these other key points:

   - Stress that in determining the appropriateness of the specific performance-appraisal rating an individual will be assigned, participants will restrict themselves to discussing only the quality of the individual's performance during the performance period as reflected in the performance assessment and ratings provided by that person's leader. Other issues, such as long-term potential, unique skills, previous successes or failures, job criticality, length of service, EEO status/diversity, and other factors that are not directly related to the specific quality of performance, will not be considered.

- When appropriate, participants may discuss their perceptions of the individual's unique strengths, needs for improvement, and suggestions for development. These factors, however, will not be considered in determining the appropriate appraisal rating.

- Confidentiality must be maintained by all participants. No disclosure of any comments made by oneself or others about individuals whose performance is reviewed in a performance-calibration session is permitted.

5. Explain that your role is specifically to facilitate the meeting and not to be a provider of information or opinion about individuals under review. Tell the group that you will encourage discussion, ask for examples, and challenge the group or specific participants when it appears that unproductive behaviors are showing up.

- Leaders arguing inappropriately hard for the upgrading of a favored subordinate's tier placement.

- Participants disengaging themselves from the process by checking e-mail, etc.

- Leaders with higher overall performance assessment ratings ("easy graders") excessively resisting adjusting their people downward to a lower tier.

### Session Process

1. Tell the group that they have two tasks to accomplish in this meeting:

- First, they will discuss and come to agreement on what the appropriate performance-appraisal rating for each person under review should be.

- Second, they will make sure that the distribution of performance-appraisal ratings conforms with the company's guidelines.

2. Explain that the flipcharts have the names of the five different performance-appraisal rating labels and the distribution requirements for each rating level.

3. Tell the group the total number of people who will be reviewed in this session. (Confirm with the group that the number is accurate.)

4. Write the actual number of individuals who must end up in each category on the flipchart next to the percentage figure based on the total number of individuals under review and the percentages for each category. (In the event that the number of people for a given category is other than a whole number, it is best to round up to the next whole number for the two higher performance levels and to round down to the next whole number for the two lower performance levels.)

5. Point out to the group that at the end of the session there must be a specific number of names on the "Unsatisfactory" flipchart, a specific number of names on the "Needs improvement" flipchart, and so on. (*Note:* This is commonly a point at

which resistance to the process arises. Expect to get some complaints and excuses from the group.)

6. Tell the group that it will first work on ensuring that the performance-appraisal ratings recommended by the individuals' immediate supervisors are accurate and will then confirm that the number of people in each performance-rating category meets the performance-distribution guideline. However, encourage group members to work toward achieving the distribution requirement as they are assigning their ratings.

## Ensuring Rating Accuracy

1. Give each person a different colored marker and a pad of large sticky-notes. Explain that this will make it easy to identify each manager's subordinates once the names and ratings are posted on the flipcharts. (*Note:* Using a different colored marker for each supervisor also will make it easy for you and the group as a whole to immediately identify any supervisor whose performance-appraisal ratings are significantly skewed in a positive or negative direction.)

2. Ask all the participants to write down on sticky-notes the names of each person they manage and that person's proposed performance-appraisal rating. When everyone has finished writing, tell them to put their sticky-notes on the appropriate flipcharts to indicate the performance-appraisal rating they feel is appropriate. (*Note:* There is a double-check mechanism here. The performance-appraisal rating is written on the sticky-note, and the sticky-note is then put on the appropriate flipchart for that rating. Check to make sure that all the rating categories on the flipcharts correspond with the rating categories written on the sticky-notes. Also check to make sure that the participants in the session are using the correct rating labels for each level of performance.)

3. Tell group members that they can put their sticky-notes either in the middle of the appropriate flipchart or close to the edge of the chart if the person's performance is either just barely into the rating area or just short of the next-higher rating.

4. Explain the procedures they will follow:

   - Once all the names have been posted, the group will start by looking over all the names and proposed ratings.

   - Each participant will explain the rationale for the proposed rating to the other participants. The role of the other participants is to ask questions and provide additional information and insights in order to make sure that everyone is applying similar standards in making performance-appraisal judgments.

   - In both explaining their rating recommendation and providing information or asking questions about the ratings proposed by other supervisors, managers must limit themselves specifically to the performance of the individual against his or her key job responsibilities, competencies, goals, and other elements assessed on the performance appraisal.

5. Tell the group that the most effective way of discussing ratings is to offer and ask for actual examples of performance that are illustrative of particularly effective or ineffective performance in one of the results/goals or behaviors/competencies areas.

6. As soon as the group has completed posting all the sticky-notes and looking over the results, point out to the group the variance (if there is any) between the number of names that are currently in each of the rating categories and the number that need to be in each one in order to meet the performance-distribution curve. (*Note:* This is another point in the process where objections are likely to arise.)

7. Tell the group that the most effective way to accomplish the task is to begin with the people at the extremes (outliers) and move toward those in the center.

8. Ask the manager of the individual with the highest rating (one of the ones in the "Distinguished" category) to begin by explaining how he or she came up with that rating.

9. Invite the rest of the participants to help confirm or question the appropriateness of the rating.

10. Once the appropriate ratings for the individuals in the "Distinguished" category have been tentatively established, move to the bottom end of the ratings. Conduct the discussions for those individuals in the "Unsatisfactory" and "Needs improvement" categories.

11. Continue the discussions until every person under review has been discussed and assigned what appear to be the most appropriate rating.

### Tips for Success

- During this process, it is likely (and healthy) that there will be a good deal of movement of sticky-notes as participants reconsider the most appropriate ratings. Encourage this. Explain that nothing is final until it is final—that participants can always move a lowered rating back up again.

- Encourage the participants to move the sticky-notes themselves. Do not do it for them. This helps to ensure that each manager is accountable for the accuracy of his or her postings.

- Encourage participants not only to identify any person who should move to a different performance-appraisal rating but also to identify the individual who should be moved out of that rating and assigned a higher or lower rating in order to meet the distribution requirements. It is likely, however, that participants will have strong feelings (and a stronger base of knowledge) about their own people whom they want to move to a higher rating and care much less about who has to move out of that rating to make way for them.

- As participants in the calibration session gain additional data from the discussions about their employees and insights into their own toughness or leniency in assessing performance, it may be appropriate for them to change their overall ratings for several employees to bring their standards for appraisal ratings into line with those of the rest of the group.

- Participants in a calibration session are likely to lose sight of the concept of *relative performance* ("Joe is better than Tom or Mary") and instead argue for the reassignment of an individual to a higher performance rating based only on the individual's *absolute performance* ("Joe does a really terrific job"). Most facilitators find that they are frequently reminding participants that the purpose of the calibration session is to explore the individual's performance not only in absolute terms but also in relative terms. Encourage use of the additional performance differentiators to help make appropriate decisions about relative performance.

### *Meeting the Performance-Distribution Guidelines (If Applicable)*

1. Once all the ratings of the employees under review have been discussed and everyone has been assigned a final rating, point out any discrepancies between the number of people assigned to each rating category and the number required by the distribution requirement.

2. If there is no variance between the required and the actual distribution of ratings, congratulate the group and remind group members of the ground rule of confidentiality.

3. If there is a variance, point out to the group the changes that are needed to meet the required distribution of appraisal ratings. Unless there is an immediate suggestion on changes to be made to meet the target, ask the group what needs to be done to reach the target.

4. Continue to explain to the group that the targeted distribution must be met. (*Note:* If you encounter severe resistance to meeting the company's distribution curve, explain that although the group will be allowed to report a distribution of ratings that is at variance with the company performance-distribution requirement, the fact that it chose not to meet the distribution curve will be reported to the head of the business unit. As the facilitator, it is inappropriate for you to be required to force the group to meet the curve.)

5. As changes are suggested to meet the targeted distribution, test to make sure that the changes recommended are genuinely based on performance and not on either a persuasive manager's ability to inappropriately sway the group or a weak manager's willingness to move someone to a lower rating just to get the meeting over.

6. When the distribution has been met, congratulate the group and close the meeting.

### *Closing the Meeting*

1. Remind the group of the ground rule regarding confidentiality.

2. Ask group members if there are any performance-appraisal rating assignments that they will find difficult to explain to employees. If there are, ask other members of the group what suggestions they have for how to handle this discussion.

3. Ask group members if there are any other issues they need to deal with as part of the performance-calibration meeting. Answer any questions that come up.

4. Remind the group of the next steps in the company's performance-management process.

5. Dismiss the meeting.

6. After the group has left, make sure that all appropriate comments have been recorded and that the final assignments to the performance-appraisal ratings have been saved. Either make notes of the information and positions of all of the sticky-notes or (better) take a digital camera picture of the flipcharts.

## Performance-Calibration Factors

The individual's performance-appraisal rating recommended by that employee's immediate supervisor, together with the examples that support that rating, usually will be the only data needed to determine the most appropriate performance-appraisal rating. However, if additional data are needed to make more exact comparisons among employees and assign the most appropriate appraisal ratings, the following factors may be helpful.

### Primary

- Examples of both effective and ineffective performance provided by other calibration session participants
- Comparisons of the quality of this individual's performance with that of other employees whose ratings already have been determined

### Secondary

- *Potential.* The individual's capability for successfully performing a job at a higher organizational level (vertical stretch) or a job in a significantly different area (horizontal stretch) in the next two to three years, provided that "potential" has been agreed on as an appropriate calibration factor.
- *Job complexity.* Degree of the job's complexity and difficulty relative to others; demonstrated willingness to seek stretch assignments.
- *Engagement.* Demonstrates ownership; actions benefit organization; proactively addresses issues and identifies/implements solutions; assumes additional responsibilities; independent, timely completion of assignments.
- *Productivity.* Manages a level-appropriate workload; work is accurate, timely, and complete; prioritizes tasks; develops good work procedures; manages time; handles information flow.
- *Versatility.* Demonstrates a variety of skill sets beyond those required in the current role that are uniquely valuable to the organization relative to others; openness to new ideas; handles pressure more effectively than others.
- *Citizenship behaviors.* Willingness to help a newcomer learn the ropes; work outside his or her normal hours for a special project; representing the organization well in the community.
- *Demonstrates technical/professional knowledge.* Demonstrates proficiency in his or her job domain; serves as a resource for others; models excellence; finds and resolves root causes of problems.

### Questionable

- Previous years' performance-appraisal ratings
- Education
- Unique/unusual skills (skills other than those required to successfully perform the position)
- Years of service
- Additional capabilities
- Flight risk
- EEO factors
- Job criticality

## Performance Calibration: Ground Rules

*Participation.* When an individual is under review, participants in the session who are directly knowledgeable of that employee's performance will actively participate in the discussion, providing examples to confirm or question the rating recommended by the individual's immediate supervisor.

*Engagement.* When an individual is under review, participants in the session who are not directly knowledgeable of that employee's performance will remain engaged in the discussion, listening and asking questions to ensure that similar standards of performance are being applied by different leaders and enhancing their familiarity with the performance of employees they do not know. Engaging in side conversations, checking e-mails, and daydreaming are inappropriate behaviors.

*Discussion Focus.* In determining the appropriateness of the specific rating to be assigned, participants will restrict themselves to discussing the quality of the individual's performance during the appraisal period against goals/results and behaviors/competencies. Other issues (e.g., long-term potential, unique talents, previous successes or failures, improvement over previous years, job criticality, length of service, EEO factors, skills other than those required to successfully perform the position, flight risk, education, and other factors that are not directly related to the specific quality of the individual's performance) will not be considered in determining the performance appraisal rating.

*Performance Differentiators.* If the discussion of the performance of the individual against his or her goals/results and behaviors/competencies is not sufficient to determine the appropriate performance rating for this individual, these additional factors—tie-breakers —may be used to make the right decision about the appraisal rating: job complexity, engagement, productivity, versatility, adaptability/flexibility, and demonstrated technical/professional knowledge.

*Other Items for Discussion.* When appropriate, participants will discuss their perceptions of the individual's unique strengths, needs for improvement, long-term potential, and suggestions for development to assist that individual's supervisor. These factors, however, will not be considered in determining the appropriate performance rating.

*Oversight.* Participants will be expected to police each other to ensure that all participants remain engaged and noting when others are becoming too much of an advocate, are discussing irrelevant information, or are taking advantage of a leader's absence from the session to assign his or her employees a lower appraisal rating. Policing the discussion to make sure that the ground rules are followed is the responsibility of the participants, not the responsibility of the facilitator.

*Openness.* Leaders must be open to changing the rating of an employee when the information provided indicates that a change is appropriate.

*Consensus.* Decisions will be made by consensus—a general agreement among the group—and not by voting. *Consensus* means that all voices and perspectives have been heard. The decision is one that most feel comfortable with and all can live with and support.

*Confidentiality.* Confidentiality must be maintained by all participants.

*Accountability and Ownership.* Leaders will demonstrate ownership of calibration session results. Specifically this means taking responsibility and ownership of performance-appraisal ratings and not saying such things as, "I had you rated higher, but the calibration group forced me to lower your rating."

# 38

# Guidelines for Effective Executive Performance Appraisals

JAMES F. REDA

*Arthur J. Gallagher & Co.'s Human Resources and
Compensation Consulting Practice*

MOLLY A. KYLE

*Arthur J. Gallagher & Co.'s Human Resources and
Compensation Consulting Practice*

Although most large companies have an executive performance-appraisal process, more needs to be done to improve the process. The performance-appraisal process provides an opportunity to capture the attention of every individual in a company and point each individual toward the goals set for the organization as a whole. Executive talent is the most expensive and most important part of an organization. As such, this precious resource needs to be constantly evaluated, appraised, and encouraged to improve.

The compensation committee should create and adhere to an effective CEO evaluation program. The most important responsibility of a board of directors is evaluation of management succession, leadership development, and management evaluation, particularly for the CEO position. Although the CEO often takes the lead for hiring and succession of other management personnel, it is the board of directors that is tasked with the responsibility of CEO succession and evaluation.

Executives should be evaluated regularly using a clearly defined process and measurable evaluation criteria. All these factors should be determined based on each company's goals, objectives, size, compensation philosophy, culture/shared values, and business plan. The information presented in this chapter will assist in designing, implementing, and refining an executive performance-appraisal process that will motivate leadership to optimize the organization's competitive advantages, manage talent, and improve economic performance.

Formal appraisals of executive performance are crucial to establishing and ensuring an appropriate balance of power between the board members, the CEO, and the executive officers. By making a portion of executive compensation packages contingent on the results of this evaluation, executives are held accountable for poor performance.[1]

The goals, as set by the board and the executive team, are created, ultimately, to grow the company and, in turn, to add value to shareholders. Collectively, the board of directors, the CEO, and the executive officers (EOs) are focused on adding shareholder value.

When discussing executive performance evaluations, a distinction should be made between the CEO, EOs [executives with "broad policy-making authority that typically include the executives listed as the top five named executive officers (NEOs) in the company's proxy disclosure statement], and all other executives (collectively referred to as the *executives*) (Figure 38.1). As discussed later in this chapter, the process and oversight of each group of executives are different.

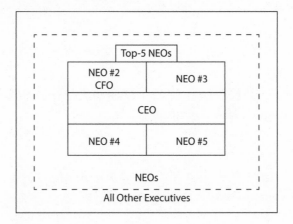

**Figure 38.1  Categories of executives.**

Because CEO performance evaluations are now required as part of the listing requirements of the New York Stock Exchange (NYSE), more and more companies are evaluating the performance of executives. Of course, this process is migrating to Nasdaq-listed companies, private companies, and even not-for-profit companies (Table 38.1). The U.S. Securities and Exchange Commission (SEC) only requires that CEO compensation be clearly outlined and justified in the compensation committee's report section of their annual proxy disclosure statement and makes no mention of the appraisal process or its implementation.

Considering that the potential gains from a performance-appraisal process are greatest for high-level executives, it is surprising that appraisals become less structured and regulated as one moves up in the organization. Thus, although executive performance appraisal is a cornerstone of good corporate governance and is widely implemented in larger companies, the information it produces is highly confidential and carefully guarded. At present, the results of such evaluations are not publicly available unless disclosure is required by subpoena or other imposed process. Although many companies conduct CEO performance appraisals to comply with NYSE requirement, many more do not have a solid process in place to conduct the appraisals.

Before discussing the evaluation process further, it is important to summarize the structure of the modern compensation committee.

| Type of Company | CEO Evaluation Requirement | Comments |
|---|---|---|
| NYSE-listed | Required | The compensation committee must review and approve corporate goals and objectives relevant to CEO compensation, evaluate the CEO's performance in light of those goals and objectives and approve the CEO's compensation level based on that evaluation. |
| Nasdaq-listed | Recommended | The compensation of the CEO and all other executive officers of the company must be determined, or recommended to the board for determination, by either a majority of the independent directors or a compensation committee comprised solely of independent directors. |
| Private | Recommended | Large private companies have compensation committees that require executive evaluations as a matter of best practice. |
| Not for Profit | Recommended | Regulatory control compels not for profits to improve corporate governance, including executive evaluations. |

Table 38.1   CEO Evaluation Requirements for Different Types of Companies

## Compensation Committee Structure

One of the most important determinants of a successful corporate strategy is the quality of the compensation committee. The committee is charged with designing and implementing a compensation system that effectively rewards key players and encourages direct participation in the achievement of the organization's core business objectives.

Outstanding, well-integrated compensation strategy does not just happen. Rather, it is the product of the hard work of independent, experienced compensation committee members. The most effective pay strategies are simple in design, straightforward in application, and easy to communicate to management and investors. The pay program for the CEO should be in line with pay programs for the company's other executives and with its broad-based incentive programs. In other words, there should be no conflict in the achievement of objectives, and the potential rewards should be as meaningful to all participants as to the CEO.

It is unusual for a public company's compensation committee to have more than five members. A compensation committee of three to five members should provide an adequate forum for a useful exchange of ideas and healthy debate.

To execute its duties responsibly, the compensation committee must be able to efficiently synthesize highly technical information and apply sound business judgment. As the field of executive compensation becomes increasingly complex and more in the focus of public attention, the committee's job grows more and more challenging. Adherence to the following six precepts will pave the way to optimal performance by the committee.

*Six Precepts for Responsible Committee Performance*

1. Get organized.
2. Get and stay informed.

3. Keep an eye on the big picture.

4. Return to reason.

5. Consider the shareholders' perspective.

6. Communicate effectively.

## Barriers to Effective Goal Setting and Appraisal

A number of factors, from ambiguous goals to a discomfort in evaluating an executive or the executive being uncomfortable about the process can inhibit the effectiveness of an appraisal. A partial list of inhibitors is as follows:

- *Discomfort.* Some executives (the board and compensation committee) in the case of the CEO or the CEO in the case of executive officers find the executive evaluation process neither enjoyable nor comfortable. Most executives being appraised feel the same way.

- *Misunderstood purpose.* Some executives misuse the evaluation to find fault rather than to provide feedback for constructive purposes.

- *Ambiguity.* This is a major impetus to implementing an effective board evaluation process. Ambiguity can come from a "squishy" statement of the organization's strategic goals, the executive's job description and goals, how the process is designed, or the way that evaluation results are shared with the executive.

- *Low priority.* Some managers have the impression that there will be a lack of time and energy to allow for an effective evaluation process.

- *Difficulty rating the executive on qualitative factors.* Factors such as the executive's ability to develop the leadership pipeline and a continuously learning organization should not be included because sometimes the board does not observe these activities directly or they are difficult to measure objectively.

- *New source of criticism for the executive.* Some companies fear the loss of an apparently good executive by the possibility of overly criticizing the executive.

However, when done properly, CEO and executive evaluations can create a sense of teamwork, mutual respect, and direct, clear lines of communication that are needed when moving forward with corporate and business goals. An effective executive evaluation system is comprised of two main components: the actual process and the evaluation criteria.

## Executive Performance-Evaluation Process

As stated earlier, the executive evaluation process needs to be segregated into three parts: the CEO, executive officers, and all other executives. Typically, the board of directors evaluates the CEO, the CEO evaluates his or her direct reports, and so forth, with all evaluations being summarized and reported upward. There is also a typical *two-up rule* that the executive's manager performs the evaluation, with the manager's manager reviewing the evaluation (before the evaluation is completed).

On the subject of CEO performance evaluation, the entire board has the final say in most matters. The compensation committee to the full board participates in gathering and presenting data. Usually, the executives take almost no part in the evaluation process, whereas outside advisors have some influence. The corporate governance committee sometimes conducts the evaluation of the CEO, but for the purposes of illustration, we show the compensation committee (see Figures 38.2 through 38.4).

| Group* | Design System | Determine Measures, Set Targets | Gather & Present Performance Data | Appraise Performance | Provide Feedback | Determine Consequences |
|---|---|---|---|---|---|---|
| Entire board | ● | ● | O | ● | ● | ● |
| Compensation committee | ◐ | ◐ | ● | ◐ | ◐ | ◐ |
| CEO | O | O | O | O | - - | - - |
| Executive officers** | O | O | O | - - | - - | - - |
| All other executives | - - | - - | - - | - - | - - | - - |
| Outside advisors | O | O | O | - - | - - | O |

\* Members of some group categories overlap.
\*\* Includes Top-5 NEOs.

Key: Approve ●
Recommend ◐
Influence O
No Role - -

**Figure 38.2 Typical CEO evaluation process.**

| Group* | Design System | Determine Measures, Set Targets | Gather & Present Performance Data | Appraise Performance | Provide Feedback | Determine Consequences |
|---|---|---|---|---|---|---|
| Entire board | O | O | - - | O | - - | O |
| Compensation committee | ● | ● | - - | O | - - | ● |
| CEO | ◐ | ◐ | ● | ● | ● | ● |
| Executive officers** | O | O | O | ◐ | ◐ | O |
| All other executives | - - | - - | - - | - - | - - | - - |
| Outside advisors | O | O | O | - - | - - | - - |

\* Members of some group categories overlap.
\*\* Includes Top-5 NEOs.

Key: Approve ●
Recommend ◐
Influence O
No Role - -

**Figure 38.3 Typical executive officer evaluation process.**

The performance-appraisal process also involves determining how the evaluation is administered, including the timing, the form the evaluation will take (written or oral), and feedback to the executive.

### Timing

The evaluation process generally should include three main stages: establishment of the evaluation goals at the beginning of the fiscal year, the midyear review, and the

| Group* | Design System | Determine Measures, Set Targets | Gather & Present Performance Data | Appraise Performance | Provide Feedback | Determine Consequences |
|---|---|---|---|---|---|---|
| Entire board | - - | - - | - - | - - | - - | - - |
| Compensation committee | O | O | - - | - - | - - | O |
| CEO | ● | ● | ● | ● | ● | ● |
| Executive officers** | ◑ | ◑ | ◑ | ◑ | ◑ | ◑ |
| All other executives | O | O | O | O | O | O |
| Outside advisors | O | O | O | - - | - - | - - |

\* Members of some group categories overlap.
\*\* Includes Top-5 NEOs.

| Key: Approve | ● |
|---|---|
| Recommend | ◑ |
| Influence | O |
| No Role | - - |

Figure 38.4 Typical evaluation process for all other executives.

end-of-the-year performance assessment and approval of compensation package. There should be multiple evaluation sessions over the year. A meaningful CEO evaluation should contain regular board executive sessions culminating in a formal annual evaluation. It should be well planned and objective, and it ultimately should be tied to the executive's pay package. The executive officer and other executive processes are similar, except that their managers (most likely the CEO in the case of an EO) are in place of the board.

At the beginning of the fiscal year, the short- and long-term objectives that will be used in the executive evaluation should be agreed on. The establishment of objectives is discussed in the section "Evaluation Criteria" later. In addition to their creation, it is important that objectives be given relative weights and that the executive is aware of which objectives are of greater importance. (See the "Example CEO Evaluation Form" at the end of this chapter for examples.) Along with the targets, the threshold and maximum performance levels and the pay adjustments associated with the different levels of performance should be discussed and defined.

The midyear review provides an opportunity to assess progress toward performance targets, isolate and address problems, and determine whether the executive is on the right path to meeting or exceeding the objectives. In some cases, it may make sense to adjust performance targets if they are no longer relevant to the company. However, it is not recommended that performance targets be changed unless there are unforeseen, unusual, or extraordinary circumstances. In a more volatile or dynamic industry (e.g., fashion or apparel), these intermediate reviews may need to be done quarterly or even on a monthly/weekly basis.

The end-of-the-year assessment is the most thorough and time-consuming part of the evaluation process. Performance results must be compared with the set targets, and the appropriate compensation package must be determined. The final evaluation typically takes place in March following the year that the work was done because it takes that long to finalize the financial statements. It is important and prudent that the audited financial statements be completed before the evaluation is completed to provide certainty to the performance data. There have been some recent examples of financial restatements that have highlighted bonuses that should not have been paid or would have been substantially less.

This final evaluation is the formal executive performance appraisal, and this should contain the following components:

- Executive completes a written self-evaluation.
- Evaluators complete questionnaires assessing performance.
- Internal and external data/information is collected.
- Committee prepares recommendations.
- Evaluators meet and discuss before approving final compensation package.

## Delivery of the Evaluation

Although it is highly recommended, there is no tax, accounting, security, or legislative rule that requires the evaluations to be in written form, which allows for the option of an oral evaluation. As with a written evaluation, the oral evaluation also should be very detailed, have outlined goals and objectives, and involve a feedback component. The oral evaluation would be conducted by the full board. Oral evaluations eradicate several of the problems with written evaluations but tend to be less thorough. Oral evaluations are much more prevalent in smaller organizations and in the case of the CEO (particularly in larger organizations that are concerned about the misinterpretation of a CEO evaluation and the discovery of the evaluation in an adverse legal proceeding).

### Advantages of Oral Evaluation

- No written comments to be misinterpreted and misused
- May help some directors to articulate their opinions
- Take less time than a written evaluation

### Disadvantages of Oral Evaluation

- Very vocal directors (in the case of the CEO and in some cases executive officers) and executives (in the case of executive officers and other executives) can more easily influence others.
- Directors and executives will tend to be less objective and fair if the evaluation is oral.
- It tends to be a less in-depth review.
- It is very difficult to implement the two-up rule.
- There will not be a good record to assist in career development and promotional opportunities.

Written, documented evaluations are preferred because a written evaluation allows for tracking of performance over multiple years. The oral process does not lend itself to this. However, CEO evaluation materials are sometimes destroyed because there is no real career development once you are CEO, and records are destroyed to avoid a plaintiff's counsel using these documents in adverse lawsuits of various types.

### Feedback to the Executive

Clear communication with the CEO and executives is necessary on the part of the compensation committee. At least two directors should deliver the CEO evaluation. The chairs of the compensation and corporate governance committees should meet with the CEO in private immediately after full-board discussions. The two-person rule is also a good practice to follow with all executives, with the immediate manager and perhaps either a representative of human resources or the manager's manager present during the evaluation.

It is paramount that great care for confidentiality be practiced during the evaluation process. The problem of confidentiality is somewhat more difficult in the case of the CEO because the evaluation process involves the completion of evaluation forms by each director. Other executive evaluations typically are completed by the manager and reviewed by the manager's manager.

In the case of CEO evaluation, all completed evaluation forms by outside directors, board members, and other sources should be returned solely to the director or person (sometimes it is an outside advisor or in some cases the corporate secretary or lawyer working in a legal group) in charge of collection of the evaluation forms and should be disposed of after the summary of the data is collected. The CEO and other executives should never see the raw data. It is easy for data and responses to be misused or misinterpreted. For cogency, a summary of the data is all that the executive should see. It is highly recommended that for further security and confidentiality, outside consultants be used to manage the evaluation process.

## Developing Evaluation Criteria

Performance evaluation criteria have evolved in the modern corporation from a trait-based, personality-centric measure to a more specific, results-oriented metric, which includes financial and nonfinancial criteria. This change began in the early 1960s and continues today as companies review their performance-measurement criteria.

Until recently, performance appraisals were based on annual *trait ratings*. Certain character traits such as degree of initiative, personality, maturity, judgment, or appearance were assessed because of their supposed relation to executive performance. Over time, executives became more hostile, defensive, and critical of this system as boards grew more critical in their assessments.[2] This trait-based appraisal system was soon replaced with the *overall performance rating*. This system, although more comprehensive, was so heavily subjective and lacking in structure that appraisals were easily influenced by insignificant factors such as personality and low golf handicap instead of more relevant factors such as growth and financial performance.[3]

Out of the shortcomings of the trait-based and overall performance rating came *management by objective*. This appraisal system is based on established long- and short-term objectives or goals that CEOs are expected to achieve in a specified period of time, and it measures the degree to which a CEO met, fell short of, or surpassed these objectives.[4]

This appraisal system was more effective than the previous models because it was

- Simple

- Focused on actual work, not personality

- Aligned executive objectives with overall company goals

- Far more accepted by CEOs

If the executive participated in the establishment of his or her objectives, it was even more motivating. Management by objective was revolutionary. Many companies rushed to augment or completely overhaul their performance-assessment systems to be in line with this new system. Management by objective is still the most used and most accepted performance-appraisal system by many companies today.

All organizations need to have a well-designed and properly focused performance plan. The performance-plan process aggregates individual goals into larger, overlapping collective goals that focus the organization to do more than it would have. A well-designed performance plan describes the preferred results, how results tie back to the company's results, weighting of results, how results will be measured, and what standards are used to evaluate results.

## Executive Performance Measures

As part of the performance plan, executives should set objectives that align with the company's culture, business strategy, and compensation philosophy. The objectives are used to define the performance measures that will be used as evaluation criteria during the performance evaluation (Figure 38.5).

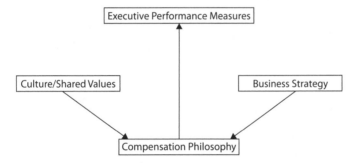

**Figure 38.5  Factors that determine executive performance measures.**

Before executive performance measures can be defined, each of the three contributing factors needs to be defined and understood so that objectives can be developed for each.

### Compensation Philosophy

The fundamental task of the compensation committee is to establish the compensation philosophy of the company. Having done so, it should design programs to advance that philosophy. The compensation philosophy takes into account the culture/shared values and business strategy. A compensation philosophy consists of four main components:

- *Peer group comparisons.* Who should the company compare itself against for salary and short- and long-term incentive opportunities?

- *Pay positioning strategy.* How should the company pay its executives in relation to the market levels of pay?

- *Internal versus external pay equity.* The culture/shared values are factored into this part of the compensation philosophy. How much weight should the company place on the internal relationships among executives (internal) versus the market (external)?

- *Performance alignment with business plan.* Specifically, how is the business strategy aligned with the compensation system, particularly the incentive strategy with emphasis on the performance measures?

The compensation philosophy should be reviewed when determining performance goals because it takes some parts from the culture/shared values (internal versus external pay equity) and some parts from the business strategy (performance alignment with the business plan). It is also important to determine the peer group with which the company needs to compete.

### Culture/Shared Values

Culture and shared values are naturally included while deciding what criteria will be considered during the appraisal process. Some of these values may include open communications, rewarding competence, preservation of integrity, openness to change, developing talent internally, loyalty, and the belief that goals should be results oriented and not process oriented. Identifying a culture and shared values will be of great value when considering how to weigh both quantitative and qualitative measures in the appraisal process. The culture and shared values will vary from company to company, as should their executive performance measures, because they should be a reflection of this culture and these values.

### Business Strategy

The corporate business strategy should be taken into account, and the board of directors and CEOs should refer to it when developing a performance-appraisal system. It is important that these strategies are set and then made clear to the executives so as to guarantee cohesion and unity of ideas and perspective over the course of the year. The appraisal process should assess how successful the executive has been in moving forward with the business strategy for that year. Midyear reviews allow for the company to reassess these strategies and alter them if they are proving to be inadequate. Business success factors should be an extension of the existing business strategy; these tend to be more concrete and narrowly focused annual goals. The executives' ability to contribute and their success in achieving these goals should be considered in the appraisal process.

### Executive Performance Measures

All the factors just discussed will be considered in the final product, the performance measures used to evaluate executives. The factors that comprise each company's background or identity will determine the route the company will take to assess the executive; it will also determine how much each area is weighted based on the relative importance or value the company believes the criterion to hold.

Because a larger portion of executive compensation has been shifting to variable pay plans, which are linked to performance, companies are placing greater value on selecting performance measures that actually have an effect on the bottom line.[5] The most obvious measurable financial results are the principal attributes[6] of profit, total shareholder return, return on invested capital, cash flow, earnings growth, and earnings stability.

Quantitative measures should work in concert with qualitative measures as appraisal criteria.[7] There is no question that qualitative data can be useful during the evaluation process, but too heavy a reliance on qualitative data can lead to a loss of valuable resources such as time, money, and energy. This fact would defeat the purpose of an appraisal because its main objective is to ensure productivity and success. Every goal specified should be quantified to the extent possible so that a third party could review the goal during an evaluation and determine whether the executive had indeed achieved the goal.

Qualitative information by nature is subjective, and quantitative data by nature are objective and thus less subject to evaluator bias. The mix of financial and nonfinancial measures is critical. If the executive evaluation is decoupled from the annual incentive plan (e.g., the bonus is paid independent of the evaluation), then nonfinancial measures should be the predominant part of the evaluation. However, if the executive evaluation is the sole determinant of the bonus, the use of quantitative data should be the main determinate of the bonus to be paid to the executive (Table 38.2).

| | Quantitative | Qualitative |
|---|---|---|
| Financial | • EPS growth<br>• ROIC<br>• TSR | • Better understanding of company strategy in investment community<br>• Achievement of IPO/spin-off/restructuring |
| Nonfinancial | • Employee turnover<br>• Diversity<br>• Employee satisfaction (survey results) | • Milestones<br>• Leadership skills<br>• Strategy implementation<br>• Communication effectiveness |

Table 38.2  Qualitative versus Nonqualitative Measures

The most effective incentive measures are return on invested capital (ROIC) and total shareholder return (TSR). However, these financial measures may not be appropriate for all executives because they may not be directly related to the executive being evaluated. Whereas there are ad hoc comments made by consultants and others that the achievement of the right nonfinancial goals such as customer satisfaction, customer retention, employee satisfaction, brand recognition, and customer loyalty will improve corporate profitability, there is no definitive proof of such claims. In addition, there are no good metrics as to the relationship between the achievement of nonfinancial goals and financial success. However, the application of nonfinancial goals is just as important as financial goals, in particular, lower in the organization.

Nonfinancial goals need to be simple, direct, and measurable. The goals should be results oriented and not process oriented—the goal should be expressed in achieving a result that will directly help the organization to achieve short- and long-term objectives.

If the performance appraisal is closely linked to compensation, then extreme caution should be exercised on the selection of nonfinancial goals. In this case, a strict financial formula should be used to fund the program to avoid wasting corporate assets by overpaying executives.

## Outcomes of the Performance Appraisal

Higher qualitative success is usually accompanied by a higher profit margin, which is, of course, the ultimate goal of any company. Qualitative criteria should be used in the executive evaluation process. Unfortunately, Internal Revenue Code Section 162(m) does not allow it to be used to set bonus amounts for the top five executives listed in the proxy disclosure statement [typically referred to as *named executive officers* (NEOs)]. We recommend that the evaluation process be used as a *negative-discretion element*. In other words, the annual executive appraisal can be used to lower the bonus for NEOs. The treatment of the other executives can vary and may include adjusting the annual incentive upward or downward depending on the executive performance appraisal.

The last and very important part of the evaluation process is to tie the evaluation process to the executive's pay package. This is especially important when corporate success is not synchronous with executive pay. For example, care should be taken to avoid large stock grants, bonus payments, salary increases, and other perceived compensation windfalls when there is an employee layoff, stock slump, or earnings drop.

One of the main objectives of assessing the performance of an executive is to ensure that the executive is being paid fairly—to gauge whether the salary for the performance is justified, overrewarded, or should be raised. It is important that executives be monitored regularly to ensure that progress is being made. The outcome of the assessment will correlate directly with the salary of the executive. Meeting expectations, whether quantitative premeditated ones or goals set relative to competition, should be rewarded.

The current CEO evaluation process is typically delinked from the CEO bonus decision. This is somewhat true for the NEOs and less true for all other executives. The bonus is typically determined using quantitative financial criteria such as earnings-per-share (EPS) growth or earnings before interest, taxes, depreciation, and amortization (EBITDA). The CEO evaluation form, as shown in the example at the end of this chapter, (per se) is 95 percent nonfinancial and is focused on such areas as leadership, communications, board relations, and management development. Companies are beginning to link these two evaluation processes.

Once performance has been appraised, the results will be considered and then used for decisions in the discourse of action. CEOs are often compared and evaluated in relation to the CEOs of other companies—the reason being that even if the CEO does meet financial goals, other companies may be doing better. If a CEO does not meet set goals or is falling behind in comparison with other companies, he or she can be put on probation or be monitored more regularly. If the CEO continues to fail to perform in the ways necessary, then a case can be built against him or her with records from multiple past appraisals, and he or she eventually can be fired. If, however, he or she meets or exceeds marks and has put the company in a good place in the market, he or she may be rewarded with a bonus or other incentives.

Clear communication with upper management is necessary on the part of the compensation committee. At least two people should deliver the evaluation (two directors in the case of the CEO). The chairs of the compensation and corporate governance committees should meet with the CEO in private immediately after full-board discussions.

The board alone should have the authority to adjust the CEO's salary and long-term incentive awards. In several companies, human resources typically gives guidelines as to salary increases. This places human resources and management in an awkward position because it may signal an action if the increase is below the recommendation. We recommend that the committee rely on outside advice for recommendations as to the range of the salary increase and incentive award.

The salary should not be adjusted as drastically as the long-term incentive award because it is important that the CEO be paid according to general market levels with respect to base salary. There is ample room to adjust the long-term incentive award opportunity based on the evaluation results.

## Final Thoughts

There are many factors to consider when designing, implementing, and operating an effective executive performance system. The performance measures (both quantitative and qualitative) are crucial to the success of the organization.

In addition, attention must be paid to the related processes for the CEO, NEOs, EOs, and all other executives. Finally, the evaluation process should be integrated into the annual incentive plan. The compensation philosophy, culture/shared values, and business plan should be considered carefully when deciding on the performance measures.

## References

Crystal, Graef S. 1968. "The Performance Appraisal Process and Its Relation to Compensation," in Russell F. Moore (ed.), *Compensating Executive Worth*. American Management Association, New York, pp. 91–105.

Hunt, Albert R. 2007. "Letter from Washington: As U.S. Rich-Poor Gap Grows, So Does Public Outcry." *International Herald Tribune: Americas*, February 18. Available at: www.iht.com/articles/2007/02/18/news/letter.php?page=1 (accessed August 7, 2007).

Conger, Jay A., David Finegold, and Edward E Lawler III. 2000. "Appraising Boardroom Performance," in *Harvard Business Review on Corporate Governance*. Harvard Business School Press, Boston, pp. 105–134.

Schneier, Craig E., and Douglas G. Shaw. 2000. "Measuring and Assessing Top Executive Performance," in Lance A. Berger and Dorothy R. Berger (eds.), *The Compensation Handbook*, 4th ed. McGraw- Hill, New York, pp. 496–498, 500.

**Example Evaluation Tools: CEO Evaluation Form**

# XYZ Company, Inc.

## Chief Executive Officer Evaluation
## For the fiscal year ending January 31, 2014

### Overview

The chief executive officer is responsible for the success or failure of XYZ and leads by providing the vision for XYZ. Develops and implements strategic and operational plans to achieve the vision. Oversees the operation of XYZ; develops management, allocates resources, and ensures control. Acts as XYZ's chief spokesperson. Works with the board to develop and maintain oversight.

The CEO or any other member of management will not view this form. A summary of your ratings and comments will be prepared that will preserve the confidentiality of your ratings and comments. This summary will be presented to the board at the 2013 board meeting. The CEO will receive a summary of your comments and feedback at the 2014 board meeting.

Please return this form to YOUR CONSULTANT, Address 1, Address 2, City, and Sate ZIP prior to DATE. You can also fax this form to YOUR CONSULTANT at FAX NUMBER.

Each question should be evaluated with the following point system and appropriate comments:

| Far Exceeded | Exceeded | Fully Met | Below | Far Below |
|---|---|---|---|---|
| Expectations/ Exceptional Performance | Expectations/ Superior Performance | Expectations/ Competent Performance | Expectations/ Performance Needs Development | Expectations/ Performance Unsatisfactory |
| 1 | 2 | 3 | 4 | 5 |

1. **Strategic Planning** *(weight 15 percent)*                     *Score:* _____

   - Ensures the development of a long-term strategy.

   - Establishes objectives and plans that meet the needs of shareholders, customers, employees, and all other corporate stakeholders and ensures consistent and timely progress toward strategic objectives.

   - Obtains and allocates resources consistent with strategic objectives. Reports regularly to the board on progress toward strategic plan milestones.

   *Comments:*

   _____

   _____

   _____

   _____

2. **Financial Results** *(weight 20 percent)*                      *Score:* _____

   - Establishes and achieves appropriate annual and longer-term financial performance goals.

   - Ensures the development and maintenance of appropriate systems to protect the company's assets and ensure effective control of operations.

   *Comments:*

   _____

   _____

   _____

   _____

**3. Succession Planning** *(weight 35 percent)*                    *Score:* _____

- Develops, attracts, retains, and motivates an effective and unified senior management team.

- Ensures that programs for management development and succession planning have the required resources and direction to grow the future leaders of the company.

*Comments:*

_____

_____

_____

_____

**4. Leadership/Communications/Board Relations**
**(weight 30 percent)**                    *Score* _____

- Develops and communicates a clear and consistent vision of the Company's goals and values.

- Ensures that this vision is well understood, widely supported, and effectively implemented within the organization.

- Fosters a corporate culture that encourages, recognizes, and rewards leadership, excellence, and innovation.

- Ensures a culture that promotes ethical practice, individual integrity, and cooperation to build shareholder value.

- Serves as a chief spokesperson for the Company, communicating effectively with shareholders, prospective investors, employees, customers, suppliers, and consumers.

- Effectively represents the Company in relationships with industry, the government, and the financial community, including major investor groups and financial services firms.

- Works closely with the Board to keep directors informed on the state of business on critical issues relating to the Company, such as the corporate strategies and the achievement of operating plan and strategic plan milestones.

- Provides effective support for board operations including board materials, and advisory services.

*Comments:*

_____

_____

_____

_____

**Final Summary**

A. Overall comments:

_____

_____

_____

_____

B. Key challenges in year ahead:

_____

_____

_____

_____

C. Thoughts and concerns:

_____

_____

_____

_____

## Notes

1.  Graef S. Crystal, "The Performance Appraisal Process and Its Relation to Compensation," in Russell F. Moore (ed.), *Compensating Executive Worth*. American Management Association, New York, 1968, pp. 91–105.
2.  Ibid.
3.  Ibid.
4.  Ibid.
5.  Craig E. Schneier and Douglas G. Shaw, "Measuring and Assessing Top Executive Performance," in Lance A. Berger and Dorothy R. Berger (eds.), *The Compensation Handbook*, 4th ed., McGraw- Hill, New York, 2000, pp. 496–500
6.  Ibid.
7.  Ibid.

# VII

# TALENT MANAGEMENT AND COMPENSATION

# 39

# Employing Novel Ways to Use Compensation to Win the Talent Wars

Deborah Rees

*Innecto Reward Consulting*

Rewarding talent in organizations has become a whirling kaleidoscope of different practices, priorities, and techniques, with some organizations sticking to tried and tested "old world" approaches and other organizations completely reviewing their approach—even going so far as to say that their business model, rather than being sales led or finance led, is now talent led.

In this chapter, my objectives are to sift through and rationalize the array of practices and attempt to combine the new with the best of the old to develop a strategic direction on how to reward talent in your organization in a way that attracts, engages, and allows talent to perform to its very best. This chapter will cover three main learning points and then provide a summary of findings, analysis, and conclusions. The learning points are

- Ensuring that compensation programs create competitive business advantage by highlighting how organizations can link their approach to rewarding talent to the bottom line through examples from Worldpay and NetFlix and ensuring that the best of the lessons of attracting and retaining gen Y are included in the strategic approach.

- Employing novel ways to win the battle for external talent, retain internal talent, and develop mission-critical skills through looking at the world of sport and other highly competitive environments. What can those hot houses of talent tell the business world about growing and rewarding talented individuals?

- Creating and maintaining a culture of innovation, engagement, leadership, and performance by taking the best of the old world and applying it to new issues: globalization, ambidexterity, and creating new ways of managing performance.

This chapter will analyze all the evidence from the conflicting models and ideas about rewarding talent effectively and close with overarching conclusions.

For organizations emerging from a frozen world of recession and downsizing, rewarding talent as a strategic policy has been overlooked, put on the back burner, and reduced to a paper exercise. The centerpiece of the Hippocratic oath is "Do no harm," and this is a policy that rewards professionals should take to heart in the complex world of talent management. Business leaders may think that they are transmitting loud and clear—that their purpose, values, objectives, goals, and performance criteria for the business are getting through. In actuality, though, many things get in the way of their transmission. My eye was caught by an article in *Rewards Magazine* in which C. McCoy (2013) says, "[P]erhaps reward specialists should be less worthy and more engaged?" Have we become too wedded to our processes without really considering where they cut across, fail to support, or actually oppose the message of the leadership of the organizations?

In the United Kingdom, consumer financial investments have words of warning attached: "Past performance is no guide to future performance"—and this is worth repeating. The last few years have led to a stagnation of talent in some organizations. Unwillingness to consider that future policy should be different from what happened in the recent past means that some organizations will be left behind as the world of business warms up. Some companies still will be in the changing rooms tying their trainers when others are out on the pitch scoring goals.

The contrast is stark: in his role as human resources director, Andy Doyle of Worldpay feels that he drives real value to the bottom line through attracting, hiring, and rewarding marquee talent that demonstrably adds to his organization's market value as a private-equity-funded organization. This contrasts with other interviewees, who acknowledged that their rewarding-talent strategy "needs to improve."

## Ensuring that compensation programs create competitive business advantage by highlighting how organizations can link their approach to rewarding talent to the bottom line

Imagine a world where human resources is not an overhead but rather a contributor to the bottom line. Imagine a world where leadership and reward are synched together in growing and retaining talent in the business—where performance management is an everyday, ongoing attempt for excellence not an annual "ache fest." In my field research for this chapter, the evidence was that the goal of rewarding talent as a strategic, accountable business investment varies in practice from a sophisticated, open, and transparent approach to one where the thinking is not yet translated into any type of distinguishable action.

For pay and reward strategies to work, there has to be clarity about the strategic requirements of the organization and how these requirements link to individual people who can deliver what the business needs. Talent-led organizations are starting to put bottom-line value on their ability to attract and retain talent in the organization and, more important, create an environment where performance is expected and rewarded and the link between talent, performance, and reward is explicit and grown up.

### The Employee Perspective

In the old world, good practice tells us talent management is based on people being rewarded through interesting work, new placements, and long-term return on their investment in a business. "Stay with us, and we'll see you right" has been the watchword.

Boom! Three major forces have shifted the grounds of this relationship for good.

*Demographics.* The world of work has changed—and so have the people inside it. Baby boomers are now aged between 50 and 70 years and are starting to leave the workplace. In their place come generation X, aged 30 to 50 years, and generation Y, aged below 30 years. Different generations have different requirements. The baby-boomer generation was strongly loyal to the company and to its teams, focused on stability and historically more likely to stay long term with a business. Generation X has a different perspective; its members put their individual needs higher—perhaps based on watching their own parents sacrifice many years to the corporate dollar—and they want to ensure that they build time for family and personal interests into their own lives. Generation Y is the global generation; its members see themselves as global citizens and have a loyalty to their tribe—but are motivated by making a difference and seeking experiences beyond work.

*Transparency.* Pay data are now more freely available on the Internet than ever before. Gag clauses in contracts have been disallowed in the United Kingdom by the Equality Act of 2010. Transparency on rewards is king—and this means that employees know their worth and want to trade their skills and experience for competitive reward.

*Psychological Contract.* For many gen X and all gen Y workers, the last years of recession have been a bucket of cold water. Once, continued career development and career options were taken as given, but resizing, redundancies, and pay freezes have fractured trust in the physiological contract. And these workers are taking control of their own destinies and futures. This means harder bargaining, more self-reliance, and less belief in the long-term promises of employers.

### The Employer Perspective

Many organizations, led by information technology (IT) innovators such as Google and Microsoft, have created an environment in which all employees are "talent." Consulting organizations now use the word *talent* to mean "employees" in the context of managing performance. However, challenging thinking and budget reductions in this area have fueled a search for a more focused approach.

Organizations are challenging their human resources and rewards teams to add value to the bottom line by

- Becoming part of a systemic approach to employee hiring decisions and linking talent, performance, and rewards together as a strategic board-level agenda item.

- Considering not just the cost of an employee but also the return on investment (ROI) that an employee brings. This requires a mind shift by rewards professionals from cost to value added and effectively presenting this concept for rewarding business-critical hires.

- Translating strategy into tactical plans by segmenting and differentiating different groups of talent and devising customized appropriate "deals" for them.

From a practical perspective, what does the development of a customized approach to rewarding talent look like? What are the models and prototypes we can examine to generate an approach to creating bespoke, realistic rewards models for our talent?

**Employing novel ways to win the battle for external talent, retain internal talent, and develop mission-critical skills through looking at the world of sport and other highly competitive environments. What can those hot houses of talent tell the business world about growing and retaining talented individuals?**

My firm has done a great deal of work recently with sporting organizations such as the Manchester City FC, the U.K. Tennis Association (the LTA), Arsenal FC, and other U.K. premiership football clubs and leading sports governing bodies. Developing talent is their business. We wanted to examine whether it is possible to learn lessons in business from sports organizations and their development of players. Adding to the debate, Jackson Samuel (2009) in its report, "The Golden Few," produced a review of talent management in highly specialized elite organizations that provides fascinating food for thought. Our high-level conclusions are as follows:

### Move to an Exclusive, Not Inclusive, World of Talent

Put in place clarity and understanding of what talent really means at the heart of your strategy—and how it is defined at different levels. For example, the LTA produces a DVD for coaches showing how a "talented" eight-year-old should hit a forehand. This level of definition keeps the talent funnel on track and does not endanger false hope at an early stage.

### Define Different Levels of Talent

We suggest creating three main categories:

- *Academy.* Your future hopefuls who have raw talent and highly developed technical ability but have not yet had the chance to hone their business skills in a really challenging situation.

- *Reserves.* Those who have cut their teeth in a business environment and have started to apply their technical expertise and develop business competence—leadership, resilience, team performance, and so on.

- *First team.* Those who have a proven track record in the "big stuff" and can demonstrate that they have a longer-term focus and history of achievement in different circumstances.

While managing these groups, it is essential to "harvest and weed" as you go; different people develop at different speeds, and some people never fulfill their early potential.

### Link Rewards to the Appropriate Level

Looping back to my original premise—that the current workforce is made of up individuals with differing overall goals than their predecessors—it is clear that different groups in your talent framework should have contrasting rewards arrangements. Moreover, crucially, the rewards should be appropriate to their level and the contribution they make to your organization (Figure 39.1).

**Figure 39.1  Link rewards to the appropriate level.**

## Academy

- *Chuck out "annual" mind-set.* Projects and growth may be happening at different times and cycles than fits comfortably with the annual pay review. Be flexible and reward according to the work completed and standards attained (e.g., an end-of-project bonus payment).

- *Keep base pay market data fresh, and keep pace with them.* Academy incumbents are characterized by patchy periods of growth and development. Annual base pay raises may be too slow to reflect new skills and value to the organization.

- *Build in recognition, not just pay.* At this level, it is important to show individuals that their contributions are important to the organization. All the emphasis should be on building experience, adding to skills, and providing challenge with a view to a long-term future.

- *Less focus on long-term pay solutions.* Traditionally, this group has been rewarded through share options and long-term plans to tie them in. The disadvantage of this approach is that there is high wastage with any academy group, and tying in a cohort at such an early stage of their career may result in a group of employees who do not make the grade, become toxic, but cannot leave because their options have not matured yet.

- *Harvest and weed regularly.* Keep an eye on your crops—accept that some will not make it out of this group, and others may mature and develop more quickly than you expect. Elite talent management is all about keeping close and flexible.

## Reserves

- *Base pay.* Individuals are visible and thus more vulnerable to competitive poachers. Keep ahead of the market, and be confident that you understand all the market pressures—particularly consider significant jumps in responsibility in a smaller firm.

- *Bonus.* This is linked to company performance and individual skills. Rotate out of slow-growth into high-growth areas where these workers can make a difference to test their skills and to create self-funded bonus opportunities.

- *Tie in the long-term stock or cash plan.* This group may be particularly attracted by newer, sexier high-growth businesses and opportunities. Give them some financial interest in the long term to help retain their focus.

- *Continue to harvest and weed regularly.*

*First Team*

- *Ensure that this really is a first-team player.* Use your talent standards to help understand the impact of these workers on the business now and the long-term value that they represent.

- *Base pay.* Make sure that you understand the relevant pay market and total remuneration mix. The mix is more important than base pay alone at this level.

- *Bonus.* This is linked to company performance—minor (20 percent) on individual performance.

- *Tie in the long-term stock or cash plan.* High upside (or downside for poor performance). Structure pay to reflect business strategy (i.e., growth or profit).

- *Know that it will not be forever.* The average tenure of a CEO in the United Kingdom is 4.5 years. The average tenure of a premiership football club manager is 2.4 years. Most of them never see the result of their five-year plan. From an employee point of view, the rewards are high during these years, but so are the risks, and some people never find another role at the highest level. It is understandable why CEOs expect and receive such high pay, but the pressure to deliver the expectation they have created is then unsustainable for many (see Table 39.1).

|  | Academy | Reserves | First Team |
|---|---|---|---|
| Base pay | Monitor closely. Move away from annual mind-set. Know pay market. Aim for median. | Vulnerable to poaching—go for UQ of your market. Know your competitors. | Important but know mix of total package is right. |
| Annual bonus | On individual achievement—milestone rewards. | On annual basis—mix between individual achievement and team/department. | Focused on operation, urgent, time-limited achievement. Medium upside. |
| Long-term plan | Less important. | Tie in your assets with options for future. | Tie into long-term growth/profit/business strategy. High upside for high performance. |
| Recognition | Highly important. Cheap/free. | In assignments to show worth. | Have to be resilient—recognition is more external. |
| Nonfinancial | Offer regular assessment and progress. Be alert to new opportunities. | "Re-recruit"—make clear where development lies in competence areas. | Benefits/pension seen as key element of package. |

**Table 39.1  Incenting the Three Talent Categories**

## Steps to Make This Happen

Business leaders have an intuitive sense that this simple model based on tried and tested approaches in the sporting world would work in their organization. To make this work in your organization, the following questions are worth considering:

- *For reward professionals.* Take a good, long, hard look at the work you have been doing in linking the talent-management team's work with your business strategy around pay. Does it make sense?

- *For senior management.* Are you proud of the way that there is clarity and clear goals around your talent-management program? Do your line managers understand the return on investment made in talented individuals in your organization? No? Why not?

- *For talent-management professionals.* Is there a simpler way of presenting and streamlining your scheme to enable a clearer line of sight between the contribution that participants make and the rewards they earn?

## Creating and maintaining a culture of innovation, engagement, leadership, and performance by taking the best of the old world and applying it to new issues: globalization, ambidexterity, and creating new ways of managing performance

In today's world, making predictions about the future is challenging. But hark back to 1894, when *The Times* of London famously predicted that by 1950, every street in London would be nine feet deep in horse manure. London was not the only city plagued by this problem. New York was predicted to have droppings three stories high by 1930. Planning meetings to discuss the issue collapsed when it was agreed that no solution could be found. And yet human ingenuity did find a solution—now we are faced with similar crises based on pollution, global warming, and energy shortages. Who could have predicted the revolution of iPads, FaceBook, apps, and Twitter only five years ago?

From a rewards perspective, our job is not to predict the future. Our job is to create rewards structures that make innovation, performance, and disruptive technologies possible in our workplaces and then get out of the way.

A good example of how rewards practices can obstruct growth is around globalization. Having a consistent approach to executive pay and rewards may be useful when all geographies share a similar place in the business life cycle. A mature market will be dominated by low growth and consolidation of players—a focus on winning market share by driving differentiation and re-skilling talent. However, in a high-growth market such as India, business growth is contingent on attracting and retaining talent. Therefore, within an overall company philosophy about pay, there should be the opportunity to differentiate rewards to meet the needs of differing markets and business life cycles in separate geographies and to develop specific tactical plans. In supporting globalization and developing a coherent performance and rewards plan linked to pay strategy, too often we can bring old world solutions to new world problems and be seen by business leaders as inflexible and dogmatic.

So how do businesses in the real world attempt to deliver a confident mix of old and new world solutions? First, organizations think carefully about their needs. They conduct audits of business requirements—how do these differ in the future? One interviewee talked about the needs of his business in requiring globally mobile talent—which differs sharply from the highly educated, academic home-country-centric traditional talent pool. Other organizations talked of the need to develop talent and leaders who are ambidextrous—able to both manage operational excellence and at the same time create an environment where innovation and disruption are flourishing.

Second, they analyze the culture and reward strengths in their businesses. The John Lewis Partnership, a major retailer in the United Kingdom and an employee-owned business with over 90,000 partners, has a common profit-sharing plan in which all partners from chairman to sales floor colleagues receive the same percentage of salary as bonus. Andrew Bridges, the rewards manager, says that for the company, varying the partnership bonus to reflect individual performance is not an option, but a strong performance-management system that is linked to basic pay progression combined with career management and a long-term commitment to development intensifies the employee deal and brand. He explains that future partners "know what they are signing up for—and for them, the value set of the business is key."

Other organizations have a more complex matrix of levers they can use to attract and retain the type of talent they need in a more aggressive marketplace. Larger organizations and those listed on the Fortune 500 list or the London Stock Exchange (FTSE) may be able to include a mix of base pay, upside to bonus based on performance, and a long-term tie-in through shares with the ongoing opportunity of career development. Sometimes, though, offering top talent a promotion along a traditional career path may not work. Rachel Stock, human resources director of Hearst Magazines in the United Kingdom, talks of her top talent, so loyal to the magazine they have helped to create that they see career advancement away from "their" brand as a negative. She says, "For some, it's so personal and the connection is so strong that their fit with the brand can limit how far they want to go."

Analyzing how useful the performance-management cycle is within the operation of the business can be helpful in evaluating how far rewards practices support rather than detract from the practice of rewarding talent. Reed Hastings, CEO of NetFlix, interviewed in an article in *Harvard Business Review* (McCord, 2014), tells us, "We've had hundreds of years to work on managing industrial firms, so a lot of HR practices are centered in that experience. We're just beginning to learn to run creative firms, which is quite different. Industrial firms thrive on reducing variation (manufacturing errors); creative firms thrive on increasing variation (innovation)." For organizations employing large numbers of gen Y employees, in a creative or technological environment where innovation and developing disruptive capital are key, using a paper-based annual appraisal system can be like a bucket of cold water over employee engagement. More innovative organizations are exploring social media–type feedback systems, where employee feedback is fast, timely, and direct. Searching for "different" solutions in the big consultancies is fruitless—universally accepted wisdom is that top-down objectives and annual reviews are a business imperative. But quiet whispers from alternative voices are challenging this construct. Good managers have always known that the quality of the conversation is king—our job is to think about devising ways to manage performance while not strangling it with annual paperwork and bureaucracy. Looking to the methods of sport, music, and media helps us to identify a dual ongoing focus on both immediate- and long-term goals. These conversations happen every day on the training pitch and in rehearsal rooms and studios.

Finally, it can come down to quantum—how much is enough? Raghavendra Rau, Sir Evelyn de Rothschild Professor of Finance at Cambridge University, has conducted a longitudinal study into payment levels versus success at named organizations between 2003 and 2009. His work noted that there was a positive correlation between the highest-paid outliers (upper decile and above relative to company size) and lower corporate performance. His hypothesis is that for very highly paid executives, their attitude toward risk becomes distorted by their own package, and they lead their organizations into financial cul-de-sacs. "Making Executive Pay Work: The Psychology of Incentives" (PwC, 2012) suggests that on a globally consistent basis, executives would accept lower rewards for the "right" job. Taken together, these studies suggest that an executive (or other talent) who joins your organization primarily for the pay package is not likely to be the best or the most fulfilled person for the job. As a head of rewards in an organization, guiding the senior decision makers away from the "we want the best and we are willing to pay top dollar for it" attitude may be the most important influence they can bring to bear.

## Conclusions

So how do we navigate a path through this challenging and warming landscape as the deep freeze of the past seven years starts to lift? The main message appears to be that business is getting serious about its need for talent and its willingness to pay for high performance. Managing performance and talent in an organization, particularly those in creative and/or global environments, is likely to become a mission-critical competence. Our expectations are that there will be pent-up demand for job moves as employees stretch their legs in new directions. However, this offers exciting opportunities in which new employees come onto the market and for organizations that have identified clear hiring and rewards strategies and have effective plans in place. Worldpay has indicated that the right talent in the right place adds bottom-line value as the business looks for funding in the future. Organizations without this topic on their agenda are likely falling behind in the competition already.

"The Next High-Stakes Quest" (Towers Perrin, 2013) suggests that organizations that have not only been able to develop an employee value proposition (EVP) but also "segment their workforce and offer customized EVPs for critical employee groups ... are nearly twice as likely to report financial performance above their peer group." The Towers Watson Global Workforce study indicates that segmenting and customizing rewards for different talent groups is key to achieving improvements in this area—but implied in this is the ability of the rewards team to have the skills and knowledge to segment appropriately. Innecto's work in sports and high-performance cultures suggests that careful segmentation and linking rewards thoughtfully to different groups can be effective in attracting, growing, and retaining talent. However, this work takes time and is resource-hungry. Human resources teams need to create space to plan effectively and spare time from the annual cycle of pay review and bonus plan to develop and implement plans coherently.

Rewards professionals are being required to develop a different range of tools—and use them in a more strategic and joined-up fashion.

- Link together in an arc with colleagues in resourcing, talent management, performance engagement, and employee engagement specialties to create the most effective process for success.

- Challenge the status quo around commonality in delivery of compensation plans and devise detailed and relevant tactical plans that meet the differing needs of employee groups, particularly supporting growth in new markets.

- Be brutal in assessing the effectiveness of the annual performance-management cycle on which so many compensation decisions rest. Think the unthinkable—is it fit for purpose?

Daniel H. Pink's book, *Drive: The Surprising Truth about What Motivates Us* (2011), has upset the status quo in assessing what truly motivates talent. He identifies autonomy, mastery, and a sense of purpose as crucial in creating engaged employees. Our job as rewards professionals is to underpin and reinforce this link, not to destroy value by complexity and bureaucracy. Think, act, and then get out of the way.

## Bibliography

Jackson, Samuel. 2009. "The Golden Few: Lessons in Talent Management from the Worlds of Entertainment, Sport, Arts and Academia." London. Available for purchase online at http://www.jacksonsamuel.com/our-research/research-paper-the-golden-few.html.

McCord, P. 2014. "How Netflix Reinvented HR." *Harvard Business Review*, Jan.–Feb. Available at https://hbr.org/2014/01/how-netflix-reinvented-hr.

McCoy, C. 2013. "Perhaps Reward Specialists Should Be Less Worthy and More Engaged." *Rewards Magazine, November-December, p. 16.*

Pink, Daniel H. Drive: *The Surprising Truth about What Motivates Us.* New York: Riverhead/Penguin, 2011.

PwC. 2012. *Making Executive Pay Work: The Psychology of Incentives.* London. Available at http://www.pwc.com/en_GX/gx/hr-management-services/publications/assets/making-executive-pay-work.pdf.

Towers Perrin. 2013. *The Next High-Stakes Quest.* WorldatWork, Scottsdale, AZ.

Towers Watson. 2014. *Global Workforce Study.* Available at www.towerswatson.com.

Veilmetter, G., and Y. Sell. 2014. *Leadership 2030: The Six Megatrends You Need to Understand to Lead Your Company into the Future.* AMACOM, New York.

# 40

# Strengthening the Link between Compensation and Return on Investment

MEL STARK
*Hay Group, Inc.*

MARK ROYAL
*Hay Group, Inc.*

From an employer perspective, there will always be a need to link rewards with return on investment (ROI). This perspective comes from the recognition that an organization must appropriately use its rewards funds to drive behavior, help to engage and motivate employees, and ensure that it is doing all that is possible to attract and retain the necessary talent for business success. In this regard, let's be clear that not all companies or all functions within any one company will require "only the very best talent." Some simply cannot afford it as a cost of doing business, whereas others will approach their people strategy with a different perspective on cash compensation and benefits because the term *rewards* covers a broad spectrum that we will explore in this chapter.

The "Conference Board Survey of CEO Challenges" (2013 and 2014) has shown human capital as a top priority, with dominant themes around growing talent internally, providing training and development, raising employee engagement, improving performance-management processes, and retaining critical talent. Further, human capital is regarded as "an enterprise-wide driver" for customer relations, innovation, and operational excellence. Thus, if human capital is on the leading edge of organizational performance and achievement, your "top talent" is critical to realizing your company's full potential, however you choose to reward such workers.

Although rewarding top talent should be a critical element of every organization's talent-management and business strategy, it is clear that one size does not fit all. Different, creative approaches to achieving the same objective are an essential "to-do" for those of us charged with rewards program management and effectiveness. Just think about what you did or the tactics that you heard were being used as the recent recession put pressure on human resources and line management alike to "do more with less" and manage budgets in a way that many in leadership roles had not previously had to do. And, most would argue, that paradigm and mind-set are still the modus operandi.

In the field of rewards, it is often said that "fair is not equal." Doing the right thing in terms of linking pay to performance—and thereby strengthening your ROI—often means treating people differently. Sometimes this is easier said than done. In research that Hay Group conducted in 2008 with *Fortune* magazine's "World's Most Admired Companies" regarding the effectiveness of their pay programs, we found that among all companies, only one-third found a way to provide top performers with two times the average salary increase (about two-thirds of the companies paid 1.5 times the average to their top performers). However, among the most admired companies, over 50 percent were able to reward top performers with a two times the average increase. One could ask, is this a "chicken or egg" question—that is, is it easier for the most admired companies to do this because they are successful and their bottom lines yield opportunities for more discretionary spending? Or are they just better at how they look at, monitor, and measure performance, which allows them to create such pay differentials and communicate about them in a more effective manner? It is really both—grounded by leadership that openly supports the development of rigorous human resources programs, line managers who understand the importance of their roles and are trained to effectively implement programs and communication to staff, and, of course, the identification, nurturing, and engagement of a workforce that drives the business to achieve objectives.

While sometimes challenging in the "corporate world," this form of differentiation has been around for decades (like it or not) in the entertainment business and in professional sports. The top talent that drives people to the box office, stadiums, and arenas, those with "star power" you can bet on are scouted, sought out, courted, engaged, and rewarded in a very conscious manner. You can argue with what is often perceived by the general public as excessive pay (especially when compared with key public-service workers such as teachers and emergency responders) but not with the concept of rewarding top talent—they do it to enhance their ability to outpace and one-up the competition, which is good business under any and all circumstances.

However, you cannot isolate or separate the idea of rewarding your top talent from how you reward all others—there needs to be "a system," a philosophy and practices that articulate the how, what, and why of your organization's approach to rewards across the board. Rewards can and should be considered in the broadest terms, including the elements that can be assigned a monetary value as well as the intangible rewards that are provided because both are keys to retention of top talent (many might argue that the intangible rewards actually carry more weight in talent retention). Thus, we will start there—with an overview and clarity around the notion of *total rewards*.

## Total Rewards

Most people's knee-jerk reaction to the idea of compensation is exactly that which they see each payroll period—their net paycheck. Beyond this, some also may include any variable pay opportunity (i.e., incentive or bonus) they may earn. Although these amounts are real and tangible, the concept of rewards is much more far-reaching.

Rewards signify different things to different people, and the meaning of the word depends on the context in which it is used (just think about old TV westerns and those "Reward" posters!). In the context of business, however, although things often can feel like the Wild West, rewards are traditionally interpreted as an employee's pay (base salary, incentives, or bonuses) and the value of benefit plans. However, when you hear the term *total rewards*, its connotation goes beyond these tangible elements. Total rewards also include intangible elements that are harder to see and touch but real enough to affect an employee's level of engagement and satisfaction while contributing to attraction and retention of key staff. A working definition of *rewards* may be to consider anything that the organization provides that is of perceived value to employees. Thus, in the spirit of rewarding your top talent, you have to be aware of and pull on all the available levers to maximize your offering and the messages you want to send.

## Total Rewards Elements

Figure 40.1 highlights these distinctions. Base salary forms the foundation for all other tangible reward elements. Beyond that, there can be bonuses, long- and short-term incentives, and, of course, a variety of considerations that contribute to the benefits plan. The message here around rewarding your top talent is to move beyond the obvious yet important elements of pay, benefits, and perquisites to explore and consider all the intangible aspects of an employee's work experience that together with tangible reward components comprise an organization's total rewards offerings—and which, when properly orchestrated, can be synergistic and a real competitive advantage that cannot be easily duplicated. As Herb Kelleher, founder of Southwest Airlines, has said, "It's the intangibles that are the hardest things for a competitor to imitate. You can get airplanes, you can get ticket counter space, you can get tugs, and you can get baggage conveyors. But the spirit of Southwest is the most difficult thing to emulate. If we ever do lose that, we will have lost our most valuable competitive asset."[1]

| | | COMMON EXAMPLES | REWARDS ELEMENTS | DEFINITION |
|---|---|---|---|---|
| Internal value or motivation | Intangible | • Career development<br>• Work/life balance<br>• Safety and security | Nonfinancial rewards | Total reward |
| Rewards to which an objective dollar value can be assigned | Tangible | • Social security | Statutory benefits | Total remuneration plus |
| | | • Retirement provision<br>• Death / disability / medical<br>• Cars<br>•Benefit allowances / loans | Nonstatutory benefits | Total remuneration |
| | | • Executive share options<br>• Restricted / performance share<br>• Long-term cash schemes | LTI | Total direct compensation |
| | | • Sales commission<br>• Annual bonus<br>• Annual incentive | Annual variable | Total cash |
| | | • Basic salary<br>• Fixed payments<br>• Near cash allowances | Guaranteed cash | |

**Figure 40.1  Total rewards options.**

In his *Harvard Business Review* article, "Leadership That Gets Results" (March–April 2000), Dan Goleman makes an analogy between professional golfers and high-impact leaders. Golf pros are armed with an array of clubs. Over the course of a match, a pro picks and chooses clubs based on the demands of the shot, sometimes pondering the options and sometimes making an automatic or instinctive selection. The same, Goleman says, is true of the high-impact leader who can pick and choose among managerial styles, making conscious or automatic decisions about the best approach to managing different situations depending on the circumstances in order to harness and extract the best from those involved.[2]

As such, Goleman's analogy can be extended to the various elements of total rewards. When total rewards are used artfully and with knowledge in differing situations, a company can effectively manage the total rewards palette to make the most of all the elements available.

Bottom line: you cannot effectively consider nor make good on how best to reward your top performers if you are looking only at the most obvious pieces of the puzzle. Sure, it will take more work and some creativity and demand more of the organization, its managers, and human resources leaders, but isn't that comparable with what you expect of your top performers?

## Promoting High Levels of Employee Engagement

Retaining top talent is a key concern in both good times and bad given the importance of such employees to a company's success and competitive edge. Many organizations turn primarily to compensation for the answer, but dissatisfaction with pay is generally not what leads employees to begin exploring job alternatives, although the prospect of better compensation elsewhere may solidify the decision to leave. To keep and motivate their talent, organizations should focus on increasing employee engagement and developing systems that provide better support for employee success.

*Engagement* refers to the commitment employees feel toward the organization (e.g., their willingness to recommend it to friends and family, their pride in working for it, and their intentions to remain a part of it). But it is also about employees' discretionary effort— their willingness to go the extra mile for the organization. Right now, as organizations need to do more with less and strive for greater efficiency, tapping into the discretionary effort of employees is all the more essential. And in the rapidly changing environments most companies now face, where roles and responsibilities are continually evolving, organizations must count on employees to act on their own in ways that are consistent with organizational culture, objectives, and values.

It has been said that "money can't buy you love"—and it will not alone buy you employee engagement either. However, a sense of balance between what employees contribute to an organization and what they get in return is fundamental to sustaining the extra efforts that come with an engaged workforce. And this means that rewards programs are an important component of effective employee engagement strategies.

Hay Group research on the factors that determine employee engagement levels in organizations has highlighted two overriding themes. First, engagement is influenced not only by employees' current work experiences but also by their view of the future. For employees to commit, especially over the long term, they need to have confidence that their companies are well led, headed in a positive direction, and well positioned to deliver products and services that are aligned with customer needs. Likewise, employees need to have a positive outlook on their own future within a company in terms of opportunities to learn, develop, and progress in their careers. Second, engagement is an exchange relationship. If organizations want employees to do and deliver more, it is essential that employees feel valued as people, that their extra efforts are recognized and appreciated, and that over time there is a balance between what they give to and get back from the organization.

It is true that numerous studies over the last several decades have suggested that nonmonetary rewards and recognition can be much more effective motivators than compensation. It's not that money doesn't matter. If employees feel that they are significantly underpaid—that their pay does not reflect their contributions to the organization—their motivation is likely to suffer. However, when it comes to encouraging employees to pour discretionary effort into their work and deliver superior performance, the chance to make a difference and be recognized for it are likely to provide a much stronger incentive. And this means that in thinking about the impact of rewards on engagement, organizations are well advised to take a total rewards perspective—focusing on both tangible and intangible elements.

This should come as a welcome message. At present, organizations are struggling to meet the pressure from employees to "show me the money." Hay Group's global employee opinion norms, comprised of the responses of over 6 million employees to employee surveys conducted worldwide, indicate that at present, just 47 percent of employees feel that they are paid fairly for the work they do. And just 44 percent believe that there is a clear link between their performance and their compensation.

The task of matching tangible rewards to employee contributions has become all the more difficult in recent years. In challenging economic environments, compensation budgets are heavily pressured, meaning that as organizations are needing to ask employees to do and deliver more, their ability to reward those extra efforts financially is particularly constrained.

How are organizations responding? To find out, Hay Group in 2009–2010 conducted a survey in partnership with WorldatWork, a global association for human resources management professionals and business leaders. Over 650 rewards professionals provided insights into how they see different rewards program elements influencing employee engagement.

In terms of financial rewards, short-term incentives and bonus programs, together with benefits and perquisites, are viewed as most impactful, ahead of base salary levels and increases, long-term incentives, and financial recognition programs. Short-term incentives may score high because of their typical direct and immediate relationship to employee contributions and performance. The value placed on benefits may seem counterintuitive to some, but it may reflect the fact that benefits, generally received most equally by all, are effective mechanisms for signaling the value placed on employees as members of the organization.

Notably, however, rewards professionals see the intangible elements of rewards programs as more consequential than the tangible components in driving and sustaining engagement. Quality of leadership, the nature of the job, the quality of work environments, career-development opportunities, and the ability to achieve a reasonable work/life balance all were rated more highly than any of the financial rewards.

What's the message for organizations and their rewards programs? We offer four key recommendations:

- *Go beyond compensation and benefits to a total rewards mind-set.* Understand that rewards extend well past compensation and benefits and build the core organizational messages, such as an employment value proposition or employer brand, around total rewards offerings. Develop tools for managers so that they can effectively reward employees beyond the confines of compensation and benefits and develop and reinforce communications around total rewards.

- *Tailor total rewards to workforce segments.* Recognize that different employee groups value different rewards, and build managers' rewards toolkits based on this understanding. Focus on the ways in which managers can use career development, organization and job design, nonfinancial recognition programs, and organizational work climate to reward employees in different roles and different stages of their careers.

- *Include employees and managers in rewards design and launch.* Rewards programs are most successful when they effectively balance the needs and wants of the organization and its employees. However, many organizations do not have a good handle on what their employees value in rewards. Most organizations listen to their customers to learn what they value in products and services. This mind-set also should apply to their most important internal customers—the employees. Rewards professionals indicate that engagement is enhanced when employees and managers are involved in the design and launch of rewards programs despite the fact that they seldom are in practice.

- *Communicate the value of what you have.* Total rewards statements are powerful tools for communicating rewards offered by the organization. The human resources function should be actively involved in helping line managers understand and communicate the value of both tangible and intangible rewards.

With today's organizations operating increasingly lean, employees are being asked to do more with less. In high-workload environments, employees generally are more influenced by rewards programs and policies. Acutely aware of all that they are contributing, employees are inclined to increase the pressure on their organizations to balance returns with contributions. In this context, it is more important than ever to ensure that rewards practices and programs are perceived as recognizing employee efforts and contributions adequately.

## Return on Investment

Earlier in this chapter we mentioned ROI and the need to maximize the return on your available rewards budget. It is often said that people are an organization's greatest asset. In truth, though, they are also one of its greatest expenses. Remuneration tends to be one of the least rigorously managed components of an organization's cost structure. With, for some organizations, up to 70 percent of total costs wrapped up in remuneration, rewards cannot be ignored, particularly in challenging economic times.

Most organizations would not purchase a $10,000 copier without calculating its ROI, but many will spend hundreds of millions of dollars on their compensation programs without considering an ROI analysis. In research conducted in 2005 by Hay Group, WorldatWork, and Loyola University Chicago, we found that approximately 62 percent of employers in a general industry survey reported that they do not even attempt to measure ROI of the compensation programs. Of the 38 percent that do, most do so informally by talking with managers and employees about their perceptions of program effectiveness. The balance of organizations that measure ROI (18 percent) use formal measures such as employee opinion surveys and comparisons of the investments in people and their resulting productivity.

There is an old saying, "If you don't know where you are going, any road will get you there," and it is especially true when it comes to rewards programs. Rewards, whether tangible or intangible, are tools that can be helpful in increasing organizational effectiveness. The employment relationship involves an exchange of organizational "carrots" for employee contributions. A well-designed rewards program focuses those offers to attract and retain the talent the organization requires and to incentivize employees to act in ways consistent with business objectives. Accordingly, a total rewards approach should be about both organizational needs and employee wants.

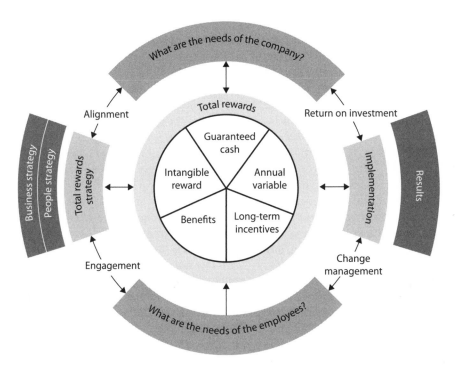

**Figure 40.2  Hay Group total rewards framework.**

*Source:* ©2008 Hay Group. All rights reserved.

Figure 40.2 highlights the Hay Group's total rewards framework. As the figure shows, a well-designed compensation program needs to focus first on developing a total rewards strategy that is aligned with and designed to support the organization's business and people strategies. Equally important, rewards programs need to be designed to maximize employee engagement levels in the organization. And changes to rewards programs need to be carefully managed and communicated during implementation to ensure adequate understanding of the rationales and implications behind decisions.

In considering the motivational impact of rewards programs, it is important to note that one size is unlikely to fit all business and employee groups. What motivates a late-career manager, for example, may not be the same as what motivates a newly hired entry-level employee. What is possible and required in a startup entrepreneurial technology organization and appeals to employees attracted to such an environment may fail in a highly regulated public-services organization. Thus, critical to the ROI of total rewards programs is first having an understanding of the needs and desires of the organization and its workforce and then tailoring the rewards offerings to particular employees or employee groups as best as possible.

## Where the Rubber Meets the Road

Although we have certainly called out the importance of total rewards as the right means to reward your top talent, there's an old adage that "cash is king." Employees may not remember all the objectives in the organization's incentive program or be able to recite the employer's core values, but they do know their base salaries and likely their variable pay opportunities, they understand what relative fairness and competitiveness are, and they probably have strong opinions about why their last raises were not big enough.

Base pay is the foundation of any compensation program and the most visible component to the vast majority of employees. Every paycheck is a reminder of the link between their efforts over the last pay period and how the organization perceives their value. Clearly, there is a critical need to "get base pay right" and to use it as one important means of rewarding your top talent. But there are a number of core elements that must work together to manage base pay and overall cash compensation effectively and that contribute to your ability to deliver effective and meaningful rewards to your top talent.

The first is having a philosophy and a set of guiding principles that highlight the organization's intent around rewards, for example, where it targets its pay—base and total cash—and why, how it balances and mixes the various rewards components, and its orientation to pay for performance. And how all of this is intended to tie back to individual employees, what they are expected to do every day, and ultimately, how they contribute to the organization's success. However, it is not sufficient to only have a sense of one's philosophy; it has to be effectively communicated and understood. Hay Group research in 2002 showed that while almost 90 percent of questioned companies said that they had a compensation philosophy, only two-thirds acknowledged that it had been committed to writing. However—and this is the point of primary concern—when asked about communication to staff, only one-third believed that they had effectively communicated about it, leading to employee understanding—a key requirement if a rewards program is intended to be motivational.

The second core element in cash compensation management is allocating salary increases relative to performance. Organizations need to ensure that performance ratings translate into differentiated rewards. Many organizations spend an agonizing amount of effort to ensure that managers comply with some sort of a distribution curve of performance ratings, but what value is this if the highest performer still receives only marginally more rewards—whether in merit pay, variable pay, or options—than the average performer? The ratings are merely a means to an end. And the end is higher rewards for the highest performance, not just a perfect distribution curve.

Most managers and employees agree that rewards should be differentiated based on performance (and the best organizations make this happen), leading to better execution and employee behaviors. In many organizations, managers want to give their stars bigger increases. But many see it as a zero-sum game. Providing larger increases to certain employees means that other employees get less, which requires managers to make some difficult decisions. Many managers choose to take the path of least resistance, giving employees roughly the same increase rather than confronting and addressing poor performance. This can be avoided by having ongoing dialogue with employees throughout the year that will pave the way for differentiating rewards. Ongoing dialogue eliminates the element of surprise, which can lessen the sting of giving a smaller increase. Managers weak in conducting performance-oriented discussions should seek coaching to improve their skills. This type of management "courage" can go a long way toward improving the climate of the organization. Nearly half of workers surveyed by Hay Group from 2009 to 2013 expressed concerns about poor performance being tolerated in their organizations.

The *merit increase matrix* provides a tool to allocate a merit budget based on individual performance and the position of an employee's salary relative to the overall salary range, which is typically a reference for the organization's desired level of competitive market pay. But the tool itself will prove insufficient, only a crutch, if managers are not prepared with the right information and the tools to communicate the company's rewards program as well as to effectively counsel employees about why they earned the increase they did and what needs to change to improve future opportunities.

The other component that is also frequently awarded as cash is that of variable pay and often is referred to, interchangeably, as *bonus* or *incentive*. However, we think that this interchangeable nomenclature is lazy and reduces the organization's quiver of rewards offerings. For purposes of clarity, we suggest that you consider the following distinctions: *incentives* should be predetermined, communicated, known about, and understood by employees. The measures should be clear and trackable so that at different points in time during the year, the company and employees might get a sense of how they are doing and so that at year end there is greater clarity about outcomes and consequences. *Bonuses*, however, may be known about but typically are determined after the fact and are highly discretionary. Accordingly, using these terms interchangeably limits an organization's ability to offer bonuses, but they may be described and awarded in addition to an incentive.

Beyond the definition of these two approaches to variable pay, in order for programs to be effective—motivating, if so intended, or simply a way to say "thank you" in recognition for something well done—they should have their roots in the organization's overall compensation philosophy and operating culture. And their amounts should be meaningful and relevant to that philosophy and culture. There's a disconnect and a lack of logic if, however, the organization promotes itself as fiercely competitive in the area of business development but then offers an incentive plan without much upside. For those who worked hard and got good results, what will be the message and the motivational intent in subsequent years?

Similarly, what is the message you are communicating if overall the organization has a "passable" year and employees do not really see their work connected to the end result but then the organization makes lavish bonus payments? We are sure that the payments will be well received, but what signal are you sending about future expectations? And are you running the risk of creating an entitlement mentality?

Cash may be king, but it has to rule actively!

## Help Me Help You

If you're a student of cinema or just someone who likes the movies, you probably will recall this memorable line, "Help me help you," as one spoken by Tom Cruise, playing the role of the high-octane super sports agent Jerry Maguire from the 1996 movie of the same name.

In it, Jerry is pleading with his one remaining client, Rod Tidwell (played by Cuba Gooding, Jr., in an Academy Award–winning role), for Rod to arm Jerry ("Help me") with what he needs to know about Rod—what makes him tick, what appeals to him, what will/will not work, what is nonnegotiable, and so on—so that Jerry can in turn negotiate and win a "right fit" contract for Rod ("Help you").

We may be stretching the analogy here a bit, but the same is true of the relationship between "the company" (Rod, the client) and its "staff" (Jerry, the agent). In order for members of your staff to do the best job they can for you, they too need to be armed with information—in part, of course, about their roles, company expectations, and the like. However, our emphasis here is that we think that members of your staff also can benefit from information about themselves, their strengths, and their development needs. This is especially true of top performers because research has shown that we tend to focus on development plans for those who fall short, thinking that the top performers have what they need and can fend for themselves when, in fact, the truth is that there's more in the tank of the top performers if you can identify blind spots and channel their development of same. In this context, we think that assessments can work for both the company and the staff.

To begin with, companies should be challenging themselves on what processes or systems they currently use to initially identify top performers or high potentials. We all have seen systems that are rooted in historical or cultural biases that, when closely scrutinized, cannot be connected directly to a "formula for success" for people or past performance that truly drives organizational results. Many organizations struggle with decisions about selection. Identifying top talent, or those with promise and high potential, is critical to driving performance. Using research-based competency assessment and modeling, with a more direct line of sight to the characteristics of those who truly make a difference in the organization, is one approach that can help. And research has shown that approaches such as these can add significant organizational value.

In the context of this chapter, though, assessments can be seen as another way to reward your top talent. It is clear that not every organization offers and certainly not every person gets the opportunity to have a professional assessment of skills and development needs. Done well, this is worth its weight in gold and is often seen as "a gift" by those who participate. The process can yield some very revealing information and needs to be managed in the most professional way, especially as it relates to feedback that can be quite sensitive. Still there are a wealth of applications to fit a variety of needs and budgets. Hay Group has developed and makes extensive use of some very effective tools in this domain, such as the "Inventory of Leadership Styles," the "Organizational Climate Survey," and the "Emotional and Social Competency Inventory."

If we go back to Jerry Maguire, assessment information is a way to help those invited to participate ("Help them") to determine the best way to contribute on a higher level for the company ("Help you"). And if you choose to focus this type of opportunity on a top performer, it certainly can be promoted and seen as a piece of his or her total rewards offering. The top performer gets the chance to obtain insights that otherwise would have gone unnoticed and use those to enhance his or her self-awareness and focus his or her development efforts. It also has happened that after involvement in an assessment process, people simply connect the dots and make a decision that "this is not the right place for me." Is it not better for all concerned, though, to have this epiphany earlier in their career or at least before more and more time and money are spent on a less-than-desirable situation and employment track rather than waking up one day too late to change horses? This could be the best gift of all.

## Further Enabling Employees to Succeed

The assessment process just described is an example of what the Hay Group would describe as one element of enablement. Our research shows that employee engagement alone does not guarantee an organization's effectiveness. Studies we have conducted in hundreds of companies in diverse industries worldwide confirm that many enjoy high levels of engagement yet still struggle in terms of performance. What is missing is real *employee enablement* to position motivated employees to succeed.

If employee engagement is about the "want to" (the desire to do and deliver more), employee enablement is about the "can do" (the ability to get things done effectively). It involves matching people with roles in ways that take best advantage of what they can offer. It also involves ensuring that employees are operating in supportive work environments (where they have what they need to be effective, and barriers to performance are minimized). A cross-industry analysis conducted by the Hay Group in 2009 involving over 400 companies represented in our global employee opinion database suggests that while organizations in the top quartile on engagement demonstrate revenue growth 2.5 times that of organizations in the bottom quartile, companies in the top quartile on both engagement and enablement achieve revenue growth 4.5 times greater—a strong case for "reward ROI."[3]

Unfortunately, most organizations employ a sizable number of "frustrated" workers—individuals who are highly engaged but are not sufficiently enabled to be fully effective and successful. Frustration is a significant problem for organizations and employees, especially in a challenging economic environment. Organizations trying to squeeze out every drop of productivity cannot afford to squander the energy of motivated employees. And employees who are being asked to work harder and do more with less understandably want to work in smart and efficient ways. In the short term, these motivated but poorly enabled employees may suffer in silence. Over time, though, many can be expected to turn off and disengage—or tune out and leave.[4]

## Today and Tomorrow

There are bound to be weak links in rewards program design and implementation. Given what should be dynamic systems, there will always be some modicum of change and therefore uncertainty around what fits, what makes sense for an organization at any one point in time. But those weak links create great opportunities in human resources and rewards. To this point, based on recent Hay Group research, human resources professionals tell us that they see a lack of robust reward strategies and that reward components are managed in isolation of one another.[5] Given the CEO priorities and concerns referred to in The Conference Board reports (2013 and 2014 cited earlier), the chance to "seize the day" and take aggressive action toward holistic thinking and practice around rewards program management (and even linkage to broader human resources policies and practices) could not be more attractive.

Further to the above-referenced research, aside from wanting to effectively promote differentiated pay, human resources professionals say that moving forward they hope to see a substantive focus on reward communications so that employees appreciate that their rewards program consists of total rewards, leaders regularly sustain reward and performance communications, and they can generate more manager and employee involvement in rewards program design and feedback.

We would add to this the need for greater emphasis on the design and communication of variable pay programs given their critical link between defined objectives—company, department, individual—being measured and what employees need to do to help the organization do well and be rewarded in kind.

## Bottom Line

There are basic dictionary definitions of *rewards* that, paraphrased, suggest that they are "something given in return for some service or attainment." We believe that the takeaway from this chapter should be that rewards are considerably more than "some thing"; in fact, rewards that the organization can and should provide are numerous and come in various forms—monetary and otherwise. In order for rewards to be effective, responsible management should be aware of all such reward opportunities and actively manage the money, mix, and message in order to make rewards the dynamic management tools they are meant to be.

## Notes

1. Doug Jensen, Tom McMullen, and Mel Stark, *The Manager's Guide to Rewards: What You Need to Get the Best for—and from—your Employees.* AMACOM, New York, 2007, p. 61.
2. Daniel Goleman, "Leadership That Gets Results." *Harvard Business Review* 78(2):78, 2000.
3. Mark Royal and J. Yoon, "Engagement and Enablement: The Key to Higher Levels of Individual and Organizational Performance." *Journal of Compensation and Benefits*, Sept.–Oct. 2009. Available at https://atrium.haygroup.com/downloads/marketingps/nl/secure/PS_WW_EES_The_Key_to_Higher_Levels_of_Performance.pdf
4. Mark Royal and Tom Agnew, *The Enemy of Engagement: Put an End to Workplace Frustration—and Get the Most from Your Employees.* AMACOM, New York, 2011.
5. Dow Scott and Tom McMullen, "Rewards Next Practices: 2013 and Beyond." *WorldatWork Journal*, Q4, 2013.

# 41

# Incorporating Work/Life Effectiveness into a Total Rewards Strategy

KATHLEEN M. LINGLE

This chapter shares the newest and most robust research findings from more than 700 work/life researchers across the globe. These findings suggest specific ways in which a tighter collaboration among compensation, work/life, and the rest of the elements of total rewards can be leveraged to solve a variety of workplace issues whose amelioration is within our collective grasp. In fact, the results will boost overall business success in predictable, measurable ways. This is a total rewards legacy worth building.

## Learning Points

Given the holistic perspective of the work/life portfolio and increasingly robust research underpinnings, the practice of work/life effectiveness offers methodologies and well-honed tools that address many of the same themes that preoccupy compensation professionals: sustainability of high-quality performance, application of more powerful analytic approaches with the advent of "big data," defining and creating workplace determinants of engagement and innovation, and developing strategy and tactics that help leaders to adapt to rapidly changing business conditions. Another business outcome in which work/life most publicly demonstrates its specialized expertise involves strengthening the competitive advantage of employers who actively compete for national and local recognition in their markets and industries as "employers of choice."

The specific learning points for this material include the following:

- *The key objective of the compensation function overlaps with the raison d'etre of the work/life endeavor.* A deeper understanding of this reality opens new avenues for collaboration that will more quickly and effectively dissolve specific barriers that are inhibiting business success today.

- *In business as in politics, mind-set can either inhibit appropriate responses to changing events, marketplaces, and processes or create motivation and productivity.* An exploration of the relationship between mind-set and corresponding impact measures brings forth several examples where compensation and work/life professionals have the potential to define and resolve issues of mutual significance.

- *Certain static notions about work, workers, and the work environment are obstacles to organizational agility and need to be dissolved.* An empirically based definition of the prerequisite elements of an "effective workplace" is given, clarifying a manageable subset of people strategies that have been demonstrated to provide maximum organizational impact.

- *Thinking out of the box is not a skill set isolated in any one organizational function; it is generated through expert teamwork across disparate mind-sets and bodies of knowledge.* Business sustainability demands even heavier doses of innovative thinking and solutions today.

## What Work/Life Effectiveness Is

*Work/life effectiveness* refers to the intersection of self (the worker), career (work), family, and community (Figure 41.1).

*Workplace* is seldom as static as the word implies because work today refers less to a place than to a set of tasks and goals to accomplish. *Community* (whether local, national, or global) is where workers live and from where employers draw both customers and their labor force. Employer organizations also earn their reputation or goodwill within the community, the maintenance of which is vital to positive business outcomes. Thus community is an important base of operations as well as a major stakeholder for both the employer and employee. *Family* is the core unit of society, the glue that holds civilization together, and the engine that creates the future supply of labor and customers, the pipeline and quality of which are of great interest to employers.

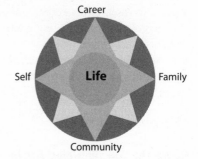

**Figure 41.1 Work/life effectiveness model.**

As a person moves through his or her *career*, predictable conflicts arise among these domains. There is inevitable spillover between what goes on at home, in the community, and in the workplace, and vice versa. These conflicts require active management for the mutual success of employees and employers. For example, having a child is a major life event that requires significant changes in the expenditure of time and energy both off and on the job, especially (but not exclusively) for the primary caregiver. The declining health of an aging parent may have a similar effect. Everyone who works is a juggler, perpetually navigating his or her way through an ever-changing variety of often conflicting priorities at the critical intersections between work and other aspects of life.

## The Work/Life Portfolio

In the past several decades, employers have developed specific organizational practices, policies, and programs to support the efforts of employees to achieve success within and outside the workplace, and they continue to innovate in response to twenty-first-century challenges.

These employer-sponsored initiatives comprise a strategic framework referred to as the *work/life portfolio*, a key element of any organization's total rewards strategy to attract, motivate, and retain the talent required to achieve its business goals. These people practices cluster into seven major categories that are designed to address the predictable life events encountered by everyone who works throughout the career life cycle, from career entry into retirement (Figure 41.2).

**Figure 41.2 The work/life portfolio.**

The bidirectional arrows in the figure indicate that none of the clusters is linear, isolated, or random. Rather, the categories interrelate in complex ways that work/life research is making great strides to untangle. For example, workplace flexibility practices are strongly associated with better health and wellness outcomes. Implementing workplace flexibility inevitably requires some retrofitting of workplace culture because few organizations are designed from the outset to remain flexible as they age. Physical and financial well-being is understood today to be far more interdependent than we understood even six years ago. Ensuring that employees' dependents are well taken care of not only enhances employee productivity but also affects the health and wellness of the entire family system. At the same time, support for dependent care improves employee financial security and stimulates the creative application of paid and unpaid time-off practices.

The process of engineering and managing a multifaceted work/life portfolio involves both art and science. The work/life professionals who do this work possess a variety of skills, including

- Child- and elder-care assessment techniques
- Work/life needs-assessment design
- Culture change-management and change-communication expertise
- Mastery of the technical aspects of design and management of flexible scheduling
- Implementation of nonlinear career-pathing
- Mentoring program design and implementation
- Pilot program implementation
- Work/life training development and delivery
- Research design
- Metrics and analytic assessment

If this sounds like a tall order, it is. However, since the 2003 merger of Alliance for Work-Life Progress into WorldatWork, the first work/life certification has been developed, so new entrants to the field now can receive training for some of the most critical aspects of the work, such as increasing organizational agility to withstand the whiplash of today's rapidly changing business conditions.

## What Work/Life Does

Work/life experts divide into three primary groups: researchers, practitioners, and consultants. Prior to 1990, there were no corporate practitioners. Work/life research preceded practice by more than a decade, and the number and quality of researchers are very much on the upswing today. In fact, the Work Family Research Network held its second global conference in mid-June 2014, and it featured nearly 1,000 researchers.

Contrary to uninformed opinion, therefore, work/life is heavily data driven in both the popular and academic press. The pursuit of work/life recognition by employers of all sizes and industries leads to highly visible national competitions, most notably vetted by two magazines, *Fortune* and *Working Mother*. Anyone can find the top 100 employers for work/life effectiveness in a few keystrokes. The same cannot be said for any other human resources function, with the exception of diversity management.

On the academic side, approximately 2,000 work/life research articles are published each year in refereed journals with stringent standards. This intellectual productivity is also channeled competitively, resulting in the annual Rosabeth Moss Kanter Award for Excellence in Work/Family Research, named after the illustrious business leader at Harvard University.

There are prestigious nonacademic work/life research centers as well, the best known of which is the Families and Work Institute (FWI), famous for conducting in tandem nationally representative longitudinal studies of both employers and employees that yield unique insights into the changing work experience of the U.S. labor force in the past three decades ("National Study of the Changing Workforce"). This is juxtaposed on the perspective of employers about the status of their work/life initiatives ("National Study of Employers," the most recent report published in April 2014).

## What Work/Life Knows

The confluence of three important research efforts has empirically defined seven factors that are universally present in the most effective workplaces. The discussion that follows will concentrate all potential total rewards collaboration in these well-documented areas. The *effective workplace* (a term coined by the FWI from its extensive longitudinal research) is characterized by optimal levels of these elements:

- Job challenge and learning
- Climate of respect and trust
- Supervisor task support
- Economic security
- Work/life fit
- Autonomy
- Minimization of status distinctions ("We're all in this together")

The first six are best encapsulated by FWI; the last of these is derived from two additional non-work/life sources, Watson Wyatt's (now Towers Watson's) "human capital index" research [Pfau and Kay, *The Human Capital Edge: 21 People Management Practices Your Company Must Implement (or Avoid) to Maximize Shareholder Value*, McGraw-Hill, New York, 2002] and *Fortune* magazine's "trust index," the research instrument used to select the annual *Fortune* list of the "100 Best Companies to Work for in America." The fact that research conducted across multiple disciplines and methodologies points to the same conclusions adds the important element of convergent validity, which confers a high level of credibility to the findings.

Of course, there are many more things that the work/life field knows empirically about work, workers, and the workplace, but these cannot be adequately summarized here. Rather, additional proof points will be integrated where appropriate into the recommendations that follow.

## What Work/Life and Compensation Expertise Can Accomplish through Collaboration

### First, a Word about the Importance of Mind-Set (Carol Dweck, *Mind-Set: The New Psychology of Success*, Ballantine Books, New York, 2007)

*Mind-set* is a fixed mental attitude that predetermines responses to and interpretations of situations, habits of mind formed by previous experience, a belief. We all operate cognitively and emotionally from a core set of assumptions and beliefs in order to make sense of what we encounter. We categorize by separating objects, resources, tasks, and people into manageable units, and then we place them into neatly arranged boxes in our mind. This creates a useful shorthand, the lens through which we view the world. Once established, a mind-set is hard (but not impossible) to change. In the workplace, mind-set discrepancies are most evident with regard to the nature of work and the nature of workers—the people who do the work. The underlying assumptions in these two directions are seldom openly discussed but manifest in specific patterns of behavior that are considered acceptable—"the way things are done here." These are the determinants of organizational culture, the seventh ball that work/life experts must juggle, because predictable elements of every workplace culture get in the way of optimizing the kind of agile, flexible organizational style that undergirds an effective workplace, as previously defined.

The compensation and work/life disciplines share a unity of intention. They are also bound by the strength of common empirical data that suggest that some courses of action are demonstrably more effective in eliciting motivation than others. Here are recommendations for specific collaborative effort between the compensation and work/life practices:

*Create a More Flexible, Agile Organizational Culture to Ensure Business Sustainability.* This objective often is the central plank of an employer-of-choice business strategy. As the term implies, the goal is to turn the normal employment relationship on its head by creating a work environment so compelling that the high-performing talent required for success chooses to apply.

On the work/life front, this can involve participating in one or more award competitions. The information and data required are heavily skewed in two directions: distribution of compensation and culture cues.

Beyond award applications, there are many other issues of mutual interest, such as the implementation of flexible work options that require alterations in schedule, triggering potential adjustments in pay. When users are women, who may in some instances be earning less than their male counterparts to begin with, prorating pay by the same ratio for both genders potentially could penalize women even further.

In many organizations, flexible work options are only made accessible to exempt professional staff, although a growing body of research suggests that organizations actually gain higher productivity and engagement from workers at the bottom rungs of the corporate ladder than from their more affluent colleagues (Jody Heymann, *Profit at the Bottom of the Ladder: Creating Value by Investing in Your Workforce,* Harvard Business Press, Boston, 2010).

It is lower-paid employees who are most often on the front lines of client and customer interaction. They acquire a great deal of relationship capital and therefore exert a disproportionate degree of influence on customer retention and loyalty, considering the compensation and respect they earn. As Heymann explains, "Employees determine 90 percent of a company's profitability. Yet many firms assume that only their highest-skilled, best-educated workers are worth investing in and that cutting wages and benefits for the workers at the bottom of the corporate ladder is a fast and effective way to improve the bottom line." The multiple examples she provides from employers who have excelled financially by offering their least-skilled workers higher wages, flexible scheduling and leave time, better healthcare benefits, profit sharing, and career advancement opportunities should not go unexamined. This would be a productive conversation opener for compensation and work/life practitioners to share and challenge aspects of a mind-set that might be out of touch with economic reality in the twenty-first century.

Another critical issue in establishing an employer-of-choice strategy is to define the quality of the employer's reputation. What will compel people to stand in line to become employed at one firm over another? Reputation will always be affected by the elements of the total rewards mix. Concocting just the right recipe for success requires the sharing and challenging of collective knowledge across multiple functions.

*Tackling the "Motherhood Penalty."* National data illustrate that in the aggregate, full-time working women earn somewhat less than men at comparable levels. Nested within these statistics is a lesser-discussed pattern of systematic compensation imbalance: mothers earn less than their unmarried peers (Melanie A. Hulbert, "Unveiling Gendered Assumptions in the Organizational Implementation of Work-Life Policies," *WorldatWork Journal*, First Quarter, 2009; Joan Williams, "Litigating the Maternal Wall," UC Hastings College of the Law, 2006; Robert Drago, "Striking a Balance: Work, Family, Life," Economic Affairs Bureau, Washington, DC, 2007).

Women with children are also offered employment and promotions at a significantly lower rate [Shelley J. Correll, Stephen Benard, and In Palk, "Getting a Job: Is There a Motherhood Penalty?" *American Journal of Sociology* 112(5):1297–1339, 2007].

This untenable situation might qualify as low-hanging fruit, an issue that a united effort between compensation and work/life could ameliorate by gathering the relevant data in our workplaces and taking appropriate remedial action. Where no such discrepancy exists, there is cause to celebrate, which will draw more qualified women into the organization. Either outcome of this type of an investigation would qualify as a win.

*Gender Pay Gap.* The larger, more well-known discrepancy between the compensation of women and men is not widely discussed in compensation circles in my experience. It does preoccupy work/life practitioners, most of whom are women themselves and often have oversight for their employers' affinity groups, which almost always include a women's network. This issue is particularly thorny because its roots run deep in the larger national culture. As Adam Grant points out in an April 13, 2014, *New York Times* article, "Raising a Moral Child," achievement (those who earn) is valued over caring (those who engage in care giving) in this country to a level not common elsewhere in the world. Nowhere is this more obvious than in the American workplace, where compensation is distributed in extremely differential patterns from the top to the bottom of the organization.

Taking on this challenge would require grappling with disparate mind-sets head-on, but the payoff would be worth it because the World Economic Forum in Davos has estimated that closing the remaining employment gender gap in the United States would increase gross domestic product by up to 9 percent (Klaus Schwab, "The Global Competitiveness Report 2011–2012," World Economic Forum, SRO-Kundig, Switzerland, 2011). What is there to lose by at least debating a path forward to such a contribution to the nation's productivity?

There is additional incentive to address the systematic underpaying of women. There is growing evidence that companies with a higher proportion of women in leadership ranks perform significantly better than those dominated by men. Two studies by Catalyst have examined the link between women leaders and the performance of the Fortune 500 companies. The group of companies with the highest average representation of women in their top management teams had 35 percent higher return on equity and 34 percent higher return to shareholders. This outperformance was greater when there were three or more women on the board of directors (Avivah Wittenberg-Cox and Alison Maitland, *Why Women Mean Business: Understanding the Emergency of Our Next Economic Revolution*, Jossey-Bass, San Francisco, 2008). Are we well advised to continue to let an outdated mind-set about the lesser value of women as caregivers put them at financial disadvantage earlier in their careers?

*Achievement of Wellness Goals in the Workplace.* A great deal of time, effort, and money is currently devoted to enticing employees to engage in healthier behaviors, taking greater accountability for their own health outcomes. A litany of studies suggests that this enterprise is not going as well as anticipated (National Institute for Health Care Reform Research Brief 1, "Employer Wellness Initiatives Grow, but Effectiveness Varies Widely," July 2010; "All Is Not Well," *Workforce*, February 2014). The United States pays more per employee for prescription benefits and healthcare than anywhere else in the world, but quality continues to fall short versus the expenditure.

Collaboration between work/life and compensation experts could be just what the doctor ordered. The application of family systems theory, incorporation of community resources into the workplace (and vice versa), a united frontal assault on overwork, a retrofitting of pay for performance that favors leading by example—there are many skill sets and tools that we could collectively bring to this table.

Total rewards professionals can apply their considerable talents to resolving work/life issues that are obstacles to business success and keep us from being the best that we can be. They can accomplish this by promoting a frank discussion of the issues, committing to a reexamination of our closest held beliefs, providing transparency of data, and sharing methodologies, tools, and strategic thinking about work, workers, and the workplace.

# 42

# A Methodology for Effectively Communicating Compensation Programs

John A. Rubino

*Rubino Consulting Services*

A clear compensation methodology is a critical component of a compensation program. Even the most elegantly designed program will not achieve its desired purpose unless employees and managers understand and accept its provisions.

What is surprising is the lack of attention many companies place on communicating compensation. They should, however, pay more attention to communications because studies show that pay is consistently cited as one of the primary reasons, though not the only one, for accepting a position or staying with a company. Moreover, compensation can be either a powerful job performance motivator or an equally powerful de-motivator depending on how it is designed—and, most important, how well it is communicated to the workforce.

Nonetheless, the reasons many companies do not communicate well are varied. Some companies, unfortunately, have compensation plans that are not designed properly or administered consistently, so communicating them would result in confusion or dissension among employees. Other companies with well-designed and company-aligned programs choose to maintain secrecy because "That's the way the culture is around here," or "It's management's responsibility to determine pay; the employees just have to accept it," or (an actual comment from a compensation professional) "The more communicating that I do, the more questions I get, and the more explaining and convincing I have to do. I don't have time to do my job!" It is important to remember, however, that a major part of every compensation professional's job is answering questions and clarifying the details of the compensation program and, most important, trying to get management and employees buy-in.

This chapter discusses the following learning points:

- Comprehensive and transparent employee communication is essential to the successful design and implementation of all compensation programs.

- Compensation communication is a qualitative and human exercise and, as such, requires the use of a structured approach to ensure the following: (1) all important communication elements are properly designed and implemented, (2) the communication design team stays focused and on track, and (3) all key employee communication objectives are realized and implemented effectively.

- A pragmatic six-step communication methodology is outlined with a proven record of success. First, a general description and key attributes of each step are presented, followed by an illustration of the six communication steps in action using a real-world case-study example.

In today's highly competitive global business and human resources environment, many companies are beginning to change their way of thinking. They are finding that carefully designed and thoroughly communicated compensation programs are the key ingredients for motivating employees and increasing profitability. Because of this, many of them are abandoning an antiquated "mushroom" mentality of keeping employees in the dark and telling them nothing constructive about their compensation programs.

As a result, there is an increasing number of companies that devote a great deal of time and effort to communicating their compensation programs. However, many organizations do not approach the task in a structured manner. Some believe that the "medium is the message" and start the process by choosing the tools of communication, such as brochures, plan descriptions, videos, and the Internet/intranet. This is a mistake because a well-designed plan description, a beautiful, multicolored brochure, or an elegantly designed human resources website may not communicate in a consistent or coherent manner—or worse, may communicate unintended messages. Another common mistake companies make is to view communication as an after-the-fact exercise; that is, design the compensation program first and then communicate. However, the most effective communication programs are developed and implemented *in tandem* with the compensation design project.

To avoid these problems and to help achieve success, it is important to develop a structured, step-by-step approach for communicating compensation programs effectively. I have found through my global consulting experiences that executing the following six steps will help to ensure that compensation communication will be accomplished in a systematic, "managed" way. I will first present a general description of the communication methodology, followed by the six steps in action using a real-world case-study example.

1. Analyze the current situation.

2. Define the objective and key messages.

3. Conduct the audience research.

4. Choose the media.

5. Design and implement the strategy.

6. Evaluate the communication program.

## Step 1: Analyze the Current Situation

This first step includes analyzing the current state of the compensation system. This is to ensure that everyone involved in the execution of the program has a clear picture of what is working and what needs to be changed. Moreover, in situations where major changes will take place, the business case needs to be made for why a new compensation strategy is necessary. In addition, it is important to "play newspaper reporter" by answering the following questions: who, what, where, when, how, and why. That is, *who* will be affected by the new compensation strategy; *what* will be communicated; *where* will the communication take place; *when* will this happen; *how* will it get done; and most important, *why* this needs to be accomplished. In this step, these questions should be answered in a general way, with more details provided in the steps to follow.

## Step 2: Define the Objective and Key Messages

This step may seem obvious, but it is often overlooked. Defining the objective and key messages means figuring out what needs to be communicated, the major points to be emphasized, as well as what the company hopes to accomplish through the communication. This is very necessary in order to stay "on message."

When companies institute a new or revised compensation program, more often than not this involves some changes in compensation philosophy or approach. It is important that the communication program not only convey new information but also that it effects some change in employee attitude and behavior. Therefore, one key objective of the program should be not only to "tell them" but also to "sell them." This "tell and sell" approach will affect every aspect of the design and implementation of the communication program.

The three mega-objectives of all compensation communication programs are

- To ensure understanding

- To change perceptions/get buy-in

- To motivate the right behaviors

With slight variations, these objectives can be used in a variety of compensation communication programs. Furthermore, within the framework of these mega-objectives, it is important to customize the goals to fit the specific programs to be communicated and to support the objectives the company hopes to achieve. Next, the key messages are the content and action plans that are linked directly to the specific objectives. They typically are written in bullet format and number no more than three or four.

## Step 3: Conduct the Audience Research

After the objectives and key messages have been identified, the next step is to collect information from executives, managers, and employees concerning their current understanding and perceptions of the compensation programs. This includes the attitudes they have regarding current programs, in addition to any knowledge they may have of anticipated changes. Use of this information, combined with the stated objectives and key messages, will ensure that the needs and concerns of both the company and the employees will be addressed.

Asking employees for their opinions and perceptions and assessing knowledge and attitudes (in effect, "taking their temperature") indicate that the company cares about what and how they think. Moreover, the employees become involved in the design of the program and, as a result, feel a sense of ownership and commitment. This goes a long way toward ensuring a successful communication program.

An example of questions to be addressed:

- Who are the audiences?
- What is the current level of understanding regarding the compensation program?
- Is there a perceived alignment of the compensation program with corporate culture and philosophy?
- How does the compensation program fit with any other recent or upcoming changes?
- Are communication messages clear and consistent?
- Do managers have the necessary people skills?
- Do employees know what is expected of them regarding job performance?
- Do employees believe that there is a connection between performance and the reward system?
- How does senior management view communication?
- What is the current employee relations climate?
- Are global considerations an issue?

These questions represent general topic areas to be addressed and are only an example of the type of information that needs to be collected and assessed. More detailed questions need to be articulated and more specific information needs to be obtained depending on the particular compensation program being communicated.

Gathering as much information as possible on knowledge, attitudes, perceptions, and opinions is important not only in designing communications but also in developing an anchor point from which to later evaluate the effectiveness of the communication program. Research methods include questionnaires, focus groups, informal networks, one-on-one interviews, and interviews with senior management.

## Step 4: Choose the Media

As mentioned earlier, many companies inappropriately begin at this step when developing communication programs. However, only after analyzing the situation, defining the objective and key messages, and conducting the audience research can a company choose effective communication "tools"—that is, determine what would be the most appropriate media to use.

There is a wide variety to choose from, ranging from the relatively simple to the technologically complex. Most of the various types of media can be slotted into one of four major categories: audiovisual, print, personal, and electronic. It is important to note, however, that these categories are not mutually exclusive. Virtually every successful communication program uses a number of media methods in various combinations.

Audiovisual media include PowerPoint presentations, flipcharts, videotape, and teleconferencing. Examples of print media are brochures, booklets, letters, memos, summary-plan descriptions, compensation policy manuals, and paycheck stuffers. Personal communications can be large meetings, small gatherings, one-on-one counseling, and manager-employee sessions. Finally, all computer-based communication technology is in the category of electronic media. These include human resources websites/intranet, interactive PC programs, e-mail, and webcasting, as well as personalized total compensation statements.

When deciding on which media (and media combinations) are most appropriate, it is important to consider the development and production costs as well as the media's communication effectiveness. In general, the most effective methods of communication are those that require a good deal of face-to-face human interaction (allowing for real-time two-way communication), as well as those that convey a personalized message. This is particularly important to keep in mind as computer-based technologies continue to play an increasingly greater role in communications. It is essential that the communication process not become dehumanized. After all, compensation is a highly emotional people-management exercise. We cannot lose sight of the critical importance of human beings in the same room conversing with each other!

In most instances, people absorb and respond to spoken messages better than they do to the written word. More "senses" are at work, which, in turn, heighten attentiveness, improve retention, and increase buy-in. Also, tailoring a message to meet the specific needs of an individual or group virtually ensures that it will be understood and accepted. However, some of these methods can carry relatively high development, production, and/or time costs.

## Step 5: Design and Implement the Strategy

The next step is to develop and implement a communication strategy within the framework of the defined objectives and to incorporate the most aligned media techniques within that strategy. The following is a generic example of a communication strategy that can be tailored to other specific compensation situations:

- An e-mail from the CEO will be sent to all employees before the new compensation design project begins. The memo generally will outline the process as well as stress the company's commitment to the project's success.

- Principal managers will meet to discuss specific responsibilities for the compensation project and subsequent communication sessions.

- To keep employees informed throughout the process, information will be communicated at key stages through "live" presentations and discussions, strategic e-mails, and the human resources website.

- As the project progresses, all managers will participate in training courses on interpersonal and team-building skills. Also, important elements of the compensation project will be discussed, particularly the performance criteria and evaluation programs.

- Formal communication sessions will be conducted for all employees at the conclusion of the compensation project, which will include an extended questions and answers section.

## Step 6: Evaluate the Communication Program

The final step in communicating compensation programs is evaluating the effectiveness of the communications effort. This statement is somewhat misleading because obtaining feedback should occur not only after the formal sessions but also throughout the course of the communication program. For example, the company should be evaluating the extent to which the communication objectives and key messages are realistic and attainable, whether the information collected on employee attitudes and perceptions is valid and indicative, whether the strategies developed are effective, whether the media chosen are the most appropriate for conveying the message, whether the communication sessions are targeting the appropriate audiences, and most important, whether the messages are being assimilated. Some of this information will become readily apparent as the communication program progresses, and ongoing adjustments in strategy and implementation may be required.

It is best to evaluate the effectiveness of the entire communication effort four to six months after the formal sessions. This allows time for employees to assimilate the information and adjust to the new system. Generally, the same approach can be used to evaluate the program as was used to conduct the audience research in step 3. This includes the use of questionnaires (with additional questions relating specifically to the communication program), focus groups, interviews, and the informal network. Ideally, the employees surveyed should be the same ones who participated in the initial information-gathering process.

As a result, a comparison of the "before" and "after" responses to questions such as the following will provide a wealth of information on whether the communication program was effective:

- What is the current level of understanding regarding compensation and benefit plans?
- How well do managers and employees communicate with each other?
- Are consistent messages being communicated by top management?
- Do employees believe that there is a connection between performance and the reward system?

The following is a synopsis of a real-world case-study example using the six-step communication methodology.

## Managed Communication Methodology for a New Compensation Strategy

### 1. Analyze the Current Situation

The organization is transforming its reward strategy this year away from a traditional job-based system (merit increases) to incentive compensation for all employees. This will require significant cultural change as well as the establishment of new behaviors that define success. The intent is to abolish the entitlement mentality and institute monetary rewards that will be variable based directly on performance: establishing a marked distinction between those who go "above and beyond" in their job duties and those who do not. Executives and managers will model the new behaviors and establish performance goals that are discernible, valid, and measurable. The organization must make these changes in order to remain competitive, as well as to attract, retain, and motivate a top-quality workforce.

The communication will take place within the next six months in every company operation and location and will use an aligned combination of media methodologies and techniques to ensure effectiveness. To be comprehensive and to increase buy-in by everyone, a cross section of executives, middle managers, and human resources representatives will be directly involved in the communication effort.

## 2. Define the Objective and Key Messages

*Objective Statement.* To ensure understanding and acceptance by all employees of the changes in the organization's reward strategy, we will effectively communicate the benefits to both the employees and the organization of the new compensation incentive program. We will emphasize compensation variability based on performance and deemphasize the entitlement mentality for the purpose of aligning the new desired behaviors with the new organizational values.

*Key Messages*

- Communicate the new behavioral models that must be demonstrated by all employees. These behaviors are aligned directly with the articulated organizational values and core competencies.

- Communicate the importance of job ownership and personal responsibility with regard to work performance.

- Thoroughly explain the new incentive compensation reward mechanisms, emphasizing variability based on performance.

## 3. Conduct the Audience Research

Because the introduction of the new incentive compensation plan represents significant cultural change, it is imperative that management and employee acceptance and buy-in be accomplished in a complete and systematic manner. The first step to achieve this objective is an audience research approach that "casts a wide net" and will serve both as an information-gathering exercise and an educational forum.

- A written questionnaire (paper and/or intranet based) will be distributed to all employees. The survey will capture the degree of understanding and acceptance by the employees of the new behaviors and reward strategies.

- Using the tabulated survey results, focus groups will be formed to delve deeper into the topic areas of most concern.

- Manager and employee study groups will be formed to get brainstorming input on the implementation of the new reward strategies.

### 4. Choose the Media and 5. Design and Implement the Strategy

To support the new culture, behaviors, and reward strategies, the media and strategy must be thorough and "human" oriented.

- *A video.* Recognizing and demonstrating the emotionality of the subject matter.

- *Written materials (plan documents).* A detailed explanation of the new incentive compensation program, with examples.

- *Face-to-face meetings throughout the organization conducted by well-trained managers and assisted by program designers from human resources.* In order to help achieve the stated objective, all employees will have an opportunity to participate in two-way real-time presentations.

- *Working/training/education sessions for all managers and employees.* To help them establish performance goals and behavioral guidelines under the new reward strategies.

- *Additional information and Q&A follow-up.* Through additional live sessions as well as the human resources website.

### 6. Evaluate the Communication Program

Four to six months after the new incentive compensation plan goes live, we will resurvey the managers and employees and reconvene the focus groups to conduct a "before and after" comparison. Also, all managers will submit a written assessment to human resources on the degree of success of the communication effort.

Strategic questions to be answered by citing specific examples:

- Are employees demonstrating and internalizing the new competencies and behaviors?

- Is the new incentive compensation program perceived as fair?

- Are the performance goals and criteria being adhered to, and most important, are they being accomplished?

- Are employees taking ownership of their jobs and career development?

In closing, it is important to note that the compensation system must first be well designed in order for positive results to occur, that is, improved employee motivation, increased productivity, and so on. However, given that the system is sound, these and other positive results will *not* occur unless the communication program is successful. Using a strategic and structured approach will go a long way toward ensuring positive results.

# PART VIII

# GLOBAL
# COMPENSATION

# 43

# Critical Expatriate Compensation Issues and Practices

Roger Herod

*Mercer LLC*

This chapter provides readers with a guide to the fundamental issues that organizations face in paying employees they transfer between countries. Compensation systems for *expatriates*, as such employees are often known, are complex and generally expensive. The original policies developed by companies to encourage employees to take international assignments were often very generous, sometimes even lavish, because international assignments were not part of the mainstream in terms of career progression within many companies. However, the globalization of many business activities has created a rapidly changing environment in which companies have found that successful business growth depends on their ability to deploy skilled resources globally. For many companies, the number of international assignments continues to increase significantly, leading to pressure to implement more cost-effective compensation policies for assignees. It is a very different environment from the old "let's make a deal" challenge to persuade employees to take ad hoc assignments to deal with problem situations.

As companies' international assignment populations increase, the need to create a competitive business advantage by ensuring that assignment policies are properly balanced in terms of attractiveness to employees and cost-effectiveness to the company becomes crucial. Benchmarking of policies against appropriate competitive practices needs to be an ongoing exercise rather than a once-off exercise every 5 or 10 years. Company policies, such as assignment incentives and housing support for expatriates, have, for example, seen significant changes in recent years, and it is all too easy for companies to find their policies out of line and overly costly.

In terms of compensation philosophy, there might appear to be some simple answers to paying an expatriate. For those not totally familiar with the issues involved, the first response might be simply to place the expatriate in the salary structure of the country in which the employee is working. Unfortunately, for the typical expatriate, working on a temporary assignment of two to five years, this may not allow the expatriate and his or her family to be able to maintain a standard of living similar to that in their home country. An alternative response might be simply to pay the employee the same salary for the position as would have been paid at home and to make no other adjustments. Once again, this usually is not an equitable solution in terms of being able to maintain an equivalent standard of living.

Because neither of the obvious simplistic approaches is satisfactory, companies have over the years devised more sophisticated pay systems. Although no two organizations pay their expatriates in exactly the same way, a pattern has emerged that allows generalizations to be made about expatriate pay practices.

This overview of expatriate pay practices covers the following:

- The key issues that create the complexity in expatriate pay systems
- The major options for determining the base pay structure for assignees
- The most significant cost-related elements of expatriate package design
- The choices involved in the provision of incentives to assignees
- The issues related to benefits and pay delivery

The underlying factors such as assignment length and pattern, the nationality of the assignee, and the type of job involved need to be considered in choosing between alternative approaches.

## What Are the Issues?

There are eight key factors that drive pay practices:

1. Gross and net compensation levels for the same position vary between countries.
2. The purchasing power of any nominal salary varies from one country to another.
3. Comparisons of home and assignment-location income will be affected by changes in exchange rates between the two countries.
4. Expatriates on temporary assignments typically have to compete for rental housing at their new assignment country that is frequently expensive and in short supply.
5. Many employees (and their families) do not welcome the disruption to family and social life caused by an international move.
6. Some locations to which employees may be transferred are not necessarily considered intrinsically desirable places to live.
7. There are difficulties in addressing benefit provisions, especially in relation to pensions, health insurance, and social security, across two countries.
8. There is a need to provide for certain special circumstances such as education for the children of expatriates and the need to assist the employee and family in returning to their home location periodically during the expatriate assignment.

# Compensation Options: Salary Base

The key decision in compensation design is the designation of base salary. This decision affects most other areas of the package in a very direct manner. The primary choices are to retain the employee in the home-country salary structure, to put the employee into the assignment-country structure, or to adopt some other salary base.

## Expatriate Compensation Practices

*Option 1: Home Salary.* Most organizations retain employees in the home salary structure, especially when they are on assignment for a limited duration and they are expected to return to their home country. Retention in the home structure makes it easier to bring employees back at the end of the assignment because they have never lost contact, in practical or psychological terms, with their home salary. Most organizations also wish to retain employees in home-country benefit programs, and the home salary structure retention facilitates this. The major drawback of retaining employees in their home-country structure is that, by definition, the expatriate will have a different income and standard of living from comparable local peers and from expatriates of other nationalities working in the assignment location. A company with expatriates mostly of one nationality may not worry about this latter issue. Even when the nationality mix is greater, the degree of concern about comparability with local nationals varies by organization. Retaining employees in the home-country structure requires the company to review the employee's base salary in accordance with home-country salary policies and merit increase guidelines. This ensures that employees on expatriate assignment do not suffer a disadvantage from holding an international position compared with employees who remain in the home country.

*Option 2: Host Salary.* Fitting employees into the host-country salary structure is administratively straightforward and would appear to address the issue of comparability with local employees. The prime drawback is that, in many cases, the attraction for the employees to accept the assignment disappears. A move from the United States to Nigeria on local pay is unlikely to attract employees to relocate because Nigerian local salaries are significantly lower than comparable U.S. salaries. However, a move from Nigeria to the United States on a local U.S. salary could be very attractive. A move from the United States to the United Kingdom on an equivalent British salary also could represent a reduction in purchasing power because of the higher level of income taxes in the United Kingdom. Even a move to a country with higher nominal gross salaries, such as a move from the United States to Switzerland, may turn out to be less attractive when the higher cost of living and rental housing costs in Switzerland are taken into account. Thus integration into the local salary structure works only where it involves an increase in real purchasing power. Therefore, a move from a low-wage country to a high-wage developed country is feasible on this basis, and many companies pay people a host salary in the case of transfers, for example, from the Philippines or India to the United States. Even then, some companies keep a link to the home salary because it provides a base for benefits and helps to ensure that employees keep in mind the salary structure to which they will potentially return.

This problem of different purchasing power can be overcome if the employee is placed in the assignment salary structure but paid other allowances to compensate for the higher costs. However, this approach can become complex because it involves tracking the relationship of the home-country pay to the assignment-country pay level, and it can undermine the value of equalizing expatriates with local employees.

*Other Options.* Some companies opt for an approach that is neither pure home nor pure host. A rare approach is to create an entirely separate pay scale for international employees. A few companies use this approach but usually only for a small group of their employees who are highly mobile and no longer have any real link to any home country. This approach is much more common in organizations such as the United Nations, in which almost all professional employees work outside their home country. Another approach that is more common is to link all employees who are being expatriated to the salary structure of one country, usually the country in which the company is headquartered. This approach is used by some companies that have few expatriates other than those from the headquarters country. It is also used, however, by some companies with a large multinational workforce to overcome the problem of expatriates of multiple nationalities having different compensation packages in the same assignment location.

Another variant, particularly popular in Europe, is the so-called higher-of-home-or-host approach. In this model, the company calculates a pay package based on home pay plus allowances to compensate for differences in housing, taxes, and cost of living and compares the net pay of the employee with the net pay of the peer position in the assignment location. The higher of the two will be paid. The precise calculation methods used vary considerably, but the perceived advantage is that there is the potential for integration in the host pay structure but with a guarantee that the employee will not suffer a reduction in standard of living. Depending, however, on the demographics of assignment locations, companies can find in some cases that the majority of their employees are actually being paid based on the home calculation, so the advantage of integration into the host pay structure becomes diluted.

## Compensation Options: Cost Allowances

In conjunction with retaining the expatriate in the home-country salary structure, most companies pay the employee a set of allowances designed to deal with additional costs that the employee could incur. The most significant elements of these costs are in relation to goods and services (e.g., food, clothing, recreation, etc.), housing, personal taxation, and education.

### Goods and Services

Where the costs of purchasing a similar range of day-to-day goods and services in the assignment location are higher than costs at home, most organizations pay a cost-of-living or a goods-and-services allowance, usually based on information from external consultants. There are numerous ways of comparing such costs, and they need to be monitored regularly to reflect the impact of the exchange rate between the two assignment locations.

Typically, the external consultant provides an index that compares costs in the two locations, where 100 indicates that costs are the same in the two locations. The allowance is usually paid at each pay period. The purpose of the allowance may be viewed in two slightly different ways. It may be seen as a protection against higher costs, or it may be seen as part of an attempt to ensure that the employee neither gains nor loses in living standard from accepting the assignment other than from changes in direct pay. In principle, companies following the balance-sheet approach should make a deduction when the cost-of-living index for the assignment location compared with the home country is less than 100. However, probably less than 20 percent of North American multinationals apply negative cost-of-living allowances. Thus an employee sent to a much lower-cost country will receive an additional windfall unrelated to the amount of money needed in the location; another employee sent to a higher-cost location is protected but does not enjoy any such windfall. If costs suddenly rise in the low-cost location, the employee may perceive a decline in standard of living when, in reality, there has merely been a reduction in the windfall gain. Because of this, some companies that do not reduce the employee's pay in lower-cost locations choose to show the employee the windfall gain to avoid complaints if costs rise.

It should be emphasized that this approach should be used in conjunction with retention in the home-country salary structure. When companies decide to integrate transferees into the host-country salary structure, they generally will make a comparison of relative living costs between the home and host countries as part of the initial determination of an appropriate host-country salary. Once the transferee is integrated into the host-country structure, the need to continue to compare local living costs with those of the employee's home country is generally no longer necessary.

If a company uses a headquarters approach and retains all expatriates on the salary structure of the headquarters country, the cost comparison still should be made but between the headquarters country and the assignment location. The result will be that the salary reflects the headquarters living costs, not the actual home location of the employee. It also ensures that expatriates of different nationalities receive the same pay, which is often the underlying objective of those using a headquarters approach.

## Housing

Housing is affected by two considerations. Most companies prefer their expatriates to rent rather than purchase housing in the assignment location. This is felt to be administratively simpler, to protect against possible losses if the host housing market falls, and to provide greater flexibility in disposing of the home on return. In addition, consideration needs to be paid to the employee's house in the home country. The most common approach is that the company encourages the employee to retain the home if the expectation is that the employee will return to the same location. In this case, the company usually provides assistance in renting out and managing the property. In the assignment location, the company will assist the employee in finding a home and will pay the rental cost either directly to the landlord or as an allowance to the employee. Some companies pay an allowance equal to the actual rent of the property; others pay a defined amount but leave the employee to select the property and to keep any amount by which the housing allowance is more than the actual rent or to pay out of their own pocket any amount by which the rent exceeds the allowance. Whatever approach is adopted, companies need to decide how much they are willing to pay for the employee's housing. Many companies use external consultants to set housing allowance levels, which often vary by family size and by job level.

Traditionally, most U.S. companies could take a "housing deduction" to reflect the savings that the employee is realizing in home housing costs. However, U.S. companies have increasingly begun to take a "hands off" approach to expatriates' home-country housing because of the high costs of realtors' fees and legal expenses when expatriates sell their homes, often having to reimburse significant equity loses on sale. As a result, about one-third of U.S. companies no longer deduct housing norms or provide home sale assistance to their expatriates. European companies are also less likely to take this deduction largely because they do not assume that the employee will rent out the home property while on assignment. Once again, the philosophy of most companies is to equalize costs for the employee, and whether this is done by requiring a home deduction or not depends on the circumstances of the employee. Some companies will allow the policy to vary depending on individual circumstances; others choose a policy that reflects the majority of their expatriate population.

The payment of host housing costs is a policy that most companies adopt regardless of whether they use home, host, or headquarters pay as a base. Again, in one sense, this undermines the logic of host pay systems because it represents a clear distinction between expatriates and local nationals. However, it is a pragmatic reflection of the need to help employees find and pay for rental housing when on limited-term assignments.

### Personal Taxation

In the area of taxes, the equalization philosophy is firmly entrenched. Most companies use an external accounting firm to prepare expatriate tax returns. This is particularly important for U.S. citizens and U.S. permanent residents because they are taxed by the United States even when they are not residents. For most other nationalities, tax liability depends not on citizenship but on residence and the source of income. Thus a British expatriate working in the United States is not taxed by the United Kingdom on U.S. earning but only on residual British earnings (interest, etc.) as long as the expatriate is not in the United Kingdom for more than a certain number of days in the year. Despite this, the principle of tax equalization is usually followed for other nationalities, although practice is more varied than for Americans.

For the employee, the normal approach is that the company will pay all personal taxes that arise from employment income; increasingly, companies also pay all or a portion of the liability related to nonemployment income. In return, the employee pays the company through regular payroll deductions an amount usually termed a *hypothetical tax deduction*, equivalent to what would have been paid in taxes at home.

### Education

An international assignment is disruptive for expatriates with children. Where the language of the assignment country is different from the home country, most expatriates want to send their children to a school in the assignment location that provides teaching in the home-country language. Even if the language is the same, if the curriculum does not match that of the home country, it may disrupt the child's ability to progress through the home curriculum. This is especially true for children in secondary education. Such international schools are usually private and therefore charge tuition and fees, which can be very costly. Companies generally will meet at least the direct tuition costs and often other additional costs. For U.S. expatriates, this usually means the American schools that exist in many cities around the world; similar schools exist for French, Japanese, and British children, although in smaller numbers. If no school is available in the assignment location, most companies will pay for boarding schools in the home country or in a third location. The cost impact for companies is therefore quite high if they send expatriates with children on assignment. This has led some companies to seek to persuade expatriates to send children to local schools if the languages of the assignment and home countries are the same. This is sometimes acceptable for younger children, but differences in the curricula and in university entrance requirements make this difficult for older children. As with housing, most companies pay for education regardless of the salary base for expatriates.

## Compensation Options: Incentives

In addition to allowances to reflect specific costs, companies frequently pay direct cash incentives to expatriates that are unrelated to cost. Historically, many companies paid a *foreign-service premium*, usually expressed as a percentage of base pay. The most common formula has been 10 to 15 percent of pay, sometimes capped at an upper salary level, paid along with each regular paycheck. An alternative approach consists of providing a lump-sum incentive payment, usually termed a *mobility premium*, paid in two amounts at the beginning and end of the assignment.

Among U.S. companies, there has been an ongoing decline in the percentage of companies that pay foreign-service premiums or lump-sum incentive premiums. Practice varies considerably by industry, however, with energy and energy-related service companies, for example, far more likely to pay incentive premiums than, say, consumer-goods companies. For many multinationals, international assignments are being seen as a requisite for advancement within the company. As a result, well over 50 percent of U.S. companies no longer pay any type of incentive premium for expatriate assignments.

Most companies, however, feel the need to pay an incentive if the employee is moving to a "difficult" location. Such payments are often termed *hardship premiums*, although some companies see this terminology as vaguely insulting to local employees in the assignment country and may use more neutral language such as *location premium*. The payment is usually expressed as a percentage of salary varying by location; a common approach is to make payments that vary in 5 percent increments from 5 percent for slightly undesirable locations to 35 percent (or more) for very problematic locations. It is rarely paid in lump-sum form. Because the types of locations that attract a hardship premium are not those in which a host-pay approach could be used, the issue of paying hardship along with host pay almost never arises.

## Employee Benefits

For expatriates going on assignment for a limited duration, the main benefit issue that companies face is in relation to both company and state pensions. Most companies sending employees for limited-duration assignments try to keep the employees in their home-country company pension plan. This is usually feasible, although it may raise administrative and tax problems. It is also usually possible to retain an employee in the home-country social security program; in addition, companies would like to exempt assignees from required payments to the host-country system. This is usually possible for up to five years when the home and assignment countries have a bilateral social security agreement (often termed a *totalization agreement*). Retention in home benefit plans is clearly consistent with retention in home salary structures, but not with host-pay approaches. Notwithstanding the apparent anomaly, most companies using a host approach for base pay continue to opt for a home approach to benefits.

Issues also arise with other benefit plans, particularly medical plans. The company needs to decide how to cover the employee when on assignment because many home-country medical plans cannot provide coverage to employees working in a different country. As a result, most companies will include expatriates and their families in special international medical plans provided by global insurance companies.

## Home Leave

The cost of providing home leave for the expatriate and family, usually once a year, can be significant, particularly if companies provide business-class airfares. Competitive practice in terms of class of airfare is very mixed. Most U.S. companies provide economy airfares for home leave trips, but many of the same companies allow for upgrades to business class for long flights, typically specified as being at least 8 to 10 hours. In addition, in particularly difficult or hazardous locations, many companies also pay for one or possibly more rest-and-recreation (R&R) leave trips to a third location.

### Relocation Assistance

Costs of relocation to the assignment country are normally reimbursed by the company. Typical provisions include preassignment visits, relocation airfares, shipment of household goods, property management or home sale assistance, reimbursement of losses on sale of personal vehicles, temporary living, and storage fees. Depending on the assignment location and family size, relocation expenses can be considerable. In addition, companies generally also will provide a lump-sum payment, usually of about one month's salary, to cover miscellaneous additional relocation expenses.

### Pay Delivery

Companies must decide how much of the compensation package to deliver in home currency and how much in host currency. Because of the complexity of delivering pay to expatriates in multiple currencies, about half of U.S. companies pay their expatriates entirely in home currency, leaving the employee to decide when and in what quantities to exchange home into host currency. Typically, companies will reimburse the cost of one or more wire transfers per month to assist expatriates in transferring funds to their assignment country. Other companies find that there are advantages to delivering in local currency the amount required by the employee to buy goods and services (and housing if the company does not pay this directly). This protects the employee against exchange-rate fluctuations and prevents delivering pay in constantly varying amounts. The rest of the pay package then will be delivered in home currency. This so-called split-pay approach is used by about one-quarter of U.S. companies but does require a significant level of administration.

## Summary of Expatriate Options

From the preceding discussion, the most common approach to paying expatriates is the following:

1. To retain the employee in the home-country salary structure
2. To pay a cost-of-living allowance if costs in the assignment location are higher than at home
3. To pay the employee's housing costs in the assignment location, with or without a direct contribution from the expatriate
4. To use a system of tax equalization that ensures as nearly as possible that the employee pays no more and no less tax than if he or she had remained in the home country
5. Depending on industry competitive practice, possibly to pay an incentive to the employee above base pay for accepting and remaining on the assignment
6. To pay a special additional incentive to employees transferring to designated "difficult" locations
7. To pay for private education in the assignment location for the children of expatriate employees

This combination of policies has become known in the compensation area as the *balance-sheet approach* to expatriate compensation or in Europe as the *home buildup approach*. In recent years, there has been much discussion as to whether this approach is the most appropriate, but it remains the dominant model.

The main alternative to a home approach in practice has been a headquarters approach. For all practical purposes, this makes the employee an "honorary citizen" of the headquarters country and then works in exactly the same way as a home approach. The host-country pay approach is a more fundamental change, but some of its advantages are undermined by providing many of the elements that an expatriate employee paid under a home approach would receive.

## The Underlying Variables

There are several variables that lead organizations to differing answers to the question of how to design an expatriate program. Some of these are factors springing from the organization's human resources strategy or from deeply entrenched cultural factors. Others have a more concrete origin. In designing a policy, it is important to look at all these factors and assess their impact.

### Assignment Length

Most expatriate assignments fall in the range of two to five years, and most compensation systems are predicated on the assumption of this length. If assignments are intended from the outset to be much longer, an attempt should be made to place the employee in the assignment-country salary structure. Unfortunately, this does not work in situations where the local salary structure is much lower than that of the home country, so it is not uncommon to retain elements of the more typical shorter-term expatriate package. In addition, many organizations find that what was initially intended as a shorter assignment turns into a longer one. The employer then faces the challenge of converting the assignee from one type of compensation package to another.

Many organizations have a policy provision that states that employees should be "localized" after five years on assignment in the same location. This involves the removal in phases or in a single step of the expatriate package. Despite the policy provision, many organizations do not actually put this into practice unless the decision to remain on assignment is clearly the wish of the employee.

A different situation arises with short assignments of under one year. Such assignments have grown steadily for most organizations as a percentage of their total assignee population. As a result, most organizations have special policies for such assignments. A major factor is that many of these assignments take place without the whole family relocating to the assignment location, and this simplifies or alters some of the elements of package design in areas such as education and housing.

### Assignment Patterns

In many companies, the typical assignment pattern is for an employee to go out on assignment and return to the home country, perhaps going on another assignment at some future point in his or her career. The mainstream solutions to expatriate policy design are based on this pattern. If employees are on a sequential assignment pattern, moving from one location to another but not necessarily back to a home country, the compensation design may need to be different. Many companies pay the "global nomads" by placing them on the salary structure of the headquarters country. Others use an international pay scale. Benefits may be funded on an offshore basis because one of the major concerns for this group lies in the provision of pensions.

## Type of Assignee

Some organizations have a strong philosophy that all assignees should be covered by one policy. Others distinguish among employees based on the type or level of job performed, on the business unit for which the employee works, or on the geographic pattern of movement. Thus some companies have one policy for management-development assignments and another for technical transfers. Some distinguish between a European employee transferring within the region and one transferring out to another region. The advantages that derive from multitier policies are that they may help to reduce overall costs by matching compensation elements to clear needs, and they may allow business units with different economic circumstances to reflect these in the level of compensation.

The disadvantages are more complex administration and potential employee resentment if they are on a less generous package than some of their perceived peers. Companies that have used such an approach find that it works best when there is little movement of employees from one expatriate policy to another, when the economic reasons for differences can be clearly explained, and when the categories of policy can be clearly defined. The last is a problem where policy is based on a judgment whether an assignment is for management development versus specific business project purposes, where there may be room for differences of opinion about the real objectives of the assignment. Assignment types also clearly influence the differences in policy from one organization to another. A company that sends only high-level executives may adopt a different strategy from one that sends primarily project engineers.

## Country of Origin

Established pay systems work well for assignees from developed countries, who have generally formed the overwhelming majority of expatriates. In recent years, however, there has been a significant increase in assignees drawn from countries such as China and India. This can create specific compensation challenges because pay levels for more junior transferees may be too low to make the traditional balance-sheet approach work effectively. However, the shortage of available talent at higher managerial levels means that some potential higher-level assignees from these countries are actually highly paid and have a very different lifestyle from typical local employees in their country. In this case, if higher-level assignees come from a country where the general cost of living is low, the normal method of comparing typical living costs between the home and host countries may not be an appropriate method of computing cost-of-living differentials for them, particularly if their lifestyle in the home country is already at a very high standing. Given these challenges, the design of an appropriate pay policy for transferees from less-developed countries requires a thorough analysis of the types of employees being moved and may require multiple pay policies.

## Industry

The industry in which an organization operates will have some impact on policy. The oil industry requires specialized expatriates to work in a variety of often remote locations; an investment bank is likely to send employees mainly to more developed locations.

## Globalism

An organization employing and transferring employees who are predominantly of one nationality faces a different set of challenges from an organization transferring employees of multiple nationalities.

## Summary

The dominance of the balance-sheet approach to expatriate compensation has been achieved in the face of frequent criticism that it is too expensive and complex. The problem, however, is that the complexities are inherent in the process of transferring employees internationally, and no simple solution has been advanced that allows companies to attract employees to go on assignment and to pay them in a fair and cost-effective manner when there. Pay administration requires the company to track many more payments than it does for a domestic employee; moreover, such payments may be in two currencies, and some of them, such as the goods-and-services allowance, are subject to frequent change. Compensation professionals used to working with pay structures in a single country will find that expatriate compensation has unusual challenges. Addressing these challenges, however, is fundamental to those companies wishing to operate successfully on a global basis.

## References

Herod, R. (ed.). 2013. *International Human Resources Guide*. Thomson/West, Eagan, MN.

Herod, R. 1995. *Compensating Globally Mobile Employees*. WorldatWork, Scottsdale, AZ (reprinted in 2014).

Hsu, Y. S. 2000. "Expatriate Compensation: Alternative Approaches and Challenges." *WorldatWork Journal*, First Quarter.

Latta, G. W. 2005. "Addressing Pay Issues for Nontraditional Expatriate Assignments." *Benefits and Compensation International*, March.

Latta, G. W. 2005. "High Mobility International Employees." *WorldatWork Journal*, Second Quarter.

Latta, G. W. 2006. "The Future of Expatriate Compensation." *WorldatWork Journal*, Second Quarter.

Schell, M. S., and C. Marmer Solomon. 1997. *Capitalizing on the Global Workforce*. Irwin Professional, Chicago.

# 44

# Global Local National Compensation Issues and Practices

Jordan Blue
*Mercer LLC*

Ed Hannibal
*Mercer LLC*

Ilene Siscovick
*Mercer LLC*

The greatest challenge of chief executive officers (CEOs), their chief human resources officers (CHROs), and global business leaders is finding the right candidate for the right role at the right time. Research from the World Economic Forum and Mercer has identified global shortages of qualified workers and the gap between supply and demand for such talent. A well-crafted international compensation strategy is a critical component in any organization's global talent strategy.

With the increasing globalization of business and this shortage of qualified talent, there has been a corresponding interest in the more effective management of local national employees and in rationalizing the ways in which they are compensated. *Local national employees* are defined as those who are employed within a given country and whose conditions of employment are established and dictated by local norms. As such, a local national can be of any nationality as long as he or she is eligible to work in a given location. The conditions of employment for the local national employee reflect the local statutory requirements, customs, and practices found in the marketplace. This is in contrast to the expatriate, who would be working with local nationals in a given location but whose compensation and conditions of employment typically are tied to a home location where he or she is expected to return at the end of the expatriate assignment.

Expatriate assignments typically extend from one to five years, but many long-term, or permanent, expatriate assignment policies have processes to integrate individuals to the local national conditions of employment over a period of time. As organizations extend their global reach, the management of an increasingly international workforce becomes more complicated, which forces many organizations to reconsider their compensation strategy on a global scale. This is not without its challenges, the biggest of which is ensuring an appropriate balance between global consistency and local market compatibility. Although a global compensation strategy offers internal equity and facilitates international mobility, it also must reflect and be responsive to local market conditions.

Pay levels for local national employees vary based on traditional compensation practices and values inherent in the concept of pay in that particular country. Influencing factors may include

- Statutory requirements
- National and/or sector collective-bargaining agreements
- The type and number of specific pay elements
- Group versus individual performance incentives
- International work experience (which may carry a "pay premium" in the country)

The situation is complicated by the supply of and demand for labor in any local market—an excess of labor will cause pay levels to drop, whereas a shortage of labor will cause pay levels to rise. This is further influenced by a number of factors, including the geographic location of the organization and the industry sector within which it operates.

The following section is an overview of the complexities and challenges associated with achieving a consistent and effective global compensation strategy while maintaining local compensation practices and culture. The effective management of both expatriate and local national employees is more critical than ever before because compensation and human resources practitioners are tasked with preparing their organizations to keep pace with a world of complex equity situations driven by the movement of talent within and across country borders.

## The Need for Local Compensation Data

Globalization of the marketplace has caused the compensation of local national employees to become a major focus. In an increasingly competitive business environment, the costs of equipment, materials, and labor are now all key components to successful operations.

Although an international pool of labor does exist for senior executive positions and certain highly skilled professional roles, most other roles operate in local labor markets at either a national or location-specific level. It is for this reason that the provision of compensation data at the local level is paramount to ensuring that organizations can be responsive to the external market in which they operate. In most multinational organizations, the vast majority of their payroll is based on local national compensation.

Local compensation data allow organizations to determine their level of competitiveness in the local marketplace. This is important for a number of reasons. First, many organizations openly communicate a formal compensation philosophy that specifies who they define as their competition for talent and services and where they position themselves relative to the global market. The most common statement is to "maintain competitive pay levels," usually expressed in terms of position relative to the 50th percentile of the specific market. Therefore, it is important for organizations to examine whether this is actually the case at the local level. When "new" positions are created, organizations may not be familiar with their market value. As such, accurate local compensation data are crucial in setting and ensuring appropriate and attractive levels of pay.

Another reason why reliable local compensation data are vital to talent management deals with the quality of an organization's workforce. The more competitive an organization is in relation to local pay levels, the greater is the chance that it will attract and retain high-caliber employees.

However, quality local compensation data are not always readily available. As a direct result of globalization, many compensation and human resources practitioners find themselves in need of local compensation data in countries where this information has been difficult to obtain. This point is particularly true for organizations operating in developing or remote locations, where, quite simply, no data exist. In these cases, many firms have used customized surveys because they are often the only viable approach to gathering meaningful local compensation and benefit information.

## Variations in Pay Elements

Any discussion of local national compensation needs to consider the variety of pay elements that exist in any given country. There are three initial ways in which compensation is commonly defined across the world:

- *Cash compensation.* This approach specifically includes wage rates, salary, cash bonuses, and short-term incentives but excludes the value of employee benefits, special allowances, long-term incentives, deferred compensation, contributions to savings plans, distributions through profit-sharing plans, and noncash compensation such as equities (stock). In the United States, this typically would include wage rates, salaries, and annual bonuses.

- *Gross compensation.* This approach typically includes the payroll costs of all employee benefits and allowances as well as the total of cash compensation as defined earlier.

- *Net compensation.* This approach is used when comparing the net (after-tax) calculation of compensation.

Ideally, each of these compensation definitions would identify each pay element so that said elements could be compared across borders on a like-for-like basis. Unfortunately, pay elements often vary depending on local norms, customs, and statutory requirements. The following example is based on employment in Mexico and lists the typical pay elements associated with salaried employees in that country:

- Base salary (reported monthly and annually)

- Christmas bonus (*aguinaldo* is a statutory benefit—could be considered in some companies as the thirteenth month)

- Profit sharing (*utilidades*—10 percent of company profit divided among all employees except the general director if they work a minimum of 60 days of the year)

- Savings fund (*fondo de ahorro*—reported as a percentage of the base salary with a legal cap)

- Vacation bonus (reported in currency and in number of days' pay)

- Transportation or car allowance (reported as a monthly allowance)

- Social provision (reported as a percentage of base salary with a legal cap)

- Housing fund (*infonavit*—statutory requirement to individual accounts)

Other benefits include costs associated with the following:

- Medical insurance

- Life insurance

- Pension and retirement

- Social security (IMSS), where the employer pays the employee's contribution

There is also considerable difference in the pay elements depending on the class of employee. Hourly-paid employees (craft or factory workers typically classified as blue collar) have a range of additional allowances and benefits not applicable to salaried or executive employees. Again using Mexico as an example, the following pay elements are typically provided to this class of employee (however, variations exist depending on the actual geographic location):

- Transportation provisions

- Clothing allowance

- In-house meal provisions

- Punctuality bonus

- Discounts on company products

- Seniority payments

- Cost-of-living allowance in some locations

If we now switch our attention to the Indian market, we find a different set of pay elements, many of which are used to make guaranteed cash more tax effective and to reduce retirement-related benefits (because these are not always perceived as attractive by a generation of employees that is "cash in hand" oriented). A number of cash allowances are prevalent, such as housing allowance, leave travel allowance, conveyance allowance (transportation), and a unique special allowance. This is simply the difference between the guaranteed cash compensation rate in the local market and the sum of the basic salary with all other allowances.

Many organizations in India have adopted a compensation benchmarking approach referred to as the *cost to company* (CTC). Using this methodology, organizations determine the total cost of providing the base salary (typically referred to as the *basic salary*), allowances, variable pay, and retirement benefits based on where they want the role to be positioned against the local market. The employee then is given a choice as to how he or she wants the guaranteed cash amounts distributed between base pay and other allowances, including the special allowance. Typically, only 40 to 45 percent of the total guaranteed cash of an employee's compensation is formed by base salary. Employees have a fair degree of flexibility to allocate the balance based on their own individual preferences and tax concerns.

Executive pay elements also vary from country to country. Frequently, they are the result of the tax policy for the given country. Such executive elements of compensation that have been identified in the global marketplace include

- Stock options
- Long-term deferred compensation
- Home entertainment allowances
- Housing supplements
- Low-cost or no-cost housing loans
- Company-provided car and driver
- Education allowances for dependents

In summary, there are considerable differences in pay elements throughout the world. These differences are driven by the economy, laws, and culture of the particular country, which makes cross-border pay comparisons extremely difficult.

Foreign exchange rates can be used for this purpose, but in today's global marketplace, exchange rates can be volatile and in a constant state of change. In any case, simply converting a salary at a given exchange rate is an incomplete analysis because it does not take account of factors unique to each country, such as the demand for and supply of labor, the cost of living, and the local tax rates.

## The Complexity of Using Local Compensation Data

Using local compensation data is not as straightforward as one may think. Quality market data should individually list all the appropriate pay elements for the role in the relevant country and provide unambiguous definitions. It is important to note that some surveys can be vague in their explanation of the various pay elements, which can be confusing for compensation and human resources practitioners when trying to match roles accurately against the local market. For example, many countries in Europe, Latin America, and Asia have practices of 13, 14, and up to 18 months of "extra" salary, sometimes referred to as a *fixed bonus* or *seasonal bonus*. Clearly, using only base salary comparisons potentially could lead to misleading results because base salary may be defined as including some or all of the extra months' pay (depending on the survey). In an effort to make the comparisons more usable for analysis, off-the-shelf compensation surveys conducted by a number of leading consultancies report a base salary and a guaranteed base salary (including the extra months' pay either required by statute or provided by local practice).

Traditionally, local market comparisons have taken place at base salary level. However, as variable pay or "pay at risk" becomes increasingly available to a wider employee population across the world, more organizations now require local compensation data at the total cash level in order to make meaningful comparisons against the marketplace. Again, as with base salary, it is important to ensure that comparisons are made on a like-for-like basis and that the information used is clearly defined in terms of the total cash components. For example, some surveys will include allowances and variable pay under a "total cash" heading, whereas other surveys will report "total cash" as simply the addition of base salary and variable pay (excluding allowances).

This can be further complicated by substantial pay differences (for the same role) between multinational organizations and local employers in the same country. This is usually driven by the background and work experience of the actual incumbent in the role. In China, for example, local national employees are paid significantly lower than "returning" Chinese nationals (i.e., those who have gained international experience or education in the United States or Western Europe), employees from other Asian markets (who have moved to China), and Western expatriates. In the Middle East, the working population is a mix of local nationals, Western expatriates, and contractors from the Indian subcontinent or the Philippines; again, there are marked differences in pay levels and compensation practices that are not necessarily segregated via off-the-shelf compensation surveys (e.g., completion bonuses, allowances, or foreign service premiums).

In an attempt to ease the pressure on compensation and human resources practitioners to understand all the compensation practices around the world, some consultancies produce individual customized market pricing reports based on local compensation data. By developing a composite of compensation data from a variety of published surveys for similar positions—within the same or similar industries and at similar revenue responsibility levels or organization types—these consultancies can arrive at a targeted view of compensation within a given local market.

## Current Compensation Issues for Local National Employees

### Emergence of Comprehensive Global Compensation Strategies

As companies move from single-country to multinational and eventually global operations, compensation specialists have sought to develop a consistent and comprehensive compensation philosophy that would be applicable on a global basis. Such efforts have resulted in standardized pay philosophies for expatriates and for many senior-level roles. Given the complexity of the global compensation environment, however, lower-level local national employees have been somewhat ignored. Typically, such globalized pay philosophies have been so vague and generalized as to not be very useful in the day-to-day work of compensation professionals. It has been easier and more practical to establish a strategy that encourages local compensation to be consistent with the local market practices and to ignore the inconsistencies between locations.

Traditionally, the key inhibitors to the development of comprehensive global compensation strategies have fallen into two categories. The first is in the definition of total compensation. Intercountry comparisons can be difficult, especially when one includes long-term incentive and employee benefit valuations. Benefits should include statutory requirements as well as private coverage and other benefits or perquisites. Efforts to establish global stock-option guidelines have been difficult because of the very high level of option grants typically given in the United States and the relatively low level of grants provided in other countries, where such grants may be illegal or impractical as a result of cultural concerns. Another complication revolves around the tax treatment for stock options. In some countries, these grants are not permitted, and in others, taxation rules make stock grants less attractive. In some locations, tax liability may occur at the time of the grant, over time, or is deferred until the time of exercise. Obviously, benefits and stock awards and the laws that govern these compensation elements vary greatly across the globe, which adds to the difficulty in developing a consistent global policy.

Global compensation strategies that relate to a narrower definition of compensation are gaining popularity—namely, limiting the comparison to salary and short-term bonuses or incentives. Indeed, a substantial number of multinational organizations have a global compensation strategy in place. These global strategies establish guidelines as to how the marketplace is to be defined, where in the marketplace compensation is to be targeted, and how the mix of base salary and forms of incentive is to be determined. Furthermore, the strategy establishes an internal relationship of jobs classified into job bands or grades. The global strategy encourages local adaptation of the overall global principles to the local marketplace when possible.

## International Position (Job) Evaluation (IPE)

Hundreds of the world's multinationals have embraced international position evaluation as a rational approach, methodology, and global language to articulate the value the job is expected to deliver. The language is based on a set of globally consistent job dimensions or factors such as impact, communication, innovation, knowledge, and so forth. A point-factor approach enables an organization to develop a quantitative value that can be used to create a hierarchy of jobs and a corresponding pay line. This is achieved by regressing the size of the job expressed in points to market rates expressed in country-specific currencies. This facilitates the integration of internal equity and external competiveness no matter what country or talent market the individual sits in. Country pay lines are also an effective way to extrapolate pay rates in country markets where there might not be position-based survey sources. Organizations then are able to link jobs to various sources of robust market data across the globe, harmonize compensation programs, and assess internal and external total rewards equity.

## Changes Occurring in Traditional Local Markets

The concept that each country has a fixed and consistent culture related to compensation has been a myth that was widely circulated and assumed to be accurate. As more compensation data are gathered and analyzed, it is clear that variations exist within locations and that even the most traditional cultures are changing. An example is Japan, which has had a long history of unique pay values. These traditional values show a high correlation between compensation and age—pay related more to the person than to a specific job. This pay philosophy is starting to change as a result of considerable experimentation by some very large Japanese companies.

Many multinational organizations are finding that they can be innovative in local markets in a way that is nontraditional but that makes good business sense and is acceptable to local employees. Much of the data being generated on this subject are anecdotal, but it appears that best practices in compensation (especially the concept of variable pay) are being considered in locations where such practices were not considered a few years ago. The emerging concept is that traditional local practices can be changed and that organizations need not be locked into local practices if alternative creative initiatives make good business sense. In most local markets, there is more room for creativity than was previously believed to be the case. The key question is whether a basic compensation approach might become more universally acceptable than it has been in the past. Clearly, many elements of the pay systems and remuneration innovations developed in the United States and many parts of Western Europe are being adapted in many other locations across the world.

## Development of Regionally Identified Markets

Over the past decade, many people have begun to believe that a single compensation market would begin to emerge in Europe. It has been hoped that the concept of supply and demand would create a single market in terms of pay levels as trade barriers have declined and the workers have been able to cross country borders. This has not occurred and appears to be inhibited by several major factors. The first is the difference in tax policies, which affects the level of net pay and the ways in which pay is delivered. The second is the differences in currencies, which make comparisons difficult. The euro makes comparisons easier, but not all countries in Europe use this currency. Additionally, the design of and benefit levels associated with social security and pension systems are also a factor.

Interest in the development of Latin American, South American, and Asian regional compensation polices has been a subject of interest, but the variations among country norms are frequently even wider than they are in Europe. Although there seems to be a desire for such regional compensation policies, to date, the common ground for such policies is not apparent.

### Internal Equity among All Classifications of Employees

The different levels of pay and conditions of employment between expatriates and local nationals residing in a single location have created internal equity concerns. The differences in practices have been rationalized in terms of the different markets to which each group has been compared. Each classification had a policy designed to attract and retain the necessary talent based on business need. Although conceptually consistent, the perception has been that some employment classifications receive preferential treatment. This is further complicated by expatriates who remain for long periods of time or expatriates who transfer from high-cost to low-cost locations (or vice versa). The appearance is that the expatriates live better and have a higher level of purchasing power than the locals. Although traditional expatriate assignments are common and expected to increase, some companies have begun to experiment with moving expatriates on host-based or local packages. The long-term strategy for many companies is to continually rationalize the number of expatriates, to limit assignment length, and to move long-term expatriates to local packages. Whereas the use of expatriates is unlikely to decrease in the near future, companies should focus on building an effective local workforce so as to reduce the need to rely on an expatriate workforce.

No single approach appears to be emerging, but to the degree possible, organizations are using local practices, including compensation, for certain types of expatriates.

## Anticipated Trends for Local National Compensation in the Future

There is no single trend that will affect all local national locations; each location is subject to pressures unique to its history and culture. However, some major drivers of change can be recognized:

- The concept of meritocracy, and specifically, the vehicle of variable pay (variable in terms of the relationship of pay to business success on the individual, group, or organizational level), is widely accepted in market-driven economies. In some locations it may be in the form of statutory profit sharing, whereas in others it will follow the U.S. and European models of short- and long-term incentives. There is likely to be a corresponding decrease in pay systems that are related to tying pay to age, seniority, gender, and other non-performance-related criteria.

- Traditional systems of compensation, which have been unique to a particular country's set of values, are likely to encounter a broadening variety of nontraditional initiatives. This will be led primarily by multinational organizations but likely will influence the range of acceptable pay systems for local firms as well.

- Employee retirement delivery vehicles will shift gradually. Both social security and private plans will continue to move toward defined-contribution plans rather than defined-benefit plans.

- Demands for market compensation data for local national employees will create additional and improved survey designs, and there will be an increased level of participation.

## Sources of Compensation Survey Data

There is not a single source of data for local national compensation that covers all country locations. The quality and validity of market data vary widely, and care must be taken in assessing individual market data. The availability of data falls into three broad categories:

- Published data from established survey sources, both private and public
- Annual or ongoing customized survey data available only to survey participants
- Customized surveys conducted at a sponsor's request

The following is a listing of the most widely used data sources:

*Published Data*

- Mercer—Total Remuneration Surveys and International Benefit Guidelines
- Towers-Watson—local reports on various countries
- Hay Associates—local reports on various countries
- AON–Hewitt Consulting—local reports on various countries
- U.S. Chambers of Commerce—in various country locations
- The U.S. State Department—surveys of U.S. embassy locations
- Custom reports

A note on online sources: although "free" data options can be found on the Internet, it is important to vet the source, methodology, and reliability of these data sets.

This listing is focused primarily on gathering data from multinational organizations. This reflects a bimodal market that exists in most countries. The "local" local market, which is composed of organizations that operate only within the country location, is typically smaller and represents a lower-paid market than exists for the larger multinational organizations. Care should be taken to ensure that the appropriate market has been identified and that the survey data are appropriate.

In many countries, market data show a fairly wide distribution, frequently without a strong central tendency in the data. This is a common situation in locations that are unstable from a compensation perspective or are experiencing high rates of inflation. Examples include Russia, Venezuela, and Argentina. The effective date of the survey data is critically important, and the data must be carefully "aged" to approximate current levels of compensation where the inflation rate is high. Also, the timing of salary reviews may need to be more frequent in locations with high inflation or varying economic conditions.

## Consulting Services Related to Local National Job Pricing

All the consulting organizations mentioned previously offer job pricing services. These consultants can provide clients with compensation, benefits, and pay-related policies and practices for a number of country locations using various survey sources. Typically, these services use public and custom-designed surveys for the purposes of job pricing. They also will conduct specialized surveys when requested. Compensation consultants who offer job pricing services typically have access to many local consulting organizations in various countries that conduct specialized data-gathering activities.

# 45

# Employing Novel Compensation Approaches to Compete for Expatriate Talent

Yvonne McNulty

*Singapore Institute of Management University*

Expatriate compensation is often regarded as a key and strategic component of effective international assignment management, yet as the fierce competition for foreign talent increases, compensating expatriates is undoubtedly becoming more and more complex. A survey by Ernst & Young, for example, found that 67 percent of mobility managers reported "compensation packages" as the biggest area where international assignee expectations are not met.[1] This may be due in part to fluctuating exchange rates, inflation, challenging locations in emerging markets, variable income tax rates, and a range of new compensation practices being introduced. Yet research suggests that expatriates do not seek or accept international assignments purely for financial reasons.[2] Indeed, there is compelling evidence that expatriates have many nonfinancial reasons for engaging in global mobility, with career enhancement and progression, seeking a personal or family adventure, and fulfilling a lifelong dream among them. Why, then, is expatriate compensation such a challenge?

This chapter examines new approaches to expatriate compensation in the battle to win external talent and retain internal talent, including the opportunity costs associated with these new approaches to assignee remuneration. I will look closely at changes in the assignee profile in terms of the types of employees who are willing to engage in global mobility, increases in turnover when expatriates leave their job during an assignment and join a competitor, and an increasing number of *third-country nationals* and *self-initiated expatriates* who are willing to accept localized employment, thereby reducing organizations' reliance on *parent-country nationals* (terms that are explained at the end of this chapter).[3] Key takeaways from this chapter include (1) the top issues that create problems in expatriate compensation, (2) an overview of new types of expatriate compensation, including local plus and localization, (3) the opportunity costs associated with new expatriate compensation approaches, and (4) how to link expatriate compensation to talent management.

## Key Issues in Expatriate Compensation

A successful compensation strategy involves keeping expatriates motivated while maintaining a competitive advantage through the meeting of an organization's corporate goals and budgets. Although this seems achievable in theory, in practice, there are many challenges with expatriate compensation that cause problems for organizations. The most prevalent is compensation disparity between expatriates and local employees, which has been identified as a key determinant of dissatisfaction and lower morale among local employees who work directly with international assignees.[4]

A second challenge is that expatriate compensation using the balance-sheet approach is expensive relative to the fact that a very small proportion of a company's overall total employee workforce (e.g., perhaps 5 percent of employees in total) may be incurring 60 or 70 percent of total salary costs. For example, over and above base salary, balance-sheet packages include cost-of-living allowances (COLAs), hardship premiums, relocation bonuses, lifestyle allowances (e.g., housing, schooling, car), and other perquisites (e.g., country club memberships, home leave, home-country storage costs, and home sale reimbursement). To be fair, for many years, this was a major reason why expatriates agreed to go: few people are willing to uproot their lives, families, established networks, and familiarity of home simply to "break even" in terms of home-country salary. There is also the tax-equalization expense when assignees relocate from low-tax to high-tax countries. Given that there are an unlimited number of home- and host-country combinations, the administrative burden on global mobility staff to transact the functional aspects of expatriate compensation can be onerous, leaving little time for new strategic initiatives such as return on investment (ROI) or talent management.

Another challenge is that the heightened competition for foreign talent has not driven assignee salaries up, as one would logically expect, but actually has driven salaries down. Consider, for example, that in years gone by, companies have used "rich" compensation packages to create a "home away from home" as an incentive for employees to relocate (predominantly the balance-sheet or full-package approach), but with the availability of more employees willing to relocate abroad to gain valuable international experience, particularly younger employees, there has been a steady decline in the need for full-package approaches, especially in Asia, where reduced packages are becoming the norm.[5]

Lastly, perhaps the biggest challenge in expatriate compensation is not only that the balance-sheet approach is becoming an outdated and overly expensive model, but it is also ineffective for moving companies' global competitive advantage to where it should be. Consider, for example, that the balance-sheet approach is based on a repatriation model that insists on maintaining a link to expatriates' home country or headquarters despite the fact that many expatriates may never return there. As a result, if compensation is strategically geared toward an expatriate who will one day return to his or her home country, it is not then capable of effectively supporting the high demand for career expatriates whose continual movement across borders—often over decades—helps to facilitate true global staffing. A further disadvantage for the career expatriate is that the balance-sheet approach also does not enable expatriates to fully acculturate to local norms and customs.

## New Types of Expatriate Compensation

There are a number of approaches to expatriate compensation, as illustrated in Table 45.1, some of which are well established. The focus in this chapter is on the third and fourth categories of package, *local plus* and *localization*, which have emerged as viable and popular alternatives to the traditional balance-sheet approach.

*Local plus* is an approach in which expatriate employees are paid according to the salary levels, structure, and administration guidelines of the host location, as well as being provided, in recognition of the employee's foreign status, with special expatriate benefits such as transportation, housing, and the costs of dependents' education. It is worth noting that not all expatriates on local plus receive the full range of additional benefits, these being at the discretion of the employing organization and largely determined by the location of the assignment (e.g., hardship versus nonhardship location), among other factors.[6] *Localization*, however, is an approach in which assignees are paid according to the salary levels, structure, and administration guidelines of the host location where they are being sent or are already living and working. Localization involves the removal or absence of an assignee's expatriate status from a policy standpoint, including benefits and allowances. In practical terms, it means that ties back to the home country from where an assignee has come or from where they may have originally been remunerated are severed, and the assignee becomes a "local" in the host country.[7] It almost always involves replacing a salary package (e.g., base salary, incentives, allowances, perquisites, social security, and retirement plans) with compensation comparable with that offered to locally hired employees.

Local plus and localization are offered in one of two ways. When it is *delayed*, an expatriate commences an international assignment on a balance-sheet approach and then, after a period of between three and five years, transitions to local plus or is fully localized directed by either the employer or employee. Some assignees relocate, for example, with full knowledge that local plus will be offered or localization will occur after two years in the host country, as predetermined in their contract, whereas other assignees may not be transitioned to local plus or localized until completion of the initial or subsequent extension(s) of the assignment, which may be 5 to 7, or even 10, years after it first began. Transitioning to a reduced compensation package usually involves a phasing-out period during which special expatriate benefits (e.g., transportation, housing, healthcare, and the costs of dependents' education) are reduced over a wind-back period (e.g., 50 percent phased out in year 1 and 50 percent in year 2). For fully localized assignees, it is essential for them to resign from their home-country office and be formally hired by the host-country office of the same company for accounting purposes. This is also a typical requirement for local-plus assignees but not always enacted.

Reduced compensation also can be offered immediately at the onset of an assignment, typically in the form of a *permanent* or *one-way transfer*. In this scenario, employees know from the outset that they will be on local plus or fully localized, which removes the company's obligation to repatriate or reassign them elsewhere.

Companies typically use reduced-compensation approaches as a cost-cutting measure in terms of maximizing both talent management *and* cost containment. A recent study found that reduced expatriate compensation is used when the assignment has a combination of (1) a permanent position in the host country, (2) the assignment location is in the same region as an employee's home country, (3) there is not likely to be a suitable role in the home country for an employee to return to, and (4) cost reduction is a priority.[8]

| Policy Name | Strategy | Description of Policy | Purpose |
|---|---|---|---|
| Balance sheet (full package, home based) | Development | • Full bells and whistles, i.e., generous remuneration (including bonus and incentives) and benefits (including tax equalization, look-see trip, COLA, housing, education, spousal allowance, car, home leave, club memberships)<br><br>• Designed to ensure employee lifestyle in comparison with home; not disadvantaged by relocating<br><br>• Based on notion that there is a home country from where the expatriate originates | • Targeted at executives for career development who possess universal skills and are considered high potential<br><br>• Used for "cadre" approach to develop careers of elite group of high performers whose permanent mobility is a long-term strategic goal<br><br>• Used for retention purposes where goal is to repatriate to corporate headquarters or business-group headquarters<br><br>• Used sparingly as reward for key individuals<br><br>• Complex to administer with many home-country–host-country combinations |
| Balance sheet (light package, home based) | Skills/secondment | • Reduced version of full package, i.e., generous remuneration with/without bonus and incentives and inclusion of some benefits (e.g. housing, education, car, home leave) but not others (e.g. club memberships, spousal allowance, COLA) | • Expatriates with deep technical skills or competencies<br><br>• Specific goal is to transfer skills and knowledge for duration of assignment only (no more than two years)<br><br>• Expatriate relocates for fixed period and repatriates with no intention to relocate again unless a specific skill need arises<br><br>• Used to service clients in locations where local skills are not available |

**Table 45.1  Overview of Compensation Strategies for International Assignments**

| Policy Name | Strategy | Description of Policy | Purpose |
|---|---|---|---|
| Local plus (host based) | Cost savings | • Provides some benefits of developmental strategy but on greatly reduced basis<br>• Expatriates often localized with some additional benefits provided to sustain retention<br>• No ongoing allowances (e.g., COLA)<br>• Initial allowances typically phased out over period of assignment (50 percent benefit year 2, 20 percent benefit year 3) | • Combination of developmental and skills/secondment expatriates but generally targeted at middle-management executives who are specialized, functional people or broad business managers and/or generalists who move between a variety of different positions (and locations) throughout their career<br>• Typically offered to managers initiating relocation or indicating willingness to relocate |
| Localization (host based) | Cost savings, functional retention | • Initial allowances from any of above phased out over period of assignment (50 percent benefit year 2, 20 percent benefit year 3) to achieve full "local" remuneration | • Offered to managers initiating relocation and long-term assignees exceeding term of contract (i.e., beyond initial assignment) but who wish to remain in location or firm does not wish to repatriate |
| Permanent transfer (host based) | Self-initiated transfers | • One-way relocation package to host destination<br>• Salary, incentives, and benefits from local payroll | • Self-initiated/employee-initiated relocation |

*Source:* Y. McNulty and K. Inkson, *Managing Expatriates: A Return on Investment Approach.* Business Expert Press, New York, 2013.

**Table 45.1  Overview of Compensation Strategies for International Assignments** (*continued*)

A recent assignment trend directly related to reduced compensation is the increase in *permanent transfers* resulting in the localization of expatriates. Brookfield, for example, found that more than one-third of the 123 participating firms in its survey used permanent transfers, which are viewed as a cost-effective alternative to the traditional (balance-sheet) international assignment.[9] A survey by Cartus identified skills shortages in host-country locations as an additional reason for using permanent transfers.[10] A *permanent transfer* is one in which an employee resigns from his or her home-country office and is hired by the host-country office of the same company but for which there is no return (repatriation) to the home country and no guarantee of company-sponsored reassignment elsewhere.[11] Permanent transfers are "one-way moves" directed by the company in which employees operate as a "local" in the host country. When a permanent transfer is used, host-country compensation and benefits are applied, with relatively few, if any, typical expatriate package benefits made available over the long term.[12] In some instances, a local-plus compensation package may be offered to a permanent transferee during an initial transfer period of up to two years to facilitate his or her transition. Importantly, employees undertaking a permanent transfer are still considered expatriates, given their nonimmigrant status and lack of citizenship (passport) of the host country. The prevalence of permanent-transfer opportunities among companies is to be expected and is consistent with cost-containment efforts. Reports by KPMG and ORC Worldwide, for example, show that more than three-quarters of companies have some form of permanent-transfer and localization policy in place.[13] Indeed, Brookfield found that half the firms in its survey were switching employees to localized conditions, with a marked increased in permanent-transfer and localization activity overall.[14]

Reduced compensation also can be used as a proxy retrenchment tool for expatriates whose performance in the host location no longer warrants the expense that the balance-sheet approach demands. Additionally, reduced compensation helps to minimize perceived inequities between expatriates working with local staff, many of whom perform similar roles but whose salary and benefits often vary significantly. Reduced compensation, especially localization, can further facilitate a company's strategy of local responsiveness, particularly when there is a need to demonstrate long-term commitment to a particular host country or region. It is worth noting, however, that reduced-compensation practices are not always driven by companies. Employees are increasingly seeking out permanent transfers as a step toward fulfilling their own career development abroad, even though doing so may not increase the financial rewards they receive as substantially as their full-package colleagues.[15]

The upside of these new approaches to expatriate compensation is that while the traditional reasons for needing expatriates (e.g., skills transfer, career development) remain, more partially and fully localized assignees now have a level of managerial talent that they can compete for jobs with full-package expatriates. This reduces global mobility costs for companies, widens the talent pool and sourcing opportunities, and provides employees with more job opportunities on the international labor market. In sum, new compensation approaches such as local plus and localization offer an alternative, less-expensive solution to global staffing, buoyed by the availability of more and more employees willing to accept partially or fully localized terms and conditions in exchange for valuable international experience.

## Opportunity Costs of Expatriate Compensation

Although reduced-compensation approaches offer many benefits to companies, the question remains whether they enable organizations to achieve their long-term strategic goals regarding talent management and knowledge sharing. Surprisingly, very little is known about the implications arising from new forms of expatriate compensation despite the prevalence with which they are being used. What we do know, in practice, is that local plus and localization create many problems not just for companies but also for assignees. This section examines some of these problems and how they can be overcome.[16]

## Expect and Manage Reduced Assignee Loyalty

Whereas generous compensation packages tend to bind expatriates to their company, local plus and localization put expatriates on a level playing field akin to their domestic counterparts in the host country, meaning that job movement in and out of the organization can be facilitated with greater ease. In other words, the opportunity cost of local plus and localization is reduced loyalty among assignees because the financial sacrifices required to leave their employer and join a competitor are significantly reduced. Reduced compensation therefore facilitates less job commitment and higher levels of risk taking by assignees because there are fewer perks (e.g., allowances and benefits) they need to give up when seeking alternative employment. Because money is no longer the defining factor, the opportunity cost of reduced compensation becomes crystal clear: although it brings very direct benefits to companies via cost savings, among expatriates, it often leads to increased tension and frustration and reduced job satisfaction and commitment. Companies therefore may save money by adopting local-plus and localization practices, but they also risk losing high-potential global staff to competitors. Hence short-term financial return-on-investment (ROI) gains can be undermined by long-term strategic losses in talent.

## Fix Process Untidiness

There are likely to be different implications for assignees localized from the outset of an assignment or those who are partially or fully localized within a two-year time frame but who knew from the outset that some form of localization would occur versus those assignees who do not initially undertake an international assignment with local plus or localization in mind. In the latter case, assignees will no longer have access to allowances and incentives when their compensation is reduced, ultimately resulting in unplanned lost income and financial disadvantages. A recent study found that this then affects assignees' psychological contract, leading to resentment, thoughts of leaving, and decreases in engagement.[17] What is meant by this?

Expatriates' psychological contract fulfillment is linked to perceptions about the obligations and promises owed to them by their organization.[18] This is the "currency" or "content" of the psychological contract, the "things that matter," and they generally fall into two categories: (1) *economic* currency in benefits such as tax equalization, bonuses, paid home leave, housing and education costs, and medical insurance and, (2) *development* currency in the form of, for example, increased levels of job autonomy and challenge and mobility opportunities (including reassignment) that can help assignees to build an international or global career. When companies reduce expatriate compensation, they are shrinking the psychological contract pie by asking assignees to redefine their sense of worth, perhaps their lifestyle, and probably their commitment to the organization.

Although it is true that some assignees welcome the opportunity to engage in international work experience irrespective of the compensation offered (i.e., balance sheet, local plus, localization), there are just as many assignees who accept reduced compensation as a means of staying employed and/or staying abroad because they perceive that there is no alternative, particularly for assignees whose reduced compensation is unplanned. However, although many expatriates accept reduced compensation, a recent study found that there is widespread dissatisfaction with the process by which it is enacted.[19] The most significant issue raised is that companies change compensation contracts *during* an assignment rather than waiting until the end of the assignment (e.g., by withdrawing or reducing a housing allowance, school allowance, or home leave), thereby leaving many expatriates feeling that they are backed into a corner financially. Others resent that once they are established as career expatriates, senior management then "moves the goal posts" by reducing compensation packages at the point of reassignment or assignment extension, knowing that assignees have few alternative employment opportunities in their home country. Doing so creates a heightened sense of unjustified loss, not necessarily because assignees are unhappy with their salary package but rather with the process. Denise Rousseau, author of *I-deals: Idiosyncratic Deals Employees Bargain for Themselves*, gets right to the point when she says that "changing the deal while keeping the people" is one of the greatest challenges in today's employment landscape.[20] The best way to alleviate tension relating to reduced compensation is to engage in a much closer dialogue with assignees and to ensure absolute transparency about the process.

*Manage the Inevitable Organizational Hierarchy* Localization frequently creates an *organizational hierarchy or hierarchical pecking order* whereby companies treat assignees differently on the basis of those considered expatriates versus those considered local from a policy standpoint. Traditional balance-sheet expatriates, for example, typically represent the elite class of international assignees being of higher strategic value, whereas partially or fully localized assignees are often viewed as lower-order expatriates stuck beneath a type of expatriate glass ceiling—a limbo status of being neither a traditional expatriate nor a true local employee. This glass ceiling frequently presents strategic and operational restrictions to assignees in terms of career advancement, therefore resulting in reduced morale. Indeed, assignees who perceive that they are not sufficiently supported or valued by a company, in comparison with other types of expatriates, are at risk of looking for job opportunities with competitors because they are working in a business environment in which there are lucrative career opportunities available elsewhere. In fact, a recent study of expatriates found that 89 percent of respondents perceived an international assignment to be of benefit not only to their current employer but to also increase their external marketability to other international employers.[21] The fact remains, however, that although localized assignees are viewed and treated differently by companies in terms of their status and compensation, they are still expatriates and still likely to face the same adjustment challenges as balance-sheet expatriates, albeit without the same level of support. This is so because, like balance-sheet expatriates, partially or fully localized assignees are not citizens of the host country.

## Linking Compensation to Talent Management

Are the various new approaches to expatriate compensation the "magic bullet" many companies perceive it to be? The latest research suggests that the use of "cheaper" assignments that seem appealing to many companies also can lead to unintended outcomes in terms of unforeseen opportunity costs (e.g., loss of critical talent) arising from "shortsighted decisions."[22] Furthermore, if expatriation is so critical to an organization's competitive advantage, why is it so difficult to link global mobility to global talent management? In their ground-breaking article about the seven myths of global talent management, Dana Minbaeva and David Collings show that the connection between global mobility activities and talent-pool acquisition remains weak: many companies continue to engage in global mobility without linking it to developing future global leaders or to meeting their assignees' career-development expectations.[23] Nonetheless, it is these same companies that espouse the hiring of global staff as broadening their organization's understanding of global markets and helping it to develop a global mind-set. What, then, can companies do to overcome the problems that new compensation approaches create in relation to effective talent management?

One way to overcome the disconnect is to align and integrate expatriate compensation with broader talent-management initiatives. This requires transitioning from *expatriate* to *global* compensation. The shift in terminology reflects a shift in mind-set, first, that although expatriates clearly perform in an international context, many are nonetheless employed in jobs similar to those of their local counterparts or in jobs that locals also can do at some point in the future. Additionally, local employees often relocate domestically for much the same reasons as expatriates do internationally (e.g., for career development and promotion), yet even when the standard of living of local is affected, they are not compensated for it like expatriates. The distinction, then, is to focus less on *expatriate status* as the defining criteria for compensation and more on the international nature of the job. Essentially, global employees engaged in international work require global compensation. This suggests that global compensation needs to move away from remunerating assignees to instead remunerating *international employees*. How can this be done?

Expatriate compensation works best when it avoids being based on an assignee's home-country status but instead on the role that the assignee performs. This is so because it is the *worth of the position* that should be aligned with strategic objectives, not whether an employee has assignee status. Furthermore, it is the role that expatriates perform that ideally should dictate whether they are compensated according to local, regional, or global wage and salary considerations. In this way, a global compensation approach enables companies to find the most appropriate candidate and then compensate him or her accordingly not because of who he or she is but according to what he or she is expected to achieve. A global compensation approach, then, is more equitable because it is performance based, thereby eliminating overpaying and perceived unfairness. In reality, global compensation is much simpler to administer than a balance-sheet approach because it represents an extension of most organizations' already existing domestic (home-country) pay-for-performance model.[24]

Although a global compensation approach will, in some instances, also reduce expatriates' compensation when partially or fully localized approaches are used, one advantage is that it allows organizations to expand their global talent pool by targeting candidates eager to pursue international and global careers, that is, candidates who are willing to expatriate not just because of the compensation being offered but often *in spite of it*. This includes career and self-initiated expatriates for whom many have already acquired the intercultural competencies, cultural intelligence, and language abilities necessary to succeed in an international role and who also have the necessary desire, skills, and attitudes. A global compensation approach therefore resembles less the traditional and same-across-the-board balance-sheet approach that has been the mainstay of expatriation for decades and moves instead toward a more innovative and strategic approach that is customized according to regional or local concerns and to the demand, location, cost, and other strategic and operational concerns of the organization.

A further advantage of a global compensation approach is that it is inherently more flexible than the balance-sheet approach because, being based on pay for performance, it can continue even after an assignee repatriates or decides to relinquish his or her expatriate status. Unlike the balance-sheet approach, which can only be used for employees deployed abroad, global compensation is not necessarily location or status specific but can be leveraged over the long term to facilitate the retention of employees—global or otherwise—as a means of ensuring a better ROI from global mobility and talent-management programs. For example, an employee who expatriates, relocates back to the home country, and expatriates again as part of his or her overall career progression need not change compensation status during each move if a global compensation approach is used. This alleviates not only a heavy transactional burden on the global mobility department in terms of administering pay and benefits for each subsequent change in host or home location but also contributes to and fosters a type of "dynamic global career" that is likely to become a normal part of global talent management over the next two decades.[25]

## Policy Best Practice for Expatriate Compensation

One of the main problems associated with the balance-sheet approach is the compensation disparity between traditional full-package expatriates versus partially and fully localized expatriates despite the fact that many may be doing the same job. All are expatriates, none are true locals, yet the former are nearly always paid according to home-country standards and the latter on local terms and conditions with few, if any, home-country links. Consider though, that if partially or fully localized assignees can do the same job for half the cost, then a radical shakeup in expatriate compensation is overdue to ensure that a small link to the headquarters or home-country standard of living is maintained, but a larger emphasis is placed on the local market context that expatriates are sent to support.

From this perspective, local-plus and localization practices represent more cost-effective means by which companies can manage various types of expatriate staff while simultaneously attempting to meet their organizational objectives. In advocating for reduced-compensation approaches, though, it is important that expatriates are not treated like local host-country or domestic employees: clearly, assignees incur more substantial expenses and greater disruption to their lives than employees who choose not to work abroad. As such, they should be compensated accordingly and subjected to a different set of policies, but only insofar as the compensation approach remains appropriate to the job that expatriates actually do rather than the status they hold because of their home-country ties. When deploying local plus or localization, consider the following guidelines:

- When reducing compensation, enter into discussions early, and put all agreed items in writing via an assignment letter, letter of understanding, policy document, or formal contract.

- Provide solutions to address assignee's concerns about retirement plans and healthcare coverage, typically two of the biggest challenges when compensation is reduced. One way to handle social security, health and life insurance, and employer-provided pension plans is to enroll the employee in the local plan immediately.

- Be mindful to consider requests to continue the payment of international school fees for children. This is often a highly emotional issue for assignees because the local school system may not be a viable alternative because of language barriers or curriculum challenges.

In addition to formal policy elements, it is important to recognize that reducing expatriates' compensation requires careful management, aside from only financial considerations, in terms of how assignees can adjust to their new status and are integrated among a local workforce permanently. Consider the following:

- Local plus and localization frequently imply a one-way transfer with little or no opportunity for repatriation. In practical terms, it is important to facilitate realistic expectations among assignees as to the potential career paths likely to arise from their now-permanent stay in the host country.

- Mentoring specifically related to acculturation into the host culture seems essential on the basis that local-plus and localized assignees are not "true" locals despite their status as localized assignees.

- There is a need to recognize the vital role to be played by local employees in helping partially and fully localized assignees to adjust.

## Conclusion: Is It Just About the Money?

Decades of research about expatriates have assumed that the fundamental driver for assignees to accept international assignments has been the financial gain, mostly as a result of the substantial benefits and allowances they receive over and above their base salary. To be fair, for many years, this was indeed a major reason why expatriates agreed to go: few people are willing to uproot their lives, families, established networks, and familiarity of home simply to "break even" in terms of home-country salary. The latest research shows, however, that the five top criteria for expatriates when making the decision to accept an international assignment go beyond only financial reasons.[26] Although base salary (71 percent) and a location bonus (to incentivize the move; 32 percent) are important, so too is accompanying partner support to assist in adjustment and the dual-career issue (finding employment; 60 percent), reintegration guarantees for an expatriate's career (58 percent), and the quality of schooling for children (whether fully or partially funded by the company; 41 percent).

Clearly, money *does* matter to some extent: expatriates, like everyone else, need to earn their keep, pay their bills, and support their families. Expatriation—and global mobility in general—is often a fast-track way to earn more money more quickly to meet this need and sometimes to save money as well, making mobility attractive to many employees, at least in the short term. Employees close to retirement may be especially focused on money, particularly maintaining home-country retirement plans, yet this aspect of remuneration remains one of the most challenging aspects particularly for career expatriates; only 12 percent of companies in a Mercer survey had established international pension plans to ensure long-term expatriates their continuity of benefits.[27] But money is not everything. As noted earlier, "job guarantees" on return to the home country, "partner support," and "children's schooling" are also ranked as important criteria. This tells us a lot about modern expatriation, wherein we are witnessing a change in the drivers that motivate expatriates to go abroad, with corresponding changes in companies' strategies to attract the right people into global employment and to keep them employed over the long term.

For more and more expatriates, compensation, then, is a "means to an end"—it matters only to a point. Most organizations are therefore mistaken in their belief that financial gain is expatriates' overriding motivation when they go abroad. In fact, a recent study found that financial gain becomes most important to expatriates only when a sudden change in remuneration causes them undue hardship or they are close to retirement.[28] Furthermore, traditional balance-sheet approaches to assignee compensation cannot be used to the same extent as they have in the past to motivate expatriates to perform and to remain with an organization. In accepting this new reality about compensation, it is not the type of compensation that matters most to expatriates but the *process* by which compensating them takes place and how they are subsequently treated because if the financial ties that bind them to their organizations are lessened by local plus or cut altogether by localization, then using only money to retain them seems somewhat futile. This is particularly true when competitor organizations can match or exceed an assignee's existing remuneration package as a means of poaching him or her.

The point here is that it is not *just* about the money. In fact, for some millennial expatriates as well as those climbing the ladder to middle management, it is often *never* about the money. To fully link global mobility with talent management, companies need to deploy compensation approaches that engage and motivate their expatriates. This is where the psychological contract can have real power in terms of (1) when and how reductions in expatriate salary are communicated, (2) when changes in benefits are likely to occur, and (3) the alternatives that are offered to offset the inevitable financial shortfall in relation to the assignee's financial obligations and responsibilities as family breadwinner. There is something else here to consider: the power of the psychological contract is determined not by how much money is spent or thrown at a problem but rather by the intent behind the action or behavior. It costs companies nothing to treat their assignees well by communicating with them openly and thereby fostering harmonious and committed relationships through mutual respect and understanding.

## Glossary

**Assignee**   An employee of an organization who voluntarily chooses to be sent from his or her country of origin and/or permanent residence to a foreign country to work temporarily but does not take up citizenship of that country; see *expatriate*.

**Balance-sheet approach**   A compensation approach that links the base salary of an expatriate to the salary structure of his or her nominated home country with the intention of "keeping him or her whole," i.e., not disadvantaging him or her compared with living standards in the home country; often referred to as *full package*.

**Career expatriates**   Reassigned expatriates who spend most of their careers in assignments in countries other than that of their citizenship or of the headquarters country of their employer.

**Cost-of-living allowance (COLA)**   Payment by a company to compensate an expatriate for differences in daily living expenses between his or her nominated home and host country. Examples include the cost of transportation, groceries, furniture and appliances, medical care, and domestic help.

**Expatriate**   An employee of an organization who voluntarily chooses to be sent from his or her country of origin and/or permanent residence to a foreign country to work temporarily but does not take up citizenship of that country.

**Global staffing**   The critical issues faced by multinational corporations with regard to the employment of home-, host-, and third-country nationals who are required to fill positions in their headquarters and subsidiary operations.

**Hardship premium**   A salary premium (typically calculated as a percentage of base salary) offered by companies to induce employees to accept an international assignment to a challenging or undesirable location in terms of physical, cultural, social, or other conditions, e.g., China, Russia, or South Korea.

**Home country/parent country**   Country of origin from where an expatriate has been recruited prior to undertaking an international assignment; the home country may or may not be the headquarters country of the organization, just as it may or may not be the country of citizenship of the expatriate.

**Home leave**   A provision whereby employers cover the expense of one or more trips back to the home country for expatriates and their family members.

**Home sale reimbursement**   Monies reimbursed to expatriates by their company for part of the loss incurred from the sale of their home when electing to sell their primary residence in the home country as a result of relocating abroad.

**Host country**   Country to which an expatriate is temporarily assigned but for which he or she usually does not have citizenship.

**Host-country nationals (HCNs)**   Mostly nonexpatriate employees residing in the host location as citizens of that country.

**Housing allowance**   A monetary provision whereby employers provide expatriates with a specified monthly sum to cover all or part of their rental accommodation costs in the host location; the monthly sum is typically determined by family size and job level and paid directly to the expatriate or the landlord.

**International assignment**   The project or temporary role in another country to which an expatriate is dispatched by his or her employing organization in service of corporate goals, typically for a period of one to five years.

**International labor market**   Defined as the total global supply of the labor force (the number of people in a particular country or area who are able and willing to work) that interacts with the world of commercial activity (*capital flows*) where goods and services are bought and sold; relies on an exchange of information between employers and job seekers about wage rates, conditions of employment, level of competition, and job location and represents the invisible factors of production associated with human capital (people) that contribute to corporate and national performance. Companies and countries compete on the international labor market to attract the best and brightest highly skilled labor and knowledge workers.

**Millennials**   A term used to describe individuals who are members of generation Y, i.e., those born between 1982 and 2000.

**Parent-country nationals (PCNs)**   Citizens of the headquarters-country location of a company, from which they are then sent abroad.

**Permanent transferee**   An employee who resigns from his or her home-country office and is hired by the host-country office of the same multinational corporation at the time of relocation but for which there is no return to the home country and no promise or guarantee of repatriation or reassignment elsewhere; employees are expected to operate as a local in the host country. Also known as *one-way moves*.

**Perquisites**   A payment, benefit, privilege, or advantage over and above regular income, salary, or wages paid to expatriates as a special right or privilege arising from their position.

**Psychological contract**   An indirect, unwritten, and often unspoken agreement between an employer and employee.

**Reassignment** or **sequential expatriation**   An international assignment that is undertaken at the immediate conclusion of a prior international assignment.

**Repatriation**   The reintegration of an expatriate into his or her original home operation from whence he or she undertook his or her (first or only) international assignment.

**Self-initiated expatriate (SIE)**   Qualified people who move to new countries of their own volition, without company support, and seek to "see the world" or develop their careers there.

**Talent management**   The strategic management of people identified as having the potential for high performance as a critical component of an organization's business success, including their recruitment, selection, identification, development, and retention.

**Tax equalization**   A compensation approach for calculating an expatriate's share of his or her worldwide tax burden by striving to ensure that he or she is financially no worse or better off than he or she would have been had an assignment not been undertaken and he or she had remained in his or her nominated home country.

**Third-country nationals (TCNs)**   Also referred to as *foreign local hires*, TCNs originate from neither the home country where corporate headquarters is located nor the host country where they are employed but a third country where they have lived either temporarily or permanently before agreeing to move to the host country.

## NOTES

1. Ernst & Young, "Global Mobility Effectiveness Survey," London, 2010.
2. Y. McNulty, "Are Self-Initiated Expatriates Born or Made? Exploring the Relationship between SIE Orientation and Individual ROI," in V. Vaiman and A. Haslberger (eds.), *Talent Management of Self-Initiated Expatriates: A Neglected Source of Global Talent*. Palgrave-Macmillan, London, 2013, pp. 30–58.
3. Y. McNulty and K. Inkson, *Managing Expatriates: A Return on Investment Approach*. Business Expert Press, New York, 2013.
4. K. Leung, Z. Wang, and A. Hong, "Moderating Effects on the Compensation Gap between Locals and Expatriates in China: A Multi-level Analysis." *Journal of International Management* 17(1):54–67, 2011.
5. F. Diez and K. Vierra, "Why Companies in Asia Are Changing Their Approach to Pay," WorldatWork, Scottsdale, AZ, 2013; ORC Worldwide, "Survey on Local-Plus Packages in Hong Kong and Singapore," New York, 2008.
6. P. Stanley, "Local-Plus Packages for Expatriates in Asia: A Viable Alternative." *International HR Journal* 3:9–11, 2009.
7. It is important to note here that there has been some confusion about the exact meaning of the term *localization* in reference to expatriation. Some articles refer to localization as the "extent to which jobs originally held by expatriates are filled by local employees who are competent to perform the job" (Selmer, 2003, p. 43) or "displacing expatriate managers with local talent" (Fryxell, Butler, and Choi, 2004, p. 269). These definitions assume that "local employees" are nationals of the host country, where localization is linked to their career development (i.e., they are offered a job that an expatriate used to do). Technically, this is not correct given that *localization* as defined and practiced among mobility consulting firms determines "local employees" as constituting *both* nationals of the host country *and* localized expatriates. Localization is not, therefore, the replacing of expatriates with nationals of the host country but the transitioning of assignees onto local terms and conditions who then join the "local employee" workforce. See G. Fryxell, J. Butler, and A. Choi, "Successful Localization Programs in China: An Important Element in

Strategy Implementation." *Journal of World Business* 39(3):268–282, 2004; and J. Selmer, "Staff Localization and Organizational Characteristics: Western Business Expatriates in China." *Asia Pacific Business Review* 10(1):43–57, 2003.

8. E. Tait, H. De Cieri, and Y. McNulty, "The Opportunity Cost of Saving Money: An Exploratory Study of Permanent Transfers and Localization of Expatriates in Singapore." *International Studies of Management and Organization* 44(3), 2014.

9. Brookfield Global Relocation Services, "Global Relocation Trends Survey Report," Woodridge, IL, 2012.

10. Cartus, "Global Mobility Policy and Practices Survey: Navigating a Challenging Landscape," Wilmington, NC, 2010.

11. J. Yates, "Putting Down Roots: How Localization Can Help Reduce Expatriate Program Costs." *Mobility*, October:92–97, 2011.

12. ORC Worldwide, "Survey of Localization Policies and Practices," New York, 2004.

13. KPMG, "International Assignment Policies and Practices Survey," New York, 2003; ORC Worldwide, "Survey of Localization Policies and Practices," New York, 2004.

14. Brookfield Global Relocation Services, "Global Relocation Trends Survey Report," Woodridge, IL, 2012.

15. D. Collings, H. Scullion, and M. Morley, "Changing Patterns of Global Staffing in the Multinational Enterprise: Challenges to the Conventional Expatriate Assignment and Emerging Alternatives." *Journal of World Business* 42(2):198–213, 2007.

16. See also Y. McNulty and G. Aldred, "Local Plus: Winning the Compensation Battle but Losing the Talent War." *Strategic Advisor* 4(9):1–5, 2013.

17. Y. McNulty, H. De Cieri, and K. Hutchings, "Expatriate Return on Investment in Asia Pacific: An Empirical Study of Individual ROI versus Corporate ROI." *Journal of World Business* 48(2):209–221, 2013.

18. A *psychological contract* is an indirect, unwritten, and often unspoken agreement between an employer and employee. It is subjective, defined by the individual within the context of his or her employment, and idiosyncratic, or unique to each employee. The psychological contract represents an exchange agreement: organizations have expectations regarding performance outcomes and other actions from their employees, and employees have reciprocal expectations from employers regarding such things as support, communication, and equity.

19. Y. McNulty and K. Inkson, *Managing Expatriates: A Return on Investment Approach*. Business Expert Press, New York, 2013.

20. D. Rousseau, *I-deals: Idiosyncratic Deals Employees Bargain for Themselves*. ME Sharpe, Armonk, NY, 2005.

21. Y. McNulty, H. De Cieri, and K. Hutchings, "Expatriate Return on Investment in Asia Pacific: An Empirical Study of Individual ROI versus Corporate ROI." *Journal of World Business* 48(2):209–221, 2013.

22. Y. McNulty and K. Inkson, *Managing Expatriates: A Return on Investment Approach*. Business Expert Press, New York, 2013; E. Tait, H. De Cieri, and Y. McNulty, "The Opportunity Cost of Saving Money: An Exploratory Study of Permanent Transfers and Localization of Expatriates in Singapore." *International Studies of Management and Organization* 44(3), 2014.

23. D. Minbaeva and D. Collings, "Seven Myths of Global Talent Management." *International Journal of Human Resource Management* 24(9):1762–1776, 2013.

24. A. Salimaki and R. Heneman, "Pay for Performance for Global Employees," in L. Gomez-Majia and S. Werner (eds.), *Global Compensation: Foundations and Perspectives*. Routledge, Milton Park, UK, 2008, pp. 158–168.

25. Y. McNulty and C. Vance, "Dynamic Global Careers: An Internal/External Model for Understanding International Career Self-Management," EURAM Conference, Valencia, Spain, European Academy of Management, 2014.

26. D. Warneke and M. Schneider, "Expatriate Compensation Packages: What Do Employees Prefer?" *Cross Cultural Management: An International Journal* 18(2):236–256, 2011.

27. R. Herod, *Benefits Challenges and Trends for Expatriates and Internationally Mobile Employees.* Mercer, Geneva, 2012.

28. Y. McNulty and K. Inkson, *Managing Expatriates: A Return on Investment Approach.* Business Expert Press, New York, 2013.

# PART IX

# BIG DATA

# 46

# A Guide to Realizing the Value of Big Data

Lance A. Berger

*Lance A. Berger & Associates, Ltd.*

Organizations collect, connect, analyze, use, and store large quantities of data pertinent to their business and employees. This gives them a foundation for integrating multiple data elements into a smaller set of cogent decision points. These decisions pertain to the design, implementation, and audit of the effectiveness of compensation strategies. Technology makes this process more accurate, easier, faster, and cheaper than ever before. This technological phenomenon has been titled *big data*.

To many compensation practitioners, big data remains ambiguous, confusing, and intimidating. However, successful practitioners will find a way to realize value from their big data capabilities. The purpose of this chapter, therefore, is to help practitioners to realize the value of big data at a level appropriate to their organizations. It is organized into five parts:

1. Starting with foundational knowledge

2. Selecting a level of big data

3. Identifying the competencies of big data practitioners

4. Identifying compensation value-creating outcomes

5. Creating a big data program

## Foundational Knowledge

A foundational knowledge is necessary to create and implement an approach to collecting, connecting, analyzing, using, and storing big data. This foundational knowledge includes a definition and a set of criteria.

### Definition

Dan Weber, in Chapter 47, writes that big data involves the process of "collecting, compiling, and analyzing human capital information, using statistical methods and processes to generate data-driven insights for business management and strategic planning." David Turetsky, in Chapter 48, states that big data "leverages disparate system data together to form a union of unlikely confederations into a symphony of knowledge and intelligence." Ezra Schneier, in Chapter 49, defines compensation big data as "the means of creating new insights through the analysis of data, or aggregating data from different sources, to achieve compensation planning and management goals."

Collectively these definitions suggest that *big compensation data* involves the integration of data elements from different disciplines using a variety of analytical tools and technologies to identify and address important human resources issues.

### Big Data Criteria

The six criteria that follow are mandatory components of a big compensation data project:

*Outcomes.* Before embarking on big data, practitioners should clearly define the issues they seek to address. Collectively, these issues seek to answer the question, "Does the organization's compensation strategy align with its business strategy, culture, and talent-management strategies?

Examples of specific issues are

- Do organization-wide salary increases based on performance-appraisal systems correlate with organization and unit performance?

- Is employee compensation appropriately distributed to critical groups, including high performers, backups for key positions, and those demonstrating high levels of key competencies?

- Is pay a contributor to turnover in critical employee groups?

- Is pay perceived as fair and consistent with organization values?

- Are compensation strategies appropriate and administered effectively?

- Does the level of variable pay reflect the pace of organizational growth and the risk acceptance level of the cultures associated with each plan?

*Types of Data.* Once outcomes are defined, the data necessary to address them must be identified. The data required typically will come from documented business strategies and performance, compensation strategies and practices, talent-management strategies and practices, and culture surveys.

*Quality.* Once big data sources are identified, their accuracy, consistency, and comprehensives for identifying and/or solving targeted compensation issues and solutions such as just listed are determined.

*Timeliness.* After relevant data are identified and their quality ensured, they are harvested and made available in the time frame necessary for identifying and/or solving active and future issues. Time frames range from periodic to real time.

*Worth.* After determining whether their data meet the criteria listed earlier, practitioners must determine whether engaging in a big data process is worth its cost and time of implementation or whether simpler processes could be used by the organization to address compensation issues.

*Credibility.* In order to implement solutions based on big data, an organization must ensure that its employees trust and believe in its capabilities for addressing compensation issues. This means that an organization must have a formalized and timely employee communications program that honestly presents the role of data in its compensation decisions.

## Level of Big Data Selection

A foundational understanding of big data enables an organization to classify its current and potential level of implementation. Table 46.1 provides practitioners with a way to categorize their current and potential level of use of big data at various levels of problem solving in four stages and at six levels. Given the distribution of organization sizes in the United States, it is likely that the vast majority will be at stage II or stage I.

*Definitions for Table 46.1 Outcome Levels*

> *Descriptive.* Descriptive big data involves the systematic approach to identifying, collecting, organizing, and analyzing high-quality business and compensation data to unearth valuable insights that help to guide compensation decisions and actions.

> *Analytical.* Analytic big data involves the blending and integration of business, compensation, and talent-management data into cogent and useful pieces of information that can be used to make valid compensation decisions.

> *Predictive.* Predictive big data is used to make more effective compensation decisions through the extensive mining of all relevant data to create paradigms that provide a clear understanding of the relationship between organization strategies and practices and current and future outcomes.

> *Prescriptive.* Prescriptive big data is complex and sophisticated. It draws on historically valid paradigms. It enables the organization to make highly accurate decisions involving specific actions necessary to achieve desired short and long outcomes.

## Big Data Practitioners' Competencies Identification

To implement a big compensation data program, organizations require practitioners with specific competencies geared to their target stage of implementation. Table 46.2 presents three levels of ten competencies for big data practitioners. They can serve as a useful starting point for developing big data position descriptions, incumbent requirements, and performance standards.

| Stage | Organization Size by Employees | Outcome Level (See definitions on p. 523.) | Data Types | Quality (Level of Scrutiny) | Timeliness | Worth to Organization (Seven-Point Scale, 7 = highest) |
|---|---|---|---|---|---|---|
| | | | Level | | | |
| I | Small, up to 100 | Descriptive | Simple business and pay data | High | Periodic | 4 |
| II | Medium, 100–500 | Analytical | Basic business, pay, and talent-management, reporting | High | Scheduled | 5 |
| III | Large, 500–1,000 | Predictive | Medium business strategy and reporting, pay strategy and salary administration, talent management and culture | Very high | Real time | 6 |
| IV | Very large, 1,000+ | Prescriptive | Advanced business strategy and reporting, pay strategy and salary administration, talent management and culture | Extensive | Real time | 7 |

Table 46.1 Level of Big Data Selection

| Competency | Level | | |
|---|---|---|---|
| | Level III: Senior Professional | Level II: Professional | Level I: Analyst |
| Analysis and creativity | Identifies important issues and provides significant value-added solutions to improve processes, methods, and systems usually at a strategic level | Develops fundamental analyses and conclusions regarding key organization issues involving the improvement of organization operating processes, methods, and systems | Accurately and efficiently collects, tabulates, and summarizes data and information pertinent to improving the content of the program in accordance with organization needs |
| Organization focus | Demonstrates ability to know and respond effectively to a variety of organization perspectives and needs; influences organization positively to take constructive actions to address complex big data strategic issues | Establishes and maintains strong continuous relations with organization based on credible ability to constructively address basic big data issues | Develops positive working relationship with organization during big data projects through credibly addressing organization needs |
| Communications (oral) | Is articulate and persuasive in all forms of oral presentation; gains high level of organization support through strong professional and credible demeanor | Provides clear, sound, and cogent presentations reflecting knowledge of how big data can address specific organization needs | Accurately and effectively presents big data in a clear, persuasive, and organization-engaging manner |
| Communications (written) | Delivers high level of well-conceived prose communications that clearly describe issues, approaches, and recommendations for complex as well as simple content | Writes persuasive, logical communications in both narrative and presentation styles that are readily understandable and credible to the organization | Writes clear, concise, and grammatically correct and descriptive reports and/or other material required by big data program |
| Fact finding | Collects, analyzes, and accurately interprets organization data of a high degree of clarity and complexity | Understands and uses the types of data required to analyze organization issues | Provides simple, accurate, and speedy fact finding in accordance with established program, processes, and procedures |
| Industry knowledge | Recognized as having a substantial knowledge of organization's industry and business dynamics | Recognized as having sound knowledge of organization's industry and business dynamics | Has a basic knowledge of organization's industry and business dynamics |

**Table 46.2  Big Data Practitioners**

| Competency | Level | | |
|---|---|---|---|
| | **Level III: Senior Professional** | **Level II: Professional** | **Level I: Analyst** |
| Leadership | Envisions solutions to complex issues; uses knowledge of people, systems, and operations to gain support for big data programs | Envisions issues and outcomes and consistently demonstrates and communicates the highest professional standards and expertise to gain support for implementing solutions | Envisions issues, outcomes, and simple solutions; demonstrates high professional, personal, and work behaviors that enable strong acceptance of applicable programs |
| Project results | Sets high goals and performance standards and develops, implements, and monitors big project plans to achieve goals | Assembles and implements big data basic project plan | Delivers high-quality and timely programs meeting expectations |
| Technical knowledge | Recognized as an expert on big data | Recognized as having strong knowledge of big data | Recognized as having a sound basic knowledge of big data |
| Value added | Identifies and develops new and/or innovative solutions to address significant organizational needs; develops paradigms that help to make accurate decisions involving specific actions necessary to achieve desired outcomes now and in the future | Identifies and presents major issues or areas of concern to make more effective compensation decisions through the extensive mining of all relevant data and the creation of paradigms that provide a clear understanding of the relationship between organization strategies and practices and current outcomes | Provides recommendations for adaptations to big data programs |

**Table 46.2  Big Data Practitioners (*continued*)**

## Value-Creating Outcomes

Regardless of each stage of solution development, the transformative power of big data for compensation practitioners lies in identifying and managing the relationship between pay and three basic key activities and value-creating outcomes. These are business results, culture, and talent management. The following list provides some basic examples of how practitioners can create value by linking big data to specific outcomes:

*Business.* Do incentive plan payouts vary directly with competitive business performance?

*Big data needs:* Competitive business performance measures, compensation data competitive levels, competitive-level targets of incentive plans

*Output:* Correlation between level of competitive targets and actual incentive plan pay and competitive business performance

*Culture.* Do the employees' perception of the compensation fairness and organization value align with actual practice; that is, does it reinforce a success culture of innovation, creativity, engagement, leadership, motivation, and equity?

*Big data needs:* Culture questionnaire covering fairness and effectiveness of pay, compensation practice linkages to employee performance appraisal, career advancement, and competencies

*Output:* Multiple correlations of employee perception of pay practices with actual linkages of compensation to performance appraisals, career advancement, and competencies

*Talent management.* Does the compensation system support the talent-management strategy?

*Big data needs:* A talent-management program that includes an administrative system based on a clear philosophy, strategy, and process that covers the assessment of employee performance, potential, backup status, career targets, and competencies; a system that links every compensation action to an element of the talent-management program and tracks all compensation activities including those affecting new hires and terminations

*Output:* Multiple correlations that link pay to turnover in critical employee groups, competitive levels of pay to employees in critical pay groups, pay allocated to core competencies, and tracking of pay and performance of promotees, terminees, and new hires over time

### Outcomes

Output from big data analyses such as those just listed will lead big data practitioners to ensure positive outcomes such as the following:

1. Organization-wide employee evaluation and total salary increases are based on performance-appraisal systems correlated with organization and unit performance.

2. Compensation is appropriately distributed to critical groups (high performers, high potentials, backups for key positions, and employees with demonstrated high levels of key competencies).

3. Pay is not a cause of turnover in critical employee groups.

## Big Data Program Creation

The creation of a compensation big data program begins with a written statement of the principles that guide the direction and actions of the organization. This organizational blueprint contains

- Organizational strategies encompassing long-term plans for maximizing value based on the institution's vision, philosophy, values, mission, goals, and priorities. It includes success measures for each strategy.

- Organization values that guide institutional behaviors in implementing strategies toward stakeholders, including customers, employees, vendors, government, and media. Values typically include ethics, beliefs, institutional competencies, and behaviors.

- Talent-management strategies that describe the types of the people in whom the organization will invest based on their values and current and potential contribution to organizational success. People with high achievement, replacements for key positions, high potentials, and critical-competency employees are usually those receiving the highest compensation package.

- Compensation strategies that indicate how an organization will allocate employee pay based on its business and talent-management strategy.

Each component of this blueprint should identify the specific outcomes associated with each strategy, including the data required to identify and analyze its outcomes. Examples of outcomes were cited earlier.

Once a blueprint is established and data are collected for each outcome, the results can be analyzed. The focus is on the degree to which actual outcomes are consistent with targeted outcomes. This will enable practitioners to adjust their compensation and related policies, processes, and/or strategies so that they better achieve targeted outcomes. This approach to big compensation data provides for the integration of data elements from different disciplines using a variety of analytical tools and technologies to identify and address important human resources issues.

## Summary

This chapter has highlighted the fact that organizations now collect, connect, analyze, use, and store large quantities of data pertinent to their business and employees. This process gives them a foundation for integrating multiple data elements into a smaller set of cogent decision points. These decisions pertain to the design, implementation, and audit of the effectiveness of compensation strategies. Technology helps practitioners to make this process more accurate, easier, faster, and cheaper than ever before. This chapter was designed to help practitioners realize the value of big data at a level appropriate to their organizations by following this five-step process:

1. Start with a foundational knowledge.

2. Select a level of big data.

3. Identify the competencies of the big data practitioners associated with your level of big data.

4. Identify compensation value-creating outcomes.

5. Create a big data program.

# 47

# Using Workforce Analytics to Make Effective Compensation Decisions

Dan Weber

*Radford, an Aon Hewitt Company*

In today's rapidly changing economic environment, businesses looking to improve operational efficiency and better strategic planning are increasingly seeking to leverage the concept of *big data*—combining information obtained from external and third-party sources, customer and client interactions, and internal processes—to analyze new opportunities, test and refine business models, and make decisions. Using sophisticated software and transactional data from such diverse sources as customer loyalty programs, web communities, and social media, companies are experimenting with changes to products, processes, and client interactions and tracking and analyzing the results in real time. This allows organizations to increase brand awareness and customer satisfaction, decrease time to market for new products and services, and reduce operational costs and inefficiencies.

The application of big data methodologies in business and the demand for greater information and insights for decision making have led to an increased interest in human capital data and analysis. *Workforce analytics* is the process of collecting, compiling, and analyzing human capital information using statistical methods and processes to generate data-driven insights for business management and strategic planning. These insights can be applied across all human resources programs and activities to measure progress and drive improvements in key organization cultural behaviors, attraction and retention of talent, and overall business success. In particular, workforce analytics can provide a quantitative assessment of the expense, effectiveness, and return on investment (ROI) of compensation programs.

One of the ways in which workforce analytics supports business operations is in the establishment and validation of metrics. *Metrics* are established and consistent measurements used to track and evaluate quantitative components of company and organizational performance. A common example of a metric is turnover, or attrition rate; this is a quantitative measure of the percent of total employees who have left an organization within a given time period. A useful metric is *repeatable*, meaning that it can be calculated on a regular basis; *reliable*, meaning that the formula used generates consistent results; and *valid*, meaning that it measures and is descriptive of the desired aspect of business performance. Workforce analytics can be used to identify and validate meaningful data points that can then be established as metrics for ongoing measurement of business activity.

## Compensation and Workforce Analytics

Compensation professionals are often called on to respond to business inquiries that can be best answered by the use of workforce analytics. To prepare for these types of questions, compensation professionals should be familiar with four areas:

- Where and how the business currently generates value (current operations)
- Where the business anticipates growth, expansion, and change (strategic plan)
- The data currently available within company compensation and human resources information systems (HRIS)
- External sources of data, such as market surveys, government agencies, and other organizations

Compensation professionals should take into account the growing importance of workforce analytics when planning for future development of the compensation function and systems. Enhanced data-management and reporting capability in the HRIS and increasing the knowledge and understanding of statistical and data analysis methods among compensation staff are examples of improvements that can be made in anticipation of further use of workforce analytics.

## Establishing the Workforce Analytics Framework

The initial step in designing workforce analytics is establishing a framework and parameters for analysis. The first consideration for the framework should be that the information produced will be meaningful and useful to the business in reflecting activity and providing insights. This is important in ensuring that workforce analytics are not seen simply as a "human resources number" or as irrelevant to business operations. Soliciting feedback and participation from business leaders and internal stakeholders, such as the corporate finance group, on what analyses and metrics they would find useful and their preferred methods of calculation and valuation can provide an initial list of analyses and metrics for evaluation.

The second consideration for the analytics framework should be the nature and type of data available. The most common sources of data used are those normally collected within the human resources department and HRIS, such as compensation history, job structures and leveling, and employee performance. This can be combined with information obtained from other internal functions and business groups to increase data robustness and provide a greater degree of business alignment.

In addition to internal data, companies also may wish to perform comparisons with other companies, such as industry peers or competitors for talent. When considering sources of external workforce analytics data, it is important to keep in mind that peers used for compensation benchmarking may not be suitable for workforce analytics comparisons. For example, a small software design company may choose to benchmark itself for compensation purposes to a group of large e-commerce companies with which it competes for talent; however, the organizational structure of these companies is likely to be very different because of their different sizes and industries, which may result in misleading comparisons if the same group of peers is used for workforce analytics. The most effective comparisons can be made from external sources that reflect data from companies that match as closely in headcount, industry type, and product as possible.

A third consideration for the analytics framework is the staffing and technology resources that are available for performing analytics. Key points to evaluate include the ease of extracting and organizing source data, the software and other technological tools available for performing analysis and calculating metrics, and the experience and knowledge of data management and statistical analysis of the assigned staff.

Once the desired metrics and analyses and available data sources are known, a feasibility review can be performed to identify and rank analyses and metrics based on business usefulness, data availability and consistency, and resources required. The feasibility review also may be used to identify gaps in business knowledge, data sources, and resources and provide insight into where improvements can be made. The goal in creating the framework should be to provide the most useful and reliable information to the business at the lowest possible resource cost.

## Common Applications of Workforce Analytics

The applications of workforce analytics are already numerous and continuing to grow as companies and human resources professionals develop greater experience with methodologies and the means of using them. This section discusses common business questions relating to talent and compensation spending and introduces a series of core workforce analyses that can be used to provide guidance for and insight into managing these challenges.

### How do we distribute compensation across the organization?

Compensation spend distribution analysis takes the total compensation spent on a defined set of employees (i.e., a group) and calculates the percent of the total spend that is allocated to each group. Groups can include business organizations, such as departments, teams, or functions; they also can include levels and types of employees, such as management versus individual contributors; technical versus nontechnical, client-facing versus business-facing, and high-performing versus lower-performing employees; and others. Total compensation spend can be calculated based on any single pay component or combination of components; some typically used components are base salary, total cash compensation (i.e., base salary plus short-term incentive pay), and total direct compensation (i.e., base salary, short-term incentive pay, and long-term incentive value).

The analysis begins by calculating the compensation cost for the desired pay component(s) for each individual group (e.g., department) and for the overall organization. For example, if *spend* is defined as base salary, then the percent of salary expense in each department represents the metric used to analyze compensation spend. The first calculation step is to sum the salaries of employees in each department. The percentage of total salary expense allocated to each department then can be calculated by taking the sum of employee salaries in each department and dividing that by the total of all employee salaries in the whole organization.

The distribution of compensation spend across an organization can provide significant insight into the operating cost and relative efficiency for a business. Viewed from an internal focus, this analysis can assist in identifying disconnects between operating cost and perceived value of a group or department; evaluated against external data, it can highlight areas of competitive advantage or disadvantage in terms of cost relative to market peers.

### How is our talent distributed across the organization?

Talent distribution analysis reviews the percent of total organizational population represented by employees in a designated group. As with compensation spend analysis, groupings can be based on internal organization alignment, functions, performance rankings, or any other means by which employees can be classified.

To perform this analysis, the total headcount for each group and organization must be calculated. This can be done on a per-capita basis simply by adding up the number of employees in a group and then summing the total number of all groups; the percent per group is equal to the total headcount of the group divided by the total headcount of the organization. For example, an organization may wish to evaluate what percent of its population is in sales roles as opposed to technical roles; the percent of each is the sum total of the headcount for the role divided by the total headcount for the organization.

The distribution of talent across an organization can be used to provide a useful view into several areas of human capital management. The percent of employees by performance rating, ratio of managers to individual contributors, and number of employees per human resources staff are all examples of typical human resources metrics derived from talent distributions. Evaluating the distribution of employees across job level can assist in identifying organizational structure issues that are restricting opportunities for employees or otherwise out of alignment with business needs.

### How productive is our workforce?

Workforce productivity analysis is normally performed as a per-capita calculation involving a standard company-wide financial or output value divided by the number of employees. Annual revenue, total sales, and operating expense per employee are commonly used metrics of productivity; these are calculated by taking the total fiscal year revenue, sales amount, or operating expense and dividing by the average annual number of employees. A particular advantage of productivity analyses is that the values needed to calculate them are normally provided as part of annual financial disclosures and regulatory filings for publicly traded companies, greatly increasing the ease of benchmarking to external peers.

## Expanded Applications of Workforce Analytics

Once the framework for workforce analytics has been established and core analyses produced, it is possible to begin probing more deeply into specific business questions and testing hypotheses based on available data by combining analyses and using different views of data. For example, when evaluating why costs for manufacturing in one group are significantly higher than in another as shown by a compensation spend analysis, the analyst may wish to test the hypothesis that the more costly group has more higher-level employees than the less costly group using a talent-distribution analysis based on job level. For another view, a comparison of productivity between the two groups can be made by calculating the total compensation spend as a percentage of product revenue or per unit of output. The data may show that whereas the total cost of compensation is higher for a manufacturing unit with more senior employees, the compensation spend as a percent of product revenue or per unit of output may be lower, indicating that the higher-cost employees are producing more value and ROI for compensation spend.

Other data and information also may be combined with core analyses to produce a richer and more robust set of insights for business. A company with several call centers may wish to test the hypothesis that employee engagement and productivity can be increased by a system in which raises are provided earlier for better performers. In this case, data from employee engagement surveys or measurements and turnover data are integrated with compensation and productivity analyses to identify changes that occur over a period of time.

In addition to describing the organization as it currently exists, which is known as *descriptive analytics*, workforce analytics also can be used to model different scenarios for changes to the organization (*predictive analytics*). An organization in the process of expanding may perform a talent-distribution analysis to determine its current ratio of managers to individual contributors; using the ratio as a guideline, the company can predict the number of managers necessary for the total amount of headcount to be added. Similarly, an organization that is trying to increase revenue growth through increased sales may perform a productivity analysis based on units and cost per salesperson and then model the number of additional salespersons and the added cost necessary to reach revenue growth targets.

The total scope and number of different workforce analyses that can be performed are theoretically infinite. Practitioners must be aware that simply because an analysis can be performed, or a metric calculated, a useful result is not a guarantee. To assist in ensuring that analyses are both valid and valuable, three general guidelines should be followed when designing analyses and metrics.

The first guideline is to understand the issue to be analyzed. How is it characterized? What is the specific outcome desired? What are the perceptions and concerns of the stakeholders? For example, the human resources department may have as one of its goals to reduce organizational turnover. The analytics designer must understand not only what turnover is but also what kinds of turnover are of interest and if turnover of one type carries a different organizational impact than another. The goal is to be able to express the outcome of the analysis in a specific, measurable, and meaningful way.

The second guideline is to look at both the typical and expanded areas that can influence the desired outcome. Returning to the example of turnover, exit-interview data may show that highly skilled and good-performing employees are primarily leaving the organization for better opportunities at other companies. A typical direction for analysis would be to review which areas in the organization are losing the most employees; an expanded analysis would look for other external factors that may tie to employees locating elsewhere, such as an improving local economy, an increase in seed capital or government tax incentives for startup businesses, and positive or negative reviews of competitors' products and potential. This outside-the-box analysis is essential for providing the largest and most descriptive data set for integration and analysis, which will, in turn, tend to produce more relevant and robust insights.

The third guideline is to think beyond the numbers. Although human resources data are "big data" in the sense of being large data sets containing high volumes of information, one also must keep in mind that employee decisions and attitudes are influenced by many factors, not all of which can be easily tracked or accounted for in analyses. With this in mind, analysis results always should be interpreted in the context of guidance rather than as absolute answers or numbers. In addition, one must honestly and realistically evaluate the information and the possible solutions in the context of the entire business. Whereas an organization may have a higher percentage of managers at the senior level than is preferred or in line with market practice, rather than immediately terminating or demoting managers, the better solution from an organization standpoint may be to understand the reality and aim to explain it. For example, was promotion or hiring of managers done without much thought in the past? Was an overstaffing of managers by design, or because of forecasted growth that did not occur? The plan may be simply to accept the increased cost as a necessary expense at this time but to change ongoing practices regarding hiring and promotion to prevent the issue from recurring absent appropriate planning and justification. In all cases, the objective of analysis should be to provide reliable and valid information and insights that are relevant to the business and its issues.

## Other Considerations

Whenever you use or analyze employee data, it is important to ensure that measures are taken to protect data security and confidentiality. Workforce analytics systems and records should be managed, transmitted, and stored in compliance with company policy and all applicable local and country or regional laws and requirements pertaining to employee data privacy and security, including notification of any breaches. When possible, analytics should be designed to eliminate the use or display of information such as U.S. Social Security numbers or other personally identifiable information for which inadvertent or deliberate release could result in identity theft. It is also a best practice to limit or significantly restrict the communication and use of employee data that are not relevant to business decision making, such as age, gender, or minority status. In addition to protections for internal data, companies should validate and ensure that data from external sources are properly collected and handled in order to remain compliant with country and international regulations governing business communication, collusion, and antitrust laws.

## Summary

The rising use of big data, workforce analytics, and metrics will significantly increase the capability of human resources practitioners to better use information to make faster and more-informed business decisions This approach will resonate with business leadership because it will be based on the type of consistent and meaningful information necessary to drive sound operational and strategic decision making and planning.

## Key Learning Points

- Workforce analytics is the process of collecting, compiling, and analyzing human capital information using statistical methods and processes to generate data-driven insights for business management and strategic planning.

- Workforce analytics are used to assess current organizational and employee performance, identify trends and patterns that may affect business operations, and model possible outcomes of strategic planning initiatives.

- Metrics are established and consistent measurements that are used to track and evaluate quantitative components of company and organizational performance.

- Common applications for workforce analytics include talent and spend distribution (which involve looking at how employee headcount and total compensation spending are distributed across geographies, business areas and functions, and job levels) and workforce productivity analyses (which use financial and other metrics to identify cost per unit and other measurements of workforce efficiency).

- Workforce analytics can be used both descriptively to describe the current organization and predictively to model the financial and organizational implications of proposed changes.

# 48

# Making Better Compensation Decisions in the Age of Big Data

DAVID B. TURETSKY

*ADP Strategic Advisory Services*

It is hard to imagine that we once lived in a world before ubiquitous computing power was available at our fingertips. Data manipulations that used to take days for mainframe computers that filled large, environmentally controlled rooms now can happen almost in an instant . . . on our smart phones.

Compensation has lived in a world of massive data sets for many years. In support of programs such as modeling incentives, merit increases, market surveys, and job evaluations, the compensation department has developed skills to manage such programs through a heavy reliance on analytically minded professionals. Whether the need arose out of a request from a finance stakeholder or from supporting a manager with a complex rewards issue, compensation has relied on data to tell stories to help facilitate the successful implementation of business strategy.

It was not too long ago that the compensation department was filling in manual forms of data into survey participation sheets that then went to survey firms that had to manually enter the data and that then sent back reams of paper—reams of paper that often contained pages of errors. These papers then were sent back to the survey firms with corrections. Then, when the surveys arrived, they came in binders, which served as the gospel of the competitive market.

Now this process is all done via interconnected Internet applications or data file transfers between clients and vendors with barely a page printed. Of course, although computers have become much more powerful since the days of paper input, many of the processes in which we participate have not changed. They still focus on completing a singular purpose—that is, quantifying human capital.

## A Look Back

The computing power used today was originally created to manipulate data. Even the name *computer* is an analogy to mathematical computational power. What had been done using sticks, bones, rocks, or an abacus evolved slowly. Data, in this environment, were used with manual processes through tremendous efforts involving many manipulations and special hardware and software.

In the age of the PC, data became easier to access, although the skills needed to transform the data varied greatly and fell on the software tools to help gain true information from masses of data. PC users kept dozens of spreadsheets filled with analytics on their desktops, constantly juggling windows of data and formulas. This continues today, although the needs are changing.

In the age of smart, always connected devices, the appetite for data is insatiable. People now have access to complete pictures of their social lives, health, wealth, security, children, and work lives in their hands. They can walk around and hold global meetings without ever making a call, sitting down, or having access to a computer. They can do all of this through a web conferencing system while on vacation from their tablet device.

These devices can show the data from the cloud in analytical dashboards that show a complete picture of a manager's business at a moment's notice. They do not need to manipulate spreadsheets into pivot tables. They do not need to communicate with anyone from human resources. The data are just there in a form that enables them to make better business decisions.

## And Now for the Revolution

This emphasis on secure cloud storage for data and on-demand data usage provides enormous opportunities for the business world to exploit. Examine each process, measure it, and find areas of improvement in order to optimize each investment in every way. This was truly a revolution. It led to massive business model changes. Some companies changed the very nature of their businesses, such as IBM, HP, and Xerox, from manufacturing to services as this new economy grew.

The new economy generated new jobs to help deal with the influx of data and interconnected devices. The newest and most demanded skills came in the form of people who could look at the data in ways that functional experts could not. The problem was that the data that are available are so disparate and varied that they required special technical and mathematical skills. This led to a new demand for statistical analysts. These people are the heart and soul of the new economy. They are the *data scientists*. The skills they possess enable them to provide a complete picture of the world of data that surrounds them.

Think of them as Olympic swimmers in an ocean of data swimming in search of good currents that will help them find stories to tell. They are the bridge or interface between enterprise data and the questions being asked or not yet asked of the data.

Typically, these people have the following skills (from various job postings):

- Degrees in applied statistics, mathematics, computer science, engineering, or the physical sciences

- Master's degrees in statistics, mathematics, or computer science

- At least five years of experience, for example, analyzing data and/or building analytical models using statistical software

- Demonstrated ability to apply statistical or data-mining techniques to solve business problems

- Ability to extract and prep data from relational databases and Excel and text files for use with statistical software

- Excellent verbal and written communication skills

- Ability to

  - Communicate with people of various technical and business backgrounds, including the ability to explain difficult technical concepts in simple terms to business users

  - Work independently in all aspects of data modeling, from sourcing through final presentation of the findings

  - Work with the business users and information technology

  - Work independently and within a team environment

*Harvard Business Review* called the data scientist the "Sexiest Job of the 21st Century" (Thomas H. Davenport and D. J. Patil, "Data Scientist: The Sexiest Job of the 21st Century," *Harvard Business Review*, October 2012). Although this is impressive, consider that IBM estimates that every day we create 2.5 quintillion bytes of data—so much that 90 percent of the data in the world today has been created in the last two years alone.

## How Business Can Use Big Data

Data reside everywhere throughout a business. They start on employee devices. Tablets, computers, and smart phones have lists, spreadsheets, calendars, notes, and documents that are created for a singular purpose; whether for computing a budget or analyzing machine utilization purposes, the employee holds those data locally. These data are singular in purpose and disconnected. This is *small data*. It is as prolific as it is important for a business. Having the power for an individual user to create data out of observations in his or her environment provides that individual with the capacity to do more than just calculate an end result. It gives the individual an unsophisticated way to create sophisticated models at his or her fingertips.

Now consider that there are more multiuser platforms that were built for a singular purpose. These are customer relationship management (CRM) systems, general ledger (GL), or order-processing systems. They have much more value to a business, and their sophistication comes in the support of a process or major business initiatives. Additional value comes from the ability of multiple users to have access to the data underlying the application for their unique purposes. Whether that is resource planning, sales planning, or reporting, these "data" platform systems generate the outputs that satisfy the process analysis of its particular functional area.

Big data leverages the small data and the data platforms to build a more complete picture of the enterprise. It leverages disparate system data together to form a union of unlikely confederations into a symphony of knowledge and intelligence. The value of the big data effort is greater than the sum of the parts of the lower-level interconnections. It is for the data scientists to find the patterns—the "currents of data"—that provide the answers to questions that business leaders have yet to ask.

The opportunities are there for businesses to have a chance in every process to learn, improve, and grow based on this information. Consider that if we are not using these tools to improve our processes, they are not as efficient as they could be, and thus we are wasting money. Your competition is using these tools, and the next bid, the next product, and the next customer sale will have improvements found in the data. Consider the consequences of not knowing what they know. This is the *big data advantage*.

## The Intersection with Human Resources

The small data–data–big data model plays out every day in the human resources world. In human resources, our processes generate thousands, if not millions, of transactional records. These transactions are stored in disparate systems all across the spectrum of the human resources world.

Human resources practitioners use spreadsheets, documents, and pieces of paper to store important facts about people in disconnected or offline ways more often than the more connected data or big data ways. The processes built to support the human resources functions were created that way. In fact, physical employee files are required in many processes through country or works council regulations.

If spreadsheets are the keys to employee productivity, then compensation takes that to the extreme. The compensation function is awash with extreme sets of data from HRIS, market information, and business results. Spreadsheets and simple database tools are the keys to help feed data-driven addiction. They can be considered the "warm blanket" of every analytical compensation professional. Not a new day goes by where compensation professionals in an organization will use a spreadsheet to analyze the simple to the complex—from job evaluation, to market pricing, to program cost models, to merit-matrix development and incentive-planning worksheets.

> "Human resources has been disadvantaged regarding Big Data with unstructured data and limited use of their data" (Tom Davenport, "Big Data at Work: Dispelling the Myths, Uncovering the Opportunities," *Harvard Business Review Webinar*, March 3, 2014.

Another key to compensation process data has been the human resources information systems or enterprise resource planning systems (ERP) that are built to provide the next level of connectivity to the human resources business processes. Yet their reach is only as broad as the process definitions that were implemented at the time they were installed. Access to them has been as tightly guarded as Fort Knox. This paradigm has played out for decades. As our business systems and human resources processes have evolved, the need for data has changed.

Big data for human resources purposes has been evolving and currently stands as an effort to display dashboards for executives and managers with several key performance indicators (KPIs). Advanced dashboard efforts even go as far as leveraging benchmarks to provide managers with comparator KPIs from general industry or competitors to help set context. The problem with these dashboards is that they do not help the manager understand the context in terms of his or her business decisions. It is up to the manager and his or her comfort level with the underlying business problems to draw conclusions and make better decisions as a result.

The key to big data success in human resources comes from the connection of all these small data sources. The connections, collections, and correlations drawn from the hidden value in those data structures are the keys to answering complex questions that we have yet to ask. The problem starts in the hidden nature of the small data sources and continues to expand with data sources beyond that collected by human resources.

## Major Challenge to Big Data: Synchronicity

If there are challenges to supporting big data initiatives within an organization, they start with the systems that hold the data we are hoping to use. As discussed earlier, the data reside on many different platforms, including paper, individual data sets in spreadsheets, and systems designed for singular purposes. But this is just the beginning of the problem. These business systems are disconnected, yes, but they are also out of synchronization.

From a timing perspective, each system has its own life cycle. A CRM system deals with the life cycle of a client, from prospect through former client. A GL system deals with financial transactions from budget through payments. An ERP system deals with supplies of raw product through production and then distribution of finished goods. An HRIS is no different because it deals with prospective candidates through exiting employees.

The use of these data sets together provides a complete picture of the enterprise, but the timing of the data in the simplest example is not intended to be synchronous. Ask any senior human resources executive to run a headcount report from the HRIS and then try to match that with a GL system headcount report and then an ERP system headcount report. It is a nightmare of epic proportions for the leader reading and interpreting the report, as it is for the support staff scrambling to try to fill in the holes when the numbers do not match. In many cases, it is a timing issue, but there is also a definitional issue.

Definitions of simple yet important model elements are not designed to be the same. The example to examine is that of a "full-time employee." This concept within ERP, GL, CRM, and HR systems is completely different unless designed with one definition in mind from the start. Such systems are almost never given this consideration unless they are built from the ground up with the common definition in mind.

Any system of record designed for global support will need to take a currency model that enables conversion to a common currency for global consolidation, budgeting, and reporting. This leads to a different discussion about the precision, accuracy, and timeliness of currency rates. Then consider older values and whether they need to be converted at current or past rates. The appropriateness of presenting historical data in a common currency for consolidation then takes on a new complexity. These systems were not meant to consider these complexities beyond support of their original purpose.

The discussion of global analyses also brings up truly global definitions. If a system is built to examine employees sitting in multiple countries, there must be definitions that contemplate global regulations and cultural issues. In Europe, data privacy regulations determine what data can be exported off the continent for what purposes without express consent from the employee. In the United States, we are expressly prohibited from using age in determining pay. Asia has many languages and different character sets. All these issues complicate the ability of human resources to bring data together in a cohesive story. The first exposures to this are typically jarring for human resources information technology (HRIT) professionals.

Ask HRIT professionals for a global report on anything, and the immediate question back will be, "You want that when?" The complications do not just end with the preceding differences. Typically, there is no one database with this information. A global human resources database has been a desired goal of HRIT professionals for decades. The years have simplified certain aspects of global storage, allowing for differences in country and regional data models.

A deeper concern is that when human resources systems change, they are typically reactionary. Serious business issues drive the changes without changing the underlying processes that were implemented in the system. They are also typically data-driven changes with some small exception to normal business processes. Some of these include

- " . . . Integrate 500 acquired associates."
- " . . . Reduce our people costs by 5 percent within six weeks."
- " . . . Consolidate sales, marketing, and product teams."
- " . . . Reengineer our service-delivery model."
- " . . . Relocate our plant."

These disruptions are aberrations that must be remembered in the context of reports and analytics; otherwise, they will seemly be blips in a historical view of data.

## Strategy Supported by Data

Every good business idea gets started with a business plan. Going back to grade school, we may remember the scientific method (Figure 48.1). Well, in this context, a good business plan is simply the scientific method. The key is having good data to measure and support our conclusions. As described earlier, the business develops the context of the model based on the strategy as defined in the problem statement of the business strategy. The measurements of the problem then are based on this statement and are directly related to the issue. The proof or disproof then is not a function of the data, but the results as described against the goals stated in the plan.

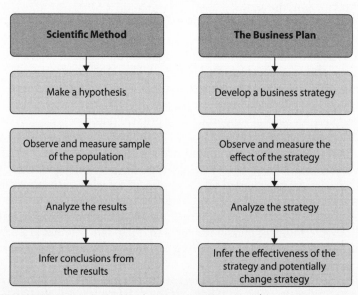

**Figure 48.1 Scientific method versus the business plan.**

As the strategy requires change as a result of business environmental conditions or otherwise, the goals, data, and measurements must change as necessary. The model is dictated by the strategy, not by the constraints of the data owing to the methods of capturing the data.

An example of the business-plan strategy change is the location of a distribution center. In order to start, we first have to make a hypothesis. Then we make observations about where the distribution center is located. Look at the measurements of the potential move, and analyze the results against the expectations. Then make an inference about the observations. The key here is that we need to understand what the tolerances are of the change to affect the key business drivers that led to the business strategy change. Without this information, we cannot complete the analysis and recommend that the change happen.

This is a key part of any successful business strategy—understanding how the change affects the fundamentals of the business and how much variation can be seen as a success versus a failure. The hypothesis is, "We must locate a distribution center closer to our stores in order to minimize costs, reduce shortages, and drive logistics costs lower."

In the scenario as described, we are going to look at the analysis presented in Table 48.1:

| Questions to Ask | Potential Answers |
|---|---|
| • What is the business goal of the move?<br><br>• What are we hoping to accomplish? | • Realize savings of getting product to stores<br><br>• Minimize time to get product to stores |
| • What criteria will we use to judge the strategy? | • Cost savings (over three years)<br><br>• Time to implement strategy<br><br>• Time to get inventory to store<br><br>• Effort to build out<br><br>• Maximizing safety risk |
| • What measurements will we use? | • Cost savings of the effort to bring product closer to stores<br><br>• Time to build out the location<br><br>• Distance from location to stores<br><br>• Effort expended in build-out<br><br>• Safety incidence |
| • What are the methods we will entertain in implementing this strategy? | • No additional build-out, but add staff to current location<br><br>• Locate new facility near stores<br><br>• Halfway between current and new locations<br><br>• Locate near to the towns where stores are located |

**Table 48.1  Scenarios for Locating Distribution Centers**

After careful consideration of each of these questions, we will lay out our model. The easiest method is a spreadsheet. Table 48.2 is the spreadsheet in its raw form.

| Measurements | Savings (3-yr.) | Time to Improvement | Distance | Effort | Safety |
|---|---|---|---|---|---|
| **Methods** | + | – | – | – | + |
| Current state | | | | | |
| Near new locations | | | | | |
| Halfway there | | | | | |
| Outskirts of new locations | | | | | |

**Table 48.2  Example Spreadsheet**

Note that each measurement is expected to correlate in some way with the change. This is critical in understanding the results because it leads us to evaluate the data more effectively.

After making observations and highlighting the best alternatives, Table 48.3 shows the spreadsheet in its completed form.

| Measurements | Savings (3-yr.) | Time to Improvement | Distance | Effort | Safety |
|---|---|---|---|---|---|
| **Methods** | + | – | – | – | + |
| Current state | $0 | Immediate | 15 miles | Low | Medium |
| Near new locations | $3.4M | Long term | 1 mile | High | Medium |
| Halfway there | $3.4M | Midterm | 7.5 miles | Medium | Medium |
| Outskirts of new locations | $4.8M | Midterm | 3 miles | Medium | High |

**Table 48.3  Completed Example Spreadsheet**

After a review of the data and the preceding criteria, we see that locating a new facility on the outskirts of town where the store is located will be the best selection because it fits the business strategy detailed earlier. Cost savings, short distance, and higher safety make the new facility on the outskirts of the town where the store is located the best alternative given the criteria.

As the implementation of the initiative starts to take shape, if any of the criteria or measurements against the methods change, then the decision should be reevaluated. As the environment changes, new alternatives become available, and then the best decision is to react to the new solution. This is the measure-evaluate-repeat methodology of business strategy.

## Intersection of Business Strategy and Compensation

This scientific method of business planning happens every day in evaluating business alternatives. Typically, the criteria that businesses use relates to KPIs that are published in scorecard metrics across the organization: earnings per share (EPS), net income (NI), and earnings before interest, taxes, depreciation, and amortization (EBITDA). They are the language of the business, and this language is spoken freely when evaluating decisions through the business-plan process, as discussed earlier.

When evaluating compensation processes in light of the business-plan process, the closest correlation comes in the factors used to judge performance against goals for short- and long-term incentive programs. Those eligible for these schemes are directly or indirectly able to affect the results by which they are being judged. These factors are weighted most often in an arrangement based on level, function, and industry (Table 48.4).

| Incentive Scheme Weightings | Factor | | |
|---|---|---|---|
| Level | Company | Business Unit | Personal |
| C-suite | 80% | | 20% |
| Senior executive | 20% | 40% | 40% |
| Senior management | 40% | 40% | 20% |
| Management | 30% | 30% | 40% |
| Junior management/professionals | 20% | 30% | 50% |

**Table 48.4  Incentive Scheme Weightings by Factor**

The definition of company and business-unit performance is directly related to the performance against the business KPIs. Because incentive programs are designed to share success of the business with participants, their alignment is built into the incentive mechanism. A higher spend on the incentive plan comes directly in relationship to the success of the business. It is a direct alignment.

That is theory, at least. In practice, management discretion and the structure of the personal goals may affect the intent of the incentive program and thus affect the extent to which the program incentivizes the right behaviors. There are plenty of discussions today on the real impacts of pay for performance on corporate goal achievement. Some high-profile organizations have fled from traditional forced-distribution mechanisms in the mid-2010s. In an article in *Talent Management Magazine* ("The Pay-for-Performance Fallacy," *Talent Management Magazine*, May 13, 2014), Sebastian Bailey focused on pay for performance as isolated from purpose, stretch goals, appreciation, coaching, and consistent differentiation. He argued that pay for performance is seen as a quick fix that "adds a few digits to an employee's paycheck." I agree—if the other factors just mentioned are not considered as part of pay for performance as well. A holistic strategy for pay for performance should be tested to ensure that its alignment with business strategy is working as the business requires.

Typically, the measurement of the pay-for-performance compensation plan alignment starts during the budget process for the focal event. This is a great opportunity to examine the appropriateness and effectiveness of the process toward meeting business objectives. In its most basic form, the analysis can start where most compensation analyses do—a spreadsheet. Compensation experts can use data to start the analyses in raw form and then build the business case for pay for performance through examination of the goals of the organization and the relevant KPIs used to measure the incentive plans.

Today, the questions usually asked are

- Can I have an employee list with base salary, target incentive, and last year's incentive results sorted high to low?
- What is the draft budget for merit increases and incentives for my organization?
- Are my jobs evaluated correctly?
- Do we have enough benchmark jobs with market data?

These are not the wrong questions, but they are not the questions that we want our data to help us answer. They are not focused on the business goals as stated earlier. They are important yet tactical. To have a meaningful business discussion with senior leaders, find the answers to the following questions, as outlined in Table 48.5:

| Base Salary | Incentives | Pay Equity |
|---|---|---|
| • Is our merit increase program effective? <br><br> • If we increased our merit increase budget by 1 percent, can we expect a 1 percent increase in performance? | • Are we rewarding the right behaviors? <br><br> • Do our goals reflect the organizational objectives? | • Do we pay too much for certain roles? <br><br> • What does pay equity mean for our organization? |
| **Market Position** | **Succession** | **Grades/Structures** |
| • Do we know how much it would cost in salary and incentive to get everyone to the market on total cash compensation? <br><br> • Do the reward programs, as currently designed, achieve the goals of the organization? | • Are our high potentials on track to be able to achieve the minimum of the range for the job for which they are successors? <br><br> • Are we compensating the right people? | • Do our grade levels represent the appropriate groupings of job responsibility and impact to the organization? <br><br> • Do our salary structures represent the market for the current job market? |

**Table 48.5  Compensation Decision-Making Considerations**

Some of these questions are simpler than others to answer. The question they raise is, "Where do we find the data to answer them?" This is the hardest question of all because answers are found in various places, and bringing the data together takes art as much as science. These questions may not even be the right questions based on the industry, maturity of the business, and market environment.

## Human Resource's Use of Metrics

The latter questions are by far the better questions to ask a big data initiative. The real question is, "Who will ask them?" If the fundamental issue is that the KPIs of the business are not being used as the central focus of the data initiatives, then the problem may be that the people who need to use them are not comfortable with them. As seen many times, human resources professionals have a great handle on the business and the functional area, but are they comfortable with the business drivers and metrics that should drive their program designs? In most cases, the answer is no.

To erase this deficit, the compensation group should start by learning about the KPIs that the company uses to measure success. Next, they should start a dialogue with each business unit to understand how each unit interprets the results of the KPIs for their particular situation. Then they should facilitate ongoing discussions with the business leaders throughout the year to stay abreast of any changes or disruptions in the business plans. At this point, the compensation group can start to develop programs that align with the business strategies.

Now that its members are conversant in the business strategies, language, and plans, the compensation group can make deeper alignments between human resources data and the business KPIs. At this point, they are ready to answer the questions posed earlier. They should be able to look at the data with a keen eye toward the business need and ask other questions that show insightful expertise.

With an understanding of the business and the metrics that drive business decisions, the compensation group also can start to redevelop its processes. As the redesign occurs, group members will look at the data generated by the process in light of the end result. This focus generates more useful data answering the questions posed of the data more directly. Such questions as "Are we rewarding the right behaviors?" are now answerable directly from the process by building those criteria into the compensation guidance or the performance-evaluation processes. Bypassing any interpretation of anecdotal data enables the compensation function to prove the value of greater investments in programs, processes, and technologies. It is like a teenager with great grades asking for a new smart phone relative to the same teenager with average grades.

The key is now that these programs are no longer human resources programs. Because the compensation group has now developed them based on the business KPIs, they have become business processes. As these new programs are rolled out, their language, purpose, and results will be aligned with the business. Managers and employees will recognize this and value the effort relative to the human resources programs that are sent to them with no consideration of their unique needs.

## Compensation Driving Business Value

Now consider an example of a business-plan strategy change that causes a focus on cost management. This is a very common business strategy in an era of constant cost pressures at many organizations. Instead of the common tactics used in cost-reduction scenarios, consider alternatives that may produce similar results but yet preserve the precious human capital investments already made in current resources. The challenge then becomes how to prove that these alternative scenarios may be as effective as others such as reducing staff, cutting back on training programs, or reducing merit increases and incentives.

As we did earlier, we first have to make a hypothesis. Then we make observations about how to control costs. We look at the measurements of potential changes and then analyze the results against the expectations. Then we make an inference about the observations. The key here is that we need to understand what the tolerances are of the change to affect the key business drivers that led to the business strategy change. Without this information, we cannot complete the analysis and recommend that the change happen. Now that we know more about the business, the recommendations will be closer to what the business would expect.

The hypothesis is, "To reduce costs and improve profitability, we need to drive better cost-conscious behaviors, improve manager training, increase investments in safety, and reduce our merit budget." In the scenario as described, we are going to examine some possible considerations, as outlined in Table 48.6.

| Questions to Ask | Potential Answers |
|---|---|
| • What is the business goal of the new focus? What are we hoping to accomplish? | • Reduce costs to improve profitability<br>• Drive results that investors are going to appreciate |
| • What criteria will we use to judge the strategy? | • Significant cost savings<br>• No reduction in productivity<br>• No impact to customer service |
| • What measurements will we use? | • Turnover statistics<br>• Customer-service scores<br>• Impact of change |
| • What are the methods we will entertain in implementing this strategy? | • Safety incentives that save on reduced workers' comp claim costs and improve quality<br>• Add goal to "Manage costs" that focuses managers on the right ways to save<br>• Reduce merit budget, which directly lowers fixed costs<br>• Increase manager training for compensation awards, which enables managers to make better decisions |

**Table 48.6  Strategy Change Considerations**

After careful consideration of each of these questions, we will lay out our model. The easiest method to do so is a spreadsheet. Table 48.7 is the spreadsheet in its raw form.

| Measurements | Turnover | Customer Satisfaction | Employee Engagement | Impact of Change |
|---|---|---|---|---|
| **Methods** | – | + | + | = |
| Safety incentives | | | | |
| Add goal to "manage costs" | | | | |
| Reduce merit budget | | | | |
| Increase manager training | | | | |

**Table 48.7  Raw Spreadsheet**

In evaluating each of the methods against the factors, we will notice that there will be a corresponding correlation with the objective of reducing costs. Turnover has a positive correlation: an increase in turnover should increase retention and talent-acquisition costs. An increase in customer satisfaction should result in lower costs to procure new and repeat business. A big impact of change likely will have a bigger effect, although as a variable it should be neutral to net income. After making observations and highlighting the best alternatives, Table 48.8 shows the spreadsheet in its completed form.

| Measurements | Turnover | Customer Satisfaction | Employee Engagement | Impact of Change |
|---|---|---|---|---|
| **Methods** | – | + | + | = |
| Safety incentives | Low | High | High | Medium |
| Add goal to "manage costs" | Medium | Medium | Medium | High |
| Reduce merit budget | High | Low | Low | Medium |
| Increase manager training | Low | Medium | High | Low |

**Table 48.8  Completed Spreadsheet**

After review of the data and the preceding criteria, we see that implementing a safety incentive program would be the best selection because it fits the business strategy detailed earlier. Lower turnover, higher employee engagement, and higher customer satisfaction make the safety incentives the best alternative given the criteria.

As the implementation of the initiative starts to take shape, if any of the criteria or measurements against the methods change, then the decision should be reevaluated. As the environment changes, new alternatives become available, and then the best decision is to react to the new solution. As said earlier, this is the measure-evaluate-repeat methodology to business strategy.

## Bringing This Strategy to Life

In order for this to be successful as a foundational business strategy, it is important to realize that data alone cannot be used to tell stories or persuade managers to act. The key to success using data is that they must be relevant to the business and they must answer practical yet complex questions that may not be possible without a change to the underlying process that produced the data. Those process changes can occur only after compensation professionals fully understand the factors involved in the business success.

Once there is a good understanding of the business variables that drive decisions and results, then the compensation processes supporting the business can evolve to measure the right things to prove the success or failure in aligning with the business strategy. The result provides managers and employees with comfort that the time they invest on these processes is drawn with direct correlation with their business outcomes.

In the end, stakeholders are provided with data that support the goals of the business. And then it is clear that the stories derived from these compensation process data answer real business questions that came from human resources—most impressive!

# 49

# Using Big Data to Enhance the Value of Compensation Programs

Ezra Schneier

*HRsoft, Inc.*

Big data is coming at us from a wide range of sources at a rapid pace. Many choices we face every day are influenced by big data. Big data is affecting the way consumers and businesses make decisions. Consider Amazon, Netflix, and Google as examples of the power of big data.

The expanding volumes of data we generate and have access to can provide valuable insights for compensation professionals. In fact, in the near future, big data likely will become a prominent ingredient in compensation planning and aligning pay with performance.

This chapter examines ways to use big data to improve compensation decisions and drive high performance for our organizations. We will use the term *compensation big data* to refer to the general area of how big data enters into compensation decisions. Looking ahead, we see compensation big data as playing a growing role in the way compensation is planned and managed. It will allow us to create value and be more innovative. Today, as practitioners, we need to be up to speed on how compensation big data can be harnessed to make better decisions, improve business results, and increase value for our organizations.

Compensation big data will elevate the role of compensation managers and analysts. Traditionally, compensation planning and management have been episodic, with a flurry of activity during the annual planning cycle. This is shifting to a more frequent flow of evaluating and determining compensation. Big data is allowing for continuous adjustments and measurements. At the same time, employees are receiving a clearer understanding of how their compensation is determined—and how they can control or influence its level. Of course, compensation professionals are in the forefront of this transformation. With growing visibility, there is more pressure and the need to stay current and adapt to these changes.

Human resources and compensation practices are well suited to take advantage of big data. We can use data to gain a perspective on what associates desire in regard to employment, make better decisions to meet those desires, and as a result, improve employee satisfaction. Understanding and acting on aspects of the employer-employee relationship can lead to greater productivity, engagement, and retention. Compensation plays a key part in this equation.

This chapter looks at a few practical ways that big data can be applied in the area of compensation planning and management. The goal is to discuss how big data can be used to enhance compensation decisions today.

By embracing big data, employers can gain a competitive advantage through their compensation practices. After all, compensation is a means to make an employer more successful. Compensation big data is a huge enabler—a tool of the trade available for compensation professionals.

## Defining Compensation Big Data

In the highly acclaimed book on the subject, *Big Data*,[1] authors Viktor Mayer-Schoenberger and Kenneth Cukier describe big data as three connected shifts of mind-set: "The first is the ability to analyze vast amounts of data about a topic rather than be forced to settle for smaller sets. The second is a willingness to embrace data's real-world messiness rather than privilege exactitude. The third is a growing respect for correlations rather than a continuing quest for elusive causality."

*Compensation big data*, for the context of this chapter, is the means of creating new insights through the analysis of data or aggregating data from different sources to achieve compensation planning and management goals. At its core, the goals of any employer's compensation practice is to allow the company to attract and retain top talent, engage employees, align associates with the employer's strategic goals, and drive high performance. There can be one human resource goal or more than one. What matters is absolute clarity. Having a specific human resources goal or set of goals that are completely understood is critical for any employer. For example, a company may have as its primary goal retention and engagement of employees. In this case, the employer is focused on efforts to reduce turnover and increase the sense of engagement among associates.

Compensation big data can be a useful ingredient in achieving these goals. It is my belief that employers must have a clear compensation strategy that supports the company's human resources agenda that, in turn, supports the company's business goals. After this is clear, then there can be a course to follow to reach that destination. And compensation big data can play a meaningful role.

## Areas to Be Examined

In *Big Data at Work*,[2] Thomas Davenport, a thought leader on business analytics and big data, notes: "There are two primary activities relative to big data analysis, based roughly on the stage of development involved. One is *discovery*, or learning what's in your data and how it might be used to benefit the organization. The other is *production*."

In the following pages, we will look at discovery and production with three specific ways that compensation big data is being used today to help employers be more successful. These approaches are presented as examples that I hope will lead readers to consider opportunities in their own company. The examples we will examine are

- Evaluating compensation along with other elements of rewards to determine what matters to employees

- Increasing the frequency of evaluating compensation and the mix of factors considered in determining compensation levels and awards

- Communicating total rewards and walk-away value to improve retention and engagement

## Evaluating Compensation along with Other Elements of Rewards to Determine What Matters to Employees: The Effect of Pay on Retention

An interesting application of compensation big data is determining when compensation levels are—and are not—the main consideration for employee retention and engagement, that is, helping to identify the role of compensation versus other issues that may be more important to employees when deciding to stay in a position. For decades, employers have gathered salary data based on industry, job category, and geography. These data are used to ensure that associates are being paid competitive wages relative to what is going on in the broader market. This is an important element of compensation planning and design. Compensation big data allows us to expand our perspective and base decisions on other elements of total rewards that can matter as much as or more than compensation level. Such items as career-advancement potential, work/life balance, what employees are learning, company culture, management issues, and community service can play a part.

An article in the *Wall Street Journal* entitled, "Big Data Upends the Way Workers are Paid,"[3] quipped, "never let money get in the way of a good pay package." Journalist Rachel Silverman reported: "Companies armed with an array of analytic tools are changing the way they pay and keep their workers. Some of these data-driven findings seem counterintuitive: Rotely paying workers more may not be enough to prevent defections. The key may be a flexible work schedule, or simply a nice boss." The author describes a large regional bank with high turnover among customer-service representatives. In an effort to improve retention, the bank gathered data on salaries, turnover, promotions, and job transfers to create a model showing why employees left the bank. Although there were frequent pay raises in the neighborhood of 10 percent, this did not have a meaningful impact on turnover. It turns out that the problem was that employees felt dissatisfied, not underpaid. By implementing more frequent job changes and transfers even without salary increases, high performers were more satisfied, and retention improved.

The large gaming company Caesars Entertainment looked at the impact of pay on retention. A detailed analysis was conducted looking at pay and employee engagement scores for about 5,000 associates who separated from the company. Caesars found that attrition was as high as 16 percent for corporate employees who earned less than the midpoint of their salary range, according to Sean Phillips, who led the effort. Increasing an employee's salary up to the midpoint reduced attrition to 9 percent. But increasing salary level above the midpoint had no additional benefit. Caesars feels that the effect of this analysis is that pay increases can be given more selectively, such as to high performers, as needed. Greater discretion by managers to make decisions based on where the impact will be felt the most can lead to significant advantages for an employer.

Well-known human resources researcher Josh Bersin, president of Bersin by Deloitte, has thoroughly analyzed aspects of big data and talent management. In "Big Data in Human Resources: A World of Haves and Have-Nots,"[4] Bersin reported on the turnover and retention behavior of employees based on pay raises. He suggested that employers reconsider the traditional compensation approach, where pay is based on a normal curve and gives top performers higher raises than second-tier performers. According to Bersin: "It turns out [that] this 'normal distribution' curve of pay is a big mistake. What the research found was that employees in the second and third quintiles of performance (good solid performers) would stay with the company even if their raise was as low as 91 percent of average increases in their job class. So these folks were being overpaid." However, people at the top of the performance curve would leave the company unless they received 115 to 120 percent of the average pay increase for their job class, indicating that compensation budget dollars should be applied here to retain high performers.

Bersin concluded: "As most managers know, top performers outdeliver midlevel performers by a wide margin, so paying top people 'much more' is a huge advantage if it prevents them from leaving."

Using compensation big data, managers can determine how to allocate their compensation budget to yield the greatest return. With data, decisions can be made with a higher likelihood of accuracy rather than searching for possible results based on less informed approaches.

### Frequency and Mix: Increasing the Frequency of Evaluating Compensation and the Mix of Factors Considered in Determining Compensation Levels and Awards

The annual focal and planning cycle is going away. It is being replaced by more frequent salary reviews and incentive determinations based on a variety of milestones, goals, and performance metrics. These metrics are measured with increasing frequency, bringing greater activity and heightened visibility to the compensation professional. Big data makes this possible, and compensation professionals are leading the charge.

Company performance measured by key financial metrics such as earnings per share, free cash flow, sales, and return on capital are used in establishing compensation in many organizations with a pay-for-performance culture. In some organizations, a portion of at-risk compensation is being determined by individual or business-unit performance related to strategic and operational objectives, that is, not just conventional quantitative financial metrics.

These metrics may be specific to the current goals of the organization, such as safety results, customer satisfaction and retention, employee productivity, market share, growth of a company's research and development (R&D) pipeline, and on-time delivery. The result is better alignment of efforts with key company objectives that drive business success. The compensation department coordinates design of the plans and tracking and measuring of the metrics. And there is a great need for accuracy in determining the awards for employees and managers based on actual performance versus targets. Executive compensation has used this approach for a long time, where compensation is more weighted toward variable compensation. The trend is to give other managers a total rewards or compensation plan with similar characteristics.

Of course, what is being measured is critical. The goal is to attract, retain, and motivate talented people. In these cases, managers should have some control over the results being measured. Different goals may apply based on department, job category, geography, and other factors. Developing and maintaining plans with a mix of performance metrics and components require careful planning. Appropriate data are likely to be housed and come from a variety of sources. The involvement of operational and finance managers is needed along with possible assistance from information technology to track results and analyze the correct data.

A recent article in the *Wall Street Journal* entitled, "When the Annual Raise Isn't Enough,"[5] looked at the issue of how companies are using frequent bonuses to motivate and retain employees. "As companies try to retain top employees and hit growth targets, some are ditching the annual salary review and doling out raises and bonuses several times a year. This practice can be risky, compensation experts and executives say, since workers who respond well at first could grow unhappy if the rewards slow down. But as the race for top technology talent escalates, bosses at some companies say [that] frequent raises are one way to keep engineering talent from leaving for giants such as Google and Facebook."

The concept of frequent raises is to break the annual merit increase or bonus into smaller amounts to keep employees motivated and engaged—and less likely to separate. For instance, Shutterfly, Inc., associates are eligible for bonuses four times a year. The quarterly check-ins let managers address employee concerns, including dissatisfaction with compensation, on a routine schedule.

Seattle-based Zulily, Inc., a web retailer, also assesses the pay of the company's 1,380 employees each quarter. CEO Darrell Cavens said that he would do it more often if he could. Quarterly raises at the company range from 2 percent to over 15 percent. Some employees receive three raises a year, and others might go 18 months without an increase. The process makes a lot of work for managers, but employees stay focused on the company's goals because the next payoff is right around the corner.

Frequent compensation evaluations and calculated bonus payouts require a greater level of work by compensation professionals and the use of big data derived from different areas of the company. Retailers have used the frequent-measurement and bonus method for a long time. As soon as the monthly sales for a store are tallied, the bonuses to the store manager and associates are ready to go based on the actual level of sales realized. Now other types of employers are applying this approach, too.

## Communicating Total Rewards and Walk-Away Value to Improve Retention and Engagement

*Total rewards communication* is the practice of sharing information with employees about compensation and other elements of employment that are pulled together in one aggregated view. Total rewards communication can help employers to improve business results by having more engaged and better informed associates. What used to be an annual printed statement is being replaced with an online experience, thanks to big data.

Total rewards communication is a way to improve the relationship between employers and employees. Companies use the communication to emphasize

- You are a valued employee. We supply you with this compensation and other benefits in recognition of all you do.
- Here is how our incentive and benefit programs work.
- We want to have an open, candid dialogue about compensation, benefits, and employment.
- We are committed to having a strong employer-employee relationship and meeting your expectations.
- We value results and believe in pay for performance.

Total rewards communication should not be a one-time event. Big data lets the relevant information be presented continuously to associates in a fresh and convenient way, even though that data may reside in separate locations. Smart companies attach a clearly stated purpose and a commitment to ongoing communication to their total rewards programs. The ability to pull together data from different sources, make them available online 24/7, keep the data fresh, and do this at relatively low cost is a game changer for compensation professionals.

Compensation professionals can design great plans and create innovative ways to reward associates. But sharing the results with employees so that they fully understand and appreciate the information can be weak. Total rewards communication, enabled with big data, analytics, and a little bit of planning, can be worthwhile for many employers.

Total rewards communication shows the full value of employment. It is tempting for employers to make the communication a self-serving message about the company's generosity. This misses a much greater opportunity. The larger goals include

- Enhanced engagement and retention
- Better alignment of individual efforts and organizational goals
- Improved business results

The communication shares with an associate the value of working for the employer during a specific period of time in the past—and can provide a look into the future as well.

What's more, the communication allows employees to more clearly understand how an incentive program works and see the value of retirement savings plans and healthcare benefits, among other elements. Employers use total rewards communication as a way to engage employees. It is not just a list of financial items. Instead, it is a way to express and reinforce the company's strategy about talent, compensation, pay for performance, and rewards.

The online method of total rewards communication allows for the presentation of current data in the manner employees want to receive information. It also gives greater flexibility than printed statements and the ability for easier personalization. The benefits of total rewards communication can be summarized this way:

- Restates and reinforces the value of people to the success of an organization
- Provides a clear message on human capital investments and their alignment with business strategies and goals
- Challenges the notion of the competitor's "grass is greener"
- Provides a discussion framework for managers to value their employees

Total rewards communication can be thought of as the "central hub" for information about compensation, benefits, and other items associated with employment.

Planning total rewards communication involves identifying the items to be presented to associates and the best source for each data element. The next step is developing an interface to pull that data into the total rewards communication site and determining the layout and frequency for refreshing the data. Additional content, design, usability, and promotion of the site are given attention as part of the effort.

Deploying an online total rewards communication site for employees is a way for compensation professionals to leverage data and deliver continuous value for associates. One element to consider with total rewards communication is a method for employees or managers to easily calculate the walk-away value associated with a position. Again, big data makes this feasible.

*Walk-away value* is the full economic value of employment today and the potential future value based on certain assumptions. The variables or assumptions can be adjusted or created by an employee to create a personalized model.

Christopher Ford, a thought leader and human resources and information technology executive in the San Francisco Bay Area, says: "Walk-away value creates a long-term engagement connection with employees. When employees think about leaving a company for better compensation, they tend to think about total compensation at a point in time. An employee who realizes [his or her] walk-away value thinks about total rewards versus total compensation and thinks about a period of time (three to five years) versus a point in time. Walk-away value could become a powerful retention tool."

Enabled by the use of data, the concept of walk-away value involves putting a self-service model right at the fingertips of associates and their managers and letting associates judge the value of their employment. This helps to answer the question on the minds of every employee: "Is this position going to meet my expectations over the next few years?" Why not recognize that this question exists and provide the tools to associates as part of the total rewards communication?

Walk-away value is the amount of money you are leaving behind if you separate from your current employer. When considering another position, it lets the associate understand exactly what he or she is walking away from (based on certain financial assumptions). The walk-away value model presents a standard list of reward elements to the associate. Then it calculates the estimated future value of those elements and their sum based on assumptions about growth made by the employee.

The model is easy for employees to use. It works like this:

1. Take your current compensation, incentive awards, and other reward items such as company-paid benefits and profit sharing.

2. Apply a growth factor to these items (e.g., salary increase, appreciation of stock value associated with restricted stock units (RSUs) or option grants, etc.).

3. Aggregate the value of these items looking ahead three, four, or five years.

4. The sum is the projected walk-away value.

Figure 49.1 is an illustration of how walk-away value can be presented. First, the employee makes assumptions about future salary and bonus increases, equity value, and other relevant elements.

The output is a model showing the value of these elements based on the assumptions entered. It also aggregates the values annually and for a set period. In the example in Figure 49.2, that period is four years. The result can be eye opening.

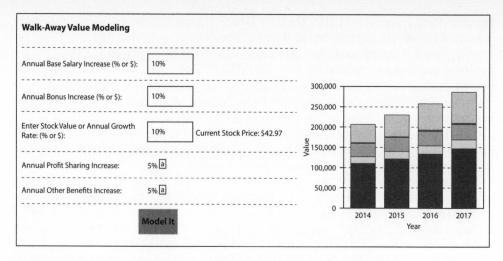

**Walk-Away Value Modeling**

Annual Base Salary Increase (% or $):     10%

Annual Bonus Increase (% or $):     10%

Enter Stock Value or Annual Growth Rate: (% or $):     10%     Current Stock Price: $42.97

Annual Profit Sharing Increase:     5% [a]

Annual Other Benefits Increase:     5% [a]

Model It

Figure 49.1   Entering variables to calculate an associate's walk-away value.

| | 2014 | 2015 | 2016 | 2017 ▬ |
|---|---|---|---|---|
| ■ Base Salary | $ 110,275.00 | $ 121,302.50 | $ 133,432.75 | $ 146,776.02 |
| ☐ Bonus | $ 15,250.00 | $ 16,775.00 | $ 18,452.50 | $ 20,297.75 |
| ▨ Profit Sharing [a] | $ 2,400.00 | $ 2,520.00 | $ 2,646.00 | $ 2,778.30 |
| ■ Other Benefits [b] | $ 31,820.32 | $ 33,411.34 | $ 35,081.90 | $ 36,836.00 |
| ☐ My LTIP | $ 43,012.97 | $ 51,718.69 | $ 64,519.45 | $ 75,678.76 |
| Unvested Shares | 910.00 | 1,003.00 | 1,155.00 | 1,258.00 |
| **Total** | **$ 205,994.30** | **$ 229,201.59** | **$ 257,864.25** | **$ 286,377.33** |
| **Accumulated Total** | **$ 205,994.30** | **$ 435,195.90** | **$ 693,060.15** | **$ 979,437.48** |

Your total walk-away value for **4 years** will be **$ 979,437.48.**

[a] Profit Sharing and Other Benefits are based on an assumed 5% increase. Past results are not indicative of future gains, and actual increase or decrease of these values cannot be guaranteed.

[b] Other Benefits are based on total of year-to- date employer contribution for 401 (K), Health & Benefits, My Defined Benefits Pension, Paid Time Off, and State & Federal Insurances.

Figure 49.2   The projected values of each element and the sum of an associate's walk-away value based on the variables entered.

## Summary

Without question, big data is already changing the way compensation decisions are made at many organizations. Although big data and data analytics are still in an early stage of development, it is time for compensation professionals to give serious thought to how they can take advantage of the emerging area of compensation big data.

# Notes

1. Viktor Mayer-Schonberger and Kenneth Cukier, *Big Data.* Houghton Mifflin Harcourt, Boston, 2013, p. 19.
2. Thomas H. Davenport, *Big Data at Work.* Harvard Business Review Press, Boston, 2014, p. 70.
3. Rachel Emma Silverman, "Big Data Upends the Way Workers Are Paid," *Wall Street Journal*, September 20, 2012, pp. B1–B2.
4. Josh Bersin, "Big Data in Human Resources: A World of Haves and Have-Nots," *Forbes*, October 7, 2013.
5. Rachel Feintzeig, "When the Annual Raise Isn't Enough," *Wall Street Journal*, July 16, 2014, pp. B1–B5.

# 50

# Turning Data into Compensation Information

Martin G. Wolf

As more organizations take advantage of the availability of all types of big data, the data flow can feel as if you are drinking from a fire hose. If they are to make compensation decisions that can increase competitive advantage and lead to greater business success, what compensation practitioners need is *appropriate data* and *valid information*—something not easily achieved.

This chapter will assist readers in the difficult task of extracting usable information from data in four ways, by

1. Reviewing some basic statistics useful for understanding compensation data

2. Identifying ways to avoid misleading or erroneous data

3. Recognizing the difference between data that are readily available and data that are truly appropriate for the task at hand

4. Identifying psychological barriers to data interpretation

## Basic Statistics for Understanding Compensation Data

Raw compensation data, as with any collection of data points, not only can be overwhelming but also can be misleading. It is all too easy to be distracted by the extremes and to misinterpret the real meaning of the totality of the data. This is where *summary statistics* and *measures of central tendency and dispersion* can be of great value.

*Summary statistics* are particularly valuable when dealing with salary survey results. This chapter uses the analysis of actual (now historical) data from four widely used contemporaneous compensation surveys covering the Long Island, New York, area to illustrate some of the issues involved in statistical data analysis.

However, before one even gets to statistical analysis, there is a data problem occasioned by differences in the survey levels used by the different surveys. To keep the illustrations manageable, comparative job level data are reviewed only for three job families: the exempt programmer/systems analyst job family and two nonexempt families, general clerks and secretaries.

Survey A has two levels of programmers and three levels of systems analysts (total = 5); survey B has three levels of programmers/analysts and three levels of systems analysts (total = 6); survey C has five levels of programmers, five levels of systems analysts, and five levels of programmers/analysts (total = 15); and survey D has three levels each of programmers, programmers/analysts, and systems analysts (total = 9). Cross-survey comparisons are tenuous at best!

Things are a little better among the nonexempt families. Surveys A, B, and C each have three levels of general clerks, although each uses a different title for what appears to be the same job, whereas survey D has two levels. In the secretarial area, things get quite confusing. Survey A has three levels, survey B has five, survey C has seven(!), and survey D manages with two.

The user is left to extract information from the profusion (and confusion) of data. One effective way to do this is to match each survey to a single, comprehensive set of job descriptions, that is, a model. The model provides a structure into which the various surveys can be placed. The use of a model can help to turn the mass of raw data into meaningful information, but the cost is some loss of data because not every bit can be matched to the model. The amount of data lost generally grows as the survey data become more fragmented as a result of an increased number of alternative position variations.

There are several approaches to choosing a model. One approach is to develop your own model based on the descriptions of a number of key jobs in your own organization. Key jobs are generally either multi-incumbent or otherwise significant and are of a type found in a number of surveys that you get. Another approach is to pick one survey that matches your organization's jobs quite well and then use that survey's positions as the model. Alternatively, you can select a model that someone else has already developed (assuming, of course, that it matches your organization's jobs). Many human resources consultancies have such a model.

### Using Measures of Central Tendency

One of the biggest problems most users have with survey data is knowing which summary statistical data to use. Most surveys report a number of summary statistics for each position. One of the most common is the *mean*, the arithmetic average of the data. Means may be weighted (large-company data are counted more than small-company data in proportion to their number of incumbents) or unweighted (each company's data are counted as if they represented one incumbent, no matter how many incumbents they actually have). The unweighted means may not be representative of the true market if a few companies dominate a position.

For example, the survey D data for a level 2 systems analyst had a total of 141 incumbents from eight companies. Two of those companies accounted for 120 of the incumbents (85 percent of the total). One company had 55 incumbents with an average salary of $31,600, whereas the other large employer had 65 incumbents with an average pay of $37,100. The unweighted mean for this position was $42,800, whereas the weighted mean was $36,500. The unweighted figure clearly did not represent "average" pay for this job!

Another common statistic is the *median*, the middle figure when the data are arrayed from high to low. The median is generally more stable than the mean, which can be affected by a few very low or very high data points when the sample is relatively small. The survey D data for a level 1 customer-service clerk, which had a total of 127 incumbents from 19 companies, was skewed by two companies. One of these two companies had eight incumbents paid an average of $41,400, whereas the second had three incumbents averaging $44,000. The unweighted mean for this position was $21,600, the weighted mean was $22,000, and the median was $18,800. The largest single employer (35 of the 127 total incumbents, or 27.6 percent of them) paid an average wage of $17,000 and had a job maximum of $18,920!

However, the median can be misleading when it is the median of the reporting organizations, not the median of all incumbents. (This is analogous to the unweighted mean versus the weighted mean issue discussed earlier.) For the level 2 systems analyst discussed earlier, the reported median (based on organizations, not incumbents) was $41,300, close to the unweighted mean and well above what the two companies that make up 85 percent of the market paid.

Another measure of central tendency is the *mode*. It is the single most frequently reported value in the data. The mode obviously is easily subjected to distortion, hence its lack of common usage.

### Using Measures of Dispersion

There are a number of indicators of dispersion of the data. The most common is probably the various percentiles. These are named by the percentage of the data that fall at or below them. Thus 10 percent of the data fall at or below the *10th percentile* (also called the *first decile*), 20 percent fall at or below the *20th percentile* (the *second decile*), and so on.

Commonly used terms, especially in salary surveys, are the *Q1* (the 25th percentile) and the *Q3* (the 75th percentile). (The *median* is technically the *Q2*, although it is rarely referred to that way.) The difference between the Q1 and the Q3 is the *semi-interquartile range*, sometimes called the *middle 50 percent range*. It covers the middle half of the population (assuming that it is incumbent, not company, based) and is a relatively stable measure of the true dispersion of the data.

Some surveys report the *average high* and the *average low*. These measures of dispersion are less consistent because they can be affected by a few extremes (because they are the mean of the highs and the lows).

### Avoiding Data that Mislead

I first got into computerized data analysis while at IBM in the mid-1960s. One of the first lessons I learned, one that still holds true a half century later, was *GIGO*—garbage *in*, garbage *out*. No type of data analysis, no matter how statistically sophisticated, can offset bad data.

It is important to be on the alert for inaccuracies in the data you receive. Apply the test of logic before you proceed to your statistical or other analyses. For example, the reported survey A median weekly pay for the executive secretary was $593, whereas the top of the reported middle 50 percent range (the Q3 or 75th percentile) was $576. Because the median is the 50th percentile (or Q2), it cannot have a greater value than the 75th percentile (the Q3)! Based on the middle 50 percent range for that job, I concluded that the entry was a typo and should have been $543 rather than $593.

In addition to typos, erroneous survey data due to poor job matching often can be identified by looking at the range of compensation reported for a position. For example, survey D data for level 3 engineers were really a mixture of at least two levels. The level 3 mechanical engineer data showed a range from $37,400 to $70,000. Of 136 incumbents, 10 averaged under $40,000, whereas 3 averaged over $60,000. All survey D level 3 engineering positions had the same problem probably because the survey had only three levels of engineer, whereas most companies have at least four.

*It is best to ignore data that are questionable. Not having any data is better than having erroneous data.*

## Using the Right Data, Not Just the Readily Available Data

Organizations tend to value quantitative data highly, but sometimes quantitative data may be misleading and/or less than truly informative. Changes in the macroeconomic environment associated with entering into or exiting from a recession may significantly affect some quantitative performance measures (e.g., sales volume) typically used for compensation decisions, thus making "objective" year-to-year comparisons uninformative. At such times, subjective measures such as customer attitudes may be truer measures of individual or unit performance than "hard" data.

External changes in specific areas, such as the recent decline in natural gas prices due to fracking, may significantly affect some quantitative performance measures (e.g., conversion costs as a percentage of total production costs) typically used for compensation decisions, thus making traditional comparisons uninformative. Here it may be necessary to switch from comparisons based on total current or historical *costs* to ones based on *units of energy used* (e.g., cubic feet or British thermal units of gas or kilowatt-hours of electricity).

## Addressing Psychological Barriers to Data Interpretation

Studies in behavioral economics have shown that people tend to continue with interpretative approaches to data that have worked well in the past long after changing conditions have rendered them ineffective or just plain wrong. In compensation administration, this is commonly seen in the difficulty in changing managers' mind-sets as to what is an "appropriate" raise when macroeconomic conditions affecting the price of labor change dramatically.

The late twentieth and early twenty-first centuries have constituted such a period. For a long time, even predating the recent Great Recession, wages have declined or remained stagnant. Various authors have offered a variety of reasons for this—global competition and outsourcing, technology reducing the need for job skills in routine operations, and so on. Although employers increased the hiring of college graduates in the 1980s and 1990s to assist them in adapting to technological changes, the pace of such hiring shifted as information technology (IT) matured and as basic computer skills became more widespread.

For workers with a bachelor's degree, real (inflation-adjusted) wages rose slightly (a little less than one-half of 1 percent annually) from 1979 to 1995, whereas real wages declined for those with lesser education. Between 1995 and 2000, real wages grew for both groups. Since 2001, real wages once again have declined for the non-college-educated, and the better-educated group has shown little change. Table 50.1 presents data (in 2013 dollars) from the Economic Policy Institute for salaried and hourly workers with a bachelor's degree.

|  | 2001 | 2013 |
|---|---|---|
| Men | $33.60 | $33.71 |
| Women | $25.33 | $25.35 |

Table 50.1  Average Hourly Wages ($000)

Although the data show that, with the exception of the late 1990s, average real wages have been stagnant at best for most of the last 35 years, traditional salary ranges have remained relatively wide.  Although it is standard practice to set range midpoints at a "competitive" level based on one's favorite salary survey(s), the 80 to 120 percent of mid-point pay ranges developed in the earlier days of substantial annual pay increases have remained in vogue.

The typical organization sets its pay ranges for the coming year ($x$ percent increase in midpoints) based on survey data and develops a salary increase budget ($y$ percent of pay-roll) as part of the organization's overall budgeting process, not necessarily in that order. In times of budget constraints and limited external wage pressure, both $x$ and $y$ tend to be rather small. As a result, the change in the organization's overall *compa ratio* (CR, or aver-age pay as a percent of average midpoint) is minimal at best, as is the CR of most individual employees. Because an employee's pay range represents a promise by the organization for higher pay for good performance over time, it can be quite demoralizing when employees experience no substantial movement through their pay ranges year after year.

### Anatomy of a Pay Range

Although most organizations espouse some form of a merit pay or pay-for-performance model, each employee's salary increase (SI) actually has three components: an amount to offset the movement of the range [the range adjustment factor (RAF)], some movement in CR through the range [the merit increase factor (MIF)], and a small amount to offset the initial drop in CR when the range was increased (equal to RAF × MIF).

Thus the formula is

$$SI = RAF + MIF + (RAF \times MIF)$$

Solving algebraically for MIF, this becomes

$$MIF = (SI - RAF)/(1 + RAF)$$

If we assume an SI of 10 percent and an RAF of 7 percent, the calculation becomes

$$MIF = (0.10 - 0.07)/(1 + 0.07) = 0.03/1.07 = 0.02804 = 2.804 \text{ percent}$$

Likewise, with an SI of 3 percent and an RAF of 2 percent, the calculation becomes

$$MIF = (0.03 - 0.02)/(1 + 0.02) = 0.01/1.02 = 0.00980 = 0.980 \text{ percent}$$

As the RAF becomes smaller, the range movement offsetting factor (1 + RAF) becomes less significant. At today's RAFs, it probably can be ignored when looking at individual employees, although when looking at large populations it can be a significant number even while remaining a tiny percentage of total payroll. Where it has some meaning, however, is in looking at employees' annual movement through the salary range from minimum to midpoint to maximum. Even when the offsetting factor is just a small percentage each year, it can compound substantially over many years.

Using the preceding formula for the MIF, Appendix 50A presents the details of a hypothetical employee's change in CR each year from minimum to maximum at various SIs for RAFs of 0, 1, 2, 3, and 4 percent. Obviously, SIs equal to or less than the RAF will result in unchanged, or lower, CRs. Table 50.2 Summarizes the key details found in Appendix 50A for various SI – RAF combinations.

| SI | RAF | 80–100% | 80–120% |
|----|-----|---------|---------|
| 1% | 0% | 22 | 40 |
| 2% | 0% | 11 | 20 |
|    | 1% | 22 | 40 |
| 3% | 0% | 7 | 14 |
|    | 1% | 11 | 20 |
|    | 2% | 23 | 40 |
| 4% | 0% | 5 | 10 |
|    | 1% | 7 | 14 |
|    | 2% | 11 | 20 |
|    | 3% | 23 | 40 |
| 5% | 1% | 5 | 10 |
|    | 2% | 7 | 14 |
|    | 3% | 11 | 21 |
|    | 4% | 23 | 40 |

**Table 50.2  Years through the Pay Range**

Examination of Table 50.2 reveals that an SI that is only 1 percent greater than the RAF (SI – RAF = 1 percent) results in a very slow increase in CR, with movement from a CR of 80 percent to approximately midpoint taking 22 or 23 years and movement from a CR of 80 percent to approximately maximum taking a whole working career—some 40 years! At (SI – RAF = 2 percent), movement from a CR of 80 percent to approximately midpoint takes 11 years, and movement from a CR of 80 percent to approximately maximum takes 20 or 21 years. These times fall to 7 and 14 years at SI – RAF = 3 percent and to 5 and 10 years at SI – RAF = 4 percent.

## Practicing Information-Driven Salary Administration

Each organization must decide for itself what time frame it considers reasonable for progression through the pay ranges. Unless it is felt possible to have SIs *at least* 2 percent larger than RAFs on a consistent basis, you should consider using narrower pay ranges if you use midpoints as your "competitive" pay target. Otherwise, unless you regularly promote or hire people into positions well above minimum range, you will fail to fulfill your targeted competitive position. (I have consulted with a number of organizations whose overall CRs had remained stuck in the low nineties year after year.)

Another option is to continue to use the 80–120 percent pay ranges but set the desired "competitive" pay target at a CR of perhaps 90 percent, thus significantly reducing the time required to move a new employee to the target pay level. Retaining the 120 percent maximum allows for extraordinary pay for extraordinary performers while holding out a large potential "carrot" for all incumbents. (Those who use such an approach probably should drop the term *midpoint* and describe their pay ranges using *minimum, market,* and *maximum* instead.)

Only in fictional Lake Woebegone can everyone be above average. Yet few organizations dare to set a target competitive pay position that is below average. Because top-paying organizations must move their pay ranges aggressively to stay ahead of all those striving to become above average, a pay strategy that targets 5 or 10 percent or more (in dollars) *below* the survey median often can allow for SIs that are noticeably greater than the lower RAFs required to maintain that reduced competitive position. It also can result in greater employee satisfaction and lower turnover than an *above*-survey-average pay target, where most of the available pay budget necessarily goes to the greater RAFs year after year, leaving little for MIFs.

Given how difficult it is for compensation professionals to get accurate information on what others actually pay for a given position, it is unlikely that many, if any, individual employees have detailed information on the true "market price" of their jobs. What they do usually have is information on the pay range for their jobs and, to a lesser degree, on what others in the organization are making. When they see themselves (and others) moving through their pay ranges, they are more likely to feel well paid than if their range goes up so fast that they do not ever really progress through it. Competitive pay is in the eye of the beholder!

# Appendix 50A

## SIs, MIFs, and Movement through the Pay Range

| SI = RAF + MIF + (RAF * MIF) | | | |
|---|---|---|---|
| MIF = (SI - RAF)/ (1+RAF) | | | |
| Range Adjustment Factor = 4.0% | | | |
| | | Salary Increase: | |
| | 4.5% | 5.0% | 5.5% |
| Merit Increase Factor > | 0.48% | 0.96% | 1.44% |
| Year | | Compa Ratio | |
| 0 | 80.0 | 80.0 | 80.0 |
| 1 | 80.4 | 80.8 | 81.2 |
| 2 | 80.8 | 81.5 | 82.3 |
| 3 | 81.2 | 82.3 | 83.5 |
| 4 | 81.5 | 83.1 | 84.7 |
| 5 | 81.9 | 83.9 | 85.9 |
| 6 | 82.3 | 84.7 | 87.2 |
| 7 | 82.7 | 85.5 | 88.4 |
| 8 | 83.1 | 86.4 | 89.7 |
| 9 | 83.5 | 87.2 | 91.0 |
| 10 | 83.9 | 88.0 | 92.3 |
| 11 | 84.3 | 88.9 | 93.6 |
| 12 | 84.7 | 89.7 | 95.0 |
| 13 | 85.1 | 90.6 | 96.4 |
| 14 | 85.6 | 91.5 | 97.8 |
| 15 | 86.0 | 92.3 | 99.2 |
| 16 | 86.4 | 93.2 | 100.6 |
| 17 | 86.8 | 94.1 | 102.1 |
| 18 | 87.2 | 95.0 | 103.5 |
| 19 | 87.6 | 96.0 | 105.0 |
| 20 | 88.1 | 96.9 | 106.5 |

|  | Salary Increase: | | |
|---|---|---|---|
|  | 4.5% | 5.0% | 5.5% |
| Merit Increase Factor > | 0.48% | 0.96% | 1.44% |
| Year | Compa Ratio | | |
| 21 | 88.5 | 97.8 | 108.1 |
| 22 | 88.9 | 98.7 | 109.6 |
| 23 | 89.3 | 99.7 | 111.2 |
| 24 | 89.8 | 100.7 | 112.8 |
| 25 | 90.2 | 101.6 | 114.4 |
| 26 | 90.6 | 102.6 | 116.1 |
| 27 | 91.1 | 103.6 | 117.8 |
| 28 | 91.5 | 104.6 | 119.5 |
| 29 | 91.9 | 105.6 | |
| 30 | 92.4 | 106.6 | |
| 31 | 92.8 | 107.6 | |
| 32 | 93.3 | 108.7 | |
| 33 | 93.7 | 109.7 | |
| 34 | 94.2 | 110.8 | |
| 35 | 94.6 | 111.8 | |
| 36 | 95.1 | 112.9 | |
| 37 | 95.5 | 114.0 | |
| 38 | 96.0 | 115.1 | |
| 39 | 96.5 | 116.2 | |
| 40 | 96.9 | 117.3 | |

# 51

# Exploring New Technologies that Enhance Compensation Programs

Mykkah Herner

*Manager of Professional Services, PayScale, Inc.*

In a rapidly changing global economy, some compensation practices are dated. New technologies provide compensation data that are broad, deep, and real time. With such information at our fingertips, we are able to shift our focus as compensation professionals from crunching numbers and building pivot tables to creating new ways for compensation to support our organizations' business objectives. This chapter first explores new technologies and methods enabling more nimble compensation execution. These include the emerging availability of big data insights for compensation benchmarking and analysis and the crowdsourcing model for data collection. Next, it discusses compensation planning and design as a keystone strategy for organizations. Lastly, it explores the impact of new technologies on measurement and the pulse of the market, linking it to the art of communication to use compensation excellence for competitive advantage.

## New Technologies

The human resources profession has evolved in recent decades from the "personnel department," to "human resources management," to the "human resources business partner" and more recently to an emerging moniker—"people operations." Implicit in each of these shifts in nomenclature is an increase in the strategic value provided by these professionals and their desire, if not their ability, to have a "seat at the table"—a phrase often used by human resources people to indicate that they are participating in strategic decisions. People operations are no longer solely focused on attracting and retaining talent; they have an emphasis on strategy, metrics, data, and engaging top talent to accomplish business objectives. The new human resources professional advances the business goals of the organization.

Compensation is making a similar shift. Previously, the "science" of compensation consisted primarily of long, paper-based surveys requiring hours to complete and summarize.

The summarized data then were sold at high cost to employers to offset the high volume of work required to prepare and interpret them. Because of the time-intensive nature of gathering, aggregating, refining, and reporting the information, compensation surveys typically were delivered annually at best, providing employers with a snapshot of how compensation looked at the time the surveys were distributed.

The increased use of computers brought advancements to the methods of compensation survey analysis because larger amounts of data could be aggregated and summarized using spreadsheets. The advent of the Internet then made it possible to collect and report the salary surveys online. Behind the scenes, however, many of the old methodologies continued to predominate. The maturation of the web and especially the emerging understanding of the potential power of big data have forever changed the world of compensation.

What is *big data*? The term has become perhaps overused, but the key idea that large data sets can provide unique insights quickly will remain powerful far into the future. Big data has many definitions, but an example might illustrate the benefits more elegantly.

A simple constraint of the traditional method of acquiring salary information (data points) was the inherent bottleneck created by asking companies to provide the data on behalf of their employees. This was the best that could be done in the age before the Internet because the ability for purveyors of salary benchmark data to reach individuals who held jobs was limited. Therefore, a relatively small number of organizations submitted data on behalf of their employees every year.

Although this often allowed some insights and companies benefited from having some information rather than none, the biases that crept in also would require further manipulation of the data to try to mitigate those biases. Data would come from companies that had the resources to allocate time and energy to responding to a survey—often meaning larger companies. Furthermore, the time required from this process meant that data would be old by the time they could be redistributed to survey participants.

The modern ability to use the Internet to source data from millions or billions of jobholders rather than hundreds or thousands of companies answering on behalf of individuals was a radical innovation and a precursor to creating the benefits of big data. However, in order to have big data, you actually need a lot more data. This is what the Internet enabled—collecting quantities of data vastly larger than could ever be possible from targeting a few companies and then extrapolating from them to the rest of the business world.

The fundamental shift in data acquisition also enables a second key innovation—removing the middleman by going directly to the incumbent for information, the person who knows that information best.

What starts to emerge from an analysis of the relationships between these pieces of data illustrates the ultimate power of big data in the world of compensation—the ability to match a job with a title and a set of requirements for education, skills, experiences, certifications, and so on to a salary that is competitive or will attract and retain that person for your company.

Once you have big data, you also have a new set of challenges. In the past data collectors relied on front-end vetting of participants who would provide data to a salary survey. Today the vetting of data happens on the back end using algorithms to identify outliers and the power of large data sets to reduce the impact of outliers on the "correct" answer. Big data also requires the ability to move beyond the relational database structures that enabled the first wave of business software innovation starting in the 1970s. These new, large data sets require a new set of organizational tools and software, including technologies to make sense of not just rows and columns but also relationships and affinities that can be pulled from large data sets given the right programming and modeling skills.

In the decades prior to the Internet's emergence, collecting data was hard and time-consuming. Given the difficulties inherent in getting data from companies, consultants and data aggregators ultimately developed data-manipulation techniques that were designed to mitigate the downside of small sample sizes. In this era, the accepted wisdom was that an organization hoping to benchmark effectively would need to acquire data from multiple sources. Of course, this served to mitigate the risk of using data from any one provider when that provider's sample was small or represented a tight segment such as Fortune 500 companies or only a small geographic area. The Internet changed this. It is now perhaps not only logical but preferred to think of a large data set sourced from the Internet as inherently reliable because, if collected with a rigorous and sound methodology, it will represent a significantly larger segment of the market and thus provide many more data points for companies that perhaps are not located in a major metropolitan market or differ in another important way from the traditional respondents to consultant-led salary surveys.

The other recent innovation that has emerged on a parallel path to the emergence of big compensation data is the wave of SaaS software technology that has brought the power of easy-to-use and easy-to-access software to many business processes, including human resources and compensation. SaaS is an acronym for *software as a service*, and it was pioneered by Salesforce.com in what was referred to as the customer relationship management (CRM) market—essentially software to manage marketing and selling to new customers. SaaS solutions have since emerged to fit the needs of a wide variety of business processes from the front office to the back office. Human resources software is often grouped under the category of *human capital management* (HCM) software. The primary reasons that SaaS solutions have become so popular is that they are accessed on the Internet using a standard browser and that they require no upgrading or reinstallation by the customer. SaaS vendors improve their software and frequently update the experience and features for the end customer. SaaS or cloud software is typically bought by organizations as a subscription, providing access to the latest technology and sometimes fresh market data for the term of the subscription.

## Compensation Planning and Design

A *keystone* is the final stone in the apex of an arch; it ensures that the arch is structurally sound and will hold weight. Compensation is similar to a keystone in that it holds together business strategy and enables the organization to withstand the weight of the competition. In the past, compensation plans often were developed separately from the business strategy for the organization. Keeping compensation in mind as an enabling tactic can help us to accomplish our business goals.

Compensation affects many organizational processes, including recruitment, retention, performance measurement, and employee engagement. Additionally, rewards systems continue to evolve to include elements beyond base pay. Now we develop an appropriate compensation mix, which can be explained using a tiered cake as a metaphor. The base, or foundational level of the cake, is the compensation philosophy and strategy held by the organization. It is in this base layer that the compensation mix itself is identified, along with other critical factors, such as how the talent market is defined, how competitive the organization aims to be relative to that market, and what benefits will round out base and incentive pay within the organization. The second tier includes the base pay plan, which remains competitive with the talent market. It includes salary, hourly, and piece-rate pay plans and is used to provide a stable way of rewarding employees for their contributions to the organization. On top of the base pay plan is the variable pay plan. This third tier includes bonus plans, commission plans, and other performance-related perks. The final tier of the cake is individualized rewards and recognition, both monetary and nonmonetary, used to reward and incent behavior. Together the full cake becomes the compensation plan that feeds the organization to make it thrive.

Compensation done right enables companies to retain top talent. A successful compensation strategy and program builds the right employees for your organization. If your organization requires fresh new ideas, you may recruit talent directly from college. In that case, your retention plan may focus on articulating clear career paths rather than a strong 401(k) plan. Perhaps your organization operates in an industry that requires years of knowledge before proficiency. In that case, your retention strategy may involve ongoing training and education. Maybe your organization cannot afford to pay at the top of the market, preferring instead to hire people at a lower wage to offset the costs of training. In that case, you may develop a retention strategy that involves letting most people naturally transition to other organizations but identifying the true stars for promotion. Whatever your goals, the design of your compensation plan will help you to accomplish the right types of retention for your organization.

A trend that continues is the desire by management to link pay to performance. Many people think of that link as existing solely at executive levels, solely for sales staff, or solely in bonus plans. According to the PayScale 2014 "Compensation Best Practices Report," increasingly, organizations are offering performance-based incentives further down in the organization. It is a continuation of a trend that began several years ago.

Also of note is the link between equitable, competitive, and clearly communicated compensation programs and high employee engagement. Engaged employees are more committed to day-to-day work, their team, their direct manager, and their organization as a whole. Engaged employees also have lower turnover rates. This also means that they have a much higher impact on key business drivers such as innovation of products and services, quality of products and services, customer satisfaction, cost/efficiency, and revenue growth.

Compensation provides a way of ensuring that organizations are able to create a competitive advantage when their strategies and goals are linked to pay. Organizations have varied business goals, including staying ahead of competitors, keeping the business afloat, or growing quickly. Big data can facilitate sound linkages between business metrics and pay.

Another approach organizations must employ to retain their competitive advantage is to build flexibility into their compensation plans. One way organizations can remain flexible is to know how they are doing relative to the market at all times. Creativity in structuring the compensation mix also can be a strong differentiator—allocating more to variable rather than fixed costs where possible. Every organization has critical roles without which it cannot operate. One way of maintaining flexibility is to be creative about rewarding the people in these critical roles. Big compensation data that uses live market information arms employers to pay people in critical roles better. Organizations must have multiple compensation tools in their toolbox, be ready to roll them out at any time, and use the best possible data to identify key decision-making moments so that they know which tools to deploy.

Everyone in the organization has a role in communicating issues concerning compensation, including executives, managers, human resources and/or compensation professionals, and employees. Big data and analytics better equip managers and executives to communicate about compensation at every level. Executives are responsible for communicating the organization's compensation philosophy.

Managers are responsible for communicating the details of the compensation program directly to employees. They are uniquely positioned to accomplish this task because they work directly with employees. They have a sense of what will motivate them. They also act as agents of the organization, carrying out key strategies within their purview. This requires that organizations adequately prepare managers to fulfill these roles. Training, education, background, and even tools for communicating to employees can radically improve the ability of managers to fulfill their role in compensation effectively.

Human resources and/or compensation professionals both develop key messaging strategies and support executives and managers in delivering their various messages throughout the organization. Human resources and compensation professionals alike need access to big data and analytics to enable them to make strategic decisions about how to adjust the compensation plan in preparation for market changes.

Finally, employees have a role in communicating their concerns regarding compensation; they should be encouraged to communicate directly and honestly with their managers about both what motivates them and their satisfaction with compensation. Managers should provide employees with total compensation reports detailing the full spectrum of rewards afforded to employees, including benefits, time off, cash compensation, and any other elements involved in their compensation mix. Employees are better equipped to make critical decisions to stay with organizations when they are provided with this information.

## Impact of New Methods on Business Strategy

New technologies enable organizations to design better compensation programs, to implement and communicate better compensation programs, and finally, to assess the impact of their compensation programs on a regular and ongoing basis. Additionally, organizations should regularly measure the impact of their compensation plan on driving their business objectives. It is critical that the correct drivers of performance be identified so that the organization does not inadvertently incent the wrong behaviors.

It is also important to measure the impact of the compensation program in terms of business performance. A few key measures can be selected to determine the impact of compensation on recruitment, retention, performance, engagement, and ultimately, the financial success of the organization. These measures should be easy to identify, explain, and calculate so that they can be gathered on a real-time, quarterly, or at least annual basis as necessary.

In the past, compensation professionals were focused on developing analyses. New methods automate large parts of analysis using standard measures, the power of cloud software, and big data. Using modern methods to gather data and run appropriate analyses will help to shift the work of compensation professionals from crunching numbers to advising the management team on actions to course-correct and navigate today's dynamic and competitive markets.

The newest incarnation of human resources professional, the people operations head, is concerned with the people part of the business, is data driven, numbers savvy, and comfortable with strategy. Whereas earlier human resources professionals often shied away from numbers, the new people operations professionals are using data to create and interpret valuable insights for the entire business. They are also using this data-informed approach to take action, to design solutions, and to comprehend the impact of those solutions.

When using new methods of gaining compensation data and measuring the impact of compensation design based on this knowledge, organizations can stay nimble and competitive in a rapidly changing business environment. They need to view compensation as one of many interdependent elements for achieving business goals.

# Contributors

**Linda E. Amuso,** President, Radford, an Aon Hewitt Company, San Francisco, California (Chapter 15)

**Michael Armstrong,** Founder, E-reward.co.uk Limited, Cheshire, United Kingdom (Chapters 8, 10)

**Dorothy R. Berger,** Partner, Lance A. Berger & Associates, Ltd., Bryn Mawr, Pennsylvania (Chapter 4)

**Lance A. Berger,** Managing Partner, Lance A. Berger & Associates, Ltd., Bryn Mawr, Pennsylvania (Chapters 1, 46)

**Jordan Blue,** Senior Associate, Mercer, San Francisco, California (Chapter 44)

**Mark Graham Brown,** President, Mark Graham Brown & Associates, Manhattan Beach, California (Chapter 34)

**Tim Brown,** Partner, Radford, an Aon Hewitt Company, San Jose, California (Chapter 11)

**Seymour Burchman,** Managing Director Semler Brossy Consulting Group, LLC, Los Angeles, California (Chapter 26)

**Ben Burney,** Senior Advisor, Exequity LLP, Libertyville, Illinois (Chapter 22)

**Ted Buyniski,** Partner, Radford, an Aon Hewitt Company, Framingham, Massachusetts (Chapter 21)

**Mark D. Cannon, Ph.D.,** Associate Professor of Leadership and Organizational Studies Peabody College, Vanderbilt University, Nashville, Tennessee (Chapter 36)

**Jerome A. Colletti,** Colletti-Fiss, LLC, Scottsdale, Arizona (Chapter 17)

**Paul Davis, M.L.I.R,** Scanlon Steward and Advocate, EPIC-Organizations.com, Lansing, Michigan (Chapter 20)

**Bruce R. Ellig,** Noted Compensation Specialist and Author, New York, New York (Chapter 29)

**Christian M. Ellis,** Enterprise Effectiveness Consultant, Speaker, Author, and Adjunct Faculty Member, University of St. Thomas Opus College of Business, Minneapolis/St. Paul, Minnesota (Chapter 35)

**Charles H. Fay,** Professor of Human Resources, Rutgers the State University of New Jersey, Piscataway, New Jersey (Chapter 32)

**Mary S. Fiss,** Colletti-Fiss, LLC, Scottsdale, Arizona (Chapter 17)

**Iain Fitzpatrick,** Vice President and Global Pay Leader Productized Services, Hay Group, Philadelphia, Pennsylvania (Chapter 12)

**Monica Franco-Santos, Ph.D.,** Cranfield School of Management, Cranfield University, Bedford, United Kingdom (Chapter 19)

**Bill Gentry,** Managing Director, Grant Thornton LLP, Dallas, Texas (Chapter 22)

**Luis R. Gomez-Mejia, Ph.D.,** Ray and Milann Siegfried Professor of Management, Medoza College of Business, Notre Dame, Indiana (Chapter 19)

**Steven E. Gross,** Senior Partner, Mercer Human Resources Consulting, Philadelphia, Pennsylvania (Chapter 2)

**Dick Grote,** President, Grote Consulting Corporation, Frisco, Texas (Chapter 37)

**Ed Hannibal,** Partner, Mercer, Chicago, Illinois (Chapter 44)

**Myrna Hellerman,** Senior Vice President, Sibson Consulting, Chicago, Illinois (Chapters 9, 25)

**Mykkah Herner,** Manager of Professional Services, PayScale, Inc., Seattle, Washington (Chapter 51)

**Roger Herod, SPHR,** Principal, Mercer, Chicago, Illinois (Chapter 43)

**Sue Holloway, CCP, CECP,** Associate Director, Practice Leadership, WorldatWork, Scottsdale, Arizona (Chapter 5)

**Blair Jones, CBP, CCP, CECP, GRP,** Managing Director, Semler Brossy Consulting Group, LLC, Los Angeles, California (Chapter 26)

**James Kochanski,** Senior Vice President, Sibson Consulting, Raleigh, North Carolina (Chapter 9)

**Molly A. Kyle,** Consultant, Arthur J. Gallagher & Co.'s Human Resources & Compensation Consulting Practice, New York, New York (Chapters 31, 38)

**Gerald E. Ledford, Jr.,** Senior Research Scientist, Center for Effective Organizations, University of Southern California, Los Angeles, California (Chapter 13)

**Kathleen M. Lingle,** Architect of Change, Scottsdale, Arizona (Chapter 41)

**Joseph J. Martocchio, Ph.D.,** Professor, University of Illinois at Urbana-Champaign, School of Labor and Employment Relations, Champaign, Illinois (Chapter 6)

**Nora McCord,** Managing Director, Steven Hall & Partners, New York, New York (Chapter 28)

**Tom McMullen,** Vice President and North American Reward Practice Leader, Hay Group, Chicago, Illinois (Chapter 12)

**Yvonne McNulty, Ph.D.,** Associate Faculty, Singapore Institute of Management University, Singapore (Chapter 45)

**Brian Moore, CCP, CSCP,** Market and Customer Research, WorldatWork, Scottsdale, Arizona (Chapter 5)

**Erin C. Packwood,** Principal, Mercer's Talent Business, Houston, Texas (Chapter 16)

**Jane Park,** Vice President, Pearl Meyer & Partners, New York (Chapter 27)

**Andrea S. Rattner,** Partner, Proskauer Rose LLP, New York, New York (Chapter 24)

**James F. Reda,** Managing Director, Arthur J. Gallagher & Co.'s Human Resources & Compensation Consulting Practice, New York, New York (Chapters 31, 38)

**Deborah Rees, BSc, FCIPD,** Director of Consulting, Innecto Reward Consulting, Wiltshire, United Kingdom (Chapter 39)

**Robert H. Rock,** President, MLR Holdings LLC, Philadelphia, Pennsylvania (Chapter 30)

**Mandy Rook,** Principal, Mercer Human Resources Consulting, Philadelphia Pennsylvania (Chapter 2)

**Andrew S. Rosen,** Principal, Compensation Leader, Buck Consultants, Berwyn, Pennsylvania (Chapter 7)

**Mark A. Royal,** Senior Principal, Hay Group, Chicago, Illinois (Chapter 40)

**John A. Rubino,** President, Rubino Consulting Services, Pound Ridge, New York (Chapter 42)

**Rebecca Sandberg,** Director of Consulting Services, SalesGlobe, Alpharetta, Georgia (Chapter 18)

**Ezra Schneier,** Corporate Development Officer, HRsoft, Inc., Philadelphia, Pennsylvania (Chapter 49)

**Dow Scott, Ph.D.,** Professor of Human Resources, Loyola University, Chicago, Illinois (Chapter 20)

**Ilene Siscovick,** Partner, Mercer, Seattle, Washington (Chapter 44)

**Mel J. Stark,** Vice President, Hay Group, Jersey City, New Jersey (Chapter 40)

**Yelena Stiles,** Senior Consultant, Sibson Consulting, Princeton, New Jersey (Chapter 25)

**David Swinford,** President & CEO, Pearl Meyer & Partners, Rochester, New York (Chapter 27)

**Paul Thompson,** Founder, E-reward.co.uk Limited, Cheshire, United Kingdom (Chapter 10)

**David B. Turetsky,** Vice President, Talent Management Consulting, ADP Strategic Advisory Services, Marlborough, Massachusetts (Chapter 48)

**Frank P. VanderPloeg Esq.,** Partner, Employee Benefits and Executive Compensation, Dentons US, LLP, Chicago, Illinois (Chapter 23)

**Melissa Van Dyke,** President, The Incentive Research Foundation, St. Louis, Missouri (Chapter 14)

**Carrie Ward,** Director of Consulting Services, SalesGlobe, Alpharetta, Georgia (Chapter 18)

**Dan Weber,** Associate Director, Radford, an Aon Hewitt Company, San Francisco, California (Chapter 47)

**Thomas B. Wilson,** President and CEO, Wilson Group, Concord, Massachusetts (Chapter 3)

**Martin G. Wolf, Ph.D,** Compensation Specialist, Jalisco, Mexico (Chapters 33, 50)

# Index

Classifications
  allocations with employee, 40
  job, 100
Clawback provisions, 279–280
Closed-loop cards, 147
Cluster analysis method, midpoints, 68–69
COBRA, 275
Codified methodologies, 5–7, 40
COLA. *See* Cost-of-living allowance
Collaboration
  team incentives and, 199–207
  work/life, 468–470
Collings, David, 510
Commitment, 215, 218
Committees, 322–323, 349. *See also* Compensation
    committee
Communication
  compensation program and methodology for
    explanation of, 471–472
    steps, 473–476
    strategy, 476–478
  connection and, 49
  incentive compensation and, 166–167
  pay programs, 312–313
  philosophy of pay and, 181
  ROI methodology and, 196–197
  total rewards communication, 555–558
Community, 326, 464
Compa ratio (CR), 565, 567
Companies, 59
  BSC, 327
  CEO evaluation requirements for different types
    of, 425
  cost, 331
  CTC, 496
  LTIs in private, 281–286
  size and type with salary surveys, 109
  top, 35, 452
  with total rewards strategy development, 32–33
Comparisons, 99, 181, 365–366, 374–375
Compensation. *See also* Benchmarking; Board
    compensation; Executive compensation
    regulation; Executive compensation strategy;
    Expatriate compensation practices; Global
    local national compensation; Incentive
    compensation; Long-term incentives; Sales
    compensation
  big data and compensation programs, 544–549,
    551–558, 561–569
  board of directors performance and, 328
  business value linked to, 383–390, 547–549
  data, 106, 123–127, 336–338, 494–495, 497–498,
    501–502, 561–562, 564–566
  executive employment agreement and,
    268–271
  knowledge, 47

philosophy, 5, 293, 431–432
  attract, retain, motivate, 330
  degree of acceptable risk, 330
  market-stage significance, 329–330
principles, 182–183
professional training in, 47, 59–60
technical skills in, 47
with total rewards strategy design, 19
"U.S. Compensation Planning Survey"
    (2014–2015), 170–171, 175
vehicles, 228
"Compensation Best Practices Report" (PayScale),
    574
Compensation committee
  accountabilities, 291
  benchmarking data, 336–338
  board of directors and, 329, 333–341
  calendar, 304
  chair of, 334
  charter, 301
  compensation plans, 338–340
  composition, 333
  deliberations, 338
  discussion and analysis, 340
  duties and responsibilities, 303, 335–336
  executive pay and, 289–306
  issues facing, 332
  outside consultants, 336
  pay philosophy, 338
  role of, 250–251, 328, 334–335
  scrutiny, 340–341
  structure, 425–426
Compensation discussion and analysis (CD&A),
    252, 309, 329, 335, 340
Compensation information
  central tendency measures, 562–563
  dispersion measures, 563
  information-driven salary administration, 567
  legal concerns with sharing, 128–129
  misleading data avoided, 563–564
  psychological barriers to data interpretation, 564
    average hourly wages, 565
    pay range, 565–566
  with right data, 564
  salary increases, MIFs, and movement through pay
    range, 568–569
  statistics for understanding, 561–562
Compensation issues
  China's rising wages, 58–60
  compensation-productivity gap, 54–55
  FLSA
    minimum wage, 55–57, 254
    overtime pay protections, 57–58
  Great Recession, 53–55
  productivity and real hourly compensation growth
    (2007–2011), 54–55

Groups, 180, 399. *See also* Hay Group
  advisory, 116
  incentives, 175–176
  peer, 123, 229, 431
  skills, 372
  travel, 147, 149
Guidelines
  board compensation and ownership, 320–321
  calibration and session facilitator, 414–420
  executive performance appraisal, 423–438
Gupta, N., 97

Hardship premium, 514–515
*Harvard Business Review*, 448, 539
Hastings, Reed, 448
Hawaii, 56
Hawk, Elizabeth, 211
Hay Associates, 501
Hay Group, 131, 133
  with ROI, 452, 454–461
  total rewards framework, 457
HCNs. *See* Host-country nationals
Health
  health care consumers, 399–400
  health care providers, 398–399
  life event program, 31
  plans
    COBRA, 275
    medical, vision, and dental care, 31
Healthways, 399
Hearst Magazines, 448
Herman Miller, 218
Heskett, J., 217
Hewlett-Packard, 401–402
Heymann, Jody, 468
Hierarchy, organizational, 510
Hippocratic oath, 442
Hired hand pay model, 282, 283
Hodgson, Paul, 344
Hofstede, G., 205
Home buildup approach, 488
Home country/parent country, 515
Home leave, 487, 515
Home ownership, 219
Home salary, 483
Home sale reimbursement, 515
Host country, 515
Host salary, 483
Host-country nationals (HCNs), 515
Hourly compensation, 54–55
Hourly wages, 565
Housing, 485–486, 496
  allowance, 515
*How to Be a Star at Work: 9 Breakthrough Strategies You Need to Succeed* (Kelley), 50, 52n3
HP, 538

HR. *See* Human resources
HR Chally Group, 180
HRIS. *See* Human resources information system
HRIT. *See* Human resources information technology
Human resources (HR)
  big data and, 540–541, 553–554
  goals with compensation vehicles, 228
  managers on, 131–132
  metrics, 546–547
  objectives with compensation principles, 182
  professionals and business acumen, 46
Human resources information system (HRIS), 530, 540, 541
Human resources information technology (HRIT), 541–542

IBM, 35, 383, 538, 539, 563
*I-deals: Idiosyncratic Deals Employees Bargain for Themselves* (Rousseau), 510
Identity/education, 214, 216
IDP. *See* Individual development plan
Immigration, reduced, 212
Incentive compensation
  administrative rules
    communication, 166–167
    plan adjustments, 166
  award opportunities, 164
    frequency, 166
    target, 165
  characteristics, 158
  corporate performance metrics, 163
  design considerations, 159–160
  eligibility, 163–164
  explanation of, 157, 159, 167–168
  issues, 159
  market-based cost model, 161
  performance metrics, 160, 162–163
  plan cost as percentage of competitive levels, 161
  plan funding and affordability, 160
Incentive Marketing Association, 148
Incentive Research Foundation (IRF), 152
Incentives, 144, 449. *See also* Long-term incentives; Team incentives
  cash, 145
  executive employment agreement and annual, 269
  with executive pay strategy, 299–300
  expatriate compensation practices, 486–488
  with expatriate compensation practices, 486–488
  group or individual, 175–176
  incentive scheme weightings by factor, 545
  incentive system design, 150
  LTIPs, 122, 339
  mechanics, sales compensation plan design, 185–186
  organizations with, 170

McAdams, Jerry, 211
McCoy, C., 442
McGregor, Douglas, 214, 219
Mean, 110, 562
Mechanics, incentive, 194
Media
    communication, 474–475, 478
    social, 14, 152, 447, 555
Median, 110, 125, 563
Medical insurance, 496
Medical plan, 31. *See also* Health
Meetings, 263, 321, 414–415, 419–420
Melville, Herman, 211
Mercer, 170–171, 175, 493, 501, 513
    reports, 15, 18
    surveys, 14, 18, 19, 20–21
Merchandise electronics, 152
Merit
    budgets, 92
    increases, 359
        as investment spending, 93–94
        matrix, 459
        salary administration, 7
    matrix, 78, 79
Merit increase factors (MIFs), 565–569
Merit pay
    alternatives, 5, 43–44
    as compensation strategy, 42–43
    merits of differentiation, 89–90
    pay actions
        as investment spending, 93–94
        with managers and performance ratings,
            92–93
        merit budgets and annual bonus pools, 92
        with performance evaluation process simplified,
            94–95
        performance expectations, 91
        performance outcomes, 91–92
        top performer set-aside pool, 90–91
    sales talent retention and, 187
    SKC pay and, 136, 137, 138, 139–140
Meritocracy, 500
Metrics, 18, 193
    defined, 529–530, 535
    with executive pay, 298–299
    HR, 546–547
    performance, 160, 162–163, 227
    productivity, 391, 393–394
Mexico, 59, 495–496
Microsoft, 35, 443
Middle East, 498
Midpoints, salary structure and, 67, 68–69, 83
MIFs. *See* Merit increase factors
Military bonuses, 137
Millennials (Generation Y), 46, 515
Minbaeva, Dana, 510
Mind-set, work/life, 467–468

Minimum wage
    FLSA, 55–57, 254
    Obama on, 55–56, 58
    productivity and, 392–393
Minnesota, 56, 400
*Moby Dick* (Melville), 211
*Moneyball* (film), 193
Monitoring, compensation practice, 10–11
Mosley, Eric, 359
Motherhood penalty, 469
Motivate, 149, 330, 372, 401, 450
Motivation tool, variable pay as, 171–172
MRPs. *See* Market reference points
MRRs. *See* Market reference ranges
Multifaceted structure. *See* Global structure
Multigraded structures, salary, 83–84, 87
Myers, Charles A., 214

NACD. *See* National Association of Corporate
        Directors
Named executive officers (NEO), 252–253,
        345–346, 434
Nasdaq, 270, 333, 347
National Association of Corporate Directors
        (NACD), 317, 341
National Business Group on Health, 399
NCR Corporation, 59
NEO. *See* Named executive officers
Net compensation, 495
Net promoter scores (NPS), 195
Netflix, 441, 448, 551
New York, 57, 278, 400–401, 561
New York Stock Exchange (NYSE), 270,
        333, 424
"The Next High-Stakes Quest," 449
Nielsen, Niels, 98
Nonmonetary awards
    application, 145–146
    efficacy of, 144–145
    IRS and, 154n13
    plan design, 149–150
    rewards options mix of business today, 143
    sourcing and fulfillment
        awards catalog administration, 148–149
        gift card administration, 149
        group travel administration, 149
    taxes and, 150–152
    trends
        corporate social responsibility, 152
        gamification, 152
        measurement techniques, 152
        merchandise electronics, 152
        points-based systems, 152
        procurement, 152
        social media, 152
        travel quality over quantity, 152–153
        wellness, 152

# About the Editors

**Lance A. Berger** is managing partner of Lance A. Berger & Associates, Ltd., in Bryn Mawr, Pennsylvania. He is a recognized consulting authority specializing in compensation, talent management and change management. He cowrote and coedited the third, fourth, and fifth editions of *The Compensation Handbook*, the first and second editions of *The Talent Management Handbook*, *Management Wisdom from the New York Yankees' Dynasty*, *The Change Management Handbook*, and *Deengineering the Corporation*.

**Dorothy R. Berger** is a partner of Lance A. Berger & Associates, Ltd. She coordinates all organizational activities for the firm and is also a talent management consultant. She cowrote and coedited the fourth and fifth editions of *The Compensation Handbook*, the first edition and second editions of *The Talent Management Handbook*, *Management Wisdom from the New York Yankees' Dynasty*, *The Change Management Handbook*, and *Deengineering the Corporation*.